FUNDAMENTALS OF
INVESTMENTS

We work with leading authors to develop the strongest educational materials in business and finance, bringing cutting-edge thinking and best learning practice to a global market.

Under a range of well-known imprints, including Financial Times Prentice Hall, we craft high quality print and electronic publications which help readers to understand and apply their content, whether studying or at work.

To find out more about the complete range of our publishing, please visit us on the World Wide Web at: **www.pearsoneduc.com**

FUNDAMENTALS OF INVESTMENTS

HAIM LEVY

The Hebrew University of Jerusalem
and Zicklin School of Business,
Baruch College, New York

FINANCIAL TIMES
Prentice Hall

An imprint of **Pearson Education**

Harlow, England · London · New York · Reading, Massachusetts · San Francisco
Toronto · Don Mills, Ontario · Sydney · Tokyo · Singapore · Hong Kong · Seoul
Taipei · Cape Town · Madrid · Mexico City · Amsterdam · Munich · Paris · Milan

To Romi, Neta, Tamar, Shira and Tal

Pearson Education Limited

Edinburgh Gate
Harlow
Essex CM20 2JE
England

and Associated Companies throughout the world

Visit us on the World Wide Web at:
www.pearsoneduc.com

First published 2002

ISBN 0 273 65169 2

British Library Cataloguing-in-Publication Data
A catalogue record for this book is available from the British Library.

Library of Congress Cataloging-in-Publication Data
A catalog record for this book is available from the Library of Congress.

10 9 8 7 6 5 4 3 2 1
06 05 04 03 02

Typeset by 68 in 10/12 pt Sabon
Printed and bound in Great Britain by Ashford Colour Press Ltd, Gosport

BRIEF CONTENTS

CONTENTS

Part I
THE MARKET ENVIRONMENT AND SECURITIES

Part II
RISK AND RETURN

Part III
BONDS AND STOCKS

Part IV
DERIVATIVES

Part VI
MARKET EFFICIENCY, MUTUAL FUNDS
AND TECHNICAL ANALYSIS

PREFACE

The picture on the cover of this book illustrates that the stock market has bearish and bullish periods. The lower part of the picture best illustrates the bearish status of most capital markets in February 2002. Although a bearish market prevailed before September 2001, we must distinguish between the period before 11 September 2001 and after this date. On 11 September the US suffered a horrific terrorist attack which inflicted severe damage to the Pentagon and completely demolished the two buildings of the World Trade Center, well known as the twin towers. These two buildings without question symbolized the strength of the US economy. The US financial markets were immediately closed and all trade was suspended until Monday, 17 September 2001. The world financial markets panicked, with an immediate drop in the leading stock indices of 6.47% in the UK, 7.3% in France, 8.5% in Germany, 4.5% in Spain, 7.79% in Italy, 6.95% in Holland, 7.63% in Sweden and 7.07% in Switzerland. When such panic occurs, investors move into gold and other raw material; indeed the price of gold went up by 7% and of crude oil by 5.5%. Investors and policymakers were afraid of the market reaction on the opening of the US financial markets on 17 September. To moderate the predicted stock prices drop in the USA, Mr Alan Greenspan, the Chairman of the Federal Reserve Bank, announced an interest rate cut from 3.5% to 3%. Europe and Japan followed: the European central bank cut the interest rate from 4.25% to 3.75% and the UK cut the interest rate from 5% to 4.75%. Japan cut the interest rate by only 0.10% because it was already very low, only 0.2% before the new cut. Despite this good news for the stock market, both the Dow Jones and the Nasdaq indices dropped on 17 September by about 7%. The drop in stock prices continued also after that date in the US, Japan and Europe alike. In the first week of trade after the terrorist attack, the Dow Jones index dropped by about 14% and the Nasdaq index by about 16%. The stock markets in Europe continued their dive also after 17 September. As the US and other capital markets recovered from the trauma of the 11 September terrorist attack, the US market again suffered in early 2002 from the Enron scandal, which was considered by many as an 'economic terrorist attack'. Enron, the largest US energy company, reported 12 months' earnings almost $1 billion higher than should have been repoted! Enron's auditors, Andersen, did not spot this. As a result, investors cast doubt on the financial statements, inducing pessimistic investment atmosphere, making the bears stronger than the bulls.

A bearish market means that the bears are out and the bulls are quiet, a metaphor for very pessimistic investors. The US capital market, the biggest in the world, had started showing a slowdown in the economy even before the terrorist attack. The Nasdaq index dropped from about 5,000 points to less than 1,700 points in a relatively short time. Even the well-established companies started to lay off employees, and the unemployment rate in the US increased by 0.4% in August 2001 to 4.9%. Mr Greenspan had already lowered the interest rate from 4% to 4.75%, hoping to avoid possible recession. As mentioned above, after the terrorist attack the interest rate was reduced further to 3%. While in August 2001 it was not clear which way the US economy would turn, Japan, the second largest capital market in the world, had been in deep trouble for a long time. In July 2001 the unemployment rate in Japan reached 5%, the highest level in 50 years! And at the beginning of 2002 the Japanese stock index fell to 9,500 points, the lowest level since 1983. In Europe the picture was not rosy either. Germany, the third largest capital market in the world, showed a sharp decrease in the gross domestic product per capita. Italy, also reported a shrinking production per capita. This is the nature of the capital markets; there are bearish and bullish periods, and it is hard to predict when one ends and the other starts.

This bearish market by no means implies that studying the capital market is worthless. First, one has to invest the wealth somewhere and in a pessimistic market there are always investments which yield a positive, albeit not very high, rate of return, e.g. US Treasury bills, savings accounts, etc. All those who sold their stock after the terrorist attack needed to invest their money in other and probably safer investment alternatives. Indeed, after 17 September 2001, many investors preferred to invest in US Treasury bills, hence their prices went up and the yield to two-year maturity Treasury bills dropped to 2.82%. We discuss in this book the available safer investment instruments and the various factors that should be taken into account in selecting among the various relatively safe alternatives. However, secondly, some investment strategies may earn money precisely in a bearish market (e.g. short positions, buying put options, etc.). Unfortunately, some of the news media claimed that the terrorist Osama bin Laden was in a short position, or bought put options, in particular of insurance and airline companies, which, if true, gave him a very large profit after 17 September when the price of many stocks dropped sharply, some by more than 50%. Though not yet proved, the short sales position in United Airlines increased by 40% before the terrorist attack and after 17 September its stock price dropped from $30.82 to $17.10, i.e. the short seller could make a profit of $13.72 per share in only a few days. If the news media claims are true, the Biblical phrase '*Have you murdered and also taken possession?*' (Kings 21: 19) best describes this situation. In this book we will explain how short sales and holding put options may yield a profit in a declining market. Thirdly, we should be ready to invest in stocks or call options because, even while this book is on your desk, a bullish market may start.

Even without such events as war or terrorist attacks, the capital market is full of surprises. New stars shine and fall rapidly. Internet, technology and communication stocks shone in recent years, and some small and unknown companies were suddenly sold at a valuation of several billion dollars. After a year, and sometimes less than a year, the value of these companies was very low and in some cases dropped to zero. The rise and fall of these companies is reflected in the Nasdaq index, which rose from 1,000 points to about 5,000 points in a very short time and then fell to less than 1,700 points in September 2001 before the terrorist attack. Thus, in a very short time we observed a profit of 400% and then a decline of more than 60% in value. The last few years emphasized what has been well known for years: investing in stocks and, in particular, in venture capital stocks and in small company stocks may be very rewarding but may also be very risky.

The capital market is very complex with many financial instruments such as stocks, bonds and options. Moreover, the introduction of the euro in January 2002 is a source of additional confusion to about 302 million citizens of 12 countries who have switched to real euro notes and coins. Are the prices in stores in euros right? Are we being ripped off by merchants? Definitely, at least in the short run, the switch to the euro has added complexity to the capital market, which was already very complex. This book is devoted to understanding this complex capital market and the financial instruments which exist in the market, and also to the investment analyses and valuation of these available financial instruments.

The three main tasks of the professional as well as the individual investor are:

(a) *security selectivity*;
(b) *investment timing*, namely the recommended changes in portfolio composition over time, known as *dynamic asset allocation* (with emphasis on three classes of assets: stocks, bonds and cash);
(c) *portfolio diversification* (the portfolio composition of the selected securities).

One school of thought believes that the market is *efficient*, implying that asset selectivity and asset allocation cannot create abnormal profit or extraordinary profit. If indeed the market is *efficient*, the fundamental and technical analyses commonly employed in security selectivity are worthless. Similarly, the use of industry and macro-economic analyses to predict the market (that is, the stock market's peaks and troughs), which is needed for dynamic asset allocation, is a waste of time. Therefore, what is left in efficient markets is the risk reduction that is due to portfolio diversification. Mark Twain probably belongs to this school of thought, saying that he hated to make predictions – in particular...regarding the future. However, if the market is inefficient or even partially inefficient, then security analyses, as well as industry and macro-economic analyses, may be financially beneficial. Is the market efficient? Let us start with an anecdote regarding this issue.

A university professor who wrote his doctoral dissertation on the topic of market efficiency was walking past the New York Stock Exchange at 11 Wall Street with his 10-year-old son when the boy suddenly exclaimed, 'Look, there's a $100 bill on the sidewalk!' 'That's impossible,' replied the professor. 'The market is efficient, and in an efficient market, $100 bills cannot be found on the sidewalk!' This anecdote serves to illustrate the main implication of the belief in market efficiency: if the market is indeed perfectly efficient, there will be no bargains in the market; there will be no $100 bills lying around just waiting to be found. In an efficient market, all risky assets will be correctly priced, and all available information on a given stock will be duly reflected in its current market price. Under such circumstances, valuation models of stocks, bonds and options will not be helpful in security selection. In other words, such models cannot be applied to obtain abnormal profits. Similarly, a dynamic asset allocation incurs transaction costs, with no benefit.

The story of the $100 bill also illustrates the absurdity of the concept of market efficiency pushed to the extreme. There is a $100 bill on the sidewalk, and you are the first one to find it. You cannot believe your eyes! True, everyone agrees that it is impossible for the $100 bill to remain on the sidewalk for very long. However, it is equally true that if it happens to be lying there, you might be the first one to see it and pick it up. Is there a moral to this story?

Even if the market is not perfectly efficient, sophisticated investors who succeed in reaping a profit from undervalued assets will push the stock prices up to an equilibrium price, as predicted by the efficient market hypotheses. For the ordinary investor, the market is usually very efficient. For you, the student taking this course – the sophisticated investor of the future – the market is probably inefficient, so you may succeed in reaping a profit.

Indeed, some well-known professional investors do not believe in efficient markets and claim they are reaping a profit because the markets are inefficient. This view is summarized in an article published in *Fortune* in which Sequoia Fund's William Ruane, Berkshire Hathaway's Charles Munger and Warren Buffett, and money manager Walter Schloss all say that they do not believe in efficient markets. Says Buffett, '*I'd rather be a bum on the street with a tin cup if the market were efficient.*'[1]

---

[1] Terrence P. Pare, 'Yes, you can beat the market', *Fortune*, 3 April 1995, p. 47.

Although the common view among academics in the past was that investors could not beat the market, recently some academics have expressed the opposite view, which enhances the importance of studying these valuation models. In fact, a study by Josef Lakonishok of the University of Illinois, Andrei Schleifer of Harvard University and Robert W. Vishny of the University of Chicago showed that stock-picking strategies using simple measures outperform both a strategy emphasizing growth stocks and the market as a whole.[2] Thus, on the one hand some professional investors claim that they make a lot of money due to market inefficiency, but on the other hand we see how difficult it is to predict market trend. There is one strong example (but not a proof) in favour of market efficiency. Even sophisticated people who not only understand the macro-economic factors well but also directly affect them sometimes cannot predict future stock prices. For example, Mr Alan Greenspan, the chairman of the Federal Reserve Bank, said in April 1998 that stock prices are based on forecasts. He stated that the US economy had entered a new era of continuous steep gains in productivity and noted that, as a central banker, he has already been highly sceptical about new eras and changing structures of how the world functions.[3] Greenspan may be right this time in his prediction, but in a 5 December 1996 speech he rattled his audience when he asked whether the market might be exhibiting 'irrational exuberance'. By 1998 we knew that he had been wrong in 1996, because at that time the Dow Jones stood at 6,400 points and during 16 months it escalated to 9,100 – a 42% gain during that period. However, more than three years later, in February 2002, the Dow Jones was at 9,900, i.e. it had shown a capital gain of only about 6% during that period of more than three years. Thus market efficiency is still an open question.

This book has been organized and written around the new developments and challenges facing the capital market. Indeed, recent years have witnessed a threefold revolution in the field of finance and investment in the capital market.

First, the argument as to whether the market is efficient or inefficient has resurfaced. This issue is crucial, because it carries implications regarding the value of some of the topics taught in investment courses as well as the justification for many of the jobs of financial analysts (which, basically, do not believe in market efficiency). I accept that there is disagreement on this issue and, in writing this book, I have maintained an open mind and tolerance towards the views expressed by both the proponents and the antagonists of market efficiency.

Second, the capital market has been bombarded with new investment strategies. Derivatives have hit the headlines and the role of options as a speculative investment tool, as well as a hedging risk investment tool, has expanded rapidly in the last few years. Investing in derivatives is very risky. One of the biggest losses (over a billion dollars) was by Barings Bank, then England's oldest bank (after its collapse, Barings Bank was purchased by Holland's ING Group). Therefore, one part of this book focuses on the role that derivative securities, such as options and futures, play in portfolio management. This discussion will help readers gain a better understanding of these popular, but often misunderstood and sometimes mismanaged, financial instruments. All these rapid changes can make the field of investments more difficult for students to understand and for professors to teach. At the same time, however, the changes also make the field more challenging and interesting.

---

[2] Josef Lakonishok, Andrei Schleifer and Robert W. Vishny, 'Contrarian investment, extrapolation and risk', *Journal of Finance*, 49(5), December 1994. This study was also cited in *Fortune*, 3 April 1995.
[3] *USA Today*, 3 April 1998.

Third, the market has become truly global. Because of fast-flowing communication systems, transactions between all parts of the planet can be executed with a computer keystroke. This fast communication system and market globalization is noticed in particular when short-run panic occurs in the market, as in the October 1987 crisis and the October 1997 crisis, and of course in the panic due to the terrorist attack of 11 September 2001 on the USA. The 1997 crisis started in Asia, and the effects reverberated throughout most stock markets around the world. In those two events, almost all major stock markets worldwide fell sharply. After the terrorist attack the stock prices crashed in Europe and Japan and only later in the US market (which was closed until 17 September). The same co-movement of price around the world has occurred with the rise and fall of the new technology stocks.

The lower the correlation between stock price movement, the greater the gain from diversification, because diversification induces stability to the value of the portfolio. In crises such as the terrorist attack all markets go down, hence diversification cannot help much. Unfortunately, also the long-run correlation between stock market movements of some countries, in particular European countries, is very high, which limits the potential gain from international diversification. However, for some countries there is zero correlation, or even a negative correlation, between stock prices in the long run, and not all markets rise or fall in tandem. Thus, for some pairs of capital markets, in the long run investors can gain from international diversification. In particular, in recent years the two largest economies in the world, the United States and Japan, generally moved sharply in different directions (that is, there was a negative correlation). To demonstrate, in the early 1990s the Dow was at the 3,000 level. In February 2002 it reached approximately the 9,900 level, that is, more than a 230% rate of return in a relatively short time. In contrast, investing in Japan during this period was devastating to Japanese investors, let alone to US investors. In 1989, the Nikkei index was close to 40,000 points. By February 2002, it had fallen to 9,800. This represents about a 75% drop in the index. In 17 September 2001 both indices fell, the Dow Jones to 9,605 points and the Nikkei index to 10,516 points. For Americans who invested in the Nikkei, the rates of return were affected by both the Nikkei index fall and the changes in foreign exchange rates. A depreciation of the yen added to the losses. For example, from 1995 to 1998, the Nikkei index did not change much. However, in 1995 one yen was worth 1.2 American cents, whereas in February 2002 it was worth about 0.75 cents. Thus, even with no change in the Nikkei index, the investor who invested $1.20 in 1995 in Japan (100 yen) could withdraw only 0.75 cents in 2002. Hence, there was a loss of 42% on the foreign exchange even with no change in the Nikkei index, and the loss was intensified with any additional drop in the Nikkei.

Short-run panics do not necessarily reflect the weakness of the economy, but long-run movements in stock prices do reflect the weaknesses and strengths of the economy. For example, the sharp drop in the Nikkei index and the deterioration of the yen relative to the dollar reflect the recent slow growth in the Japanese economy. Between 1987 and 1991, Japan had an annual growth in gross domestic product (GDP) in the range of 4% to 6%. This growth rate dropped sharply in recent years (with the exception of 1996), reaching a mere 0.9% in 1997 and even a negative growth in 2001. The sluggish economy induces financial distress and a flow of bad debt, which in turn affect the bankruptcy rates in Japan. In contrast, in the US up to 2002 the economy has been rapidly expanding, which was reflected in the bullish stock market. In 2002, a sluggish US economy started, and indeed the Dow Jones index dropped from about 11,000 points to about 9,900 points in early February 2002. Thus, one must distinguish between short-term shifts in the stock market, and in particular short-term panic, and long-term trends (which are not necessarily in the same direction but rather reflect the fundamental characteristics of the various economies).

Investors' panic and euphoria, new developments such as the Internet and the human genome research, short position, options, international diversification and foreign exchange rates all make the field of investments more difficult for students to understand and for professors to teach. At the same time, however, such changes also make the field more challenging and interesting.

Finally, most evaluation methods studied in this text are based on the evaluation of future cash dividends. In some cases cash dividends are not paid and reported earnings are used rather than cash dividends. The Enron scandal emphasises the importance of cash flow rather than reported earnings. Therefore, when earnings are employed to evaluate a stock, it should be done with great care. Remember that earnings can be distorted but cash dividends cannot, at least not for many years. Hence the saying 'a bird (dividend) in the hand is worth two (earnings) in the bush'.

INTENDED READERSHIP

This book is geared to the needs of undergraduate students. The subject matter can be covered in a two-semester course, but the text can also be used for a one-semester course by selecting the chapters considered most important. Generally, this course is taken after principles of finance have been studied. However, in order to achieve a self-contained text, the concepts needed for this book (such as discounting) are discussed in Appendix A. With regard to mathematics, no more than high school-level algebra is assumed.

The student who studies principles of finance before taking an investments course will probably wonder why some of the material, such as risk and return analysis, appears in both courses. Many issues are common to both areas. Both the corporate manager and the portfolio manager face the problems of asset evaluation and risk reduction by diversification. However, there is one distinction: portfolio managers diversify the portfolio across many stocks available in the market, whereas corporate managers focus their activities on a relatively small number of projects contained in the firm's portfolio of projects. The selection of a portfolio from a large number of securities requires specialized tools, and these tools are introduced and discussed in this book.

ORGANIZATION OF THE BOOK

Some investment texts devote early chapters to modern portfolio theory and some relegate this material, which is quite complicated, to the end of the book. This material quite often is not being taught to undergraduate students because it is relatively more quantitative. In this text we suggest a compromise: the fundamentals of risk reduction via diversification are given in Chapter 6, and the more quantitative risk–return equilibrium relationship is postponed to Chapter 14. Market efficiency is covered in the last part of the book. This by no means reflects its importance. The reason for its location is that only after studying the risk–return relationship and the capital asset pricing model (CAPM) can one describe the empirical tests of market efficiency, which rely on the definition of an abnormal return (or excess return). This, in turn, cannot be understood before studying the CAPM.

Part I (Chapters 1–3) is devoted to the market environment and to a description of the various securities and how they are traded. Part II (Chapters 4–6) covers risk and return in he capital market with an emphasis on the gain or risk reduction due to diversification. Part III (Chapters 7–11) is devoted to bonds and stocks with an emphasis on valuation and management of these assets. Part IV (Chapters 12 and 13) covers derivatives, focusing on forwards, futures, and options. In Part V (Chapters 14 and 15) we expand the analysis of risk-reduction due to diversification, and the risk return equilibrium relationship achieved under optimal diversification. We also discuss the benefit from international diversification. Finally, the last part of the book, Part VI (Chapters 16–18), is devoted to market efficiency, mutual funds performance and technical analysis, which explicitly assume that the market is inefficient.

SPECIAL FEATURES

■ Investment in the news

This text and its special features were carefully developed by the author and evaluated by a dedicated panel of reviewers. The goal throughout has been to spark the interest of students and enhance their motivation to learn about the field of investments. Included are articles and discussions from sources such as the *Wall Street Journal, Barron's, Business Week, Fortune*, the *New York Times* and *Financial Times*, as well as the financial statements of corporations. This material introduces students to real-life scenarios that will give them the opportunity to apply and develop investment techniques. Each chapter opens with one newspaper article highlighting the main topic discussed in the chapter, and called *Investment in the news*.

■ Present and future value calculations

Appendix A to the book provides the basic mathematics and formulas needed to understand the book. Actually, these are present and future values formulas studied in basic courses in corporate finance or foundations of finance. However, for students who did not take corporate finance before taking the course, reading the Appendix is all that is needed to make this a self-contained book.

■ International websites

Appendix B, at the end of the book, provides a list of Internet sites where the student can get financial and macro-economic information data. The list is quite extensive and covers many topics that students as well as lecturers might use.

■ Questions

At the end of each chapter there is a list of questions, for which solutions are given in the *Instructor's Manual*, which is available free of charge to lecturers adopting the text, upon application to the publishers. It is also available to download from the lecturer's section of the website http://www.booksites.net/levy.

■ Quiz

For each chapter there is also a multiple-choice quiz on the website http://www.booksites.net/levy which can be used for self-instruction or as a class exercise.

A NOTE TO THE STUDENT

What are the potential benefits of studying investments?

Why study investments? There are several reasons why it is worthwhile to study finance and, in particular, investments. First, nowadays you can hardly go through life totally oblivious to terms such as *swaps, options, bonds, stocks* and *yields*. The media will not let you. To understand the financial news, you need some understanding of such terms.

Second, no matter what job you eventually get, you hope to be able to save some of your income. Should you buy mutual funds, or should you personally diversify across various stocks? Should you play it safe and buy certificates of deposit, or should you take on risk and invest in emerging markets? The material in this book will help you make decisions regarding your own investment.

Third, studying finance is very challenging. It is a practical field in which highly sophisticated models are applied. For example, the *beta* risk index is used and published by Value Line and Standard & Poor's in ranking stocks. The Black–Scholes *option pricing model* is employed regularly by practitioners and traders in the financial markets. Thus, the topics covered in this book are not only intellectually challenging but also important in day-to-day decision making.

Indeed, the theoretical underpinnings of this field finally received recognition by the Nobel Committee in 1990, when it awarded the Nobel Prize in economics to financial economists Harry Markowitz, Merton Miller and William Sharpe. A large part of this book relies on the work of Markowitz and Sharpe, which laid the foundation for portfolio decision-making models and equilibrium risk–return relationships. (Miller's main contribution is in the area of corporate finance.) In 1997, Robert Merton and Myron Scholes won the Nobel Prize in economics for their contribution to research in derivatives with an emphasis on options valuation models.

Yet, perhaps the most important reason for studying this subject is the hope that the yield will be truly profitable. Indeed, the rewards of a career in this area can be awesome. Moreover, a job on Wall Street as well as in the European exchanges and brokerage houses spells prestige. To acquire such a job – and the competition is stiff – you will usually need an MBA degree. The following table will give you an idea of what to expect in pursuing a career in investments.

'Still making out on Wall Street'

Position	Total compensation: salary and bonus (in thousands)	
	Junior professional (3–5 years' experience)	Senior professional (10+ years' experience)
Stock research analyst	$150–$250	$350–$500
Bond trader	$300–$500	$650–$850
Corporate finance generalist	$250–$400	$700–$1,000
Institutional bond salesperson	$200–$300	$600–$800

Generally, these financial compensations go up in a bullish market and down in a bearish market. Yet, they are considered to be high relative to other professions, and many people want to be included in this statistic! But what's the catch? To receive these high salaries, you need three to five years or more than 10 years of experience. The 'catch-22' here is this: how can you get a job when you have no experience, and how can you get experience without a job? The aim of this book is to provide you with enough knowledge for your first job, even with no experience. Indeed, it is hoped that mastery of the material presented in this book will be a good substitute for the experience needed to acquire your first position and to be successful in your job. Who knows, within no time, you may be part of the salary statistics appearing in the table!

Haim Levy
January 2002

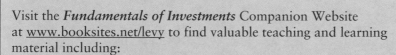

A Companion Website accompanies FUNDAMENTALS OF INVESTMENTS

Visit the *Fundamentals of Investments* Companion Website at www.booksites.net/levy to find valuable teaching and learning material including:

For Students:
- Study material designed to help you improve your results
- Multiple choice questions to test your learning

For Lecturers:
- A secure, password-protected site with teaching material
- A downloadable version of the full *Solutions Manual*
- PowerPoint slides to use in your lectures
- A syllabus manager that will build and host your very own course web page

GUIDED TOUR

Practice boxes
Problems and worked Solutions are
provided to demonstrate principles.

Learning Objectives
are given for each
chapter

Investment in the news
brings each chapter to
life by featuring a
recent relevant
topical news article

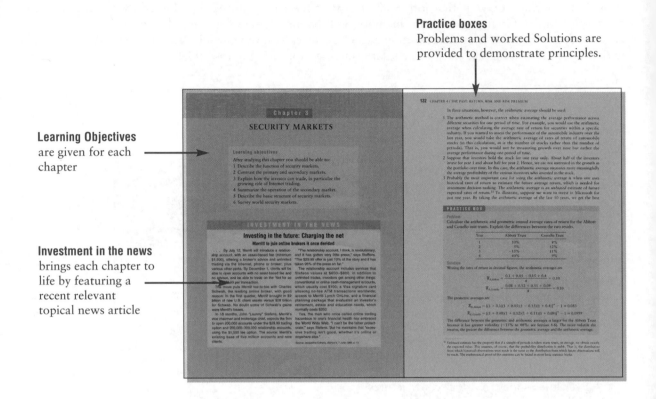

Exhibits
Extracts from the
financial press, such
as the *Financial
Times*, are included
throughout the book to
emphasize the relevance
to real-world events.

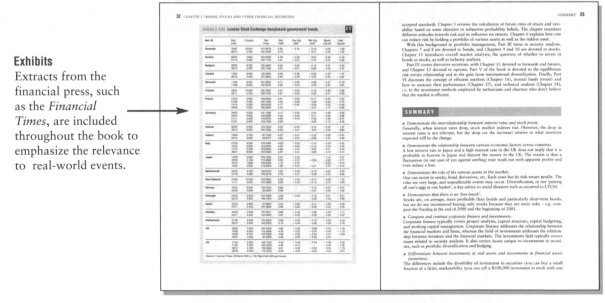

Summaries
Each chapter concludes with a summary
of the main topics covered.

GUIDED TOUR

Appendices
provide the basic mathematics
and formulae needed to use
this self-contained book.

Key terms
are recapped at the
end of each chapter
and definitions are
given in the Glossary
at the end of the
book.

Questions
detailed questions are
provided after each
chapter for class
discussion.

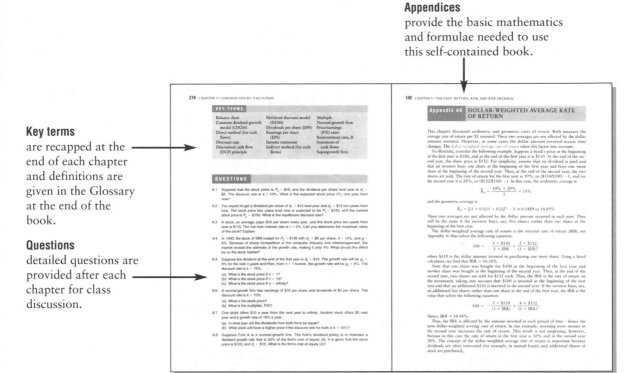

Website
Visit the website on
www.booksites.net/levy.

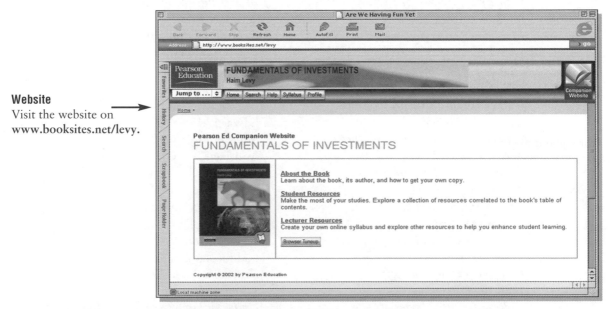

Screen shot reprinted by permission of Microsoft Corporation.

ACKNOWLEDGEMENTS

This project could never have been completed without the help of many colleagues and friends. I would like to thank the many reviewers who provided valuable feedback for earlier material which serves as the basis for the text.

Michael J. Alderson
St Louis University

Yakov Amihud
New York University

Hames J. Angel
Georgetown University

Sung C. Bae
Bowling Green State University

Kegian Bi
University of San Francisco

Avi Bick
Simon Fraser University

Gilbert Bickum
Eastern Kentucky University

Richard H. Borgman
University of Maine

Denis O. Boudrequx
University of Southern Louisiana

Stephen Caples
McNeese State University

John Clark
University of Alabama

John Clinebell
University of Northern Colorado

Charles J. Corrado
University of Missouri-Columbia

Arthur T. Cox
University of Northern Iowa

Richard F. DeMong
University of Virginia

Giorgio De Santis
University of Southern California

Elroy Dimson
London Business School

John W. Ellis
Colorado State University

Thomas H. Eysell
University of Missouri at St Louis

Daniel Falkowski
Canisius College

James Feller
Middle Tennessee State University

J. Howard Finch
University of Tennessee at Chattanooga

Adam K. Gehr, Jr
DePaul University

Deborah W. Gregory
University of Otago

Deborah L. Gunthorpe
University of Tennessee

Frank M. Hatheway
Pennsylvania State University

David Heskel
Bloomsburg College

Stan Jacobs
Central Washington University

Vahan Janjigian
Boston College

Hazel J. Johnson
University of Louisville

Edward M. Kaitz
Marymount University

Andrew Karolyi
Ohio State University

Mike Keenan
New York University

Yoram Kroll
Hebrew University

Ladd Kochman
Kennesaw State College

Thomas Krueger
University of Wisconsin LaCrosse

Yoram Landskroner
Hebrew University

Graham K. Lemke
Pennsylvania State University

Azriel Levy
Hebrew University

K.C. Lim
City Polytechnic, Hong Kong

K.C. Ma
Investment Research Company

Steven V. Mann
University of South Carolina

Ralph D. May
Southwestern Oklahoma State University

William M. Mayfield
Northwestern Oklahoma State University

Michael L. McBain
Marquette University

Robert McConkie
Sam Houston State University

Robert McElreath
Clemson University

Bruce McManis
Nicholls State University

Edward Miller
University of Texas at San Antonio

Lalatendu Misra
University of Texas at San Antonio

Santhosh B. Mohan
Ohio Northern University

Eli Ofek
New York University

Joseph P. Ogden
State University of New York at Buffalo

Rajeev N. Parikh
St Bonaventure University

Ros Prasad
Michigan State University

Hugh M. Pratt
University of Manitoba

Jerry Prock
University of Texas

Shafiqur Rahman
Portland State University

Venkateshward K. Reddy
University of Colorado, Colorado Springs

William Reichenstein
Baylor University

Stan Reyburn
*Commercial Investment Counselor,
Professional Realty Associates*

Meir Schneller
Virginia Polytechnic Institute

Latha Shanker
Concordia University

Neil Sicherman
University of South Carolina

Raymond W. So
Louisiana State University

Meir Statman
Santa Clara University

Stacey L. Suydam
Montana State University, Billings

Antoinette Tessmer
University of Illinois

David E. Upton
Virginia Commonwealth University

Gopala K. Vasudevan
Suffolk University

Joseph D. Vu
DePaul University

William Wells
Merrimack University

Darin While
Union University

James A. Yoder
University of South Alabama

I would also like to thank Hyla Berkowitz and Maya Landau for their editorial help, as well as Yael Ben-David, Daniel Berkowitz, Natali Eisof, Allon Cohen, Eitan Goldman and Doran Lavee for their assistance in preparing the manuscript. I want to extend special thanks to Boaz Leibovitch for his significant contribution in updating and revising this text. He spent countless hours on this task.

PUBLISHER'S ACKNOWLEDGEMENTS

We are grateful to the following for permission to reproduce copyright material:

Table p. xxii from 'Still making out on Wall Street,' *Fortune*, 6 April, p. 71, © 1992 Time Inc., all rights reserved (Worthy, F.S. 1992); Exhibits 1.4, 15.1 from www.fibv.com, reprinted with permission of the World Federation of Exchanges, http://www.world-exchanges.org; Exhibit 1.6(b) data from http://finance.yahoo.com, and 3.4(b) from www.amex.com © copyright 2002, The Nasdaq Stock Market, Inc., reprinted with the permission of The Nasdaq Stock Market, Inc.; Exhibit 1.9(a) from International Data Corporation, reprinted with permission of IDC; Exhibits 2.3(a), 2.5, 2.6, 2.7(a), (b), 2.8(c), 2.11, 12.1, 12.3, 13.1, 13.2, 18.8 from *Barron's* 2 July 2001, pp. 29, MW47, MW48, MW17, MW16, MW55, F8, MW52, MW52-3, MW50; Exhibit 3.18 from *Barron's* 6 October 1997, p. 64, Chapter 15 inset from *Barron's* 20 July 2001, p. MW6, Exhibits 17.2, 17.4, 17.7 and 17.10 from *Barron's* 30 July 2001, p. F3, F3, F23, F21; Exhibit 17.6 from *Barron's* 15 July 1999, p. F38, Barron's Online by Barron's; Exhibits 3.2(a) from *Wall Street Journal* 5 August 1997; p.C1, Exhibit 3.4(a) from *Wall Street Journal* 24 June 1999; p.C2, Exhibit 15.8 from *Wall Street Journal* 7 July 1999; p. MW72; Exhibit 17.5 from *Wall Street Journal* 2 January 1998, p. 34, Wall Street Journal (Online) by Wall Street Journal, Exhibit 7.8 from *Wall Street Journal* 3 August 1992, p. C17, Wall Street Journal (Online) by Merrill Lynch Securities Research, Exhibit 14.1 from www.dowjones. com, 28 August 2001, Wall Street Journal, Online (staff produced copy only), copyright 1992, 1997, 1998, 1999, 2001 by Dow Jones & Co Inc, reproduced with permission of Dow Jones & Co Inc in the format *Fundamentals of Investments* via Copyright Clearance Center; Exhibits 3.2(b) and 3.5(c) from www.londonstockexchange.com/newissues/brokers/ brokers.asp, 27 May 2001, Exhibit 3.5(a), (b) from www.londonstockexchange.com/join/default.asp, 27 May 2001, Exhibits 4.1 (a) and (b) from FT Investor, www.ftinvestor.com (formerly www.ftmarketwatch.com), 29 January 2002. © Financial Times Limited 2002. Exhibit 4.2 from www.bigcharts.com. © 2000 Big Charts. Exhibit 3.8(c) from www.amex.com/about/amex_listnonu.stm, 27 May 2001, reprinted with permission of the American Stock Exchange; Exhibit 3.10 from *Financial Market Trends*, No. 65, November 1996, copyright OECD 1996; Exhibit 3.11 from *Bloomberg*, 15 June 1999, © 1999 Bloomberg L.P. All rights reserved. Reprinted with permission. Visit www.bloomberg.com; Exhibit 7.6 from 'The implications of corporate bond ratings drift,' *Financial Analysts Journal*, May–June, p. 71 (Altman E.I. and Duen Li Kao, 1992), Exhibit 15.6(a), (c), from 'The benefits of international diversification in bonds,' *Financial Analysts Journal*, September–October, pp. 56–64 (Levy, H. and Lerman, Z., 1988), Exhibit 15.7 from 'Why not diversify internationally rather than domestically?' *Financial Analysts Journal*, July–August, p. 50 (Solnik, B., 1974), Exhibits 17.13 and 17.14 adapted from 'Is a long-term time frame for investing affordable or even relevant?' in the *Investing for the Long Term* seminar proceedings (Bogle J.C. Sr, 1992), copyright 1974, 1988, 1992, Association for Investment Management and Research, reproduced and republished from *Financial Analysts Journal* with permission from the Association for Investment Management and Research, all rights reserved; Exhibit 8.7 from www.capitalgainsincorp.com/hottopic.htm, 1 September 2000, copyright 2000, Capital Gains Incorporated, all rights reserved, this article is being distributed with the permission of Capital Gains Incorporated, www.capitalgainsincorp.com; Exhibit 10.1 from *Money*, Vol. 28, © 1999 Time Inc., all rights reserved (Rose, S., 1999); Exhibit 10.3 from 'Break the barrier between you and your analyst,' *Financial Executive*, September, p. 19 (Chugh, L.C. and Meador, J.W., 1984); Exhibit 11.2 from A. Abel/B. Bernanke, *Macroeconomics*, 2nd edition (figure 9.1 from p. 291), © 1995 by Addison-Wesley Publishing Company, Inc., reprinted by permission of Pearson Education, Inc.; Exhibit 11.8 from 'A bureaucrat with a head for oil,' *Forbes*, 5 July, pp 54–6, reprinted by permission of Forbes Global Magazine © 2002 Forbes Global Inc. (Christy, J.H., 1999); Exhibits 15.2(a), (b) from http://www.yeske.com/articles/mkt-correlations.htm, 2 September 2001, Exhibits 15.3 and 15.4 from http://www.yeske.com/articles/international.htm, reprinted with permission of David Yeske; Exhibit 15.6(b) from 'International diversification of investment portfolios,' *American Economic*

Review, September, p. 673 (Levy, H. and Sarnat, M., 1970); Exhibit 16.4 from *Journal of Finance Economics*, Vol. 3, R. Rendleman *et al*. 'Empirical abnormalities based on unexpected earnings and the importance of risk adjustment,' p. 285, copyright 1982, with permission from Elsevier Science; Exhibits 1A.1 from http://www.euro.gov.uk/rate.html, 10 October 2000, 1A.2 from http://www.euro.gov.uk/will/time.html, 10 October 2000, © Crown Copyright 1999, 2000; Crown copyright material is reproduced with the permission of the Controller of Her Majesty's Stationary Office and the Queen's Printer for Scotland; Exhibit 10B.1 from 'Use it because it works', *Fortune*, 8 September 1997, reprinted with permission of Stern, Stewart & Co; Exhibit 1.8 from *Global Finance*, March 1999. Reprinted with permission; Exhibits 1.2 and 1.3 and graphs in 'Investment in the News' Chapters 1 and 11 from Thomson Financial Datastream; Exhibits 1.6 (a), 3.19, 3.20, 3.21, 3.22, 4.6, 4.7, 16.8 and 4B from http://ibbotson.com/news/dow.forecast.asp, http://www.ibbotson.com/research/wealth.htm and *Stocks, Bonds, Bills and Inflation® Yearbook*, © Ibbotson Associates, Inc., based on copyrighted works by Ibbotson and Sinquefield, all rights reserved, used with permission; Exhibit 1.6(b) lower figures from http://finance.yahoo.com, 2 October 2000; Exhibit 1.6(c) from http://finance.yahoo.com, 2001 (CAC data only) and Exhibit 4C.2 from http://finance.yahoo.com, 25 March 2001. CAC 40 is a registered trademark of Euronext Paris SA, which designates the index it calculates and publishes. Euronext Paris SA makes no warranty as to the figure at which the said index stands at any particular time. Reprinted with permission; Exhibit 1.9(b) from Forrester Research Inc, reprinted with permission; Exhibit 3.5(a) and (b) from www.londonstockexchange.com/join/default.asp, 27 May 2001; Exhibit 3.6 from www.wrhambrecht.com/ind/auction/openipo/completed.html, 10 February 2002, reprinted with permission of WR Hambrecht & Co; Exhibit 3.17 from www.brownco.com, 12 March 2002, reprinted with permission of Brown & Co; Exhibit 11.1 'Measuring inflation and components of the GDP and when they are reported' and Exhibit 11.4 'The actions of the Federal Reserve Bank and its influence on the economy' from *The Atlas of Economic Indicators* by W. Stansbury Carnes and Stephen D. Slifer, copyright © 1991 by HarperCollins Publishers Inc, reprinted by permission of HarperCollins Publishers Inc, Exhibit 14.3 from *The Value Line Investment Survey*, 9 January 1998, p. 5424, reprinted with permission of Value Line Publishing, Inc; Exhibit 16.7 from 'The cross section of expected returns' in *The Journal of Finance*, 47, pp. 427–65 (Fama, E.F. and French, K.R., 1992); Exhibits 9.A1, 9.A2 and 9.A3 from http://www.microsoft.com/MSFT/history.htm, copyright © 2001 Microsoft Corporation, One Microsoft Way, Redmond, Washington 98052-6300, USA, all rights reserved; Exhibit 13B.1 from the *Pocket Options Margin Guide*, reprinted with permission of The Options Clearing Corporation; AIMR for extracts from 'The stock valuation process: the analysts' view' published in *Financial Analysts Journal*, November/December 1984, copyright © 1984 by Association for Investment Management and Research, and 'Report of the Performance Presentation Standards Implementation Committee, 1991' published in *Financial Analysts Journal* 1991, copyright © 1991 by Association for Investment Management and Research. All rights reserved; *Barron's* for an extract adapted from 'Investing in the future: charging the net' by Jacqueline Doherty published in *Barron's*, 7 June 1999; Premier Magazines for an extract adapted from 'A world of investment information' by Tony Levine published in *High Life*, May 2001. We are grateful to the Financial Times Limited for permission to reproduce the article and graph on pp. 3–4, the article on pp. 197–8, the box 'Secondary yield spreads widen' on p. 215, the article and graph on pp. 305–6, the article on pp. 487–8, and the article on p. 115 from FT Investor. Exhibit 17.9 from Kanon Bloch Carré and *The New York Times*, 4 July 1999, p. 28, reprinted with permission; Exhibit 7.9 data from *The High-Yield Debt Market: Investment Performance and Economic Impact* (Altman, E.I., 1990) and Exhibit 18.6 from *Technical Analysis Explained* (Pring, M.J., 1991), copyright. The McGraw-Hill Companies, Inc; Exhibit 10.4 from http://www.quicken.com, reprinted with permission of Intuit Ltd.

Whilst every effort has been made to trace the owners of copyright material, in a few cases this has proved impossible and we take this opportunity to offer our apologies to any copyright holders whose rights we may have unwittingly infringed.

ABBREVIATIONS

ADR	American Depository Receipt		GNP	gross national product
ADS	American Depository Share		GS	gross spread
AIMR	Association for Investment Management and Research		GTC	good-till-cancelled (order)
			IM	initial margin
AM	actual margin		IPO	initial public offering
AMEX	American Stock Exchange		IRR	internal rate of return
APT	arbitrage pricing theory		IRS	Internal Revenue Service
BMV	beginning-of-period market value		IV	intrinsic value (of an option)
BSOPM	Black–Scholes option pricing model		LEH	local expectations hypothesis
BVPS	book value per share		LIBID	London Interbank Bid Rate
CAPM	capital asset pricing model		LIBOR	London Interbank Offer Rate
CAR	cumulative abnormal rate of return		LPH	liquidity preference hypothesis
CAR	cumulative average (excess) return		LSE	London Stock Exchange
CBOE	Chicago Board Options Exchange		LTCM	Long-Term Capital Management
CBOT	Chicago Board of Trade		M/B	market-to-book (value)
CD	certificate of deposit		MM	maintenance margin
CDGM	constant dividend growth model		MSH	market segmentations hypothesis
CF	cash flow		MV	market value
CME	Chicago Mercantile Exchange		MVC	mean–variance criterion
CML	capital market line		MVP	minimum variance portfolio
CP	commercial paper		NASD	National Association of Securities Dealers
CPI	consumer price index		Nasdaq	(or NASDAQ) NASD Automated Quotations
CPPS	Committee for Performance Presentation Standards (of the AIMR)			
			NAV	net asset value
CV	convertible bond		NH	not-held (order)
DCF	discounted cash flow		NL	no-load
DDM	dividend discount model		NMS	National Market System
DJI	Dow Jones index		NPV	net present value
DJIA	Dow Jones Industrial Average		NYSE	New York Stock Exchange
D/P	dividend/price (ratio), or dividend yield		OCC	Options Clearing Corporation
DPS	dividends per share		OTC	over the counter
ECB	European Central Bank		PCP	put–call parity
EMH	efficient market hypothesis		P/E	price/earnings (ratio)
EMT	efficient market theory		PHLX	Philadelphia Stock Exchange
EMU	European Monetary Union		P&L	profit and loss
EMV	end-of-period market value		PSE	Pacific Stock Exchange
E/P	earnings/price (ratio)		PV	present value
EPCoR	equal percentage contribution rule		REPO	repurchase agreement
EPS	earnings per share		ROE	return on equity
EU	European Union		SEC	Securities and Exchange Commission
EVA	economic value-added (model)		SEE	standard error of the estimate
FCF	free cash flow		SIM	single index model
FCFM	free cash flow model		SIPC	Securities Investor Protection Corporation
FCM	futures commission merchant		SML	security market line
FED	Federal Reserve Bank		S&P	Standard & Poor's (index)
FNMA	Federal National Mortgage Association		SUE	standardized unexpected earnings
FRA	forward rate agreement		T-bill	Treasury bill
FT	*Financial Times*		TSE	Tokyo Stock Exchange
FTSE	*Financial Times* Stock Exchange (index)		TV	time value (of an option)
GCAPM	general capital asset pricing model		UEH	unbiased expectations hypothesis
GDP	gross domestic product		WSJ	*Wall Street Journal*

Part I

THE MARKET ENVIRONMENT AND SECURITIES

Chapter 1

INTRODUCTION

Learning objectives

After studying this chapter you should be able to:

1 Understand that short-term and long-term interest rates, stock indices and foreign exchange rates are all related, and affect both bonds and stocks prices.

2 Understand the potential profits and losses of stocks with reference to the recent collapse of the Nasdaq index.

3 Understand the important role of the European and American capital markets in the world capital market.

4 Compare the historical average rates of return on various assets and the forecast of the average rates of return for the years 1999–2025.

5 Understand the growing role of online trading.

6 Compare and contrast corporate finance and investments.

7 Understand the difference between investments in real assets and investments in financial assets (securities).

8 State some good reasons for the study of investments.

9 Summarize the overall investment process.

INVESTMENT IN THE NEWS

Market falls are worst in decade

By Alex Skorecki in London and Gary Silverman in New York

The curtain came down yesterday on the worst year in a decade for world stock markets.

The Dow Jones Industrial Average, the leading US index, has fallen 6 per cent from its opening level of 11,497 on January 1, its worst performance in 20 years.

The total return on the Standard & Poor's 500 stocks was minus 10 per cent – the worst performance since 1977.

In Frankfurt, Germany's benchmark Xetra Dax index has been relatively resistant to decline, but is still 20 per cent off its March peak. And the high-technology Neuer Markt has fallen by about two thirds.

The Paris CAC 40 index of blue chip shares has closed at much the same level as it started 2000, despite its high exposure to technology, media and telecommunications shares (TMTs), reflecting the strength of the French economy. Nonetheless, it is about 15 per cent off its peak for the year.

In London, the FTSE 100 index closed at 6,222.5, 10 per cent lower on the year. The last time it fell more sharply was in 1990.

▶

INVESTMENT IN THE NEWS

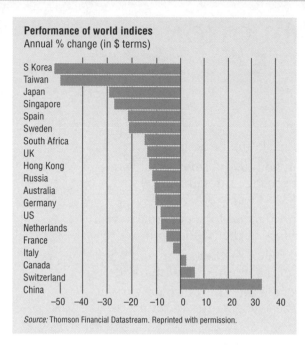

Performance of world indices
Annual % change (in $ terms)

Source: Thomson Financial Datastream. Reprinted with permission.

Tokyo's benchmark index, the Nikkei 225 average, had its worst year of the decade, falling more than 27 per cent and closing yesterday at 13,785.

It is all a far cry from the buoyant mood in which the year began, in the midst of a frenzied rush for TMT shares and wide-spread optimism about the sustaining power of the US-led economic boom.

Nasdaq, the US market dominated by high-technology shares, surged until early March, but ended the worst year in its three-decade life 39 per cent down and 51.8 per cent off its peak.

The decline has been a two-stage process, according to Theodore Varelas, equity strategist at ABN Amro in London. 'First, we had the bursting of the TMT bubble as the high equity valuations proved to be unsustainable. Then in the second half of the year we saw the US economy slowing down.'

The best performer among markets in developed economies has been Copenhagen, though it made a mere 3 per cent gain. It was followed by Zurich on 2 per cent. At the other end of the spectrum was Wellington in New Zealand, with a fall of 33 per cent.

The rise and fall was sharper in Europe than the US, with European markets packing the same order of growth into six months that US markets had seen over 18 months. Europe's telecoms companies and telecoms equipment markers, such as Nokia and Ericsson, were the focus of huge inflows of capital, pegged to the prospects for third-generation mobile phones.

The constituents of the FTSE 100 index reflected the boom-bust picture. In March nine TMT stocks, including Freeserve and Psion, were added to the blue chip index, but they and others were ejected at quarterly revisions because their market capitalisations had fallen so far.

In Asia, where markets are also driven strongly by technology and electronics shares, there was a spring surge followed by bitter disappointment. Tokyo share prices are down to the level of two years ago while Seoul has halved over 12 months. Hong Kong fared relatively well, thanks to a balance of new and old economy stocks, but is still down 12 per cent.

As the gloom deepened, investors retreated to less volatile sectors. Larry Wachtel, market analyst at Prudential Securities in New York, said: 'The areas that flourished this year were the defensive stocks like drugs, energy and utilities.'

Source: *Financial Times*, 30 December 2000, p.1. Reprinted with permission.

INVESTMENT IN THE NEWS

Exhibit 1.1(a) Equity market developments

Major indices[1]

- Standard & Poor's Composite
- Nikkei 225
- Deutscher Aktienindex (DAX)
- FTSE 100

Emerging market indices[2]

- Asia
- Latin America

Exhibit 1.1(b) International short- and long-term interest rates

Weekly averages, in percentages

Short-term rates[3]

- US dollar
- Euro[5]
- Yen
- Sterling

Long-term rates[4]

Exhibit 1.1(c) Bilateral exchange rates

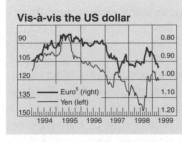

Vis-à-vis the US dollar

- Euro[5] (right)
- Yen (left)

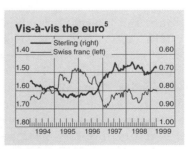

Vis-à-vis the euro[5]

- Sterling (right)
- Swiss franc (left)

[1] Weekly averages; indexed to the average for the first week of 1994.
[2] IFC indices in US dollar terms; indexed to the month-end observation for December 1993.
[3] Three-month euromarket interest rates.
[4] Yields in annual terms on the basis of 10-year benchmark government bonds.
[5] ECC before 1999.

Sources: (a) International Finance Corporation (IFC); BIS; (b) and (c) Thomson Financial Datastream; BIS.

INVESTMENT IN THE NEWS

Exhibit 1.2 Short-term interest rates in various currencies

Period average	UK	USA
1990	14.76	8.28
1991	11.51	5.98
1992	9.63	3.83
1993	5.92	3.30
1994	5.50	4.75
1995	6.70	6.04
1996	6.05	5.51
1997	6.87	5.74
1998	7.35	5.56
1999	5.44	5.41
1999		
July	5.07	5.31
August	5.15	5.45
September	5.33	5.57
October	5.94	6.18
November	5.76	6.10
December	5.95	6.13
2000		
January	6.05	6.04
February	6.14	6.10
March	6.14	6.20
April	6.19	6.31
May	6.19	6.75
June	6.11	6.79
July	6.09	6.73
August	6.13	6.69

Source: Thomson Financial Datastream. Reprinted with permission.

Exhibit 1.3 The euro vs. other currencies

Progress of the euro

Euro vs leading currencies (rebased Jan 1 199=100)

The euro tumbled to fresh life-time lows against the yen and the dollar after Gerhard Schröder the German chancellor, said he was not concerned by the currency's fall

Euro exchange rates

Dollar	0.8664
Yen	91.934
Sterling	0.6088
Swedish krona	8.3551
Danish krona	7.4571
Greek drachma	338,199
Swiss franc	1.5481

Source: Thomson Financial Datastream. Reprinted with permission.

No doubt the Internet, communications and new inventions have pushed the Western economy to new heights. For example, the Nasdaq[1] index, which is composed of many such firms and new start-ups, jumped from 1,000 points in 1999 to 5,048 points in March 2000. This large profit was almost completely wiped out when the Nasdaq index dropped from 5,048 points in March 2000 to 1,820.6 in March 2001.[2] Such a loss made many firms and individuals much less willing to spend money, which in turn raised fears of a recession in the US and in the Western world.

In the long run, investors make a substantial gain in the stock market above what they can make by investing their money in bonds, or depositing their money in the bank.

---

[1] Nasdaq Index – National Association of Securities Dealers' Automated Quotations. Nasdaq is a computerized system that provides brokers and dealers with price quotations for securities traded over the counter as well as on the New York Stock Exchange.

[2] It is interesting to notice how volatile was the Nasdaq in that period: it fell by more than 5% in one day 17 times during that year and it rose by more than 5% 15 times during the year.

However, the investment in stocks is very risky, as the *Investment in the news* article reveals. The year 2000 was one of the worst in the stock market, and this phenomenon was felt across most countries. It is interesting that China was the outlier with a positive rate of return of more than 30% in that year (see the bar chart in the article).

These fears induced the chairman of the US Federal Reserve Bank to cut the interest rate from 6.5% to 5% to jump-start the economy. In April 2001, another half per cent cut in interest rate was announced (to 4.5%), and the Nasdaq index reacted with an 8% jump in one day. The drop in interest rate continued and in August 2001 it was reduced to 3.5% (in January 2002 it was 1.75%). With this drop the stock market reacted with a decrease in prices. From these events we see that interest rates, recession and stock prices are all related factors. Also, while there is a potential large profit on these new inventions or so-called start-ups, a large loss may also show its ugly face when these start-ups do not fulfil expectations or fail completely.

The figures that follow illustrate the main issues which are important to investors and which are extensively dealt with in this book.

The following is a sample of questions raised by looking at these figures:

1 What are stock indices and what do they measure? Why do some of the indices rise and some fall? (See Exhibit 1.1(a).)
2 Why interest rates may vary across time? Why are short-term interest rates generally lower than long-term interest rates (see Exhibit 1.1(b))? Does the interest rate difference reflect risk? Expected inflation? As an investor who would like to invest in bonds, should you invest in long-term higher interest rate investments rather than short-term lower interest rate investments? We will explain in this book why such a conclusion may be wrong. Apart from interest, the bonds investor is also exposed to possible capital gains and capital losses. In addition, the short-term interest rate in the UK dropped from 14.76% in 1990 to only 6.13% in March 2001! In the US there was a decline from 8.28% in 1990 to about 1.75% in January 2002. What induced such a large drop in short-term interest rates? Why is there such a big difference in the drop in the two countries? How is this related to the rate of inflation? To currency exchange rates?
3 How can one explain the differences in interest rates across countries? Given these interest rate differences, why not borrow in Japan at almost zero interest rate and deposit the money in the UK or the US and make the interest rate difference (see Exhibit 1.1(b))?
4 Related to question 3 above, the figures given in Exhibit 1.1(c) reveal that the exchange rates are not fixed across time. Thus, borrowing in Japan and depositing the money in the UK may be risky to the British investor because the British pound may be weaker, which will eat up all the profit from the interest rate difference. Moreover, investors can also induce a money loss on such transactions. To see this, assume that the British investor borrows 100,000 yen, exchanges them to pounds and deposits the pounds in the UK. He or she may find that when converting the pounds back to yen (in order to pay back the loan), a much larger number of pounds has to be paid for the 100,000 yen; hence, a loss occurred on the transaction.

The euro is a relatively new currency. On 1 January 1999 the following European countries introduced the euro: Germany, France, Italy, Spain, Portugal, Finland, Ireland, Belgium, Luxembourg, the Netherlands and Austria. The euro thus supersedes the German mark, French franc, Italian lira, Spanish peseta, Portuguese escudo, Finnish markka, Irish punt, Belgian and Luxembourg franc, Dutch guilder and Austrian schilling. The conversion rate of each of these currencies was decided in advance (see Appendix 1A). In 2002 these European national currencies continue to exist in parallel with the euro. The timetable for the euro can be seen in Appendix 1A. In September

2000, the Danish voted for not joining the euro. The people of the UK will probably decide on this issue after 2002. Unfortunately, the euro turned out to be very weak relative to the other currencies. Exhibit 1.3 shows what happened to an investor who decided to invest in the euro in 1999. The euro fell by 15% against sterling, by about 20% against the US dollar and by more than 30% against the yen. This situation caused the European Central Bank to intervene in the market, as you can see in the press release from 22 September 2000 shown in the box.

PRESS-SERVICE 22 September 2000

The ECB announces joint intervention in the exchange markets

On the initiative of the European Central Bank, the monetary authorities of the United States and Japan joined with the European Central Bank in concerted intervention in exchange markets because of their shared concern about the potential implications of recent movements in the euro exchange rate for the world economy.

European Central Bank: Internet: http://www.ecb.int

---

5 Exhibits 1.1(a) and (b) reveal that as the long-term interest rate declines, the stock markets respond with a sharp rise, with the exception of the Nikkei index (the Japanese stock index). What is the relationship between interest rates and stock prices? It is not that simple. In January and March 2001, Mr Alan Greenspan, Chairman of the American Federal Reserve Bank, announced a decrease in the interest rate from 6% to 5%. Despite these interest cuts, the Dow Jones index dropped by 12% and the Nasdaq index dropped by 25% in the first quarter of 2001. On the other hand, in April 2001 when Greenspan surprised the market with another half per cent cut, which was announced on an earlier date than expected, the Nasdaq reacted by a jump of 8.2% on one day. We will argue that it is important to compare the *expected* interest rate changes to the actual changes. In the case of the recent cut in interest rate in the US, it is possible that investors were disappointed because they expected a larger interest rate cut.

6 How does the decline in long-term interest rates affect bond prices?

Most of this book deals with valuation of stocks, bonds and derivatives; a large portion of the book is devoted to answering questions like the six described above. For example, we see that interest rates fluctuate over time: in the US, the *long-term* interest rate fell to about 4.3% in January 1999 and jumped back to about 6.25% in August 1999[3] (not shown in the graph). Generally, when the US Federal Reserve Bank or any national bank in Europe changes the interest rate, this also affects stock and bond prices, as well as foreign exchange rates. We discuss in this book how changes in interest rates affect bond and stock prices as well as foreign exchange rates.

Nowadays, we have a global capital market with almost completely free movement of capital across countries, with a low transaction cost due to Internet trading. Thus, any macro-economic change (in inflation, interest rate, etc.) in one major country directly affects other countries' markets because investors can buy assets in most major capital markets, and by switching capital from one market to another, they affect asset prices as well as foreign exchange rates.

---

[3] In August 2000 the long-term interest rate fell to 5.92%. It continued to fall during 2001 and in January 2002 the rate was 5.46%.

There are other macro-economic factors which affect the stock and bond market. One crucial factor is the expected rate of inflation. For example, in August 1999, fears of an increase in inflation in the US forced the Federal Reserve Bank to increase the interest rate. In August 1999, data revealed that the wage per hour increased by 3.5% on an annual basis, less than the expected 3.8% rate. As a result, the fears of an inflation and interest rate hike faded out, the Dow Jones industrial index jumped by 2% and the Nasdaq index jumped by 4% in one day. Similarly, the interest rate on long-term bonds fell from 6.18% to 6.02%, and the price of the bonds jumped by 1.8% on that same day. In 2001 fears of a recession prevailed, triggering a series of interest rate cuts.

Exhibit 1.2 shows that such an effect also occurred in the UK. The Bank of England raised the interest rate in the second half of 1999 (which was about 5%) by more than 1%.

Thus, we can see that many macro-economic factors affect inflation and interest rate expectation, and hence also stock and bond prices.

The above figures are related to macro-economic factors. This does not mean that a firm's specific performance is not important for stock and bond valuation. Allocating assets between stocks and bonds and the allocation of funds to various foreign countries is greatly affected by the macro-economic factors illustrated above. However, selecting the stocks to be included in the stock portion of the portfolio is determined mainly by the firm's specific factors, e.g. expected future rate of return and risk. Thus, macro-economic factors determine the *asset allocation*, and firms' specific factors determine the *stock selectivity*, or the composition of the equity component of the portfolio. We deal in this book with both macro-economic factors as well as a firm's specific factors.

1.1   A FEW FACTS ON THE CAPITAL MARKET

First, the US market is by far the largest, and in the US the New York Stock Exchange (NYSE) is the largest. Exhibit 1.4 shows the stock market capitalization (i.e. equity) at the end of 1998. NYSE, Nasdaq and Chicago account for 62% of the world market capitalization. It is interesting that Japan accounts for only 10%; before the collapse of the Nikkei index (which in the past had reached almost 40,000 points, compared to about 10,000 points in January 2002) it had a much bigger portion of the market capitalization.

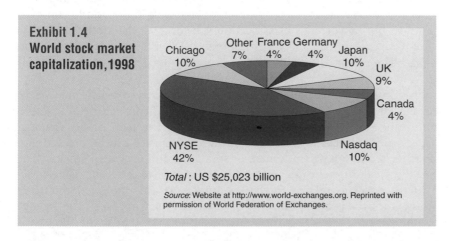

**Exhibit 1.4
World stock market
capitalization,1998**

Chicago 10%
Other 7%
France 4%
Germany 4%
Japan 10%
UK 9%
Canada 4%
Nasdaq 10%
NYSE 42%

Total : US $25,023 billion

Source: Website at http://www.world-exchanges.org. Reprinted with permission of World Federation of Exchanges.

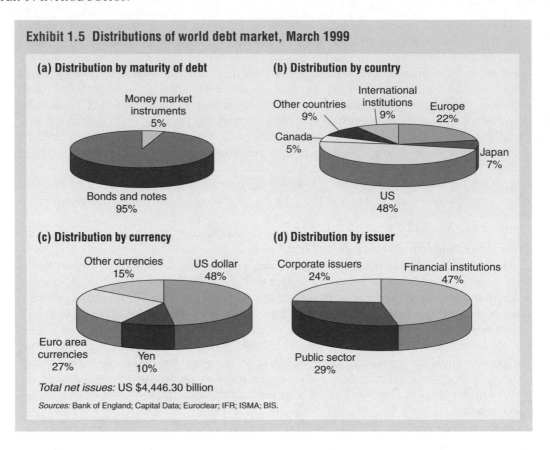

Exhibit 1.5 Distributions of world debt market, March 1999

(a) Distribution by maturity of debt

Money market instruments 5%

Bonds and notes 95%

(b) Distribution by country

International institutions 9%

Other countries 9%

Europe 22%

Canada 5%

Japan 7%

US 48%

(c) Distribution by currency

Other currencies 15%

US dollar 48%

Euro area currencies 27%

Yen 10%

(d) Distribution by issuer

Corporate issuers 24%

Financial institutions 47%

Public sector 29%

Total net issues: US $4,446.30 billion

Sources: Bank of England; Capital Data; Euroclear; IFR; ISMA; BIS.

Exhibit 1.5 reveals the stock of the various issues of the outstanding debt at the end of March 1999. Exhibit 1.5(a) distinguishes between short-term money market instruments and long-term bonds and notes. It reveals that the debt market is mainly long-term (more than one year), with bonds and notes making up about 95% of the debt market.

Exhibit 1.5(b) provides a breakdown of the debt market by countries. Here we see that Europe accounts for 22% of the outstanding debt and the US accounts for 48%. Exhibit 1.5(c) provides the breakdown of the debt by currency showing the central role that the US dollar plays in the debt market. Note that if a British firm issues bonds in London and the bonds are nominated in US dollars, then by country classification the bond belongs to the category of 'Europe' but by currency classification it belongs to the 'dollar' category. Finally, Exhibit 1.5(d) reveals that financial institutions (i.e. commercial banks) account for 47% of the outstanding debt, the public sector accounts for 29% and corporations account for 24%.

The assets described in Exhibits 1.4 and 1.5 are available for investment. The investor has to make a selection of portfolios composed of these assets. The investor can invest in bonds (which constitute a 'debt' from the point of view of the firm or government issuing the bonds) or equity (stocks). Also, each of these categories can be divided into subgroups (i.e. short-term and long-term bonds, or small cap and large cap stocks). The various assets generally yield different rates of return and also have different risk characteristics. Exhibit 1.6(a), which is related to the US market, reveals the *average* rate of return on various assets for the period 1926–1998, as well as the forecast of the average rates of return for the period 1999–2025. It is interesting to note that if the forecast is

Exhibit 1.6(a) Average rate of return for the period 1926–1998 and forecast for the period 1999–2025

	1926–1998	1999–2025
Forecast total return of small cap Stocks	12.4%	12.5%
Forecast total return of large cap Stocks	13.2%	11.6%
Forecast total return of government bonds	5.7% (long-term)	4.7%
Forecast total return of treasury bills	3.8%	4.5%
Forecast of inflation	3.2%	3.1%

Source: Website at http://www.ibbotson.com/news/dow.forecast.asp and *Stocks, Bonds, Bills and Inflation® Yearbook*, © Ibbotson Associates, Inc. Based on copyrighted works by Ibbotson and Sinquefield. All rights reserved. Used with permission.

correct, the Dow Jones index is expected to be at 120,362 points in the year 2025 (compared to about 11,000 in 1999 and 9,800 in January 2002).

Exhibit 1.6(b) shows the returns for the UK (FTSE 100), Germany (DAX) and France (CAC 40) stock indices in the last 10–15 years (up to June 2000).

Past performance as well as future forecasts have one thing in common: they are both characterized by a high average rate of return on stocks. Bonds, on the other hand, and in particular Treasury bonds, hardly beat inflation.

Does this mean that investment in stocks is better than investment in bonds? Not necessarily so. Stocks are also riskier than bonds. When you invest, say, for one year, you get the realized return for this year but you do not receive the 'average' return. Thus, you may lose a lot of money despite the reported high average returns. For example, investors around the world lost more than 20% on stock investment in October 1987 in only one day. Such losses do not generally occur with bond investment. For the investors who needed their money in October 1987, the 'average' return was not very appealing.

Up to March 1999, investing in the Nasdaq was far better than the other investment. Can we recommend investing in the Nasdaq in the future?

Exhibit 1.6(c) shows the rate of return of some major indexes against the US Nasdaq index in the period January 2001–December 2001. The crash in the Nasdaq was more severe than the crash of other indexes. Thus, a profit in one period does not necessarily indicate a success in the future. The boxed article 'Investors: Is the worst over?' (on p. 13) shows that the Internet stocks crash raised a lot of questions about the future of investment in the stock markets.

Thus, in this book we consider average returns as well as risk of the various **assets**, with the goal of constructing a portfolio of assets which generally includes stocks (for their relatively high return) as well as bonds (for their relatively high safety).

Sometimes you wish to take a position with a potentially high reward, but you do not wish to be exposed to a high risk. For example, consider an American investor who is bullish on UK stocks, and hence wishes to invest in UK stocks but does not wish to be exposed to foreign exchange currency risk. **Derivatives** can be employed to reduce this risk. In our specific example, currency options can be bought or currency swaps can be employed. Exhibit 1.7 shows the growing role of derivatives (not including stock options), increasing from a $196 billion daily turnover in 1995 to a $362 billion daily turnover in 1998.

The derivatives in the international market are very colourful with currency and interest rate swaps, interest rate and currency options, and forward agreements (FRAs), which are swap-of-cash-flows agreements that will start sometime in the future, say

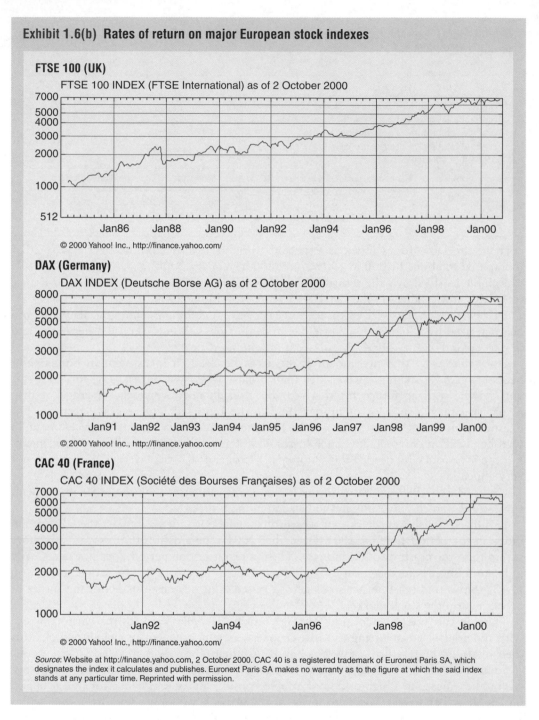

Exhibit 1.6(b) Rates of return on major European stock indexes

FTSE 100 (UK)

FTSE 100 INDEX (FTSE International) as of 2 October 2000

© 2000 Yahoo! Inc., http://finance.yahoo.com/

DAX (Germany)

DAX INDEX (Deutsche Borse AG) as of 2 October 2000

© 2000 Yahoo! Inc., http://finance.yahoo.com/

CAC 40 (France)

CAC 40 INDEX (Société des Bourses Françaises) as of 2 October 2000

© 2000 Yahoo! Inc., http://finance.yahoo.com/

Source: Website at http://finance.yahoo.com, 2 October 2000. CAC 40 is a registered trademark of Euronext Paris SA, which designates the index it calculates and publishes. Euronext Paris SA makes no warranty as to the figure at which the said index stands at any particular time. Reprinted with permission.

two years from now. Two chapters of this book are devoted to derivatives, which have nowadays become a very important investment vehicle (see Chapters 12 and 13).

The capital market is full of surprises and unexpected events. There are two basic approaches to handling these events:

(a) Trying to forecast future events, e.g. a cut in the interest rate by the Federal Reserve Bank or the National Central Bank, and capitalizing on it if the forecast is correct.
(b) Constructing a portfolio of assets to reduce risk of unforeseen future events.

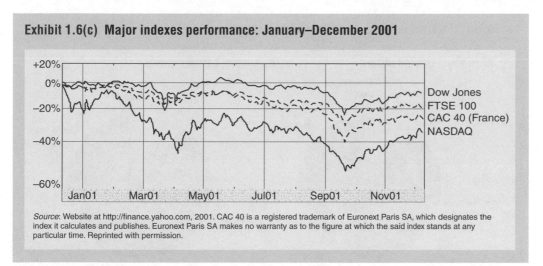

Exhibit 1.6(c) Major indexes performance: January–December 2001

Source: Website at http://finance.yahoo.com, 2001. CAC 40 is a registered trademark of Euronext Paris SA, which designates the index it calculates and publishes. Euronext Paris SA makes no warranty as to the figure at which the said index stands at any particular time. Reprinted with permission.

Investors: Is the worst over?

By Pierre Belec

NEW YORK (Reuters) – They're Wall Street's walking wounded, the masses of investors in shock after the stock market went from slow correction to freefall frenzy. Twelve months after 'The Big One' started, people are only now beginning to ask themselves 'What could I have been thinking?'

Many have lost their shirts after throwing money into 'New Economy' stocks, those technology high-flyers.

A lot of tech stocks have crashed and some have burned. Internet stocks that went through the roof two years ago are now selling for pennies a share after having their 15 minutes of fame.

The optimists say the technology-laced Nasdaq market, which has been the hardest hit, appears to have hit bottom and they think that months from now Wall Streeters will be kicking themselves for not scooping up stocks after the tumble. They say the bullish ingredients are coming together, i.e., the media have discovered that there is a bear market, which is usually a good time to start buying.

But there's the scary realization the market is still overpriced, despite its heart-stopping drop.

Source: Website at http://biz.yahoo.com/rb/010324/business_markets_stocks_dc_330.html, 25 March 2001.

Exhibit 1.8 reveals 20 unexpected events which occurred in 1998 that were totally unpredicted. Russia's default, the loss on derivatives, the **Long-Term Capital Management (LTCM)** which was near collapse, the Nikkei index sharp decline, and a negative interest on yen deposits, are only a few examples demonstrating the risk involved in investing in the capital market all over the world. Of course, if such events are forecast, the investor can be wealthy. However, given that it is hard, if not impossible, to predict such events, we teach you in this book how to protect yourself from possible negative events. For example, the Long-Term Capital Management (LTCM) near bankruptcy (due to speculation on changes in interest rates on various types of bonds) could be avoided if one would adhere to the principle of diversification: if you speculate on some change in interest rates, take into account the possibility that you may be wrong. Hence, allocate only a limited proportion of your investment to this position. This is the main idea of portfolio diversification, advocating not to 'put all your eggs in one basket'. By similar reasoning, if you invest some proportion of your assets in Japan and some in the UK or the US, the unpredicted losses in Japan may be offset by the gains from investing in other countries. Thus, international diversification may stabilize your portfolio, without necessarily reducing the average

Exhibit 1.7 Global turnover in OTC derivative instruments*

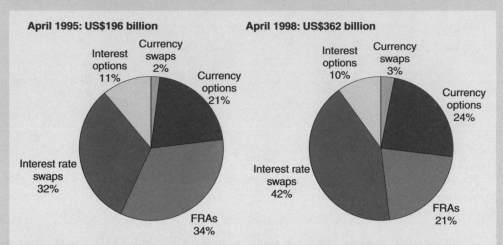

April 1995: US$196 billion

Currency swaps 2%
Interest options 11%
Currency options 21%
Interest rate swaps 32%
FRAs 34%

April 1998: US$362 billion

Interest options 10%
Currency swaps 3%
Currency options 24%
Interest rate swaps 42%
FRAs 21%

* Daily averages of notional amounts, excluding traditional foreign exchange instruments (outright forwards and foreign exchange swaps) and adjusted for local and cross-border double-counting ('net–net').

Exhibit 1.8 Twenty unexpected events of 1998

Capital Markets Risk Advisors, a New York risk management consultant, keeps an informal list of 'first-time' market events – events that risk models relying on historical data can't foresee. Normally, four or five such events occur each year. In 1998 CMRA recorded 77. Here are some that had the greatest impact on markets.

Apr 7	Citicorp and Travelers agree to a $82.9 billion merger.
May 18	Indonesia's rupiah collapses, to 17,000 to the US dollar.
Aug 17	Russia defaults on some debt; rouble collapses.
Aug 31	The Dow plunges 512.61 points, or 6.37%.
July–Sept	US banks suffer worst derivatives losses ever – $445 million.
Sept 24	Hedge fund Long Term Capital Management is bailed out to the tune of $3.6 billion.
Sept 27	Japan Leasing files for bankruptcy with $17.9 billion in liabilities – biggest financial failure since World War II.
Oct 5	30-year US treasury yield hits record 4.74% low.
Oct 7	The US dollar plunges 7.8% against the yen, largest one-day loss in 12 years.
Oct 8	China's yuan soars to an all-time high of 8.2777 to the US dollar.
Oct 9	Japan's Nikkei Index sinks to 11,542, lowest since 1984.
Oct 13	London's FTSE-100 index soars a record 214.2 points.
Nov 2	The US savings rate sinks to a miserably low 0.2%.
Nov 5	Some leading Western banks cut yen deposit rates to below zero – a negative interest rate.
Nov 11	Shares of the globe.com skyrocket more than tenfold in first day of trading.
Nov 23	7 M&A megadeals ($1 billion plus) are announced the same day.
Nov 30	US mortgage rates fall to 6.64%, lowest since 1967.
Dec 3	11 European countries cut interest rates simultaneously.
Dec 4	Exxon and Mobil announce $86.3 billion merger, largest industrial deal ever.
Dec 10	World oil prices slide below $10 a barrel, lowest since 1986.

Source: Global Finance, March 1999.

portfolio return. We devote Chapters 6 and 14 to this diversification idea, and Chapter 15 to international diversification.

1.2 ONLINE TRADING

The trading system has been through a revolution. Online trading has grown rapidly since its onset. You can sit at home in front of your computer and sell and buy stocks several times a day (hence the name day-trader). You do not need to call your broker, and after opening an account with your broker, with a push of a button you conduct a transaction. Online trading reduces transaction costs and has attracted many new investors to the stock market.

Exhibit 1.9(a) shows that the proportion of online investors increased from 1997 to 1999 with a forecast for a continuation of this growth up to 2002. For example, in 2002, there is an expectation that out of about 80 million investors, 20 million will be online investors. Exhibit 1.9(b) explains the reasons why investors choose to invest online.

In this introduction we mention the fascinating revolution that is taking place in the trading system. Chapter 3 is devoted to the various trading mechanisms employed in the capital market.

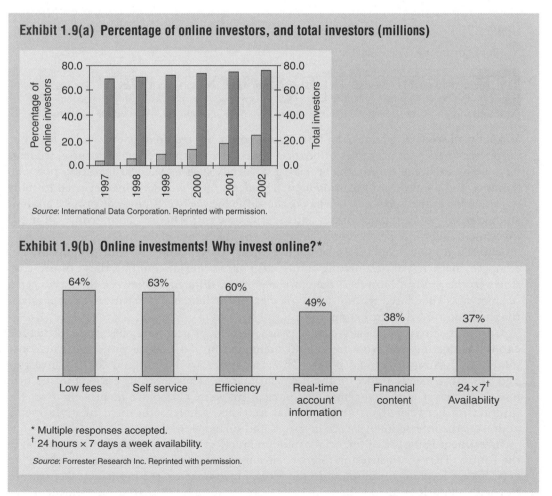

Exhibit 1.9(a) Percentage of online investors, and total investors (millions)

Source: International Data Corporation. Reprinted with permission.

Exhibit 1.9(b) Online investments! Why invest online?*

* Multiple responses accepted.
† 24 hours × 7 days a week availability.

Source: Forrester Research Inc. Reprinted with permission.

1.3 FACTORS AFFECTING ASSET PRICES

In this book we examine models for determining the value of various financial assets (for example, bonds and stocks) and show how changes in expected earnings, dividends and risk, or changes in inflation rate and in the interest rate, affect the current price of these assets.

Thus, what affects the asset's value is a firm's specific factors (earnings and risk), as well as macro-economic factors such as inflation, interest rate, etc. Generally, academics and practitioners agree on the effects of the most important economic factors on the prices of stocks and bonds. For example, almost all agree that when the Federal Reserve cuts interest rates *more than expected*, or when it announces no increase in the interest rate when such an increase is expected, the overall stock market will go up. If the Federal Reserve cuts interest rates less than expected, the overall stock market will go down. Similarly, investors routinely observe that when a firm announces greater-than-expected quarterly earnings and dividends, the stock price of the firm goes up. The only questionable issue is the extent to which such news will or should affect prices. Indeed, the valuation models presented in the following chapters attempt to evaluate both stock and bond prices and the effect of various levels of interest rates, dividends, earnings and risk on these prices.

Some of the information in this book will be familiar to readers from studies in other classes – particularly corporate finance. In the next section, we compare corporate finance and investments. We then compare investments in physical and financial assets.

1.4 THE DIFFERENCE BETWEEN CORPORATE FINANCE AND INVESTMENTS

Virtually all students who take an investments course are required to have had at least one corporate finance (or principles of finance) course. In a corporate finance course, students have some exposure to investment-related concepts, such as yield to maturity, portfolio variance and the dividend valuation model. Students often wonder why they need to study investments again. Specifically, what is the difference between physical project analysis studied in corporate finance classes and security analysis? After all, both involve an initial investment and the hope of getting the largest possible return in the future.

There are many similarities between project analysis and investment analysis. For example, both rely on estimating future cash flows and discounting these future cash flows to the present. However, there are also many differences between these two types of analysis. Therefore, specific tools are needed in financial asset investment analysis that are not needed in project analysis.

Corporate finance typically covers issues such as project analysis, capital structure, capital budgeting and working capital management. To finance projects, firms raise money by issuing stocks and bonds. These securities are bought and sold by investors and are subsequently traded in the financial market. Thus, both investors and the firm have an interest in the workings of financial markets. Corporate finance involves the interaction between firms and financial markets, whereas the field of investments addresses the interaction between investors and financial markets.

Investment is the use of financial capital in an effort to create more financial capital in the future. That is, an investor forgoes consumption today in an attempt to achieve an even higher level of consumption in the future. Investment in the **money market** (securities with maturities of less than one year) can be distinguished from investment in the

Exhibit 1.10 Examples of financial securities by market classification

Money market securities

- Treasury bills
- Commercial paper
- Negotiable certificates of deposit
- Eurodollars
- Banker's acceptance
- Repurchase agreements

Capital market securities

- Fixed-income securities: debt instruments by the European Treasury, federal agencies, municipalities, and corporations
- Equity securities: common stock and preferred stock

Derivative market securities

- Options
- Future contracts

capital market (securities with maturities greater than one year). Exhibit 1.10 provides examples of the securities in each of the three main market categories.

Some investments are **speculative**, meaning they involve a high degree of risk. However, many investors in speculative vehicles undertake strategies to **hedge** against the risk of a major loss. Hedging is a technique used to limit loss potential. Risk reduction can also be achieved by holding a portfolio of assets or by investing in derivative assets. A **portfolio** is a group of securities that are held together in an effort to achieve a maximum future consumption (or rate of return) for a given level of risk.

The primary focus of this book is on the relationship between financial markets and investors. Hence, issues related to corporate finance will be addressed only to the extent that they influence prices and perceptions of riskiness in financial markets. The basic formulas employed in both areas – corporate finance and investments – are covered. In fact, some of the same techniques used to evaluate assets in project analysis are used in financial assets analysis. Therefore, Appendix A at the end of the book reviews the basic formulas – present value, internal rate of return and so forth – that you studied in your corporate finance course. This review will serve as a bridge between the two courses and will help later, because stock and bond valuation formulas are based on present value and internal rate of return methods.

1.5 THE DIFFERENCE BETWEEN PHYSICAL AND FINANCIAL ASSETS

There are two categories of assets: **financial assets**, which are intangible, such as corporate stocks and bonds, and **physical assets**, also called **real assets** or **tangible assets**. Examples of tangible assets are precious metals, real estate and textile machines. Although financial assets are typically represented by tangible certificates of ownership, the financial asset itself is intangible. Financial assets are also called **securities**. A key distinction between financial and real (physical) assets is that real assets are income-generating assets used to produce goods or services. Financial assets, in contrast, represent claims against the income generated by real assets.

Investment in real assets differs from investment in financial assets in several ways. Investing in the capital market typically involves a commitment of money to various financial assets, such as bonds and stocks, as opposed to real assets, such as machines. The use of the term *investment* in this book is confined strictly to investments in financial assets.

Financial assets are **divisible**, i.e. you can buy a few shares of BMW on the German exchange. Physical assets are not divisible: you cannot buy some fraction of a machine. Financial assets are marketable, i.e. they can be easily bought and sold. You can sell stocks that you hold with a phone call to your broker, but it is difficult to quickly sell a physical asset, e.g. a house. **Marketability** refers to the ease with which you convert the asset into cash, while **liquidity** reflects the feasibility of converting an asset into cash quickly and without significantly affecting its price. Stocks with a large number of outstanding shares that are actively traded are very liquid. These securities are preferred by investors who trade large quantities of securities, because their trading activity will have no (or minimal) impact on the security's price. Many financial assets are very easy to buy and sell. However, most real assets are not very liquid and hence are described as illiquid. An investor who owns textile machines and who wants to sell them will generally have difficulty doing so.

Financial assets can be held for a relatively short period of time. But when investors acquire a real asset, they normally plan to hold it for a relatively long period. Buying new steel-producing machines, for example, requires large installation costs. Therefore, no-one would plan to hold these machines for a month or even just a year. However, the transaction costs of buying securities are relatively low, and investing for a month or a year may be reasonable. Thus, the planned **holding period** of securities can be much shorter than the corresponding holding period of most real assets.

Finally, there is a difference in **information availability**. There is plenty of information on financial assets, while on physical assets there is much less information. For example, suppose you enquire about buying an oil-drilling machine. Where would you get information on the value of the machine? What are the transportation and installation costs of the machine? Probably only a few people in the oil industry have the information to determine these costs. The situation is different with stocks and bonds. Anyone can open the *Financial Times* or call a broker to find out how much a share of BMW stock costs. Similarly, a person who wants to buy shares of BMW stock can obtain information (at almost no cost) on earnings, dividends and so forth. Today, almost every large firm has an Internet site, and an investor can obtain all needed information free of charge with just the push of a button. Because this information is publicly available, the impact of many published factors on the value of the financial asset can be analyzed. This type of analysis cannot be easily done with real assets.

Four factors – divisibility, marketability (also called liquidity), holding period and information availability – make investments in financial assets different from investments in real assets. Thus, we need different tools to analyze these types of investments. In particular, because of the divisibility property of financial assets, this book will focus on how to build portfolios of securities.

1.6 THE BENEFITS OF STUDYING INVESTMENTS

Studying investment can lead to a rewarding career. As the financial markets become increasingly complex, job opportunities for professional investors increase. Even though

Exhibit 1.11 Job opportunities in investments

Title	Typical firms	Description
Broker, registered representative, account executive	Brokerage firms, financial institutions	Provide sales and financial planning services
Analyst	Brokerage firms, financial institutions	Conduct research and security analysis
Financial planner	Private firms, certified public accountant (CPA) firms	Advise individual investors
Portfolio manager	Mutual fund groups, pension funds, money managers	Perform asset allocation and security selection
Asset/liability and risk manager	Insurance companies, financial institutions, banks	Perform research, actuarial work and asset allocation
Auditor	All firms	Monitor and devise internal controls
Regulator	Government agencies, exchanges	Oversee and police market activity
Surveillance	Exchanges	Oversee and monitor trading behaviour

job opportunities declined after the October 1987 stock market crash, the overall trend has been expansion. Increasingly, firms are looking for people with specialized skills. In 1999, the stock indices in the United States hit an all-time high, with the Dow Jones index passing the 11,000-point mark. This bull market increases the demand for finance majors with specialized skills. Exhibit 1.11 provides a sampling of job opportunities in the investments field, and Exhibit 1A.3 in Appendix 1A lists some job opportunities that were available at the European Central Bank.

1.7 THE INVESTMENT PROCESS

The study of investments is never completed. The investment process is dynamic and ongoing. Thus, the job of the investment analyst is never finished. However, there are always five basic components in the investment process: investor characteristics, investment vehicles, strategy development, strategy implementation and strategy monitoring.

1.7.1 Investor characteristics

Exhibit 1.12 shows the relationship of the components in the investment process. The first element in the investment process is the investor. The investor may be an individual or an institutional investor, such as a manager of an employee retirement account or bank trust department. The investor should first establish the investment policy, a written document detailing the objectives and constraints (characteristics) of the investor.

The investment policy should have specific objectives regarding the return requirement and risk tolerance. For example, the investment policy may state that the portfolio's target average return should exceed 8% and the portfolio should avoid exposure to more than

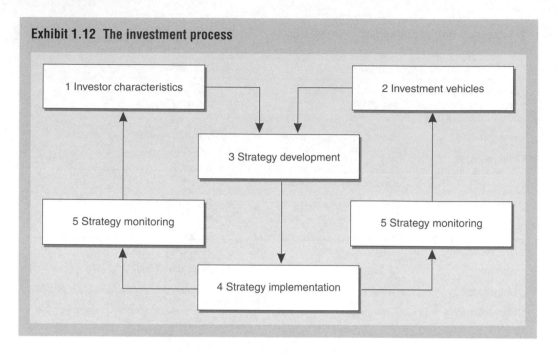

Exhibit 1.12 The investment process

10% in losses. Typically, identifying the tolerance for risk is the most important objective, because every investor would like to earn the greatest return possible. The investment policy should also state any constraints that will affect the day-to-day management of the funds. Constraints include any liquidity needs, projected time horizons, tax considerations, and legal and regulatory considerations.

1.7.2 Investment vehicles: the trade-off between risk and return

After an assessment has been made of the investor's characteristics, the available investment opportunities can be explored. Financial assets are broadly classified as money market capital market and derivative market securities.

Let us look at three categories of investment vehicles: bonds, stocks and derivative securities. Bonds are financial assets that represent a creditor relationship with an entity. They are debt instruments of a firm. Stocks represent an ownership position in a corporation. Derivative securities (also called contingent claims), such as options and futures, are tied to the performance of another security (hence the term derivative). Of the three categories, bonds are generally the least risky and also offer the lowest return. Stocks offer a higher return on average; however, they are generally riskier than bonds. Derivative securities have the highest potential risk level, as well as the highest potential return. Exhibit 1.13 describes these three major classes of investment opportunities and gives some general information about them. Of course, the information in Exhibit 1.13 is general and therefore not true for every security.

1.7.3 Strategy development

The next element in the investment process is to optimize the competing constraints of the various investment vehicles and the investor's characteristics. Investors generally

Exhibit 1.13 Summary of investment vehicles

Vehicle	Potential risks	Potential return	Marketability	Dividend and interest cash flows
Bonds	Low	Low	Low/moderate	High
Stocks	Moderate/high	Moderate/high	Usually good	Low
Derivative securities	Very high	Potentially high	Low	None

seek an investment strategy that provides the highest possible expected return within the constraints of the desired cash flow, risk level and other important variables (such as liquidity).

The precise strategy developed depends on the investor's perception of how good capital markets are at processing information. If the capital markets process information quickly and accurately, we say that the markets are efficient. An **efficient market** is one in which stock prices reflect all relevant information about the stock.

If an investor believes that the market is efficient, the investment focus will be on designing well-diversified portfolios. (The investor sees no benefit in trying to uncover mispriced securities.) However, the investor who does not believe that the markets are efficient may wish to acquire all of the latest information and attempt to buy under-priced securities and sell overpriced securities.

Chapters 6 and 14 of this book address the development of strategies when the investor believes that the market is efficient. Chapters 9, 10 and 18 address the development of strategies when the investor does not believe that the market is efficient. Most investors fall somewhere between these two extreme views. They typically believe the market is somewhat efficient, so they diversify and try to design optimal portfolios, as discussed in Chapter 6. However, investors are ever watchful for securities that may be temporarily mispriced due to some unforeseen event.

When developing a strategy, some investors like to avoid as much risk as possible. For example, investors who need money to pay tuition next year would put all their money in very safe securities, such as short-term bonds. Some investors who are not willing to miss a possible high return are willing to expose themselves to the risk and put all or most of their money in stocks or derivative securities. However, it is not necessary to go to the extreme and put all available money in one security. The investor can buy a little of each category of asset. By doing so, the investor may benefit from a relatively high return but not be exposed to a very high risk. This concept is known as asset allocation.

Asset allocation is the apportioning of an investment portfolio among various asset categories, such as cash, bonds, stocks and real estate. Asset allocation plays a key role in investment management. Securities within each asset class – for example, stocks – tend to move together over time. This co-movement is called **correlation**. Thus, asset allocation is essential, because assets in different classes do not tend to move together. This lack of co-movement helps reduce portfolio risk.

After the asset allocation decision has been made, the investor can turn to the task of individual security selection. **Security selection** is the decision-making process used to determine the specific securities within each asset class that are most suitable for a client's needs.

1.7.4 Strategy implementation

After a strategy has been developed, the asset allocation decisions are implemented and the specific securities selected. Successful implementation of the asset allocation decision is difficult in practice, because it involves changing securities in the portfolio frequently. One problem is transaction costs: changing the asset allocation decision is costly because it requires liquidating many securities.[4] These costs directly reduce the benefits expected from the allocation strategy.

A second problem is changing economic and market factors. Economies and markets are in constant flux, which changes the optimal allocation strategy. These changes result in assets either being allocated in a suboptimal fashion or incurring transaction costs induced by the need to change the asset allocation. Thus, constantly changing circumstances result in the need of investors to constantly change their asset allocations.

A third problem is changing investor objectives and constraints. Over time, the needs of an individual or fund change, requiring reallocation of assets. For example, an investor's degree of aversion to risk may change if he or she inherits a large sum of money.

An investor must also decide the best course of day-to-day strategy implementation – that is, the most cost-effective way to acquire the desired financial assets.

1.7.5 Strategy monitoring

Once the investment process has begun, it is important to periodically re-evaluate the approach. This monitoring is necessary because financial markets change, tax laws change, and other events alter stated goals. For example, in 1997, a reduction in the capital gains tax from 28% to 20% took place. How should this reduction affect an investor's asset allocation strategy? Perhaps a much better security than was previously available is created. Investors must regularly examine and question their strategy to make sure it is the best. Primarily, they need to monitor goals and objectives and review the available financial assets.

1.8 WHERE DO WE GO FROM HERE? A BRIEF OVERVIEW OF THE BOOK

This book has six parts. The remainder of Part I provides an overview of the investment environment. Chapter 2 introduces the basic securities used in the investment process: stocks, bonds and derivative securities. Chapter 3 surveys the security markets, focusing on the practical issues investors encounter when they actually implement an investment strategy.

Part II focuses on the basic components of risk and return. Chapter 4 surveys the methods used for calculating the historical rates of return, focusing on the professionally

---

[4] A recent solution to avoiding these costs is to use futures and options contracts on broad-based indices. Also, the recently implemented Internet trading sharply reduces these transaction costs.

accepted standards. Chapter 5 reviews the calculation of future rates of return and variability based on some objective or subjective probability beliefs. The chapter examines different attitudes towards risk and its influence on returns. Chapter 6 explains how one can reduce risk by holding a portfolio of various assets as well as the riskless asset.

With this background in portfolio management, Part III turns to security analysis. Chapters 7 and 8 are devoted to bonds, and Chapters 9 and 10 are devoted to stocks. Chapter 11 introduces overall market analysis, the question of whether to invest in bonds or stocks, as well as industry analysis.

Part IV covers derivative securities, with Chapter 12 devoted to forwards and futures, and Chapter 13 devoted to options. Part V of the book is devoted to the equilibrium risk–return relationship and to the gain from international diversification. Finally, Part VI discusses the concept of efficient markets (Chapter 16), mutual funds (trusts) and how to measure their performance (Chapter 17), and technical analysis (Chapter 18), i.e. to the investment methods employed by technicians and chartists who don't believe that the market is efficient.

SUMMARY

■ *Demonstrate the interrelationship between interest rates and stock prices.*
Generally, when interest rates drop, stock market indexes rise. However, the drop in interest rates is not relevant, but the drop (or the increase) relative to what investors expected will be the change.

■ *Demonstrate the relationship between various economic factors across countries.*
A low interest rate in Japan and a high interest rate in the UK does not imply that it is profitable to borrow in Japan and deposit the money in the UK. The reason is that a fluctuation (in our case of yen against sterling) may wash out such apparent profits and even induce a loss.

■ *Demonstrate the role of the various assets in the market.*
One can invest in stocks, bond derivatives, etc. Each asset has its risk–return profile. The risks are very large, and unpredictable events may occur. Diversification, or not 'putting all one's eggs in one basket', is key advice to avoid disasters such as occurred to LTCM.

■ *Demonstrate that there is no 'free lunch'.*
Stocks are, *on average*, more profitable than bonds and particularly short-term bonds, but we do not recommend buying only stocks because they are more risky – e.g. compare the Nasdaq at the end of 2000 and the beginning of 2001.

■ *Compare and contrast corporate finance and investments.*
Corporate finance typically covers project analysis, capital structure, capital budgeting, and working capital management. Corporate finance addresses the relationship between the financial markets and firms, whereas the field of investments addresses the relationship between investors and the financial markets. The investments field typically covers issues related to security analysis. It also covers issues unique to investments in securities, such as portfolio diversification and hedging.

■ *Differentiate between investments in real assets and investments in financial assets (securities).*
The differences include the divisibility of investment in securities (you can buy a small fraction of a firm); marketability (you can sell a $100,000 investment in stock with one

phone call to a broker); the investment holding period (which can be shorter for financial assets); and the more abundant information available on financial assets as compared with real assets.

■ *Summarize the overall investment process.*

The investment process consists of five components: investor characteristics, investment vehicles, strategy development, strategy implementation and strategy monitoring.

KEY TERMS

Asset	Holding period	Physical asset
Asset allocation	Information availability	Portfolio
Capital market	Investment	Real asset
Correlation	Investment policy	Security
Derivatives	Liquidity	Security selection
Divisible	Long-term capital	Speculative
Efficient market	management (LTCM)	Tangible asset
Financial asset	Marketability	
Hedge	Money market	

SELECTED REFERENCES

Ayling, David E. *The Internationalisation of Stockmarkets*. Brookfield, VT: Gower Publishing, 1986.

de Caires, Bryan, and David Simmonds, (eds). *The GT Guide to World Equity Markets 1989*. London: Euromoney Publications, 1989.

Downes, John, and Jordan Elliot Goodman. *Dictionary of Finance and Investment Terms*, 2nd edn. New York: Barron's Educational Series, 1987.

Eatwell, John, Murray Milgate, and Peter Newman (eds). *New Palgrave Dictionary of Money and Finance*. New York: W.W. Norton, 1989.

Erb, Claude B., Campbell R. Harvey, and Tadas E. Viskanta. 'Expected return and volatility in 135 countries'. *Journal of Portfolio Management*, Spring 1996, pp. 46–58.

Global Finance, 'What if Wall Street crashed?', January 2000, Vol. 14, No. 1.

Global Finance, 'What if the EMU falls apart?', January 2000, Vol. 14, No. 1.

Global Finance, 'What if emerging markets dollarized?', January 2000, Vol. 14, No. 1.

Global Finance, 'What if the Internet bubble burst?', January 2000, Vol. 14, No. 1.

Huang, Roger D., and Hans R. Stoll. *Major World Equity Markets: Current Structure and Prospects for Change*. Monograph Series in Finance and Economics, Monograph 1991–3. New York: New York University Salomon Center, 1991.

Johnson, Mark, 'The euro gets physical as the ECB prepares new coins and notes', *Global Finance*, July 2001.

Malkiel, Burton. *A Random Walk Down Wall Street*, 5th edn. New York: W.W. Norton, 1991.

Appendix 1A   # THE INTRODUCTION OF THE EURO

Exhibit 1A.1 Euro conversion rates for currencies participating in EMU

1 euro equals:	
1.95583	German marks
6.55957	French francs
1936.27	Italian lira
166.386	Spanish pesetas
200.482	Portuguese escudos
5.94573	Finnish markka
0.787564	Irish punt
40.3399	Belgian/Luxembourg francs
2.20371	Dutch guilders
13.7603	Austrian schillings

Source: Website at http://www.euro.gov.uk/rate.html, 10 October 2000. © Crown Copyright 1999. Crown copyright material is reproduced with the permission of the Controller of Her Majesty's Stationery Office and the Queen's Printer for Scotland.

Exhibit 1A.2 Timetable for countries that introduced the euro on 1 January 1999

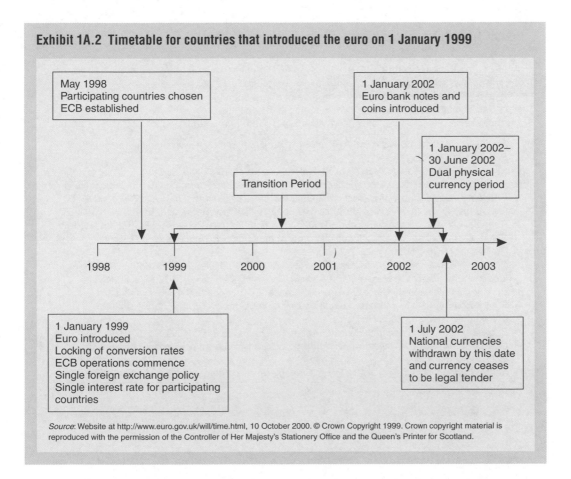

Source: Website at http://www.euro.gov.uk/will/time.html, 10 October 2000. © Crown Copyright 1999. Crown copyright material is reproduced with the permission of the Controller of Her Majesty's Stationery Office and the Queen's Printer for Scotland.

The changeover can be divided into three distinct phases:

- **Spring 1998–31 December 1998** – Phase 1 started with the decision in May by EU governments on which countries qualify to join. The European Central Bank (ECB) was then set up.
- **1 January 1999–31 December 2001: the 'transition period'** – The conversion rates between currencies of qualifying countries and the euro were legally fixed on 1 January 1999. The euro then became the legal currency in those countries. The ECB became responsible for interest rates. National currencies continued to exist in parallel to the euro, but changed in status. They are temporary 'denominations' or 'units' of the euro. No euro banknotes or coins are available, so national banknotes and coins are being used for all cash transactions.
- **1 January 2002–30 June 2002 (at the latest): the 'dual circulation period'** – Euro banknotes and coins will be introduced in participating countries on 1 January 2002. They will circulate alongside national currency banknotes and coins. By the end of the period, national banknotes and coins will be withdrawn from circulation. Old national banknotes will remain convertible into euros according to national practice.

Source: Website at http://www.euro.gov.uk/will/time.html, 10 October 2000. © Crown copyright 1999.

Exhibit 1A.3 Job opportunities at the European Central Bank

The European Central Bank (ECB), established in Frankfurt am Main on 1 June 1998, is currently recruiting staff to fill existing vacancies within the organisation.

The ECB has its own terms and conditions of employment, including a competitive salary structure, retirement plan, health insurance and relocation benefits.

Candidates must be nationals of a Member State of the European Union.

- *Senior Accounting Assistant in the Financial Reporting and Policy Division* (Reference: ECB/221/2000/II NET)
- *Economist in the Middle Office Division* (Reference: ECB/229/2000/II NET)
- *Accountants in the Financial Reporting and Policy Division* (Reference: ECB/234/2000/II NET)
- *Economist-Statistician in the Directorate General Statistics* (Reference: ECB/278/2000 NET)
- *Messenger/Driver in the Office Services and Security Division* (Reference: ECB/279/2000 NET)
- *Research Analyst in the Money and Banking Statistics Division* (Reference: ECB/280/2000 NET)
- *Senior Organisation Expert / Strategic Planner in the Organisational Planning Division* (Reference: ECB/281/2000 NET)
- *System Integrator in the IT Business Development Division* (Reference: ECB/282/2000 NET)
- *Messenger in the Office Services and Security Division* (Reference: ECB/283/2000 NET)
- *Economist in the Middle Office Division* (Reference: ECB/284/2000 NET)
- *Senior Economist in the Monetary Analysis Unit of the Monetary Policy Stance Division* (Reference: ECB/285/2000 NET)
- *Bookkeeper in the Accounting Division* (Reference: ECB/287/2000 NET)
- *German Translator in the Language Services Division* (short-term position) (Reference: ECB/288/2000 NET)
- *Senior Economist in the Monetary Policy Strategy Division* (Reference: ECB/289/00 NET)

Source: Website at European Central Bank, 2 October 2000.

Chapter 2

BONDS, STOCKS AND OTHER FINANCIAL SECURITIES

Learning objectives

After studying this chapter you should be able to:

1 Describe basic characteristics and types of bonds and stocks.
2 Explain how to read the securities quotes.
3 Compare different types of derivative securities.
4 Explain the risks involved in bond and stock investment.
5 Describe investment opportunities in international securities and mutual funds.

INVESTMENT IN THE NEWS

Treasuries lower on price data

Bond prices fell yesterday after the Labor Department reported that consumer prices posted their largest gain in 10 months in January, raising some concerns that inflation might not be as mild as many had thought.

But losses were modest as stock prices continued to slide, and analysts said inflation was not enough of a threat to keep the Federal Reserve from cutting interest rates further.

The Consumer Price Index, the benchmark gauge of inflation, rose 0.6 percent last month as energy costs soared after a gain in December of just 0.2 percent.

Inflation erodes the value of long-term securities, and 30-year bonds shed more than half a point by late afternoon. But economists maintained that the risk of a recession – not inflation – represented the greatest threat to the economy.

Of more immediate concern, traders said, slumping equity markets might be expected to stem losses by Treasuries ...

Source: *The New York Times*, Thursday 22 February 2001.

Inflation erodes the value of long-term bonds. Also stocks (the equity market) are affected by inflation. And as we see, the price of 10-year Treasury notes fell but their yield rose.

What are bonds and stocks, and how are their prices related to inflation? And why, when bond prices fall, does the yield rise?

This chapter describes the basic characteristics of bonds and stocks, describes the cash flows attached to each of these two important securities, discusses inflation, and shows why low inflation is expected to have a positive effect on bond prices and relatively high inflation has a negative effect on bond prices. This chapter also illustrates how to read the financial quotes as they appear in the financial media. We show the relationship between yield and bond prices. We discuss options in this chapter only briefly; separate chapters in Part IV (Chapters 12 and 13) discuss the valuation and management of options, and forward and futures contracts, as well as providing more detailed analyses of each.

2.1 BONDS

A **bond** is a financial contract.[1] The bond issuer, such as a corporation, will pay the bond's buyer periodic interest. Then, at the end of the specified term, the issuer pays the principal, also called the par value. In return, the bondholder pays the firm a given sum of money today. Bonds are traded in the bond market and have a market price that may change over time. A bond is a security that is basically an IOU from the issuer. It carries no corporate ownership privileges. For example, a 10-year AT&T bond gives you the right to receive periodic coupon (interest) payments and the principal (or face value) at maturity. As a bondholder, you have no voice in the affairs of the corporation. Most bonds are **fixed-rate bonds** or fixed-income securities, because the stated payments are contractual and constant over time. However, some bonds pay variable income and are referred to as **floating-rate bonds**. For example, in July 1999, Ford Unit (Ford Motor Credit Co.) launched the largest corporation bond issue in US history ($8.6 billion) at a floating rate which holds for 32 years at 140 basis points (i.e. 1.4%) over the Treasury rates. Shorter maturity bonds were issued by Ford 26 basis points (0.26%) over the three-month LIBOR (see Section 2.1.2) rate. With a floating-rate or fixed-rate bond, the issuer is obligated to pay the bondholder specified amounts of money at specified dates. As long as the maturity of the bond is not too long, and there is no risk of bankruptcy (e.g. government bonds and gilts), the risks of bonds are generally low, with correspondingly low returns. Bonds are usually less liquid than stocks and generate relatively high periodic cash flows (to the bondholders in the form of interest payments).

Bonds are interest-bearing obligations of governments or corporations. With every passing day, investors are offered new types of bonds with different characteristics. Among the newest types of bonds are century bonds, which mature in 100 years. Dresser Industries issued $200 million worth of century bonds in 1996, which will mature in 2096.[2] On 23 March 2001, the Grantite Company issued 350 million bonds nominated in sterling that will mature in January 2041. This section examines common characteristics of bonds and the most popular types of bonds traded today.

---

[1] It is common to make a distinction between bonds and fixed-income securities. Fixed-income securities include all interest-bearing securities, whereas bonds refer only to securities that are long-term.

[2] *Barron's*, 17 May 1999, p. MW54.

2.1.1 Basic characteristics of bonds

Bonds have three major identifying characteristics. First, they are typically securities issued by a corporation or governmental unit. Second, they usually pay fixed periodic interest instalments, called **coupon payments**. Also available are variable coupon payment bonds, or bonds whose coupon payment changes as market interest rates change. Third, bonds pay a lump sum at maturity that is called the **par value, face value** or **principal**.

Bonds are typically classified into two groups based on their length of time to maturity. **Money market securities** are short-term (less than 1 year) obligations (e.g. Treasury bills) and usually require a minimum of $25,000 to purchase. In contrast, **capital market securities** are long-term securities (more than 1 year) such as Treasury bonds (usually having initial maturities in excess of 10 years). The term *capital market securities* also applies to stock.

Exhibit 2.1(a) shows the cash flow characteristics of a bond in general. Exhibit 2.1(b) shows an example of cash flows from a particular bond. The downward-pointing arrows in Exhibit 2.1 depict the cash payments from the investor, and the upward-pointing arrows depict cash receipts to the investor. Hence, by investing the current market price of the bond today ($Price), there is a promised stream of cash receipts in the future, called coupon payments ($C), and principal payment (or par value, $Par).

The bond price today is the present value of its future coupons and par value. Note that if inflation increases the discount rate will increase and the present value of the future cash flows ($C and $Par) will decrease, thus decreasing the price of the bond. The

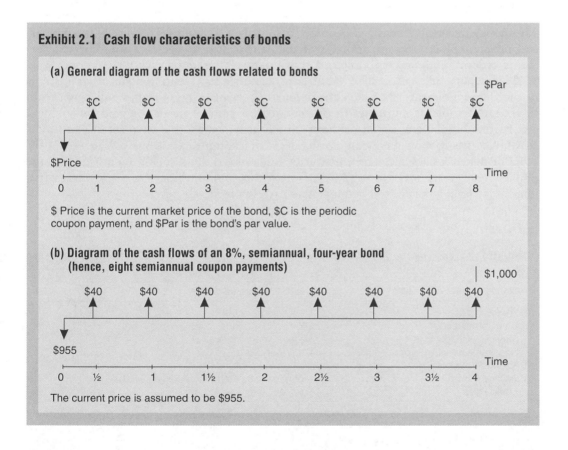

Exhibit 2.1 Cash flow characteristics of bonds

(a) General diagram of the cash flows related to bonds

$ Price is the current market price of the bond, $C is the periodic coupon payment, and $Par is the bond's par value.

(b) Diagram of the cash flows of an 8%, semiannual, four-year bond (hence, eight semiannual coupon payments)

The current price is assumed to be $955.

opposite holds when the interest rate decreases. For example, on 23 March 2001, the bonds of IBM with $8^3/_8\%$ interest (coupon) and maturity in 2013 were traded at $\$115^1/_2$ while the par value is only $100. Due to a decrease in the interest rates, the discount rate decreases and the present value of future cash flows on IBM's bonds increases, which explains the gap between the market value and par value of these bonds. Thus, bond prices are sensitive to interest rate changes. The larger the change in the interest rate, the larger the potential losses or gains. However, as the *Investment in the news* article reveals, stocks are also sensitive to changes in rates induced by interest changes.

The advantages of bonds to an investor relative to stocks are that they are good sources of current income, at least for short-term bonds, and their investment is relatively safe from large losses (unless, of course, the bonds have a large risk of default by the issuing company). Another advantage is that bondholders receive their payments before shareholders can be compensated. A major disadvantage of bonds relative to stocks is that the potential profit is limited.

2.1.2 Types of bonds

Several types of bonds are available to investors, including short term and long term, high risk and low risk, and taxable and nontaxable. Exhibit 2.2 lists the different types of bonds, classified by whether they are money market securities or capital market securities. The following section provides a brief description of various types of bonds.

■ Money market securities

The money market includes a wide range of securities, including Treasury bills, commercial paper, bankers' acceptances, negotiable certificates of deposit, repurchase agreements, federal funds and eurodollars. Let us briefly elaborate on each type of bond.

US Treasury bills (also called **T-bills**) are securities representing financial obligations of the US government. They have the unique feature of being issued at a discount from their stated value at maturity. In other words, a sum of money is paid today for a greater fixed dollar amount in the future at maturity; usually the payment at maturity is $100,000 (no coupon payments are made). For example, Treasury bills may sell for $98,000 when issued and have a maturity value of $100,000 in six months. Thus, the dollar return to the investor is $2,000. During this six-month period, the investor earns interest, although the interest is not paid in cash but is merely accrued.

Exhibit 2.2 Types of bonds

Money market securities	Capital market securities
Treasury bills	US Treasury notes
Commercial paper	US Treasury bonds
Bankers' acceptances	Federal agency bonds
Negotiable certificates of deposit	Municipal bonds
Repurchase agreements	Corporate bonds
Federal funds	Mortgages and mortgage-backed securities
Eurodollars	

Exhibit 2.3(a) US Treasury bills

Maturity		Days to Mat.	Bid	Asked	Fri. Chg.	Ask Yld.
Jul	05 '01	3	3.07	2.99	− 0.19	3.03
Jul	12 '01	10	3.38	3.30	+ 0.02	3.35
Jul	19 '01	17	3.41	3.33	−	3.38
Jul	26 '01	24	3.38	3.30	− 0.03	3.35
Aug	02 '01	31	3.41	3.37	+ 0.03	3.43
Aug	09 '01	38	3.44	3.40	+ 0.01	3.46
Aug	16 '01	45	3.46	3.42	−	3.48
Aug	23 '01	52	3.50	3.46	− 0.04	3.53
Aug	30 '01	59	3.53	3.49	− 0.03	3.56
Sep	06 '01	66	3.58	3.56	+ 0.02	3.63
Sep	13 '01	73	3.57	3.55	+ 0.02	3.63
Sep	20 '01	80	3.57	3.55	+ 0.02	3.63
Sep	27 '01	87	3.57	3.56	+ 0.02	3.64
Oct	04 '01	94	3.57	3.55	+ 0.03	3.63
Oct	04 '01	94	3.57	3.56	+ 0.03	3.64
Oct	11 '01	101	3.56	3.54	+ 0.02	3.63
Oct	18 '01	108	3.56	3.54	+ 0.02	3.63
Oct	25 '01	115	3.56	3.54	+ 0.02	3.63
Nov	01 '01	122	3.55	3.53	+ 0.01	3.62
Nov	08 '01	129	3.53	3.51	− 0.01	3.60
Nov	15 '01	136	3.53	3.51	−	3.61
Nov	23 '01	144	3.53	3.51	−	3.61
Nov	29 '01	150	3.54	3.52	−	3.62
Dec	06 '01	157	3.53	3.51	−	3.61
Dec	13 '01	164	3.52	3.50	− 0.01	3.61
Dec	20 '01	171	3.51	3.49	− 0.03	3.60
Dec	27 '01	178	3.52	3.51	−	3.62
Jan	02 '02	184	3.53	3.52	+ 0.02	3.63
Feb	28 '02	241	3.51	3.50	+ 0.04	3.62

Source: *Barron's*, 2 July 2001, p. 29. Barron's Online by *Barron's*. © 2001 by Dow Jones & Co., Inc. Reproduced with permission of Dow Jones & Co., Inc. in the format *Fundamentals of Investments* via Copyright Clearance Center.

Treasury bills have maturities of less than one year. T-bills are issued on an auction basis. The US Treasury accepts competitive bids and allocates bills to those offering the highest prices. Noncompetitive bids are also accepted. A noncompetitive bid is an offer to purchase the bills at a price that equals the average of the competitive bids. The yields on T-bills are closely watched in the money market for signs of interest rate trends. Many floating rate loans have interest rates tied to the yield on T-bills. By the end of 1998, the short-term Treasury securities market exceeded $370 billion.[3]

Gilts are bonds issued by the British government and are equivalent to the Treasury securities in the US in that they are perceived to have no risk or default.

Exhibit 2.3(a) shows recent quotes for US Treasury bills. The first two columns give the maturity date and the number of days left to maturity. Next, the bid and asked discount rates are given, followed by the change from the previous day. Note that the bid and ask discount rates, as well as the yield (see Ask Yld.), are on an annual basis. The **bid rate** is the discount rate at which you, the investor, can sell a T-bill. The **asked rate** is the discount rate at which you can buy it from a dealer. The higher the discount

---

[3] *Economic Report of the President* (Washington, DC: US Government Printing Office, 1999), p. 398.

Exhibit 2.3(b) London Stock Exchange benchmark government bonds   FT

Mar 23	Red Date	Coupon	Bid Price	Bid Yield	Day chg yield	Wk chg yield	Month chg yld	Year chg yld
Australia	10/02	10.000	107.9219	4.62	+ 0.10	+ 0.15	− 0.26	− 1.65
	06/11	5.750	105.0780	5.10	−	+ 0.01	− 0.29	− 1.32
Austria	05/02	4.625	100.2500	4.39	+ 0.02	− 0.05	− 0.36	− 0.16
	01/10	5.500	104.1100	4.91	+ 0.02	− 0.05	− 0.24	− 0.55
Belgium	06/02	8.750	105.2900	4.25	+ 0.02	− 0.12	− 0.37	− 0.35
	09/10	5.750	105.7400	4.97	+ 0.01	− 0.06	− 0.23	− 0.51
Canada	12/02	6.000	102.4000	4.49	+ 0.08	− 0.04	− 0.43	− 1.47
	06/10	5.500	101.9900	5.22	+ 0.08	+ 0.03	− 0.25	− 0.67
Denmark	11/02	6.000	101.9500	4.71	+ 0.02	− 0.08	− 0.31	− 0.19
	11/09	6.000	107.6700	4.88	+ 0.03	− 0.03	− 0.25	− 0.67
Finland	09/01	10.000	102.4500	4.37	+ 0.03	− 0.16	− 0.28	+ 0.06
	02/11	5.750	106.7400	4.87	+ 0.02	− 0.05	− 0.21	− 0.53
France	07/03	4.500	100.6000	4.21	+ 0.05	− 0.11	− 0.37	− 0.22
	01/06	5.000	102.7350	4.35	+ 0.03	− 0.09	− 0.33	− 0.75
	10/10	5.500	105.5000	4.77	+ 0.02	− 0.04	− 0.23	− 0.54
	04/29	5.500	102.3600	5.34	−	− 0.07	− 0.14	− 0.28
Germany	09/02	5.000	101.1300	4.17	+ 0.02	− 0.15	− 0.36	− 0.23
	08/05	5.000	102.8896	4.26	+ 0.02	− 0.11	− 0.35	− 0.86
	01/11	5.250	104.8000	4.63	+ 0.03	− 0.05	− 0.23	− 0.57
	01/31	5.500	103.7599	5.25	−	− 0.06	− 0.12	− 0.28
Greece	02/03	5.900	102.7200	4.34	− 0.04	− 0.14	− 0.40	− 1.87
	05/10	6.000	105.7000	5.20	+ 0.01	− 0.04	− 0.20	− 0.94
Ireland	10/02	2.750	97.7300	4.27	+ 0.01	− 0.12	− 0.35	− 0.21
	04/10	4.000	93.8781	4.85	+ 0.01	− 0.05	− 0.22	− 0.58
Italy	01/03	4.500	100.4300	4.25	+ 0.03	− 0.13	− 0.39	− 0.30
	12/05	5.250	103.0500	4.52	+ 0.02	− 0.12	− 0.33	− 0.55
	11/10	5.500	103.8500	4.99	+ 0.01	− 0.07	− 0.21	− 0.43
	05/31	6.000	104.8000	5.67	+ 0.01	− 0.05	− 0.10	− 0.10
Japan	12/02	4.800	108.1500	0.07	+ 0.02	−	− 0.16	− 0.27
	03/06	3.100	112.6380	0.52	+ 0.07	+ 0.05	− 0.22	− 0.71
	12/10	1.800	106.4204	1.10	+ 0.07	−	− 0.29	− 0.70
	12/20	2.500	116.0200	1.55	+ 0.07	− 0.01	− 0.33	− 0.74
Netherlands	02/03	4.750	100.9100	4.23	+ 0.03	− 0.13	− 0.39	− 0.23
	07/10	5.500	105.4818	4.75	+ 0.01	− 0.06	− 0.23	− 0.62
New Zealand	03/02	10.000	104.0620	5.59	+ 0.08	+ 0.11	− 0.28	− 1.26
	11/11	6.000	100.0680	5.99	+ 0.03	+ 0.14	− 0.12	− 0.94
Norway	10/02	9.500	103.7500	6.88	−	− 0.12	+ 0.07	+ 0.51
	05/09	5.500	96.9500	5.98	−	− 0.07	− 0.08	− 0.06
Portugal	04/03	4.812	101.0000	4.29	+ 0.02	− 0.16	− 0.41	− 0.21
	05/10	5.850	106.1000	5.00	−	− 0.06	− 0.23	− 0.50
Spain	01/03	3.000	97.8600	4.23	+ 0.02	− 0.14	− 0.39	− 0.39
	07/11	5.400	101.5800	4.98	+ 0.02	− 0.06	− 0.22	− 0.45
Sweden	04/02	5.500	101.6071	3.88	+ 0.02	− 0.08	− 0.26	− 1.11
	03/11	5.250	104.4930	4.67	+ 0.02	− 0.05	− 0.26	− 0.07
Switzerland	07/02	4.500	101.8500	2.99	− 0.05	− 0.10	− 0.28	− 0.43
	08/10	3.500	102.5000	3.19	+ 0.04	− 0.05	− 0.28	− 0.76
UK	06/02	7.000	102.4300	4.88	+ 0.03	− 0.08	− 0.34	− 1.43
	12/05	8.500	115.5600	4.76	+ 0.03	− 0.07	− 0.40	− 1.15
	12/09	5.750	107.5500	4.68	+ 0.05	+ 0.02	− 0.31	− 0.53
	06/32	4.250	97.5600	4.39	+ 0.02	+ 0.05	− 0.07	−
US	11/02	5.625	102.1242	4.29	+ 0.08	− 0.03	− 0.38	− 2.22
	11/05	5.750	105.2578	4.48	+ 0.10	−	− 0.43	− 1.92
	08/10	5.750	106.2699	4.91	+ 0.09	+ 0.03	− 0.35	− 1.18
	05/30	6.250	112.3750	5.40	+ 0.05	+ 0.02	− 0.24	− 0.51

Source: *Financial Times*, 26 March 2001, p. 30. Reprinted with permission.

rate, the lower the price. The difference between the bid and asked rates is called the bid-asked spread. The bid discount rates exceed asked discount rates, because dealers are willing to sell only at prices higher than they are willing to buy. The final column gives the internal rate of return of the asked price of the T-bill.

Exhibit 2.3(b) lists the government bonds traded at the London Stock Exchange.

Another type of money market security is **commercial paper**, which is a vehicle of short-term borrowing by large corporations. Large, well-established corporations have found that borrowing directly from investors via commercial paper is cheaper than relying solely on bank loans. The lenders are generally investors with temporarily idle cash. Commercial paper is unsecured notes of corporations, usually issued at a discount. *Unsecured* means that these loans are not backed by specific assets. That is, the only thing backing the loans is the 'full faith and credit' of the firm. Commercial paper is issued either directly from the firm to the investor or through an intermediary.

Issuers of commercial paper are typically corporations that have a high credit rating. However, other firms can use the commercial paper market if they 'enhance' the credit quality of the commercial paper. Firms can enhance their credit by purchasing a guarantee from another, more well-established firm or by pledging collateral of quality assets with the issue.

Commercial paper is riskier than Treasury bills, because there is a greater risk of default by a corporation. (There is virtually zero probability of default by the federal government.) Also, commercial paper is not easily bought and sold after it is issued, because most investors in commercial paper hold it until maturity. The majority of investors in this market are institutions such as money market mutual funds and pension funds. By the end of September 1998, the commercial paper market in the United States exceeded $715 billion.[4]

Bankers' acceptances are short-term obligations that are based on a customer's request to pay a supplier at a future date. Bankers' acceptances arise from the financial needs of corporations engaged mainly in international commerce. The supplier desires immediate payment, and the customer desires to pay once the goods are delivered and inspected. A bankers' acceptance allows both the supplier's and the customer's desires to be achieved, but not without cost.

To demonstrate how a firm and its customer use bankers' acceptances, suppose a US firm ships a 3-ton engine to a UK firm, and delivery takes two months. The US firm would like payment from the sale today, and the UK firm wants to wait until the engine is delivered. Neither the US firm's bank nor the UK firm's bank wants to provide the capital for this loan. The Swiss firm's bank provides the UK firm with a short-term loan. The bank pays the US firm a discounted amount now. The UK bank (which will be paid by the UK firm in two months) could then sell this short-term loan contract to an outside party, recouping its initial outlay. This short-term loan contract, called a banker's acceptance, will typically have a higher interest rate than similar money market securities, making it attractive to investors. Because of its complexity, the market for bankers' acceptances does not have active trading of its securities. Its market, which is much smaller than that for commercial paper, was only about $14 billion in October 1998.[5]

Negotiable certificates of deposit (CDs) are debt instruments issued by banks and usually pay interest. Most CDs cannot be traded, and they incur penalties for early withdrawal. To accommodate large money market investors, financial institutions allow

[4] *Economic Report of the President*, p. 379.
[5] *Ibid.*

their large-denomination CD deposits to be traded as negotiable CDs. Negotiable CDs can be as small as $100,000, but tend to trade in increments of $5 million. The maturity ranges from a few weeks to several years. The largest investors in this market are money market mutual funds and investment companies. By the end of 1998, the large-denomination CD market was approximately $624 billion.[6]

The repurchase agreements (repos) market affords additional liquidity to the money market. Firms are able to raise additional capital by selling securities held in inventory to another institution with an agreement to buy them back at a specified higher price at a specified time. The securities are usually government securities. In effect, a repurchase agreement is a short-term loan. Because of concerns about default risk, the length of maturity of a repurchase agreement is usually very short. Typically, repos are used for overnight borrowing needs.

As an example of how repos work, suppose that for cash management purposes, Ford Motor Corporation holds $4 million in three-month US Treasury bills yielding 5%. Now Ford has an immediate need for $4 million so it can purchase a specialized piece of equipment being offered at a bankruptcy liquidation. Ford's cash manager also knows that in a week, Ford will receive a $4 million payment for auto sales in Canada. What can Ford do?

One solution would be to take a bank loan at, say, 11%. Ford could also sell the T-bills and buy them back in one week. Ford would incur two transaction costs when the bills had to be repurchased. In addition, there would be a price risk in this transaction: the price of the T-bills could rise in a week. Alternatively, Ford could enter into a repurchase agreement using its T-bills. Ford could sell the T-bills to an outside firm with a guarantee to buy them back in two weeks at a specified price. From the difference between the sale price and the purchase price, an implied interest rate, known as the *repo rate*, can be computed. Obviously, Ford should employ the transaction that is the cheapest after all transaction costs are considered.

There are many variations in the design of repurchase agreements. A term repo has a longer holding period. A reverse repo is the opposite of a repo. In this transaction, a corporation buys the securities with an agreement to sell them at a specified price and time. The repo market was about $283 billion at the end of 1998.[7]

The firm that holds short-term financial assets and, in particular, bank deposits can invest in the repo market. The firm can make more money than it can earn in deposit accounts, and with a lower risk. How is this possible? Security dealers who need to borrow money are not allowed to enter the deposit market. Therefore, they are willing to pay a firm that lends them money in a repo agreement at a relatively high interest rate. In addition, a firm that lends money to dealers holds the securities as collateral, whereas the deposits in the bank are uninsured. Thus, a higher return and a lower risk on the firm's money is obtained compared with a bank deposit. For example, by investing in repos, Dupont/Canoco reports an annual income increase of $2 million.

The federal funds market helps banks place reserves on deposit at the Federal Reserve Bank. Banks that do not have sufficient funds on reserve can borrow from other banks that have excess reserves. Most of this borrowing is for one day, although some agreements are for as long as six months.

Finally, eurodollars are US dollar deposits held outside the United States. These deposits are not subject to the same regulations as bank deposits held within the United

---

[6] *Ibid.*
[7] *Ibid.*

Exhibit 2.4 Money rates (%)

	US	UK
Discount rate	1.25	3.75
Prime rate	4.75	4.00
T-bills rate (3-month)	1.68	$3^{29}/_{32}$
CDs rate (6 months)	1.87	$4^{1}/_{32}$
Commercial paper rate (3 months)	1.71	$4^{1}/_{8}$
LIBOR rate (6 months)	1.92	4.10875

Sources: *Wall Street Journal Europe*, 24 January 2002, p. 21, and *Financial Times*, 25 January 2002, p. 23.

States. Hence, the interest rate offered on eurodollar deposits is typically different from the rate offered in the United States. The interest rate quoted for these deposits between major banks is referred to as the LIBOR, or London Interbank Offer Rate. It is the rate that one bank asks from another bank for borrowing. London is the main trading centre for eurodollars. The LIBID, or London Interbank Bid Rate, is the rate at which major banks will offer eurodollars as deposits to other banks. The interest on loans is sometimes linked to the LIBOR. Quotes such as 'LIBOR +1%' or 'LIBOR +2%' are very common, where the riskier the borrower, the higher the increase in the interest rate above the LIBOR.

Exhibit 2.4 provides the various short-term interest rates in the US and UK. The differences between the rates reflect the risk difference as well as market imperfection; namely, the bank lends at a higher rate than it borrows in order to earn money.

The **discount rate** is the interest rate the Federal Reserve charges member banks for loans (with collateral usually in the form of government securities). This is the lowest interest rate on the floor, since banks set their loan rate a notch above the discount rate. When the Federal Reserve changes the discount rate, the other market rates adjust in the same direction. The **prime rate** is the interest rate banks charge their most creditworthy customers. Thus, for less creditworthy customers, the interest rate is high, e.g. prime + 2%, prime + 3%, etc. When the banks borrow from customers by selling CDs, they pay the investors in the CDs only 1.87%, and the difference between the prime rate and the CDs rate accounts for the banks' costs and profit. Individuals who buy stocks on margin borrow part of their investment from their brokers. The broker loan call rate is the rate at which the brokers borrow from banks to finance these loans to the customers. Because these loans are callable by the banks on a 24-hour notice, they are called call rates.

■ Capital market securities

Like T-bills, **US Treasury notes** and **US Treasury bonds** are government securities used to finance the government debt. In contrast to T-bills, which have maturities of less than 1 year, US Treasury notes and bonds have maturities greater than 1 year at the time they are issued. They pay stated coupon amounts semiannually and are exempt from state and local taxes. When first issued, *notes have maturities of 2 to 10 years, and bonds have maturities of more than 10 years*. The minimum denomination is $1,000.

Exhibit 2.5 illustrates Treasury bond and Treasury note quotes. The bid price of the August 2001 bond is quoted as 100:14, which means $100\frac{14}{32}$ of par value. (Recall that par value is the lump sum paid at maturity.) If par is $1,000 (which is standard), then

Exhibit 2.5 US notes and bonds

Rate	Mo/Yr	Bid	Asked	Fri. Chg	Ask Yld.
$5^1/_2$	Jul 01n	100:04	100:06	...	3.08
$6^5/_8$	Jul 01n	100:07	100:09	...	3.02
$7^7/_8$	Aug 01n	100:16	100:18	...	3.14
$13^3/_8$	Aug 01	101:06	101:08	−1	2.91
$5^1/_2$	Aug 01n	100:08	100:10	...	3.51
$6^1/_2$	**Aug 01n**	**100:14**	**100:16**	**...**	**3.34**
$5^5/_8$	Sep 01n	100:14	100:16	...	3.52
$6^3/_8$	Sep 01n	100:19	100:21	−1	3.62
$5^7/_8$	Oct 01n	100:21	100:23	−1	3.63
$6^1/_4$	Oct 01n	100:25	100:27	−1	3.61
$7^1/_2$	Nov 01n	101:12	101:14	...	3.53
$15^3/_4$	Nov 01	104:13	104:15	−1	3.43
$5^7/_8$	Nov 01n	100:27	100:29	−1	3.63
$6^1/_8$	Dec 01n	101:05	101:07	...	3.62
$6^1/_4$	Jan 02n	101:13	101:15	...	3.66
$6^3/_8$	Jan 02n	101:15	101:17	−1	3.68
$5^1/_2$	May 09n	100:30	101:00	−12	5.34
$9^1/_8$	May 04–09	111:19	111:23	−7	4.71
6	Aug 09n	104:01	104:03	−13	5.37
$10^3/_8$	**Nov 04–09**	**116:23**	**116:27**	**−14**	**4.89**
$4^1/_4$	Jan 10i	105:29	105:30	−18	3.44
$6^1/_2$	Feb 10n	107:15	107:17	−13	5.40
$11^3/_4$	Feb 05–10	122:14	122:20	−9	4.86
10	May 05–10	117:10	117:14	−13	4.99
$5^3/_4$	Aug 10n	102:15	102:16	−11	5.40
$12^3/_4$	Nov 05–10	129:29	130:03	−15	4.99

Source: Barron's, 2 July 2001, p. MW47. Barron's Online by *Barron's*. © 2001 by Dow Jones & Co., Inc. Reproduced with permission of Dow Jones & Co., Inc. in the format *Fundamentals of Investments* via Copyright Clearance Center.

this quote results in a price of \$1,004.3 because $\frac{14}{32} = 0.43$. Thus, the price is 100.43% of par when 100 is the par. Because the par value is \$1,000, if we buy the bond we pay $(100.43/100) \times \$1,000 = 1,004.3$ today and get only \$1,000 in the future. We do not lose money, because we also receive coupon payments every semiannual period up to the maturity date. Note, however, that the price of bonds as quoted in the financial media is not equal to the cash flow the investor has to pay for the bond. The investor also has to pay the accrued interest because bond prices are quoted without the accrued interest. Accrued interest is found by multiplying the fraction of the semiannual coupon period that has elapsed by the coupon payment. For example, if 142 days have elapsed since the last coupon has been paid and the semiannual coupon is worth \$45, one has to add to the quoted price of a bond $(142/184) \times \$45 = \$34.73$, where 184 days represent half a year. Investors sometimes neglect the fact that the bond is worth more than the quoted price, and hence may lose money in financial deals. The following story taken from *Barron's* illustrates such an error made by investors:

'...For example, a group known as KN Financial tendered for the bonds of May Department Stores. The group offered to pay 104.75, according to one person who had seen the offering documents. And at first glance, such a bid doesn't seem bad, considering that the bonds were trading around 104.375.

It's only by reading the fine print that investors would realize that they're getting less than meets the eye. KN's offer includes accrued interest. But the bonds are quoted in the market without accrued interest, as is the convention.

And wouldn't you know, an interest payment is due in just a few weeks. With that accrued interest added in, a fair value for the bond would be closer to 108. All of which means KN financial would be able to turn a quick $40 profit (per $1,000) on any tendered bond, with very little risk ....'

(See 'The return of mini-tenders at micro prices: Just for Feet's bondholders feel down at the heel', by Jacqueline Doherty, *Barron's*, 31 May 1999, p. MW17.)

Thus, when you buy or sell bonds, always remember that the accrued interest should be added.

A **callable bond** can be bought back by the issuing entity at a stated price in the future. The notation 04–09 for the November $10^3/_8$ bond in Exhibit 2.5 means that the bond is first callable in 2004 (i.e. 04) and, if not called, it matures in November 2009. The Change (Chg) column is in 32nds. Hence, the bond decreases $^{14}/_{32}$ from the previous day.

The US government also issues also *Inflation Indexed Treasury Securities*. The coupons and the principal (the par value) are linked to the cost of living index. For example, on 2 July 2001, *Barron's* reports that this linked bond which matures on 29 April had a yield of 3.875%. This means that this is the real annual rate of return the investor will get. No wonder, then, that the yield is relatively low, because with inflation of 2–3% per year the nominal yield will be about 6–7%.

The Federal National Mortgage Association (FNMA – pronounced 'Fannie Mae') issues **federal agency bonds**. Publicly owned and sponsored by the government, it was chartered in 1938 to purchase mortgages from lenders and resell them to investors. They are usually in $100,000 denominations.

Agency securities differ from Treasury securities. Agency securities are issued by federal government-sponsored corporations, such as the Federal Home Loan Banks, and not directly from the US government. Agency securities are perceived to be slightly more risky than Treasuries from a default risk viewpoint. The US government may not be as likely to come to the rescue of an agency as it would be for securities issued by the US Treasury.

State and local governments issue **municipal bonds** to finance highways, water systems, schools and other capital projects. There are two basic types of municipal bonds: general obligation bonds and revenue bonds. **General obligation bonds** are backed by the full faith and power of the municipality. **Revenue bonds** are backed by the income generated from a specific project, such as a toll bridge. The income from these bonds is exempt from federal, state and local taxes if the investor lives in that locality, but the income is subject to state and local taxes if the investor does not live in the locality issuing the bonds. Because investors are interested in after-tax returns, we would not anticipate the yields to be as high as those from their fully taxable counterparts. Everything else being equal, investors would prefer a tax-free bond.

Corporate bonds are issued to finance investment in new plant equipment (real assets). These bonds usually have a par or face value of $1,000. Corporate bonds vary in their riskiness and their returns to investors. Some highly rated bonds are very safe but pay low interest. **Junk bonds**, in contrast, are very risky and thus pay much higher interest. For such bonds, there is a higher risk that the firm will go bankrupt and the investor will lose the entire investment – hence the name junk bonds.

Some bonds do not pay any interest and are called **zero-coupon bonds**. For example, Alza Zr 14 is a bond which does not have any coupons. Thus, this bond matures in

Exhibit 2.6 Corporate bond quotes

52-Wk High	52-Wk Low	Name and Coupon	Cor yld	Sales	Weekly High	Weekly Low	Last	Net Chg
101	88⅞	AES Cp 8s8	8.2	540	98⅛	96	98	−1⅝
109	100	AMR 9s16	8.7	107	107½	103⅝	103⅝	−⅜
101³¹/₃₂	98⅛	ATT 7⅛02	7.1	128	101	100⅝	100⅝	−1/32
103⅛	97¼	ATT 6½02	6.4	83	102⅛	101⅛	101½	−¾
103⅛	96½	ATT 6¾04	6.6	165	102⅝	101⅝	102⅛	+¼
100¾	93⅜	ATT 5⅝04	5.6	386	100¾	99½	99⅞	−¾
104	96⅝	ATT 7s05	6.8	116	103⅞	103½	103¾	+⅛
106⅞	97½	ATT 7½06	7.2	42	105	103¼	104½	−½
106⅞	99⅛	ATT 7¾07	7.4	442	106⅛	105	105¼	−¼
95½	86½	ATT 6s09	6.4	761	95¼	93½	93½	−1⅜
103	91⅝	ATT 8⅛22	8.0	412	102	101⅛	101¼	−1
103¾	92¼	ATT 8⅛24	8.0	443	102⅛	101⅝	101⅞	−⅛
104½	95	ATT 8.35s25	8.1	1177	103⅞	102⅝	102⅝	−1
90	78	ATT 6½29	7.7	2054	87¼	84⅞	84⅞	−2¼
105¼	95	ATT 8⅝31	8.4	339	104⅛	103⅜	103⅜	−⅞
134	70	Alza zr14	...	4	134	134	134	+2¼
61	56⅛	AForP 5s30	8.5	2	59	59	59	−1
80	63	ARetire 5¾02	cv	175	78	76	76	−2
105	101⅛	Apache 9¼02	8.9	25	104½	103¼	104½	+1½
104	16½	vjArmW 9¾08f	...	31	48	44	44	+1½
123⅞	113⅝	ARch 10⅞05	8.9	2	122½	122½	122½	+4
105	97¾	BkOne 7¼04	7.0	15	103½	103½	103½	+½
...	...	...	...	...	...	...	...	...
...	...	...	...	...	...	...	...	...
...	...	...	...	...	...	...	...	...

2014 (see Exhibit 2.6). Bonds that make coupon payments during the life of the bond are **coupon-bearing bonds**. For example, 'ATT 7s05' denotes ATT's 7% semiannual coupon-bearing bonds that mature in 2005. This means that AT&T pays coupons at a rate of 2.5% of the stated maturity value each semiannual period. Other bonds, such as the Aretire bonds listed in Exhibit 2.6, are convertible into common stock. Convertible bonds (denoted by CV) are discussed in more detail below.

Mortgages are bonds in which the borrower (the mortgagor) provides the lender (the mortgagee) collateral, which is usually real estate.[8] You are probably most familiar with mortgages on homes. In the US, default risk related to mortgages can be insured either privately or through government insurance agencies such as the Federal Housing Authority (FHA) or the Veterans Administration (VA). Mortgages are typically pooled (packaged together in portfolios) and sold. These pools of securities are called **mortgage-backed securities**. The originator of the mortgage will sell the mortgage through another firm (called a **conduit**), such as the Federal National Mortgage Association (FNMA). Mortgage-backed securities may or may not be backed by a federal agency. The most difficult aspect of managing a mortgage portfolio is assessing the risk that the mortgages will be prepaid. Mortgage holders generally prepay when interest rates are down.

---

[8] Other mortgage bonds are collateralized by corporate assets, such as property and equipment.

2.2 STOCKS

This section covers the basic characteristics of common and preferred stock. It compares and contrasts the different types of stock issues and concludes with a description of published stock quotations.

2.2.1 Basic characteristics of common stock

A **common stock** represents part ownership in a firm. A stock certificate is evidence of this ownership share. Common stocks are also referred to as *common shares* or *equity*. Typically, each common stock owned entitles an investor to one vote in corporate stockholders' meetings. Stockholders vote on such issues as who will be in senior management positions, who will be the outside auditor, and what to do with merger offers. Historically, common stocks on the whole have provided a higher return than bonds, but they also have higher risk. For example, in the stock market crash of 19 October 1987, the overall value of the market declined more than 20% in one day.

With common stocks, the ownership of the firm is residual; that is, common stockholders receive what is left over after all other claims on the firm have been satisfied. Because they are residual claims, common stocks have no stated maturity. In other words, unlike corporate bonds, common stocks do not have a date on which the corporation must buy them back. If you own common stock and wish to sell it, you must find a willing buyer.

Also, **cash dividends** are paid to stockholders only after other liabilities such as interest payments have been paid. Cash dividends are cash payments made to stockholders from the firm that issued the stock. The stockholder receives these residual benefits in the form of dividends, capital gains or both. Typically, the firm does not pay all its earnings in cash dividends. Usually the firm will retain some of its earnings to reinvest in other projects in an effort to enhance the firm's value. For example, a pharmaceutical company will take some of its earnings and invest them in research and development in an effort to discover new and better drugs, thereby earning future profits.

Corporations try to maintain a constant dividend payment, because this situation tends to enhance share prices (or at least it is perceived by some investors to do so). An investor earns **capital gains** (the difference between the asset's purchase price and selling price, when this difference is positive) when he or she sells stocks at a price higher than the purchase price. If the stock is sold at a price below the purchase price, a **capital loss** is incurred. The tax consequences of capital gains are discussed in Appendix 2A.

Several dates are important when investing in dividend-paying common stock. Dividends are typically paid quarterly, although there are many other payment methods. The **declaration date** is the day when the board of directors actually announces that stockholders on the date of record will receive a dividend. The **date of record** is the day on which the stockholder must actually own the shares to be able to receive the dividend. The date of record is usually several weeks after the declaration date. The **ex-dividend date** is the first day on which, if the stock is purchased, stockholders are no longer entitled to receive the dividend. Stocks on the New York Stock Exchange (NYSE) go ex-dividend four trading days before the date of record. This allows for the official records to be adjusted. The **payment date** is the day that the company actually mails the dividend cheques to its stockholders. The payment date is about three weeks after the ex-dividend date. Finally, some corporations pay cash to their stockholders by purchasing their own shares. These are known as **buyback shares**.

2.2.2 Classifications of common stocks

Stocks are usually classified using the following categories: (1) growth, (2) income, (3) blue chip, (4) speculative, (5) cyclical, and (6) defensive. A stock may be classified in more than one category. For example, WalMart stock is rated as both growth and blue chip. Some stocks may fall into only one or two categories, and other stocks may avoid classification because of their unique features.

Growth stocks are usually common stocks of firms having sales and earnings growth in excess of the industry average. The company pays very low or no dividends and reinvests its earnings for expansion. For example, Microsoft Corporation had recorded sales and earnings growth rates in excess of 20% per year from 1988 to 1998. To date, Microsoft has not paid any cash dividends.

Income stocks are common stocks of older, more mature firms that pay high dividends and are not growing rapidly. Stocks of utility companies are examples of income stocks. Income stocks are usually in low-risk industries, and their price increases little, if at all. For example, Duke Power Company has paid dividends consistently for at least the last 20 years without ever decreasing the amount paid. In the last 10 years, Duke has consistently increased its dividends at a rate of about 5% per year.[9] Hence, Duke Power Company has been a solid source of income and a very stable firm.

Blue chip stocks are common stocks of large, financially sound corporations with a good history of dividend payments and consistent earnings growth. These stocks tend to have very little risk of default. Blue chip stocks typically have more capital gains potential than do income stocks. For years, IBM has been well known as a blue-chip stock.

Speculative stocks are the opposite of blue chip stocks. These are stocks with a higher than average possibility of gain or loss, due to the fact that they are very risky and have considerable short-term volatility. Generally, stocks with a big difference between the high and the low price corresponding to the last 52 weeks are considered speculative stocks.

Cyclical stocks are common stocks that tend to move with the business cycle. When the economy is doing well, these stocks do well. When the country is in recession, these stocks do poorly. Ford Motor Company is a cyclical stock, as are other automobile makers. Automobile sales are typically a leading indicator of economic activity. Hence, as the economy slips into a recession, so do the earnings of automobile companies. Ford recorded large income gains during the expansion years in the late 1980s, but the company experienced sizable losses in the recession of the early 1990s.

Defensive stocks are the opposite of cyclical stocks, in a sense. Defensive stocks tend to do relatively well in recessionary periods but do not do very well when the economy is booming. These stocks are more difficult to find than cyclical stocks. Stocks of automobile-parts makers may be defensive. When the economy is in a recession, consumers are much more likely to attempt to maintain their motor vehicles rather than purchase new ones. Hence, sales by auto-parts makers tend to increase in recessions and decrease in expansions.

2.2.3 Preferred stocks

Preferred stocks typically pay a stated dividend and have preference over the payments to common stockholders. Thus, preferred stock is a 'hybrid security' that has some properties of bonds and some properties of stocks. Investors are attracted to this type of

---

[9] This means that if Duke paid a $1 dividend last year, then on average, it will pay $1.05 this year.

investment, but they sometimes overlook the risk. It is true that preferred stocks may provide a relatively high yield, but this high yield is not guaranteed. Also, if the firm goes bankrupt, the preferred stockholder stands in the credit line behind bondholders. A company's failure to pay preferred stock dividends, however, does not result in bankruptcy. Sometimes the firm can even call back the preferred stock, thus avoiding the high dividend. Finally, owners of preferred stock do not enjoy the same benefits as owners of common stock when the firm is doing well. That is, the common stock price could increase sharply, offering stockholders high capital gains. However, the preferred stock price gains are limited, much like the earning potential of bonds.

Cumulative preferred stocks are preferred stocks whose dividends accumulate if they are not paid. That is, before common shareholders can receive a dividend, the preferred shareholders receive all prior dividends that are due. **Participating preferred stocks** are preferred stocks whose dividends are tied to the success of the firm according to some stated formula in the earnings of the firm.

Dividends on preferred shares are not tax deductible. However, in 1995, the Internal Revenue Service (IRS) approved a new type of preferred shares whose dividends are tax deductible. Thus, the firm can enjoy a cheaper source of obtaining funds to finance operations.[10]

2.2.4 Reading the stock pages

Exhibit 2.7(a) shows a stock page from the financial pages of a newspaper. The first two columns give the 52-week high and low stock prices, followed in the third column by the company's abbreviated name. For example, AT&T had a 52-week high of 35.19 and a 52-week low of 16.50. The *s* by AMCOL means the firm has recently had a stock split. A **stock split** occurs when a company issues more new shares in return for existing shares. For example, a 2-for-1 split means that a company issues two new shares for every one share currently outstanding. Stock splits are a method that firms use to control the per-share price of its stock. After a 2-for-1 split, a firm's stock will trade at about half of its previous value.

Notice that in the explanatory notes in Exhibit 2.7(b) *pr* stands for *preference shares*, and *pf* stands for *preferred stock*. **Preference shares** are preferred stocks with a higher claim to any dividend payments than other preferred stock issues. That is, in hard times these shares' dividends are paid before any other dividends are paid (see ABN stock in Exhibit 2.7(a)).

The fourth column in Exhibit 2.7(a) gives the company's unique ticker symbol. The fifth column gives the volume of shares trading in 100s, and the sixth column gives the dividend yield. The dividend yield is found by dividing the annual (52-week) dollar dividend, D, by the closing price per share (denoted by P, see Column 10). The dividend yield is stated as a percentage. For example, the dividend yield = $(D/P) \times 100$ for ASA (see Exhibit 2.7(a)) is 3%.

The seventh column gives the price/earnings (P/E) ratio, which is the closing price divided by the past four quarters' earnings per share. The P/E ratio is a widely used ratio in evaluating common stocks. A firm that is expected to experience significant growth in the future will have a higher P/E ratio. That is, the current price will reflect this perceived growth, but the earnings per share, E, does not reflect this growth (because it is last year's earnings per share). Therefore, a relatively high P/E ratio is expected to be found in growth firms.

---

[10] See Andrew Bary, 'What a deal: new breed of preferred issues helps everybody but the tax man', *Barron's*, 27 February 1995.

Exhibit 2.7(a) Extract from *Barron's* Stock Tables

Mkt Sym	52-Wk High	52-Wk Low	Name	Tick Sym.	Vol. 100s	Yld	P/E	Week's High	Week's Low	Last	Net. Chg	Dividend Rec.Date
						A						
▲	**17.10**	**9.75**	**AAR**	**AIR**	3448	2.0	25	**17.10**	**14.50**	**17.10**	**+ 2.55**	**05–01–01**
	38.20	21.75	ABM Indus	ABM	4922	1.8	19	37.75	34.00	37.25	– 0.03	07–13–01
	26.50	16.81	ABN Am ADR	ABN	5305	4.3	...	19.10	18.32	18.93	+ 0.54	05–11–01
▲X	**25.60**	**21.13**	**ABN Am pfA**		4145	7.5	...	**25.60**	**25.02**	**25.10**	**+ 0.15**	**06–29–01**
▲X	25.65	20.25	ABN Am pfB		5764	7.3	...	25.65	24.50	24.55	+ 0.15	06–29–01
X	28.50	23.50	ACE CapTr		151	8.4	...	27.00	26.01	26.56	+ 0.12	06–29–01
X	43.94	27.13♣	ACE Ltd	ACE	51489	1.5	19	40.00	36.05	39.09	+ 1.75	06–29–01
	89.00	59.75	ACE LtdPRIDES		625	5.1	...	80.55	78.00	80.55	+ 4.30	05–15–01
▲	8.89	7.13	ACM GvtFd	ACG	15560	9.6	...	8.89	8.68	8.72	+ 0.03	07–06–01
▲	9.00	6.75	ACM OppFd	AOF	491	8.3	...	9.00	8.65	8.70	– 0.20	07–06–01
	9.38	6.19	ACM MgdDlr	ADF	2231	12.7	...	8.12	7.81	8.05	+ 0.15	07–06–01
	6.56	4.35	ACM MgdInco	AMF	1659	10.9	...	4.86	4.61	4.66	– 0.10	07–06–01
	13.50	11.50	ACM MuniSec	AMU	361	6.7	...	12.97	12.81	12.97	+ 0.07	07–06–01
	72.81	39.95♣	AES Cp	AES	109220	...	36	44.50	40.75	43.05	+ 1.99	...
	110.00	64.01	AES Tr		3712	4.9	...	70.50	65.41	69.00	+ 2.60	07–13–01
s	37.47	22.53	AFLAC	AFL	78823	.6	24	33.16	30.50	31.49	– 0.96	05–17–01
	13.25	7.90	AGCO Cp	AG	23117	.4	65	9.15	8.14	9.15	+ 0.84	02–15–01
n	25.15	24.85	AGL Cap TruPs		1640	...	...	25.15	25.00	25.15	+ 0.10	...
	24.25	15.63	AGL Res	ATG	7089	4.5	12	24.00	22.51	23.75	+ 0.80	05–18–01
	20.00	10.44	AgSvcAm	ASV	208	...	12	14.06	13.25	13.45	– 0.52	...
	19.74	11.25	AICl Cap Tr pf		155	13.2	...	17.25	17.00	17.10	– 0.19	06–15–01
▲	46.75	15.00	AIPC	PLB	5498	...	30	46.75	40.57	46.40	+ 5.94	...
	15.00	7.50♣	AK Steel	AKS	28485	2.0	15	13.46	12.00	12.54	– 0.72	05–01–01
	49.00	38.13♣	AK Steel pfB		2	7.7	...	47.00	47.00	47.00	...	06–01–01
	26.06	22.50♣	AMB Prop	AMB	8461	6.1	17	25.80	25.29	25.76	+ 0.56	07–05–01
▲	25.25	20.38♣	AMP Prof pfA		177	8.5	...	25.25	25.06	25.16	+ 0.06	07–05–01
s	**7.81**	**2.50**	**AMCOL**	**ACO**	3323	1.0	1	**6.10**	**5.15**	**6.00**	...	**05–28–01**
	25.31	20.13♣	AMLI Resdntl	AML	2579	7.6	9	24.60	24.00	24.60	+ 0.45	05–11–01
	43.94	26.00	AMR	AMR	71837	...	9	36.22	32.50	36.13	+ 1.77	03–15–00
	25.05	21.31	AMR PINES		383	7.9	...	25.04	24.75	24.89	– 0.03	07–15–01
X	25.69	21.75	ANZ pf		1026	8.0	...	25.57	24.95	25.14	+ 0.29	07–01–01
X	25.75	21.88	ANZ II pf		1031	8.0	...	25.65	25.12	25.18	– 0.09	07–01–01
	63.25	31.50	AOL Time	AOL	608358	...	dd	53.84	51.51	53.00	– 0.10	...
	5.31	2.63	APT Satelt	ATS	282	5.5	...	4.12	3.85	3.85	– 0.15	05–15–01
n	49.88	5.00♣	APW		8107	...	...	10.15	8.54	10.15	+ 0.95	...
	22.90	**14.06♣**	**ASA**	**ASA**	1935	3.1	...	**19.80**	**18.80**	**19.14**	**+ 0.37**	**05–18–01**
	29.56	15.29	AT&T Wrls	AWE	307900	...	...	16.79	15.45	16.35	+ 0.15	...
X	**35.19**	**16.50**	**AT&T**	**T**	470319	.7	dd	**22.00**	**20.50**	**22.00**	**+ 1.03**	**06–29–01**
	26.35	23.63	AT&T 8 1/4 PNS		536	8.0	...	26.05	25.37	25.65	– 0.30	07–03–01
	25.88	23.63	AT&T 8 1/8 PNS		1297	8.0	...	25.55	25.33	25.33	– 0.27	04–30–01
	31.75	15.13♣	AVX Cp	AVX	13729	.7	7	21.00	18.00	21.00	+ 3.08	05–04–01
s	40.47	24.58	AXA ADS	AXA	11135	1.8	...	29.34	27.40	28.17	– 0.22	...
▲	25.00	14.63	AZZ	AZZ	663	.6	15	25.00	22.52	25.00	+ 2.40	04–13–01
	4.00	0.44	AamesFnl	AAM	375	...	dd	1.44	1.25	1.35	+ 0.08	...
	19.50	11.47	AaronRent	RNT	2339	.2	12	17.50	15.86	17.00	– 0.50	06–01–01
	16.50	12.13	AaronRent A	RNTA	5	.3	12	15.87	15.87	15.87	– 0.13	06–01–01
...	...	...	...	...	...	...	...	...	...	...	...	...
...	...	...	...	...	...	...	...	...	...	...	...	...
...	...	...	...	...	...	...	...	...	...	...	...	...

The current P/E ratio is 25 for AAR; in other words, the stock price is 25 times larger than the annual earnings per share. With the P/E ratio and the closing price, we can infer an earnings per share (EPS). That is,

$$P/E = P/EPS$$

and therefore

$$EPS = P/(P/E)$$

Exhibit 2.7(b) How to read *Barron's* Stock Tables

The stock tables reflect issues that changed hands during last week's trading through 4 p.m. Eastern Time. Stock ticker symbol codes appear for common stock listings. Sales volume figures are the unofficial weekly total for shares traded, quoted in hundreds. The 52-week high/low range columns show the highest and lowest intraday stock price. These ranges are adjusted to reflect stock dividends of 1% or more and cash dividends of 10% or more.

Yield is determined by dividing the company's latest 12-month dividend by the last current market price.

The price-earnings ratio is determined by dividing the closing market price by the company's diluted per-share earnings, as available, for the most recent four quarters. Charges and other adjustments usually are excluded when they qualify as extraordinary items under generally accepted accounting rules. The price/earnings ratio (P/E) reflects the relative value of a company by showing the number of times its latest 12-month earnings would have to be multiplied to equal its stock price.

As a general rule, to be eligible to receive a newly declared cash dividend or stock dividend of less than 25% on a listed security, shareholders must have purchased their stock before the ex-dividend date, which is two business days (days on which the exchanges *and* banks are open) prior to the record date.

For distributions of 25% or more, the ex-dividend date is still one business day after the payment date (the day when the new shares begin trading).

All securities listed in the Nasdaq system are identified by a four- or five-letter symbol. The fifth letter indicates the issues that aren't common or capital shares, or are subject to restrictions or special conditions. Below is a rundown of stock ticker code symbol fifth letter identifiers and a description of what they represent.

Stock ticker code symbols

A Class A.
B Class B.
C Exempt from Nasdaq listing qualifications for a limited period.
D New issue.
E Delinquent in required filings, with SEC, as determined by the National Association of Securities Dealers.
F Foreign.
K Non-voting.

L Miscellaneous situations, second class units, third class warrants or sixth class preferred stock.
M Fourth preferred, same company.
N Third preferred, same company.
O Second preferred, same company.
P First preferred, same company.
Q In bankruptcy proceedings.
R Rights.

S Shares of beneficial interest.
T With warrants or rights.
U Units.
V When issued and when distributed.
W Warrants.
Z Miscellaneous situations, including second class of warrants, fifth class preferred stock and any unit, receipt or certificate representing a limited partnership interest.

Market transaction symbols

▲ Indicates a new high intraday price for the preceding 52 weeks.
▼ Indicates a new low intraday price for the preceding 52 weeks.
cc P/E Ratio is 100 or more.
cld Called.
dd Indicates loss in the most recent four quarters.
f Indicates two zeros are omitted from volume figure.
g Indicates the dividend or earnings is expressed in Canadian money. The stock trades in U.S. dollars. No yield or price/earnings ratio is shown unless stated in U.S. money.
gg Special sales condition; no regular trading.
h Indicates a temporary exception to Nasdaq qualification.
n Indicates new stock listing issue within the past trailing 52-weeks. The high-low price

range begins with the start of trading and does not cover the entire 52-week period.
nt Not traded this week.
pf Preferred stock.
pp Holder owes installment(s) of purchase price.
pr Preference shares.
rt Rights.
s Indicates a stock split or stock dividend amounting to 10% or more within the past trailing 52 weeks. The high-low price range is adjusted from the old stock.
un Units.
v Trading halted on primary market.
vj In bankruptcy or receivership or being reorganized under the Bankruptcy Code, or securities assumed by such companies.
wd When distributed.
wi When-issued trading for new issues, stock splits, or large

stock dividends where the settlement date is determined after the securities become available.
wt Warrant.
ww With warrants.
x Ex-dividend or ex-rights. Shareholders must have purchased their stock before the ex-dividend date to receive a newly declared dividend – the price of the share drops automatically by the amount of the dividend and the week's net change for the share price is exclusive of the ex-dividend.
xw Without warrants.
z Sales in full, not in hundreds.
♣ Free annual/quarterly report or prospectus available. See details below

Dividend Rec. Date **06-14-01** Boldface and underline indicates a revised or recently reported dividend.

Source: Barron's, 2 July 2001. p. MW16. Barron's Online by *Barron's*. © 2001 by Dow Jones & Co., Inc. Reproduced with permission of Dow Jones & Co., Inc. in the format *Fundamentals of Investments* via Copyright Clearance Center.

For example, we find AAR EPS to be

$$EPS = \$17.10/25 \cong \$0.68$$

Thus, AAR's EPS over the past year is approximately $0.68. This is an approximation, because the reported P/E is rounded. When the earnings are negative or very close to zero, the P/E ratio is meaningless and hence not reported. Columns 9 and 10 give the previous day's high and low prices, respectively. Column 11 gives the closing price, which is the price of the last trade. Column 12 gives the change from the previous trading day, and the final column gives the date of the recently reported dividend.

When you wish to know whether the stock market is tending to go up or down, you cannot look at prices of one stock but should rely on an index of stocks or some average price of many stocks. There are many indices that measure the changes in the price of various groups of stocks. Probably the most well-known indices you hear on the daily news are the Dow Jones index, the Standard & Poor's index, the FTSE 100 and the Nasdaq index. Exhibit 2.8(a) shows that on 23 March 2001 the closing price of the FTSE 100 was 5402.3. Exhibit 2.8(b) lists the other FTSE indices. Exhibit 2.8(c) shows the major US indices such as the Dow Jones index (DJI), the S&P, the Nasdaq, etc.

Originally, the DJI average was calculated as a simple average of the stock prices included in the average, because when there is a stock split or stock dividends, the stock price artificially falls. In order to correct for this technical decline in price, the sum of all the 30 prices is divided by a number smaller than 30, such that the average will not change due to splits and stock dividends. The denominator which adjusts over time is called the *divisor*.

The DJI is a *price-weighted index* because the rate of return on the index is the rate of return that would be obtained if one share of each of the 30 stocks will be held in a portfolio. The Standard and Poor's 500 Index (S&P 500) is a *value-weighted index* rather than a price-weighted one. It measures the rate of return that would be earned on a portfolio of the 500 stocks held in proportion to their market values.

Similarly, the New York Stock Exchange index, the NYSE index, is a value-index of all listed NYSE stocks; and the American Stock Exchange index, derived from

---

Exhibit 2.8 Some stock market indices

(a) FTSE 100 and other FTSE indices   **FT**

	Mar. 23	Mar 22	Mar 21	Mar 20	Mar 19	2000/01 High	2000/01 Low	Since comp High	Since comp Low
FTSE 100	5402.30	5314.80	5540.70	5646.80	5551.60	**6798.10**	5314.80	**6930.20**	986.90
FTSE 250	5943.80	5929.70	6104.20	6218.90	6219.40	**7149.60**	5929.70	**7149.60**	1379.40
FTSE 250 ex IT	6040.40	6037.60	6208.00	6322.60	6330.90	**7166.20**	5987.20	**7166.20**	1378.30
FTSE 350	2658.30	2620.10	2726.90	2778.90	2738.40	**3325.30**	2620.10	**3546.40**	664.50
FTSE SmallCap	2869.14	2859.34	2931.38	2979.85	2975.87	**3629.06**	2859.34	**3629.06**	1363.79
FTSE SmallCap ex IT	2860.47	2857.14	2919.96	2963.54	2960.52	**3575.63**	2857.14	**5554.10**	1363.79
FTSE All-Share	2609.40	2573.07	2676.31	2727.15	2688.78	**3265.95**	2573.07	**3265.95**	61.92

Source: Financial Times, 26 March 2001, p. 28. Reprinted with permission.

Exhibit 2.8 (continued)

(b) FTSE share indices (European series)

Mar 23	Euro Index	Day's %	change points	Yield% gross	xd adj ytd	Total retn (Euro) €
FTSE Eurotop 300	1308.65	+ 2.32	+ 29.68	2.21	4.89	1403.42
FTSE E300 Eurobloc	1437.26	+ 2.76	+ 38.66	2.05	2.49	1520.95
FTSE E300 Ex-Eurobloc	1190.82	+ 1.83	+ 21.37	2.39	7.07	1291.96
FTSE E300 Ex-UK	1400.87	+ 2.74	+ 37.30	2.00	1.98	1476.32
FTSE Eurotop 100	2972.87	+ 2.43	+ 70.64	2.13	10.80	1107.86
FTSE Eurobloc 100	1176.30	+ 2.84	+ 32.45	2.06	1.85	1237.17
FTSE EuroMid	1346.06	+ 1.15	+ 15.27	2.51	3.90	1474.70
FTSE EuroMid Eurobloc	1257.97	+ 1.35	+ 16.75	2.31	1.50	1357.01
FTSE EuroMid Ex-UK	1291.47	+ 1.45	+ 18.50	2.20	2.24	1380.07
FTSE Eurotop 300 Industry Sectors						
RESOURCES	1283.78	− 1.85	− 24.21	2.63	5.05	1417.03
Mining	1629.83	+ 2.45	+ 39.05	3.11	31.44	1812.45
Oil & Gas	1212.19	− 2.23	− 27.69	2.58	3.04	1307.28
BASIC INDUSTRIES	1213.15	+ 0.21	+ 2.50	2.95	6.77	1312.69
Chemicals	951.94	+ 0.22	+ 2.09	2.91	2.30	1023.81
Construction & Bld Matls	1115.62	+ 1.01	+ 11.11	2.58	1.36	1174.02
Forestry & Paper	1112.08	− 3.09	− 35.47	4.79	53.31	1314.44
GENERAL INDUSTRIALS	1253.23	+ 3.44	+ 41.72	2.31	4.80	1333.17
Aerospace & Defence	713.49	+ 1.27	+ 8.94	1.99	0.00	759.06
Diversified Industrials	872.31	+ 3.20	+ 27.06	2.91	0.00	930.53
Electronic & Elect Equip	1605.23	+ 4.60	+ 70.60	1.80	8.77	1666.08
Engineering & Machinery	827.52	+ 2.13	+ 17.26	3.35	7.52	892.37
CYCLICAL CONS GOODS	1193.57	+ 2.07	+ 24.20	2.69	0.87	1282.51
Automobiles & Parts	796.67	+ 2.05	+ 16.01	3.08	0.82	845.52
Household Goods & Texts	1782.25	+ 2.12	+ 36.92	1.72	0.00	1855.82
NON-CYC CONS GOODS	1368.12	+ 1.72	+ 23.09	1.72	4.25	1458.26
Beverages	1052.33	− 1.40	− 14.90	2.62	8.35	1143.20
Food Producers & Procesrs	1005.68	+ 0.78	+ 7.83	2.00	1.67	1057.10
Health	1110.44	+ 0.79	+ 8.69	1.49	0.00	1160.47
Personal Care & Hse Prods	1394.80	+ 2.90	+ 39.25	0.97	2.59	1437.73
Pharmaceuticals	1241.44	+ 2.35	+ 28.46	1.42	2.07	1288.09
Tobacco	1760.66	+ 1.14	+ 19.77	5.09	54.76	2005.77
CYCLICAL SERVICES	1155.36	+ 1.90	+ 21.58	2.02	3.09	1235.95
Distributors	1021.47	+ 3.90	+ 38.38	2.18	0.00	1090.97
General Retailers	873.30	+ 0.90	+ 7.81	2.40	1.07	930.85
Leisure Entertmt & Hotels	909.80	+ 1.62	+ 14.47	2.45	6.24	971.29
Media & Photography	1367.42	+ 2.37	+ 31.60	1.76	4.18	1424.12
Support Services	886.33	+ 4.00	+ 34.08	1.30	1.67	920.25
Transport	733.19	− 0.18	− 1.31	2.75	0.00	793.41
NON-CYCLICAL SERVS	1219.18	+ 2.97	+ 35.16	1.77	0.41	1283.88
Food & Drug Retailers	1218.07	− 0.07	− 0.88	1.86	0.00	1280.04
Telecommunication Servs	1163.46	+ 3.59	+ 40.29	1.76	0.47	1205.94
UTILITIES	1361.60	+ 2.12	+ 28.24	3.64	9.63	1551.88
Electricity	982.67	+ 1.99	+ 19.19	3.91	8.44	1095.67
Gas Distribution	1320.67	+ 2.60	+ 33.44	2.30	2.37	1507.52
Water	810.50	+ 2.22	+ 17.64	4.22	0.00	974.48
FINANCIALS	1382.51	+ 3.13	+ 41.92	2.61	7.90	1491.78
Banks	977.18	+ 2.94	+ 27.88	2.97	8.36	1050.95
Insurance	1070.87	+ 3.42	+ 35.41	1.79	1.04	1119.38
Life Assurance	1005.66	+ 3.21	+ 31.24	2.65	0.00	1057.10
Investment Companies	1524.24	+ 1.81	+ 27.07	1.85	0.00	1617.27
Real Estate	767.75	+ 0.40	+ 3.05	3.68	0.00	846.12
Speciality & Other Fin	1208.40	+ 7.51	+ 84.40	1.31	2.26	1273.02
INFORMATION TECH	1392.42	+ 7.62	+ 98.65	0.84	4.51	1417.91
Information Tech Hardware	1678.07	+ 8.40	+ 129.99	0.96	6.99	1711.91
Software & Computer Serv	708.66	+ 5.28	+ 35.52	0.48	0.24	717.37

Source: Financial Times, 26 March 2001, p. 28. Reprinted with permission.

Exhibit 2.8 (continued)

(c) The major US stock market indices

	12-Month		Weekly		Friday		Weekly	12-Month		Change From	
	High	Low	High	Low	Close	Chg.	% Chg.	Chg.	% Chg.	12/31	% Chg.
Dow Jones Averages											
30 Indus	11337.92	9389.48	10566.21	10434.84	10502.40	-102.19	-0.96	54.51	0.52	-284.45	-2.64
20 Transp	3145.65	2368.65	2833.56	2643.49	2833.56	157.07	5.87	188.19	7.11	-113.04	-3.84
15 Utilities	416.11	306.91	359.68	352.57	359.34	2.84	0.80	52.43	17.08	-52.82	-12.82
65 Comp	3392.23	2882.28	3143.60	3083.60	3143.60	24.93	0.80	152.76	5.11	-173.81	-5.24
US Tot. Mkt	358.00	252.46	284.75	280.69	284.75	1.45	0.51	-54.44	-16.05	-22.13	-7.21
Internet	326.99	54.21	84.41	79.96	84.41	6.40	8.20	-203.74	-70.71	-52.08	-38.16
New York Stock Exchange											
Comp	677.58	566.35	621.76	616.00	621.76	-3.61	-0.58	-21.17	-3.29	-35.11	-5.35
Indus	851.94	696.58	767.50	760.82	765.92	-7.35	-0.95	-57.91	-7.03	-37.37	-4.65
Utilities	504.91	365.58	376.61	365.58	376.61	7.36	1.99	-102.96	-21.47	-63.93	-14.51
Transp	494.71	379.37	469.65	443.16	469.65	21.34	4.76	84.97	22.09	6.89	1.49
Finan	657.52	520.11	627.21	620.55	626.65	-5.36	-0.85	106.54	20.48	-20.30	-3.14
American Stock Exchange											
Amex Corp	974.18	832.24	917.80	902.88	917.80	11.82	1.30	-18.09	-1.93	20.05	2.23
Major Mkt	1110.28	941.21	1054.49	1043.09	1051.15	-12.51	-1.18	23.56	2.29	-26.41	-2.45
Standard & Poor's Indexes											
100 Index	829.83	560.99	635.58	626.69	632.02	-4.13	-0.65	-158.23	-20.02	-54.43	-7.93
500 Index	1520.77	1103.25	1226.20	1211.07	1224.42	-0.93	-0.08	-230.18	-15.82	-95.86	-7.26
Indus	1874.50	1260.17	1410.09	1392.44	1407.46	1.08	0.08	-411.18	-22.61	-120.40	-7.88
Transp	764.16	563.43	713.55	661.59	713.55	35.66	5.26	150.12	26.64	15.90	2.28
Utilities	353.03	256.96	303.12	295.40	303.12	4.73	1.59	46.16	17.96	-47.49	-13.54
Finan	168.30	131.06	159.53	157.49	159.24	-2.06	-1.28	28.18	21.50	-5.48	-3.33
MidCap	548.60	433.70	519.12	503.06	519.12	13.03	2.57	37.35	7.75	2.36	0.46
SmallCap	236.76	192.86	232.41	217.90	232.41	12.97	5.91	21.72	10.31	12.82	5.84
Nasdaq Stock Market											
Comp	4274.67	1638.80	2160.54	2050.87	2160.54	125.70	6.18	-1805.57	-45.52	-309.98	-12.55
100 Index	4099.30	1370.75	1832.75	1743.90	1832.75	105.28	6.09	-1931.04	-51.31	-508.95	-21.73
Indus	2319.28	1114.27	1516.53	1434.35	1516.53	91.96	6.46	-590.03	-28.01	33.54	2.26
Insur	2314.75	1700.16	2295.45	2258.67	2277.93	24.47	1.09	577.77	33.98	84.56	3.86
Banks	2108.94	1497.35	2108.94	2062.41	2108.94	35.18	1.70	611.59	40.84	169.49	8.74
Computer	2538.43	779.72	1083.72	1024.01	1083.72	78.81	7.84	-1260.25	-53.77	-211.25	-16.31
Telecom	935.90	280.27	311.18	292.79	311.18	17.29	5.88	-559.52	-64.26	-152.26	-32.85
NNM Comp	1946.26	744.04	981.66	931.73	981.66	57.25	6.19	-823.54	-45.62	-142.84	-12.70
NNM Indus	957.32	458.13	624.60	590.70	624.60	37.99	6.48	-243.94	-28.09	12.31	2.01
Russell Indexes											
1000	813.71	577.85	647.22	638.78	646.93	0.86	0.13	-122.75	-15.95	-53.16	-7.59
2000	545.18	425.74	513.13	484.19	513.13	24.48	5.01	-4.11	-0.79	29.60	6.12
3000	841.47	601.74	677.36	667.71	677.36	3.31	0.49	-119.08	-14.95	-48.39	-6.67
Value-v	609.20	527.09	583.80	577.72	583.80	-2.07	-0.35	45.39	8.43	-12.75	-2.14
Growth-v	919.26	470.23	554.97	544.93	553.61	4.57	0.83	-318.11	-36.49	-93.10	-14.40
MidCap	667.87	534.19	610.97	594.91	610.97	12.96	2.17	-2.57	-0.42	-16.65	-2.65
Others											
Value Line-a	1306.62	1045.40	1254.80	1203.81	1254.80	46.37	3.84	192.04	18.07	130.03	11.56
Value Line-g	439.78	346.50	399.93	384.68	399.93	13.58	3.51	-7.92	-1.94	6.46	1.64
Wilshire 5000	14329.94	10068.63	11407.15	11229.02	11407.15	94.69	0.84	-2211.35	-16.24	-768.73	-6.31
Wilshire SC	905.05	629.27	763.29	727.73	763.29	30.49	4.16	-81.66	-9.66	11.10	1.48

a-Arithmetic Index. G-Geometric Index. V-Value 1000 and Growth 1000.

Source: Barron's, 2 July 2001, p. MW55. Barron's Online by Barron's. © 2001 by Dow Jones & Co., Inc. Reproduced with permission of Dow Jones & Co., Inc. in the format Fundamentals of Investments via Copyright Clearance Center.

stock listed in the AMEX and the Nasdaq index, relates to about 3,000 stocks which are traded over the counter (OTC). There is a broader index called the Wilshire 5,000 index which includes stocks of the NYSE and AMEX plus many stocks traded OTC.

2.3 DERIVATIVE SECURITIES

A derivative security is one whose value depends directly on, or is derived from, the value of another asset. Four types of derivative securities are stock options, convertible bonds, futures and swaps.

2.3.1 Stock options

A **call option** on common stock gives the holder of the option (the buyer) the right to buy a specified stock at a specified price on or before a specified date. A **put option** gives the holder the right to sell a specified stock at a specified price on or before a specified date. Investors buy call options in the hope that the stock price will rise so they may buy the stock at a discount. Investors buy put options hoping that the stock price will fall so they may sell the stock at a premium.

For example, the following data corresponding to options on Motorola stock was reported in *Barron's*, 2 July 2001:

Call option

Strike	*Call price*
$15	$2.0

Put option

Strike	*Put price*
$15	$0.35

This means that you could buy a call option on Motorola stock for $2. This option entitled you to buy, up to the end of July, Motorola stock for $15. The market price of Motorola on this date was $16.56. Thus, if the stock price had increased until July, say to $19, you would have bought the stock for only $15 (i.e. exercised the call option) and earned $4 less than the price you had paid for the call option, giving you a profit of $4 − $2 = $2. If you had bought a put option, and paid $0.35, it would have given you the right to sell the stock for $15. If the stock price of Motorola had dropped to, say, $10, you would have gained $5 less than the price paid for the put option ($0.35).

The advantage of call options is that when stock prices rise, these options provide a much higher return than the comparable return from stock ownership. However, there is a risk that the call option will expire worthless if the stock price falls, and a put option may expire worthless if the stock price rises. In these cases you lose all your investment, i.e. − 100% rate of return. Options are useful tools in managing the risks of a portfolio. For example, options can be used to insure the downside risk of a stock portfolio. We examine this issue in Chapter 13.

2.3.2 Convertible bonds

Convertible bonds provide a unique investment opportunity. A **convertible bond** is a corporate bond with an option to convert the bond into stock. The bondholder receives coupon payments that generally have a higher yield than the dividend yield of the underlying stock but lower than the yield on nonconvertible bonds with the same risk. Because the bond is convertible, it provides the opportunity to participate in any rise in stock price. In essence, a convertible bond is an ordinary bond with a call option attached.

Suppose Cray Research $6^1/_8$, 2011 convertible bonds were trading at $85^3/_4$. That is, the bonds offer a $6^1/_8\%$ coupon and will mature in 2011. The price of $85^3/_4$ refers to the percentage of par. The par value of the bonds is $1,000; hence, the quoted price of the bond is $857.50 (or $0.8575 \times \$1,000$).

To understand the price of the Cray Research bond, we need more information. We need the **conversion ratio**, the number of common shares a bondholder will receive if the bond is tendered for conversion. For Cray Research convertible bonds, the conversion ratio is 12.82. That is, each bond with $1,000 par is convertible into 12.82 shares of stock. The **conversion price** is the par value of a bond divided by the conversion ratio, which for Cray is about $78 (that is, $1,000/12.82). Cray Research stock is currently trading at $42 per share. The **conversion value** is the current value of a bond if it is converted. If we converted the Cray bonds, our equity would be worth $538.44 (that is, 42×12.82), which is far less than the bonds' current trading price of $857.50. The **conversion premium** is the value of the option to convert the bond into stocks, which is the difference between the current market value of the bonds and the comparable market price of a nonconvertible bond. In this case, the option to convert the bond to stocks at price of $78, when the stock is presently trading at $42, is not worth very much. We will study how to value such an option in Chapter 13.

2.3.3 Futures

A futures contract is a security that *obligates* one to buy or sell a specified amount of an asset at a stated price on a particular date. For example, the buyer of a 50,000 libras cotton futures contract that matures in three months agrees to buy 50,000 libras of a specified grade of cotton at a specific location at a specific price (the futures price).

For example, on 2 July 2001, the price of cotton futures in March 2002 was 44.20 cents per libra. This means that if you buy a 50,000 lb (which is the minimum in the case of cotton) contract, you are obligated to pay on the delivery date 50,000 $\times$ $0.4420 \cong \$22,100$ regardless of the cotton price which will prevail in March 2002.

Futures contracts exist on most major commodities: metals, energy products, interest rates, currencies, and various (mainly stock) indices. Futures are used to hedge financial price risk and to speculate on the direction of future prices. For example, a multinational corporation that has large accounts receivable in Japanese yen may sell yen futures contracts to hedge against a weakening yen relative to the dollar. A speculator who believes the dollar will weaken against the yen may buy yen futures in the hope of profiting. Thus, futures provide the ability to transfer financial price risk from the hedger to the speculator. Futures will be discussed in Chapter 12.

2.3.4 Swaps

A newer type of financial security is the swap. A **swap** is an agreement to exchange specific assets at future points in time. For example, a currency swap is an agreement to exchange currencies – say, US dollars for euros – at specific dates and for specific amounts in the future. The first major swap occurred between IBM and the World Bank in 1981. IBM held fixed-rate debt in German marks (DM) and Swiss francs (SF). Because of recent changes in the foreign exchange rates, IBM wanted to convert its DM and SF liabilities to US dollar liabilities. In August 1981, the World Bank issued fixed-rate bonds in dollars with the exact maturities of the IBM debt. The World Bank and IBM then agreed to 'swap' the interest payments. The interest payments were calculated based on the par value of the bonds. This par value is referred to as the **notional principal**. The net result of these transactions was that the World Bank would, in effect, make IBM's debt payments in DM and SF, and IBM would make the World Bank's debt payments in US dollars. Thus, IBM eliminated its currency risk. Why did the World Bank take this currency risk? Probably, it had assets in Germany and Switzerland that generated DM and SF cash flow. These assets could then be used to pay the World Bank's debts with no concern about changes in exchange rates. Thus, both sides of this transaction benefited.

2.4 RISKS OF BONDS AND STOCKS

Exhibit 2.9 compares the risk and average (or expected) return characteristics of the financial securities introduced in this chapter. If held in isolation, options and futures are the most risky, but they also provide the highest potential return. Short-term government bonds are the safest, but they also offer the smallest return. Between these two extremes are securities offering different levels of risk and return. Although stocks are typically riskier than bonds, they also offer a higher return on average. Long-term bonds have a higher risk and generally also a higher return than short-term bonds. Finally,

Exhibit 2.9 Risk and return on various assets

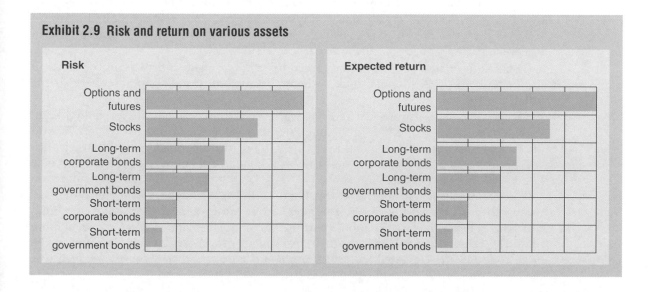

corporate bonds must offer a higher return on average to induce investors to take on default risk.

Investing in bonds and stocks has nine major sources of risk. (The order of coverage here does not suggest priority of risks, as risks vary among different securities.) The risk sources follow.

■ 1 Default risk

One risk that affects bond investors is that of default. The municipality or corporation may fail to pay either the coupon payment or face value at maturity. Bond investors in the Seabrook Nuclear Power Plant suffered from default risk when the plant's owner, the New Hampshire Power Company, failed to pay the coupon payments. Firms may default if they have too much debt (relative to the cash flows they generate). In this event, both stockholders and bondholders may lose. Of course, federal government bonds do not have default risk, because the Treasury Department can print money. Corporate bonds, municipal bonds and stocks are exposed to default risk.

■ 2 Interest rate risk

A second source of risk to bond investors is that of a change in interest rates. Would you want to buy a bond offering an annual 8% coupon rate when the market is paying 10% on newly issued bonds? Recall that bonds typically have a fixed coupon. If you have an 8% coupon bond, it is an agreement to pay you 8% of par value every year. Now suppose interest rates increase to 10%, and you are locked into a bad agreement; then you lose money. To be more specific, investors will sell the 8% bond and buy the 10% bond, causing the price of the 8% bonds to fall. The falling price will result in rising yields. For example, if an 8% coupon bond is selling for 90% of the price of the new 10% bond, for the same investment you can buy more of the old bond and earn more interest. The selling will continue until both the old and new bonds yield 10%. These higher yields imply that you can reinvest the coupon payment at a higher yield. However, if the interest goes down, the coupon reinvestment rate will be smaller and hence the terminal value of the investment will be smaller. This possible decrease in the reinvestment rate is called the **reinvestment rate risk**. In contrast, the change in the bond price because of an increase in the interest rate described above is called the **price risk**. In this case, the relatively low coupon rate (8%) causes you to lose money.

The rise in interest rates could be caused by factors outside a firm's control: a rise in the Federal Reserve discount rate, a change in monetary policy, or a change in the inflation rate.

Of course, changes in interest rates may also be a source of gain. If you hold a bond with a fixed coupon of 8% and the interest rate goes down in the market to 6%, you are locked into a good agreement. Everyone will buy the 8% bond, and its market price will go up (which gives you a capital gain as a bondholder) until both the old and new bonds yield the same return of 6%.

For example, suppose a government bond with $8^3/_4$% coupon and maturity date of August 2020 is traded for 131.5. The interest rate fell to about 6.06% since the bond was issued, hence the large coupons (plus the par value) discounted at 6.06% yield more than 31% capital gain. However, the reinvestment risk shows its ugly face: when the large coupons are reinvested the profit on them is 6.06% rather than $8^3/_4$% which was the reinvestment rate when the bond was issued.

Although changes in the interest rate may result in a gain for bondholders, interest rate changes are usually referred to as *interest rate risk*, because the uncertainty caused by these changes in general is undesirable to investors. In other words, if investors could buy one of two bonds, where the first bond's price did not change and the second bond's price would have a $50 gain or a $50 loss with equal probability, most investors would choose the first bond.

Stockholders also can lose or win when interest rates change. Specifically, higher interest rates make bonds relatively more attractive, causing some investors to sell stocks and buy bonds. This stock selling results in lower stock prices.

■ 3 Inflation rate risk

Interest rate changes may be caused by many factors that are very hard to predict. One of these factors is a change in the inflation rate, which is referred to as the *inflation rate risk* or *purchasing power risk*. These terms refer to the risk of losing the purchasing power of future cash receipts. That is, the value of the dollars received in the future in real terms decreases, hence the investor is unable to purchase as many goods and services as anticipated.

For example, suppose a one-year bond is offering a 5% yield, but inflation is 6%. At the end of the year, investors would be able to buy *less* with the bond's proceeds than they could with the initial investment at the beginning of the year. Inflation is a threat to the future benefits provided from investing. Inflation risk also affects stocks; generally, an increase in inflation induces an increase in the interest rate which, in turn, induces a decline in stock prices.

Recently, new bonds called inflation-indexed Treasury securities, discussed above, have been issued. The interest and principal of the bonds are linked to the cost of living index, which shields these bonds from inflation rate risk.

■ 4 Risk of call

Another potential risk to bondholders is the risk of call. Many bonds contain a call provision that allows the issuing firm to repurchase its bonds at a stated price after a stated date. The purchase price is usually the face value plus one year of coupon payments. This call provision can adversely affect the value of the bonds if interest rates decline dramatically.

For example, an 8% coupon bond with a face value of $1,000 that matures in 15 years may have a call provision after eight years. According to the call provision, the firm could repurchase the bonds any time after the eighth year if it is willing to pay the face value ($1,000) plus one year of interest ($80), or $1,080.

If interest rates fall to 5%, a non-callable bond gains from having an 8% coupon. However, for a callable bond there is a risk that the bond will be taken away from the investor, who then will not fully benefit from the drastic change in the interest rate. The firm could call the bonds and issue new ones at 5%, saving 3% per year. Thus, in the case of a sharp decrease in interest rate, the callable bonds will not provide the capital gain as will the non-callable bonds, because they can be called back at $1,080. Also, the investor faces an investment decision of what to do with the proceeds from the bond at the time the firm chooses to buy the bond back. Bonds are typically called after interest rates have fallen substantially. Thus, bond investors will be reinvesting the proceeds at a time when rates are low.

On the one hand, a callable bond, like all other bonds, also suffers losses when interest rates go up (because the price falls). On the other hand, as shown above, a callable bond's price will not go up in the same way as a noncallable bond's price. Thus, why would anyone want to buy such bonds, which seem to be an inferior investment? The reason is simple. The firm issuing the bonds must issue them at a higher interest rate than the rate for noncallable bonds; otherwise a rational investor will not buy the callable bonds. Thus, in the event that the interest rate does not go down and the bonds are not called, the bondholder enjoys a relatively high interest rate.

■ 5 Liquidity risk

Another risk of investing in certain bonds and stocks is that they may not be liquid. That is, if the bonds or stocks have to be sold unexpectedly, it could be very costly to the investor. There may be no-one who wishes to buy the securities at that time. To get a buyer quickly, the investor may have to sell the security at an unreasonably low price relative to its true value and thus incur a substantial price concession. Investors typically do not have a liquidity risk problem with government bonds and actively traded bonds of larger corporations, such as those issued by AT&T and GM. However, investors must anticipate a liquidity risk with the bonds or stocks of small firms, because they are not actively traded. To compensate for the lack of liquidity, small firms must offer investors a higher yield on bonds and a higher expected return on the stock. No one would buy them otherwise.

■ 6 Political and regulatory risk

Bonds and stocks are also exposed to political risk. This risk refers to unforeseen changes in the tax or legal environment that have an impact on stock and bond prices. For example, suppose Congress decided to double the income tax rate and cut the capital gains tax rate in half. What impact would this have on coupon-bearing bonds? In such a case, the tax liabilities of the coupon payments would double, and investors would have an incentive to buy stocks rather than bonds because the change in capital gains tax would favour stocks. Therefore, coupon-bearing bonds would decline in value as a result of the new tax laws.

The collapse of the Soviet Union illustrates a case of a political risk. In such a case, the government may be unable to or may refuse to pay its foreign debt, which induces a loss to a foreign investor who buys Soviet bonds.

■ 7 Business risk

Stocks and corporate bond prices are influenced greatly by the prosperity of the particular company, as well as by the economy in general. Stock and bond prices are directly influenced by how well a company is performing. Furthermore, because the firm is often involved with risky research and development projects, stocks are influenced by company performance much more than bonds. The higher volatility of sales and profit of the firm, the higher the business risk. Company performance is usually directly linked to the performance of the overall economy.

■ 8 Market risk

Much of the research conducted on securities markets has documented that the prices of all securities in a particular market tend to move together. For example, the US Treasury bond market exhibits a high level of co-movement of its bond prices. This principle is also true for corporate bonds and stocks. Even a good stock tends to perform poorly when the overall market is going down.

■ 9 Exchange rate risk

As an American investor, why would you buy US bonds yielding only 4.12% when you could earn 10.15% in the United Kingdom? The answer is simple: when you invest in the United Kingdom, you have to convert your US dollars to sterling. However, when you want your money back – say, at the end of the year – you must sell the UK bonds for sterling and then convert the proceeds to US dollars. Of course, there is a risk that for each pound you receive, you may get fewer dollars because of changes in the exchange rate. In dollars, you may end up with a yield much lower than 10.15%; indeed, the yield may be even less than the 4.12% that you can get on the US bonds. Thus, the high yield of 10.15% may be an illusion. Bonds are bought and sold in local currencies, not in US dollars. This exchange rate risk adds one more layer of risk for the international investor.

The risks of investing in government and corporate bonds, as well as in common stocks, are summarized in Exhibit 2.10. Corporate bonds of similar maturities to government bonds have a higher yield because of default risk. Stocks do not induce default risk, because not paying dividends does not cause the firm to be declared in default. However, stockholders are exposed to risk of default by the firm from other factors (for example, a big financial loss or lawsuit).

Exhibit 2.10 Risk exposure for bonds and stocks

Risks	Government bonds	Corporate bonds	Common stocks
Default	No	Yes	Yes
Overall level of interest rates in the economy	Yes	Yes	Yes
Inflation rate	Yes	Yes	Yes
Call	Some issues	Most issues	No
Liquidity	Little	Yes	Yes
Political and regulatory	Yes	Yes	Yes
Business	No	Yes	Yes
Market	Yes	Yes	Yes
Foreign exchange rate	Yes	Yes	Yes

Yes: Investors in bonds or stocks of this category are exposed to this risk.
No: Investors in bonds or stocks of this category are not exposed to this risk.
Little: Investors in bonds of this category are exposed to some, but not much, of this risk.

Changes in interest rates influence both the bond market and the stock market. Typically, if the interest rates fall, both the bond market and the stock market rally. Inflation risk has exactly the same influence as interest rate risk. Stocks are not callable, whereas most corporate bonds are. The call feature introduces an *opportunity loss* if interest rates fall. Liquidity risk is present in all securities; however, the government market is the most liquid. Political and regulatory risk, market risk and foreign exchange risk are present in both the bond and the stock markets. However, business risk applies only to corporate securities, not to securities issued by governments.

PRACTICE BOX

Problem

A government bond sold at $1,000. It pays an annual interest of 5% a year at the end of each year, and it matures in exactly two years. The par value is $1,000, and the bond has a yield of 5%. What is the capital gain if interest rates go down to 3%? What is the capital loss if interest rates go up to 7%? How would your results change if the bonds had 10 years to maturity? Which bond is riskier, the two-year bond or the 10-year bond?

Solution

Using present value tables, a calculator or software, we calculate the present value of the bonds' cash flows. The results are:

Interest rates (discount rate)	Market price of two-year bond	Market price of 10-year bond
3%	$1,038	$1,171
5%	$1,000	$1,000
7%	$964	$860

Thus, the two-year bond provides a $38 capital gain when rates fall to 3%, whereas the 10-year bond provides a $171 capital gain. However, the loss differences are similar in magnitude to the gain differences ($36 and $140, respectively), making the 10-year bond riskier.

2.5 INTERNATIONAL SECURITIES

International securities include stocks and bonds issued in foreign countries by foreign firms (e.g. a Japanese firm issues in the US) as well as securities issued by some domestic firms that pay interest or dividends in a different currency. For example, McDonald's Corporation issued bonds that pay interest in New Zealand dollars. International securities are increasing in importance for several reasons. First, as technologies are improving, the costs of trading international securities are declining. These costs include the cost of actual trading, taxes and other market impediments. Second, markets are dominated more and more by institutional investors. Institutional investors – such as banks, pension funds, insurance companies, endowments and mutual funds – trade large quantities of securities. These larger firms have the economies of scale to invest the energy needed to explore foreign markets. Third, technological advances in communications have been astounding. Fibre-optic telecommunication lines now link several trading firms directly to each other, as well as to multiple securities exchanges. Nowadays, with the Internet, detailed information on most major firms is available. These lines allow information to be communicated at a rate nearing the speed of light.

The major benefits of investing in international securities include the possibility of higher returns and diversification. For example, many international bonds offer a higher yield than similar US bonds. However, the investor must also consider how the bond's price will change over time, as well as how changes in the foreign exchange rate will influence the return on international bonds.

People can invest in international securities in three ways. First, investors can buy foreign bonds or stocks directly in their own markets traded in foreign currency. Second, many domestic exchanges trade **American Depository Receipts** (ADRs),[11] which are receipts for foreign shares held in a US bank. ADR holders are entitled to the dividends and capital gains of the foreign shares. ADRs trade just like shares of common stock. For example, ADRs trade on the NYSE for Honda Motor Company, a Japanese-based automobile manufacturer. Honda Motor's ADRs trade on the NYSE with ticker symbol HMC, and Honda Motor also trades on the Tokyo Stock Exchange (TSE) in yen. Each ADR allows the holder the rights to two common shares. For example, on a given day HMC was trading at $61^7/_8$ on the NYSE, and Honda Motor was trading at 3,630 yen on the TSE. The price difference can be explained in the following fashion. On this particular day, the dollar exchange rate for yen was 0.00846 dollar per yen. Because one ADR equals two common shares, the dollar value of two Honda common shares is about $61.42 \cong 2 \times 3,630$ yen $\times \$0.00846$. Although stock in Honda Motor can be bought in two ways, either on the TSE or on the NYSE, the price is about the same.[12] Finally, some mutual funds specialize in international markets. It is now possible to buy a portfolio of international securities with one phone call.

2.6 MUTUAL FUNDS/TRUSTS

Many investors choose to invest their money in **mutual funds**, which receive money from investors with the common objective of pooling the funds and then investing them in securities. There are many different types of mutual funds, as well as a range of ways to classify them. For example, there are **open-end funds**, which can issue additional shares upon demand and eliminate shares when they are redeemed. The shares of the open-end funds are not traded in the market, hence the investor buys and sells shares from the mutual funds themselves. The price is not determined by demand and supply but rather by the net asset value (NAV) per share. Investors can buy or sell shares of open-end funds like any other stock in the market. Conversely, **closed-end funds** cannot increase or decrease the number of shares easily.[13] Closed-end funds sell their shares on stock exchanges.

Some open-end funds are no-load (NL), and some are load. The load is a sales charge paid by an investor who buys a share in a load mutual fund. A fund that does not charge this fee is called a no-load fund. On a closed-end fund, the investor pays transaction costs exactly as paid on stocks bought in the stock market.

Exhibit 2.11 provides a sampling of data for mutual funds. The most important figure in the exhibit is the NAV, which is similar to the price quotation for other assets, such as stocks. 'NAV' stands for **net asset value**, which is the current market value of the assets per share (based on the market value of the underlying securities in the mutual fund). For example, the NAV of Brinson Global Fund is $11.16 million dollars

---

[11] American Depository Receipts are also sometimes referred to as American Depository Shares, or ADSs.

[12] Also, there are enough traders watching the relationship between these securities. In their desire to make any possible profit from price differences, these traders, who are known as *arbitrageurs*, ensure that the pricing differences will not be too great. By trading large blocks between markets, arbitrageurs influence prices, drawing them closer together.

[13] A closed-end fund, with shareholder approval, can undertake a new issue or change the nature of the fund (for example, change it to an open-end fund).

Exhibit 2.11 Sample of mutual funds data

52 Week High	Low	Fund Name	Close NAV	Wk's Chg.	—% Return — YTD	3-Yrs
		BlackRock Funds A:				
21.27	14.06	BalanceA p	14.86	− 0.16	− 7.4	+ 2.9
29.13	21.15	IndexEqA p	23.50	NA	NA	NA
15.51	13.16	LgCpValA p	14.38	− 0.02	− 3.4	+ 8.5
47.91	18.29	MicroCapA p	23.42	+ 1.72	− 6.3	+ 227.6
36.41	13.37	SmCpGrA p	15.50	+ 0.76	− 19.1	+ 23.1
		BlackRock Funds B&C:				
21.09	13.94	BalanceB t	14.73	− 0.14	− 7.8	+ 0.5
28.75	20.83	IndexEqB t	23.12	NA	NA	NA
28.75	20.82	IndexEqC t	23.11	NA	NA	NA
25.59	8.16	MdCpGrB t	8.85	+ 0.19	− 25.1	+ 52.8
47.15	17.78	MicroCapB t	22.73	+ 1.67	− 6.6	+ 220.6
47.13	17.77	MicroCapC t	22.72	+ 1.67	− 6.6	+ 220.5
21.94	12.14	SelectB t	13.22	− 0.06	− 13.2	− 7.6
34.94	12.53	SmCpGrB t	14.18	NA	NA	NA
		BlackRock Funds Svc:				
21.30	14.07	BalancedS	14.87	− 0.17	− 7.4	+ 3.3
9.85	9.20	CoreBd	9.63	− 0.13	+ 2.9	+ 18.6
29.16	21.17	IndexEqS	23.51	NA	NA	NA
15.44	9.29	IntlEqS	9.50	− 0.03	− 14.9	− 10.2
26.37	10.56	LgCpGrS	11.84	+ 0.09	− 24.4	− 13.6
15.53	13.18	LgCpValS	14.39	− 0.03	− 3.3	+ 8.9
10.46	9.75	ManagedS	10.23	− 0.15	+ 3.2	+ 17.7
22.46	12.55	SelEqS	13.70	− 0.06	− 12.8	− 5.0
36.84	13.63	SmCpGrS	15.47	NA	NA	NA
		BNY Hamilton Instit:				
18.19	13.11	EqInc	14.09	− 0.04	− 9.9	+ 12.6
15.70	10.21	IntEq	10.58	− 0.04	− 15.4	− 4.0
10.06	9.37	IntmGvt	9.85	− 0.13	+ 2.8	+ 17.6
10.32	9.76	IntlnGrd	10.09	− 0.12	+ 2.6	+ 15.8
10.20	9.62	Int TE	10.11	− 0.01	+ 3.0	+ 14.0
19.10	10.43	LgCapGth	11.45	− 0.04	− 17.4	+ 16.3
26.98	14.35	SmCapGth	17.19	+ 0.78	− 3.6	+ 89.5
29.42	24.23	BostonBalanced n	25.28	− 0.30	− 3.3	+ 5.5
		Boston Partners:				
13.19	10.81	MidValInst	12.82	+ 0.25	+ 6.6	+ 5.3
32.48	22.07 ♣	BramwellGr n	23.23	NA	NA	NA
23.91	16.62	BrandesInstIE	17.23	+ 0.07	− 7.2	+ 55.4
		Brandywine Funds:				
41.47	22.88	BlueFd n	24.21	− 0.24	− 12.2	+ 33.6
51.06	24.31	Brandywine n	26.26	+ 0.12	− 10.6	+ 41.0
		Brazos Funds:				
27.46	16.02	MicroCap	20.89	+ 1.77	+ 11.5	+ 142.6
13.94	9.73	MidCap Y	11.81	+ 0.26	− 4.2	NS
21.47	14.66	MultiCap	17.31	+ 0.45	− 4.6	NS
10.45	8.92	ReEst	10.45	+ 0.08	+ 8.0	+ 11.7
23.99	15.78	SmCap	19.50	+ 0.65	− 4.9	+ 34.4
10.22	9.61	BremerBd n	10.07	− 0.11	+ 3.8	+ 16.9
19.40	13.89	BermerGrStk n	15.46	+ 0.03	− 7.2	+ 16.1
44.71	31.20	BridgesInvest n	33.81	NA	NA	NA
		Bridgeway Funds:				
58.03	35.75	AggrGrwth n	41.94	+ 0.50	− 3.3	+ 159.0
		Brinson Fnds:				
11.63	**10.68**	**Global**	**11.16**	**NA**	**NA**	**NA**
9.48	7.84	HiYldI	7.90	+ 0.01	+ 1.6	+ 3.1
13.70	10.12	IntlEq	10.64	− 0.05	− 11.4	− 2.0
10.61	9.98	USBond	10.36	− 0.12	+ 3.5	+ 18.8
17.24	14.34	USEqty	16.00	+ 0.13	+ 2.2	+ 6.1
		Brinson Fnds Class A:				
33.57	24.17	FnSvA p	28.33	− 0.41	− 2.8	+ 3.7
9.60	5.24	StrtgyA p	5.99	+ 0.01	− 14.6	NS
35.65	25.03	TctAllA p	27.81	− 0.02	− 7.0	+ 16.7
		Brinson Fnds Class B:				
32.25	22.99	FnSvB t	26.88	− 0.40	− 3.2	+ 1.3
9.55	5.18	StrtgyB p	5.91	+ 0.01	− 15.1	NS
34.98	24.59	TctAllB p	27.27	− 0.02	− 7.3	+ 14.1

Exhibit 2.11 (continued)

| 52 Week | | | | | —% Return — | |
High	Low	Fund Name	Close NAV	Wk's Chg.	YTD	3-Yrs
		Brinson Fnds Class C:				
35.19	24.76	TctAllC	27.46	− 0.02	− 7.4	+ 14.1
9.55	5.19	StrtgyC p	5.91	+ 0.01	− 15.1	NS
		Brinson Fnds Class Y:				
35.98	25.26	TctAllY	28.08	− 0.03	− 6.9	+ 17.7
16.16	8.61	BrownIASmCpGr n	12.54	+ 1.02	+ 1.0	NS
34.06	24.94	BrownSmColnst	32.61	+ 1.85	+ 4.4	+ 79.0
24.24	17.04	BrundgEq xn	18.34	+ 0.01	− 8.9	+ 21.0
		Baffalo Funds:				
18.48	13.99	SmCap n	18.48	+ 0.79	+ 21.3	+ 123.2
14.73	13.88	BldProLoan	14.37	− 0.17	+ 2.9	+ 14.9
50.77	31.78	Burnhm p	35.40	− 0.07	− 8.5	+ 30.1

Source: Barron's, 2 July 2001, p. F8. Barron's Online by *Barron's*. © 2001 by Dow Jones & Co., Inc. Reproduced with permission of Dow Jones & Co., Inc. in the format *Fundamentals of Investments* via Copyright Clearance Center.

(see Exhibit 2.11). Investors will receive the net asset value if they sell an open-end mutual fund share. From time to time, detailed data on mutual funds is published, including data on performance in the last five years.

In closed-end funds, market supply and demand drive the trading prices. Closed-end funds trade at a premium above, or at a discount below, net asset value, depending on a range of factors (including how well the fund is run, the expenses charged, and the particular focus of the fund). Mutual funds are discussed in more detail in Chapter 17.

New investment vehicles have recently begun to compete with mutual funds. On January 1998, the American Stock Exchange began trading unit trusts called **Diamonds**. Each of these unit trusts represents a stake in the 30 stocks that make up the Dow Jones index. In effect, Diamonds turn the Dow into publicly trading stock, thus enabling investors to buy and sell the index at any time during the trading day. Each Diamond is sold for the equivalent of 1% of the value of the index. Thus, if the index is traded for, say, 8,000, the Diamond price is determined as $80. Diamonds complement the Amex's popular **Spiders**, which are unit trusts based on the stocks included in the Standard & Poor's 500 Index. Diamonds and Spiders provide a solid alternative to mutual funds.

SUMMARY

■ *Describe basic characteristics and types of bonds and stocks.*
Bonds are instruments that are useful primarily when investors have specific income requirements, whereas stocks are purchased primarily for growth potential. Money market securities are short-term obligations, including Treasury bills, commercial paper, bankers' acceptances, negotiable certificates of deposit, repurchase agreements, federal funds and eurodollars. Capital market securities are long-term obligations, including Treasury notes and bonds, federal agency bonds, municipal bonds, corporate bonds, mortgages and mortgage-backed securities, and stocks.

■ *Compare different types of derivative securities.*

A derivative security is a security whose value is derived from the value of another asset. Examples of derivative securities include stock options, convertible bonds, futures and swaps. A call option gives the holder the right to buy, whereas a put option gives the holder the right to sell, a specified stock at a specified price on or before a specified date (for an American option). A convertible bond is just like a regular bond, but with an added feature: if you own a convertible bond, you can convert the bond into a specified number of stocks. A futures contract is a security that obligates the investor to buy or sell a specified amount of an asset at a stated price on a particular date. A swap is an agreement to exchange specific assets at future points in time.

■ *Explain the risks involved in bond and stock investment.*

There are nine categories of risks related to bonds and stocks: default risk, interest rate risk, inflation rate risk, risk of call, liquidity risk, political and regulatory risk, business risk, market risk and exchange rate risk. US government bonds do not have default risk or business risk. Common stocks are not callable. Understanding the risks related to investments is an important first step in successful money management.

■ *Describe investment opportunities in international securities and mutual funds.*

International securities increase the investor's opportunities. International securities can be purchased directly from an international stock exchange, indirectly through an American Depository Receipt, or indirectly through a mutual fund. Mutual funds receive money from investors with common objectives, pool the funds together, and then invest them in securities. Shares of open-end funds are purchased and sold exclusively with the fund, whereas shares of closed-end funds are traded on stock exchanges.

KEY TERMS

American Depository
  Receipt (ADR)
Asked rate
Bankers' acceptance
Bid rate
Bid-ask spread
Blue chip stock
Bond
Buyback shares
Call option
Callable bond
Capital gains
Capital loss
Capital market security
Cash dividend
Closed-end fund
Commercial paper
Common stock
Conduit
Conversion premium
Conversion price
Conversion ratio
Conversion value
Convertible bond
Corporate bond
Coupon-bearing bond
Coupon payment

Cumulative preferred
  stock
Cyclical stock
Date of record
Declaration date
Defensive stock
Diamonds
Discount rate
Eurodollar
Ex-dividend date
Face value
Federal agency bond
Federal funds
Fixed-rate bond
Floating-rate bond
General obligation bond
Growth stock
Income stock
Junk bond
Money market security
Mortgage
Mortgage-backed security
Municipal bond
Mutual fund
Negotiable certificate of
  deposit
Net asset value

Notional principal
Open-end fund
Par value
Participating preferred
  stock
Payment date
Preference share
Price risk
Prime rate
Principal
Put option
Reinvestment
  rate risk
Repurchase agreement
  (repo)
Revenue bond
Reverse repo
Speculative stock
Spiders
Stock split
Swap
T-bill
Term repo
US Treasury bill
US Treasury bond
US Treasury note
Zero-coupon bond

QUESTIONS

2.1   What are the advantages and disadvantages of investing in bonds?

2.2   What are the major identifying characteristics of bonds?

2.3   Explain what is meant by the statement: 'The ownership of the firm is residual in nature'.

2.4   Explain the dates that are important in relation to the dividends paid on common stocks.

2.5   What is the P/E ratio, and how is it calculated?

2.6   What is a derivative security?

2.7   Give an example of how futures are used to hedge financial price risk and to speculate on the direction of future prices.

2.8   Why are international securities increasing in importance?

2.9 Joe-Bob from L.A. decided to invest $950 (price) in a 12% semiannual, 3-year bond. What is the yield to maturity (internal rate of return or IRR) if the par value is $1,000?

2.10 A bond is sold for $700 and matures in 5 years. It pays $20 at the end of the year. The par value is $1,000. Calculate the yield to maturity (IRR) on the bond using a calculator or software.

2.11 A junk bond is trading for $800 and matures exactly one year from now at $1,000. There is no interest paid between now and maturity.

(a) Calculate the yield to maturity on the bond.
(b) How do you explain your results, knowing that the interest rate on government bonds is only 5% a year?

2.12 The bid and asked yields on zero-coupon bonds with a $1,000 par value are 6.2% and 6%, respectively. The maturity is 5 years. What are the implied bid and asked prices of these two bonds? (Assume annual interest compounding.)

2.13 You have two different bonds, both of which were just issued for 10-year maturities: (1) a zero-coupon bond with a par value of $1,000, and (2) a bond that pays $50 interest at the end of each year with a par value of $1,000. Both of these bonds have the same 10% annual yield to maturity.

(a) Calculate the market price of these two bonds, and explain your results.
(b) Suppose that immediately after the issue of the bonds, the interest rate goes up to 12%. Which bond will suffer larger losses? Why?

2.14 The P/E ratio of a stock is 10. The price is $100 per share. What is the implied earnings per share?

2.15 The net asset value of a mutual fund is $12. The share price is $13.

(a) Is it an open-end fund or a closed-end fund?
(b) Calculate the premium or discount.

2.16 The dividend yield on IBM stock is 2%. The yield to maturity on IBM bonds is 8%. Does this mean that you will be better off buying the bonds than buying the stock?

2.17 A municipal bond and a corporate bond offer you the same yield of 8%. Both have the same risk of default.

(a) Which bond would you prefer if you were a tax-exempt investor?
(b) Which bond would you prefer if you pay 31% tax on interest received? Explain.

2.18 Suppose you buy a stock for $100. You receive $4 as a cash dividend at the end of the year. The stock price at the end of the year is $95.

(a) What is the rate of return on your investment?
(b) What is the dividend yield as measured at the beginning of the year? At the end of the year?
(c) What is your total dollar return on this investment?

2.19 Suppose you buy a stock on 1 January for 100 and consider selling it on 20 December. The stock price is $150. Your income tax rate is 31%. Is it worthwhile for you to wait a few days before selling? How many days should you wait, assuming the stock price will remain at $150? What will be your gain from waiting?

2.20 You have the following data regarding two firms (all numbers are in millions):

Year	Firm A		Firm B	
	Earnings	Dividends	Earnings	Dividends
1	$1.0	$0	$100	$50
2	1.2	0	101	50
3	1.5	0	98	50
4	1.7	0	100	55

Which firm would be classified as a growth firm, and which would not? Calculate the annual growth rate of earnings and dividends of each of these two firms.

2.21 Suppose you buy a bond that matures in one year, pays no interest, and has a par value of $1,000. You buy the bond for $950. The inflation rate was 10% for this year. What did you earn on this bond? Explain.

2.22 You hold a bond that matures in 20 years. The yield to maturity is 10%, and the coupon rate is 10%. The market, as well as the face value of the bond, is $1,000. Suppose the yield to maturity drops to 5% after you buy the bond. Determine your immediate gain under the following conditions:

(a) If the bond is not callable.
(b) If the bond is callable at $1,100 and the firm does call the bond whenever the price is above $1,100.

SELECTED REFERENCES

Fabozzi, Frank J., and D. Fabozzi. *Bond Market Analysis and Strategies*. Englewood Cliffs, NJ: Prentice-Hall, 1989.

Fabozzi, Frank J., and Irving M. Pollack (eds). *Handbook of Fixed Income Securities*. Homewood, IL: Dow Jones–Irwin, 1987.

Kelly, Jonathan M., Luis F. Martin, and John H. Carlson. 'The relationship between bonds and stocks in emerging markets'. *Journal of Portfolio Management*, Spring 1998, pp. 110–22.

Kihn, John. 'To load or not to load? A study of the marketing and distribution changes of mutual funds'. *Financial Analysts Journal*, May/June 1996, pp. 28–37.

Lederman, Jess, and Keith Park (eds). *Global Bond Markets*. Chicago: Probus, 1991.

Lederman, Jess, and Keith Park (eds). *Global Equity Markets*. Chicago: Probus, 1991.

Stigum, Marcia. *The Money Market*, 3rd edn. Homewood, IL: Dow Jones–Irwin, 1989.

SUPPLEMENTARY REFERENCES

Caglayan, Mustafa Onur, and R. Edwards Franklin. 'Hedge fund and commodity fund investments in bull and bear markets'. *The Journal of Portfolio Management*, Summer 2001, Vol. 27, No. 4.

Carrieri, F. 'The effects of liberalization on market and currency risk in the European Union'. *European Financial Management*, 2001, Vol. 7.

Schwartz, Roberta, and Daniel G. Weaver. 'What we think about the quality of our equity markets'. *The Journal of Portfolio Management*, Summer 2001, Vol. 27, No. 4.

Appendix 2A TAXES

In 1997 a new US tax law was completed after long discussion in Congress. The main item in the new law is a reduction in capital gains tax from 28% to 20%. If an asset is held for 5 years before it is sold, the capital gains tax is reduced, according to the new law, to only 18%.

Taxes are an important consideration in the investment process, because they affect an investor's net income. Investments differ in how they determine an investor's tax bill. For example, selling a stock that has greatly appreciated in price and buying a different stock will result in an investor's having to pay tax on the stock that has appreciated. No taxes would have to be paid yet, if the investor did not sell the stock.

Unfortunately, taxes are very complicated. Tax rules change often and typically the tax rates are determined more by political negotiation than by economic forces. This appendix briefly reviews some of the major tax consequences of investing in bonds and stocks.

Although there are many different taxes, the most significant tax is the federal income tax. State and local income taxes take a smaller percentage of an investor's return.

The tax rate applied to investment profits depends on whether the profits are classified as ordinary income (or loss) or capital gain (or loss). Most profits related to interest or cash dividend payments are considered ordinary income. If you own 1,000 shares of CWE, Inc., which paid $3 per share in cash dividends, then you have $3,000, or $3 × 1,000, in ordinary income. Most profits or losses related to price changes are considered capital gains or losses. If you purchased 100 shares of ABM at $30 and subsequently sold them at $35, you have a capital gain of ($35 − $30) × 100 = $500 or $5 per share (ignoring commissions).

Capital gains and losses are further divided into short-term and long-term gains and losses. If a security is held for no longer than 18 months (according to the new 1997 law), the proceeds are classified as a short-term capital gain or loss. If a security is held for more than 18 months, it is classified as a long-term capital gain or loss. Before the new 1997 law was employed, net long-term gains were taxed at a maximum rate of 28%. If your ordinary income tax rate was lower than 28%, net long-term capital gains were taxed at the ordinary income tax rate. Short-term capital gains are taxed at the ordinary income tax rate. With the new 1997 tax law, the 28% rate was reduced to 20% (or 18% if the investment is held for 5 years or more).

Commissions paid to brokers for making security transactions are deducted only after a security is sold. Commissions paid to buy a stock, for example, are considered a increasing the purchase price of the security. If 200 shares purchased at $30 resulted in a $60 commission then the price, including commission (known as the *basis*), is

$$\text{Basis} = \frac{(\$30 \times 200) + \$60}{200} = \$30.30 \text{ per share}$$

If an investor sells 100 shares for $33 (with a $30 commission) after four weeks, the investor's short-term capital gain is

$$(\$33 \times 100) - \$30 - (\$30.30 \times 100) = \$240$$

Exhibit 2A.1 lists the marginal tax rates – the amount of tax imposed on an additional dollar of income – for the four different categories of taxpayers, as well as the corporate tax rates. The tax rates are progressive, because they increase with a taxpayer's income. Hence, tax planning increases in importance as income increases. Exhibit 2A.2 lists the maximum capital gains for various holding periods. The investor can use these various rates to help decide what the holding period should be.

Exhibit 2A.1 Individual and corporate US tax rates

(a) Tax rates for individual investors in 1997

Single—Schedule X

If line 5 is: Over—	But not over—	The tax is:	of the amount over—
$0	$24,650	....................15%	$0
24,650	59,750	$3,697.50 + 28%	24,650
59,750	124,650	13,525.50 + 31%	59,750
124,650	271,050	33,644.50 + 36%	124,650
271,050	....	86,348.50 + 39.6%	271,050

Married filing jointly or Qualifying widow(er)—Schedule Y-1

If line 5 is: Over—	But not over—	The tax is:	of the amount over—
$0	$41,200	....................15%	$0
41,200	99,600	$6,180.00 + 28%	41,200
99,600	151,750	22,532.00 + 31%	99,600
151,750	271,050	38,698.50 + 36%	151,750
271,050	....	81,646.50 + 39.6%	271,050

Head of household—Schedule Z

If line 5 is: Over—	But not over—	The tax is:	of the amount over—
$0	$33,050	....................15%	$0
33,050	85,350	$4,957.50 + 28%	33,050
85,350	138,200	19,601.50 + 31%	85,350
138,200	271,050	35,985.00 + 36%	138,200
271,050	....	83,811.00 + 39.6%	271,050

Married filing separately—Schedule Y-2

If line 5 is: Over—	But not over—	The tax is:	of the amount over—
$0	$20,600	....................15%	$0
20,600	49,800	$3,090.00 + 28%	20,600
49,800	75,875	11,266.00 + 31%	49,800
75,875	135,525	19,349.25 + 36%	75,875
135,525	....	40,823.25 + 39.6%	135,525

Source: US Internal Revenue Service.

(b) US corporate tax rate schedule for 1997

Tax rate	Taxable income
15%	$0–50,000
25%	$50,001–$75,000
34%	$75,001–$100,000
39%[a]	$100,001–$335,000
34%	$335,001–$10,000,000
35%	$10,000,001–$15,000,000
38%[b]	$15,000,001–$18,333,333
35%	Over $18,333,333

[a] Includes additional 5% recapture tax under 1986 law.
[b] Includes additional 3% recapture tax under 1993 law.
Source: US Internal Revenue Service.

2A.1 Bonds

In general, bond coupon payments are considered ordinary income for tax purposes. When a bond is sold before maturity, the bond price changes are treated as capital gains and losses. However, not all bonds are taxable. The most important consideration is whether the bond's coupon payments are subject to federal income taxes. Municipal bonds are exempt from federal income tax. Because of this exemption, municipal bonds typically trade at higher prices (lower yields) than comparable corporate bonds (see

Exhibit 2A.2 US Capital Gains Tax summary*

Holding period of asset or stock	Maximum Capital Gains Tax as of 1997	Maximum Capital Gains Tax prior to 1997
If held between 0 and 12 months	39.6%	39.6%
If held between 12 and 18 months	28%	28%
If held between 18 and 60 months	20%	28%
If held more than 60 months but acquired after 2000	18%	28%

* The 20% rate applies to assets sold between 6 May 1997 and 29 July 1997 and held for between 12 and 18 months. Investors should confirm the applicable tax rates relevant to their situation with the Internal Revenue Service Tax Code.

Chapter 7). Investors in the highest tax bracket may find municipal bonds attractive on an after-tax basis.

Numerous other minor issues should be examined. For example, municipal bonds are typically also exempt from state or local income taxes in the locality where they are issued. Municipal bonds issued by, say, the state of Alabama are exempt from Alabama income tax. Also, investment in some bonds issued at a deep discount (for example, zero-coupon bonds) requires that income tax be paid on the interest accrued each year, even though the interest is not paid until the bond matures. The worst of both worlds can occur with such bonds. An investor might buy a 20-year zero-coupon bond, pay taxes each year on the implied interest (even though the investor receives no interest), and then have the bond default in the last year.

2A.2 Stocks

The cash dividends received from stocks are considered ordinary income. However, stock splits are not considered ordinary income. When a stock splits (say, two shares for each one share owned), the cost basis is adjusted.

For example, if you purchase 100 shares of Microsoft for $90 per share and pay a $50 brokerage commission, your cost basis is

$$\text{Basis} = (\$90 \times 100) + \$50 = \$9,050$$

or $90.50 ($9,050/100) per share. If Microsoft splits 2-for-1, you receive two new shares for every old share. The new basis per share is $45.25($9,050/200), and you own 200 shares. If 100 shares are sold after nine months at $50 per share (with a commission of $30), you will have the following short-term capital gain:

$$\text{Capital gain} = (100 \times \$50) - \$30 - (100 \times \$45.25)$$
$$= \$5,000 - \$30 - \$4,525$$
$$= \$45$$

Like dividends on common stocks, preferred stock dividends are not tax deductible for the company (whereas interest payments are tax deductible). However, 70% of the dividend on preferred stocks is tax exempt to most corporate owners. Thus, companies that purchase preferred shares do not have to pay taxes on 70% of the preferred dividends, although individuals must pay the full income tax rate. Therefore, corporations have an incentive to hold preferred stock, and preferred stock is most suitable for corporate clients.

This appendix has described only the major tax consequences of investment in bonds and stocks. For more information, see Ray Sommerfeld's *Essentials of Taxation* (Reading, Ma: Addison-Wesley, 1989).

Chapter 3

SECURITY MARKETS

Learning objectives

After studying this chapter you should be able to:

1 Describe the function of security markets.
2 Contrast the primary and secondary markets.
3 Explain how the investor can trade, in particular the growing role of Internet trading.
4 Summarize the operation of the secondary market.
5 Describe the basic structure of security markets.
6 Survey world security markets.

INVESTMENT IN THE NEWS

Investing in the future: Charging the net

Merrill to join online brokers it once derided

. . . By July 12, Merrill will introduce a relationship account, with an asset-based fee (minimum $1,500), offering a broker's advice and unlimited trading via the Internet, phone or broker, plus various other perks. By December 1, clients will be able to open accounts with no asset-based fee and no advisor, and be able to trade on the 'Net for as little as $29.99 per transaction.

The move puts Merrill toe-to-toe with Charles Schwab, the leading online broker, with good reason: In the first quarter, Merrill brought in $9 billion of new U.S. client assets versus $28 billion for Schwab. No doubt some of Schwab's gains were Merrill's losses.

In 18 months, John "Launny" Stefens, Merrill's vice chairman and brokerage chief, expects the firm to open 200,000 accounts under the $29.99 trading option and 200,000–300,000 relationship accounts, using the $1,500 fee option. The source: Merrill's existing base of five million accounts and new clients.

"The relationship account, I think, is revolutionary, and it has gotten very little press," says Steffens. "The $29.99 offer is just 10% of the story and it has taken 95% of the press so far."

The relationship account includes services that Stefens values at $600–$800. In addition to unlimited trades, investors get among other things: conventional or online cash-management accounts, which usually cost $100; a Visa signature card allowing no-fee ATM transactions worldwide; access to Merrill Lynch OnLine, and a financial planning package that evaluates an investor's retirement, estate and education needs, which normally costs $250.

Yes, the man who once called online trading hazardous to one's financial health has embraced the World Wide Web. "I can't be the father protectorate," says Stefens. But he maintains that "excessive trading isn't good, whether it's online or anywhere else." . . .

Source: Jacqueline Doherty, *Barron's*, 7 June 1999, p. 13.

Commission fees are one of the main sources of income of brokerage houses. Buying stocks with Merrill Lynch as a broker in the past, you had to pay about a 2% commission fee. Thus, with a $100,000 transaction, paying a fee of $2,500 was very common. High fees have been relegated to history. With the Internet service, Merrill Lynch suggests a commission fee of $29.99 per transaction. No wonder the brokerage firms and, in particular, Merrill Lynch objected in the past to online electronic trading. However, competition is the name of the game. Merrill lost business to brokers such as Charles Schwab and had no choice but to join the Internet trading revolution.

This chapter is a study of security markets – the markets where investors buy and sell the financial assets described in Chapter 2. This task is not as simple as it might seem, because security markets have changed dramatically as technology has improved and Internet investing is increasing. In a sense, learning about security markets is like aiming at a moving target.

As this chapter's *Investment in the news* illustrates, Internet investing is taking off. In many ways the Internet is ideal technology for investment tasks. It's *dynamic*: an investor can get stock quotes that are ahead of those on the 'crawler' ticker at the bottom of the television screen and daily NAVs before they are printed in the next morning's paper. The Internet is *inexpensive*: brokerages often offer lower trade commissions online, because it is cheaper for them to accept trades that way. It's *automated*: normal office hours do not apply, which is crucial in an era when everyone leads hectic lives. It's *searchable*: you can find a wealth of free, sophisticated information that was once available only to wealthy individuals, investment analysts and larger corporations.

Regardless of the changes in security markets, these markets are designed to allow firms to raise funds for growth and capital investment. They are the arenas in which investors – both individual investors and institutional investors – execute their buying and selling decisions. It is this aspect of security markets that we study in this chapter.

Our investigation of markets begins with Section 3.1, a discussion of the reasons why markets exist and the benefits they offer to society. Sections 3.2 and 3.3 explain the institutional structure of security markets. They describe the primary market, where securities are first sold, and the secondary market, where securities are subsequently traded. Section 3.4 describes and compares different methods of trading. In Section 3.5, world security markets are discussed. Finally, security markets are viewed in terms of historical development.

3.1 THE ROLE OF SECURITY MARKETS

A **market** is the means by which products and services are bought and sold, directly or through an agent. A market need not be a physical location. Indeed, it can be a computer network or a telecommunications system, as described in *Investment in the news*. In a security market, you do not have to possess the security you wish to sell; you can sell a security that you do not own but that you can borrow.

A security market that functions effectively provides society with two benefits. First, it allocates scarce resources – in this case, investors' funds – to those firms that will make the best economic use of them. That is, a well-functioning security market helps suppliers of funds find those who demand funds and will make the best use of them. For example, consider two firms that both need several hundred million dollars for investment. Firm A can make 20% on this investment, whereas Firm B can make only 15% (assume the risk is similar). Suppose there is a limited supply of funds. If the market is efficient and all information is available to potential investors, these investors will be more inclined to buy Stock A than Stock B. Therefore, more money will be allocated to the more profitable firm. Second, a well-functioning security market will reduce the cost of moving in and out of securities, which in turn enlarges the set of investors willing to supply funds; hence, firms will have more funds to invest in production.

A well-functioning security market also benefits buyers and sellers in three ways: by making information available, by establishing prices, and by increasing the liquidity of the assets being bought or sold.

3.1.1 Information availability

Buyers and sellers must be able to communicate with each other and have access to timely and accurate information in a well-functioning security market. Notice that neither criterion requires the buyer and seller (or their representatives) to meet at a physical location.

3.1.2 Price setting

In a well-functioning security market, prices should reflect all the available information. That is, the market price should not misrepresent known information. Price setting has its costs, and for a market to function well, these costs should be minimal. We call these costs of price setting **execution costs**, and they include *transaction costs, market impact effects* and *inaccurate price discovery*.

Transaction costs include the costs related to communication systems, the costs related to the party who is willing to buy or sell the securities, and any other fees or expenses. When transaction costs are low, more investors are willing to participate in the market.

Market impact effects are price changes that result from buying or selling pressure. For example, a stock may be quoted at $100, but if it has to fall to $90 for an investor to be able to sell 10,000 shares, this market impact effect represents a major cost to the investor.

Inaccurate price discovery refers to securities trading at prices that do not reflect true value. Clearly, buying a stock that is 10% overpriced will be costly. In a well-functioning security market, prices adjust quickly to new information, and securities are correctly priced. If there is a lag between the time when information is available and a price change, price discovery will be inaccurate during this period.

3.1.3 Liquidity

The liquidity of a security market is the ease with which securities can be purchased or sold without a dramatic impact on their prices. When markets are liquid, transactions are completed quickly. For example, the market for US Treasury bills is more liquid than the market for real estate, because $10 million in US Treasury bills can be traded in seconds at their fair market price, whereas trading real estate may take months. The market for stocks and bonds of big companies is more liquid than the market for securities of smaller firms. When markets are liquid, market participants execute trades at existing prices or at prices which are very close to the existing prices. This certainty of quoted prices is called **price continuity.** If prices are fairly certain and only small changes occur when a trade takes place, we say we have price continuity.

We can measure the liquidity of different security markets by looking at the depth, breadth and resiliency of transactions that occur in each market. If a sufficient number of orders exist at prices above and below the price at which shares are currently trading, the transaction has **depth.**[1] Otherwise the market is **shallow.** If a large volume of orders exist at prices above and below the current price, the transaction has **breadth.** Otherwise, it is called a **thin market.** If new orders come into the market rapidly when prices change due to an imbalance of orders, the transaction has **resiliency.**[2]

Exhibit 3.1 illustrates this concept when the current price is assumed to be 99\frac{1}{8}$. The exhibit shows hypothetical stock orders at various bid prices as they appear in the Market Maker limit order book. (The concepts of bid price, market maker and limit order will be explained later in the chapter.) Column A demonstrates a thin and shallow market; Column B, a thin and deep market; Column C, a broad and shallow market; and Column D, a broad and deep market. If the market for a given stock is broad and deep, as well as resilient, it is considered to be a relatively liquid market. A transaction can be made in such a market quickly, with no significant price change.

3.2 THE PRIMARY SECURITY MARKET

Securities are traded on two basic markets: the primary market and the secondary market. The **primary market** is the mechanism through which a firm can raise additional capital by selling stocks, bonds and other securities. All securities are first traded in the primary market, and the proceeds from the sale of securities go to the issuing firm. The issuers of new securities include both corporate and government entities. The **secondary market** is where previously issued securities trade among investors. Note that the issuing firm does not receive any funds when its securities are traded in the secondary market. However, the secondary market provides liquidity for the newly issued securities in the

Exhibit 3.1 Hypothetical stock orders*

Bid price	Alternative hypothetical orders			
	A	B	C	D
$100	100	100	1,000	1,000
99$\frac{1}{8}$	100	100	1,000	1,000
99$\frac{3}{4}$	10	50	0	1,200
99$\frac{5}{8}$	5	20	0	1,400
99$\frac{1}{2}$	0	10	0	1,500
99$\frac{1}{8}$	0	5	0	1,600
99	0	5	0	1,700
Market condition	thin and shallow	thin and deep	broad and shallow	broad and deep

* For simplicity of the discussion, all orders are assumed to be of equal volume. Hence the larger the number of orders, the larger also the volume of orders.

---

[1] These orders are known as *limit orders* and are covered in Section 3.4.7.
[2] For more information, see Robert A. Schwartz, *Equity Markets: Structure, Trading, and Performance* (New York: Harper & Row, 1988).

primary market. Investors are much more willing to buy securities in the primary market when they know there will be a market in which to trade them in the future. The existence of a well-functioning secondary market thus makes buying securities in the primary market more appealing.

Historically, new issues have been a profitable investment over the short run. To attract willing investors, new issues have been underpriced; that is, they have been sold at a small discount from their fair market value. Thus, the appeal of buying securities in the primary market over the secondary market is the potential for making above-average returns.

Securities traded in the primary market for the very first time are referred to as **initial public offerings (IPOs)**. A company can have only one IPO. If a company has sold stock previously, a new stock offering is called a **primary offering** or a **seasoned new issue**. After the initial trading, the securities move to the secondary market. To issue securities in the primary market, a firm must provide a **prospectus**, a legal document containing the business plan and other information that will help investors make prudent investment decisions.

3.2.1 Investment bankers and underwriting

Security issues in the primary market are usually handled by **investment bankers**, who assist firms needing funds by locating individuals and firms wanting to invest funds. Investment bankers act as **underwriters** of a new issue – intermediaries between the buyers and sellers of a new issue, who may also provide a guarantee (for a certain fee) that the new issue is successful.

Underwriters perform different services to firms. Of course, the more services they provide, the larger the underwriting fee. Underwriters may do the following:

1 *Give advice*. Underwriters provide advice as to the type and terms of security to offer and the timing of the issue.
2 *Provide a firm commitment*. In this arrangement the underwriter buys the issue at a predetermined price from the issuing corporation with the expectation of reselling shares of the issue at a higher price.
3 *Make a best effort*. In this arrangement the underwriter markets the new issue as best it can and takes no price risk. The underwriter does not take ownership of the securities.
4 *Issue a standby commitment*. In this arrangement the underwriter buys the remainder of an issue that could not be sold above a specified price. The price that the underwriter must pay is substantially less than the market price; hence, the standby commitment is less risky than the firm commitment (see below).

The largest underwriters are listed in Exhibit 3.2(a). In terms of equity capital, Morgan Stanley/Dean Witter are the largest; however, Goldman Sachs earned the highest profit in 1996. Exhibit 3.2(b) lists some of the new issues brokers in the UK.

Underwriters generate revenues from the firm commitment arrangement, through the difference between the firm commitment price (P_{FC}) and the price received when issued (P_I). The difference between these two prices is referred to as the **gross spread (GS)** or the **underwriter's discount**. Thus,

$$\text{Gross spread} = \text{price received by the issue} - \text{firm commitment price}$$

or

$$GS = P_I - P_{FC} \tag{3.1}$$

Exhibit 3.2(a) How they stack up: profits at some of Wall Street's biggest securities firms (in billions)

Firm	1996 Profit	Equity capital
Goldman	$2.60[a]	$5.40
Morgan Stanley, Dean Witter	1.96[b]	12.20
Merrill Lynch	1.62	7.30
Salomon	0.62	5.90
Bear Stearns	0.58[c]	3.28
Lehman	0.42	4.10
Paine Webber	0.36	1.84

[a] Goldman profits are stated before taxes and payments to partners.
[b] Morgan Stanley, Dean Witter's profits have been restated to reflect the 1997 merger.
[c] Annualized net income for the 12 months ended 31 December 1996.

Source: Wall Street Journal, 5 August 1997, p. C1. Wall Street Journal (Online) by *Wall Street Journal*. © 1997 by Dow Jones & Co., Inc. Reproduced with permission of Dow Jones & Co., Inc. in the format *Fundamentals of Investments* via Copyright Clearance Center.

Exhibit 3.2(b) Some new issues brokers on the London Stock Exchange in May 2001

Brewin Dolphin Securities Ltd
Capital International Ltd
Charles Stanley & Co Ltd
Durlacher Ltd
Fyshe Horton Finney Limited
Goodbody Stockbrokers
I A Pritchard Stockbrokers Ltd
Keith, Bayley, Rogers & Co
Kyte Securities, a division of The Kyte Group Ltd
Lloyds TSB Stockbrokers Ltd
Numis Securities Ltd
Peel, Hunt plc
Rathbone Neilson Cobbold Ltd
Redmayne-Bentley
Robson Cotterell Ltd
St Paul's Square Stockbrokers Ltd
Stocktrade, a division of Brewin Dolphin Securities Ltd
The Share Centre Limited
Walker, Crips, Weddle, Beck plc
Wilkinform Stockbrokers Ltd
Wise Speke, a division of Brewin Dolphin Securities Ltd

Source: Website at http://www.londonstockexchange.com/newissues/brokers/brokers.asp, 27 May 2001. © London Stock Exchange 2001. Reprinted with permission.

To illustrate how an investment banker profits from a firm commitment, consider the following example. Morgan Stanley helped issue 100,000 $1,000 par Gulf Stages Inc. 20-year bonds. The firm commitment price was 98.5% of par (P_{FC} = $985), and the issuing price turned out to be 100.50% of par (P_I = $1,005.00). The gross spread per bond was GS = $1,005 − $985 = $20, or $2,000,000 for the issue ($20 × 100,000).

The gross spread, given as a percentage of the total proceeds to the firm, varies with the type of issue and its size. The gross spread for IPOs of bonds is about 14% for small issues (less than $1 million) and drops to about 1% for large issues ($50 million or more). For preferred stocks, the range (for the corresponding issue size) is 1.5% to 17%; for common stocks the range is 4% to 22%. If the issue has already traded in the market, the gross spread is much smaller: for stocks, about 15% for an issue of less than

$1 million and about 4% for large issues of more than $50 million. For stock right issues, the fees are much smaller: about 8% for small issues and 4% for large issues. (A stock right issue is an issue of a common stock to existing shareholders at a discount from the market price.) The reason why the spread is smaller for right issues is that rights are offered to the public at a price much lower than the current market price; hence, the underwriter's risk is relatively small. If the stocks are sold as best efforts, the underwriter does not take any risk, and the fee is about one-third (or much less, for large issues) of the gross fee. Usually, even a relatively small fee covers the administrative costs of handling the issue and makes a profit for the investment bank. The main risk faced by underwriters with firm commitments is the possibility of enormous losses between the time the underwriter makes a firm commitment and the time the underwriter sells the securities to the public. If the underwriter is wrong in the anticipated issue price, it could prove costly. Exhibit 3.3 lists the entry fees in the major US stock exchanges.

In an IPO there is no market price of the stock, hence the underwriter may be very wrong in the estimate of the value of the firm, and is therefore vulnerable to a big loss.

Exhibit 3.3 Entry fee comparison: major US stock markets

Number of Shares	Nasdaq National Market	NYSE	Amex	The Nasdaq SmallCap Market
Up to 1 million	$34,525	$51,550	$10,000	$6,000
1+ to 2 million	$38,750	$51,550 – $66,300	$15,000	$6,000 – $7,000
2+ to 3 million	$48,750	$66,300 – $73,700	$20,000	$7,000 – $8,000
3+ to 4 million	$53,750	$73,700 – $81,100	$22,500	$8,000 – $9,000
4+ to 5 million	$60,000	$81,100 – $84,600	$25,000	$9,000 – $10,000
5+ to 6 million	$63,725	$84,600 – $88,100	$27,500	$10,000
6+ to 7 million	$66,875	$88,100 – $91,600	$30,000	$10,000
7+ to 8 million	$69,375	$91,600 – $95,100	$32,500	$10,000
8+ to 9 million	$72,875	$95,100 – $98,600	$35,000	$10,000
9+ to 10 million	$75,625	$98,600 – $102,100	$37,500	$10,000
10+ to 11 million	$78,875	$102,100 – $105,600	$42,500	$10,000
11+ to 12 million	$81,625	$105,600 – $109,100	$42,500	$10,000
12+ to 13 million	$84,875	$109,100 – $112,600	$42,500	$10,000
13+ to 14 million	$87,000	$112,600 – $116,100	$42,500	$10,000
14+ to 15 million	$88,500	$116,100 – $119,600	$42,500	$10,000
15+ to 16 million	$90,500	$119,600 – $123,100	$50,000	$10,000
16+ to 20 million	$95,000	$123,100 – $137,100	$50,000	$10,000
20+ to 25 million	$95,000	$137,100 – $154,600	$50,000	$10,000
25+ to 50 million	$95,000	$154,600 – $242,100	$50,000	$10,000
50+ to 75 million	$95,000	$242,100 – $329,600	$50,000	$10,000
75+ to 100 million	$95,000	$329,600 – $417,100	$50,000	$10,000
100+ to 125 million	$95,000	$417,100 – $500,000[a]	$50,000	$10,000
More than 125 million	$95,000	$500,000[a]	$50,000	$10,000

Fees include one-time initial listing charges of $5,000 for the Nasdaq National Market®, $36,800 for NYSE, $5,000 for Amex®, and $5,000 for The Nasdaq SmallCap Market.

The original fees for the Nasdaq National Market and The Nasdaq SmallCap Market are based on total shares outstanding. The original listing fees for NYSE and Amex are based on the total number of shares outstanding plus any shares reserved for a specific future issuance.

[a] The initial fee component of the original listing fee for common shares is capped at $500,000 including the $36,800 special charge.

Source: The American Stock Exchange, New York Stock Exchange, The Nasdaq Stock Market (March 2000).

The risks of an IPO are demonstrated by the experience of Orbital Science Corporation, a space technologies firm. Orbital Science Corporation specializes in launching satellites into orbit from underneath the wing of a large plane. The firm and underwriter originally scheduled an IPO of stock to occur a month before the first rocket launch. Then an article appeared in the *Wall Street Journal* describing how this first launch could make or break the company. Obviously, there was a risk that the launch would fail and the stock's value would diminish. To reduce the price risk, Orbital Science and the underwriter delayed the issue until the outcome of the launch was known. On 5 April 1990, at 12:10 Pacific Daylight Time, Orbital Science successfully launched its first rocket. On 24 April 1990, Orbital Science sold about 2.4 million shares of stock at $14 per share during its initial public offering.[3] Clearly, an unsuccessful launch would have greatly influenced the issuing price.

If the IPO had not been deployed and the launch had failed, the underwriter could have suffered a very big loss. To reduce this risk exposure, underwriters form **syndicates** (purchase groups), groups of investment bankers that agree to participate in the risk related to the sale of an IPO. Participation includes accepting part of the risk, as well as part of the potential revenues. The syndicate also forms a selling group that includes the investment bankers in the syndicate, as well as others whose sole focus is distribution of the shares in the IPO. The selling group typically does not take any risk. Exhibit 3.4(a) shows an announcement of an IPO. The syndicate (purchase group) is Bear, Stearns & Co., Inc., Hambrecht & Quist and Wit Capital Corporation (the lead investment bankers). The remaining firms listed make up the selling group. Such an announcement is called a *tombstone*. The IPO is for selling 10,781,250 common shares of drkoop.com, at a price of $9.00 per share. On 2 August 1999, the price of drkoop.com (symbol: 'Koop'), was $21 per share, a rise of 133% from its IPO date.

Exhibit 3.4(b) shows two companies which had gone public in 1999 at the Nasdaq. The exhibit describes all the relevant data of the two stocks, IVGN and BIGI. It is very interesting to look at the price of the stocks in May 2001. The IPO price of IVGN was $15 and the price in May 2001 is $75. But for BIGI the story is not the same. The price of the IPO was $14 but in May 2001, the price of the stock is only $6.

Exhibit 3.4(c) lists some of the IPO filings in the US market in May 2001. The investment banking industry also underwrites issues that are not IPOs, namely stocks of firms that have outstanding shares. In this case, the market price is known. Generally, when additional shares are issued, the price of identical shares outstanding is temporarily depressed, and the underwriter must take this into account. The firm is trying to sell a large number of shares at one time, and there may not be willing buyers. Price pressure from the new supply of shares can result in a significant stock price reduction. For example, when General Motors announced its plans to issue $2.9 billion in new stock, the stock price sank $2.7 per share, to $39.625 (a decline of more than 6%).

In response to this type of problem, in 1982 the Securities and Exchange Commission (SEC) allowed for *shelf registration* under Rule 415 for certain types of securities. This rule allows large firms to register security issues and sell the issues in pieces during the two years following the initial registration (possibly on short notice). Thus, firms can reduce the losses due to price pressure by issuing the shares when the market is strong.

---

[3] Based on several articles appearing in the *Wall Street Journal*, 13 February, 23 March, 26 March, 6 April, and 25 April 1990.

PRACTICE BOX

Problem

Suppose Kidder Peabody was the underwriter of a 3 million common stock issue under a firm commitment. The IPO was issued at $10 per share, and the firm commitment for $9.875 per share. What was Kidder Peabody's gross spread? What was the gross spread as a percentage of the firm's proceeds?

Solution

The gross spread is the difference between the issue price and the firm commitment price (see Equation 3.1), or $10 − $9.875 = $0.125 per share, or $0.125 × 3 million = $375,000. The firm's proceeds are $9.875 × 3 million = $29.625 million. Hence, the percentage gross spread is $375,000/$29,625,000 = 0.01266, or 1.266%.

Exhibit 3.4(a)

This announcement is neither an offer to sell nor a solicitation of an offer to buy any of these securities.
The offering is made only by the Prospectus.
New Issue
10,781,250 Shares

Common Stock
Price $9.00 Per Share

Copies of the Prospectus may be obtained in any State in which this announcement is circulated from only such of the Underwriters, including the undersigned, as may lawfully offer these securities in such State.

Bear, Stearns & Co. Inc.	**Hambrecht & Quist**	**Wit Capital Corporation** *as e-Manager*™
Banc of America Securities LLC	BancBoston Robertson Stephens	Deutsche Banc Alex. Brown
Goldman, Sachs & Co.	ING Baring Furman Selz LLC	Merrill Lynch & Co.
Warburg Dillon Read LLC	Thomas Weisel Partners	SG Cowen, B.C. Ziegler and Company
Access Financial Group, Inc.	William Blair & Company	Cantor, Weiss & Friedner, Inc.
Chatsworth Securities LLC	Friedman, Billings, Ramsey & Co., Inc.	Josephthal & Co. Inc.
Kenny Securities Corp.	Leerink Swann & Company	Southwest Securities
Vector Securities International, Inc.	Volpe Brown Whelan & Company	Wunderlich Securities, Inc.

Exhibit 3.4(b) Two US listings from the 1999 Nasdaq IPO case studies

Invitrogen Corporation IVGN
Carlsbad, CA

Develops, manufactures, and sells products designed to facilitate molecular biology research.

SIC 2836	Biological Products
CEO	Mr. Lyle C. Turner
CFO	Mr. James R. Glynn
Lead Manager	Donaldson, Lufkin & Jenrette
Co-Managers	Warburg Dillon Read
	U.S. Bancorp Piper Jaffray Inc.
IPO Price	$15.000
IPO Shares	3,500,000
Closing price on first day of trading (26/02/99)	$15.375
Closing price on 31/12/99	$60.000*
Price appreciation from first day traded to year end	290%
Market Makers	8
IPO Market Value	$189,363,150
Market value at end of first day of trading	$194,097,229
Market value as of 31/12/99	$970,920,000

Pinnacle Holdings, Inc. BIGI
Sarasota, FL

Provides wireless communications tower space, primarily in the Southeastern United States.

SIC 4899	Communication Services
CEO	Mr. Robert Wolsey
CFO	Mr. Steven Day
Lead Manager	Deutsche Banc Alex. Brown
Co-Managers	Salomon Smith Barney Inc.
	Banc of America Securities
	Raymond James & Associates, Inc.
IPO Price	$14.0000
IPO Shares	20,000,000
Closing price on first day of trading (19/02/99)	$14.0625
Closing price on 31/12/99	$42.3750†
Price appreciation from first day traded to year end	201%
Market Makers	13
IPO Market Value	$419,999,314
Market value at end of first day of trading	$421,874,311
Market value as of 31/12/99	$1,741,400,625

* The price in May 2001 was $75.
† The price in May 2001 was $6.

Source: Website at http://www.finance.yahoo.com. Nasdaq data © 2002, The Nasdaq Stock Market, Inc. Reprinted with the permission of The Nasdaq Stock Market, Inc.

Exhibit 3.4(c) Some IPO filings in May 2001

Company Name	Symbol	Market	IPO Date	Price	Shares	Received	Form Type
QUANTUM BRIDGE...	QBCI	Nasdaq National Market	–	–	–	5/25/2001	RW
GPC CAPITAL COR ...	GPA	New York Stock Exchange	–	–	–	5/24/2001	RW
ECHAPMAN COM IN...	ECMN	Nasdaq National Market	6/20/2000	13.00	1,260,000	5/23/2001	424B3
SMITH & WOLLENS...	SWRG	Nasdaq National Market	5/23/2001	8.50	5,295,972	5/23/2001	424B4
SMITH & WOLLENS...	SWRG	Nasdaq National Market	5/23/2001	8.50	5,295,972	5/23/2001	S-1MEF
PEABODY ENERGY ...	BTU	New York Stock Exchange	5/22/2001	28.00	15,000,000	5/22/2001	424B1
NATUS MEDICAL I...	BABY	Nasdaq National Market	–	$10.00–$12.00	4,500,000	5/22/2001	S-1/A
PEABODY ENERGY ...	BTU	New York Stock Exchange	5/22/2001	28.00	15,000,000	5/22/2001	424B1
FMC TECHNOLOGIE...	FTI	New York Stock Exchange	–	$19.00–$21.00	8,840,000	5/21/2001	S-1/A
GLOBAL POWER EQ...	GEG	New York Stock Exchange	5/18/2001	20.00	7,350,000	5/21/2001	424B4
PRINCETON REVIE...	REVU	Nasdaq National Market	–	$11.00–$13.00	5,400,000	5/21/2001	S-1/A
KRAFT FOODS INC	KFT	New York Stock Exchange	–	$27.00–$30.00	280,000,000	5/21/2001	S-1/A
MULTILINK TECHN...	MLTC	Nasdaq National Market	–	$10.00	8,000,000	5/18/2001	S-1/A
CHARTER FINANCI...	–	Nasdaq National Market	–	$10.00	5,157,750	5/18/2001	S-1/A
INSTINET GROUP...	INET	Nasdaq National Market	5/18/2001	14.50	32,000,000	5/18/2001	424B1
PEABODY ENERGY ...	BTU	New York Stock Exchange	5/22/2001	28.00	15,000,000	5/17/2001	S-1/A
TELLIUM INC	TELM	Nasdaq National Market	5/17/2001	15.00	9,000,000	5/17/2001	424B4
BIRCH TELECOM I...	–	Nasdaq National Market	–	0	1	5/17/2001	RW
TELLIUM INC	TELM	Nasdaq National Market	5/17/2001	15.00	9,000,000	5/17/2001	S-1MEF
WEBGAIN INC	WEBG	Nasdaq National Market	–	$10.00–$12.00	6,000,000	5/17/2001	S-1/A
KRAFT FOODS INC	KFT	New York Stock Exchange	–	$27.00–$30.00	280,000,000	5/17/2001	S-1/A
INSTINET GROUP ...	INET	Nasdaq National Market	5/18/2001	14.50	32,000,000	5/17/2001	S-1MEF
GLOBAL POWER EQ...	GEG	New York Stock Exchange	5/18/2001	20.00	7,350,000	5/16/2001	S-1/A
INSTINET GROUP...	INET	Nasdaq National Market	5/18/2001	14.50	32,000,000	5/16/2001	S-1/A
SMTC CORP	SMTX	Nasdaq National Market	7/21/2000	16.00	11,000,000	5/16/2001	424B3

Source: Website at http://www.nasdaq.com/reference/IPOs.stm, 27 May 2001. Nasdaq data © 2001, The Nasdaq Stock Market, Inc. Reprinted with the permission of The Nasdaq Stock Market, Inc.

3.2.2 IPOs versus private placement

An alternative way to raise capital in the primary market is through a private placement. A **private placement** is an offering of a security directly to one investor or group of investors.

For example, on 21 January 1998 the Macerich Company (MAC) raised $100 million from a private placement with Security Capital Group Incorporated (SCZ). A private placement bypasses the public marketplace and is therefore generally less costly than IPOs. Why do firms sometimes select private placements rather than public issues? In the United States, private placements do not require a prospectus. However, a **private placement memorandum**, which provides information regarding the new issue, is required. A private placement memorandum is less exhaustive than a prospectus. Prior to April 1990, private placements could not be resold for two years. This restriction greatly hampered the private placement market by effectively eliminating any liquidity. In April 1990, however, the SEC adopted Rule 144A, which allows 'large' institutions to trade private placements with other 'large' institutions without having to wait two years or register the placement with the SEC.

Initial public offerings in the United States require prior review by the SEC, as well as compliance with a large number of costly regulations. Section (2) of the Securities Act of 1933 exempts 'nonpublic' or private offerings. Regulation D adopted by the SEC in 1982 gave specific guidelines for what is exempt under Section 4(2) of the 1933 act. These guidelines require no general advertising for private issues. However, the sale must be to 'sophisticated' investors who can evaluate the risk and return and who have substantial economic resources.[4]

Exhibit 3.5(a) shows the instructions for joining the London Stock Exchange. Exhibit 3.5(b) shows the list of rules and regulatory guidance of the London Stock Exchange, and Exhibit 3.5(c) shows the new issues list as of 27 May 2001.

3.2.3 Underpricing IPOs and price discovery

If IBM were to consider issuing stocks when its stock is already traded in the market at $80, the underwriters as well as potential investors would know that the issuing price could not be much further away from $80. IPOs, on the other hand, have no pre-existing market price. Thus, the underwriter has to evaluate and estimate the 'fair' price for the stock. Pricing IPOs is very complicated and requires tools that are covered in the remainder of this book. Setting aside the issue of determining the appropriate value of a security, let us examine why underwriters tend to underprice IPOs relative to their 'fair' value.

Underwriters face a dilemma in pricing IPOs. If they overprice the issue, then the investors who buy the IPOs will lose both money and trust in the investment bankers. If they underprice the issue, then the issuing firm will lose both capital and trust in the investment bankers. On average, underwriters historically have underpriced IPOs.[5] For example, during the week 14–18 June 1999, 10 IPOs came to the market, raising $1.2 billion. Because of the underpricing, these 10 IPOs averaged a 35% gain on the first day of trade, with 'PHONE.COM' picking up 150.8% on the first day of trade!

Several explanations are often given for IPO underpricing:

1 *Information asymmetry*. Differences in the information available to the firm, investment banker and potential investors is known as **information asymmetry**. For example, the firm and the investment banker may have better information than investors. If this is the case, the investors who are less informed will have greater

---

[4] For more details, see Frank J. Fabozzi and Franco Modigliani, *Capital Markets Institutions and Instruments* (Englewood Cliffs, NJ: Prentice-Hall, 1992).
[5] See Clifford W. Smith, 'Investment banking and the capital acquisition process', *Journal of Financial Economics*, 15 (January–February 1986): 3–29.

Exhibit 3.5(a) Instructions for joining the London Stock Exchange

HOW TO JOIN OUR MARKETS

We provide a range of markets for UK and international companies of all sizes to facilitate capital raising and trading in their shares. This section gives companies an overview of the markets and information on how to join them.

The London Stock Exchange plays a vital role in maintaining London's position as one of the world's leading financial centres. As the national stock exchange for the UK and the world's main marketplace for listing UK and international equities, the Exchange provides an environment where the trading of securities can flourish.

The Exchange provides a choice of markets – allowing companies large and small to raise capital and to have their shares traded publicly. Companies can join either the main market or the **Alternative Investment Market (AIM)**. Technology companies joining the main market may also be eligible to join **techMARK**, the Exchange's new market for innovative technology companies. The companies on the Exchange's markets represent over 60 countries from around the world. By listing in London, these companies have been able to reach a substantial and diverse investor base and to raise funds in the world's most heavily traded international market.

The Exchange regulates capital raising, assessing the applications of companies, monitoring listed and AIM companies' ongoing compliance with the rules, and dealing with any rule breaches. In the secondary market, in its role as a Recognised Investment Exchange (RIE), the Exchange is responsible for maintaining orderly markets and protecting against market abuse.

A two-stage admission process applies to companies that list in London. A company's securities need to be admitted to the Official List by the UK Listing Authority (UKLA), a division of the Financial Services Authority, and also admitted to trading by the Exchange. Once both processes are complete, the securities are officially listed on the Exchange. In parallel to the UKLA's listing process, the Exchange has its own set of Admission and Disclosure Standards which are designed to sit alongside the UKLA's Listing Rules to make access to the Exchange as straightforward as possible.

The Standards, which can be downloaded **here** contain admission requirements and ongoing disclosure requirements to be observed by companies seeking admission, or already admitted, to trading on our markets for listed securities. They do not apply to companies seeking to be admitted to AIM, our market for unlisted securities.

For further information about the admission process, please contact the Company Services Help Line on 020-7797-1600.

The Exchange has revised its 'Admission and Disclosure Standards'. The revised standards, which detail the Exchange's role in the admission of securities to trading, will come into effect on 1 June 2001. The Exchange has made a number of changes including:

- the techMARK eligibility and admission criteria have been incorporated into the Standards and revised to enable the inclusion of listed international equity securities and retail depositary receipts;
- a requirement that techMARK securities must be eligible for electronic settlement and admitted to trading on the London Stock Exchange's Domestic Equity Market ("DEM"); a requirement that all applications for admission to techMARK must be supported by a written submission;
- an obligation to submit information for the New Issues List with consequent inclusion of the New Issues Form in the Standards; and
- the removal of the requirement for the Block Admission Six Monthly Return (Schedule 2) to be submitted.

The changes to the techMARK eligibility criteria are supported by an extension of the arrangements for the admission of international companies to the DEM announced in January 2001. From 1 June 2001 international companies will be eligible for admission to the DEM where:

- they are either joining techMARK or are constituents of the Eurotop 300 or S&P 500 indices;
- they are admitted to the UK Listing Authority's Official List (either primary or secondary listing);
- there are adequate arrangements for electronic settlement by UK investors; and
- the issuer pays fees at the UK rate.

All trading and reporting obligations, as set out in the Rules of the London Stock Exchange, will apply to any security admitted to the DEM. The platform (SETS, SEAQ etc) used to trade the securities will depend on the same measures, including liquidity, as for securities issued by companies incorporated in the UK.

As a domestic company with equity lines of stock listed on the London Stock Exchange, you will be provided with free access to our new Company Report Service. This is a secure website that provides high quality interactive reports of your company's market performance, covering share price, trading and market value movements over the previous month and in the last 12 months. It allows you to select up to 5 key competitors/peers to benchmark your company's performance against. For more details of this service, select the 'Your Company Report', button.

For more information on the markets, please see the **Regulatory Guides** section and the **Stock Exchange Notices** section. Notices are issued periodically throughout the year and contain information of a regulatory nature and amendments to rules and/or guidance.

Source: Website at http://www.londonstockexchange.com/join/default.asp, 27 May 2001. © London Stock Exchange 2001. Reprinted with permission.

Exhibit 3.5(b) Rules and regulatory guidance for the London Stock Exchange

RULES & REGULATORY GUIDANCE

This section provides details about the regulatory role of the London Stock Exchange as well as Stock Exchange Notices, Regulatory Guides and Making a complaint.

<u>Overview of the Exchange's regulatory role</u>.

<u>Regulatory Forms</u> contains a number of standard forms in PDF format, which are used by member firms for regulatory purposes. Each form can be downloaded, printed, completed and returned to the relevant Exchange department.

<u>Market Rules</u> contains all chapters of "Rules of the London Stock Exchange" and rule update pages issued this year – Intended audience – member firms.

<u>Stock Exchange Notices</u> provides a search engine for new and historic Notices together with a <u>registration facility</u>. Intended audience – member firms and market professionals.

<u>Regulatory Guides</u> provide rules and guidance for the markets of the London Stock Exchange. Intended audience – member firms and market professionals.

<u>Global lending agreement</u> contains the prescribed agreement for on-exchange stock borrowing and lending transactions – intended audience member firms and market participants.

<u>Making a complaint</u> explains what to do if you have a complaint and how to make it. Intended audience – private investors.

<u>List of Member Firms</u> provides both an alphabetical and a regional list of member firms of the London Stock Exchange. Intended audience – member firms, market professionals and private investors.

Source: Website at http://www.londonstockexchange.com/regulation/default.asp, 27 May 2001. © London Stock Exchange 2001. Reprinted with permission.

Exhibit 3.5(c) London Stock Exchange new issues list on 27 May 2001

NEW ISSUES

The New Issues List is a list of all new companies which are either seeking admission to one of our markets or have been admitted to trading within the last seven days. This list provides basic information on the company, terms of the offer and its sponsors.

Company name ▼▲	Market ▼▲	Expected first day of trading ▼▲	Expected offer price (p)	Method of issue
Pursuit Dynamics plc	AIM	23/05/2001	N/A	N/A
Imprint Search and Selection plc	AIM	23/05/2001	80p	Placing
Transware plc	techMARK	21/06/2001	N/A	Introduction
Friends Provident Group Plc	Main	09/07/2001	N/A	N/A
Atlantic Global Plc	AIM	May 2001	25p	Placing
Cytomyx Holdings plc	AIM	TBC	TBC	TBC
Digital Broadcasting Corporation Plc	AIM	TBC	TBC	TBC
Picardy Media Group Plc	AIM	TBC	N/A	N/A

Source: Website at http://www.londonstockexchange.com/newissues/brokers/brokers.asp, 27 May 2001. © London Stock Exchange 2001. Reprinted with permission.

uncertainty about the issue and therefore will not buy it unless they are offered a lower price. Higher potential returns must be offered to attract investors to participate in the IPO market. These higher returns translate into underpricing.

2 *Scalping.* Higher returns have to be offered, because investment bankers and their affiliates tend to buy the really 'good' issues and leave the 'scraps' to the investing public. This skimming of quality issues is called **scalping.** To compensate the public for buying the 'scraps', a higher return should be offered, which again implies underpricing.

3 *Liquidity.* One benefit provided by the secondary market is liquidity. Investors will not buy IPOs that subsequently are hard to sell. One argument for why IPOs are underpriced is that underpricing is compensation for the relatively low liquidity. Also, there is uncertainty regarding the degree of liquidity that a security will subsequently command. Will there be any active trading in the future? This lack of liquidity is paid for by the firm by underpricing its IPO.

4 *Appraisal costs.* Assessing the fair value of an IPO has a cost. This cost has to be compensated. The prospectus must be studied, market data have to be collected and evaluated, and industry analysis is usually performed. If only one investor had to incur this cost, perhaps it would be negligible. Unfortunately, stock exchanges require a wide ownership of shares to facilitate trading and limit corporate control. Thus, every IPO must be evaluated by many investors. The more investors there are, the higher the total appraisal cost will be.

For example, if one investor buys the entire $100 million IPO and has $1,000 appraisal costs, the IPO should be underpriced by 0.001% ($1,000/$100,000,000). However, if 1,000 investors each buy $100,000 of the IPO, each investor's cost will be 1% ($1,000/$100,000), so the IPO likewise must be underpriced by 1%. In this case, the total appraisal cost is $1,000,000, or 1,000 × $1,000. Thus, private placements are less costly because they are evaluated by only one investor.

Obviously, when an IPO is substantially underpriced, the issuing firm suffers a loss because it could issue the stocks at a higher price and obtain more cash inflow per share. The underwriter has an interest in underwriting the issue to protect itself from potential loss. Recently, firms have broken the tradition and go through OpenIPO. Exhibit 3.6 provides the details of some companies who completed the process of an OpenIPO. By opening an account, every individual can bid for the IPO through the Internet. The first main feature of this OpenIPO is that it is sold at an auction in a price range of $10.50–$13.50 per share. Thus, if the stock is relatively highly evaluated by the investor, it will be sold close to the upper bound and the loss to the issuing firm is minimized. If the investor thinks that the stock is not worth much, it will end up closer to the lower bound. The second feature is that large institutional investors and individual investors have an equal chance to bid for the IPO.

3.3 THE SECONDARY SECURITY MARKET

In the secondary market, previously issued securities are traded between investors. The proceeds of selling a security go to the current owner of the security, not to the original issuing company. The secondary market provides liquidity to individuals who acquire securities in the primary market. The secondary market consists of major stock exchanges and over-the-counter markets. The most well-known and active stock exchanges are the New York Stock Exchange (NYSE), the American Stock

Exhibit 3.6

Completed OpenIPOs

$16,000,000	$26,400,000	$42,000,000	$82,800,000
		NOGATECH	AND**O**VER
Briazz, Inc. (BRZZ)	Peet's Coffee & Tea (PEET)	Nogatech, Inc. (NGTC)	Andover.net (ANDN)
OpenIPO Lead Manager Offering Price: $8 Date: 5/02/01	OpenIPO Lead Manager Offering Price: $8 Date: 1/25/01	OpenIPO Lead Manager Offering Price: $12 Date: 5/17/00	OpenIPO Lead Manager Offering Price: $18 Date: 12/8/99

$27,300,000	$11,550,000
salon.com	RAVENSWOOD
Salon.com (SALN)	Ravenswood (RVWD)
OpenIPO Lead Manager Offering Price: $10.50 Date: 6/22/99	OpenIPO Lead Manager Offering Price: $10.50 Date: 4/9/99

Source: Website at http://www.wrhambrecht.com/ind/auctions/openipo/completed.html, 10 February 2002. Reprinted with permission. OpenIPO levels the playing field in initial public offerings, allowing individuals and institutional investors to bid online for shares in an IPO. All investors end up paying the same price – a price determined by the auction. WR Hambrecht & Co, for example, founded in 1998 by William R. Hambrecht, is a financial services firm committed to using the Internet and auction process to level the playing field for investors and issuers. The firm's impartial Internet-based auctions, which allow the market to determine pricing and allocation, are dramatically changing the financial services landscape.

Exchange (AMEX) and the Tokyo Stock Exchange (TSE). In over-the-counter (OTC) markets, transactions are conducted by the National Association of Securities Dealers' Automated Quotations (Nasdaq) system, interbank markets, and major commodity and derivative exchanges. The Chicago Board of Trade (CBOT) and the Chicago Mercantile Exchange (CME) are exchanges where commodity and derivative securities such as stock options are traded.

The New York Stock Exchange is the oldest (established in 1792) and the largest stock exchange in the United States. Stocks were auctioned alongside bonds and lottery tickets whenever wealthy investors needed some cash. They signed the Buttonwood Agreement, named after a buttonwood tree in Wall Street under which securities traders met. The pact obligated them to 'give preference' to one another in stock trading and collect a minimum fixed commission on stock sales. Buttonwood's effect became clear when winter came. The 24 brokers moved their business to a cosy back room of Wall Street's Tontine Coffee House, leaving other auctioneers and brokers shivering in the cold. The NYSE is also called the Big Board or simply The Exchange. The NYSE is a corporation governed by a board of directors composed of 27 individuals representing the public and the exchange membership. The chairman and presidents are appointed and the remaining board of members are elected by the members of the exchange. The total number of voting members is fixed at 1,366 'seats', which are owned by individuals, usually officers of security firms. When members die or retire, the seats are usually auctioned to bidders approved for membership by the NYSE. The price of the seats varies from as low as $35,000 in 1977 to more than $2.6 million in 2002. In comparison, a seat on the AMEX sold for $260,000 on 13 February 2002 – considerably less than for a seat on the NYSE.[6] The higher the potential income of the member because of the ownership of a seat, the higher the price of the seat (for example, in January 2002 the daily average volume of stock traded on the NYSE was 1,426 billion compared with about 51 million on AMEX).

About 28,000 corporations are listed on the NYSE,[7] with nearly $16 trillion in global market capitalization. The stocks, bonds, options, rights and warrants of these corporations are traded in 20 trading posts, each representing the market for all securities located on the *floor*.

A large range of trading activities is conducted in the secondary market. Transactions in this market are categorized as follows.

First market transactions are trades of securities that are actually made on the floor of the exchange on which the security is listed. For example, AT&T is a stock that is traded on the NYSE. When AT&T is traded on the NYSE, it is said to be traded in the first market. Similarly, when Carmel (less well known than AT&T) is traded on the AMEX, it is said to be traded on the first market. Exhibit 3.7 shows a post of a specialist (left corner) as well as the various people involved with the trade and the various screens with current information on the traded stocks. As we can see, nowadays the scene of trading is more like a beehive than a quiet buttonwood tree.

Exhibit 3.7 Part of the NYSE trading floor

Source: Used with permission of the New York Stock Exchange.

---

[6] See 'AMEX STATS' at http://www.AMEX.com.
[7] We recommend that you visit the NYSE website at www.nyse.com for the most recent information.

Second market transactions are over-the-counter (OTC) trades that are made in the over-the-counter market. The OTC is not a formal exchange. There are no membership requirements, and thousands of brokers register with the SEC as dealers on the market. The NASD (National Association of Securities Dealers) is a nonprofit organization formed under the joint sponsorship of the Investment Bankers' Conference and the Securities and Exchange Commission. NASD members include virtually all investment houses and firms dealing with the OTC market. The NASD establishes and enforces fair and equitable rules for security trading on the OTC. The NASD owns the Nasdaq, which is a computerized system that provides brokers and dealers with price quotations for securities traded on OTC markets as well as for many NYSE-linked securities. A security traded on OTC must, however, be listed on the computer-linked network called Nasdaq. Thus, the **over-the-counter market** is a telephone- and computer-linked network for trading securities. Securities listed on the OTC market are not listed on an exchange. Generally, securities of small firms which do not meet the requirements of the NYSE or AMEX (earlier) listings are traded on the OTC market (the OTC market will be discussed in more detail later in the chapter).

Third market transactions are trades in *exchange-listed* issues that take place off the exchange floor with the aid of brokers. An example would be an AT&T trade that is conducted through an OTC market. (Recall that AT&T is listed on the NYSE.)

Fourth market transactions are trades in exchange-listed issues that are arranged by the buyers and sellers off the exchange floor, without the aid of brokers. An example would be trading AT&T with your uncle.[8]

Upstairs market transactions are trades that are arranged from a network of trading desks that negotiate large block transactions.

Securities can be listed on more than one exchange. This is known as **dual listing.** Dual listing enhances the level of competition and is thought to lower the cost of trading.[9] Dual listing in international markets, as well as on the east and west coasts in the United States, expands the hours when trading can occur. There are various regulations restricting dual listings. For example, securities listed on the NYSE cannot also be listed on the AMEX.

The NYSE is the most important US exchange, and it celebrated its 200th birthday in 1992. Institutional investors play a major role in trading on the NYSE. (The ownership of shares by households and non-profit organizations fell from 91.3% in 1950 to 47.7%

Exhibit 3.8(a) Listing requirements for the NYSE, AMEX and Nasdaq

Characteristic	NYSE	AMEX	Nasdaq
Minimum shares publicly held	1.1 million	0.5 million	1.0 million
Minimum number of shareholders	2,000	800	300
Minimum pre-tax income last year	$2.5 million	$0.75 million	–
Minimum market capitalization	$10 million	$3 million	$50 million

[8] The back of a stock certificate, like a title to an automobile, contains the appropriate forms for transferring ownership. The stock certificate is then mailed to the corporate registrar, who will issue a new certificate.
[9] Some argue that dual listing actually increases the cost of trading, because multiple dealers all have to cover the same fixed expenses with lower volume.

Exhibit 3.8(b) New York Stock Exchange listing requirements

Minimum Distribution Criteria	Requirements
Shareholders[A]	
Round-lot holders (holders of a unit of trading – generally 100 shares)	2,000
or	
Total shareholders together with	2,200
Average monthly trading volume (for the most recent six months)	100,000 shares
or	
Total shareholders together with	500
Average monthly trading volume (for most recent twelve months)	1,000,000 shares
Public shares[B]	1,100,000 outstanding
Market value of public shares[B,C]	$60,000,000 (IPOs, spin-offs & carve-outs)
	$100,000,000 (public companies)

Minimum Quantitative standards		Requirements
Earnings		
Aggregate for the last three years achieved as	Pre-tax earnings[D]	$6,500,000
Most recent year	Pre-tax earnings[D]	$2,500,000
Each of the two preceeding years	Pre-tax earnings[D]	$2,000,000
or		
Most recent year (all three years must be profitable)	Pre-tax earnings[D]	$4,500,000
or		
Operating cash flow		
For companies with not less than $500 million in global market capitalization and $100 million in revenues in the last 12 months:		
Aggregate for the last three years[E] (each year must be a positive amount)	Adjusted cash flow	$25,000,000
or		
Global market capitalization		
Revenues for last fiscal year		$100,000,000
and average global market capitalization[F].		$1,000,000,000

[A] The number of beneficial holders of stock held in "street name" will be considered in addition to the holders of record. The exchange will make any necessary check of such holdings that are in the name of exchange member organizations.

[B] In connection with initial public offerings (including spin-offs and carve-outs), the NYSE requires a letter of undertaking from the company's underwriter or representations from a financial advisor in the case of a spin-off to ensure that the offering or distribution will meet or exceed NYSE standards.

[C] Shares held by directors, officers or their immediate families and other concentrated holdings of 10% or more are excluded in calculating the number of publicly held shares. If a company either has a significant concentration of stock, or if changing market forces have adversely impacted the public market value of a company which otherwise would qualify for listing on the exchange, such that its public market value is no more than 10 per cent below $60,000,000 or $100,000,000 as applicable, the exchange will generally consider $60,000,000 or $100,000,000, as applicable, in stockholders' equity as an alternate measure of size and therefore as an alternate basis on which to list the company.

[D] Pre-tax earnings is adjusted for various items as defined in the NYSE Listed Company Manual.

[E] Represents net cash provided by operating activities excluding the changes in working capital or in operating assets and liabilities, as adjusted for various items defined in the NYSE Listed Company Manual.

[F] Average global market capitalization for already existing public companies is represented by the most recent six months of trading history. For IPOs, spin-offs, and carve-outs it is represented by the valuation of the company as demonstrated in the case of a spin-off, by the distribution ratio as priced or, in the case of an IPO/carve-out, the as priced offering in relation to the company's total valuation.

Source: Website at http://www.nyse.com/pdfs/04_LISTEDCOMPANIES.pdf, 12 March 2002. Used with permission of the NYSE.

Exhibit 3.8(c) AMEX listing guidelines for international companies	
Regular financial guidelines	
Pre-tax income	$750,000 latest fiscal year or in 2 of most recent 3 fiscal years
Market value of public float	$3,000,000
Price	$3
Operating history	–
Stockholders' equity	$4,000,000
Alternative financial guidelines	
Pre-tax income	–
Market value of public float	$15,000,000
Price	$3
Operating history	2 years
Stockholders' equity	$4,000,000
Distribution guidelines (applicable to regular and alternative guidelines)	
Alternative 1	
Public float	500,000
Public stockholders	800
Average daily volume	–
Alternative 2	
Public float	1,000,000
Public stockholders	400
Average daily volume	–
Alternative 3	
Public float	500,000
Public stockholders	400
Average daily volume	2,000
Alternative 4	
Public float	1,000,000 worldwide
Public stockholders	800 worldwide
Average daily volume	–

Source: Website at http://www.amex.com/about/amex_listonu.stm, 27 May 2001. Reprinted with permission.

in the third quarter of 1996).[10] Shares are owned primarily by institutional investors, including mutual funds. As will be discussed later, the stock exchanges responded to this changing composition by catering more to institutional investors (although not neglecting the needs of individual investors).

In order for stocks to trade on exchanges, minimum requirements have to be met. Exhibit 3.8(a) presents the minimum listing requirements for the NYSE, AMEX and Nasdaq. Exhibit 3.8(b) shows the full listing requirements at the NYSE, Exhibit 3.8(c) shows the listing requirements for international companies, and Exhibit 3.8(d) is a short list of some of the international companies that joined the AMEX in 1999.

[10] See 'Mutual funds: navigating the future', *Fortune*, 24 November 1997, p. S4.

Exhibit 3.8(d) Some of the international companies that joined the AMEX in 1999

Issuer	Country	Market[1]	Offer Price	Global Offering Value[2]	Market Value	Offer Date	Lead Managers	Co-Managers	Issuer Legal Counsel
Ebookers.com	United Kingdom	NNM	18.000	70,380,000		11/10/1999	J.P. Morgan Securities	Commerzbank AG Salomon Smith Barney Inc. SG Cowen Securities Corporation	Brobeck Hale and Dorr International
QXL.com	United Kingdom	NNM	16.150	90,440,000	367,489,729	10/07/1999	Credit Suisse First Boston	Robertson Stephens SG Cowen Securities Corporation Warburg Dillon Read	Rogers & Wells
i-Cable Communications Ltd	China	NNM	27.000	522,450,000	2,160,000,000	11/18/1999	Merrill Lynch & Co.	Lehman Brothers Morgan Stanley Dean Witter	Rogers & Wells
MIH Limited	Virgin Islands	NNM	18.000	187,830,000	898,051,950	04/13/1999	Merrill Lynch & Co.	Donaldson, Lufkin & Jenrette	Harney, Westwood & Riegels Cravath Swaine & Moore
PrimaCom AG	Germany	NNM	16.250	163,569,000	641,177,940	02/19/1999	Morgan Stanley Dean Witter Dresdner Kleinwort Benson North America	LB Rheinland Pfalz Lehman Brothers Paribas Corporation	Baker & McKenzie
United Pan Europe Communications NV	Netherlands	NNM	32.780	1,461,988,000	4,085,899,912	02/12/1999	Goldman, Sachs & Co. Morgan Stanley Dean Witter	Donaldson, Lufkin & Jenrette	Holme Roberts & Owen LLP
ECtel Ltd	Israel	NNM	12.000	42,000,000	186,750,000	10/26/1999	Chase H & Q	Salomon Smith Barney Inc. CIBC World Markets	Fulbright & Jaworski L.L.P.
Qiao Xing Universal Telephone, Inc.	China	NNM	5.500	8,800,000	52,800,000	02/17/1999	Barron Chase Securities, Inc.		
Optibase Ltd.	Israel	NNM	7.000	30,450,000	57,001,000	04/07/1999	C.E. Unterberg, Towbin Co.	Needham & Company, Inc. Nomura Securities International, Inc. Oddo Et Enterprise	
China.com	China	NNM	20.000	96,600,000	422,138,400	07/12/1999	Lehman Brothers	Bear, Stearns & Co.	Rogers & Wells
El Sitio Inc	Argentina	NNM	16.000	150,880,000	617,191,360	12/09/1999	Credit Suisse First Boston Lehman Brothers	Merrill Lynch & Co. Salomon Smith Barney Inc. WIT Capital Corporation	Conyers, Dill & Pearman Paul, Hastings, Janofsky & Walker
Freeserve	United Kingdom	NNM	23.670	362,254,000		07/25/1999	Credit Suisse First Boston	Robertson Stephens Cazenove Incorporated Donaldson, Lufkin & Jenrette Merrill Lynch & Co. Warburg Dillon Read	Shearman & Sterling
Korea Thrunet Co., Ltd	Korea	NNM	18.000	209,070,000	1,186,508,592	11/16/1999	Lehman Brothers	Bear, Stearns & Co. CIBC World Markets	Shearman & Sterling
Satyam Infoway Ltd	India	NNM	18.000	86,423,000	380,808,000	10/18/1999	Merrill Lynch & Co.	Salomon Smith Barney Inc.	Latham & Watkins
Infosys Technologies Limited	India	NNM	34.000	70,380,000	1,119,769,600	03/11/1999	Banc of America Securities	Robertson Stephens Deutsche Banc Alex. Brown Thomas Weisel Partners L.L.C.	Wilson Sonsini Goodrich & Rosat
Radware Ltd	Israel	NNM	18.000	81,900,000	262,875,762	09/29/1999	Salomon Smith Barney Inc.	CIBC World Markets U.S. Bancorp Piper Jaffray Inc.	
E-Cruiter.com	Canada	SCM	6.000	14,700,000	44,283,666	12/07/1999	Whale Securities Co., L.P.		Weil Gotshal & Manges

Source: Website at http://www.amex.com

The NYSE and the AMEX are national exchanges; they trade securities that command a national, and sometimes international, investor following. There are other stock exchanges in the United States besides the NYSE and the AMEX that cater to securities that have only regional interests. The trading volume on these exchanges is much lower. Regional stock exchanges include the Midwest Stock Exchange, the Pacific Stock Exchange, the Boston Stock Exchange and the Philadelphia Stock Exchange.

An alternative to trading on a stock exchange is the OTC market. As mentioned above, the OTC market is traditionally for securities of smaller companies. However, there are exceptions, such as Intel, Microsoft, Netscape and Apple Computer, which are large firms whose stocks trade on the OTC market. The decision of where to list a security is primarily made by the company issuing stock to the public.

Stocks are traded on the OTC market in several ways. First, the OTC traded stocks are generally less active issues that are usually traded in regional brokerage offices. For example, a small Alabama firm's stock may trade only within the Southeast. This firm could opt for a regional stock exchange. Second, the OTC market trades less active issues that have national trading activity. For these issues, quotations are reported daily on 'pink sheets' that are mailed to national brokers by the National Quotations Bureau. Third, the OTC market trades issues that are listed on the Nasdaq. Trade on the Nasdaq system, however, is not limited to only the OTC stocks. Actually, the Nasdaq is an electronic trading system and stocks linked on NYSE and AMEX can also be traded on this system.

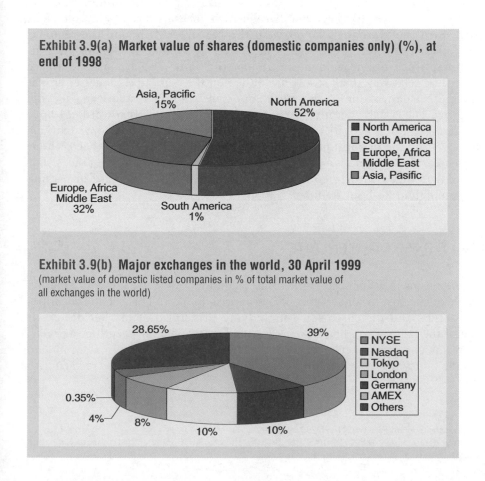

Exhibit 3.9(a) Market value of shares (domestic companies only) (%), at end of 1998

Exhibit 3.9(b) Major exchanges in the world, 30 April 1999
(market value of domestic listed companies in % of total market value of all exchanges in the world)

The Nasdaq lists over 5,540 domestic and foreign companies. In 1996, the share volume was 138.1 billion shares, with a dollar volume of $3.3 trillion, surpassing the other markets.[11] Finally, the OTC market's most actively traded issues are listed on the Nasdaq's more sophisticated system, called the National Market System (NMS).

Exhibit 3.9(a) shows the market value of various regions in the world as a percentage of the total value in the world. The exchanges in North America have 52% of the total world value, while Europe, Africa and the Middle East have 32%. However, Europe's total value is growing faster than the North American value. The value of Europe's exchange rose by 27.4% in 1998, while in North America the total market value rose by 19.2%. Exhibit 3.9(b) shows the market capitalization distribution of the major exchanges. Once again, the NYSE dominates the market for equity, with 39% of the total equity.

In 1998 a possible merger between Nasdaq and AMEX was discussed. If approved by the membership of both exchanges, as well as the SEC, the make-up of the financial markets will change. Among the benefits cited are better quality trades and lower costs. In April 1998 the merger was approved by both the Nasdaq and AMEX boards of directors.

The secondary market must be sensitive to investor needs. Providing a secondary market is a competitive business, with the market shares going to those exchanges that best serve the investors at the lowest cost. An exchange is constantly trying to attract firms that will allow it to trade their shares. Exchanges have distinguished themselves in many different ways. For example, the NYSE and the AMEX cater to larger firms, whereas the OTC market primarily caters to smaller firms. To understand the importance of the various exchanges, note that when we measure size by the volume of shares traded, then the Nasdaq is larger than the NYSE, AMEX and the regional exchanges together. However, when size is measured by volume in dollars, its proportion declines (since dollar values are almost the same size for all the above exchanges), because relatively small stocks are traded on the Nasdaq. No matter how it is measured, the Nasdaq is one of the most important trading systems and its role continues to grow. The NYSE and other exchanges are moving quickly towards 24-hour trading to increase trading activity and respond to investor demand. Some markets already offer investors the opportunity to trade 24 hours a day. The idea that 24-hour trading will increase trading activity has been validated in many circumstances. For example, US dollar index futures contracts experienced a 35% increase in trading during the first month of 24-hour trading.[12]

3.4 TRADING MECHANICS

The actual mechanisms in a financial market that facilitate trading are known as **market microstructure,** or the institutional setup of a securities market. This section identifies some typical setups and discusses some underlying principles of market design. It reviews some of the goals of trading systems, various participants in securities markets, and the establishment of market prices. Also included is an overview of automated trading systems and various issues important to investors when they are trying to execute a trade.

---

[11] See the Nasdaq website at http://www.NASDAQ.com.
[12] Based on a letter dated 31 March 1992 by Peter Burton, director of Financial Instruments Exchange (FINEX), a division of then New York Cotton Exchange.

3.4.1 Securities trading systems

The trading of securities is conducted by members of the exchange or by an official of the exchange. However, trades are not conducted in the same manner in all stock exchanges around the world (or even in the United States). The three main trading systems are the call market, continuous market and mixed market.

In the **call market,** trading and prices are determined at a specified time during the day by a designated person collecting all of the buy and sell orders and then determining the equilibrium price (that is, the price where supply and demand are equal). For example, suppose that by 2:00 p.m. the total accumulated buy orders by all investors in Sabra stock is as follows:

- Buy 60 shares at $13 per share or less
- Buy 70 shares at $12 per share or less
- Buy 80 shares at $11 per share or less
- Buy 100 shares at $10 per share or less.

Note that the higher price is associated with a smaller number of shares demanded. Similarly, the following might be the aggregate supply of orders:

- Sell 10 shares at $11 per share or more
- Sell 40 shares at $12 per share or more
- Sell 70 shares at $13 per share or more
- Sell 150 shares at $14 per share or more.

Note that the higher the price, the more shares are made available to sell. From the aggregate supply and demand information, we see that the equilibrium price is $13 per share and 60 shares traded. Those investors wanting to sell securities at a higher price than $13 will be unable to find a buyer, and those wishing to buy securities at a price less than $13 will be unable to find a seller. Also note that in our example a total of 70 shares were offered for sale at a price of $13; however, the investors were willing to purchase only 60 shares at this price, leaving 10 sell orders not executed. In practice, demand is always equal to supply at a given price. If the investors wish to sell these 10 shares, they must decrease the price to, say, 12\frac{1}{2}$ in order to create new demand and supply functions until equilibrium is reached. When trade in one security is finished, trade in the second security takes place, and so on until all securities are traded. All unfulfilled orders can be resubmitted the following day or the next time the security is traded. Call market trading usually occurs once a day, but in some countries it can occur two to three times a day.

Call market trading is common in Hong Kong, Austria and Norway. In most large exchanges (for example, in the United States, Canada and the United Kingdom), where the volume of trading and the number of listed securities is large, the **continuous market** system of trading is employed. As the name indicates, trades in each security occur at any time when the stock exchange is open. If there are a seller and a buyer of IBM shares at an agreed price, for example at 10:00 a.m., the transaction is conducted in a matter of minutes. Five minutes later, another transaction in the same stock may be executed at a different price. For example, on some of the business television news networks in the United States, you can view the NYSE and Nasdaq transactions occurring throughout the day by watching the information scrolling across the television screen. This information includes, for example, the ticker symbol of the stock, volume traded, last price, and change in price from the previous one.

In some countries (for example, Switzerland and France), a **mixed market** exists. In this system, a group of stocks is traded continuously for, say, half an hour, and then another group of stocks is traded continuously for half an hour, and so forth throughout the day.

Exhibit 3.10 summarizes the impact of automation on the regulated exchanges around the world. Several of the exchanges have adopted automated systems modelled after the Nasdaq (developed in 1971). For example, the Easdaq (Nasdaq Europe), which is a subsidiary of the Nasdaq stock market, was developed in 1996 (see www.easdaq.be). Others (for example, German exchanges) combine a number of different trading structures. Below, we elaborate on the Nasdaq trading system.

3.4.2 The Nasdaq trading system

As will be explained below, trade on the NYSE and AMEX is done by market makers who organize all the trade in a given stock in one post. On the Nasdaq the trade is done in a different way: by the use of computers. There is no one physical place where all trades are conducted. Dealers can trade with the public by posting bid and ask quotes. An investor who wishes to buy or sell shares calls a broker who tries to locate a dealer on the Nasdaq with the best deal. The dealer trades on his or her account and makes a profit due to the spread.

Exhibit 3.10 Trading characteristics of stock exchanges

Exchange site	Exchange characteristics
United States	Largest single marketplace is the NYSE, which is principally a floor-based system; the OTC market introduced an automated system in 1971 (Nasdaq), which is an interdealer quotation system; real-time trade reporting was established in 1982; National Market System (NMS) legislation was enacted in 1975.
Japan	Among the eight stock exchanges, 80% of the trading volume occurs on the Tokyo Stock Exchange (TSE), which is principally a floor-based system; equities may trade through the Jasdaq, which was modelled after Nasdaq; the bulk of bond trading occurs on the OTC market.
Europe	Quote-driven dealer market; screen-based trading system (EASDAQ, a subsidiary of Nasdaq) allows dealers to disseminate price quotes; in September 1995, Tradepoint, a new trading system, went into effect in the United Kingdom at the London Stock Exchange (LSE), and permits investors and broker-dealers to trade directly and anonymously with one another.
Paris	Continuous order-driven screen-based trading system replaced the periodic call auctions with open outcry in 1986; a new exchange was established in Paris in 1996 for young, innovative, high-risk companies to trade; similar markets have opened in Germany, Belgium and the Netherlands.
Germany	Combines three different trading structures: (1) floor trading (still used in eight regional exchanges, Frankfurt being the most important); (2) electronic trading system; and (3) off-exchange telephone market; an interesting feature is that many companies are listed on several exchanges, and prices often vary across exchanges.

Source: Financial Market Trends, No. 65, November 1996. © OECD, 1996. Reprinted with permission.

Exhibit 3.11 illustrates the bid–ask spread (which is the difference between the bid and asked price of the stocks, see Section 3.9.1). provided by various dealers, as well as the best bid–ask offer for Microsoft, as quoted by Bloomberg on 15 June 1999. The best quotes are at the top of the table. Five dealers are ready to sell at $84^3/_4 (see SLKC for example), and one dealer (see MASH) is ready to buy at $84^{13}/_{16}. The rest of the quotes made by various dealers are worse, as the bids are at a lower price than $84^3/_4 and all ask quotes are for higher prices than $84^{13}/_{16}.

Note also that some dealers who are obligated to suggest bid–ask quotes are not really trading in the market, hence suggesting residual quotes: e.g. AXCS has a bid–ask quote of $10–$300. Obviously, the best quotes (at the top of the table) may change continuously, when a trade takes place or a dealer suggests new quotes.

In 1994 the Justice Department announced an investigation of the Nasdaq stock market. It was found that Nasdaq stock traded at a bid–ask spread of odd eighths, that is $^1/_8$, $^3/_8$, $^5/_8$ and $^7/_8$, very rarely. Thus, the spreads are commonly $^1/_4$, $^1/_2$, etc., which implies a relatively large profit to the dealers. It raises the suspicion that there is collusion among dealers who decided to maintain these large spreads, which is a violation of the anti-trust laws. In 1996 the Justice Department and the SEC settled with the dealers. The dealers agreed not to refrain from making transactions with dealers who suggest cutting the spread and to make sure that no collusion occurs.

Exhibit 3.11 Bid–ask spreads and best offer for Microsoft, 15 June 1999

HELP for explanation, MENU for similar functions. P183 **Equity CQ**
MSFT US $ Market Q **84** $^3/_4$ **84** $^7/_8$ Q 10×10 Vol 19, 700 Prev 84$^{15}/_{16}$
Competing Quotes Monitor
MSFT   US   MICROSOFT CORP

Prev 84$^3/_4$–84$^{13}/_{16}$

Vol: 0

5 SLKC MLCO GSCO FBCO NFSC 84$^3/_4$ –84$^{13}/_{16}$ MASH   1

Name	Bid	Ask	Name	Bid	Ask	Name	Bid	Ask	Name	Bid	Ask
						LEHMp	84$^1/_2$	–84$^7/_8$	PIPRp	84$^1/_4$	–85$^1/_4$
AANAp	84$^1/_4$	–86	DLJPp	84$^5/_{16}$	–84$^7/_8$	MADFp	84$^9/_{16}$	–84$^7/_8$	PRUSp	84$^1/_4$	–84$^7/_8$
AGISp	83$^7/_3$	–84$^7/_3$	EVRNp	83$^3/_4$	–86	MASHp	84$^{11}/_{16}$	–84$^{13}/_{16}$	PUREp	51$^7/_8$	–140
ALLNp	83$^7/_8$	–95$^3/_8$	FBCOp	84$^3/_4$	–85$^1/_4$	MDSNp	82	–88$^3/_{16}$	PWJCp	84$^1/_4$	–85
ALWCp	40	–120	FCAPp	83	–90$^1/_2$	MHILp	82	–92	RAGNp	83	–85$^1/_2$
AXCSp	10	–300	FEDEp	50	–200	MHMYp	83$^1/_2$	–85$^1/_2$	RAJAp	84	–87
BARDp	83$^1/_4$	–85$^9/_{16}$	GKMCp	84$^1/_4$	–85$^3/_8$	MLCOp	84$^3/_4$	–85	RAMSp	84$^1/_4$	–90
BESTp	84$^1/_{16}$	–85$^1/_{16}$	GSCOp	84$^3/_4$	–85$^1/_{16}$	MONTp	84$^1/_4$	–85$^1/_4$	RSSFp	84$^1/_8$	–90$^3/_{10}$
BUCKp	84$^1/_4$	–88$^5/_8$	GVRCp	83$^1/_2$	–87$^1/_2$	MSCOp	84$^7/_{16}$	–84$^{15}/_{16}$	SBSHp	84$^1/_3$	–85
CANTp	84$^1/_4$	–86$^1/_4$	HRCOp	1	–300	MWSE	84$^1/_2$	–85$^3/_4$	SELZp	84$^1/_4$	–85$^1/_2$
CIBCp	84	–85$^1/_4$	HRZGp	84$^1/_4$	–84$^7/_8$	NEEDp	83$^{13}/_{16}$	–87$^1/_2$	SHWDp	84$^1/_4$	–85
COSTp	84	–85	ISLD		–	NFSCp	84$^3/_4$	–85$^3/_4$	SLKCp	84$^3/_4$	–85$^3/_4$
COWNp	83$^1/_8$	–85$^1/_8$	JBOCp	75	–95	NITEp	84$^1/_4$	–84$^{15}/_{16}$	SNDSp	83$^3/_4$	–85$^1/_4$
CWCOp	84$^7/_{16}$	–85$^5/_8$	JEFFp	84$^1/_4$	–86$^1/_4$	NTRD	80	–91	SNDVp	84$^1/_{16}$	–86$^1/_{16}$
DBKSp	83$^3/_4$	–85$^1/_8$	JOSEp	82$^3/_4$	–85$^3/_4$	OLDEp	84$^1/_4$	–85$^1/_8$	STAFp	75	–105
DEANp	84$^1/_4$	–86$^1/_4$	JPMSp	84$^9/_{16}$	–84$^{15}/_{16}$	PERTp	83$^7/_8$	–85$^5/_8$	SWSTp	83$^3/_4$	–85$^1/_2$
DKNYp	84$^1/_2$	–84$^{15}/_{16}$	KCMOp	84$^1/_4$	–85$^1/_4$	PFSIp	83$^1/_2$	–85$^1/_2$	TWPTp	84	–87

© 1999 BLOOMBERG L.P. Frankfurt Hong Kong London New York Princeton Singapore Sydney Tokyo São Paulo

Source: 'Competing quotes monitor for US equity: MSFT (Microsoft) 06/15/99' accessed from the BLOOMBERG PROFESSIONAL® service on 15 June 1999. © 1999 Bloomberg L.P. All rights reserved. Reprinted with permission. Visit www.Bloomberg.com.

■ Trading firms

On 9 August 1999 the *Wall Street Journal of Europe* reported that British funds intended to form a trading firm. The top managers could trade between themselves, a move akin to steps being taken in the US by securities brokerage firms to expand the role of electronic trading systems. The new company, called E-crossnet Ltd, will save traders about 80% of the transaction costs. Apart from cost savings, the new trade between funds will eliminate to some degree the effect that large stock market transactions can have on share prices. E-crossnet will still need, however, the London Stock Exchange to quote prices. However, when one fund's manager wants to sell stocks and another manager wants to buy them, this can be done anonymously and without affecting the stock market. Such a move puts more pressure on the big exchanges, because like electronic trading it is challenging the Nasdaq, the NYSE and other major exchanges for business.

3.4.3 Goals of trading systems

Markets facilitate trading, and investors will trade on the market that provides the best service at the most competitive price. When a new market is being developed, several questions need to be addressed by the market designers. There is no clear-cut answer to all these issues, and not all exchanges around the world adopt the same policy. The important questions are:[13]

1 *Should all information be made public?* For example, how can information known only to insiders, such as corporate executives, be used? Exchanges in the USA do not permit insider trading, because it is illegal.
2 *If all information is not made public, then should at least the trading record be public information?* For example, should you be able to know who is doing the trading? On the NYSE, investors may trade without revealing who they are. Thus, the NYSE has decided that it is in the best interest of investors to be able to trade in secret. Although corporate executives must report their trading activities to the appropriate regulatory agencies, they do not have to reveal their trading activities until *after* the trade has been executed.
3 *Are prices allowed to gyrate wildly, or are there constraints on how much prices can move?* Are there daily price limits? The NYSE has adopted a circuit breaker system in response to the stock market crash of 1987. By Rule 80B, when the Dow Jones Industrial Average (DJIA) falls by 350 points from the previous day's close, trading is stopped for half an hour. If the DJIA continues to fall to 550 points below the previous day's close, trading is stopped for one hour.[14] The idea is that these trading halts will give potential buyers an opportunity to assess the market and be willing to place orders to buy.
4 *Will the market attract a large number of traders who will provide the necessary liquidity?*
5 *Will this market require an individual to specialize in providing liquidity for a particular security?* For example, the NYSE has such a person, whereas the OTC market does not.

Several of these issues are conflicting. For example, how can there be an informationally efficient market (Question 1) and, at the same time, a market that disallows large

---

[13] Based on Joel Hasbrouck, 'Security markets, information and liquidity', *Financial Practice and Education* 1 (Fall–Winter 1991): 7–16.

[14] *NYSE Fact Book for the Year 1996* (New York: New York Stock Exchange, Inc., 1996), pp. 22–23.

price swings (Question 3)? This is impossible, because information can arrive in a dramatic fashion. Consider the possible effect on a market of the news of an earthquake, a major accident or a political event.

3.4.4 Participants in securities markets

All participants in security markets are referred to generically as *traders*. The most important traders are the **market makers,** or the individuals determining the bid and asked price quotes. The **bid price** is the price at which the public can sell securities and the market maker must buy securities. The **asked price** is the price at which the public can buy securities and the market maker must sell securities. Clearly, for the market maker to make a living, the bid price must be less than the asked price. Exhibit 3.12, taken from the Internet, shows the bid and ask prices of IBM's shares in June 1999 as quoted by Charles Schwab. We see that the dealer is ready to buy some shares of IBM at $119^5/_8$ and to sell some shares at $119^3/_4$ Thus, the spread in this case is $\$^3/_4 - \$^5/_8 = \$^1/_8$ per share. That is, the market maker must be buying at the bid price for less than what he or she is selling at the asked price. Brokers who know at which post of the floor a given stock is traded sometimes meet and enact a transaction between themselves 'inside the quotes'. For example, if the bid quote of Xerox is $113 and the asking price is $113^1/_4$, they can conduct the transaction at $113^1/_8$. Such a transaction is called an 'inside the quotes' transaction.

The members of the exchange are involved in transactions in the listed securities. They have various functions, and hence various sources of income. The main players

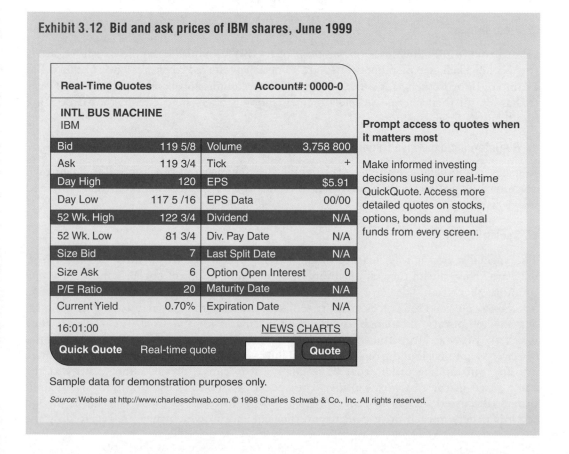

Exhibit 3.12 Bid and ask prices of IBM shares, June 1999

Sample data for demonstration purposes only.

on the floor of most exchanges, such as the NYSE, include commission brokers, dealers, floor brokers, registered competitive traders and specialists. Some exchange members buy or sell for their own account. Some function as **brokers** (now also called *registered representatives*). Generally, brokers are persons who act as intermediaries between a buyer and a seller, a service for which they charge a commission. Brokers must register with the exchange where the stocks are traded (hence the name *registered representative*).

■ Commission brokers

Commission brokers buy and sell securities for clients of brokerage houses. They are connected to the brokerage houses (for example, Merrill Lynch) by either telephones or computer terminals, and they receive requests to buy or sell securities, execute the trade, and then send back a confirmation message to the brokerage firm. For this service, they charge a commission fee. Of course, commission brokers also trade for their own accounts and thus also act as dealers (discussed next).

■ Dealers

Dealers maintain their own inventory of securities and buy and sell securities from this inventory; thus, dealers are market makers. In this capacity, they do not serve as intermediaries but rather take the risk of holding the securities in their own account. Because most brokerage firms operate both as commission brokers and as dealers, the term *broker-dealer* is often used. Dealers earn their incomes from selling securities they own at a higher price than they initially paid for them.

■ Floor brokers

Floor brokers are individuals on the floor of the NYSE who handle the overflow orders from other exchange members. They are sometimes referred to as freelance brokers. For example, floor brokers, for a fee, will work with commission brokers who get too busy to handle all their clients' orders on time. Floor brokers help ensure that orders are handled in a timely fashion.

■ Registered competitive traders

Registered competitive traders own seats on the exchange and buy and sell for their own accounts. Like dealers, they earn their incomes solely by profiting from their buy and sell decisions.

■ Specialists

The **specialist** is a unique feature of the NYSE. Specialists are members of the NYSE who are charged with the responsibility of maintaining a fair and orderly market for one or more securities. They are called **registered equity market makers** on the AMEX. Specialists buy and sell (or even short-sell) securities for their own accounts to counter-act any temporary imbalance in supply and demand for the stock. In this way, they work to prevent large fluctuations in the price of the stock in which they trade. Specialists are prohibited from buying or selling securities for their own accounts if there are any outstanding orders that have not been executed for the same security at the same price in the *specialist's book*. The specialist's book is essentially a log of limit orders (discussed later in this section) that have been received by the specialist; the log records orders in each price category in the sequence in which they are received by the specialist. Each stock is traded only by one specialist who has a post on the floor of the exchange. However, one specialist can handle the trade of several stocks. The specialist who maintains an inventory of stocks publishes quotes of bid and ask spreads and is obligated to execute (even from his or her portfolio) at least a limited number of market orders at these quotes. Then, the specialist may decide to have another bid–ask quote to which once again they are obligated. The specialist has to use the highest outstanding purchase price and the lowest outstanding offered selling price when he or she makes a trade. Thus, it is an auction market, because all buy–sell orders are concentrated in one place and the best offers are executed, i.e. win in the auction. When a transaction is executed, the specialist reports it and it appears on the screen (see the bottom of your TV set when you watch the CNN news).

The specialist has an important role in making the market a continuous one. To illustrate, suppose that the highest limit order to buy IBM stock is $120, whereas the lowest limit order to sell is $122. As market buy and sell orders come to the floor, the market price of IBM stock fluctuates from $120 to $122. The specialist is expected, and has agreed, to reduce this relatively large fluctuation by stepping in and buying and selling IBM stock for his or her own account at bid and ask prices between these two prices, such that the range would be only between $1/4$ and $1/2$. In this way, the specialist provides continuity.

Specialists earn income in two ways. First, as brokers, they receive commission fees for executing orders. Second, as dealers, they receive income by selling securities held in their own inventory at prices greater than the original purchase price.

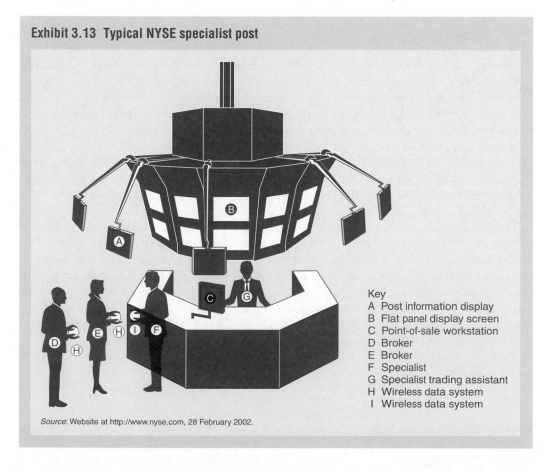

Exhibit 3.13 Typical NYSE specialist post

Key
A Post information display
B Flat panel display screen
C Point-of-sale workstation
D Broker
E Broker
F Specialist
G Specialist trading assistant
H Wireless data system
I Wireless data system

Source: Website at http://www.nyse.com, 28 February 2002.

Exhibit 3.13 illustrates a typical post of a specialist of the NYSE, with the data screens available to customers and with the trading assistant who helps the specialist, as well as other people with whom he or she conducts business.

3.4.5 Establishing market prices

The difference between the asked price and the bid price – what determines the market maker's income – is known as the **bid–ask spread.** For example, Microsoft stock may be quoted at 83 bid and $83^1/_8$ asked. Thus, the bid–ask spread is $^1/_8$ of a dollar, or $0.125 per share.

The bid–ask spread set by the market maker is determined by several factors:

1 Fixed operating costs (such as leasing an office and computer terminals) and anticipated volume of activity.
2 Nonfinancing variable cost per transaction (labour and supplies).
3 Cost of financing the inventory of securities.
4 Risk of price depreciation if inventory is held, and risk of price appreciation if sales have exceeded inventory.[15]
5 Likelihood of trading with those who have superior information (insiders). Because the first three factors are relatively stable, many investors monitor the size of the bid–ask spread for clues regarding how the market maker views the volatility of a stock. Larger bid–ask spreads signal larger uncertainty.

3.4.6 Automated trading

All traders will probably rely more heavily on technology in the years ahead. As technological advances continue at top speed, the potential for computerized trading has become a reality (see this chapter's *Investment in the news*). The changes have sparked an intense debate on the efficiency of floor traders versus traders who use computerized machines. To determine which is most efficient, we need to determine the primary tasks that exchanges seek to accomplish.

The primary task of an exchange is determining the current price that will support the quantity of trading desired. That is, whatever trading framework is adopted, one must be able to identify efficiently the current price and the quantity with which trading can occur at that price.

One innovation used to carry out this task using automated trading is a strategy known as **program trading,** which is the simultaneous purchase or sale of at least 15 different stocks with a total value of $1 million or more. The computer program constantly monitors the stock, futures and option markets. It gives a buy or sell signal when opportunities for arbitrage profits (sure profits with no risk) occur, or when market conditions warrant portfolio accumulation or liquidation. Program trading was blamed for the large decline in the stock market that occurred on Black Monday (19 October 1987), because when the market was down, the computer program triggered a sale order that enhanced the price fall.

Program trading does not necessarily have to be transacted via computer. The idea of trading 'baskets' of securities has been around for a long time; however, it was not until the advent of computerized trading that it became very efficient. The volume of program

---

[15] See the discussion of short selling later in this section. The market marker is short if the sales have exceeded the inventory.

trading is enormous. For example, program trading on the NYSE averaged 16.8% of the average daily trading volume for 10–14 November 1997.[16]

The GLOBEX trading system, which was developed by a joint venture between the Chicago Mercantile Exchange and Reuters (a British information distribution company), promises to be the security exchange of the future. GLOBEX is a global OTC market where many different types of securities trade. Reuters has more than 200,000 terminals in more than 120 countries. Hence, GLOBEX has a phenomenal degree of direct access to trading.

3.4.7 Types of orders

Investors can use different types of orders to buy and sell securities. The most common is a **market order,** which is an order to buy or sell a specified quantity of a specified security *at the best price currently available.* In contrast, a **limit order** is an order to buy or sell a specified quantity of a specified security *at a specified price or better.* The trade will occur only when the specified price is available.

For example, suppose the current bid and asked prices for Microsoft stock are 89^7/_8$ bid and 90^1/_8$ asked. A market order to buy Microsoft stock would be executed with the market maker at 90^1/_8$. A market order to sell Microsoft stock would be executed at 89^7/_8$. Rather than issue a market order, the investor could issue a limit order to buy, say, 100 shares (one round lot) of Microsoft common stock at $89. This order would not be executed until the asked price dropped to $89 or lower. If the price did fall – say, to $89 – then the market maker would sell 100 shares of Microsoft at $89 to the investor. In the same fashion, a limit order to sell Microsoft stock could be placed at $91. This sell order would not be executed until the bid price rose to $91 or higher.

All orders are **day orders** unless otherwise specified. That is, all limit orders expire at the end of the trading day if not executed. Market orders are day orders by definition, because they are executed very quickly. An alternative to a day order is the **good-till-cancelled (GTC) order**, a limit order that remains in effect until it is executed or cancelled.

Other specialized orders include the not-held order and the stop order. A **not-held (NH) order,** given to a floor broker, allows the broker to try and obtain a better price, but the broker is not held responsible if he or she is unsuccessful. For example, on a NH order to sell, the broker is not liable if the price falls sharply and the broker does not successfully sell an order at the higher price. A **stop order** is an order to sell if the price falls below a specified price or to buy if the price rises above a specified price. Stop orders are used to limit losses or protect accumulated gains. If you purchased Microsoft when it was trading at $50, and it rose to $200, you could limit your risk of losing this gain with a stop order to sell if the price falls below $190. Thus, you protect your accumulated gain by a sell stop order.

Similarly, if the stock price of, say IBM, rises about $120 you can give a buy order to stockholders. Such an order is usually given by investors who are in short position (see Section 3.4.9) in IBM stocks, hence they lose money when the stock price rises. By buying the stock if it goes above $120, they put a limit on the losses in the short position. Exhibit 3.14 lists other unusual types of orders that currently exist.

---

[16] See 'NYSE program trading averages 16.8 percent of volume', at
http://www.f2.yahoo.com/finance/finance/971120/NYSEprogram_trading_1.html.

Exhibit 3.14 Specialized orders for securities

Type of order	Definition
All-or-none order	Partial execution of an order is prohibited. For example, assume you have a seller wishing to sell 1,000 shares of IBM stock at $80 per share, and the buy limit order is for 2,000 shares at $80. Because the order would be only partially filled, it would not be executed.
Minimum-fill order	Execution of the order will take place at a prespecified minimum volume of trading.
Market opening/closing order	Order is executed only at the opening or closing of the market.
Last-sale-price order	Order must be executed at a price equal to or better than the last sale price.
Mid-market order	Execution of this order must be at the middle of the most recent bid–offer spread only.
Basket trade	Purchase (or sale) of a given security may be executed only in conjunction with the sale (or purchase) of another security.
Index-related trade	The execution price is related to the value of a specified market index (could be considered a type of limit order).
Spot/future trade	Execution of a cash position is permitted only if a prespecified and simultaneous execution occurs in a futures market.

Finally, although most orders are for **round lots** (increments of 100 shares), trading can be in **odd lots,** which is any number of shares not in increments of 100. For example, a 50-share trade would be an odd-lot trade. Odd-lot trades, however, incur substantially higher fees; thus, it is more economical to trade round lots. In 1996, 104.6 *billion* shares in round lots traded on the NYSE, whereas only 381,932 *million* odd-lot shares were purchased.[17]

3.4.8 Placing an order: call your broker or trade via the Internet

Investors can place buy or sell orders in one of three ways. The standard method is a phone call to a broker, who executes the trades. Investors can also trade from their personal computers. Trading through a personal computer is typically done with a modem and dial-in capabilities with a broker. Trades can also be initiated with a call on a touch-tone phone to a broker's computer.

Nowadays, electronic trading via the Internet plays a very large role in securities trading. Exhibit 3.15 shows how you can fill an order. After having your account with the broker, you fill in the type of order you submit, concerning shares you want to buy and at what price.

Although there are different ways to initiate a trade, the path the trade takes after the order is given is typically the same (Exhibit 3.16). The client contacts the broker with an order (1). The broker keys the order into the firm's computer (2). The computer is programmed to locate the exchange with the best available price to make the trade (3). Depending on the type of order, the trade will be executed either electronically (4) or by

---

[17] *NYSE Fact Book for the Year 1996* (New York: New York Stock Exchange, Inc., May 1997), p. 11.

Exhibit 3.15 Placing trade orders

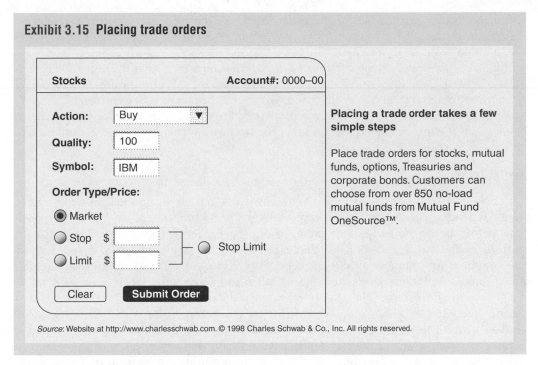

Exhibit 3.16 The path of a stock trade

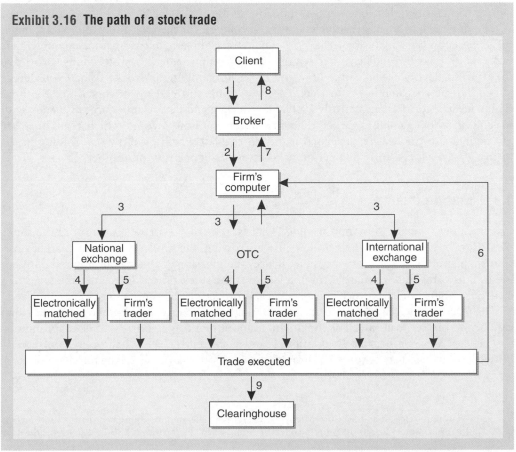

the firm's trader responsible for the order (5). Once the trade is executed, the relevant information is sent back to the firm via a computer network (6) and given to the broker (7), who passes it on to the client (8).

All orders are settled on the *settlement date*, which is three days after the order is executed. At this time, the brokerage firm remits the proceeds from the sale of securities to the client, or the client must remit the funds to the brokerage firm for the purchase of securities.

Each exchange has a clearinghouse (or is affiliated with a clearinghouse) that keeps track of all the intricate details of trading. The trading information is also communicated to the clearinghouse (9).

■ Day traders

There are day trading brokers which allow investors to trade using the firm's computers. The **day trader** usually buys a stock and sells it several times a day and closes the position before he or she leaves the trading room. Such clients 'think' they discover some pattern in the stock, e.g. its price fluctuates within the day between $98 and $99, so they adopt a policy to buy at $98 and sell at $99. Sitting all day in front of the computer and using some technical rates telling you when to buy or sell a stock is very similar to gambling in the casino. The clients frequently do not know what is the company's profit, nor even to which industry it belongs. On average, the stock market goes up (unlike gambling in the casino where, on average, you lose money), so one would believe that, on average, the day traders would gain. However, because they conduct many transactions within a day, they pay the day trading company transaction costs; hence, it is claimed that, on average, they lose money.

The day traders are not regular investors who invest for the long run presumably, based on some economic analysis of the firm. They are gamblers, and sometimes gamblers, as with other possibly addictive behaviours, do not know when to stop. Many also leave their job to devote all their time (day and night) to gambling in stocks. When you devote all your time to gambling, you may lose everything and end up in tragedy of the kind which happened in Atlanta in July 1999. Day trading and its bad influence on clients, with its emphasis on gambling rather than investment, is now a topic which regulators are discussing. No one will be surprised if the US regulators will disallow day trading in the future or at least constrain its operations to investors in one way or another.

3.4.9 Margin trading

Investors may engage in **margin trading.** That is, they may borrow a portion of the funds needed to buy stock from their brokers. By borrowing, the investor can take a larger position than otherwise would be possible; hence, the investor is able to 'leverage' the investment. One advantage of margin trading is that if the stock price appreciates, the investor's return is enhanced. If the stock price declines, however, the investor's losses are magnified.

The interest rate charged by the broker on the borrowed funds is known as the **call loan rate** or the **broker loan rate.** The maximum amount that can be borrowed is established by the Federal Reserve Board's Regulation T and is currently 50% of the purchase price.[18] However, brokers may require investors to put up more than 50% of the purchase price.

---

[18] The margin requirement has been 50% since 3 January 1974. The margin requirement had been as high as 100% (in 1946) and as low as 40% (in the late 1930s and early 1940s). (See *NYSE Fact Book for the Year 1996*, p. 79.)

As stock prices fall, the percentage of borrowed money in relation to security value will rise. If this percentage rises above the allowable limit, the investor must supply more funds to reduce the amount borrowed. When a broker calls for more money, it is a **margin call.** One factor to consider before buying on margin is at what price level a margin call will go out.

The **initial margin (IM)** is the percentage of the dollar amount originally required by the lender to be put up by the borrower:

$$IM = \frac{\text{total amount put up by investor}}{\text{total value of the shares}}$$

which can be expressed in symbols as

$$IM = \frac{\text{total purchase} - \text{borrowing}}{\text{total purchase}}$$

For example, if you purchased 200 shares of AT&T at $60 per share, then the total cost is $12,000. An initial margin of 50% would require that you borrow no more than 50% of $12,000, namely, $6,000:

$$IM = \frac{(\$60 \times 200) - \$6,000}{\$200 \times \$60} = 0.5, \text{ or } 50\%$$

The percentage of the total current market value that an investor originally put up is known as the **actual margin.** As prices fall, the actual margin will also fall. For example, if the AT&T stock price falls to $55, then the investor's actual margin (AM) is

$$AM = \frac{\text{value of stock} - \text{borrowing}}{\text{value of stock}} = \frac{(200 \times \$55) - \$6,000}{200 \times \$55} = 0.45, \text{ or } 45\%$$

To minimize the risk of default by the investor, the broker has a minimum margin requirement, known as the **maintenance margin,** which is the percentage of the dollar amount of the securities market value that must always be set aside as margin. If the margin falls below the maintenance margin, the investor pays the broker cash to reduce the amount of borrowing. The maintenance margin is always less than the initial margin. The maintenance margin (MM) can be written as

$$MM = \frac{(N \times P') - B}{N \times P'} \qquad (3.2)$$

where P' is the price at which a margin call will be issued. Solving for P', we find

$$P' = \frac{B}{N(1 - MM)} \qquad (3.2')$$

Suppose you purchased 100 shares ($N = 100$) of Microsoft common stock for $90 by borrowing $4,500 and providing $4,500 of your own funds (because of the initial margin of 50%). Now suppose the maintenance margin is 40% (MM = 0.4). The price below which you will receive a margin call is

$$P' = \frac{4,500}{100(1 - 0.4)} = \frac{4,500}{60} = \$75$$

Hence, you will not receive a margin call as long as the price remains above $75. If the price suddenly falls to $60, how much will you have to add in cash to hold this position? To reduce the amount of money borrowed, you will have to add the amount of cash that will bring the maintenance margin back to 40%, or from Equation 3.2:

$$MM = 0.40 = \frac{(100 \times 60) - \$4,500 + cash}{100 \times \$60}$$

$$cash = (0.40 \times 100 \times \$60) - (100 \times \$60) + \$4,500 = \$900$$

where $4,500 is the borrowing and $60 is the new market price of the stock.

Indeed, the amount borrowed decreases to $4,500 − $900 = $3,600, and the maintenance margin (MM) is:

$$\frac{(100 \times 60) - \$3,600}{(100 \times 60)} = \frac{6,000 - 3,600}{6,000} = \frac{2,400}{6,000} = 0.40, \text{ or } 40\%$$

as required.

Most investors buy securities with the expectation that they will appreciate in value. Margin trading is one method to enhance the return when a security's price rises.

PRACTICE BOX

Problem
Suppose you purchased 1,000 shares of GE common stock for $65 by borrowing $30,000. Thus, the initial margin is $35,000 [($65 × 1,000) − $30,000], or 53.85% ($35,000/$65,000). Now suppose the maintenance margin is 25%. What is the price below which you would receive a margin call?

Solution
Given the information above, N = 1,000, B = $30,000 and MM = 0.25. Therefore, from Equation 3.2', you have:

$$P' = \frac{\$30,000}{1,000(1 - 0.25)} = \$40$$

If the stock price fell below $40, you would receive a margin call.

3.4.10 Short selling

How can you profit when stock prices are falling? Is selling your own stocks the best that you can do? **Short selling** is a method that allows you to profit when a stock's price falls by selling securities that you borrow. Actually, your broker borrows these securities from the inventory of other clients. If the price falls, the short seller can buy the securities back at a lower price. By selling high and buying low, the short seller can make a profit. Thus, the short seller is hoping prices will fall.

To demonstrate how a short sale works, assume you borrow from your broker 100 shares of GM stock, and you sell them for $40. Assume further that the price falls to $38. Now you buy the stock back and return it to the broker. From this transaction, you make a profit of $2 per share. However, if the price goes up to $42, you have to pay $42 to buy it, and you lose $2 per share.

The short seller must pay any dividends due to the original owner of the shorted securities. Also, the proceeds from the short sale are held by the broker as collateral for the borrowed securities and the short seller receives interest on the held proceeds. The short seller must provide additional money to insure against default. If 100 shares of GM are sold short at $40, and GM's stock price rises to $50, then the brokerage firm will lose $1,000, or $100(\$50 - \$40)$, if the short seller defaults. The current minimum initial margin requirement for short selling set by the Federal Reserve is 50%.[19]

Stocks can be sold short only if prior to the short sale they have traded on an **uptick** or **zero-plus tick**. Trading on an uptick refers to a security's last trade price exceeding the previous trade price (for example, $\$101^{1}/_{8}$, then $\$101^{1}/_{4}$). Trading on a zero-plus tick refers to a security's last trade price being the same as the previous trade price, but the previous trade price exceeding the one before it (for example, $\$101^{1}/_{8}$, then $\$101^{1}/_{4}$, then $\$101^{1}/_{4}$).

Short selling is a high-risk position, because the securities may continue to rise. For example, if an investor had sold short 100 shares of Microsoft when it was trading at $50 per share in the late 1980s, the investor would be required to cover this short position by buying Microsoft. Microsoft common stock is currently trading for about $250 (adjusting for splits). In this case, the investor is facing a $200 loss per share. The investor could wait, but then the price might go even higher.

When investors buy stock (a long position), the most they can lose is the investment itself (when or if the stock price falls to zero). However, when investors sell short (a short position), their loss has no bounds because there is no upper limit to the stock price. The higher the price, the larger the loss.

3.4.11 Brokers

There are two basic types of brokers: **full-service brokers** and **discount-service brokers.** Full-service brokers earn commissions based on the volume of trading they transact. At a full-service brokerage firm, an investor is assigned to a broker, and that broker notifies the investor about prospects on various securities. The broker also shares advice from the firm's research group as to the anticipated direction of security prices. Full-service brokers typically have analyses of most major corporations. The commission can be as high as 2% of the value of the transaction.

Discount-service brokers are paid a set salary. Investors do not receive any investment advice from discount-service brokers. However, the cost of trading is from 50% to 70% less than the prices charged by full-service brokers.

[19] See *Federal Reserve Bulletin*, December 1992 (Washington, DC: Board of Governors of the Federal Reserve System), p. A26.

Exhibit 3.17 Equities (stocks and warrants) transaction costs

- $5 market/$10 limit for equity orders up to 5,000 shares online, touchtone, or PC line.
- $12 additional for broker-assisted equity orders.
- Add $0.01 per share for total orders over 5,000 shares retroactive to the first share.
- For online, touchtone, or PC line option orders: $5 + $1.50/contract for market orders; $10 + $1.50/contract for limit/stop orders, $15 minimum; $25 minimum for broker-assisted orders.
- See commission and fee schedule for full details.

Note: Brown & Co. does not offer brokerage services to non-US citizens.
Source: Website at http://www.brownco.com, 12 March 2002. Reprinted with permission.

■ Commission schedule

The typical discount brokerage's equities transaction costs are listed in Exhibit 3.17.[20] For example, purchasing 400 shares of $20 stock (i.e. $8,000 investment) would cost

Exhibit 3.18

Flat Free Trading® Makes The Difference

	200 sh. @$25	300 sh. @$20	500 sh. @$18	1000 sh. @$14
Schwab	89.00	95.60	106.60	123.60
Fidelity	88.50	95.10	106.10	123.10
Quick & Reilly	60.50	65.00	81.50	94.00
NDB	24.95/ 27.95*	24.95/ 27.95*	24.95/ 27.95*	24.95/ 27.95*

BROKER-ASSISTED RATES BASED ON SURVEY DONE 8/28/97.

*DOMESTIC STOCK, MARKET ORDER VS. LIMIT ORDER, LISTED ORDERS IN EXCESS OF 5,000 SHARES WILL INCUR A 1 PERCENT PER SHARE CHARGE ON THE ENTIRE ORDER. OTHER PRODUCTS AND SERVICES ARE AVAILABLE AT OTHER PRICES AND FEES.

National Discount
BROKERS
1-800-4-1-PRICE
www.ndb.com
help@ndb.com • 1-800-888-3999• Member NASD, SIPC, MSRB and Discount Brokers Association.
A National Discount Brokers Group Company • Listed on the NYSE (Symbol:NDB)

N D B
Listed
NYSE

Source: *Barron's*, 6 October 1997, p. 64. Barron's Online by *Barron's*. © 1997 by Dow Jones & Co., Inc. Reproduced with permission of Dow Jones & Co., Inc. in the format *Fundamentals of Investments* via Copyright Clearance Center.

---

[20] This commission schedule is from Brown & Company. Full-service brokerage fees are usually much more complicated. Typically, they will be at least 100% more than the fee schedule given here.

$83, or $35 + (0.006 × 20 × 400). Most firms have both maximum and minimum fees. Trading odd lots is more expensive.

There are big differences in commission rates among firms, as the advertisement in Exhibit 3.18 reveals. For a 200-share transaction with a price of $25 per share, Schwab charges $89, which implies that the commission as a percentage of the transaction is $89/(200 shares × $25) = $89/$5,000 = 0.0178, or 1.78%. NDB charges just a little more than a quarter of Schwab's commission.

■ Brokerage services

Discount-service and full-service brokerage firms offer several services. These services vary widely, so investors should compare brokerage firms before choosing one. Most firms offer an 800 (toll-free in the US) telephone number to buy and sell securities. They also provide a toll-free number to receive current stock quotes and provide execution capabilities on all US security markets. Some brokerage firms also handle international trades and provide real-time quotes via the Internet. Several houses offer money market rates for idle cash between investments, as well as checking services. Most firms provide complete safekeeping and record-keeping services (usually monthly). Finally, most brokerage houses offer up to $500,000 in insurance through the Securities Investor Protection Corporation (SIPC). The SIPC insurance covers the risk that the brokerage firm might become insolvent. It does not, however, cover losses from a fall in security prices.[21]

3.4.12 Financial planners

Rather than dealing directly with brokers, individual investors sometimes use financial planners. Financial planners evaluate an investor's situation and formulate a strategic investment plan. The academic field of financial planning is still in its infancy. Although financial planning has gone on for centuries, the label *financial planner* is new. Just about anyone can be a financial planner in the United States simply by paying $150 and registering with the SEC. (Some states require registration with state officials as well.)

Most financial planners generate their revenues from commissions. Hence, investors must exercise care when soliciting their advice. It is now possible to call state securities departments to find out if a particular financial planner has ever been in trouble. The North American Administrators Association and the National Association of Securities Dealers (NASD) have developed a computer database of financial planners that covers all 50 states. The system, known as the Central Registration Depository, lists a financial planner's education, employment, any bankruptcy filings, any legal injunctions against his or her business, and any criminal convictions.[22]

3.5 WORLD SECURITY MARKETS

So far the chapter's description of security markets has covered only the workings of US markets. With today's technology, however, investors can routinely search the entire globe for the securities that best meet their needs. Most major brokerage firms have offices in every continent and can effectively conduct international securities transactions.

---

[21] To gain a greater understanding of the services provided by different brokerage firms, call a few local brokerage houses (see 'Stock Brokers' in the telephone book) and request information.
[22] Based on an article by Ellen E. Schultz, *Wall Street Journal*, 13 September 1990, p. C1.

The history of world security markets is long and varied. Babylonian merchants financed their activities from the savings of the rich around 2000 BC. By 400 BC the Greeks had their equivalent of a modern joint-stock company and markets for handling currencies and interest-bearing securities.[23] With the exception of the Middle Ages and major wars, the move towards more sophisticated security markets has never stopped. Today's world security markets include bond, stock and derivative markets.

3.5.1 World bond markets

The world bond market has increased more than 15-fold in the past 30 years – from $700 billion in 1966 to over $21 trillion at the end of 1994.[24] As Exhibit 3.19 illustrates, the majority of this debt is from governments. Notice that government borrowing makes up approximately 62% of the total bond market.

There have been numerous advances in the international money market. For example, Germany moved into the commercial paper (CP) market in 1991, when 'certain amendments to section 795 of the German Civil Code made it possible to issue short-dated domestic securities'.[25] The market for Deutsche Mark CP developed rapidly and was being widely used by German firms, as well as German subsidiaries of foreign firms.

US Treasury securities constitute one of the largest and most liquid capital markets in the world. Other major governments, however, also have substantial treasury issues. Exhibit 3.20 summarizes the major government bond markets and their sizes. The US

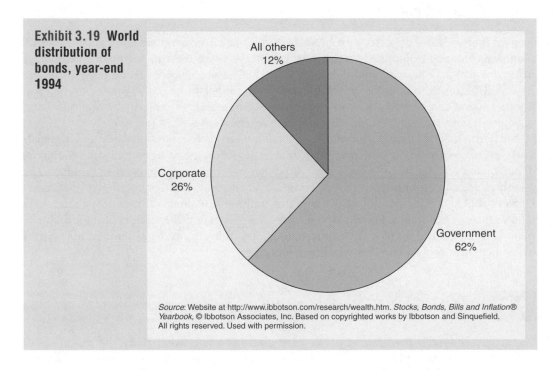

Exhibit 3.19 World distribution of bonds, year-end 1994

All others 12%

Corporate 26%

Government 62%

Source: Website at http://www.ibbotson.com/research/wealth.htm. *Stocks, Bonds, Bills and Inflation®Yearbook,* © Ibbotson Associates, Inc. Based on copyrighted works by Ibbotson and Sinquefield. All rights reserved. Used with permission.

---

[23] See D.E. Ayling, *The Internationalization of Stock Markets* (Brookfield, VT: Gower Publishing, 1986), p. 44, and http://www.ibbotson.com/research/wealth.htm, Laurence B. Siegel, 'The $40 trillion market: global stock and bond capitalization and returns'.

[24] For perspective, $1 million in tightly bound $1,000 bills makes a stack approximately 4 inches tall. Thus, $20 trillion in tightly bound $1,000 bills makes a stack approximately 1,290 miles high!

[25] See Peter Lee, 'Deutschmark CP gets into gear', *Euromoney,* August 1991, p. 51.

government bond market is the largest, making up 48.5% of the world market. The Japanese market follows, with 26.3%, and then the German market, with 10.9%. Thus, the government bond market is highly concentrated in just a few countries.

Government bonds are traded on the major exchanges and the over-the-counter market, as well as in interbank markets. For example, as of 31 December 1996, there were 640 government issues listed on the NYSE with a total par value of $2.55 billion.[26]

Country	Market value (US $ billion)	Percentage (rounded)
United States	5,489	48.5
Japan	2,977	26.3
Germany	1,236	10.9
France	513	4.5
Canada	335	3.0
United Kingdom	331	2.9
Netherlands	253	2.2
Australia	82	0.7
Denmark	72	0.6
Switzerland	37	0.3
Total	11,325	100

Exhibit 3.20 Major national government bond markets as of year-end 1994

Source: Website at http://www.ibbotson.com/research/wealth.htm. *Stocks, Bonds, Bills and Inflation® Yearbook*, © Ibbotson Associates, Inc. Based on copyrighted works by Ibbotson and Sinquefield. All rights reserved. Used with permission.

Exhibit 3.21 Global distribution of corporate bonds, 1994

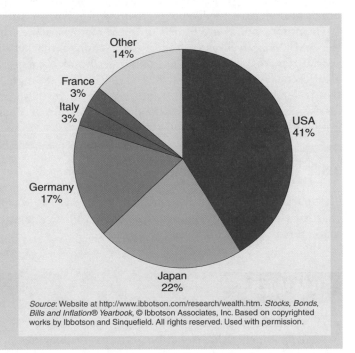

Source: Website at http://www.ibbotson.com/research/wealth.htm. *Stocks, Bonds, Bills and Inflation® Yearbook*, © Ibbotson Associates, Inc. Based on copyrighted works by Ibbotson and Sinquefield. All rights reserved. Used with permission.

---

[26] See NYSE *Fact Book for the Year 1996*, p. 84.

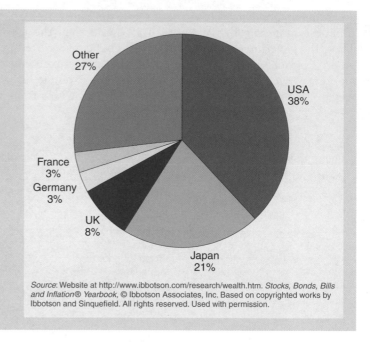

Exhibit 3.22 Global stock market capitalization, year-end 1994

The world corporate bond market stands at over $5.4 trillion. Exhibit 3.21 provides a breakdown by major country. Again, the United States dominates, with 41% of the market. Five countries capture all but 14% of the market.

Corporate bonds are an attractive means of raising capital, because the interest expense is tax deductible (whereas dividend payments are not). However, recall that corporate bonds also increase the likelihood that the firm will go bankrupt in hard economic times.

Corporate bonds are traded on most major stock exchanges, such as the NYSE and the AMEX, as well as on the over-the-counter market. The international arena has a special type of bond, called a **crossborder bond.** Crossborder bonds are bonds issued in a different country from that of the issuer. For example, a bond that a US firm issues that is denominated in Swiss francs, paying interest and principal in Swiss francs, would be classified as a crossborder bond. The crossborder bond has been one of the fastest-growing segments of the bond market.

3.5.2 World stock markets

The market value of world equities now exceeds $17.8 trillion. Exhibit 3.22 shows a pie chart of equity markets by major countries. Once again, the United States is the largest market, here closely followed by Japan.

SUMMARY

■ *Describe the function of security markets.*
A security market that functions effectively provides accurate information, accurate prices and liquidity. Buyers and sellers have access to timely and accurate information. Market prices reflect all known information. When markets are liquid, transactions are completed quickly.

- *Contrast the primary and secondary markets.*

The primary market is the mechanism through which a firm can raise additional capital by selling stocks, bonds and other securities. The secondary market is where previously issued securities trade among investors. An alternative to raising capital by an initial public offering is with a private placement. The secondary market includes national exchanges such as the New York Stock Exchange (NYSE) and the American Stock Exchange (AMEX), regional exchanges such as the Pacific Stock Exchange and the Boston Stock Exchange, and the over-the-counter (OTC) market.

- *Describe the basic structure of security markets.*

Security exchanges seek to have a trading mechanism that satisfies competing constraints. For example, determining what information must be made public and what information is to remain private is a difficult task. Market makers are individuals who set the bid and asked price quotes. The bid price is the price at which investors can sell securities, and the asked price is the price at which investors can buy securities.

- *Survey world security markets.*

The world security markets include bond, stock and derivative markets. The $21 trillion bond market is dominated by the United States. The $17.8 trillion stock market is led in size by the United States, followed closely by Japan. The world security markets also include more than 87 security exchanges that trade derivative securities, such as options and futures.

KEY TERMS

Actual margin (AM)	Gross spread (GS)	Program trading
Asked price	Information asymmetry	Prospectus
Bid–ask spread	Initial margin (IM)	Registered competitive
Bid price	Initial public offering	trader
Breadth	(IPO)	Registered equity market
Broker	Investment banker	maker
Broker loan rate	Limit order	Resiliency
Call loan rate	Maintenance margin	Round lot
Call market	(MM)	Scalping
Commission broker	Margin call	Seasoned new issue
Continuous market	Margin trading	Second market
Crossborder bond	Market	Secondary market
Day order	Market maker	Shallow market
Day trader	Market microstructure	Short selling
Dealer	Market order	Specialist
Depth	Mixed market	Stop order
Discount-service broker	Not-held (NH) order	Syndicate
Dual listing	Odd lot	Thin market
Execution cost	Over-the-counter market	Third market
First market	Price continuity	Underwriter
Floor broker	Primary market	Underwriter's
Fourth market	Primary offering	discount
Full-service broker	Private placement	Upstairs market
Good-till-cancelled (GTC)	Private placement	Uptick
order	memorandum	Zero-plus tick

QUESTIONS

3.1 What are the main explanations given for IPOs being underpriced?

3.2 How are the US secondary market transactions categorized?

3.3 Describe the three major categories of secondary markets.

3.4 Describe the market maker on the NYSE.

3.5 What factors affect the bid–ask spread?

3.6 What is margin trading and why is it considered risky?

3.7 Suppose you purchase 500 shares of Wal-Mart common stock at $75 per share by borrowing funds, and your initial margin is 65%. The maintenance margin is 55%.
   (a) How much of your own money will you have to provide?
   (b) What is the price at which you would begin to receive a margin call?

3.8 Using the commission schedules provided in this chapter, how much would you pay in commission to a discount-service brokerage firm if you bought 700 shares of Ford Motor Company's common stock at $35 per share?

3.9 Suppose IBM stock is trading for $70 a share. You borrow from your broker 100 shares and sell them. Calculate your dollar profit if IBM's stock price drops to $60 per share. Also calculate your dollar loss if IBM's stock price rises to $80 a share. Are your profits limited? Are your losses limited? Explain.

3.10 Suppose you are an underwriter who has a firm commitment to sell a million shares at $100 a share. You have an agreement to give the issuing firm $95 per share. Suppose there is a 50% chance that all shares will be sold at $100 and a 50% chance that the issue will not go well and the market price will end up being only $92 per share. What is, on average, the underwriter spread?

3.11 Suppose you invested $400,000 with your broker, and the broker went bankrupt. Are you insured? Suppose now that the value of your assets went down to $200,000 because of bankruptcies of firms that issued the shares you hold. Are you insured now?

3.12 A specialist at Xerox Corporation has an asked price of $20\frac{1}{8}$ and a bid price of $19\frac{1}{2}$. How can you explain these differences in the bid and asked prices?

3.13 The bid price of Stock A is $1, and the asked price is $1\frac{1}{8}$. The bid and asked prices of Stock B are $100 and $100\frac{1}{8}$, respectively. Which stock do you think is more volatile?

3.14 Suppose an underwriter has a firm commitment on two issues, each issue at $10 per share and for 1 million shares. Suppose the price falls to $9 in both issues. Would the underwriter be better off by having one issue of 2 million shares and having the price of the issue fall from $10 to $9?

3.15 In light of your answer to Question 3.14, why do underwriters form syndicates?

3.16 The stock price is $P = \$100$, and you bought 1,000 shares of this particular stock. The initial margin you use is 20%. How much did you borrow? (Use Equation 3.2'.)

SELECTED REFERENCES

Benos, A., and M. Crouhy. 'Changes in the structure and dynamics of European markets'. *Financial Analysts Journal,* May–June 1995, pp. 37–50.
This article provides a description of changes in European securities markets and the prevailing tracking systems in the various exchanges in Europe.

Eatwell, John, Murray Milgate, and Peter Newman (eds). *New Palgrave Dictionary of Money and Finance.* New York: W.W. Norton, 1989.
This is a detailed dictionary of financial concepts. The terms are defined and discussed by leading academics in finance.

Fabozzi, Frank J., and Franco Modigliani. *Capital Markets Institutions and Instruments.* Englewood Cliffs, NJ: Prentice-Hall, 1992.
This text provides a detailed analysis of world capital markets, with special emphasis on the United States.

Fridson, Martin S., and Gao Yan. 'Primary versus secondary pricing of high-yield bonds'. *Financial Analysts Journal,* May–June 1996, pp. 20–7.
This article analyzes the underpricing of newly floated securities vis-à-vis secondary market price levels.

Griffin, Mark W. 'A global perspective on pension fund asset allocation'. *Financial Analysts Journal,* March–April 1998, pp. 60–8.
This article provides a detailed comparison of pension fund asset allocation around the globe with an emphasis on equities versus bonds.

Hasbrouck, Joel. 'Security markets, information and liquidity'. *Financial Practice and Education,* 1 (2), Fall–Winter 1991, pp. 7–16.
This article is a good summary of market microstructure.

Lederman, Jess, and Keith K. H. Park (eds). *The Global Bond Markets State-of-the-Art Research, Analysis and Investment Strategies.* Chicago: Probus Publishing, 1991.
This book surveys the major world bond markets and addresses some of the more sophisticated global bond investment strategies.

Livingston, Miles. *Money and Capital Markets: Financial Instruments and Their Uses.* Englewood Cliffs, NJ: Prentice-Hall, 1990.
This text provides many useful technical details of capital markets, with an emphasis on pricing.

Mann, Steven V., and Robert W. Seijas. 'Bid-ask spreads, NYSE specialists and NASD dealers'. *Journal of Portfolio Management,* Fall 1991, pp. 54–8.
This article describes the salient differences between the NYSE specialist system and the NASD dealer system of making a market. The authors view these different systems as 'cousins' and not 'twins'.

Robertson, Malcolm J. *Directory of World Futures and Options.* Englewood Cliffs, NJ: Prentice-Hall, 1990.
This is an exhaustive directory of futures and options markets worldwide.

Scarlata, Jodi G. 'Institutional developments in the globalization of securities and futures markets'. *Federal Reserve Bank of St Louis,* January–February 1992, pp. 17–30.
This article provides a good survey of recent developments in globalization. Particularly helpful is the summary of computerized trading systems.

Schwartz, Robert A. *Equity Markets: Structure, Trading, and Performance.* New York: Harper & Row, 1988.
This book provides the institutional detail of US security markets and focuses on market microstructure issues and regulations.

Tucker, Alan L. *Financial Futures, Options, and Swaps.* St Paul, MN: West Publishing, 1991.
This is a detailed introduction to futures, options and swaps.

SUPPLEMENTARY REFERENCES

AMEX Fact Book. Annual. New York: American Stock Exchange.

Bancel, F. and R. Mittoo. 'European managerial perceptions of the net benefits of foreign stock listings'. *European Financial Management*, 2001, Vol. 7, Issue 2.

Bae, Sung C., and Haim Levy. 'The valuation of firm commitment underwriting contracts for seasoned new equity issues: theory and evidence'. *Financial Management,* Summer 1990, pp. 48–59.

DiNoia, C., 'Competition and integration among Stock Exchanges in Europe: Network effects, implicit mergers and remote access'. *European Financial Management*, 2001, Vol. 7.

Glosten, Lawrence R. 'Insider trading, liquidity, and the role of the monopolist specialist'. *Journal of Business*, April 1989, pp. 211–35.

Lazer, R., B. Lev, and J. Livnat. 'Internet traffic and portfolio returns'. *Financial Analysts Journal*, May/June 2001.

NASD Fact Book. Annual. Washington, DC: National Association of Securities Dealers.

NYSE Fact Book. Annual. New York: New York Stock Exchange.

Smith, Clifford W. 'Investment banking and the capital acquisition process'. *Journal of Financial Economics,* 15, January–February 1986, pp. 3–29.

Tokyo Stock Exchange Fact Book. Annual. Tokyo: Tokyo Stock Exchange.

Part II

RISK AND RETURN

Chapter 4

THE PAST: RETURN, RISK AND RISK PREMIUM – DEFINITIONS, MEASUREMENT AND THE HISTORICAL RECORD

Learning objectives

After studying this chapter you should be able to:

1 Understand how to compute past rates of return.

2 Understand how to incorporate taxes and inflation into the calculation of rates of return.

3 Understand the differences between the arithmetic average and geometric average rates of return.

4 Calculate the volatility of past rates of return by the variance and standard deviation.

5 Understand the past relationship between volatility, average rate of return and risk premium.

INVESTMENT IN THE NEWS

Media, banks, oils prop up FTSE 100

Vince Heaney

A late run on the media sector kept the FTSE 100 in the black on Monday, despite weakness in technology stocks.

The Daily Mail Group led the blue-chip leaderboard at the close, with Granada firming.

Simon Baker, media analyst at SG Securities, said of the Daily Mail: 'There were some encouraging national newspaper circulation figures for December recently and [the markets] could be looking forward to some positive statement at next month's AGM.'

Tech sentiment was dealt a fresh blow after upbeat results from chip designer ARM Holdings were followed by a drop in the share price as analysts focused on the cautious outlook.

Heavyweights

It was left to the market heavyweights in the blue-chip oils and banking sectors to prop up the market, with both sectors benefiting from positive broker comment.

The FTSE 100 closed 0.6 per cent firmer at 5,223.6, while the FTSE Techmark was 1.5 per cent weaker at 1,371.5.

Source: Website at http://www.ftmarketwatch.com, 28 January 2002. (Now www.ftinvestor.com). Reprinted with permission from FT Investor. © Financial Times Limited 2002.

INVESTMENT IN THE NEWS

Exhibit 4.1 London gainers and losers, 28 January 2002

(a) FTSE 100 Gainers

Gainers	Value	% Change
Tea Plantations...	1.25	+66.67
Rts Networks Gr...	1.25	+66.67
Transacsys	4.50	+20.00
Convergent Comm...	8.00	+10.34
Creightons	3.25	+8.33
Widney	102.50	+7.89
Howard Holdings	36.50	+7.35
M.L. Laboratorie...	39.50	+6.76
Pennant Intl Gr...	8.50	+6.25
Cabouchon Colle...	34.50	+6.15
Marlborough Int...	17.50	+6.06
Centamin Egypt	9.00	+5.88
Direct Message	5.00	+5.26
Schroder Asia P...	10.50	+5.00
Macro 4	160.00	+4.92

Source: Website at http://www.ftmarketwatch.com/tools/indices.asp?region= 100§ion=101

(b) FTSE 100 Losers

Losers	Value	% Change
Anglesey Mining	1.00	−33.33
Elementis	0.75	−25.00
Smartlogik Group	1.00	−20.00
Invesco Asia Trust	3.50	−17.65
World Travel Hldgs	3.00	−14.29
Chaucer Holdings	6.00	−14.29
Martin Currie Jap	3.00	−14.29
Gartmore Selec Jap	1.50	−14.29
Orchestream Hldgs	11.50	−13.21
Electra Inv Trust	590.00	−12.59
Pacific Horizon It	0.44	−12.50
Gameplay	0.53	−12.50
Cash Converters In	1.75	−12.50
Stockbourne	1.75	−12.50
Synigence	8.50	−10.53

Source: Website at http://www.ftmarketwatch.com/tools/indices.asp?region=100 (now www.ftinvestor.com), 29 January 2002. Reprinted with permission from FT Investor.

Exhibit 4.2 FTSE 100 index, 28 January 2002

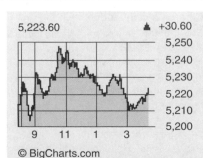

© BigCharts.com

Source: Website at http://www.ftmarketwatch.com/tools/indices.asp?region=100 (now www.ftinvestor.com), 29 January 2002. © BigCharts.com. Reproduced by permission of FT Investors and Big Charts.

Investors buy securities for their returns. In most cases there is also a risk attached to each investment. No one can guarantee that Tea Plantations will not be a loser next day or sometime in the near future, despite its performance on 28 January 2002. Being on the 'honour roll' one year or one day does not necessarily mean that the stock will appear on the 'honour roll' the next year. Uncertainty (or risk) therefore exists regarding future returns on an investment in the capital market. The main dilemma of the investor is how to choose from various available assets with different risk–return characteristics.

In this chapter we demonstrate how to calculate past **rates of return**. We then discuss the various multi-period averages of rates of return, which measure the average past profitability of an asset. We are also interested in knowing how to calculate the dispersion of rates of return around the average, which measures the historical risk or volatility of the investment. We then present the historical record of various assets in order to demonstrate that, in general, the higher the average rate of return on an asset, the higher its risk. Historical data are frequently used to estimate future expected rates of return and risk. These estimates are required for investment decision-making, a process which will be discussed in the next chapter.

4.1 RATES OF RETURN

As discussed below, one important use of rates of return is as a measure of comparison of the profitability of different investments. It is standard practice for investment managers to present the profitability of financial assets in percentages rather than in dollars or pounds. This enables investors to compare the rates of return on alternative assets whatever their price level. In this chapter we first demonstrate how to calculate rates of return on the investments.

Investors and investment analysts have three uses for past rates of return:

1 *Measuring historical performance*. Investors generally compare the rates of return on alternative investments, e.g. of alternative unit trusts. Suppose, for example, that two unit trusts are managed by two professional managers, Abraham and Alita. Fund managers are to be compensated according to performance. The historical or **realized rate of return** on a fund is an important measure of a manager's performance.

   However, rates of return are not in themselves a sufficient criterion for ranking the two managers. One would also need to know how much risk each manager has taken on.

2 *Estimating future rates of return*. Investors may use historical rates of return to estimate future *expected* rates of return and risk of various securities in order to make portfolio investment decisions.

   In general, future fluctuations in rates of return can be estimated from historical fluctuations. For example, the fluctuations in the technology stocks rate of return are higher than those of the big stocks (such as the Gas Corporation or the Electricity Corporation). These *ex-post* fluctuations can be used to estimate future (or *ex-ante*) fluctuations which, in turn, can be used in constructing an investment portfolio.

3 *Estimating cost of capital*. Finally, past rates of return can be used to estimate a firm's cost of equity, a term which is probably familiar to students who have studied corporate finance. Financial managers use the cost of equity (or cost of capital) in

capital budgeting decisions. One method of estimating the appropriate discount rate (for use in net-present-value calculations) utilizes the average historical rate of return on equity.

Similarly, investors and investment analysts who are considering buying a stock may use the *ex-post* average rate of return in order to discount the expected future dividends of the stock.

Historical rates of return, therefore, fulfil several functions for investors, analysts and financial managers.

4.2 RATE-OF-RETURN CALCULATIONS

Rates of return can be calculated in more than one way. Different methods yield different results, and money managers, who are rated on their performance, have an incentive to use those methods that make them look the best. Bearing this problem in mind, in 1992 the Committee for Performance Presentation Standards (CPPS) of the Association for Investment Management and Research (AIMR) established strict guidelines for its members to follow in presenting historical performance measures. The AIMR is the largest association of financial analysts in the world and you will most likely have to adhere to their standards if you become involved in the money management industry. This section reviews the techniques used in complying with the AIMR standards.[1]

4.2.1 Simple rate of return

Investors hold a security for a given period. The rate of return measured for this period is called the *holding period return* (HPR). There are several ways to measure security rates of return. This discussion begins with the *simple* rate of return.

The simple rate of return measures how much the value of a given investment increases or decreases over a given period of time. The **simple rate of return** (R) is given by

$$R = \frac{\text{EMV} - \text{BMV} + I}{\text{BMV}} \tag{4.1}$$

where EMV is the end-of-period market value, BMV is the beginning-of-period market value, and I is the income (generally in the form of interest and dividends) received from the investment during the period. This is the simplest and most common way of calculating the rate of return. Equation 4.1 gives rates of return in decimal form. To arrive at percentages, simply multiply by 100.

To demonstrate the simple rate-of-return calculation, assume you purchased one share of stock at the beginning of the year for £100 per share. You receive an

---

[1] Adapted with permission from the *Report of the Performance Presentation Standards Implementation Committee*. © 1991, Association for Investment Management and Research, Charlottesville, VA. All rights reserved.

£8 cash dividend per share. The stock is trading at the end of the year at £110 per share. Because EMV = £110, BMV = £100 and I = £8, the simple rate of return in this case is:

$$R = \frac{£110 - £100 + £8}{£100} = \frac{£18}{£100} = 0.18 \text{ or } 18\%$$

Note that the rate of return is the percentage change in the value of the investment; it does not matter whether you buy 200, 100 or one share of stock.

Equation 4.1 can also be written as

$$R = \frac{EMV + I}{BMV} - \frac{BMV}{BMV} = \frac{EMV + I}{BMV} - 1$$

and hence,

$$1 + R = \frac{EMV + I}{BMV}$$

which, in the earlier example, would be

$$1 + R = \frac{£110 + £8}{£100} = 1.18$$

which tells us that the value of £1 at the end of the period is £1.18. That is, £1 invested one period earlier would be worth £1.18 at the end of the period.

Determining a stock's or portfolio's performance using the simple rate of return calculation is appropriate when income is received at the end of the period. If dividends are paid during the period the simple rate of return has certain limitations.

In the next section, we calculate the adjusted rate of return. We use the simple rates of return in the calculation of the adjusted rate of return, which correctly takes into account the timing of the dividend and interest income.

4.2.2 Adjusted rate of return

The simple rate of return is easy to calculate and gives us an idea of the asset's rate of return. However, as mentioned above, it is not accurate, since it does not take into account the timing of dividends. To illustrate, consider two stocks, priced at £100 at the beginning of the year and £110 at the end of the year. The cash dividend is £10 for each stock. However, on one stock, the £10 is paid in January, while on the other it is paid in December. The simple rate of return shows a 20% rate of return on both stocks, regardless of the timing of cash dividends. However, investors are not indifferent to the timing of cash dividends. The earlier the dividends are obtained, the better off the investors are (this is the idea of 'time value of money' studied in corporate finance). The **adjusted rate of return** takes into account the timing of cash dividends and interest payments. Since the adjusted rate of return takes into account the timing of the cash flows, it is also called the **time-weighted rate of return**. This more correct measure of rate of return is used in the rest of the chapter and will be termed *the rate of return* to distinguish it from the *simple rate of return*. The rate of return assumes that all interim cash flows (in the form of dividends, interest and other cash benefits) are reinvested in the security under consideration. For example, if an investor wants to measure the rate of return on Marks & Spencer stock for the year

2001, and $10 dividends are paid in January 2001, then the method of calculation presented below implicitly assumes that the $10 is used to purchase more Marks & Spencer stock immediately upon being received. The AIMR explains the philosophy of this adjustment as follows:

> If cash flows occur during the period, they must theoretically be used, in effect, 'to buy additional units' of the portfolio at the market price on the day that they are received. Thus, the most accurate approach is to calculate the market value of the portfolio on the date of each flow, calculate an interim rate of return for the sub-period, and then link the sub-period returns to get the return for the month or quarter.[2]

Therefore, we must correctly incorporate the timing of cash flows to the investor or make adjustments to allow for the fact that dividends are in general not paid at the end of the year. The method for computing the rate of return is called the **linking method**. According to this method, we first calculate the simple rate of return for each sub-period where the cash dividend date determines the end of each sub-period, and then calculate the rate of return from these simple rates of return. The following numerical example illustrates this method.

Assume you are investing in shares of EMI Group. Exhibit 4.3(a) provides the necessary data for your calculations. Assume that EMI Group paid quarterly cash dividends and its stock price fluctuated considerably during the year.[3] Specifically, notice that the price fell early in the year, rose during the latter part of the year, and fell again to its original level by year's end.

Using the linking method, the simple rate of return (r_t) is calculated for each sub-period (t). The rate of return (R) for the entire period is then obtained by Rule 1, as follows.

Rule 1: To obtain the adjusted rate of return, first calculate the simple rate of return corresponding to each period, add 1 to it, multiply these terms and finally subtract 1:

$$R = [(1 + r_1)(1 + r_2) \ldots (1 + r_m)] - 1 \tag{4.2}$$

where m is the number of sub-periods. By this method the value of the investment at the end of the first sub-period ($1 + r_1$), including the obtained dividend, is reinvested for the second period, and so on up to the last period. This is equivalent to using dividends to purchase additional stock immediately upon receiving them.

Exhibit 4.3(b) illustrates the linking method for computing returns. The simple rate of return for Period 1 (January 1 through February 15) is [(£80 − £100 + £2)/£100] = −0.18, and for Period 2 (February 15 through May 15) is [(£95 − £80 + £2)/£80] = 0.2125. Thus, the rate of return over the period January 1 through May 15 is calculated by ([1 + (− 0.18)][1 + 0.2125] − 1) = −0.0057. Continuing this procedure, the rate of return for the whole year is found to be 0.0842, or 8.42% (see the last entry in the last column of Exhibit 4.3(b)). Note that the simple rate of return is calculated such that the final date of each period is determined by the dividend payment date (e.g. February 15). Thus, it is equal to the rate of return for this sub-period and hence is an accurate measure of profitability for the given sub-period.

---

[2] AIMR, p. 28 (see footnote 1).
[3] Dividends are typically declared about a month after the end of a fiscal quarter and paid two weeks later. Hence, most firms pay dividends in February, May, August and November.

Exhibit 4.3 Calculating a rate of return for EMI Group

(a) Table of input information

Date	Dividend per share (£)	Stock price when dividend is received (£)
January 1		100
February 15	2	80
May 15	2	95
August 15	2	105
November 15	2	120
December 31		100

(b) Calculating a rate of return by the linking method

Date	Interim period	Interim simple rate of return	Cumulative rate of return
January 1			
February 15	1	−0.18	−0.18
May 15	2	0.2125	−0.0057
August 15	3	0.1263	0.1198
November 15	4	0.1619	0.3011
December 31	5	−0.1667	0.0842

To sum up, the 8% simple rate of return method (using the simple rate of return equation given by Equation 4.1) assumes that when the dividends are received they are either left idle or spent, whereas the rate of return (8.42%) calculated using Equation 4.2 assumes reinvestment of the cash dividends. The rate of return is superior to the simple rate of return because it appropriately addresses the timing of cash flows. Investors prefer to receive money earlier rather than later, a fact that is ignored by the simple rate of return. The rate of return method guarantees that profitability on various assets is compared for the same level of pound investment. Investors want to know how well different securities have performed over time. It must, therefore, be assumed that interim cash flows are invested in the security itself. For example, suppose you want to compare the historical rates of return on two firms, A and B. You invest £100 in Firm A and £100 in Firm B. Firm A pays you £50 in dividends after one day. Firm B does not pay dividends at all. Using the simple method to calculate rates of return does not make sense, because your investment in Firm A is reduced by £50 after one day (hence the firm has less resources to invest, creating less returns). Thus, by the simple method, you actually compare the return on an investment of £100 in Firm B to £50 in Firm A. Therefore, the reinvestment of the obtained cash flow assumption is incorporated in order to reach an accurate measure of performance for a particular security, independent of its dividend policy and the size of the investment.[4]

---

[4] Appendix 4A at the end of the chapter provides a rate of return measure where the investment level changes over time. For example, suppose that an investor increases his or her investment in a given stock every month by allocating some percentage of the monthly salary to such an investment. This is a rate of return that measures the investor's percentage profit but not the rate of return on the security itself. It is affected by the rate of return on the asset in various periods as well as the amount of money invested by the investor in each period.

PRACTICE BOX

Problem

Suppose you purchased 100 shares of Misys on 1 January at £50 per share. Misys pays £2.30 annual dividend per share on 15 March, when the stock is trading at £55. Misys declares a 3-for-2 stock split effective on 30 May, when the stock is trading at £60. (A 3-for-2 stock split implies three new shares are substituted for two old shares held.) If Misys closed on 31 December at £35 per share, what would your rate of return be using the linking method?

Solution

The following table summarizes the basic data regarding Misys which is relevant for the rate of return calculation:

Date	Dividend	Split	Adjusted price Market price of stock
January 1			£50
March 15	£2.30		£55
May 30		3-for-2 shares	£40
December 31			£35

The simple rate of return for the period 1 January through 15 March is:

$$\frac{£55 + £2.30 - £50}{£50} = \frac{£7.3}{£50} = 0.1466 \text{ or } 14.6\%$$

The simple rate of return for the period 15 March through 30 May is:

$$\frac{1.5 \times £40 - £55}{£55} = \frac{£60 - £55}{£55} = \frac{£5}{£55} \cong 0.0909 \text{ or } 9.09\%$$

Note that we multiply the end of the period price of £40 by 1.5 because a 3-for-2 split implies a 50% increase in the number of shares holding. As we assume in the calculation that one share was bought at the beginning of the period, 1.5 shares are held at the end of the period due to the split. Finally, the rate of return for the last period is:

$$\frac{£35 - £40}{£40} = \frac{-£5}{£40} \cong -0.125 \text{ or } -12.5\%$$

Using the linking method (Equation 4.2), the rate of return for the year is given by

$$R = [(1 + 0.1466)(1 + 0.0909)(1 - 0.125)] - 1 \cong 0.09447 \text{ or about } 9.447\%$$

Nonetheless, in many cases cash dividends are relatively small; hence, the simple and adjusted rates of return are not that different. This explains why the simple and quick method is sometimes employed despite its lack of precision.

Notice that the various methods of calculation do not attempt to identify the best strategy for the investor but rather endeavour to measure the correct rate of return. For example, sometimes reinvesting dividends reduces the rate of return (as, for example, when the stock price falls). However, only the rate of return method gives the true historical rate of return on a given asset.

Thus far, we have demonstrated how to adjust the rate of return for cash dividends. If the firm makes other distributions to stockholders apart from cash dividends, they must obviously be incorporated into the rate of return calculation. For example, if the firm pays stock dividends of say 10%, the stock price generally drops. This reflects the fact that there are more outstanding shares, although the investor holds only 1.1 shares for each share bought at the beginning of the period (i.e. a 10% increase in the number of shares held). This fact should be incorporated into the rate of return calculation. Similarly, if the firm splits its stocks, adjustments should be made, since the investor holds more shares, albeit at a lower price. The company may also issue rights offerings, i.e. rights issued to stockholders to purchase new shares at a relatively low price (called the subscription price). These rights have a market value that also needs to be incorporated in the rate of return calculation.

Stock split

On 23 February 2001, Misys Company split its stock in a 2-for-1 ratio. This means that an investor holding 100 shares of Misys before the split holds 200 shares after the split. The investor returns the 100 old shares to the firm and gets 200 new shares instead with no additional investment. Thus, no cash flows are involved. How does such a split affect the rate of return calculation? The practice box above demonstrates how to incorporate stock split and cash dividends into the rate of return calculations.

Stock dividends

Stock dividends are incorporated into the calculation exactly as is the split. This is because the stock dividend increases the number of shares held with no cash flow involved. To illustrate, suppose that 10% stock dividends are paid, the stock price being £38 at the beginning of the period and £40 at the end. Then, for each share bought at the beginning of the period, the investor would hold 1.1 shares (due to the 10% stock dividends); hence we should multiply £40 by 1.1 to obtain the value of the investor's holding at the end of the period. The rate of return for our example at the end of the period would be

$$\frac{1.1 \times £40 - £38}{£38} = \frac{£44 - £38}{£38} = \frac{£6}{£38} \cong 0.1579 \text{ or } 15.79\%$$

Rights

Firms may raise equity by rights offerings, whereby existing stockholders have the right to buy new shares at a price lower than the market price. Rights offerings affect the end of a period stock price, and thus affect the rate of return on the stock.

Rights offerings are incorporated into the simple rate of return like cash dividends. To illustrate, suppose that for every two shares held, the investor earned the right to buy one share at a lower than market price. One right is linked to each old stock (i.e., in our specific example, for every stock the investor has a right to buy half a new share). The right has economic value and therefore we have to add the market value of the right to the end-of-period value of the investment. These rights are traded separately from the stocks and have market value. Because existing stockholders receive a right to buy new shares at a price lower than the market price of the stock, the stock price generally drops when the rights are traded separately from the stock. Suppose that the stock price at the beginning of the period on 1 January is £100 and on 10 March the rights were traded for £5 a right (thus, the value of the right attached to each share is £5). On 10 March, after the right was traded separately from the stock for the first time, the stock price was £107. Assuming no other distributions, the rate of return for this period is given by

$$\frac{£107 + £5 - £100}{£100} = \frac{£12}{£100} = 0.12 \text{ or } 12\%$$

It is assumed that investors obtain the £5 and this is treated the same as cash dividends. It is, therefore, assumed that investors will sell the stock and the right at the end of the sub-period and receive £107 plus £5.

We would like to emphasize that the price of rights as published in the media (e.g. *The Wall Street Journal*) is the value attached to each old stock regardless of the allocation ratio. Thus if, for example, the right allocation ratio is one right for each two old stocks and an investor wishes to exercise the right (i.e. buy more shares at the relatively low price), he or she needs two rights (or a value of £10) to buy one new share.

Indeed, investors who do not hold firm stocks can buy two rights for £10 and add the subscription price, say £97, to purchase one share of the firm. What is important for the rate of return calculation is that the value of the right is added to the end-of-period value exactly as cash dividends are added, regardless of whether the investor exercises the rights or simply sells them in the market.

■ Rate of return on derivatives

Call and put options are financial assets which are traded in the market. The call option holder of, say, Hilton is entitled to buy one share of Hilton at a given price for a given period. This predetermined price is called the *strike price*, and the option is intact up to a given date in the future, called the *expiration date*. A put option holder has the right to sell the stock at a predetermined price. If the stock price in the market goes up, we expect the call price to rise and the put price to decline. Call and put options pay no dividends and interest; hence, the rate of return calculation on these two assets is very simple, solely reflecting the capital gain or capital loss.

The following practice box illustrates such a calculation for options on Hilton share.

4.2.3 Bond returns on an accrual basis

Calculating the rate of return on bonds raises an additional issue regarding the timing of cash flows because of the way bond prices are quoted. Whereas the cash dividends on stocks are paid on a periodic (most often quarterly) basis, bond coupon interest accrues daily. *The bond prices quoted by the financial media and market makers do not include accrued interest in most cases.* However, the actual price paid for the bonds includes accrued interest. Thus, the equation for calculating bond returns must incorporate that accrued interest. When calculating the rates of return of bonds, the investor must, therefore, incorporate accrued interest. The CPPS of the AIMR describes the underlying philosophy of rate of return calculations for bonds:

> The Standards clearly state that an accrual basis, rather than a cash basis, should be used for calculating interest income. The guiding premise, again, should be to include that income to

PRACTICE BOX

Problem
The following data, taken from the *Financial Times*, provides the Hilton stock price, the call option price and the option price for two days, 31 and 30 December 2000. The strike price of each option is £200. Calculate the one-day rate of return on Hilton share as well as the put and the call option.

	31 December	30 December
Hilton stock	£209	£212
Hilton Feb call option	£9	£10
Hilton Feb put option	£18½	£17½

Solution
Let us calculate the daily rate of return on the stocks, on the call option and on the put option.

The rate of return on Hilton share (no dividends were paid on the day) for the one day was

$$R = \frac{£209 - £212}{£212} \cong -0.0142 \text{ or } -1.42\%$$

The rate of return on the call option was

$$R = \frac{£9 - £10}{£9} \cong -0.11 \text{ or } -11.11\%$$

and the rate of return on the put option was

$$R = \frac{£18½ - £17½}{£17½} \cong 0.0571 \text{ or } 5.71\%$$

which the portfolio was truly entitled if the security were sold at the end of the performance interval. Stock dividends do not become payable unless the stock is owned on the ex-dividend date. Dividends should therefore be accrued as income of their ex-date. Interest on most fixed-income securities becomes payable pro rata as long as the security is held. Interest should therefore be accrued according to whatever method is appropriate for the specific issue.[5]

Using the quoted bond prices to calculate the rates of return for bonds on a cash basis ignores the accrued interest (which the buyer has to pay and seller receives), and thus is not accurate. To account for accrued interest, simply add the values for accrued interest at the beginning and end of the period to the respective beginning and ending prices in Equation 4.1. Formally, the simple rate of return (R_t) can be expressed as

$$R_t = \frac{P_t + C_t - (P_{t-1} + AI_{t-1})}{P_{t-1} + AI_{t-1}} \tag{4.3}$$

[5] Adapted with permission from the *Report of the Performance Presentation Standards Implementation Committee*, December 1991, pp. 31–32. © 1991, Association for Investment Management and Research, Charlottesville, VA. All rights reserved.

where the date on which a coupon C_t is paid is determined by the end of the sub-period corresponding to the simple rate of return calculation. P_t is the price of the bond at the end of Period t, P_{t-1} is the price of the bond at the end of Period $(t-1)$, AI_{t-1} is the accrued interest as of the end of Period $(t-1)$ (investors must pay it when they buy the bonds), and C_t is the coupon paid at the end of sub-period t. If the rate of return is calculated from one coupon payout date to another, then there is no accrued interest. Similarly, if one chooses a different date for the end of the period than that of the accrued interest rate, AI_t rather than C_t should be added to P_t.

In general, for any selected period the rate of return on bonds is calculated by Rule 2.

Rule 2: Take the price of the bond at the end of the period and add to it the received or accrued interest. Subtract from it the price of the bond at the beginning of the period and the payment for the accrued period up to the bond's purchasing date. Divide this difference by the investment which is the bond price at the beginning of the period and the accrued interest.

Let us illustrate how to calculate the rate of return for bonds on an accrual basis. Consider a coupon bond that pays 8% on a semiannual basis. Assume that £40 in interest is paid on 15 November and 15 January. Exhibit 4.4 illustrates how to calculate the rate of return by the linking method. The exhibit lists the coupon payments, market prices and accrued interest for each date. Recall from Equation 4.3 that the rate of return requires calculating the beginning and ending market values. The accrual basis incorporates accrued interest in these values. For example, consider the rate of return during the period 1 January through 15 May, where the beginning market value is £1,000 (£990 + £10, where £10 is accrued interest). The accrued interest can be estimated as the fraction of the period since the last payment times the payment amount. In this case, it is (1.5 months/6 months) × £40 = £10. The 1.5 months is 15 November to 1 January. The ending market value is £1,030. The income paid in this period is the coupon payment of £40. Thus, the rate of return for the first time interval is

$$R_1 = \frac{£1,030 + £40 - (£990 + £10)}{£990 + £10} = \frac{£70}{£1,000} = 0.07 \text{ or } 7\%$$

In a similar way the simple rate of return is calculated for the other time interval. Note that for the last time interval, the investor received £10 accrued interest. The adjusted rate of return for the whole year is 9.03%.

Exhibit 4.4 Calculating the rate of return for an 8% semiannual coupon-bearing bond

Computing the rate of return by the linking method

Date (t)	Interim period	Coupon	Market price	Accrued interest	Accrued rate of return	Rate of return to date t
Jan. 1			£990	£10[a]		
May 15	1	£40	£1,030	£0	0.07	0.07
Nov. 15	2	£40	£1,020	£0	0.0291	0.1011[b]
Dec. 31	3		£1,000	£10[a]	−0.0098	0.0903[c]

[a] (1,000) (0.08) (1.5/12) = £10 (interest is paid on 15 May and 15 November).
[b] (1 + 0.07) × (1 + 0.0291) − 1 = 0.1011.
[c] (1 + 0.1011) × (1 − 0.0098) − 1 = 0.0903.

Note that the accrued interest at the end of period *t* will be zero if there is a coupon payment. That is, all interest that has been accrued was paid via the coupon payment. From Exhibit 4.4 we find that the rate of return on this bond over this year was 9.03%.

4.3 AFTER-TAX RATES OF RETURN

Taxes generally change the rate of return an investor receives. Although many pension funds and other portfolios are tax exempt, the security holdings of many investors are taxable. The procedure for calculating after-tax rates of return is conceptually similar to the simple rate of return calculations in Section 4.2. The only difference is the reduction of rates of return resulting from taxes.

To illustrate, suppose that your marginal income tax is 30%, and that you pay 20% capital gains tax.[6] You hold the stock for one year and you receive the dividend of £10 at the end of the year. The stock's price at the beginning of the year is £100 and at the end of the year £140.

The *pre-tax* rate of return is:

$$\frac{£140 + £10 - £100}{£100} = 0.50 \text{ or } 50\%$$

The *after-tax* rate of return is:

$$\frac{£140 + £10 - £100 - (£140 - £100) \times 0.2 - (£10 \times 0.30)}{£100}$$

$$= \frac{£50 - £8 - £3}{£100} = \frac{£39}{£100} = 0.39 \text{ or } 39\%$$

The investor, therefore, pays £8 capital gains tax and £3 income tax on dividends; hence the after-tax rate of return is, in this example, only 39% as opposed to 50% on a pre-tax basis.

4.4 INFLATION-ADJUSTED RATES OF RETURN

Thus far we have calculated rates of return in nominal terms, ignoring the effect of inflation.[7] Inflation causes investors to lose purchasing power when they sell their financial assets in the future and wish to buy goods with the proceeds. Investors would probably prefer that there was no inflation. The consumer price index (denoted CPI in the UK financial press) measures the inflation rate. The CPI provides the percentage change in the price of a specified basket of consumer goods.

Inflation reduces the purchasing power of an investment. That is, a person may invest £1,000 with the expectation of receiving £1,100 back within a year and using this sum

[6] By the current tax laws in the UK you have to pay capital gains tax of 10% (if you're earning up to £1,880), 20% (if you're earning up to £29,400) or 40% (if you're earning over £29,400). For all related tax issues, we recommend you to visit www.inlandrevenue.gov.uk.
[7] *Inflation* is the increase over time in the cost of goods and services. *Deflation* refers to the decrease over time in the cost of goods and services. In most years inflation rather than deflation has prevailed in the Western world.

to purchase goods and services. But, if the overall cost of goods and services rises more than 10% over the year the investment will not have been worthwhile.

The **real rate of return** is the nominal rate of return adjusted for inflation. The real rate of return (R_{real}) is calculated as

$$R_{real} = \frac{1 + R_{nom}}{1 + h} - 1 \tag{4.4}$$

where R_{nom} is the nominal rate of return and h is the inflation rate.[8] For example, if the nominal rate of return is 10% and inflation is 15%, the real rate of return is

$$R_{real} = \frac{1 + 0.1}{1 + 0.15} - 1 \cong -0.0435 \text{ or } -4.35\%$$

Note two properties of real rates of return:

1 In the case of no inflation ($h = 0$), the real rate of return is equal to the nominal rate of return.
2 If the nominal rate of return is equal to the inflation rate ($R_{nom} = h$), then in real terms, the rate of return is zero.

Let us turn to our previous example where the rate of return on the stock was 50% before tax and 39% after tax. Assuming an additional 5% annual inflation, the after-tax *real* rate of return would be:

$$\frac{1 + 0.39}{1 + 0.05} - 1 \cong 0.324 \text{ or approximately } 32.4\%$$

Thus, in our example, both inflation and taxes reduce the nominal rate of return from 50% to about 32.4%.

4.4.1 Calculating the rate of return values – an example

Let us now employ actual data to demonstrate the various rates of return on the stock of 'Hi Tech Dream' (HD) corresponding to the year 2001.

Exhibit 4.5 provides the basic data regarding HD. The table provides the stock prices at the beginning of the year, at the end of the year, and at each date where a dividend was paid. These prices are necessary for calculating the simple rate of return for each sub-period. The dividend paid in 2001 was four times £0.5, i.e. £2 for the year.

The simple rate of return for the year is:

$$\frac{(£71.5625 - £60.625) + £2}{£60.625} \cong 0.2134 \text{ or } 21.34\%$$

Note that the price of £71.5625 is quoted as £71⁹/₁₆. We thus transfer the prices here to decimals. To calculate the rate of return, we first need to calculate the rate of return

---

[8] Equation 4.4 can be approximated by $R_{real} = R_{nom} - h$, where R_{real} is the real rate of return, R_{nom} is the nominal rate of return and h is the inflation rate. This is known as the *Fisher relationship*, which was originally proposed by I. Fisher, in *The Theory of Interest* (New York: Macmillan, 1930).

Exhibit 4.5 The various rates of return on the stock of 'Hi Tech Dream' in 2001

Date (2001)	Price (close)	Dividends	Simple rates of return (%)	
			Before tax	After tax
January 2	60.625	–	–	–
February 17	64.875	0.5	7.83	7.59
May 12	73.125	0.5	13.49	13.26
August 11	69.00	0.5	−4.96	−5.16
November 9	66.00	0.5	−3.62	−3.84
December 31	71.5625	–	8.43%	5.11
Nominal rate of return for 2001			**21.55%**	**16.81%**
Real rate of return for 2001			**19.64%**	**14.97%**

---

for each sub-period ending at the date when a dividend was paid. For example, for the first period, covering 2 January 2001 through 17 February 2001, the simple rate of return is:

$$\frac{(£64.875 - £60.625) + £0.5}{£60.625} \cong 0.0783 \text{ or } 7.83\%$$

Using the data in Exhibit 4.5, the simple rate of return corresponding to the other sub-periods was calculated in a similar way. Having the simple rates of return, we can employ the linking method to obtain the before-taxes rate of return for the year as follows:

$$[(1.0783)(1.1349)(0.9504)(0.9638)(1.0843)] - 1 \cong 0.2155 \text{ or } 21.55\%$$

The before-taxes real rate of return for 2001 is given by:

$$\frac{1.2155}{1.016} - 1 \cong 0.1964 \text{ or } 19.64\%$$

where $h = 1.6\%$ is the annual inflation corresponding to the year 2001.

We employ the same method to calculate the simple after-tax rate of return and the after-tax rate of return in nominal and real terms, yielding a nominal rate of return of 16.81% and after-tax real rate of return of 14.97%. To calculate the after-tax rate of return, it is assumed that a 30% tax rate is paid on the cash dividends and 20% on capital gains. Of course, any other tax rates corresponding to the individual taxpayer rates can be used in the after-tax calculation. However, since it is assumed in this example that the holding period of the stock is one year (any other arbitrary holding period is possible), the capital gains tax is paid only at the end of the year when the stock is sold. For example, for the first sub-period (see Exhibit 4.5) the after-tax rate of return is given by:

$$\frac{(£64.875 - £60.625) + £0.5 - 0.3 \times £0.5}{£60.625} \cong 0.0759 \text{ or } 7.59\%$$

where $-0.3 \times £0.5 = -£0.15$ is the tax paid on the first £0.5 of dividends. Note that no capital gains tax is paid because it is assumed that the stock is not sold at the end of the first time interval.

The calculation of the after-tax rate of return of the last period corresponding to Exhibit 4.5 is a little more complicated because capital gains tax is paid on the difference between the price at the end of the year (when the stock is assumed to be sold) and the price at the beginning of the year (when the stock is assumed to be bought). We thus have the following after-tax rate of return for this period:

$$\frac{(£71.5625 - £66) - 0.2 \times (71.5625 - £60.625)}{£66} =$$

$$\frac{(£71.5625 - £66) - £2.1875}{£66} \cong 0.0511 \text{ or } 5.11\%$$

where £2.1875 is the capital gains tax paid on the difference between the prices at the end and the beginning of the year.

4.5 AVERAGE RATE OF RETURN: THE MEASURE OF PROFITABILITY

The past average rate of return measures the average profitability of an investment. To see why such an average is needed, suppose that you observe the following rates of return on stock A and B over the past two years:

Year	Stock A	Stock B
1	−10%	+1%
2	+60%	+45%

Which stock has a better historical record? For year 1, stock B is better, because its rate of return is 1%, while stock A suffers a loss of 10%. The opposite holds for year 2. Thus, to answer the question 'which stock has a better historical record?' we need to calculate some average rate of return which takes the two years (as in our example) into account. This average reflects the average rate of return per period; i.e. per year in our specific example.

There are two main methods for calculating the average rate of return, yielding the **arithmetic average** and the **geometric average**. Because the two methods yield different results, it is important to study them and to be able to understand the interpretation of both these averages.

This section discusses historical averages, called *ex-post* averages, to distinguish them from expected values or means, which relate to future values (*ex-ante* values). The **arithmetic method** of determining the average rate of return adds the realized rates of return over different periods[9] identified by subscript t (R_t) and divides by the number of observations (m). This is summarized by Rule 3 below.

Rule 3: To obtain the arithmetic historical mean, sum all the historical returns and divide by the number of observations. That is,

$$\overline{R}_A = \frac{\sum_{t=1}^{m} R_t}{m} \qquad (4.5)$$

[9] At this point, the length of the period (t) does not matter. It can be a year, a quarter or even a day.

where $\overline{R}_A$ is the *arithmetic* average rate of return. Note that we distinguish between the forward-looking, or *ex-ante*, expected returns (denoted as $E(R)$) and historical, or *ex-post*, returns (denoted as $\overline{R}$). The expected rate of return will be discussed in the next chapter.

The **geometric method** is an averaging method that compounds rates of return. That is, if £1 is invested in Period 1, then it will be worth £$(1 + R_1)$ at the end of Period 1. The geometric method assumes that the amount £$(1 + R_1)$ is invested for Period 2. At the end of Period 2, the investment will be worth the amount invested at the beginning of Period 2 times 1 + the rate of return in Period 2. That is, the investment at the end of Period 2 is worth £$(1 + R_1)(1 + R_2)$. Continuing this procedure over all *ex-post* periods would give us the value at the end of m periods of a £1 investment at the beginning of the period. This total return is averaged by taking the mth root. The geometric average can, therefore, be expressed as Rule 4.

Rule 4: To obtain the historical geometric mean, add 1 to the rate of return of each period, multiply all these terms, take the mth root and subtract 1. That is,

$$\overline{R}_G = [(1 + R_1)(1 + R_2)...(1 + R_m)]^{1/m} - 1 \qquad (4.6)$$

where $\overline{R}_G$ is the geometric average rate of return.

Using our previous example we have:

Stock	Arithmetic average	Geometric average
A	$\frac{-0.1 + 0.60}{2} = 0.25$ or 25%	$[(0.9)(1.60)]^{1/2} - 1 = 0.2$ or 20%
B	$\frac{0.01 + 0.45}{2} = 0.23$ or 23%	$[(1.01)(1.45)]^{1/2} - 1 \cong 0.2102$ or 21.02%

Thus, by the arithmetic average, stock A has a better historical record, while the opposite holds when the historical record is measured by the geometric mean.

Let us look at a more dramatic case to illustrate the different results obtained from these two methods. Suppose a unit trust paid no dividends and began with a market value of £100 per share. At the end of the first year, the unit trust was worth £50 per share, and at the end of the second year, the fund was once again worth £100 per share. The rate of return in the first year was $[(£50 - £100)/£100] = -0.50$, or a loss of 50%. The rate of return in the second year was $[(£100 - £50)/£50] = 1.0$, or a profit of 100%. The arithmetic average is $(-0.5 + 1.0)/2 = 0.25$, or 25%. The geometric average, however, is $[(1 - 0.5)(1 + 1)]^{1/2} - 1 = 0\%$.

Because the geometric and the arithmetic averages may drastically differ from each other, it is important to guide the reader under what circumstances each average is more meaningful. When one holds the asset for several periods (years) the geometric average is more meaningful. To see this, suppose you invest for two years in the fund. Which averaging method is correct – the 0% geometric average rate of return or the 25% arithmetic average rate of return?

In this case, you originally invested £100 and after two years ended up with £100. Clearly, from an investor's viewpoint, there was no profit, or the investor obtained a 0% rate of return. The geometric average, therefore, is the correct average because it shows a zero rate of return that reflects the change in the value to the investor over the two years. Indeed, the geometric average can be interpreted as being the actual growth rate of the asset, and the arithmetic average is meaningless in this case.

In three situations, however, the arithmetic average should be used:

1 The arithmetic method is correct when estimating the average performance across different securities for one period of time. For example, you would use the arithmetic average when calculating the average rate of return for securities within a specific industry. If you wanted to assess the performance of the automobile industry over the last year, you would take the arithmetic average of rates of return of automobile stocks (in this calculation, m is the number of stocks rather than the number of periods). That is, you would not be measuring growth over time but rather the average performance during one period of time.

2 Suppose that investors hold the stock for one year only. About half of the investors invest for year 1 and about half for year 2. Hence, we are not interested in the growth in the portfolio over time. In this case, the arithmetic average measures more meaningfully the average profitability of the various investors who invested in the stock.

3 Probably the most important case for using the arithmetic average is when one uses historical rates of return to estimate the future average return, which is needed for investment decision-making. The arithmetic average is an *unbiased* estimate of future expected rates of return.[10] To illustrate, suppose we want to invest in Microsoft for just one year. By taking the arithmetic average of the last 10 years, we get the best

---

PRACTICE BOX

Problem

Calculate the arithmetic and geometric annual average rates of return for the Abbott and Costello unit trusts. Explain the differences between the two results.

Year	Abbott Trust	Costello Trust
1	10%	8%
2	5%	12%
3	−15%	11%
4	40%	9%

Solution

Writing the rates of return in decimal figures, the arithmetic averages are

$$\overline{R}_{A,Abbott} = \frac{0.1 + 0.05 - 0.15 + 0.4}{4} = 0.10$$

$$\overline{R}_{A,Costello} = \frac{0.08 + 0.12 + 0.11 + 0.09}{4} = 0.10$$

The geometric averages are

$$\overline{R}_{G,Abbott} = [(1 + 0.1)(1 + 0.05)(1 - 0.15)(1 + 0.4)]^{1/4} - 1 \cong 0.083$$

$$\overline{R}_{G,Costello} = [(1 + 0.08)(1 + 0.12)(1 + 0.11)(1 + 0.09)]^{1/4} - 1 \cong 0.0999$$

The difference between the geometric and arithmetic averages is larger for the Abbott Trust because it has greater volatility (−15% to 40%: see Section 4.6). The more volatile the returns, the greater the difference between the geometric average and the arithmetic average.

---

[10] Unbiased estimate has the property that if a sample of periods is taken many times, on average, we obtain exactly the expected value. This assumes, of course, that the probability distribution is stable. That is, the distribution from which historical observations were made is the same as the distribution from which future observations will be made. The mathematical proof of this assertion can be found in most basic statistics books.

estimate of next year's rate of return. To see this, recall the unit trust example. Looking at past performance, we know that in one year the rate of return was −50%, and in the second year it was +100%. Suppose further that these are the only two possible outcomes for the future. Because we do not know which outcome will occur next year, our best estimate is that on average, we will make 25%, a case where the arithmetic average is relevant. Note once again that we are not addressing the issue of the long-run performance of the fund but only what we expect to earn over the next year. For portfolio investment decisions discussed in Chapter 6, we use the arithmetic average as an estimate of the expected rate of return on individual assets and on portfolios.

The arithmetic average will exceed the geometric average as long as rates of return are not constant. The difference between these two averages is greater when the **volatility** of returns is larger. If there is zero volatility across time, then the arithmetic average is equal to the geometric average. The arithmetic average is more often used in this textbook; hence, in the rest of the book, when we state 'average' we mean arithmetic average. When we refer to the geometric average, we will explicitly state it.

4.6 THE STANDARD DEVIATION: THE MEASURE OF RISK

4.6.1 Returns, average return and risk

The rates of return on some assets, e.g. government bonds, are quite stable, while the rates of return on other assets, e.g. stocks of hi-tech firms, are relatively volatile. The dispersion of the rates of return around the average rate of return is frequently used to measure the risk of the investment. If the rate of return deviates far from the average, we say that the dispersion is large and there is relatively large volatility (or risk) with such an investment.[11] Generally, the volatility of past rates of return also provides an indication for the future risk involved with the investment under consideration. The following simple example demonstrates why dispersion spells risk and how to measure the dispersion of historical rates of return. To illustrate the risk due to the volatility of returns, suppose we have the following three years' rates of return:

Year	Rates of return (%)	
	Stock A	Stock B
1	−10	4
2	0	6
3	+40	5
Average	10	5

The average rate of return on Stock A is 10% and the average rate of return on Stock B is 5%. Thus, Stock A, on average, is more profitable than Stock B. In practice, investors do not receive the average rate of return; rather they buy the stock for a given

---

[11] For simplicity, we assume here that the investor holds only the asset under consideration. In Chapter 6 we will discuss the effect of correlation between rates of return of various assets on the portfolio risk, i.e. the volatility of the portfolio's returns.

period, say a year. Therefore what is relevant for them is the rate of return realized in this particular year, not the average return across several years. Thus, it is clear that not all investors were better off in the past by buying Stock A rather than Stock B. For example, an investor who invests in year 1 lost 10% on Stock A and gained 4% on Stock B. Also, an investor who invested in year 2 was better off with Stock B rather than Stock A. Thus, because of its dispersion, Stock A was not necessarily better than Stock B. To see the negative effect of the dispersion on stockholders, suppose that there was no volatility in Stock A, i.e. the rate of return was 10% in each of the three years. In this case, there is a clear dominance of Stock A over Stock B because in each of the three years it would provide a higher rate of return. Thus, the actual dispersion of the rates of return of Stock A casts doubt on its superiority over Stock B, because with no volatility Stock A would be superior to Stock B (with a higher return in each of the three years) and with the actual dispersion such a superiority is no longer obvious. From this example, we can conclude that holding all other factors, including the mean rate of return, constant, investors dislike dispersion because the larger the dispersion (or volatility) the larger the risk involved with the investment. Therefore, in the rest of the book we use the terms volatility and risk interchangeably.

The dispersion of the past rates of return around the mean measures the historical volatility attached to the corresponding investment. It is common to measure the dispersion of rates of return by the standard deviation or by the variance of the rates of return. The **standard deviation** is denoted by the Greek letter σ and the **variance** is its squared value, denoted by σ^2. The past (or sample) variance is given by Rule 5.

Rule 5: The historical variance is calculated by the sum of the squared deviations (of the returns from the mean) divided by the number of observations minus 1. That is,

$$\sigma^2 = \frac{\sum_{t=1}^{m} (R_t - \overline{R})^2}{m - 1} \tag{4.7}$$

The standard deviation is the square root of the variance, given by $\sigma = (\sigma^2)^{1/2}$. R_t is the rate of return corresponding to period t (year t in our example), $\overline{R}$ is the arithmetic average and m is the number of years (periods) included in this calculation.[12]

Using our previous example with $m = 3$, we have the following variances for Stocks A and B, respectively:

Variance of Stock A: $[(-10 - 10)^2 + (0 - 10)^2 + (40 - 10)^2]/(3 - 1) = 700$

Variance of Stock B: $[(4 - 5)^2 + (6 - 5)^2 + (5 - 5)^2]/(3 - 1) = 1$

The dimension of σ^2 is 'percentage squared', which is meaningless. Therefore, we take the square root of these figures to calculate the standard deviations denoted by σ, which is given in percentage terms. However, note that to obtain the standard deviation we need to first calculate the variance.

---

[12] Dividing by $m - 1$ rather than by m provides an unbiased estimate of the variance which is needed for future investment decision-making. For the notion of an unbiased estimate, see footnote 10.

To sum up this example, the variance and the standard deviation of the above two stocks is calculated as follows:

Stock	Variance, σ^2	Standard deviation, σ
A	700	$\sqrt{700} \cong 26.46\%$
B	1	$\sqrt{1} = 1\%$

Thus, Stock A, with higher fluctuations than Stock B, indeed has a higher standard deviation (26.46% versus 1%), reflecting its historical volatility, which is much greater than the volatility of Stock B. Thus, historically, Stock A has a higher profitability than Stock B but also a higher risk.

4.6.2 Historical risk premium

From the above example, it is clear that volatility hurts investors. The relatively large volatility of Stock A makes it less attractive relative to the hypothetical case of no volatility but with the same average rate of return of 10%. Investors generally dislike volatility, and hence will require a relatively high average rate of return from assets with a relatively high volatility. Otherwise, they will not purchase them. Thus, generally, the higher the volatility, the higher the risk, and investors require **risk premium** to compensate them for risk. Though the concept of required risk premium has to do with the future rates of return and will be discussed in the next chapter, one can examine if in the past, with realized returns, indeed a positive risk premium prevailed. The historical risk premium is defined as:

$$\text{Historical risk premium} = \text{historical average rate of return} \\ - \text{historical riskless interest rate}$$

This relationship can also be rewritten as:

$$\text{Historical average rate of return} = \text{historical riskless interest rate} \\ + \text{historical risk premium}$$

Suppose that the average rate of return on Stock B and Stock A is 5% and 10%, respectively, and the risk-free interest is 5%. Then the historical risk premium for Stocks B and A discussed above is given by:

$$\text{Risk premium of Stock B} = 5\% - 4\% = 1\%$$

$$\text{Risk premium of Stock A} = 10\% - 4\% = 6\%$$

Thus, the greater the risk, the greater the required risk premium. The relationship between volatility and risk premium is, of course, an empirical question. In the next section we show that indeed such a strong relationship prevailed in the past.

4.7   THE HISTORICAL RECORD

Exhibit 4.6 provides the historical record on several classes of assets: large company stocks, small company stocks, bonds with long maturity (20 years), bonds with intermediate maturity (5 years) and US Treasury bills with 30 days maturity. Generally,

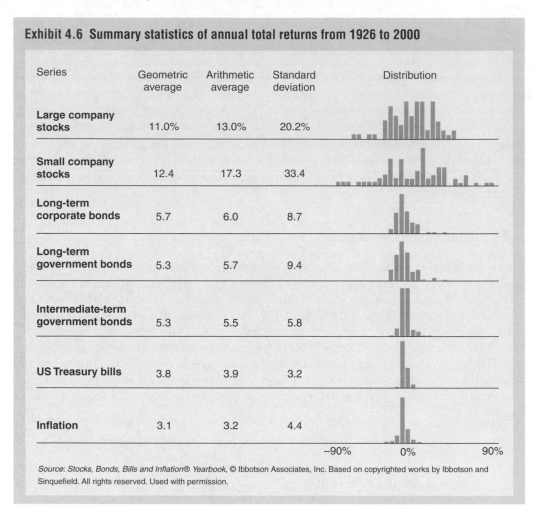

Exhibit 4.6 Summary statistics of annual total returns from 1926 to 2000

Series	Geometric average	Arithmetic average	Standard deviation	Distribution
Large company stocks	11.0%	13.0%	20.2%	
Small company stocks	12.4	17.3	33.4	
Long-term corporate bonds	5.7	6.0	8.7	
Long-term government bonds	5.3	5.7	9.4	
Intermediate-term government bonds	5.3	5.5	5.8	
US Treasury bills	3.8	3.9	3.2	
Inflation	3.1	3.2	4.4	

stocks of small firms are considered to be very risky, and therefore yield a relatively high average rate of return. Also, long-term bonds are considered to be riskier than short-term bonds, and corporate bonds are riskier than government bonds. Finally, US Treasury bills are the assets with the smallest risk, hence with the smallest average rate of return.

Exhibit 4.7 and Appendix 4B reveal the historical record regarding these assets. Focusing on the arithmetic average, the small company stocks (i.e. the average rate of return of stocks falling in this category) yielded in the period 1926–2000 the highest average rate of return: 17.3% per year. However, if an investor invested in one year selected at random from these years, he or she would also be exposed to the highest risk. This can be seen from the standard deviation corresponding to small company stocks (33.4%), as well as from the histogram given on the right-hand side of Exhibit 4.7. Years with very large negative and positive rates of return characterized small company stocks while much less dispersion is observed with the other assets. Assuming that the rate of return on Treasury bills is a good proxy to the riskless interest rate, the risk premium on small company stocks is given by 17.3% − 3.9% = 13.4% while it is only 5.7% − 3.9% = 1.8% for long-term government bonds. Exhibit 4.7 shows what happened to an investment of $1 in 1926 in

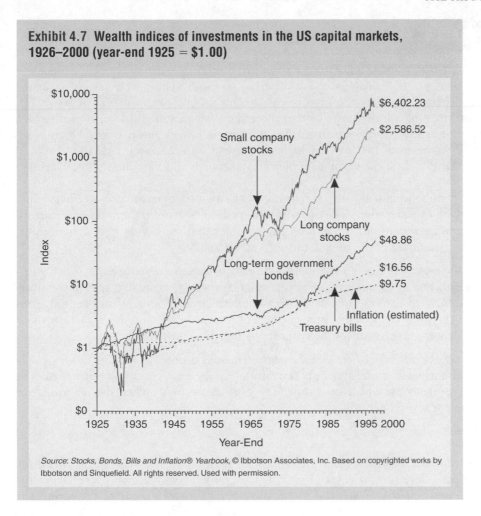

Exhibit 4.7 Wealth indices of investments in the US capital markets, 1926–2000 (year-end 1925 = $1.00)

each of these assets: for example a $1 investment in small company stocks in 1926 will yield about $6,402 in the year 2000.

The main conclusion from Exhibits 4.6 and 4.7 is that historically, the higher the volatility (standard deviation), the higher the risk, and therefore the higher the average rate of return, reflecting a higher required premium by the investors. As we shall see, this is consistent with the concept of risk aversion – investors dislike volatility or risk, and the larger the volatility, the larger the required risk premium. Based on this past observation, in the next chapter we analyze risk aversion and volatility when probabilities and future possible rates of return rather than past annual rates of return are employed. However, we keep in mind in the next chapter's analysis that history teaches us that investors dislike volatility and require compensation for the risk of fluctuation in the rates of return. Based on this historical observation, one can construct a theory regarding risk aversion and investors' preferences.

Appendix 4C shows the historical returns of some of the European indexes, relating to the Dow Jones, during 1991–2001. These charts can teach you about the level of risk and the rate of return of each European index relative to this level in the US, as described by the Dow Jones index.

SUMMARY

■ *Understand the different methods for computing rates of return.*

Rates of return can be calculated using different methods. The simple rate of return is the dollar profit divided by the investment. It ignores the time value of money. The method that uses the adjusted rate of return, or the time-weighted rate of return (which we call rate of return to distinguish it from the simple rate of return), has the endorsement of the Association for Investment Management and Research (AIMR). Rates of return are found by first calculating simple rates of return and then linking these returns together.

The idea of time-weighted rates of return is that any interim cash flow is reinvested in the asset under consideration. The appropriate method to handle the rates of return of bonds is the accrual method, which basically assumes that the bonds were actually purchased at the beginning of the period and sold at the end.

■ *Analyze the impact of taxes and inflation on rate of return calculations.*

Taxes and inflation affect the rate of return calculation and, generally, reduce the overall rate of return. In the case of taxes, there is a reduction of income and capital gains (tax payment), which reduces the after-tax rate of return. Inflation reduces the investor's purchasing power, which reduces the real rate of return to the investor.

■ *Understand the difference between the arithmetic and geometric average return.*

The arithmetic average is useful mainly for estimating the next period rate of return. The geometric average is useful for measuring the portfolio growth when the investor held the portfolio for several periods.

■ *Analyze the relationship between volatility of rates of return and the average rate of return.*

The higher the volatility the higher the risk of losing money. The volatility is measured by the standard deviation of rates of return. It is shown that, generally, the larger the standard deviation, the larger the historical average rate of return, reflecting the required risk premium by investors as compensation for the risk involved.

■ *Compare the historical risk–return trade-off for stocks and bonds.*

Historically, common stocks have been more volatile than bonds. Also, common stocks have offered a higher average rate of return than bonds. There appears to be a positive relationship between volatility and average rate of return.

KEY TERMS

Adjusted rate of return	Geometric average (or mean)	Simple rate of return
Arithmetic average (or mean)	Geometric method	Standard deviation
Arithmetic method	Linking method	Time-weighted rate of return
Dollar-weighted average rate of return (see Appendix 4A)	Rate of return	Variance
	Real rate of return	Volatility
Ex-post rate of return	Realized rate of return	
	Risk premium	

QUESTIONS

4.1 A stock that was purchased in January for £50 paid a £3 dividend in December, when its price was £55.

(a) Calculate the pound *return* on this investment if 100 shares were purchased.
(b) Calculate the *rate of return* on this investment if 100 shares were purchased.
(c) How would your answers to (a) and (b) change if 200 shares were purchased?
(d) How would your answers to (a) and (b) change if the stock split 3-for-1 before the end of the year? (Hence, the £55 is the price after the stock split was taken.)

4.2 A zero-coupon bond was purchased in January for £875 per £1,000 par. In December the bond was trading for £950.

(a) Calculate the return and rate of return on this bond.
(b) If the tax rate were 30%, what was the after-tax rate of return?
(c) If deflation of 3% occurred during the year (that is, −3% inflation), what was the real, after-tax rate of return?

4.3 Suppose a United Kingdom bond was purchased by an American investor in January for £500 when the exchange rate was $2.0/pound. Assume no coupon payments; also, the bond was sold for £475 in December, when the exchange rate was $2.2/pound.

(a) What was the rate of return on the bond in British pounds?
(b) What was the rate of return to the American investor on the exchange rate only?
(c) What was the rate of return in US dollars?

4.4 Use the data in Question 4.3, and assume that the inflation rate was 5% in the United States and 10% in the United Kingdom.

(a) What was the real rate of return in British pounds?
(b) What was the real rate of return in US dollars?

4.5 The following table gives the NYSE composite index over a 15-year period:

End of year	NYSE composite	End of year	NYSE composite
2000	71.11	2008	195.04
2001	81.03	2009	180.49
2002	95.18	2010	229.44
2003	96.38	2011	240.21
2004	121.58	2012	259.08
2005	138.58	2013	250.94
2006	138.23	2014	329.51
2007	156.26	2015	392.30

(a) Ignoring dividends, calculate the simple annual rates of return.
(b) Calculate the arithmetic average of the annual rates of return.
(c) Calculate the geometric average of the annual rate of return.
(d) Compare your answers to (b) and (c). How do you account for the difference between these averages?

4.6 The following table gives the Consumer Price Index (CPI) over a recent 10-year period:

End of year	CPI	End of year	CPI
2000	109.6	2006	140.3
2001	113.6	2007	144.5
2002	118.3	2008	148.2
2003	124.0	2009	152.4
2004	130.7	2010	156.9
2005	136.2		

(a) Compute the inflation rates for each year over this 10-year period.
(b) Compute the geometric-average inflation rate over this 10-year period.
(c) Calculate the real rate of return on the NYSE composite (using the data in Question 4.5) for each year.

4.7 Suppose we have the following information on Xerox, Inc.:

Dividends paid ($)	Date
0.75	2 February
0.75	4 May
0.75	30 July
0.75	25 October

Stock price ($)	Date
$61^{1}/_{4}$	4 January
$52^{3}/_{8}$	2 February
$64^{7}/_{8}$	4 May
$70^{1}/_{2}$	30 July
$75^{3}/_{4}$	25 October
71	30 December

(a) Calculate the simple rate of return for the period 4 January through 30 December.
(b) Calculate the rate of return for the period 4 January through 30 December using the linking method.
(c) Calculate the rate of return for the period 4 January through 30 December using the index method.
(d) Explain any differences in rates of return.

4.8 Rework Question 4.7(b), assuming that the income tax rate on dividends is 25% and the capital gains tax rate is 15%.

4.9 Using the data in Question 4.7, suppose Xerox, Inc., also had a rights issue of one share for each existing share. In a rights issue, the firm gives its existing shareholders the right to buy additional shares of common stock at a specified price. For each share owned, a shareholder receives one right. Rights were traded in the secondary market. In this case, Xerox began trading the rights on 25 October at $1 per right. Rework Question 4.7(c), incorporating the effects of this rights offering.

4.10 Suppose you purchased 1,000 shares of Hardin Bread Company on 1 January at £60 per share. Hardin pays £1.50 annual dividend on 22 April, when the stock is trading at £42. Hardin declares a 5-for-1 stock split effective 28 August, when the stock is trading at £54.

(a) If Hardin closed on 29 December at £15 per share, what was your rate of return by the index method?
(b) If the inflation rate was 7.8%, what was your real rate of return?

4.11 We are given the following information on Goodyear on 15 October 2001, 7.35% coupon-bearing bonds:

Date	Coupon	Price (in % of £1,000 par)	Accrued interest
January 3		$101^{3}/_{4}$	£15.3
April 15	£36.75	$93^{1}/_{8}$	
October 15	£36.75	$97^{3}/_{4}$	
December 27		$99^{3}/_{4}$	£15.2

(a) Calculate the annual rate of return based on the index method.
(b) How does your answer to (a) compare with the simple-rate-of-return calculation? Explain.

SELECTED REFERENCES

Association for Investment Management and Research. *Report of the Performance Presentation Standards Implementation Committee.* Charlottesville, VA: AIMR, December 1991.
This 47-page monograph explains the recently adopted standards for reporting rates of returns by the AIMR, a leading financial analysts' association.

Eiteman, David K., Arthur I. Stonehill, and Michael H. Moffett. *Multinational Business Finance*, 6th edn. Reading, MA: Addison-Wesley, 1992, p. 25.

Fisher, I. *The Theory of Interest.* New York: Macmillan, 1930.

Jakobsen, J., and O. Sorensen. 'Decomposing and testing long-term returns: an application of Danish IPO'. *European Financial Management*, 7(2), 2001.

Larsen, Glen A. Jr., and B.G. Rasnick. 'Parameter estimation techniques, optimization frequency and portfolio return enhancement'. *Journal of Portfolio Management*, 27(4), Summer 2001.

Levy, Haim, and Marshall Sarnat. *Portfolio and Investment Selection: Theory and Practice.* Englewood Cliffs, NJ: Prentice-Hall International, 1984.

Reilly, Frank K., G. Wenchi Kao, and David J. Wright. 'Alternative bond market indexes'. *Financial Analysts Journal*, May–June 1992, pp. 44–58.
This article is a detailed analysis of the major alternative bond market indexes.

Siegel, Jeremy J. 'The equity premium: stock and bond returns since 1802'. *Financial Analysts Journal*, January–February 1992, pp. 28–46.

Appendix 4A   DOLLAR-WEIGHTED AVERAGE RATE OF RETURN

This chapter discussed arithmetic and geometric rates of return. Both measure the average rate of return per $1 invested. These two averages are not affected by the dollar amount invested. However, in some cases the dollar amount invested across time changes. The **dollar-weighted average rate of return** takes this factor into account.

To illustrate, consider the following example. Suppose a stock's price at the beginning of the first year is $100, and at the end of the first year it is $110. At the end of the second year, the share price is $132. For simplicity, assume that no dividend is paid and that an investor buys one share at the beginning of the first year and buys one more share at the beginning of the second year. Then, at the end of the second year, the two shares are sold. The rate of return for the first year is 10%, or ($110/$100) −1, and for the second year it is 20%, or ($132/$110) −1. In this case, the arithmetic average is

$$\overline{R}_A = \frac{10\% + 20\%}{2} = 15\%$$

and the geometric average is

$$\overline{R}_G = [(1 + 0.1)(1 + 0.2)]^{1/2} - 1 \cong 0.1489 \text{ or } 14.89\%$$

These two averages are not affected by the dollar amount invested in each year. They will be the same if the investor buys, say, five shares rather than one share at the beginning of the first year.

The dollar-weighted average rate of return is the internal rate of return (IRR; see Appendix A) that solves the following equation:

$$100 = -\frac{1 \times \$110}{1 + IRR} + \frac{2 \times \$132}{(1 + IRR)^2}$$

where $110 is the dollar amount invested in purchasing one more share. Using a hand calculator, we find that IRR = 16.54%.

Note that one share was bought for $100 at the beginning of the first year and another share was bought at the beginning of the second year. Then, at the end of the second year, two shares are sold for $132 each. Thus, the IRR is the rate of return on the investment, taking into account that $100 is invested at the beginning of the first year and that an additional $110 is invested in the second year. If the investor buys, say, an additional five shares rather than one share at the end of the first year, the IRR is the value that solves the following equation:

$$100 = -\frac{5 \times \$110}{(1 + IRR)} + \frac{6 \times \$132}{(1 + IRR)^2}$$

Hence, IRR = 18.48%.

Thus, the IRR is affected by the amount invested in each period of time – hence the term dollar-weighted average rate of return. In our example, investing more monies in the second year increases the rate of return. This result is not surprising, however, because in this case the rate of return in the first year is 10% and in the second year 20%. The concept of the dollar-weighted average rate of return is important because dividends are often reinvested (for example, in mutual funds) and additional shares of stock are purchased.

Appendix 4B ANNUAL RATES OF RETURN, 1926–2000

Year	Large company stocks	Small company stocks	Long-term corporate bonds	Long-term government bonds	Intermediate-term government bonds	US Treasury bills	Inflation
1926	11.62	0.28	7.37	7.77	5.38	3.27	−1.49
1927	37.49	22.10	7.44	8.93	4.52	3.12	−2.08
1928	43.61	39.69	2.84	0.10	0.92	3.56	−0.97
1929	−8.42	−51.36	3.27	3.42	6.01	4.75	0.20
1930	−24.90	−38.15	7.98	4.66	6.72	2.41	−6.03
1931	−43.34	−49.75	−1.85	−5.31	−2.32	1.07	−9.52
1932	−8.19	−5.39	10.82	16.84	8.81	0.96	−10.30
1933	53.99	142.87	10.38	−0.07	1.83	0.30	0.51
1934	−1.44	24.22	13.84	10.03	9.00	0.16	2.03
1935	47.67	40.19	9.61	4.98	7.01	0.17	2.99
1936	33.92	64.80	6.74	7.52	3.06	0.18	1.21
1937	−35.03	−58.01	2.75	0.23	1.56	0.31	3.10
1938	31.12	32.80	6.13	5.53	6.23	−0.02	−2.78
1939	−0.41	0.35	3.97	5.94	4.52	0.02	−0.48
1940	−9.78	−5.16	3.39	6.09	2.96	0.00	0.96
1941	−11.59	−9.00	2.73	0.93	0.50	0.06	9.72
1942	20.34	44.51	2.60	3.22	1.94	0.27	9.29
1943	25.90	88.37	2.83	2.08	2.81	0.35	3.16
1944	19.75	53.72	4.73	2.81	1.80	0.33	2.11
1945	36.44	73.61	4.08	10.73	2.22	0.33	2.25
1946	−8.07	−11.63	1.72	−0.10	1.00	0.35	18.16
1947	5.71	0.92	−2.34	−2.62	0.91	0.50	9.01
1948	5.50	−2.11	4.14	3.40	1.85	0.81	2.71
1949	18.79	19.75	3.31	6.45	2.32	1.10	−1.80
1950	31.71	38.75	2.12	0.06	0.70	1.20	5.79
1951	24.02	7.80	−2.69	−3.93	0.36	1.49	5.87
1952	18.37	3.03	3.52	1.16	1.63	1.66	0.88
1953	−0.99	−6.49	3.41	3.64	3.23	1.82	0.62
1954	52.62	60.58	5.39	7.19	2.68	0.86	−0.50
1955	31.56	20.44	0.48	−1.29	−0.65	1.57	0.37
1956	6.56	4.28	−6.81	−5.59	−0.42	2.46	2.86
1957	−10.78	−14.57	8.71	7.46	7.84	3.14	3.02
1958	43.36	64.89	−2.22	−6.09	−1.29	1.54	1.76
1959	11.96	16.40	−0.97	−2.26	−0.39	2.95	1.50
1960	0.47	−3.29	9.07	13.78	11.76	2.66	1.48
1961	26.89	32.09	4.82	0.97	1.85	2.13	0.67
1962	−8.73	−11.90	7.95	6.89	5.56	2.73	1.22
1963	22.80	23.57	2.19	1.21	1.64	3.12	1.65
1964	16.48	23.52	4.77	3.51	4.04	3.54	1.19
1965	12.45	41.75	−0.46	0.71	1.02	3.93	1.92
1966	−10.06	−7.01	0.20	3.65	4.69	4.76	3.35
1967	23.98	83.57	−4.95	−9.18	1.01	4.21	3.04
1968	11.06	35.97	2.57	−0.26	4.54	5.21	4.72
1969	−8.50	−25.05	−8.09	−5.07	−0.74	6.58	6.11
1970	4.01	−17.43	18.37	12.11	16.86	6.52	5.49

▶

Year	Large company stocks	Small company stocks	Long-term corporate bonds	Long-term government bonds	Intermediate-term government bonds	US Treasury bills	Inflation
1971	14.31	16.50	11.01	13.23	8.72	4.39	3.36
1972	18.98	4.43	7.26	5.69	5.16	3.84	3.41
1973	−14.66	−30.90	1.14	−1.11	4.61	6.93	8.80
1974	−26.47	−19.95	−3.06	4.35	5.69	8.00	12.20
1975	37.20	52.82	14.64	9.20	7.83	5.80	7.01
1976	23.84	57.38	18.65	16.75	12.87	5.08	4.81
1977	−7.18	25.38	1.71	−0.69	1.41	5.12	6.77
1978	6.56	23.46	−0.07	−1.18	3.49	7.18	9.03
1979	18.44	43.46	−4.18	−1.23	4.09	10.38	13.31
1980	32.42	39.88	−2.76	−3.95	3.91	11.24	12.40
1981	−4.91	13.88	−1.24	1.86	9.45	14.71	8.94
1982	21.41	28.01	42.56	40.36	29.10	10.54	3.87
1983	22.51	39.67	6.26	0.65	7.41	8.80	3.80
1984	6.27	−6.67	16.86	15.48	14.02	9.85	3.95
1985	32.16	24.66	30.09	30.97	20.33	7.72	3.77
1986	18.47	6.85	19.85	24.53	15.14	6.16	1.13
1987	5.23	−9.30	−0.27	−2.71	2.90	5.47	4.41
1988	16.81	22.87	10.70	9.67	6.10	6.35	4.42
1989	31.49	10.18	16.23	18.11	13.29	8.37	4.65
1990	−3.17	−21.56	6.78	6.18	9.73	7.81	6.11
1991	30.55	44.63	19.89	19.30	15.46	5.60	3.06
1992	7.67	23.35	9.39	8.05	7.19	3.51	2.90
1993	9.99	20.98	13.19	18.24	11.24	2.90	2.75
1994	1.31	3.11	−5.76	−7.77	−5.14	3.90	2.67
1995	37.43	34.46	27.20	31.67	16.80	5.60	2.54
1996	23.07	17.62	1.40	−0.93	2.10	5.21	3.32
1997	33.36	22.78	12.95	15.85	8.38	5.26	1.70
1998	28.58	−7.31	10.76	13.06	10.21	4.86	1.61
1999	21.04	29.79	−7.45	−8.96	−1.77	4.68	2.68
2000	−9.11	−3.59	12.87	21.48	12.59	5.89	3.39

Appendix 4C   RATES OF RETURN OF SOME EUROPEAN INDEXES, 1991–2001

Exhibit 4C.1 London: the FTSE 100 index, 25 March 2001

Sunday, March 25 2001 1:27am ET – U.S. Markets Closed.

FTSE 100 INDEX (FSI:^FTSE)-More Info: News – Trade NEW!: N/A				
Last Trade	Change		Prev Cls	Volume	Div Date
Mar 23 · **5402.3**	+87.5 (+1.65%)		5314.8	N/A	N/A
Day's Range	Bid	Ask	Open	Avg Vol	Ex-Div
5314.8 – 5438.0	N/A	N/A	5314.8	N/A	N/A
YTD Range	Earn/Shr	P/E	Mkt Cap	Div/Shr	Yield
5279.6 – 6360.3	N/A	N/A	N/A	N/A	N/A

FTSE 100 Index as of 23–Mar–2001

Source: Website at http://www.finance.yahoo.com, 25 March 2001.

Exhibit 4C.2 France: the CAC 40 index, 25 March 2001

Sunday, March 25 2001 1:22am ET – U.S. Markets Closed.

CAC 40 INDEX (PAR:^FCHI)-More Info: News – Trade NEW!: N/A				
Last Trade	Change		Prev Cls	Volume	Div Date
Mar 23 · **4951.13**	+126.31 (+2.62%)		4824.82	N/A	N/A
Day's Range	Bid	Ask	Open	Avg Vol	Ex-Div
4911.54 – 4968.52	N/A	N/A	4922.39	N/A	N/A
YTD Range	Earn/Shr	P/E	Mkt Cap	Div/Shr	Yield
4804.40 – 5999.18	N/A	N/A	N/A	N/A	N/A

France CAC–40 Index as of 23–Mar–2001

Source: Website at http://finance.yahoo.com, 25 March 2001. CAC 40 is a registered trademark of Euronext Paris SA, which designates the index it calculates and publishes. Euronext Paris SA makes no warranty as to the figure at which the said index stands at any particular time. Reprinted with permission.

Exhibit 4C.3   Germany: the DAX index, 25 March 2001

Sunday, March 25 2001 1:25am ET - U.S. Markets Closed.

XETRA DAX INDEX (GER:^GDAXI)-More Info: News - Trade NEW!: N/A				
Last Trade Mar 23 . **5544.67**	Change +156.65 (+2.91%)		Prev Cls 5388.02	Volume N/A	Div Date N/A
Day's Range 5396.63 - 5574.99	Bid N/A	Ask N/A	Open 5396.63	Avg Vol N/A	Ex-Div N/A
52 week Range 5351.48 - 6795.14	Earn/Shr N/A	P/E N/A	Mkt Cap N/A	Div/Shr N/A	Yield N/A

FTSE 100 Index as of 23–Mar–2001

Source: Website at http://www.finance.yahoo.com, 25 March 2001.

Exhibit 4C.4   Sweden: the Stockholm General index, 25 March 2001

Sunday, March 25 2001 1:26am ET – U.S. Markets Closed.

STOCKHOLM GENERAL (STO:^SFOG)-More Info: N/A – Trade NEW!: N/A				
Last Trade Mar 23 · **3898.70**	Change +73.74 (+1.93%)		Prev Cls 3824.96	Volume N/A	Div Date N/A
Day's Range 3824.96 – 3931.62	Bid N/A	Ask N/A	Open 3824.96	Avg Vol N/A	Ex-Div N/A
YTD Range 3766.28 – 5036.13	Earn/Shr N/A	P/E N/A	Mkt Cap N/A	Div/Shr N/A	Yield N/A

Sweden Stockholm General Index as of 23–Mar–2001

Source: Website at http://www.finance.yahoo.com, 25 March 2001.

Chapter 5

THE FUTURE: RETURN, RISK, RISK AVERSION, RISK PREMIUM AND ASSET PRICES

Learning objectives

After studying this chapter you should be able to:

1 Compare the maximum return and maximum expected return criteria as investment selection methods.

2 Explain what a risk averter is.

3 Calculate the required risk premium.

4 Apply the mean–variance criterion in asset selection.

INVESTMENT IN THE NEWS

Why risk matters

How important is a fund's risk profile? This important: It can tell you more – and sometimes a lot more – than past performance. This year, beginning in our annual summer Retirement Guide and continuing in this year-end investment issue, we've introduced into our list of best mutual funds a statistical measure called 'standard deviation'. Even if you are only a casual follower of mutual funds, chances are you've heard of it, since standard deviation, which in this case gauges a fund's volatility, has become an increasingly popular yardstick of risk. Simply put, standard deviation tells you how much a fund's short-term results vary from its long-term average; the higher the standard deviation, the more the fund's results jump around. If investing is like a roller-coaster ride – and that's as good as any analogy – then standard deviation tells you what to expect in the way of dips and rolls. It tells you how scared you'll be.... The fact is, standard deviation can be an important tool for investors – one that can offer some insight not only into how risky a fund is but even into how it might perform in a given market environment in the future....

Source: David Whitford, 'Why risk matters', *Fortune*, 29 December 1997, pp. 147–152. Reprinted from the 29 December 1997 issue of *Fortune* by special permission. © 1997, Time, Inc.

The goal of investors is to maximize their wealth. There is a chance that this goal will not be achieved, however, because most investments are risky. This chapter's *Investment in the news* highlights not only the importance of risk but also the practical use of one measure of risk – standard deviation. Although the article focuses on the standard deviation (the square root of variance) of mutual funds, this statistical measure is also commonly used to examine the volatility of an individual stock or bond.

As the article asserts, one needs the standard deviation of *future* rates of return ('standard deviation can be an important tool for investors'). This chapter examines volatility of future rates of return, defines a quantitative measure of risk, and shows that the larger the volatility, the worse off investors are because their risk increases. The chapter formally introduces the concepts of risk, risk aversion, risk premium, and variance of rates of return. For simplicity in introducing these concepts, it is assumed that investors hold a portfolio of only one asset or one mutual fund. In Chapter 6 we will discuss the case where several assets are held.

In the previous chapter we introduced these concepts based on past data, using the realized rates of return to calculate the average and the standard deviation. In this chapter we employ probabilities which are related to future returns rather than past returns. We address the meaning of an asset's risk, its measurement, and how the market compensates investors for bearing this risk. In particular, the higher the risk of an asset, the higher is its required expected return. This future risk–return relationship hypothesis is confirmed with the past risk–return relationships discussed in the previous chapter.

To gain a clear perspective on how asset prices change when risk prevails, this chapter first examines how current asset prices change in the unrealistic case where future prices are known with certainty. Then, we discuss the risk–return relationship in the case of uncertainty of future returns.

5.1 THE CASE OF CERTAINTY

We saw in Chapter 4 that different assets can yield different average rates of return. We introduce in this chapter the concept of uncertainty and risk premium. The higher the uncertainty, the higher the average return which compensates the investor for risk; hence the higher the risk premium. However, if future value of the various investments is certain, we would expect the same rate of return on all assets and zero risk premium, simply because there is no risk. If this is not the case, investors would sell the asset with the lowest rate of return and switch their investment to the asset with the highest rate of return. Because we are now assuming that the future is known with certainty, all investors will hold the asset offering the highest rate of return. In contrast to the certainty case, we will see that when the future is uncertain, the higher the volatility the higher the expected rate of return. Therefore, with uncertainty, not all investors will invest only in the asset with the highest expected rate of return.

We start with two investments and demonstrate how current prices are established on these two assets when future prices are known with certainty. Similar trading and price changes take place with uncertain rates of return. Suppose two assets exist, A and B, each with a market price of £100. We know with certainty that Asset A's price one year hence will be £110 and Asset B's price one year hence will be £120; no dividend or interest is paid on these assets. Is the market in equilibrium? No, it is not. Because Assets A and B have the same current price of £100, and Asset B provides a higher certain future return, an investor currently holding Asset A should sell it and buy Asset B. The investor would be sure of earning £10, or £120−£110, in the future, with no additional investment. This type of trading strategy, in which profits are made with no risk and no additional investment, is known as **arbitrage**. (Remember, this is a world of certainty.) This arbitrage trading will cause the price of Asset A to fall (because there will be a glut of Asset A on the market) and the price of Asset B to rise (because it will be in great demand) until the two assets yield the same certain rate of return. To illustrate this idea, suppose that the price of Asset A falls to £95. What should the equilibrium price of Asset B be?

To answer this question we turn to the definition of *rate of return* given in Chapter 4. Recall that by assumption there are no dividends; hence the rate of return on an investment over Period 1 is (see Equation 4.1)

$$R_1 = \frac{P_1 - P_0}{P_0} = \frac{P_1}{P_0} - 1$$

where P_1 represents the price at the end of the period and P_0 represents the price at the beginning of the period. Because the rates of return for Assets A and B must be identical in equilibrium, the following should hold:

$$(£110/£95) - 1 = (£120/P_{B,0}) - 1$$

where $P_{B,0}$ is the equilibrium market price of Asset B today. Solving for $P_{B,0}$, we find that $P_{B,0} = £103.64$. For this market price, the return on Asset A is

$$(£110/£95) - 1 \cong 0.158 \text{ or } 15.8\%$$

and the rate of return on Asset B is

$$(£120/£103.64) - 1 \cong 0.158 \text{ or } 15.8\%$$

Once the certain returns on the two assets are identical, there are no more arbitrage opportunities, and the market is said to be in equilibrium for these two specific assets.

PRACTICE BOX

Problem

Suppose there are two stocks worth with certainty £110 and £200, respectively, one year from now. The current price of the first stock is £100. What is the equilibrium price of the second stock?

Solution

In equilibrium, the rate of return on both securities must be identical and be equal to 10%, because $(£110/£100) - 1 = 0.10$, or 10%. Therefore, $£110/£100 = £200/P_2$, or $P_2 = (£200 \times £100)/£110 \cong £181.82$. Notice that with this price, the rate of return on this asset is also 10%.

Rates of return on various assets actually observed in the markets, as shown in Chapter 4, are in fact different, however, which clearly indicates that future returns are uncertain. Outside the realm of textbooks, uncertainty regarding future rates of return prevails. Moreover, even average rates of return on various assets are not identical over the years. The different average returns reflect the market compensation for the differential uncertainty or risk characterizing various assets. However, average rates of return on various assets are not arbitrarily determined, and as we shall see in the next chapter as well as in Chapter 14, investors will shift from one portfolio of assets to another in a similar way to the certainty case to guarantee that each asset will have the average return such that the investor will be compensated for the risk involved. If the expected rate of return on a given asset is 'too high', investors will buy it, and the stock price will go up exactly as in the certainty case described above until equilibrium is reached.

There is one asset, however, whose rate of return is *almost* certain. US or UK short-term Treasury bills (T-bills) yield almost a certain return. Ignoring inflation and the chance of a revolution in the United States or the United Kingdom, Treasury bills will pay with certainty the stated yield. Also, because they are a short-term asset, changes in interest rates do not significantly affect the price. Therefore, it is common to refer to the yield on T-bills as the *riskless interest rate*. It is true that over time, the yield on T-bills changes. However, when you purchase a given T-bill on a given date, the rate of return you earn is fixed if you hold it to maturity. Nevertheless, we would like to emphasize that the rate of return on T-bills is almost certain but not absolutely certain, because inflation in practice cannot be ignored. For example, in January 1999 the inflation rate in the US was 0.7% and in August 1999 fears of inflation arose again. The same fears were renewed in the UK in March 2001 as you can see in the following boxed article. As we can see from this article, interest rates, stock prices and inflation are all related factors, which will be analyzed in this book. Moreover, the US, UK and other stock markets are closely related and affect each other. Yet, it is common to refer to T-bills as the riskless asset. Understanding that the rates of return on most assets are uncertain, we are now prepared to introduce risk into the investment analysis.

British investors eye CPI, fear plunge after Wall St havoc

By Peter Nielsen

LONDON (Reuters) – The nerves of British investors will be tested on Monday following Friday's bloodbath on Wall Street, renewed inflation fears and dire newspaper warnings about a plunge in share prices when the London market reopens after the weekend.

Reassuring words from Group of Seven (G7) financial leaders in Washington about solid economic fundamentals in the United States and Europe are unlikely to soothe investors rattled by newspaper headlines such as the Sunday Telegraph's 'Europe Poised for Massive Sell-off' or the Observer's 'City Set for Big Bust'.

Worries over further interest rate rises in Britain will become a focus for markets with the release of consumer prices on Tuesday, Wednesday's policy meeting notes from the Bank of England and retail sales on Thursday.

Inflation fears were stoked late Friday when Mervyn King, deputy governor of the Bank of England, spelt out the dangers of allowing domestic demand to grow significantly above its sustainable level for too long, as it has done in recent years.

King's statement is likely to spook share markets by stirring speculation the central bank will raise rates again in coming months, after pushing up the cost of borrowing four times in the past eight months to the current level of six percent.

'We could get a real bloodbath on Monday', said one share analyst, quoted by The Sunday Times.

European exchanges had closed on Friday before U.S. inflation data caused major losses on Wall Street and havoc in the technology-weighted Nasdaq index.

Stoking Friday's sell-off on Wall Street was news that U.S. inflation in March raced at its highest speed in more than five years. The fear of further U.S. interest rate rises hit the Dow Jones industrial average, which tumbled nearly six percent, following a dive of nearly 10 percent on the tech-weighted Nasdaq composite index, putting the two indices 12 percent and 34 percent respectively off their year highs.

Source: Website at http://uk.news.yahoo.com/000416/5/a35rq.html, 16 April 2001.

5.2 THE NATURE OF RISK

Suppose you invest for one year in a government bond with a zero-coupon rate and £100 face value. The price of the bond is £90. The bond matures exactly one year from today. What rate of return will you earn on this bond if you hold it to maturity? You are sure that you wish to invest for one year; hence, the bond is riskless.[1]

A simple calculation reveals that the rate of return is

$$(£100/£90) - 1 \cong 0.111 \text{ or } 11.1\%$$

Because the £100 is received with *certainty* when the bond matures one year from now, the 11.1% represents a certain rate of return. Also, because the government cannot realistically go bankrupt, there is no default risk on this investment.

Now suppose instead that you purchase a share of British Airways which was traded on 16 March 2001 for £319. Obviously, unlike the government bond that matures one year from now, the value of the stock one year from now is uncertain. Suppose no dividends are paid, and the stock price at the end of the year is either £380 with a probability (chance) of $1/2$ or £300 with a probability (chance) of $1/2$. Given that the stock price today is £319, the rate of return will also be uncertain with the following values: either $(£380/£319) - 1 \cong 0.191$ or 19.1% with a probability of $1/2$, or $(£300/£319) - 1 = -0.0596$ or -5.96% with a probability of $1/2$.

In such a case we say that the investment in the stock is risky, which means that a rate of return obtained in the future is not known with certainty. Namely, the distribution of possible rates of return is known, but which of the outcomes will occur is unknown.

These two investment examples indicate that an investor can distinguish between two alternative situations: **certainty**, the situation in which the future value of the asset (or the rate of return) is known with a probability of 1, and **uncertainty** or **risk**, the situation in which there is more than one possible future value of the asset (or more than one possible rate of return). In this case, the asset's future value is not known with certainty. In such a case we say that the future value is a *random variable*. If investors know the probability of each random outcome, they face *risk*. If the probability of each outcome is unknown to investors, they face *uncertainty*. Note that in both uncertainty and risk, more than one future value is possible. Most assets traded in the market fall in this category. In Section 5.5 we suggest to measure the risk by the variance (or standard deviation) of returns as asserted in the *Investment in the news* article.

Actual probabilities that are known (as in a coin-flipping experiment) are called **objective probabilities**. In actual decision-making by investors and, in particular, in decisions made by people in business, the true probabilities are rarely known. Normally, the investor can collect some rates of return taken from the past few years on the same stock (see Chapter 4) and, based on these data, estimate the probabilities of possible future rates of return. These probability estimates are called **subjective probabilities**. Thus, even if the objective probabilities are unknown, an investor can attach subjective probabilities to each possible future value of an asset. By doing so, the investor faces a situation defined as risk rather than uncertainty. Because an investor can always assign

---

[1] For simplicity, assume no inflation. Otherwise, the bond is risky in real terms. If there is inflation, then the rate of return on bonds whose principal and interest are linked to the cost of living index is riskless. Such bonds are issued by the US government and are called inflation-indexed Treasury securities.

subjective probabilities to the various possible outcomes, the rest of this book uses the words *uncertainty* and *risk* interchangeably.

Note that although some assets in the market yield an almost certain rate of return (short-term government T-bills), most assets (stocks, long-term debt, options, investments in real estate, and so forth) yield uncertain rates of return. Therefore, an investor must develop systematic rules to use in choosing among assets characterized by uncertain returns and, in particular, to find the best diversification strategy among such assets.

Different assets have different expected rates of return, as well as different degrees of risk, so investors need criteria for selecting the best asset. The historical record given in Chapter 4 (see Exhibit 4.6 and Appendix 4B), shows that, on average, assets with higher risk also offer higher average rates of return. This property generally characterizes future returns as well, which are relevant for investment decision-making. How does an investor go about selecting the best asset for a particular investor? We present below several investment decision criteria when both certain and uncertain returns prevail.

5.3 THE CALCULATED EXPECTED RATE OF RETURN

In the rest of this chapter and in Chapter 6 we focus on the mean–variance investment criterion. The **mean–variance criterion** (MVC), which was developed by Harry Markowitz,[2] for which he won the 1990 Nobel Prize in economics, is the foundation of modern portfolio theory. According to this investment rule, the mean measures the profitability of the investment and the variance measures the risk involved. In this section we explain how to calculate the expected rate of return.

5.3.1 Calculating the expected return

Consider the four securities illustrated in Exhibit 5.1. All four investments require the same initial outlay of, say, £10,000. If only investments A and B are considered, the choice is simple: investment in Security A clearly is better than investment in Security B, because 6% is greater than 5%. Deciding between Securities A and C, however, is not so straightforward. If we look at the − 10% return from Security C and compare it with Security A's return, then Security A is superior by this rule. However, if we take

Exhibit 5.1 Possible rates of return on four securities with a £10,000 investment

Security A		Security B		Security C		Security D	
Rate of return (%)	Probability	Rate of return (%)	Probability	Rate of return (%)	Probability	Rate of return (%)	Probability
6	1	5	1	−10	$1/4$	−20	$1/4$
				0	$1/4$	10	$1/2$
				20	$1/2$	40	$1/4$

[2] See Harry Markowitz, 'Portfolio selection', *Journal of Finance*, 7, no. 1 (1952): 77–91.

the +20% return from Security C and compare it with Security A's return, then Security C turns out to be better.

Thus, when we compare certain and uncertain choices or two uncertain choices, the selection is not simple as in the case of the trivial comparison of two certain choices. In uncertain cases, we have to identify for each asset the average profitability and the risk involved. Let us first focus on profitability as measured by the expected return.

Rule 1: To calculate the expected rate of return, multiply each possible return by the probability to obtain it and sum all these terms. That is,

$$E(R) = \sum_{i=1}^{m} P_i R_i \qquad (5.1)$$

where R_i is the rate of return on an asset in a given state (the ith return), P_i is the probability corresponding to R_i, m is the number of possible rates of return (or possible values of R), and E stands for the 'expected' return.

The **expected rate of return** is the average of all possible rates of return. The expected return is also known as the *mean return* or simply as the **mean**. Expected returns have two components: probabilities and rates of return on an asset. The probabilities and rates of return are multiplied and then summed across *states*. States refer to each estimate of probability and rate of return. To avoid confusion from now on, when past returns are employed to calculate the average return, we call it the average rate of return; when probabilities are employed (the future), we call it the expected rate of return, or the mean rate of return.

Applying this formula to the examples in Exhibit 5.1, we have:

Security	Expected return, $E(R)$
A	$E(R_A) = 1 \times 6\% = 6\%$
B	$E(R_B) = 1 \times 5\% = 5\%$
C	$E(R_C) = (^1/_4) \times (-10\%) + ^1/_4 \times 0 + ^1/_2 \times 20\% = 7.5\%$
D	$E(R_D) = (^1/_4) \times (-20\%) + ^1/_2 \times 10 + ^1/_4 \times 40 = 10\%$

Based solely on expected return, we see that Security D is the best, because it yields the largest expected rate of return (10%).

When each rate of return is equally probable – that is, $P_i = 1/m$ for each i – then for Equation 5.1 we have:

$$E(R) = \sum_{i=1}^{m} \frac{1}{m} R_i = \frac{1}{m} \sum_{i=1}^{m} R_i$$

(We can move the $1/m$ term outside the summation, because it is a constant (see also the next Practice Box).)

Finally, where we have a continuous distribution function, e.g. a normal distribution (see, for example, Exhibit 5.4), then the expected rate of return is

$$E(R) = \int_{-\infty}^{\infty} R f(R) dR$$

where $f(R)$ is the density function of the return R.

Will you choose the investment with the highest expected return? Not necessarily, because it may also be the most risky. To see this, compare Securities C and D given in the previous example. Although Security D provides the highest expected return, it also exposes the investor to the maximum possible loss, −20%. To understand the risk involved with investment D, suppose that Bobby Jones, a student at the London School

PRACTICE BOX

Problem
Calculate the expected rate of return on Boston Celtics and Boston Edison common stock, given the following historical rates of return. Suppose that the investor selects the investment by the expected rate of return. Which is better?

Boston Celtics		Boston Edison	
Rate of return (%)	Probability	Rate of return (%)	Probability
7	$1/4$	8	$1/4$
−5	$1/4$	4	$1/4$
12	$1/4$	9	$1/4$
6	$1/4$	7	$1/4$

Solution
From Equation 5.1, we have:

$$E(R_{Celtics}) = {}^1/_4\,(0.07) - {}^1/_4\,(0.05) + {}^1/_4(0.12) + {}^1/_4(0.06)$$

$$= \frac{0.07 - 0.05 + 0.12 + 0.06}{4} = 0.05 \text{ or } 5\%$$

and

$$E(R_{Edison}) = {}^1/_4\,(0.08) + {}^1/_4(0.04) + {}^1/_4(0.09) + {}^1/_4(0.07)$$

$$= \frac{0.08 + 0.04 + 0.09 + 0.07}{4} = 0.07 \text{ or } 7\%$$

Thus, Boston Edison would be selected by the expected rate of return maximization.

of Business (LSB), has an initial wealth of £10,000. To pay for tuition and living expenses next year, he needs a minimum of £9,000. If he invests in Security C for one year and the lowest return occurs, he will still have £9,000 at year-end:

$$£10,000 \times [1 + (-0.1)] = £10,000 \times 0.9 = £9,000$$

where −0.10 is the lowest possible rate of return. If Jones invests in Security D and the worst outcome occurs, he will end up with

$$£10,000 \times [1 + (-0.2)] = £10,000 \times 0.8 = £8,000$$

and he will not have the minimum funds he needs for school next year. Jones is an ambitious student; hence, he would see it as a disaster if he had to drop out of school because of a lack of money. Therefore, he will avoid investment in Security D, because it puts his college career at risk.

However, for other investors who need a minimum of, say, only £5,000 next year, Security D may be preferable. (Again, assume a £10,000 starting amount.) In a nutshell, Security D has the advantage of having the largest mean rate of return, but it also has the disadvantage of having the lowest possible rate of return, −20%. Therefore, it is also the most risky. Thus, the choice between Securities A, C and D is difficult and may vary from one investor to another, depending on the investor's future financial needs or obligations. An investor with a strong distaste for risk may prefer Security C, whereas an investor who is more willing to take risk (in pursuit of higher returns) may prefer Security D. The next section links investor preference with asset risk.

5.4 RISK AVERSION

In the example illustrated in Exhibit 5.1, a tough decision had to be made. In contrast, Exhibit 5.2 presents an easier case where the mean return on the two assets is identical. Both Security A and Security B have the expected return of £120 on a £100 investment. The return on Security A is certain (£120 with a probability of 100%), whereas the return on Security B is uncertain, because it yields £110 with a probability of 50% and £130 with a probability of 50%.

Looking at Exhibit 5.2, which investment would you prefer? Empirical evidence and data taken from the stock market reveal that most investors would prefer Security A.

5.4.1 Definition of risk averters

The investors who prefer Security A over Security B are called risk averters. Risk averters, other things being equal, are investors who dislike volatility or risk. They always prefer a certain investment over an uncertain investment (namely, they prefer Security A over Security B) *as long as* the expected returns on the two investments are identical. Thus, for risk averters to be convinced to buy Security B, they would have to be compensated by a higher expected return. The difference between the expected rate of return on a risky asset and the riskless interest rate is known as the risk premium. In Chapter 4 we discussed the concept of past or historical risk premium. This past data is the base for the hypothesis that most investors are risk averters, and as such, risk premium prevails also with future return.

To provide an intuitive explanation of why most investors are risk averters, consider Leslie Chin, a junior in the business school at the London School of Business, who gets £120 per week for food from her parents. The £120 is exactly enough for food and one movie a week (no soda or popcorn). If we offer Chin £110 with a probability of $1/2$ and £130 with a probability of $1/2$ rather than the option of getting £120 for sure, she would probably refuse the offer. The reason is that on the one hand, with £110, she would have to cut out the movie. On the other hand, with £130, she could go to two movies a week. However, because the *satisfaction* or *utility* she would derive from having a second movie per week is less than the loss of satisfaction induced by giving up one movie per week, Chin would prefer £120 with certainty. Leslie Chin is called a risk averter, because when she is faced with two alternative investments with identical expected returns, she chooses the safer one.

5.4.2 Required risk premium

In this section, we discuss the required risk premium on future investments given the future returns and probabilities, in contrast to the observed risk premiums discussed in Chapter 4. Let us return to the example in Exhibit 5.2, where investments in Securities A and B have the same expected rate of return, +20%. Suppose all investors in the market are risk averters. Then all will buy Security A and none will buy Security B. Is this possible? Of course not; someone must hold Security B. Assets in the financial markets are at times like the infamous hot potato. If you don't want it, you have to sell

Exhibit 5.2 Dispersion of returns: returns on securities A and B with a £100 investment

	Security A		Security B	
	Return (£)	Probability	Return (£)	Probability
	120	1	110	$^{1}/_{2}$
			130	$^{1}/_{2}$
Mean return (£)	120		120	
Mean return (%)	20		20	

it. To induce someone to buy an undesirable asset, you have to lower its price to make it more attractive to the buyer.

Thus, the market mechanism is similar to the one described in the certainty case (see Section 5.1): the price of Security B will fall (because it has no demand), say, to £95. At this price, some investors may find it an attractive investment. Assume that at this price, the market is in equilibrium; no one wants to sell or buy stocks. The rate of return on Security B with a current purchase price of £95 is

$$(£110/£95) - 1 \cong 15.79\% \text{ with a probability of } ^{1}/_{2}$$

and

$$(£130/£95) - 1 \cong 36.84\% \text{ with a probability of } ^{1}/_{2}$$

The mean rate of return on Security B is therefore

$$^{1}/_{2}(15.79\%) + ^{1}/_{2}(36.84\%) \cong 26.31\%$$

whereas the mean return on Security A remains 20% (or £120 per £100 invested). Suppose the market is in equilibrium. That is, at these prices there is neither excess demand nor excess supply, and all available assets are bought by investors. Because the rate of return on Security A is certain, the difference in the mean return on these two assets when the market is in equilibrium is called the *required risk premium* or simply *risk premium*. Namely,

$$\text{Required risk premium} = 26.31\% - 20\% = 6.31\%$$

This is the premium on Security B required by the market to compensate investors for the risk involved with this asset.

Thus, we can say that the mean rate of return on risky assets is composed of the following two elements.

Rule 2: The expected rate of return is equal to the riskless interest rate plus the required risk premium. Namely,

$$\begin{matrix} \text{Mean rate of return} \\ \text{on risky asset} \end{matrix} = \begin{matrix} \text{rate of return} \\ \text{on riskless asset} \end{matrix} + \begin{matrix} \text{required risk} \\ \text{premium} \end{matrix} \qquad (5.2)$$

The more risk averse investors are (for example, avoiding the dissatisfaction of not finishing college, the danger of going bankrupt, and so forth), the lower the equilibrium price of Security B and, hence, the larger the required risk premium. In Chapter 4 we introduced the past observed historical risk premium on various assets. The past risk premium can be negative if the sample of years covers periods with large negative rates of return in the stock

PRACTICE BOX

Problem

Investment A yields a 10% rate of return with certainty. Investment B yields −10% with a probability of $1/_2$, and 40% with a probability of $1/_2$, and the market is in equilibrium. Calculate the risk premium.

Solution

From Equation 5.2, we know that the risk premium is equal to the mean rate of return on the risky asset minus the rate of return on the riskless asset (Investment A). In this case, the mean return on the risky asset is

$$E(R_B) = 1/_2(-10\%) + 1/_2(40\%) = 15\%$$

Thus, the risk premium is 15% − 10% = 5%.

market. Here, in contrast, we discussed the future required, or risk, premium. Therefore, it is common to add 'required' risk premium, emphasizing that it is related to future investment. If risk aversion prevails, the required risk premium is always positive.

In Exhibit 5.2, Security B has only two possible outcomes (£110 and £130). It is clear that the larger the deviation of these outcomes from the £120 mean (for example, £100 and £140), the greater the risk. When there are more than two outcomes, however, an investor needs to find a quantitative measure for the risk. One common measure of the risk is the variability (measured by the variance or standard deviation: see *Investment in the news*) of the rates of return.

5.5 CALCULATING VARIANCE

The **variance** of returns is a measure of the dispersion around the mean and is used as a measure of risk.[3] The variance of the possible returns for an asset is denoted by σ^2 (σ is the Greek letter sigma) and is calculated as follows.

Rule 3: The variance is the sum of the probability times the squared deviations from the mean:

$$\sigma^2 = \sum_{i=1}^{m} P_i[R_i - E(R)]^2 \tag{5.3}$$

where P_i is the probability of outcome i, R_i is the rate of return on the asset in State i, $E(R)$ is the expected return on R (see Equation 5.1), and m is the number of possible states.

For example, consider an investment that has two states. In State 1 the investment offers 0% with probability of $\frac{1}{3}$, and in State 2 it offers 30% with probability of $\frac{2}{3}$ over the next year. The expected rate of return one year from now is $\frac{1}{3} \times 0.0\% + \frac{2}{3} \times 0.3\% = 0.2$ or 20%, and the variance is

$$\sigma^2 = \tfrac{1}{3}(0.0 - 0.2)^2 + \tfrac{2}{3}(0.3 - 0.2)^2 = 0.02$$

---

[3] Variance is the measure of risk of a portfolio held. The risk of an individual asset held in the portfolio is beta, which is discussed in Chapter 14.

If the probability of each return is equal, simply substitute $1/m$ for P_i, where m is the number of possible returns to obtain:[4]

$$\sigma^2 = \sum_{i=1}^{m} \frac{1}{m}[R_i - E(R)]^2 \tag{5.4}$$

For example, if the rates of return for British Airways common stock are 37%, -17% and 17% with an equal probability of $\frac{1}{3}$ then the expected return is

$$E(R_{\text{British Airways}}) = (0.37 - 0.17 + 0.17)/3 \cong 0.123 \text{ or } 12.3\%$$

and the variance is

$$\sigma^2_{\text{British Airways}} = \tfrac{1}{3}(0.37 - 0.123)^2 + \tfrac{1}{3}(-0.17 - 0.123)^2 + \tfrac{1}{3}(0.17 - 0.123)^2 \cong 0.0497$$

Note that if the rates of return are expressed in percentage figures, then the unit of variance is *per cent squared*. If the rates of return are in dollar figures, then the unit of variance is *dollars squared*. These terms are difficult to interpret. Therefore, it is common to take the square root of the variance, which is called the **standard deviation**. The standard deviation, denoted by σ, is stated as a percentage or in dollars and is expressed as

$$\sigma = \left\{ \sum_{i=1}^{m} P_i[R_i - E(R)]^2 \right\}^{1/2} \tag{5.5}$$

In the preceding example, we found the variance to be 0.0497. Therefore, the standard deviation is

$$\sigma_{\text{British Airways}} = (0.0497)^{1/2} \cong 0.223 \text{ or } 22.3\%$$

Note that if R_i is measured in percent then σ is also given in percent. If R_i is measured in dollar return than σ is given in dollars. Thus, R_i and σ (as well as the mean) have the same dimension.

Once again, when we have a continuous random variable, R (e.g. see Exhibit 5.4), the variance is given by

$$\sigma^2 = \int_{-\infty}^{\infty} [R - E(R)]^2 \times f(R)dR$$

where R is the density function of the return R. A short-cut formula for the variance is

$$\sigma^2 = ER^2 - (ER)^2$$

where

$$ER^2 = \sum_{i=1}^{m} P_i R_i^2$$

and ER is the expected return as discussed above. Using this equation to calculate the variance of British Airways we get:

$$ER^2 = \frac{0.37^2 + 0.17^2 + 0.17^2}{3} = 0.0649$$

---

[4] Note that when historical rates of return are employed to estimate the variance of future rates of return, and there are m observations, we divide the sum of the squared deviations by $m - 1$ (see Chapter 4). The reason is that by dividing by $m - 1$ we obtain the best (unbiased) estimate of σ^2. But here we do not need to estimate σ^2; we calculate it where $1/m$ is the probability of each state.

$$(ER)^2 = 0.123^2 = 0.01513$$

$$\text{and } \sigma^2 = ER^2 - (ER)^2 = 0.0649 - 0.01513 = 0.0497$$

as before.

5.6 THE MEAN–VARIANCE CRITERION

Now that we know that most investors are risk averse, we can refine our investment selection criteria. To include this risk aversion characteristic in the decision of security selection, we turn to the **mean–variance criterion (MVC)**. We see from the variance formula that the greater the uncertainty of future returns, the higher the variance. Therefore, the MVC is used to select those assets (or portfolios of assets) with (1) the lowest variance for the same (or higher) expected return, or (2) the highest expected return for the same (or lower) variance.[5]

Suppose that asset A has a greater (or equal) mean than asset B (otherwise we change the roles of A and B). In a comparison of two assets, A and B, there are then six possibilities:

1 $E(R_A) > E(R_B)$ and $\sigma_A^2 < \sigma_B^2$

2 $E(R_A) > E(R_B)$ and $\sigma_A^2 = \sigma_B^2$

3 $E(R_A) > E(R_B)$ and $\sigma_A^2 > \sigma_B^2$

4 $E(R_A) = E(R_B)$ and $\sigma_A^2 < \sigma_B^2$

5 $E(R_A) = E(R_B)$ and $\sigma_A^2 = \sigma_B^2$

6 $E(R_A) = E(R_B)$ and $\sigma_A^2 > \sigma_B^2$

Thus, we can say that by the MVC, asset A is preferred to asset B in cases 1, 2 and 4 above. In case 5, the investor is indifferent between the two assets, while in case 3 one cannot tell which asset is better because A has a higher expected return as well as a higher variance. Finally, in case 6 asset B is preferred because it has the same mean as asset A with a lower variance. We need to know the investor's preference to decide between A and B in case 5 (see Section 5.8).

Suppose that each investor holds only one asset (either A or B), or alternatively that A and B are portfolios rather than individual assets. We claim that in equilibrium, only cases 3 and 5 above prevail, i.e. no one portfolio is better than the other by the MVC. We illustrate this issue with Exhibit 5.3. Exhibit 5.3 shows that the variance can be increased with no change in the mean return. Security A yields £130 with certainty, Security B yields £120 and £140 with equal probability, and Security C yields £110 and £150 with equal probability. As we move from A to B to C, £10 is added and subtracted with equal probability, creating a larger dispersion (variance) without changing the mean return. This movement, which increases the variance but does not change the mean return, causes the risk averter to be worse off, according to the MVC.

---

[5] So far, it is assumed that only one asset or one portfolio is selected. When we discuss the risk of an asset when a portfolio is constructed, we will also incorporate correlations as important factors determining the portfolio variability (or risk) (see Chapter 6).

Exhibit 5.3 Expected return and variance: returns on Securities A, B and C with a £100 investment

Security A		Security B		Security C	
Return (£)	Probability	Return (£)	Probability	Return (£)	Probability
130	1	120	$1/2$	110	$1/2$
		140	$1/2$	150	$1/2$
Mean (£)	130	130[a]		130[b]	
Variance	0	100[c]		400[d]	
Standard deviation (£)	0	10		20	

[a] $1/2(120) + 1/2(140) = 130$.
[b] $1/2(110) + 1/2(150) = 130$.
[c] $1/2(120 - 130)^2 + 1/2(140 - 130)^2 = 100$.
[d] $1/2(110 - 130)^2 + 1/2(150 - 130)^2 = 400$.

The reason risk averters would not like this movement is that the joy or satisfaction they get from the increase of £10 is smaller for them than the sorrow or damage caused by a loss of £10 in the case where the lower income is realized. Thus, for risk averters, Security A is preferred to Security B, and Security B is preferred to Security C. Risk averters prefer to avoid the honey (higher return) not because they do not like honey but because they know there is a probability that they could get stung!

Thus, by case 2 above, asset A is preferred to asset B and asset B is preferred to asset C. Is is possible to hold in equilibrium? Absolutely not! Assuming that all or most investors are risk averters, the stock price of Security B must drop, and the stock price of Security C must drop even further relative to Security A, otherwise no one will buy them. Once all available assets have been purchased and the market is cleared, we will find that, in fact, there is a risk premium on Securities B and C and that the risk premium on Security C is larger than the risk premium on Security B.

For example, if the price of Security A is £100, the price of Security B may drop to £98, and the price of Security C may drop to £95. Suppose that at these prices, the market is in equilibrium; hence, there is neither an excess demand nor an excess supply of securities. In this case, the mean rate of return would be:

$$\text{Security A: } (£130/£100) - 1 = 0.3 \text{ or } 30\%$$

$$\text{Security B: } [1/2(£120/£98) + 1/2(£140/£98)] - 1$$
$$\cong [(1/2 \times 1.22) + (1/2 \times 1.43)] - 1 = 0.325 \text{ or } 32.5\%$$

$$\text{Security C: } [(1/2 (£110/£95) + 1/2 (£150/£95)] - 1$$
$$\cong [(1/2 \times 1.16) + (1/2 \times 1.58)] - 1 = 0.37 \text{ or } 37\%$$

After the prices dropped, case 3 above holds and one asset is not preferred over another by the MVC. Thus, we may be in equilibrium. Therefore, for these assumed equilibrium prices, the required risk premiums on Securities A, B and C are as follows:

$$\text{Security A: Certainty, hence zero risk premium}$$

$$\text{Security B: Risk premium} = 32.5\% - 30\% = 2.5\%$$

$$\text{Security C: Risk premium} = 37\% - 30\% = 7\%$$

As you can see, the larger the variance, the lower the price and the larger the required risk premium.

Finally, note that we do not claim that the market is always in equilibrium. If the investor identifies portfolios like those described in cases 1, 2 and 3 above, portfolio A should be preferred. However, when the market realizes the existence of A over B, the stock price of A will go up, and the investors who first identify this disequilibrium will have a capital gain.

Exhibit 5.4(a) illustrates two bell-shaped normal distributions with the same variance but with different expected returns corresponding to the rates of return on two stocks, A and B. In this case both stocks have the same risk but stock B is more profitable because it has a higher expected rate of return. Exhibit 5.4(b) illustrates two distributions with the same expected return but different variance. In this case stock B is worse because it has the same profitably as stock A but a higher risk. To see why a lower variance or a lower standard deviation means a greater certainty (and hence smaller risk) consider the case where both stocks have the same mean of 10%, and standard deviations $\sigma_A = 5\%$ and $\sigma_B = 20\%$, respectively. With normal distributions, there is about a 64% chance that the actual returns will deviate from the expected value by one standard deviation or less, and about a 95% chance that the deviation will be by two standard deviations or less.

Thus, we can say that in our case there is a 64% chance that the realized return on stock A will be $10\% \pm 5\%$ and for stock B it will be $10\% \pm 20\%$. Thus we see that the range of return on stock A is from 5% to 15% and for stock B from 10% to 30%. From this example we see that the returns on stock A with a lower σ are less dispersed. The same phenomenon holds for two standard deviations, and in fact any number of standard deviations one selects. When the number of standard deviations increases, we can say that the return will fall in a certain range with a greater chance or greater probability. However, the smaller the σ, the smaller will be the range of possible returns.

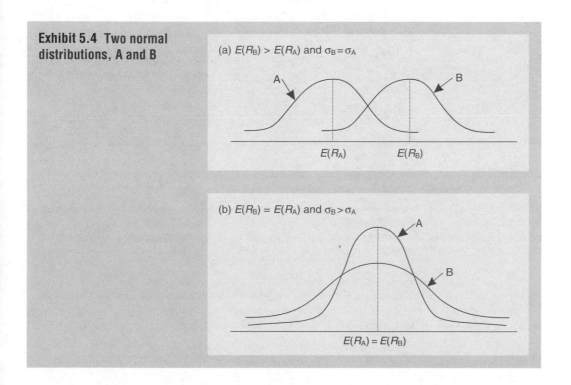

Exhibit 5.4 Two normal distributions, A and B

(a) $E(R_B) > E(R_A)$ and $\sigma_B = \sigma_A$

$E(R_A)$ $E(R_B)$

(b) $E(R_B) = E(R_A)$ and $\sigma_B > \sigma_A$

$E(R_A) = E(R_B)$

Because the return on the stock with the lower deviation is more certain, we can conclude that the higher the standard deviation, the higher the uncertainty of future return, hence σ measures the risk involved. Finally, we demonstrate calculation for normal distribution, but similar results hold for other distributions of returns.

5.7 OTHER ATTITUDES TOWARDS RISK

Investors who are **risk neutral** completely ignore an asset's variance and make investment decisions based only on the asset's expected rate of return. In the example given in Exhibit 5.3, the risk-neutral investor will be indifferent between Securities A, B and C. If all investors were risk neutral, no risk premium would be required, and Securities A, B and C would have the same market price.

PRACTICE BOX

Problem

The following are 10 states and the corresponding rates of return on Coca-Cola and Ford stocks. Assume that each state has an equal probability of $1/m = 1/10$. It is given that the riskless interest rate is 6.1%. Calculate the mean, variance, standard deviation and risk premium.

State	Coca-Cola Rate of return (%)	Ford Rate of return (%)
1	0.15%	0.08%
2	0.135	0.09
3	−0.04	0.05
4	0.16	0.10
5	0.08	0.12
6	−0.10	0.03
7	0.24	0.15
8	0.02	0.06
9	0.30	0.14
10	0.12	0.10

Solution

Using Equations 5.1, 5.4 and 5.5 we obtain:*

Average rate of return	0.1065%	0.092%
Variance	0.013	0.001
Standard deviation	0.114%	0.032%

We see that the average rate of return for Coca-Cola was higher than for Ford. However, the variance and standard deviation were also higher for Coca-Cola. The risk premium for Coca-Cola is 10.65% − 6.1% = 4.55%, and the risk premium for Ford is 9.2% − 6.1% = 3.1%. Thus, Coca-Cola offers a higher risk and a higher return than Ford.

* The average rate of return, variance and standard deviation are calculated using $P_i = 1/m$ where $m = 10$.

Investors are defined as **risk seekers** if they like risk or variance. These investors will be ready to pay a higher price for an asset whose variance increases. In Exhibit 5.3, risk seekers will prefer Security C over Security B and Security B over Security A. There is ample evidence that some people are risk seekers, at least during some periods of time and for small dollar amounts. For example, most gambling activities, such as state lotteries, have expected payoffs less than the cost to play, yet many people still buy lottery tickets.

If all investors were either risk neutral or risk seeking, there would be no positive risk premium. One way to assess whether financial markets are dominated by risk seekers or risk averters is to examine historical rates of return as was done in Chapter 4. If riskier securities earn, on average, higher returns, then we can infer that on the whole, the market participants are risk averse. It has been shown in Chapter 4 that the historical risk premium was positive. Moreover, the larger the standard deviation of rates of return, the larger the average return, implying that, at least historically, risk premium is related to the size of the standard deviation of rates of return.[6] Because positive risk premiums are found in the market, we can conclude that risk aversion is the dominating preference in the marketplace. Therefore, in the rest of the book, we assume that investors are risk averse.[7]

5.8 DEGREE OF RISK AND THE INVESTMENT CHOICE

Given the positive historical risk premium (see Chapter 4) we can safely assert that most investors are risk averters, and therefore they dislike variance. For a given expected future value of an asset, the higher the variance the less money investors will be willing to pay to purchase the asset, hence the higher the mean rate of return and the higher the required risk premium. Thus, in equilibrium we expect that case 3 in Section 5.6 holds: the mean of A and the variance of A are greater than the corresponding values of B. How would one select an investment in such a case? We need to introduce the investors' preference to make a selection in such a case. Let us illustrate. Suppose that the expected price at the end of the year of the two assets A and B is £110. The current price of asset A is £100; hence the expected rate of return is 10%. Asset B has a much higher variance than Asset A; hence, investors are willing to pay only £90 for it. Thus, the expected rate of return on asset B is £110/£90 − 1 ≅ 22.22%, reflecting the relatively high risk of this asset. Of course, each investor has his or her degree of risk aversion. For a given increase in variance, some investors will increase the required rate of return from the asset by only a little and some investors may increase it by a much larger amount, meaning that the increase in variance hurts them very much and they require substantial compensation for their loss. Investors can assign a **utility score** to the various investments, reflecting their satisfaction from the investment. The one common utility score which takes the expected return $E(R)$ and the variance σ_R^2 into account is given by

$$U = E(R) - a\sigma_R^2 \tag{5.6}$$

U is the utility score from the investment and a is a positive number reflecting the investor's attitude towards risk. When a selection between investments is done, the one

[6] See Ibbotson Associates, *Stocks, Bonds, Bills and Inflation* (Chicago: Ibbotson Associates, 1999 Yearbook).
[7] See also Jeremy J. Siegel, 'The equity premium: stock and bond returns since 1802', *Financial Analysts Journal*, January–February 1992, pp. 28–38.

with the highest utility score U is selected. The choice depends on the value of a in Equation 5.6. The larger the value of a, the more risk averse the investor is, as a given variance drastically reduces his or her utility score.

To see the meaning of the utility score, let us go back to the previous practice box, comparing Coca-Cola and Ford stocks.[8] Investors with $a = 0$ completely ignore the variance; they are not hurt by the variance, hence they will choose the asset only by the mean rate of return. These investors are risk neutral. They will choose Coca-Cola stock with the higher mean return.

Now assume that $a = 1$; i.e. the investor dislikes variance because utility (or satisfaction from the investment) will be reduced as the variance increases. For $a = 1$ we will get the utility score as follows:

Coca-Cola stock: $\qquad U = 0.1065 - 1 \times 0.013 = 0.0935$

Ford stock: $\qquad U = 0.092 - 1 \times 0.001 = 0.091$

We see that even for $a = 1$, Coca-Cola stock is still a better choice than Ford stock because it provides a higher level of satisfaction or utility score to the investor than Ford stock. For more risk-averse investors with, say, $a = 2$ we have:

Coca-Cola stock: $\quad U = 0.1065 - 2 \times 0.013 = 0.1065 - 0.026 = 0.0805$

Ford stock: $\quad U = 0.092 - 2 \times 0.001 = 0.092 - 0.002 = 0.090$

Ford stock is a better choice.

Thus, the utility score reflects the degree of satisfaction from the investment. Some investors badly dislike variance (relatively large a) and some are not much hurt by the variance (relatively low value of a). Thus, if a choice between Coca-Cola and Ford stocks (with no other assets involved) needs to be made, some investors will choose Ford stock and some will choose Coca-Cola stock. Generally speaking, the more risk averse the investor is, the less risky the selected assets will be.

Finally, the choice is simple in a case where the mean of asset 1 is larger than the mean of asset 2, and asset 1 also has a smaller variance. In such a case, any risk averter, regardless of the magnitude of a (which is non-negative for risk averters), will choose asset 1 because always $U(1) > U(2)$, where $U(1)$ and $U(2)$ stand for the utility of assets 1 and 2, respectively.

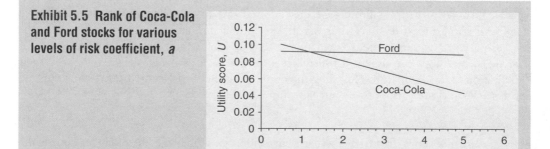

Exhibit 5.5 Rank of Coca-Cola and Ford stocks for various levels of risk coefficient, a

---

[8] We assume that the investor decides to invest either in Ford stock or in Coca-Cola stock. In practice, investors can increase the utility score by diversifying between the two stocks, or by constructing a portfolio of these two stocks. This will be covered in Chapter 6.

Exhibit 5.5 demonstrates the utility of Coca-Cola and Ford stocks for various levels of risk coefficient *a*. As we can see, for relatively low levels of *a*, Coca-Cola stock is preferred, and for higher values of *a* Ford stock is preferred. Thus, less risk-averse investors would prefer Coca-Cola, but more risk-averse investors will penalize Coca-Cola for the large uncertainty and would prefer to invest in Ford.

SUMMARY

■ *This chapter first discussed asset pricing under the assumption of certainty.*
Under certainty, in equilibrium all assets will yield the same rate of return. However, we live in a world of uncertainty, where different assets have different expected returns.

■ *Explain how to calculate the expected rate of return and the variance.*
The expected rate of return measures predictability and the variance measures risk.

■ *Explain what a risk averter is.*
A risk averter, other things being equal, dislikes volatility. Such an investor will always prefer a certain investment over an uncertain investment as long as the expected returns on the two investments are identical. To be induced to take risk, risk averters must be offered a risk premium.

■ *Calculate the required risk premium.*
Assuming that the investors hold only one asset, we show that the larger the deviations of the returns from the mean, the more risky the asset and the larger the required risk premium.

■ *Apply the mean–variance criterion in asset selection.*
Risk averters like a high expected return and dislike high variance. The mean–variance criterion (MVC) provides a simple method to assess choices between risky assets. However, in equilibrium, the mean and the variance of one asset are greater than the corresponding figures for another asset and the MVC cannot distinguish between the two assets.

■ *Compare the utility score.*
When two investments exist such that investment 1 has a higher mean and higher variance than investment 2, the choice depends on the degree of risk aversion of the individual investor. Investors with a high degree of risk aversion will tend to invest in asset 2, while the opposite holds for less risk-averse investors. The choice depends on the utility score which may vary from one investor to another.

KEY TERMS

Arbitrage	Objective probability	Standard deviation
Certainty	Risk	Subjective
Expected rate of return	Risk averter	probability
Mean	Risk neutral	Uncertainty
Mean–variance criterion	Risk premium	Utility score
(MVC)	Risk seeker	Variance

QUESTIONS

5.1 What is the difference between risk and uncertainty? How are these differences resolved?

5.2 What is an arbitrage transaction?

5.3 Suppose the market is in equilibrium, and there are no mispriced assets. What do different average rates of return in the market reflect?

5.4 When is the MRC the proper investment rule to use?

5.5 What is the relationship between an investor's level of risk aversion and the required risk premium?

5.6 You prefer to get £100 with a probability of $\frac{1}{2}$ and £200 with a probability of $\frac{1}{2}$ over getting £150 with certainty. Are you a risk averter or a risk seeker?

5.7 A firm requires at least a 12% rate of return on a project, the cost of capital is 12% and the interest rate is 5%. What can we learn about the average stockholder's risk preferences? What is the risk premium?

5.8 Consider the following rates of return on stock mutual funds:

Year	Fund A (%)	Fund B (%)
1	−10	−15
2	+20	+23
3	+10	+8
4	+12	+15

Examine whether one fund dominates the MVC.

5.9 What is the annual rate of return on a riskless two-year zero-coupon bond with a face value of £200 that cost you £70?

5.10 Suppose there are two assets, X and Y, and the current price of Asset X is £100. If it is known with certainty that in one year Asset X will be worth £120 and Asset Y will be worth £144, what is the equilibrium price of Asset Y today?

5.11 Suppose a stock that has a current price of £80 has a 50% chance of rising to £120 and a 50% chance of falling to £60 in one year. What is the expected price of the stock? What is the expected pound profit? What is the expected rate of return?

5.12 Consider the following data related to Assets A, B, C and D (given in percentages):

Asset A

Rate of return (%)	Probability
5	1

Asset B

Rate of return (%)	Probability
−10	1/4
10	3/4

Asset C

Rate of return (%)	Probability
−20	1/3
15	1/3
30	1/3

Asset D

Rate of return (%)	Probability
−20	1/4
10	1/2
40	1/4

Which asset is preferable if you decide to choose the investment with the maximum expected return? Explain.

5.13 From Question 5.12, which asset is preferable by the mean–variance criterion (MVC)? Discuss.

5.14 During a recent 10-year period, the following rates of return were earned on General Electric (GE) and Duke Power Company (DP). Assume that these are the population distributions and that each year has a probability of $1/m$, where m is the number of years.

Year	GE	DP	Year	GE	DP
1	0.11	0.10	6	−0.04	−0.01
2	0.13	0.12	7	0.34	0.12
3	−0.06	0.09	8	0.05	0.06
4	0.12	0.17	9	0.26	0.02
5	0.03	0.05	10	0.16	0.08

(a) Calculate the expected rate of return, variance and standard deviation of each stock.
(b) Assume that the riskless interest rate is 4%. What is the risk premium on these two assets? Explain your results.

5.15 Next year a security will yield £90 with a probability of $\frac{1}{2}$ and £110 with a probability of $\frac{1}{2}$. An investor is willing to pay $80 for this asset today. The risk-free interest rate is 15%.

(a) Is this investor a risk seeker or a risk averter?
(b) What is the risk premium?

5.16 Answer Question 5.15 assuming that the investor is ready to pay £95 for this asset.

5.17 Investment A costs £1,000 today, and the return next year is either £900 or £1,300, with an equal probability. Investment B costs £100 today, and the return next year is either £90 or £130, with an equal probability.

(a) Calculate the means and variances of future returns (in pounds) on these two assets.
(b) Calculate the means and variances of future *rates* of return on these two assets.
(c) Suppose Investments A and B are two stocks that exist in the market, and you can buy as much as you wish from these two stocks, but you can buy only one (A or B). Which investment would you prefer?

5.18 Suppose both Stock A and Stock B cost £100. The future returns on these two stocks are as follows:

Stock A		Stock B	
Probability	Return (£)	Probability	Return (£)
1/2	90	1/3	90
1/2	150	2/3	150

(a) Calculate the expected rates of return and the variances of the rates of return on these two assets.
(b) Which investment is better, according to the MVC?
(c) Given that the riskless interest rate is 5%, calculate the risk premium on each of these two assets.

5.19 Repeat Question 5.18 when the return on Stock B is £90 with a probability of $\frac{2}{3}$ and £150 with a probability of $\frac{1}{3}$. The information on Stock A is unchanged.

5.20 'The variance is always a larger number than the standard deviation'. Is this assertion true? Give an example to demonstrate your answer.

SELECTED REFERENCES

Arnott, Robert D., and Ronald J. Ryan. 'The death of the risk premium'. *Journal of Portfolio Management*, Spring 2001.

Arrow, K.J. 'Alternative approaches to the theory of choice in risk-taking situations'. *Econometrica*, October 1951.

Arrow, K.J. 'The role of securities in the optimal allocation of risk-bearing'. *Review of Economic Studies*, April 1964.

Good, Walter R. 'Yes, Virginia, there is a risk premium, but....'. *Financial Analysts Journal*, January/February 1994.

Hirshleifer, J.H. 'On the theory of optimal investment decision'. *Journal of Political Economy*, August 1958.

Levy, H., and A. Cohen. 'On the risks of stocks in the long run: revisited'. *Journal of Portfolio Selection*, Spring 1998.

Markowitz, H. 'Portfolio selection'. *Journal of Finance*, 7(1), March 1952, pp. 77–91.

Markowitz, H.M. *Portfolio Selection*. New York: Wiley, 1959.

Markowitz, H.M. *Mean–Variance Analysis in Portfolio Choice and Capital Markets*. New York: Basil Blackwell, 1987.

Rowe, D. 'The relevance of risk and uncertainty'. *Risk*, December 1999.

Rowe, D. 'Science and sentience'. *Risk*, December 2000.

Sharpe, W.F. 'Risk aversion in the stock market: some empirical evidence'. *Journal of Finance*, June 1976.

Suominen, Matti. 'Trading volume and information revelation in stock markets'. *JFQA*, forthcoming.

Wright, Paul. 'The FSA and a broader view on risk'. *Risk*, October 2001.

Chapter 6

RISK REDUCTION BY DIVERSIFICATION

Learning objectives

After studying this chapter you should be able to:

1 Discuss the rate of return, expected rate of return and variance of a portfolio.

2 Explain the effect of an individual asset's risk on a portfolio's risk.

3 Define and explain covariances and correlation coefficients between pairs of assets.

4 Explain the role of correlation within a portfolio.

INVESTMENT IN THE NEWS

Blue-chip stocks for gold-plated clients

How Todd Morgan manages the rest of Barbra Streisand's millions: very conservatively

Jeanne Lee

The rich are different when they are investors; they're more conservative. As Todd Morgan, chairman of Bell Air Investment Advisors, explains, 'Our clients are already rich. Our goal is not to make them rich but to keep them rich.'....

Accordingly, Morgan's approach is solidly conservative – typically 65% in equities (heavy on the blue chips) and 35% in muni bonds. In particular, he favors premium large-cap growth stocks in financial services, consumer products, health care, and technology, such as Citicorp, Gillette, Kimberly-Clark, and Abbott Laboratories. Even when he gets into tech, it's gold-plated names like Microsoft, Intel, and IBM. 'People are talking about the Internet all the time, but these big-cap names are going to be around longer than any of us,' says Morgan....

Source: Website at http://cgi.pathfinder.com/fortune/investor/1999/06/21/stx3.htm

In Chapters 4 and 5 we defined and discussed the expected rate of return and variance of rates of return of an individual asset. We also explained that the variance is a risk measure. In the above *Investment in the news* article we see that more than one asset is held in the portfolio of Barbra Streisand; it is composed of 65% in equities and 35% in municipal bonds (Muni Bonds). Moreover, the equity itself is composed of various stocks taken from various industries. Like Barbra Streisand, most other investors hold more than one asset in their portfolios. From this we conclude that diversification of the investment among various assets is probably beneficial to the investors.

In this chapter we first define what a **portfolio** of assets is. We then show:

(a) how to calculate the expected rate of return on a portfo lio;
(b) how to calculate the variance of the rate of return on a portfolio;
(c) that when a portfolio composed of several assets is held, the variance of an asset included in the portfolio is not the only indication of its risk. Rather one should also consider the co-movement of the asset's rates of return with other assets' rates of return included in the portfolios.

Thus, the risk and return of a *portfolio* of assets is the subject of this chapter.

6.1 A PORTFOLIO OF ASSETS

A portfolio is a combination of assets. However, at times, we use also the term *portfolio* also to refer to a holding of only one asset. In general, an investor has a portfolio that diversifies wealth in a number of assets, which can be combined in a variety of proportions, or weights. Because the weights are nothing but the proportion of wealth invested in each available asset, the sum of the weights must be equal to 1 (or 100%). For example, a proportion of $\frac{1}{2}$ invested in IBM stock, $\frac{1}{4}$ invested in AT&T stock and $\frac{1}{4}$ invested in T-bills constitutes a portfolio. If, for each dollar invested from the investor's own wealth, $\$\frac{1}{4}$ is *short* in AT&T, it means that the investor sells short the stock of AT&T and receives the cash flow from this sell. Hence, altogether $\$1\frac{1}{4}$ (or 125% of wealth) is to be invested in the other asset, say, IBM. Thus, a portfolio of $-\frac{1}{4}$ short in AT&T and $1\frac{1}{4}$ invested in IBM is also a portfolio with $-\frac{1}{4} + 1\frac{1}{4} = 1$ (or 100%). Any other combination of investment proportions, with negative as well as positive proportions, such that the sum of these proportions is equal to 1, defines a portfolio.

6.2 AN ASSET'S RISK WHEN HELD WITH OTHER ASSETS IN A PORTFOLIO

As Chapters 4 and 5 described, the higher the variance (or standard deviation) of the return on an asset, the higher the risk and therefore the higher the required risk premium. Hence, the variance of the returns on an asset appears to measure the risk of that asset. Although this is true if an investor holds only one asset, the variance is not the sole measure of risk if the investor holds more than one risky asset in his or her portfolio. In a portfolio, the risk of an individual asset is a function not only of its own variance but also of its degree of dependency with the other assets in the portfolio. Let us demonstrate the role that dependency of returns plays in determining the portfolio's risk.

Exhibit 6.1 Return on Assets A and B

	Return on Asset A		Return on Asset B	
	Return	Probability	Return	Probability
	+20%	$\frac{1}{2}$	+20%	$\frac{1}{2}$
	−10%	$\frac{1}{2}$	−10%	$\frac{1}{2}$
Mean	5%		5%	
Variance	225		225	
Standard deviation	15%		15%	

The degree of dependency measures how the returns on two assets move together. If both go up or down together, we say they have *positive dependency*. If one asset goes up when the other goes down or vice versa, we say they have *negative dependency*. In general, the more negative the degree of dependency between assets in a portfolio, the lower the risk of the portfolio, and hence the lower the required risk premium for each specific asset. The precise measure of risk of each asset in a portfolio context is discussed in Chapter 14. This section demonstrates that a risk-averse investor will require a risk premium on the risky portfolio held that decreases as the degree of dependency between the risky assets in the portfolio decreases.

Let us explain this dependency concept with a numerical example. Suppose there are two assets, A and B, whose returns in dollars are given in Exhibit 6.1. Each asset yields +20% and −10% with an equal probability of $\frac{1}{2}$. The expected rate of return on each asset is

$$\tfrac{1}{2}(20\%) + \tfrac{1}{2}(-10\%) = 5\%$$

and the variance is

$$\tfrac{1}{2}(20 - 5)^2 + \tfrac{1}{2}(-10 - 5)^2 = 225$$

Hence, the standard deviation is $\sqrt{225} = 15\%$.

Exhibit 6.2 lists the distributions of the returns from these two assets together, when a portfolio composed of $\frac{1}{2}$ of the assets are invested in stock A and $\frac{1}{2}$ in stock B, such that the total investment for weights is $\frac{1}{2} + \frac{1}{2} = 1$.

We make different assumptions regarding the dependency between the two assets' distributions. First, let us explain how the portfolio's rate of return is obtained. Suppose that you construct a portfolio such that $\frac{1}{2}$ of it is invested in asset A and $\frac{1}{2}$ of it in asset B. Therefore, if you earn, say, 20% on asset A, the contribution of this asset to the portfolio's rate of return is only 10% because $\frac{1}{2} \times 20\% = 10\%$. Thus, the contribution of each asset to the portfolio rate of return is calculated by the product of the investment proportion in the asset times the return on the asset.

The left column of Exhibit 6.2 assumes an extreme positive dependency between the returns on the two assets.[1] Namely, if +20% is realized on asset A, this return of 20% is also sure to be realized on asset B. Hence, 20% is obtained on each asset with a probability of $\frac{1}{2}$. Because we invest $\frac{1}{2}$ in B, the return on the portfolio in such a

---

[1] This will be measured later by *correlation*, i.e. we have here a correlation of +1 (see Section 6.4).

Exhibit 6.2 Return on portfolio composed of Asset A and Asset B
(The investment in the portfolio is $100)

	Positive dependency		No dependency		Negative dependency	
	Return	Probability	Return	Probability	Return	Probability
	20%	$\frac{1}{2}$	20%	$\frac{1}{4}$	5%	1
	−10%	$\frac{1}{2}$	5%	$\frac{1}{2}$		
			−10%	$\frac{1}{4}$		
Mean	5%		5%		5%	
Variance	225[a]		112.5[b]		0	

[a] Variance = $\frac{1}{2}(20\% - 5\%)^2 + \frac{1}{2}(-10\% - 5\%)^2 = 900.$
[b] Variance = $\frac{1}{4}(20\% - 5\%)^2 + \frac{1}{2}(5\% - 5\%)^2 + \frac{1}{4}(-10\% - 5\%)^2 = 112.5.$

case is $\frac{1}{2} \times 20\% + \frac{1}{2} \times 20\% = 20\%$ with a probability of $\frac{1}{2}$. Similarly, if an event occurs with a negative return on asset A (−10%), the same event also causes a loss on asset B of −10%. Thus, with a probability of $\frac{1}{2}$, we get −10% on each asset, or $\frac{1}{2} \times (-10\%) + \frac{1}{2} \times (-10\%) = -10\%$ is obtained on the portfolio composed of these two assets.

The right column in Exhibit 6.2 represents the distribution corresponding to an extreme negative dependency between the two assets.[2] Namely, if asset A has a return of +20%, asset B has a return of −10%, with a total rate of return of $\frac{1}{2} \times (20\%) + \frac{1}{2} \times (-10\%) = 5\%$ on the portfolio of the two assets. Similarly, if the low return is realized on asset A (−10%), a high rate of return is received on asset B (+20%), and once again we end up with a +5% rate of return on the portfolio. Hence, no matter what eventually occurs, the total rate of return obtained on the portfolio is +5%, so we get +5% with a probability of 1 (meaning certainty); therefore, in the extreme negative dependency of the right-hand column, the portfolio's variance is equal to zero.

Finally, the middle column of Exhibit 6.2 reports an intermediate case where the returns have no dependency; there is no association, either positive or negative, between the returns on these two assets. Thus, we get +20% on asset A with a probability of $\frac{1}{2}$ and +20% on asset B with a probability of $\frac{1}{2}$, ending up with 20% (i.e. $\frac{1}{2} \times 20\% + \frac{1}{2} \times 20\% = 20\%$) with a probability of $\frac{1}{2} \times \frac{1}{2} = \frac{1}{4}$. Similarly, we get 10% with a probability of $\frac{1}{4}$. Note, however, that +5% is obtained with a probability of $\frac{1}{2}$, because it encompasses two events: +20% on asset A and −10% on asset B, and −10% on asset A and + 20% on asset B. Because each event has a probability of $\frac{1}{4}$, we end up with 5% with a probability of $\frac{1}{2}$.

The bottom part of Exhibit 6.2 clearly indicates that although the mean return on the two assets combined is 5%, no matter what the assumed degree of dependency between the two assets, the variance of the portfolio returns is a function of their dependency: the lower the dependency, the lower the variance. In the case of an extreme negative dependency, the portfolio's variance is reduced to zero.

Let us return to the relationship between risk premium and variance, taking the case of the extreme negative dependency given in Exhibit 6.2 (right column). At the end of the

---

[2] We shall see in Section 6.4 that this extreme negative dependency corresponds to a correlation of −1.

investment period of, say, one year, an investor receives with certainty a rate of return of 5%. For an investment of, say, $100 ($50 in Stock A and $50 in B), the end-of-period wealth on the portfolio is $105 with certainty, because a 5% rate of return is earned with certainty. Suppose that the riskless interest rate is 5% and that the investor is offered a certain sum of money for selling his portfolio composed of assets A and B when this sum is paid at the end of the period. What should this sum be in order to make the investor indifferent between the two choices? The answer is clearly $105. If you offer the investor $106 at the end of the period for the portfolio he holds, you are 'bribing' him, and he will sell the portfolio to you, because he obtains $105 with certainty on the portfolio. Moreover, the investor can borrow $100 at 5% interest rate, buy these two stocks, sell them to you and make a $1 gain with certainty, because he or she will pay the bank $105 at the end of the period but receive $106 from you. If you offer him $104 he will not agree to sell the portfolio to you because he can sell the stock for $100, deposit it at the bank and receive $105 at the end of the period. Thus, $105 is exactly the point where he is indifferent between selling or not selling his portfolio to you. Because the return on the portfolio is 5% and the interest rate is 5%, it implies that the investor requires no risk premium at all. This makes sense: no risk is involved in holding a portfolio of these two assets, because the return on them is 5% with certainty. Of course, for a $100 investment there is $1 profit which seems negligible. But the same argument holds for a $100 million investment (or even more) which yields a $1 million profit.

The important conclusion from this example is that although each of the two assets, when held *separately*, is risky, the two assets are considered to be riskless when included in a portfolio. The extreme negative dependency between the returns on these two assets completely eliminates the uncertainty involved in the returns. Hence, an asset's own variance should be the measure of risk only when the asset is held separately. When the asset is held in a portfolio with other assets, however, the degree of dependency should be incorporated into the measurement of risk, and hence into the risk premium. Thus, in this case, the *portfolio's variance* is the measure of risk, not the individual asset's variance.

Indeed, the portfolio's variance in the extreme negative dependency of Exhibit 6.2 is equal to zero, which reflects the certainty of the future return. Exhibit 6.2 shows that as negative dependency shifts to no dependency and then to positive dependency, the portfolio variance becomes larger.

In general, the higher the degree of dependency of a particular asset with other risky assets included in a portfolio, the higher this asset's contribution to the portfolio's risk will be and the higher the risk premium required for the asset will be. Therefore, the required risk premium is a function not only of the asset's variance but also of its dependency with other assets.

The discussion so far can be summarized by the following rules:

Rule 1: If an investor holds only one risky asset, the variance is the measure of risk. The higher the variance, the higher the required risk premium from the individual assets in the portfolio.

Rule 2: If an investor holds more than one risky asset in a portfolio, the risk of each asset is a function of both the asset's own variance and its degree of dependency with the other assets held in the portfolio.

Rule 3: The larger the portfolio's variance, the higher the required risk premium on the portfolio and therefore, on average, the larger the required risk premium on each asset.

Thus, the portfolio's variance, rather than the individual asset's variance, is the key factor in determining the required risk premium. In order to further understand the concept, let us first define the portfolio's expected rate of return and portfolio variance and then turn to how the portfolio's risk can be reduced by diversifying among different assets.

6.3 THE EXPECTED RATE OF RETURN ON A PORTFOLIO

When you invest in many assets, the **portfolio expected return**, denoted by $E(R_p)$, is the weighted average of the expected returns of all the assets held in your portfolio, where the weights are the investment proportions (w_i). This is summarized by Rule 4.

Rule 4: The portfolio expected value of return is the sum of the products of the investment weighted in the individual asset by its expected rate of return:

$$E(R_p) = \sum_{i=1}^{n} w_i E(R_i) \tag{6.1}$$

where n is the number of assets in the portfolio, $E(R_i)$ is the expected rate of return on the ith asset, and w_i is the weight invested in the ith asset. (Note that the weights must sum to 1; that is $\sum_{i=1}^{n} w_i = 1$.)

For example, if there are only two assets in the portfolio $(n = 2)$ with expected rates of return of 5% on the first asset and 20% on the second asset, and if $w_1 = \frac{1}{2}$ and $w_2 = \frac{1}{2}$, we have

$$E(R_p) = \tfrac{1}{2}(0.05) + \tfrac{1}{2}(0.20) = 0.125 \text{ or } 12.5\%$$

Of course, when the investment proportions change, the expected rate of return on the portfolio also changes. For example, if $w_1 = \frac{1}{4}$ and $w_2 = \frac{3}{4}$, then

$$E(R_p) = \tfrac{1}{4}(0.05) + \tfrac{3}{4}(0.20) = 0.1625 \text{ or } 16.25\%$$

To show how to calculate the expected return on a portfolio, let us turn first to Exhibit 6.3 where three assets A, B and C are considered and there are three possible scenarios of the economy: the economy may grow, the economy may remain stable, or the economy may go into a recession (see Exhibit 6.3). Note that Asset B provides a higher return in a recession; for example, it may be a firm that produces an inexpensive, low-quality product that is in great demand in a recessionary period. For simplicity we assume that each scenario has a probability of $\frac{1}{3}$. For example, we have a $\frac{1}{3}$ probability that the economy will grow with a 5% rate of return on Asset A, 10% on Asset B and 30% on Asset C. We construct two portfolios: $\frac{1}{2}$B and $\frac{1}{2}$C, and alternatively $\frac{1}{2}$A $+ \frac{1}{4}$B $+ \frac{1}{4}$C. Of course, the return on each portfolio in each scenario is the corresponding returns on the stock times the investment proportions in these assets. For example, if the economy grows, we get on portfolio $\frac{1}{2}$B $+ \frac{1}{2}$C, the return of $\frac{1}{2} \times 0.1 + \frac{1}{2} \times 0.3 = 0.2$ or 20%. In a similar way all returns in Exhibit 6.3 are calculated.

Each scenario (stable, growth or recession) has a probability of $\frac{1}{3}$. Therefore, as in the single asset case, the expected rate of return on portfolio I $(\frac{1}{2}$B $+ \frac{1}{2}$C) can be calculated as:

$$E(R_p) = \tfrac{1}{3}(0.20) + \tfrac{1}{3}(0.10) + \tfrac{1}{3}(0.15) = 0.15 \text{ or } 15\%$$

Exhibit 6.3 Rates of return on three assets and two portfolios

1	2	3	4	5	6	7
Scenario	Probability	Asset A	Asset B	Asset C	Portfolio I: $\frac{1}{2}B + \frac{1}{2}C$	Portfolio II: $\frac{1}{2}A + \frac{1}{4}C + \frac{1}{4}C$
Growth	$\frac{1}{3}$	0.05	0.10	0.30	0.20[a]	0.125
Stable	$\frac{1}{3}$	0.05	0.05	0.15	0.10	0.075
Recession	$\frac{1}{3}$	0.05	0.15	0.15	0.15	0.10
Portfolio expected rate of return		0.05	0.10	0.20[b]	0.15[c]	0.10

Demonstration of some of the calculations:
[a] $\frac{1}{2}(0.10) + \frac{1}{2}(0.30) = 0.20$
[b] $\frac{1}{3}(0.30) + \frac{1}{3}(0.15) + \frac{1}{3}(0.15) = 0.20$
[c] $\frac{1}{3}(0.20) + \frac{1}{3}(0.10) + \frac{1}{3}(0.15) = 0.15$

Similarly, the expected rate of return on portfolio II ($\frac{1}{2}A + \frac{1}{2}B + \frac{1}{4}C$) is

$$E(R_p) = \tfrac{1}{3}(0.125) + \tfrac{1}{3}(0.075) + \tfrac{1}{3}(0.10) = 0.10 \text{ or } 10\%$$

In the calculation above we first construct the portfolio's rates of return and then calculate the expected return as we did for a single asset in Chapter 5. When a portfolio of assets is involved, we can apply Equation 6.1 to obtain the portfolio expected rate of return.

Let us verify that Equation 6.1 yields the same result, as obtained with direct calculation shown above. For portfolio I given in Exhibit 6.3 we obtain

$$E(R_p) = \tfrac{1}{2}(0.10) + \tfrac{1}{2}(0.20) = 0.15 \text{ or } 15\%$$

and for portfolio II:

$$E(R_p) = \tfrac{1}{2}(0.05) + \tfrac{1}{4}(0.10) + \tfrac{1}{4}(0.20) = 0.10 \text{ or } 10\%$$

Thus, we obtain the same result as before with the direct calculation of expected return on these two portfolios.

In summary, the expected rate of return on a portfolio can be calculated in two ways:

1 First calculate all possible returns on the portfolio, and then calculate its expected rate of return.
2 Calculate the portfolio expected rate of return using Equation 6.1.

Both methods produce the same results. Actually, one method serves as a verification of the other. The expected rate of return on a portfolio, then, is simply the sum of the expected returns of the various individual assets multiplied by the weights of each asset in the portfolio. Obviously, the higher the proportion of wealth (w_i) invested in the ith security, the higher its individual effect on the portfolio's expected return (or mean). In the extreme, when all the wealth (100%) is invested in only one security, the portfolio's mean rate of return is simply the mean rate of return on a selected security.

PRACTICE BOX

Problem

Assume the following historical rates of return for General Motors (GM) and British Petroleum (BP). Calculate the expected rate of return on a portfolio that has one-third of your wealth invested in GM and two-thirds of your wealth invested in BP. First compute the portfolio rates of return (assume that each year is equally probable), and then employ Equation 6.1 to calculate the portfolio's expected rate of return.

Year	GM	BP
1	10%	15%
2	−5%	10%
3	8%	0%
4	15%	−1%

Solution

To answer this problem, first note that the probability of each outcome is $\frac{1}{4}$, because each year is equally probable, and there are four years. Thus, construct the following table:

Year	Rates of return			Portfolio:
	Probability	GM	BP	$\frac{1}{3}$ GM and $\frac{2}{3}$ BP
1	$\frac{1}{4}$	0.10	0.15	0.1333[a]
2	$\frac{1}{4}$	−0.05	0.10	0.05
3	$\frac{1}{4}$	0.08	0.0	0.0267
4	$\frac{1}{4}$	0.15	−0.01	0.0433
Expected rate of return		0.07[b]	0.06[c]	0.0633[d]

[a] $\frac{1}{3}(0.10) + \frac{2}{3}(0.15) = 0.1333$

[b] $\frac{1}{4}(0.10) + \frac{1}{4}(−0.05) + \frac{1}{4}(0.08) + \frac{1}{4}(0.15) = 0.07$

[c] $\frac{1}{4}(0.15) + \frac{1}{4}(0.10) + \frac{1}{4}(0.0) + \frac{1}{4}(−0.01) = 0.06$

[d] $\frac{1}{4}(0.1333) + \frac{1}{4}(0.05) + \frac{1}{4}(0.0267) + \frac{1}{4}(0.0433) = 0.0633$

Using Equation 6.1 and the results in the table, we have

$$E(R_p) = \tfrac{1}{3}(0.07) + \tfrac{2}{3}(0.06) \cong 0.0633$$

which is equal to the expected rate of return obtained in the table (see the right column and footnote d).

6.4 COVARIANCES AND CORRELATIONS

We showed above how to calculate the expected rate of return on a portfolio. We turn now to calculate the variance of a portfolio. The portfolio's variance depends on the variances of each asset included in the portfolio and, as we have illustrated in Exhibit 6.2, on the degree of dependence between the assets. In Exhibit 6.2 we illustrated three cases: an extreme negative dependence, an extreme positive dependence and independence. Of course, we may have dependence which is not so extreme and we need to know how to measure it. In this section we define a **correlation** as an index of the degree of dependence

Exhibit 6.4 Rates of return for two stocks over a four-year period

Year	Stock A	Stock B
1	0.05	0.10
2	0.15	0.20
3	−0.05	−0.10
4	0.25	0.60

between the rates of return on two assets. However, to understand the correlation we first need to define a related measure of dependence called **covariance**.

Whereas the variance measures the variability of the rates of return on a given asset or portfolio, the covariance measures the 'co-movements', or degree of dependency, of the rates of return of two assets. If the rates of return of two assets tend to go up and down together, they have a positive covariance. If one asset's rate of return is relatively high and the other asset's return tends to be relatively low, the covariance is negative.

Exhibit 6.4 gives the rates of return for two stocks over a four-year period. This exhibit shows a positive co-movement or positive covariance between the two stocks. When one stock is doing relatively well, the other is also doing relatively well, and vice versa.

It is easiest to see positive co-movement in a graph. Exhibit 6.5 shows the rates of return for both stocks plotted in a single graph. Each point represents the pair of returns for both stocks in a given year. For example, in year 2, stock A's rate of return was 15% and stock B's rate of return was 20%. When stock A's rate of return is down, so is stock B's rate of return. When stock A's rate of return is up, so is stock B's rate of return. Notice that the pattern moves upward as you look from left to right (see Exhibit 6.5). This upward pattern characterizes a positive covariance which implies a positive dependence. If there is a downward pattern of the points there is a negative dependency (see next Practice Box), and if there is neither an upward nor a downward pattern, the returns on the two stocks are independent.

Exhibit 6.6 demonstrates how to calculate the covariance between the returns of asset A and asset B. To calculate the covariance of R_A and R_B, denoted by $Cov(R_A, R_B)$, we calculate first the deviation of each observation R_A from its mean $E(R_A)$ (see column 4 in Exhibit 6.6), then the deviation of each observed R_B from its mean $E(R_B)$ (see column 5 in Exhibit 6.6). For example, for year 1 the rate of return on stock A is 0.05 and the mean is 0.10; hence the deviation is $0.05 - 0.10 = -0.05$. We then multiply these deviations (see

Exhibit 6.5 A positive dependancy of returns

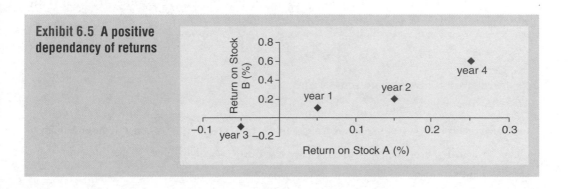

Exhibit 6.6 The covariance calculation

1	2	3	4	5	6
	Rates of return		Deviations from the expected value		
Year	Stock A	Stock B	Stock A	Stock B	(4) × (5)
1	0.05	0.10	−0.05	−0.10	0.005
2	0.15	0.20	0.05	0.00	0.000
3	−0.05	−0.10	−0.15	−0.30	0.045
4	0.25	0.60	0.15	0.40	0.060
Expected value	0.10[a]	0.20[b]			0.0275[c]

[a] (0.05 + 0.15 − 0.05 + 0.25)/4 = 0.10
[b] (0.10 + 0.20 − 0.10 + 0.60)/4 = 0.20
[c] (0.005 + 0.000 + 0.045 + 0.060)/4 = 0.0275

column 6), sum these products and divide by $n = 4$ to obtain $\text{Cov}(R_A, R_B) = 0.0275$. The covariance calculation is summarized in Rule 5.

Rule 5: The covariance of the returns on two stocks A and B, denoted by $\text{Cov}(R_A, R_B)$, is the sum of the products of the deviation of R_A from its mean $E(R_A)$ and the deviation of R_B from its mean $E(R_B)$, multiplied by the probability of obtaining the pair R_A and R_B. Using historical data with an equal probability for say, each year, or in the case where each pair (R_A, R_B) has an equal probability, the covariance is the sum of the product of the deviations divided by n, where n is the number of years (e.g. $n = 4$ in Exhibit 6.6).[3]

Positive and negative covariances tell an investor that the stocks in a portfolio either move together or move in opposite directions, but they do not tell the investor much about the strength of this association. The co-movement of two variables depends, in part, on how volatile the returns are on each asset alone. For example, suppose we find a covariance of 0.003. Is this covariance very large? Is it modestly large? Is it twice as strong as a covariance of 0.0015? If the two variables are not very volatile, then 0.003 may indicate a strong dependency. However, if the two variables are highly volatile, then a covariance of 0.003 may indicate a weak dependency.

By dividing the covariance by the product of the standard deviations of each asset, we can determine the strength of their dependency, or their **correlation**. The number we obtain is called the *correlation coefficient*, or ρ (Greek letter 'rho'); this is summarized in Rule 6.

Rule 6: The correlation is obtained by dividing the covariance by the product of the standard deviations of each asset as given by Equation 6.2:

$$\rho_{A,B} = \frac{\text{Cov}(R_A, R_B)}{\sigma_A \sigma_B} \tag{6.2}$$

The correlation is always between −1 and +1.

---

[3] Cov can formally be written as $\text{Cov}(R_A, R_B) = \sum_{i=1}^{n} P_i[R_{A_i} - E(R_A)][R_{B_i} - E(R_B)]$ where P_i is the probability to obtain the pair (R_{A_i}, R_{B_i}). When $P_i = 1/n$, it is reduced to $\text{Cov}(R_A, R_B) = \frac{1}{n}\sum_{i=1}^{n}[R_{A_i} - E(R_A)][R_{B_i} - E(R_B)]$ as calculated in Exhibit 6.6.

PRACTICE BOX

Problem

Suppose you are given the following historical data of the returns of stocks A and B. Draw a diagram like Exhibit 6.5 and calculate the covariance between the returns of stocks A and B.

	Rates of return	
Year	Stock A	Stock B
1	0.05	0.20
2	0.15	0.10
3	0.25	−0.10
4	−0.05	0.30

Solution

The figure below shows a tendency for a negative relationship between the returns on the two assets.

When the return on one asset is high, it is relatively low on the other asset. Thus, there is a tendency for the point to decline from left to right, which indicates a negative dependency between the returns on the two stocks.

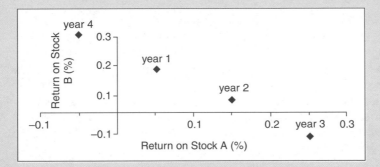

Let us turn to the covariance calculation. Following the procedures illustrated in Exhibit 6.6, construct the following table:

1	2	3	4	5	6
			Deviation from the mean		
Year	Stock A	Stock B	Stock A	Stock B	(4) × (5)
1	0.05	0.20	−0.05	0.075	−0.00375
2	0.15	0.10	0.05	−0.025	−0.00125
3	0.25	−0.10	0.15	−0.225	−0.03375
4	−0.05	0.30	−0.15	−0.175	−0.02625
Expected value	0.10[a]	0.125[b]			

[a] (0.05 + 0.15 + 0.25 − 0.05)/4 = 0.1
[b] (0.2 + 0.1 + (−0.1) + 0.3)/4 = 0.125

Therefore, $\text{Cov}(R_A, R_B) = [(-0.00375) + (-0.00125) + (-0.03375) + (-0.02625)]/4 \cong -0.01625.$

Both covariance and correlation measure the association between the rates of return on two assets. When the covariance is positive, the correlation also will be positive, and vice versa. The advantage of correlation, though, is that it is an absolute number ranging between -1 and $+1$, and it is not in units, such as dollars or percentages. Thus, correlations are directly comparable. For example, if the correlation between rates of return of stocks A and B is 0.8 and the correlation between rates of return of stocks C and D is 0.6, we can state with confidence that stocks A and B have a stronger positive dependency. If there is a *perfect positive association* between rates of return, then the correlation is $+1$. If there is a *perfect negative association*, the correlation is (-1). If the rates of return are unrelated (that is, uncorrelated), the correlation is zero.

Let us calculate the correlation coefficient for the data given in Exhibit 6.6. The standard deviations are as follows:

$$\sigma_A = \left[\frac{(-0.05)^2 + (0.05)^2 + (-0.15)^2 + (0.15)^2}{4} \right]^{\frac{1}{2}} = 0.0125^{\frac{1}{2}} \cong 0.1118$$

$$\sigma_B = \left[\frac{(-0.10)^2 + (0.00)^2 + (-0.30)^2 + (0.40)^2}{4} \right]^{\frac{1}{2}} = 0.065^{\frac{1}{2}} \cong 0.255$$

Thus, the correlation coefficient for stocks A and B, recalling that the covariance was previously found to be $\text{Cov}(R_A, R_B) = 0.0275$ (see Exhibit 6.6), is

$$\rho_{A,B} = \frac{0.0275}{0.1118 \times 0.255} \cong 0.965$$

Thus, we can conclude that the rates of return of stocks A and B have a strong positive dependency of almost $+1$. The correlation is close to a perfect positive one (of $+1$) despite the fact that the covariance is very small. Thus, the covariance is needed to calculate the correlation, but only the latter can measure the intensity of the association between the rates of return on the two assets. (Now look at the Practice Box on p. 181.)

6.5 THE PORTFOLIO VARIANCE

As in the expected return of a portfolio, the **variance** of a portfolio can also be calculated in two ways. With the first method, the rates of return on the portfolio are calculated for each period (year), and then the variance formula, as in the single asset case, is employed on the portfolio rates of return. Alternatively, one can employ a specific portfolio's variance formula, which will be discussed below, to calculate the portfolio's variance. Both methods are useful. The first method is easy to compute, whereas employing a formula for the portfolio variance calculation has the advantage of demonstrating the relationship between the portfolio variance and individual asset variances as well as the correlation between assets. Using a formula to calculate the portfolio's variance also has an advantage if one wishes to calculate the variance of various portfolios with various diversification strategies (weights). The variance of a portfolio can be calculated *directly* from the portfolio's rates of return, as shown in Exhibit 6.7 on p. 182. To calculate the portfolio's variance directly, one has to first compute the rates of return on the portfolio for each year. For example, in year 1 for portfolio 1, the rate of return is

$$R_p = \tfrac{1}{2}(0.05) + \tfrac{1}{2}(0.10) = 0.075 (\text{Year 1})$$

PRACTICE BOX

Problem
Suppose you are given the following information about stocks A and B. Calculate the correlation coefficient.

State of the economy	Probability	Rates of return	
		R_A	R_B
Growth	$\frac{1}{2}$	0.15	0.30
Stable	$\frac{1}{4}$	0.10	0.05
Recession	$\frac{1}{4}$	0.05	0.10

Solution
Following the procedures outlined in Exhibit 6.6, based on Rule 5 and Equation 6.2, construct the following table:

State of the economy	Probability	R_A	R_B	$R_A - E(R_A)$	$R_B - E(R_B)$	$(R_A - ER_A)(R_B - ER_B)$
Growth	$\frac{1}{2}$	0.15	0.30	0.0375	0.1125	0.00422
Stable	$\frac{1}{4}$	0.10	0.05	−0.0125	−0.1375	0.00172
Recession	$\frac{1}{4}$	0.05	0.10	−0.0625	−0.0875	0.00546
Expected value		0.1125	0.1875			

From Rule 5, the covariance is

$$\text{Cov}(R_A, R_B) = 0.25 \times 0.00422 + 0.25 \times 0.00172 + 0.25 \times 0.00546 = 0.00391$$

And the variances are as follows:

$$\sigma_A^2 = 0.5(0.15 - 0.1125)^2 + 0.25(0.1 - 0.1125)^2 + 0.25(0.05 - 0.1125)^2 = 0.00172$$

$$\sigma_B^2 = 0.5(0.3 - 0.1875)^2 + 0.25(0.05 - 0.1875)^2 + 0.25(0.1 - 0.1875)^2 \cong 0.0130$$

Therefore, the standard deviations are

$$\sigma_A = 0.00172^{\frac{1}{2}} \cong 0.04147$$

$$\sigma_B = 0.0130^{\frac{1}{2}} \cong 0.1140$$

Thus, the correlation coefficient (see Equation 6.2) is

$$\rho_{A,B} = \frac{0.00391}{0.04147 \times 0.1140} \cong 0.827$$

We see that stocks A and B are highly positively correlated. This is not surprising, because when growth occurs, which is likely (a 50% chance), both stocks are up, and when a stable economy or a recession occurs, both stocks are below their means. The relationship is not perfect, hence the correlation is less than +1.

Exhibit 6.7 Rates of return on Assets A and B and on various portfolios

		Individual asset		Portfolios		
				1	2	3
Year	Probability	A	B	$\frac{1}{2}A + \frac{1}{2}B$	$\frac{1}{5}A + \frac{4}{5}B$	$\frac{4}{5}A + \frac{1}{5}B$
1	$\frac{1}{3}$	0.05	0.10	0.075	0.09	0.06
2	$\frac{1}{3}$	0.10	0.05	0.075	0.06	0.09
3	$\frac{1}{3}$	0.15	0.30	0.225	0.27	0.18
Expected rate of return		0.1	0.15	0.125	0.14	0.11
Variance		0.00167[a]	0.01167	0.005[b]	0.0086	0.0026

Demonstrations of some of the calculations:

[a] $\frac{1}{3}(0.05 - 0.10)^2 + \frac{1}{3}(0.10 - 0.10)^2 + \frac{1}{3}(0.15 - 0.10)^2 = 0.00167$

[b] $\frac{1}{3}(0.075 - 0.125)^2 + \frac{1}{3}(0.075 - 0.125)^2 + \frac{1}{3}(0.225 - 0.125)^2 = 0.005$

Similarly, the rates of return of portfolio 1 for years 2 and 3 are found to be

$$R_p = \tfrac{1}{2}(0.10) + \tfrac{1}{2}(0.05) = 0.075 (\text{Year 2})$$

$$R_p = \tfrac{1}{2}(0.15) + \tfrac{1}{2}(0.30) = 0.225 (\text{Year 3})$$

Now the variance of portfolio 1 can be calculated using the single asset formula given in Chapter 5:

$$\sigma_p^2 = \tfrac{1}{3}(0.075 - 0.125)^2 + \tfrac{1}{3}(0.075 - 0.125)^2 + \tfrac{1}{3}(0.225 - 0.125)^2 = 0.005$$

Calculating the portfolio variance by this direct method is straightforward, because the portfolio is treated like any other single asset. Once a series of returns on the portfolio and the corresponding probabilities have been determined, the variance can be easily calculated. (See portfolios 2 and 3 in Exhibit 6.7.)

Calculating first the returns on the portfolio and then the variance of the portfolio as shown in Exhibit 6.7 is very simple. However, for each possible diversification strategy (or weighting of assets A and B), one has first to calculate the portfolio's returns and only then the variance of the portfolio. Moreover, the role of the correlation in determining the portfolio's variance is not transparent. Therefore, we also employ a formula to calculate the portfolio's variance which yields exactly the same result obtained above in Exhibit 6.7, but the role of the correlation in determining the portfolio's variance is explicitly shown.

This formula is given in Equation 6.3 below.

Rule 7: The two-asset portfolio's variance is given by:

$$\sigma_p^2 = w_A^2\,\sigma_A^2 + w_B^2\,\sigma_B^2 + 2w_A w_B \rho_{A,B}\,\sigma_A \sigma_B \qquad (6.3)$$

where w_A and w_B are the weights of these two assets in the portfolio. Because $\rho_{A,B}\,\sigma_A\,\sigma_B$ = $\text{Cov}(R_A, R_B)$ (see Equation 6.2), one can use $\text{Cov}(R_A, R_B)$ rather than $\rho_{A,B}\,\sigma_A\sigma_B$ in the calculation.

To employ Equation 6.3 on the data of Exhibit 6.7, let us first calculate the covariance of R_A and R_B. The covariance is given by

$$\text{Cov}(R_A, R_B) = [(0.05 - 0.10)(0.10 - 0.15) + (0.10 - 0.10)(0.05 - 0.15)$$

$$+ (0.15 - 0.10)(0.30 - 0.15)]/3 \cong 0.00333$$

Exhibit 6.8 The portfolio variance of the three portfolios in Exhibit 6.7

Portfolio	Allocations (strategy)	$w_A^2\sigma_A^2$	$w_B^2\sigma_B^2$	$2w_Bw_B\text{Cov}(R_A,R_B)$	$=\sigma_p^2$
1	$\frac{1}{2}A+\frac{1}{2}B$	$(\frac{1}{2})^2\,0.00167+$	$(\frac{1}{2})^2\,0.01167+$	$2(\frac{1}{2})(\frac{1}{2})\,0.00333$	$=0.005$
2	$\frac{1}{5}A+\frac{4}{5}B$	$(\frac{1}{5})^2\,0.00167+$	$(\frac{4}{5})^2\,0.01167+$	$2(\frac{1}{5})(\frac{4}{5})\,0.00333$	$=0.0086$
3	$\frac{4}{5}A+\frac{1}{5}B$	$(\frac{4}{5})^2\,0.00167+$	$(\frac{1}{5})^2\,0.01167+$	$2(\frac{4}{5})(\frac{1}{5})\,0.00333$	$=0.0026$

Because $\text{Cov}(R_A, R_B) = \rho_{A,B}\sigma_A\sigma_B$ (see Equation 6.2), we can employ $\text{Cov}(R_A, R_B)$ in the portfolio variance as demonstrated in Exhibit 6.8.

Exhibit 6.8 first shows numerically that Equation 6.3 indeed yields the same variance as the direct calculation given in Exhibit 6.7. To be more specific, Exhibit 6.8 demonstrates that this equation is indeed the correct equation for the three portfolios under consideration, as given in Exhibit 6.7. Namely, when we calculate the variance directly from the portfolio's return, as is done in Exhibit 6.7, or by applying Equation 6.3 (see Exhibit 6.8), we get the same results.

In the rest of the book we calculate the portfolio's variance either as demonstrated in Exhibit 6.7 or by employing Equation 6.3. (Now look at the Practice Box on p. 184.)

6.6 THE GAINS FROM DIVERSIFICATION

6.6.1 The gain with two risky assets

Suppose that you have two stocks with the following expected return and standard deviations:

	Stock A	Stock B
Expected return	10%	30%
Standard deviation	20%	40%

The correlation between the return on these two stocks is $\rho_{A,B} = -\frac{1}{2}$. Employing Equation 6.3, the portfolio's variance is given by:

$$\sigma_p^2 = \left[w_A^2(20)^2 + w_B^2(40)^2 + 2w_Aw_B(-\tfrac{1}{2})\times 20\times 40 \right]^{1/2}$$

One can change the investment proportions w_A and w_B to obtain various possible portfolios with various expected returns and standard deviations. Exhibit 6.9(b) reveals these calculations (see column corresponding to a correlation of $-\frac{1}{2}$) and Exhibit 6.9(c) shows all these portfolios in the mean standard deviation space (see curve 4).

All portfolios located on curve AMB are possible, i.e. there are diversification strategies (w_A, w_B) which yield all the portfolios located on AMB. However, as we can see, only the segment MB is *efficient*, while the segment AM is *inefficient*, and for every inefficient portfolio located on segment AM there is at least one portfolio on segment MB with the same standard deviation and a higher expected rate of return (for example, portfolio C is superior to portfolio C'). Thus, investors will choose either to buy stock B or to diversify between A and B, but not to invest solely in A which is located on the

PRACTICE BOX

Problem

Recalculate the variance of the portfolio $\frac{1}{2}B + \frac{1}{2}C$ (portfolio 1) given in Exhibit 6.3, with the following change: the probability of growth is $\frac{1}{2}$ and the probabilities of a stable economy or a recession are $\frac{1}{4}$ each. Carry out a direct calculation as in Exhibit 6.7, and then apply Equation 6.3. Do you get the same result?

Solution

The calculation by the direct method results in the following (note the change in the expected rate of return):

$$\sigma_p^2 = \tfrac{1}{4}(0.20 - 0.1625)^2 + \tfrac{1}{4}(0.10 - 0.1625)^2 + \tfrac{1}{4}(0.15 - 0.1625)^2 \cong 0.0017$$

where the rates of return on the portfolio

$$E \text{ growth} = 0.20 = \tfrac{1}{2}(0.10) + \tfrac{1}{2}(0.30)$$

$$E \text{ stable} = 0.10 = \tfrac{1}{2}(0.05) + \tfrac{1}{2}(0.15)$$

$$E \text{ recession} = 0.15 = \tfrac{1}{2}(0.15) + \tfrac{1}{2}(0.15)$$

and portfolio 1's expected rate of return is $\frac{1}{2}(0.20) + \frac{1}{4}(0.10) + \frac{1}{4}(0.15) = 0.1625$.

Using Equation 6.3, we first have to find the variances and covariances with the new probabilities. We find:

$\sigma_B^2 = \tfrac{1}{2}(0.10 - 0.10)^2 + \tfrac{1}{4}(0.05 - 0.10)^2 + \tfrac{1}{4}(0.15 - 0.10)^2 = 0.00125$

$\sigma_c^2 = \tfrac{1}{2}(0.30 - 0.225)^2 + \tfrac{1}{4}(0.15 - 0.225)^2 \cong 0.00563$

$Cov(R_B, R_C) = \tfrac{1}{2}[(0.10 - 0.10)(0.30 - 0.20)] + \tfrac{1}{4}[(0.05 - 0.10)(0.15 - 0.20)]$
$\qquad\qquad + \tfrac{1}{4}[(0.15 - 0.10)(0.15 - 0.20)] = 0$

hence $\rho_{A,B} = 0$ (see Equation 6.2).

Substituting these results into Equation 6.3, we have

$\sigma_p^2 = (\tfrac{1}{2})^2 0.00125 + (\tfrac{1}{2})^2 0.00563 + 2 \times \tfrac{1}{2} \times \tfrac{1}{2} \times 0$
$\quad = 0.0003 + 0.0014 = 0.0017$

which yields identical results to the calculation by the direct method.

---

inefficient frontier. In Exhibit 6.9(b) we add a few columns where the portfolio standard deviation is calculated under various assertions regarding $\rho_{A,B} = -1, \frac{1}{2}, 0$ or 1.

As we can see from Exhibit 6.9(c) all efficient frontiers form a parabola, apart from the case of a perfect negative and perfect positive correlation. In all cases M denotes the portfolio with the minimum possible standard deviation, called the *minimum variance portfolio* or MVP.[4] We can conclude the following from Exhibits 6.9(b) and (c):

1 As expected, the lower the correlation the more to the left is the location of the efficient frontier. This implies that the lower the correlation, the greater the gain from diversification.

2 If $\rho_{A,B} = -1$, we can reduce the portfolio risk to zero if the appropriate investment proportions are selected.

---

[4] The MVP is obtained by $w_A = \dfrac{\sigma_A^2 - \sigma_A\sigma_B\rho_{A,B}}{\sigma_A^2 + \sigma_B^2 - 2\sigma_A\sigma_B\rho_{A,B}}$

Exhibit 6.9 The efficient frontier and the efficient curve for various correlations

(a) The data

	Mean	Standard deviation
Stock A	0.1	0.2
Stock B	0.3	0.4

(b) The means and standard deviations of various portfolios

W_A	W_B	Portfolio mean	Portfolio standard deviation				
			Correlation				
			−1	−0.5	0	0.5	1
0	1	0.30	0.400	0.400	0.400	0.400	0.400
0.1	0.9	0.28	0.340	0.350	0.361	0.370	0.380
0.2	0.8	0.26	0.280	0.302	0.322	0.342	0.360
0.3	0.7	0.24	0.220	0.255	0.286	0.314	0.340
0.4	0.6	0.22	0.160	0.212	0.253	0.288	0.320
0.5	0.5	0.20	0.100	0.173	0.224	0.265	0.300
0.6	0.4	0.18	0.040	0.144	0.200	0.243	0.280
0.7	0.3	0.16	0.020	0.131	0.184	0.225	0.260
0.8	0.2	0.14	0.080	0.139	0.179	0.212	0.240
0.9	0.1	0.12	0.140	0.164	0.184	0.203	0.220
1	0	0.10	0.200	0.200	0.200	0.200	0.200

(c) The efficient frontier for various correlations

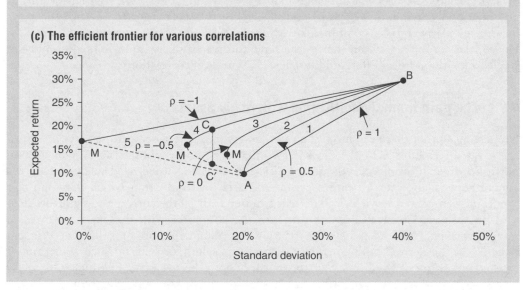

To see the latter point, recall that the portfolio variance in the case of $\rho_{A,B} = -1$ is reduced to (see Equation 6.3):

$$\sigma_P^2 = w_A^2\sigma_A^2 + w_B^2\sigma_B^2 - 2w_Aw_B\sigma_A\sigma_B$$

which can be rewritten as

$$\sigma_P^2 = (w_A\sigma_A - w_B\sigma_B)^2, \text{ or } \sigma_P = w_A\sigma_A - w_B\sigma_B$$

To have $\sigma_p = 0$ we must have

$$w_A\sigma_A = w_B\sigma_B, \text{ or } \frac{w_A}{w_B} = \frac{\sigma_B}{\sigma_A}$$

In our specific example,

$$\sigma_B = 40\% \text{ and } \sigma_A = 20\%, \text{ hence } \frac{w_A}{w_B} = \frac{40\%}{20\%} = 2$$

Because $w_B + w_A = 1$ we have

$$\frac{w_A}{1 - w_A} = 2, \text{ or } w_A = 2 - 2w_A, \text{ or } 3w_A = 2; \text{ hence } w_A = \tfrac{2}{3} \text{ and } w_B = \tfrac{1}{3}.$$

Indeed, for this investment proportion we obtain:[5]

$$\sigma_p^2 = (\tfrac{2}{3})^2 \times 20^2 + (\tfrac{1}{3})^2 \times 40^2 - 2(\tfrac{2}{3})(\tfrac{1}{3})(-1) \times 20 \times 40$$

$$= \frac{4}{9} \times 400 + \frac{1}{9} \times 1600 + \left(-\frac{4}{9}\right) \times 20 \times 40$$

$$= \frac{1600}{9} + \frac{1600}{9} - \frac{3200}{9} = 0$$

Exhibit 6.10 presents the efficient frontier of two pairs: General Motors (GM) and Ford (F), and alternatively GM and Philip Morris (MO). As can be expected, the correlation between GM and Ford is positive and high ($\rho = 0.73$) while it is negative (-0.27) between GM and MO. Indeed, the gain from diversification is much larger when one diversifies between stocks of unrelated industries (GM and MO). We see that for almost any portfolio combination of Ford and GM there is a better portfolio (with the same mean and a lower risk) combined of MO and GM (compare portfolios C and C'). Hence, the common wisdom that if you have to diversify between a limited number of stocks, pick them from different industries, i.e. with low correlations.

6.6.2 The gain from diversification with many assets

Suppose now that there are more than two assets (e.g. five assets whose rates of return are given in Exhibit 6.11). As in the two-assets case, we obtain the efficient set of portfolio diversification. To obtain the efficient frontier, all we need to do is feed the computer with the rates of return on the n assets involved, from which the computer program is employed to yield the efficient frontier with all the corresponding diversification portfolios. Alternatively, one can feed the computer with the expected rates of return, variances and all pairs of correlations to obtain the same results. The efficient frontier can be derived with constraint of no short selling or with no such constraint, a case where some of the investment proportions may be negative. Exhibits 6.11(a)–(e) below show the rates of return on five stocks for the years 1989–98 (the input to the efficient frontier calculation) as well as the computer output: the investment proportions of five points on the frontier (one can add any number of points) and the resulting efficient frontier curve, with and without short sales.

---

[5] If the correlation is $+1$, one can also achieve zero portfolio variance with the proportions $\frac{w_A}{w_B} = -\frac{\sigma_B}{\sigma_A}$ (in this case, one's assets must be sold short to obtain a zero variance portfolio).

Exhibit 6.10 Two efficient frontiers and two-stocks portfolio

(a) The data

	GM	Ford	Philip Morris
Expected return	0.156	0.24	0.249
Standard deviation	0.3	0.37	0.263

	Correlation
$R_{(GM,F)}$	0.73
$R_{(GM,MO)}$	−0.27

(b) The efficient frontiers

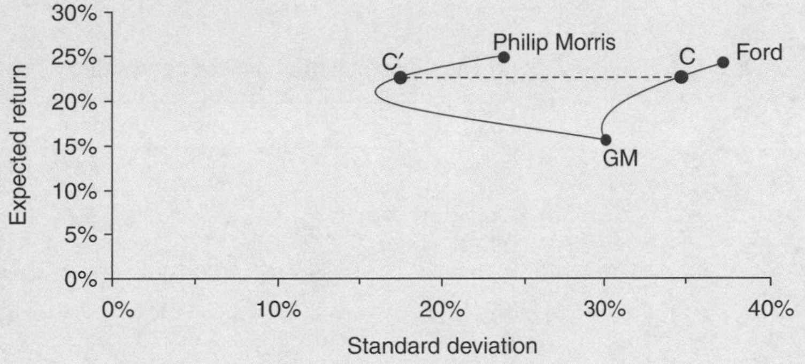

6.6.3 The gain from diversification due to the riskless asset

Suppose that you can diversify between asset A and the riskless asset whose rate of return is r. Thus, the expected rate of return on such a portfolio is

$$E(R_p) = w_A\, E(A) + w_r\, r$$

where $w_A + w_r = 1$. Because r is constant, it has a zero variance and zero correlation with R_A; hence by Equation 6.3 the portfolio variance $\sigma_{R_p}^2$ is reduced to:

$$\sigma_{R_p}^2 = w_A^2\, \sigma_A^2$$

Therefore, the standard deviation is $\sigma_{R_p} = w_A\, \sigma_A$.

By changing the investment proportion w_A, many portfolios with $E(R_p)$ and σ_{R_p} are obtained. Are these portfolios located on a curve as in Exhibit 6.11(e)? No! Because r is constant, all these portfolios are located on a straight line. To see this, employ the portfolio standard deviation formula to isolate $w_A = \sigma_{R_p}/\sigma_A$ and substitute it in the expected return formula to obtain

$$E(R_p) = \left[\frac{\sigma_{R_p}}{\sigma_A}\right] \times E(A) + \left(1 - \frac{\sigma_{R_p}}{\sigma_A}\right) \times r$$

(recall that $w_r = 1 - w_A = 1 - \dfrac{\sigma_{R_p}}{\sigma_A}$), which can be rewritten as:

$$E(R_p) = r + \frac{E(A) - r}{\sigma_A}\, \sigma_{R_p}$$

Exhibit 6.11
The efficient frontiers with and without short sales

(a) Rates of return

Year	UK	AMR	GE	MO	GM
1989	−0.195	−0.105	0.328	0.439	−0.024
1990	−0.094	0.023	0.062	0.521	−0.063
1991	0.282	0.292	0.266	0.412	−0.078
1992	0.923	−0.110	0.102	0.008	0.212
1993	0.562	0.139	0.316	−0.154	0.653
1994	0.027	−0.218	−0.015	0.064	−0.355
1995	0.690	0.354	0.532	0.604	0.388
1996	0.096	0.059	0.378	0.338	0.155
1997	−0.018	0.571	0.523	0.086	0.076
1998	−0.080	−0.071	0.373	0.174	0.595
Mean	0.219	0.094	0.286	0.249	0.156
SD	0.361	0.234	0.176	0.236	0.300

(b) The efficient portfolios with short sales

	Portfolio				
	1	2	3	4	5
Expected return	0.7815	0.6822	0.5629	0.4238	0.2648
Sigma	0.3198	0.2706	0.2155	0.1622	0.1342
X_{UK}	0.5309	0.4797	0.4028	0.3131	0.2106
X_{AMR}	−1.9085	−1.6077	−1.1565	−0.6301	−0.0284
X_{GE}	3.5580	3.0627	2.3198	1.4530	0.4625
X_{MO}	−0.0849	−0.0181	0.0822	0.1992	0.3329
X_{GM}	−1.0955	−0.9166	−0.6483	−0.3352	0.0225
Total	1	1	1	1	1

(c) The efficient frontier with short sales

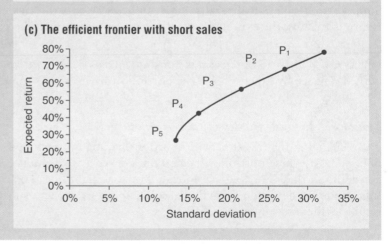

This is a straight-line formula with an intercept r with the vertical axis and a slope $[(E(A) - r]/\sigma_A$. All portfolios located on such a line with (R_p, σ_{R_p}) can be achieved by changing w_A. Exhibit 6.12 demonstrates such a line connecting asset A and the riskless asset r.

**Exhibit 6.11
(continued)**

(d) The efficient portfolios without short sales

	Portfolio					
	1	2	3	4	5	6
Expected return	0.2669	0.2676	0.2696	0.2739	0.2759	0.2864
Sigma	0.1366	0.1372	0.1393	0.1456	0.1491	0.1763
X_{UK}	0.1415	0.1355	0.1176	0.0797	0.0629	0.0000
X_{AMR}	0.0000	0.0000	0.0000	0.0000	0.0000	0.0000
X_{GE}	0.5904	0.6041	0.6444	0.7298	0.7675	1.0000
X_{MO}	0.2681	0.2604	0.2380	0.1905	0.1696	0.0000
X_{GM}	0.0000	0.0000	0.0000	0.0000	0.0000	0.0000
Total	1	1	1	1	1	1

(e) The efficient frontier without short sales

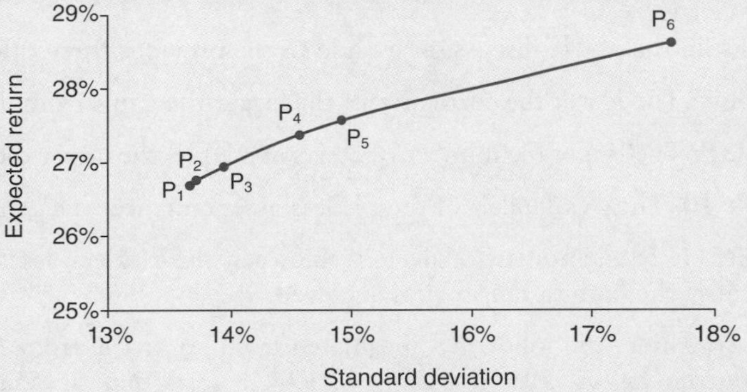

Suppose now that there is another asset B which can be mixed with the riskless asset. It is easy to see that a diversification between B and r is better than a diversification of A and r because a line with a higher slope is achieved. Thus, for any portfolio located on line rA there is a better portfolio on line rB (compare portfolios C′ and C).

By the same logic the investor's goal is to find a line with the maximum slope. Therefore, the best strategy is to diversify between portfolio m and r because by such a diversification the line with the highest possible slope is obtained. With portfolio m we obtain the line:

$$E(R_p) = r + \frac{E(m) - r}{\sigma_m} \sigma_p. \tag{6.4}$$

This line is called the *capital market line* (CML), and portfolio m, the tangency portfolio of the efficient frontier and the straight line rising from point r, is called the *market portfolio*. As we can see, for any portfolio located on the efficient frontier OMF (see Exhibit 6.12) there is a better portfolio on line rr' (e.g. portfolio D′ dominates portfolio D). Hence, by adding the riskless asset, the investor's welfare is enhanced.

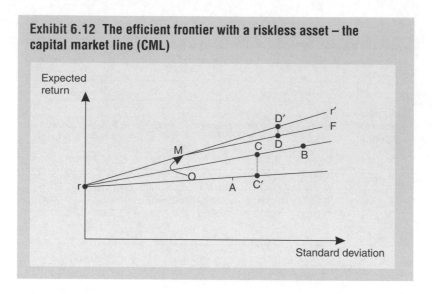

Exhibit 6.12 The efficient frontier with a riskless asset – the capital market line (CML)

From the above discussion we add to the previous three rules, the following rules:

Rule 8: The lower the correlations, the larger the gains from diversification.

Rule 9: The larger the number of assets available, the larger the gain from diversification.

Rule 10: The availability of the riskless asset enhances the gain from diversification.

Rule 11: It is optimal to diversify between the riskless asset and the market portfolio because the highest tangency is achieved.

To conclude, the following lines taken from an article from *Risk Analysis*, while examining the 1990s crisis (Russia, Mexico), asserts that the main tool to use in order to hedge against this crisis is diversification:

> '....we must realize that some crises will occur without even a reasonable basis to anticipate their possibility. In such cases, the surest source of protection is diversification. While history indicates that periodic crises are inevitable, it also indicates that they don't strike all markets and all regions at the same time. The key is to be sure that no one crisis event, no matter how unlikely, can do irreparable damage to one's institution. But be aware that correlations generally behave differently in a crisis than in day-to-day market fluctuations. Psychological contagion is a product of crisis and its behaviour is not well represented by data from more normal times. As a result, a critical eye is needed to assure that apparent diversification will hold up when markets experience extreme stress.'

Source: *Risk Analysis*, December 1999, p. 57.

SUMMARY

■ *Explain the difference between asset risk when held alone and asset risk when held in a portfolio.*

When an asset is held with other assets in a portfolio, that asset's risk depends not only on the asset's variance but also on the degree of dependency with other assets. When two assets are perfectly negatively correlated, each asset could be very risky in isolation, but when placed together with the correct weights, a riskless portfolio can be created. The dependency among assets plays an important role in determining the portfolio's risk and hence in determining the risk premium.

■ *Discuss the expected rate of return and variance of a portfolio.*
The expected rate of return of a portfolio is the sum of the weights (proportions) invested in an asset times the expected return on that asset, where we sum for all assets. The formula for the variance of a portfolio is much more complicated: the variance of a portfolio is a function of the proportions invested in each asset, the variance of each asset, and the covariances (or correlations) among assets.

■ *Explain covariances and correlation coefficients between assets.*
Covariances (or correlation coefficients) measure the degree of dependency between two assets. The correlation coefficient, ρ, is a number such that $-1 \leq \rho \leq 1$: the higher the ρ, the higher the degree of dependency between the assets. The covariance (or correlation) plays a major role in determining a portfolio's variance.

■ *Explain the role of correlation within a portfolio.*
When everything else is held constant, the lower the correlation of each pair of assets included in a portfolio, the lower the portfolio's variance will be. Low variance is an attractive feature to risk-averse investors.

■ *Explain the effect of the number of assets on the gain from diversification.*
The larger the number of assets in the portfolio, the larger the gain from diversification.

■ *Explain the importance of the riskless asset in deriving the CML.*
Diversification between the riskless asset and a risky asset creates a straight line from which each investor could select the portfolio. The line with the highest slope is called the capital market line (CML).

KEY TERMS

Correlation	Market portfolio	Portfolio
Covariance	Minimum variance	Portfolio expected return
Efficient frontier	portfolio (MVP)	Variance

QUESTIONS

6.1 Suppose you are given the following information regarding the rates of return on three assets:

State of the economy	Scenario probability	Asset		
		A	B	C
1	$\frac{1}{3}$	5%	10%	30%
2	$\frac{1}{3}$	5	5	15
3	$\frac{1}{3}$	5	15	15

Calculate the expected return, variance and standard deviation for each asset, as well as the covariances and correlation coefficients.

The following are daily price data for four stocks, which will be used for Questions 2 through 5.

Day	A	B	C	D
1	616.4000	23.0000	74.6250	59.0000
2	617.4600	22.5000	74.0000	58.1250
3	621.3200	22.8750	74.8750	59.8750
4	614.1600	22.6250	75.0000	58.7500
5	625.6200	22.1250	74.0000	57.3750

6.2 Calculate the daily rates of return for Stocks A, B, C and D.

6.3 Calculate the average rate of return, variance and standard deviation for Stocks A, B and C.

6.4 Calculate the covariance and correlation coefficient for Stocks B and C.

6.5 Suppose you had $100,000 to invest in B and C. Calculate the expected rate of return and standard deviation of a portfolio in which an equal dollar amount is invested in each security.

6.6 Suppose you invested 30% in Asset A, which returned 40%; invested 25% in Asset B, which returned −10%; and invested 45% in Asset C, which returned 15%. What was the rate of return on the portfolio?

6.7 Repeat Question 6.6, except assume that instead of rates of return, the returns given are *expected* rates of return. Thus, calculate the expected rate of return on this portfolio.

6.8 'Correlation does not really reduce the risk of a portfolio, because the underlying securities remain risky.' Evaluate this statement, and defend your answer using a portfolio of two securities with identical standard deviations of 30% and in which 50% is invested in each security.

6.9 Prove that the covariance of Asset X with $\frac{1}{2}$ X is equal to one-half the variance of Asset X.

6.10 Calculate the variance of a portfolio that is equally divided among four uncorrelated assets with standard deviation of 10%, 20%, 30% and 40%.

6.11 The following are the rates of return on Assets A and B:

Year	R_A	R_B
1	−10%	+10%
2	20	17
3	−2	0
4	4	8
5	12	19

(a) What is the rate of return on the portfolio if Year 4 occurs and when $w_A = \frac{1}{5}$ and $w_B = \frac{4}{5}$? How would you change your answer if the investment weights were $w_A = \frac{1}{2}$ and $w_B = \frac{1}{2}$?

(b) If each year has a probability of $\frac{1}{5}$, calculate the portfolio mean and variance when $w_A = \frac{1}{2}$ and $w_B = \frac{1}{2}$. First do the calculations by constructing the portfolio rates of return and calculating the mean and variance of these rates of return. Then do the calculations by employing Equation 6.3 in the text. Which method is easier?

6.12 You have two stocks, A and B, with $\sigma_A = 10\%$ and $\sigma_B = 20\%$. The investment proportions in a portfolio are $w_A = w_B = \frac{1}{2}$. It is known that the portfolio standard deviation is $\sigma_p = 5\%$. What is the covariance, or $Cov(R_A, R_B)$?

6.13 You have two stocks with the following rates of return:

Year	R_A	R_B
1	+10%	+10%
2	−5	−5
3	15	15

The probability of each year is $\frac{1}{3}$.

(a) Calculate the correlation between Stock A and Stock B.

(b) Calculate the variance of a portfolio composed of $w_A = \frac{1}{2}$ and $w_B = \frac{1}{2}$. Calculate the variance of a portfolio composed of $w_A = \frac{1}{5}$ and $w_B = \frac{4}{5}$. Explain your results.

SELECTED REFERENCES

See Chapter 5.

Part III

BONDS AND STOCKS

Chapter 7

INTEREST RATES AND BOND VALUATION

Learning objectives

After studying this chapter you should be able to:

1 Construct and interpret a yield curve.

2 Use the bond pricing equation to find bond prices and bond yields.

3 Summarize the theories that explain the shape and level of yield curves.

4 Describe the behaviour of the spread over Treasuries.

5 Describe the impact of the call feature and the convertible feature on bond prices.

INVESTMENT IN THE NEWS

Dark day for shares boosts bonds

Government bonds rose in the US and Europe yesterday as investors continued to pull money out of equity markets and shift it to the safety of government debt.

In midday trading on Wall Street, the 10-year **US** Treasury was up $\frac{19}{32}$ to $102\frac{11}{32}$, pushing its yield down to 4.69 per cent. The 30-year bond rose $\frac{27}{32}$ to $102\frac{7}{32}$, yielding 5.22 per cent, while the two-year note gained $\frac{5}{32}$ to $100\frac{29}{32}$, yielding 4.12 per cent.

The buying was triggered by another dark day for equity markets. The Dow Jones Industrial Average was down 305 points at mid-day, falling into 'bear market' territory, while the Nasdaq lost 29 points.

The losses piled up as disappointment lingered over the Federal Reserve's cutting short-term interest rates by only 50 basis points on Tuesday. Many investors had predicted the Fed would cut rates by 75bp amid the turmoil in equity markets.

Bond prices were also boosted by the Treasury's buy-back of $1.75bn in long-term securities as part of its plan to reduce the national debt.

Euro-zone government bond prices also surged yesterday, pushing yields to their lowest in two years.

Bond investors benefited from a combination of weak equity prices and the expectation of an interest rate cut from the European Central Bank.

Following the release of weak German Ifo index data on Wednesday, French economic growth was revised downwards.

There were also signs of weakening consumer confidence in the Netherlands. Some analysts expect a rate cut from the European Central Bank within weeks, following comments by its president, Wim Duisenberg, about the impact of the US slowdown.

The 10-year **German bund** future rose 52 to 110.40 in heavy trading volumes. In the crash market the two-year **schatz** yield fell 10.8bp to 4.059 per cent, while the 10-year bund yield fell 5.9bp to 4.60 per cent. These are the lowest yields since late 1999.

►

INVESTMENT IN THE NEWS

In the UK, **gilt** prices also rose as the FTSE 100 index followed US stock markets and fell to a 29-month low.

Investors are expecting an interest rate cut from the Bank of England after the Confederation of British Industry said that the slow-down of the US economy could have a more serious impact on the UK than previously thought.

In contrast, Japanese government bond prices fell yesterday on weak demand at a auction of 10-year **JGBs** with a record low coupon.

The government sold ¥1,005bn of 10-year JGBs with a 1.1 per cent coupon, resulting in 1.96 bids per value, down from 2.38 registered at last month's auction of 10-year debt with a 1.4 per cent coupon. The lowest price at Thursday's auction was 110.65.

The leading June JGB futures contract fell to 140.15 after the auction results were released. It closed at 140.42, down 0.18 from Wednesday. The yield on the benchmark 10-year cash JGB rose 0.020 to 1.065 per cent.

Source: Financial Times, 23 March 2001, p. 28.

The *Investment in the news* article illustrates the important relationship between various variables: equity markets, changes in interest rate, gains or losses to investors in bonds, the length of the maturity of bonds and the relative performance of corporate and government bonds. In this chapter, we will discuss the relationship between these variables. In particular, we focus on the relationship between interest rates, a bond's yield (called yield to maturity) and the fluctuations of the bond's price as the yield to maturity changes. We will show that the longer the maturity, the larger the risk involved in the investment in bonds.

7.1 THE YIELD CURVE

7.1.1 The yield

A bond represents borrowing by the bond's issuer and saving by the bond's purchaser. The interest earned on a bond if held to its maturity is called the **yield to maturity**. The demand and supply for bonds with given coupons and par values determine their market prices. A bond's market price, in turn, determines the yield to maturity, which is the percentage profit for the bond buyer and the percentage cost to the bond seller.

Yield to maturity is the annualized discount rate that makes the present value of future cash flows just equal to the current price of the bond. Mathematically, it is calculated from the value of y (that is, the internal rate of return of the bond) in the following equation:

$$P = \sum_{t=1}^{n} \frac{C}{(1 + y)^t} + \frac{\text{Par}}{(1 + y)^n} \tag{7.1}$$

where C is the coupon payment each period, n is the number of periods to maturity, Par is the face value of the bond (payment at maturity), and P is the current market price of the bond.

The yield to maturity is found by applying Rule 1.

Rule 1: Write the cash flow of the bond and calculate the internal rate of return (IRR) of this cash flow (see Appendix A at the end of the book for IRR calculation). The IRR of this cash flow is the bond's yield to maturity. For zero coupon bonds, $C = 0$, hence Equation 7.1 is reduced to:

$$P = \frac{\text{Par}}{(1 + y)^n} \qquad (7.1)'$$

and for a perpetuity bond the par is never paid back and Equation (7.1) is reduced[1] to:

$$P = \sum_{t=1}^{\infty} \frac{C}{(1 + y)^t} = \frac{C}{y} \qquad (7.1)''$$

If coupons are paid annually, then y is the yield to maturity. If coupons are paid semiannually, then the yield to maturity is $(1 + y)^2 - 1$. Thus, the yield to maturity is given on an annual basis. In order to compare profitability on bonds, it is common to state the yield on an annualized basis. Unless stated otherwise, all yields we refer to in the rest of the chapter as well as in the next chapter are annual yields. Because y is the internal rate of return of the bonds, it measures the profit, in percent, to the bondholder provided that the bond is held to maturity. However, if the bond is not held to maturity, the realized rate of return to the bondholder can be very different from the other yield. From Equation 7.1, it seems that lenders, i.e. bond buyers, should choose to lend for time to maturity n with the highest yield to maturity y, because by such a lending policy they obtain the highest annual interest rate (that is, the highest internal rate of return on their investment). For example, the *Financial Times* on 25 January 2002 reported a yield of 4.60% on December 2003 maturity Treasury bonds and a 4.64% yield on 30-year maturity Treasury bonds. So, should all invest in the high-yield bond? Although this is a tempting conclusion, it is generally wrong, because the lending and borrowing decisions are functions not only of the yield but also of the risk of such borrowing – lending activities. The following discussion will elaborate on this point.

The yield curve generally refers to the yield on government bonds, which are default-free. Even in the absence of a risk of bankruptcy, as the time to maturity (n) changes, the yield to maturity (y) that solves Equation 7.1 may change. The **yield curve** is the relationship between the yield to maturity and the time to maturity. That is, ideally C and Par are held constant, and P and y change as n changes.

Exhibit 7.1 illustrates some recent yield curves for US Treasury securities. Exhibit 7.1(a) shows the yield curve for US Treasury securities on 5 August 1997, when it was sloping upwards. The horizontal axis is time to maturity (n), and the vertical axis is yield to maturity (y). Exhibit 7.1(b) shows a flat yield curve as observed on 29 December 1989, and Exhibit 7.1(c) shows an *inverted* yield curve as observed on 31 December 1980, where the yield decreases as the maturity increases. These graphs show that the yield curve can have a wide variety of shapes.

Analysts seek to determine why bonds of different maturities have different yields to maturity (or why equilibrium interest rates are different for different maturities) and in particular the risk involved with each maturity. That is, they try to determine what factors influence the shape of the yield curve. The next section explains these factors.

---

[1] The present value of a perpetuity C is C/y.

Exhibit 7.1 Examples of actual yield curves
(These curves are based only on the most actively traded issues. Market yields on coupon issues due in less than three months are excluded)

(a) Upward-sloping yield curve – yields of Treasury securities, 5 August 1997 (based on closing quotations)

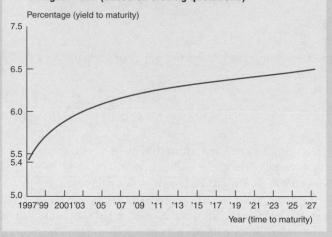

(b) Flat yield curve – yields of Treasury securities, 29 December 1989 (based on closing bid quotations)

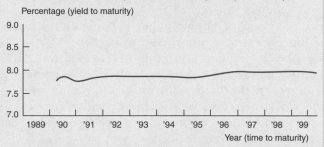

(c) Inverted yield curve – yields of Treasury securities, 31 December 1980 (based on closing bid quotations)

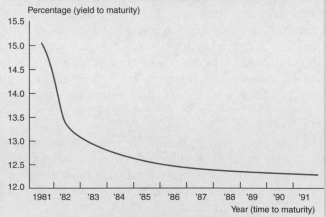

Source: *US Treasury Bulletin* (Washington, DC: Department of the Treasury, various issues).

7.1.2 The risk

Investing in the bond market is not without risks. These risks are a function of the time to maturity of the bond relative to the investor's time horizon. The lender must choose between investing in short-term bonds or long-term bonds. Consider the choices facing young parents who want to invest or lend their money to ensure that their children will have funds to attend college in 15 years' time. Should the parents invest in short-term or long-term bonds? Changing interest rates complicate this decision. If the parents invest over a short period, then they may have to reinvest the money in the near future at a different interest rate, which may be lower. This risk of declining interest rates is known as **reinvestment risk** – the risk to bondholders that in the future they will not be able to reinvest the cash flows they receive from their investment at the same rate they receive today. Of course if one invests in zero-coupon bonds, and no interest is paid, there is no reinvestment risk.

If long-term lenders expect an increase in interest rates in the future, they should lend for the short term only and reinvest later at a higher interest rate. By purchasing long-term bonds, they might miss out on the higher rates should interest rates go up. Long-term bonds would be a poor investment choice when interest rates rose, because the bond's price would decline as a result of an increase in the interest rate. The longer the length to maturity of a bond, the greater the risk exposure to large price declines. To see this, return to Equation 7.1. As y increases, then the larger is n, the larger is the decline in P, thus the larger is the loss to the investor who holds these bonds. This exposure to price declines is known as **price risk**. Bond investors experience price risk because increases in interest rates decrease a bond's price. The opposite effect occurs if the investor expects interest rates to fall. In this case, the lender could benefit by investing in long-term bonds and locking in the current higher interest rate.

To summarize, price risk is the negative effect of a possible increase in interest rates on a bond's value; that is, when rates rise, bond prices fall. Reinvestment risk is the negative effect of a decline in interest rates on the cash flows received when those cash flows must be reinvested at a lower interest rate; that is, when interest rates fall, the interest rate available for future investment of cash flows is lower.

Let's turn to the borrower's viewpoint. Assume that a borrower – maybe a corporation – needs money for long-term investment in profitable capital projects. The corporation faces the choice of borrowing for either a short-term or a long-term period. If a corporation chooses a short-term bond, it may have to refinance the bond at higher interest rates. Note that this is exactly opposite to the problem faced by lenders. If the corporation chooses the long-term bond and interest rates fall, the corporation is paying a higher borrowing rate than would have been required if the financing had been short term.

So far, we have assumed that the lender wanted to invest for a long-term period and the borrower needed the money for a long-term period. In reality, lenders and borrowers want to lend and borrow for varying lengths of time. In addition, the needs of borrowers and lenders change over time. These varied needs within the economy create the demand and supply for bonds of varying maturities. The demand and supply for bonds with different maturities determine the yield curve. For example, if pension funds wish to invest in 30-year maturities, and there is a little supply of this bond, the bond price will go up and the yield will go down (see Equation 7.1). Also, individual long-term borrowers and lenders have different preferences regarding risk and different expectations regarding changes in future interest rates. These are the factors that influence the shape of the yield curve. The next section discusses the various hypotheses regarding the role these factors have in determining the shape of the yield curve.

7.2 EXPLAINING THE SHAPE OF THE YIELD CURVE

The behavior of the yield curve, which is also known as the **term structure of interest rates**, has certain well-known patterns. First, short-term yields are generally more variable than long-term yields. Second, the yield curve is usually upward sloping. Third, inverted or declining yield curves typically occur when the overall level of interest rates is relatively high.

Several hypotheses have been developed in an attempt to explain different yield curve shapes. This section reviews each hypothesis and briefly highlights its strengths and weaknesses. However, first it is necessary to define and explain several concepts related to bonds that are used in the explanation of the shape of the yield curve.

7.2.1 Spot rates, forward rates, forward contracts and holding period rates

The **spot rate** is the yield to maturity of a zero-coupon bond that has a stated maturity, where zero-coupon bonds are sold at a discount from their par value and pay no coupons. For example, if a one-year bond is trading at $90.9 with $100 par value, we say the spot rate is about 10%, or [($100 − $90.9)/$90.9] × 100.

The **forward rate** is the yield to maturity of a zero-coupon bond that an investor agrees to purchase at some future specified date. For example, an investor agrees today to purchase *in one year* at $89.286 a bond that has one year to maturity with a par value of $100. In this case there is no cash flow today, and in one year the investor will pay $89.286 for the bond (regardless of its current market price in a year) and will receive $100 two years from today (or one year from the bond purchase date). The forward rate is about 12%, or [($100 − $89.286)/$89.286] × 100. The forward rates can be used in interpreting the information contained in the yield curve, as will be shown later.

A concept related to the forward rate is the **forward contract,** which is an agreement between a buyer and a seller to trade something in the future at a price negotiated today. A forward contract is obligatory to both the buyer and the seller. For example, a forward contract to buy $1 million of par value of Treasury bills at a 6% discount rate (which determines the bond's price) in six months obligates the buyer to purchase the T-bills at a 6% discount rate; it also obligates the seller to sell the T-bills at the same price. Suppose T-bills are selling for a 7% discount rate in six months when the forward contract matures and the buyer delivers the bills. This means that the T-bills have a lower market price. Recall that when interest rates are up, bond prices are down (that is, there is an inverse relationship between bond prices and yields, see Equation 7.1: when y goes up, p becomes lower). The seller will profit from this transaction, and the buyer will lose, because the buyer is obligated to purchase the T-bills at 6% despite the fact that a 7% rate is available in the market. At a 7% rate, the buyer could purchase the T-bills at the lower market price, but the buyer must buy them at the 6% rate (a higher price) to comply with the forward contract. A range of actively traded forward contracts are available in interest rates, currencies and energy products (such as crude oil or natural gas): see Chapter 12.

Exhibit 7.2 Spot and forward rates for annually compounded, zero-coupon bonds

Maturity (in years, n)	Spot rate (R_n)	Forward rate (f_n) (a contract which starts at year $n-1$ and matures at year n)[a]
1	5%	–
2	5.8	6.606%
3	6.3	7.307
4	6.4	6.701
5	6.45	6.650

[a] $f_2 = [(1 + R_2)^2/(1 + R_1)] - 1 = (1 + 0.058)^2/(1 + 0.05) - 1 \cong 0.06606$
$f_3 = [(1 + R_3)^3/(1 + R_2)^2] - 1 = (1 + 0.063)^3/(1 + 0.058)^2 - 1 \cong 0.07307$
$f_4 = [(1 + R_4)^4/(1 + R_3)^3] - 1 = (1 + 0.064)^4/(1 + 0.063)^3 - 1 \cong 0.06701$
$f_5 = [(1 + R_5)^5/(1 + R_4)^4] - 1 = (1 + 0.0645)^5/(1 + 0.064)^4 - 1 \cong 0.06650$

The forward interest rates can be derived from the spot rates of bonds with various maturities.[2] To see this, consider the numerical example in Exhibit 7.2. The data in the table are spot and forward rates for annually compounded, zero-coupon bonds.[3] The spot and forward rates in this exhibit are equilibrium rates, i.e. the investor is indifferent between various investment strategies, as explained below. A yield curve plotted from these data would slope upwards from 5% for one-year bonds to 6.45% for five-year bonds.

Suppose we wish to invest for two years. Consider the following investment strategies:

- Strategy 1. Invest in a two-year zero-coupon bond and earn 5.8%.
- Strategy 2. Invest in a one-year zero-coupon bond and earn 5%. Also enter into a one-year forward rate agreement (FRA) to invest in one year.

What interest rate on the FRA will make Strategies 1 and 2 equivalent?

It will be the forward rate that results in an overall annual rate of return of 5.8% for two years. To see this, consider investing $1 in each bond, and let R_i denote the spot rate and f_i denote the forward rate for each year, $i = 1, 2$.

- Strategy 1. $\$1(1 + R_2)^2 = \$1(1 + 0.058)^2 = \$1.119364$
- Strategy 2. $\$1(1 + R_1) = \$1(1 + 0.05) = \$1.05$. Then invest $1.05 in the FRA.

The forward rate that makes Strategies 1 and 2 equivalent is $\$1.05(1 + f_2) = \$1.119364$, or $f_2 = 0.06606$, or 6.606%. Thus, in equilibrium we have

$$(1 + R_2)^2 = (1 + R_1)(1 + f_2)$$

Note that if f_2 is higher than 6.606%, all investors will be better off not buying the two-year bond. Its price will fall, and R_2 will go up until the equation $(1 + R_2)^2 = (1 + R_1)(1 + f_2)$ holds. The opposite is true if f_2 is smaller than 6.606%. Similarly, for a three-year period there are three alternative strategies which in equilibrium must yield the same terminal value:

- Strategy 1. Invest in a zero-coupon bond with three years to maturity and earn 6.3%.

[2] A market exists for contracts based on forward interest rates. These contracts are known as forward rate agreements, and they are traded in the over-the-counter market primarily between banks.
[3] The following analysis could be conducted with coupon-bearing bonds, but would be slightly more complex.

- Strategy 2. Invest in a one-year zero-coupon bond, enter into a one-year FRA to invest in one year, and enter again into a one-year FRA to invest in two years.
- Strategy 3. Invest in a two-year zero-coupon bond and enter into a one-year FRA to invest in two years.

Following the same analysis as before, the return on all of these strategies must be the same. Hence, we arrive at the following equilibrium:

$$(1 + R_3)^3 = (1 + R_1)(1 + f_2)(1 + f_3)$$

However, because in equilibrium, as we have seen before,

$$(1 + R_2)^2 = (1 + R_1)\ (1 + f_2), \text{ this can be rewritten as}$$

$$(1 + R_3)^3 = (1 + R_2)^2(1 + f_3)$$

and for the given spot rates R_2 and R_3, the equilibrium rate f_3 can be determined.

This type of analysis could be conducted for n periods in order to arrive at the following general expression of equilibrium:

$$(1 + R_n)^n = (1 + R_1)(1 + f_2)(1 + f_3)\ldots(1 + f_n) \tag{7.2}$$

or

$$(1 + R_n)^n = (1 + R_{n-1})^{n-1}(1 + f_n) \tag{7.2'}$$

We can use Equation (7.2)' to calculate the equilibrium forward rate. If we know that the four-year spot rate is 6.4% and the five-year spot rate is 6.45%, then we can solve for the forward rate over the fifth year as follows:

$$(1 + 0.0645)^5 = (1 + 0.064)^4(1 + f_5)$$

Solving for f_5, we find the forward rate to be 6.65% (see Exhibit 7.2).

Thus, one can solve for the forward rate (for the nth year) by applying Rule 2.

Rule 2: Observe the yield to maturity on a zero-coupon bond for n years and for $n - 1$ years. Then, the forward rate for the nth year can be solved by employing Equation (7.2)'.

From Equation 7.2 we see that spot interest rates for various maturities can be thought of as a portfolio of agreements for forward contracts. If the yield curve is upward sloping, then the implied forward rates are higher than the short-term spot rate. Indeed, in the example, we have an upward-sloping yield curve, and we found $f_5 > R_4$, which confirms this assertion. Similarly, if the yield curve is downward sloping, then the implied forward rates are lower than the short-term spot rate. For a flat yield curve, the forward rates are equal to the spot rate.

The final bond-related concept pertinent to the slope of the yield curve is the **holding period rate**, the rate of return earned on a bond by holding it for the next period (see Chapter 4). This rate is different from the yield to maturity, because the price of the bond changes over time. Falling bond prices may cause the holding period rate to be negative. The holding period rate is uncertain, whereas the yield to maturity is a fixed number, given the price.

These basic bond and interest rate concepts can help investors understand the various hypotheses that have been developed to explain yield curves. The discussion begins with the expectations hypothesis.

PRACTICE BOX

Problem

Suppose the 10-year spot interest rate was 8%, and the 11-year spot interest rate was 7.9%. What is the equilibrium forward rate for the eleventh period?

Solution

Using Equation 7.2' and solving for f_n, we have

$$f_n = \frac{(1 + R_n)^n}{(1 + R_{n-1})^{n-1}} - 1$$

Substituting for the spot interest rates, we have

$$f_n = \frac{(1 + R_{11})^{11}}{(1 + R_{10})^{10}} - 1 = \frac{(1 + 0.079)^{11}}{(1 + 0.08)^{10}} - 1$$

$$\cong \frac{2.3080}{2.1589} - 1 \cong 0.069 \text{ or } 6.9\%$$

Once again, notice that the forward rate is less than the 10-year spot rate because the 11-year spot rate is less than the 10-year spot rate.

7.2.2 The expectations hypothesis

The expectations hypothesis, as its name implies, predicts that investors' expectations determine the course of future interest rates. There are two main competing versions of this hypothesis: the local expectations hypothesis and the unbiased expectations hypothesis.

The **local expectations hypothesis (LEH)** states that all bonds (similar in all respects except for their maturities) will have the same expected holding period rate of return. That is, a one-month bond and a 30-year bond should, on average, provide the same rate of return over the next period (e.g. next month). Thus, by this hypothesis, if you wish to invest for one month, on average, you get the same rate of return if you buy a one-month bond and hold it to maturity or buy a 30-year bond and sell it after one month. The LEH doesn't specify the length of the next period.

Empirical evidence consistently rejects this hypothesis. Specifically, holding period returns on longer-term bonds are, on average, significantly different from holding period returns on shorter-term bonds. On average, the holding period rates of return on longer-term bonds are higher and have higher volatility. Hence, longer-term bonds offer greater rewards, yet have higher risk. The LEH doesn't match our observations that investors are risk averse and require higher returns, on average, to take the higher risk related to long-term bonds. Investor risk aversion implies, in turn, that the yield curve, *on average*, will be upward sloping.

The **unbiased expectations hypothesis (UEH)** states that the current implied forward rates are unbiased estimators of future spot interest rates. Therefore, if the yield curve is upward sloping, the UEH states that the market expects the spot rates to rise. For example, from Exhibit 7.2 and the UEH, our best estimate in Year 1 of Year 2's spot rate is for it to rise to 6.606% (the implied forward rate). In contrast, if the yield curve is downward sloping, the UEH states that the market expects rates to fall.

The empirical evidence consistently shows that forward rates are biased predictors of future interest rates. Specifically, forward rates generally overestimate future spot rates.[4] This evidence leads to the next hypothesis, the liquidity preference hypothesis.

7.2.3 The liquidity preference hypothesis

The **liquidity preference hypothesis (LPH)** states that the yield curve should normally be upward sloping, reflecting investors' preferences for the liquidity and lower risk of shorter-term securities. In its purest form, the LPH is not supported by observation of the historical behaviour of the term structure. In fact, on numerous occasions the yield curve has been inverted. However, in real terms the curve may support the LPH. Let us elaborate.

An inverted yield curve does not necessarily contradict the LPH when that hypothesis is combined with the UEH. If nothing is known regarding the future (but interest rates can go up or down with an equal probability), then an upward-sloping yield curve should be expected. Suppose, however, that inflation is so high that it pushes the interest rate to 15% (which in fact occurred in 1980, when interest rates were very high, as shown in Exhibit 7.1(c)). Thus, for short-term bonds, the yield is 15%. However, no one expects this rate of inflation to continue at such a high level for a long period. Hence, for 10-year bonds the yield is only 12.5%, and we observe a decreasing yield curve. Taking these yields and dividing them by the expected inflation rate, the yield curve can be stated in real terms. The resulting real yield curve may be increasing and consistent with the LPH. Thus, the LPH may hold even if there is a decreasing (or inverted) nominal yield curve.

7.2.4 The market segmentations hypothesis

The last hypothesis, the **market segmentations hypothesis (MSH)**, evaluates the yield curve from a slightly different perspective. This hypothesis states that bonds of different maturities trade in separate segmented markets. For example, banks tend to participate exclusively in the short-maturity bond markets, whereas insurance companies or pension funds tend to participate exclusively in the long-maturity markets. The yield curve shape is a function of these different preferences. Thus, the supply and demand preferences of participants within each maturity segment determine the equilibrium yield without regard to the equilibrium interest rate in neighbouring maturities. Under this hypothesis, any shape of yield curve is possible due to the supply demand quantities for bonds with various maturities.

A modified version of the MSH, the **preferred habitat hypothesis**, states that different participants have preferred locations on the yield curve, but with sufficient incentive they can be induced to move. Thus, segmentation in the bond market affects the term structure, because short-term bonds that are riskless for banks may be risky for insurance firms, which have long-term obligations. If a bank invested in long-term

---

[4] See Eugene F. Fama, 'Forward rates as predictors of future spot interest rates', *Journal of Financial Economics*, October 1976, pp. 361–77; Eugene F. Fama, 'The information in the term structure', *Journal of Financial Economics*, December 1984, pp. 509–28; and Haim Levy and Robert Brooks, 'An empirical analysis of term premiums using stochastic dominance', *Journal of Banking and Finance*, May 1989, pp. 245–60.

bonds, it would be taking considerable price risk. If an insurance company invested in short-term bonds, it would be taking considerable reinvestment risk. Different segments have different risk premiums, but they are ready to take less preferable bonds once the price of the bonds falls below a certain level.

In summary, no theory provides a complete description of what we actually observe. Each hypothesis offers insight into what may drive the current shape of the yield curve. Expectations and risk clearly play a role in determining the shape of the yield curve.

7.3 OTHER MEASURES OF BOND YIELDS

This text uses the term *yield* to mean *yield to maturity*. Among investors and in the financial media, the term *yield* has various meanings. This section introduces five different definitions of *yield*.

The **coupon yield** or **nominal yield** is the promised annual coupon rate. For example, if the annual coupon payment is $120 and the par value is $1,000, then the coupon or nominal yield is 12%.

Current yield is found by taking the stated annual coupon payment and dividing it by the current market price of the bond. Current market prices for bonds can be found in any financial newspaper or through a broker. A 12% coupon bond selling at $900, for example, has a current yield of $120/$900 \cong 13.33\% (where $120 is 12% of $1,000 par).

The yield to maturity is a more complex yield and represents the internal rate of return of a bond investment, as discussed earlier. That is, it is y that solves the standard bond-pricing equation given by Equation 7.1.

The **yield to call** is similar to the yield to maturity, except it assumes that the bond will be called at the first possible call date. The call feature allows the bond's issuer to essentially buy back bonds at a specified price. In this case, instead of using the par value at maturity as the final payment, we use the amount to be paid to bondholders when the bond is called. Specifically:

$$P = \sum_{t=1}^{nc} \frac{C}{(1 + y)^t} + \frac{\text{call price}}{(1 + y)^{nc}} \tag{7.3}$$

where nc is the number of coupon payments until the first call date. Note that if C is paid semiannually, then y is the semiannual yield, and the annual yield is $(1 + y)^2 - 1$.

This call price is typically in excess of the par value. For example, the call price may be set at par plus one year's interest. However, the investor is not assured that the bonds will in fact be called on this date. (For more on callable bonds' features, see Section 7.6.1.)

The yield to call is summarized in Rule 3.

Rule 3: The yield to call is the bond's cash flow internal rate of return on the assumption that the bond is called on the first call date.

Finally, the **realized yield** refers to the holding period rate of return actually generated from an investment in a bond. It is the return found after the bond has matured and all risks have been resolved. The calculation of this rate of return was explained in Chapter 4.

When referring to yield, be careful to specify exactly which yield calculation you mean. The most common yield quoted is the yield to maturity. However, there are no set standards in interest rate quotations, and as the previous discussion shows, the yield calculation does make a difference in the returns.

PRACTICE BOX

Problem

Calculate the five different yields given the following information. The bond is a two-year, 8% annual coupon, and it has $1,000 par. The bond is currently trading for $1,030 and is callable at $1,050 (without interest included) in one year. After one year the bond is trading for $1,010 (without interest).

Solution

The current yield is

$$C/P = \$80/\$1,030 \cong 7.77\%$$

The coupon or nominal yield is

$$C/Par = \$80/\$1,000 = 8.0\%$$

The yield to maturity is found using software or a handheld calculator by solving the following equation:

$$\$1,030 = \sum_{t=1}^{2} \frac{\$80}{(1 + y)^t} + \frac{\$1,000}{(1 + y)^2}$$

Using a financial calculator, we get 6.36%.

The yield to call is found by solving this equation:

$$\$1,030 = \sum_{t=1}^{1} \frac{\$80}{(1 + y)^t} + \frac{\$1,050}{(1 + y)^1} = \frac{\$1,130}{(1 + y)}$$

Thus, the yield to call is 9.71%.

Finally, assuming that the bond has not been called, the realized yield if the bond was actually held for one year is

$$R = [(\$1,010 + \$80)/\$1,030] - 1 \cong 5.83\%$$

Thus, we see that none of the yields are the same.

7.4 PRICING BONDS IN PRACTICE

The price of a bond can be expressed as the present value of its coupon payments plus the present value of the par value, discounted at the yield to maturity (y) as expressed in Equation 7.1. For example, a 10% annual coupon, $1000 par bond with a yield to maturity of 12% and 30 years to maturity is worth

$$P = \sum_{t=1}^{30} \frac{\$100}{(1 + 0.12)^t} + \frac{\$1,000}{(1 + 0.12)^{30}} \cong \$838.90$$

Of course, as the market interest rate changes, the yield to maturity changes, and the bond prices change to adjust to the new yield to maturity. The longer the maturity, the more sensitive the bond price to changes in yield.

Exhibit 7.3 lists the prices of several bonds, all with 10% coupon rates, for various interest rates. At yields of 10%, all the bonds are priced at $1,000.

Exhibit 7.3 Bond prices and changes in yield to maturity

(a) Bond prices for 10% coupon bonds, par value of $1,000

Years to maturity	Yield to maturity (y)		
	12%	10%	8%
1	$982.14	$1,000.00	$1,018.52
10	887.00	1,000.00	1,134.20
30	838.90	1,000.00	1,225.16
Infinity	833.33	1,000.00	1,250.00

(b) Percentage changes, mean and standard deviation (assuming 12%, 10% and 8% are equally probable)

Years to maturity	Yield to maturity			Mean	Standard deviation
	12%	10%	8%		
1	−1.79	0.00	1.85	0.02[a]	1.49[b]
10	−11.30	0.00	13.42	0.71[c]	10.10
30	−16.11	0.00	22.52	2.14	15.84
Infinity	−16.67	0.00	25.00	2.78	17.12

[a] $1/3(−1.79\%)1/3 + 1/3(0\%) + 1/3(1.85\%) = 0.02\%$ because we assume each outcome to be equally likely.
[b] $[1/3(−1.79 − 0.02)^2 + 1/3(0.00 − 0.02)^2 + 1/3(1.85 − 0.02)^2]^{1/2} = 1.49\%$
[c] The mean and standard deviations of the other bonds are calculated in a similar manner.

Note in Exhibit 7.3(a) that longer-term bonds experience greater fluctuations in price than do shorter-term bonds. For example, when yields rise from 10% to 12%, one-year bonds drop $17.86 (or $1,000 − $982.14), whereas bonds with no stated maturity (n approaches infinity) drop $166.67 (or $1,000 − $833.33).

Exhibit 7.3(b) illustrates the percentage change (or rate of return) on a bond if it originally had a 10% yield to maturity and then immediately rose to 12%, stayed the same (at 10%), or dropped to 8% with equal probability. A couple of interesting properties can be observed.[5] First, longer-term bonds have a higher standard deviation of rates of return than do shorter-term bonds. Therefore, the longer the maturity, the larger the risk for short-term holding period investors. Second, for the same absolute change in interest rates, a rate decline produces a larger gain than a rate increase produces losses. For example, the 10-year bond gained 13.42% on a rate decline, whereas it lost only 11.30% on a rate increase. The result is a positive expected rate of return.

Exhibit 7.4 illustrates these observations with the 10-year bond and with the perpetual bond. Notice that the 10-year bond and the perpetual bond have the same price when rates are 10%. The reason is that by assumption, they are 10% coupon-bearing bonds, and when the coupon yield equals the yield to maturity the bonds will trade at par. However, when yields change, the perpetual bond price is more sensitive. Also, when rates fall, prices move up by a greater amount than when rates rise and prices fall. Hence,

[5] These properties and others will be more formally developed in Chapter 8.

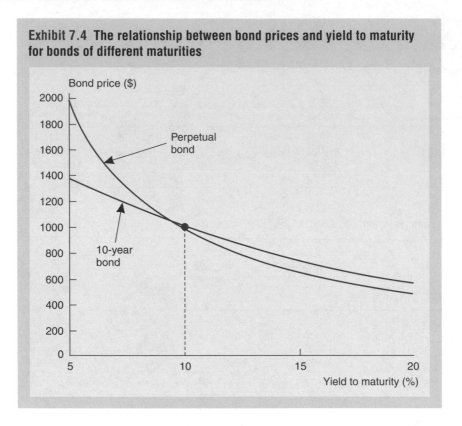

Exhibit 7.4 The relationship between bond prices and yield to maturity for bonds of different maturities

perpetuities are generally considered to be more risky. As you will see in more detail in Chapter 8, longer-maturity bonds are more sensitive to changes in yield than are shorter-maturity bonds.

7.5   SPREADS OVER TREASURIES

So far this chapter has discussed only one type of risk: the risk associated with changes in the interest rate and its effect on the price of a bond. With government bonds this is the only real risk investors face. With corporate bonds, however, there is an additional risk factor: the risk of default. The risk of default applies to both the firm's failure to pay the coupon payments and the par value at maturity. Thus, there is no guarantee that bond issuers will honour their commitments. The uncertainty over whether the lender will make coupon and principal payments is called *default risk*, and it causes the yields to maturity for corporate bonds to exceed those for Treasury bonds. This difference is known as the *spread over Treasuries*, and it is a measure of default risk.

The analyses of bond pricing and yield to maturity in the previous sections were based on the assumption that the bond's coupon and par value would be paid in a timely way. For US or UK Treasury securities, this is a reasonable assumption. However, for corporate bonds, there exists a significant risk of default. If investors believe there is a possibility the bond issuer will default, they will demand a higher yield to maturity on corporate bonds than on Treasury bonds with similar characteristics.

In July 1999 Ford Unit (the finance arm) issued the largest corporate bond offering in US history. They sold $8.6 billion in debt. The bond issue was for 32 years with a spread of 1.4% over US Treasury (140 basis points) and the portion of bonds sold for two years was only 0.17% (17 bonus points) over the three-month LIBOR rate. Thus, we see that the spread is also a function of the time to maturity of the bonds and it makes sense. The chance that Ford Unit will be unable to pay its debt in the short run is very close to zero. However, the chance of default during the next 32 years cannot be ignored, e.g. considering another possible oil crisis.

7.5.1 Bond ratings

At least four independent firms assess the credit risk of a bond issue. The most familiar rating services are Moody's Investors Service, Standard & Poor's, Fitch Investors Services, and Duff and Phelps. **Credit risk** is the risk that the interest or principal will not be paid as agreed. The firms that assess this risk are known as **rating agencies**, because they seek to 'rate' bonds on a scale from low credit risk to high credit risk. Corporations issuing bonds pay a rating fee ranging from a few thousand dollars to over $50,000.

Exhibit 7.5 lists the categories the rating agencies use. The highest-rated bonds are known as *prime-rated bonds* (Aaa by Moody's and AAA by the other three firms). These bonds are referred to as triple A and are perceived to have very little credit risk. They are described as being of high **credit quality**, indicating a low risk of default. The next level down in credit quality is a high-quality rating, or double A (Aa by Moody's and AA by the other three firms). The main difference between double A and triple A is the amount of cushion available to avoid default. Double A bonds have a smaller cushion, but are still very strong and have relatively low credit risk. Double A and triple A bonds are sometimes called **high-grade** bonds.

Single A bonds are the third level down on the rating scale, indicating slightly higher credit risk than double A. These bonds are referred to as *upper-medium-grade* bonds, and they may suffer under circumstances such as an economic downturn in the firm's industry.

The next rating category is *medium-grade bonds*, which is denoted as Baa by Moody's and BBB by the other three firms. These bonds are more vulnerable to default if the firm encounters hard times.

Triple A through triple B bonds fall under the classification of **investment grade**. Many professionally managed funds are restricted to investing solely in investment grade securities. For example, the Vanguard Bond Market mutual fund must invest in investment grade bonds.[6] Because of these restrictions, firms strive to keep the ratings on their bonds at or above triple B in order to maintain greater demand for their bonds and hence also maintain a lower required yield to maturity.

Bonds rated below investment grade (below triple B) are referred to as **speculative grade bonds** or **junk bonds**. At the upper end of speculative grade bonds are Ba, BB or double B. These bonds are considered to have 'major ongoing uncertainties'. That is, they face considerable risks in an economic downturn. Single B bonds are slightly more risky than double B. Bonds in categories CCC and below are bonds nearing default or in default. Also, triple C and double C sometimes refer to bonds that are subordinated to bonds holding B ratings that are not already in default (the term **subordinated bonds**

---

[6] See *The Individual Investor's Guide to No-load Mutual Funds*, 10th edition, 1991, p. 433.

Exhibit 7.5 Bond rating categories by company

Category	Moody[a]	S&P[b]	Fitch[b]	DP[b]	Description
Prime	Aaa	AAA	AAA	AAA	Best quality, extemely strong
High quality	Aa	AA	AA	AA	Strong capacity to pay
Upper medium	A	A	A	A	Adequate capacity to pay
Medium	Baa	BBB	BBB	BBB	Changing circumstances could affect ability to pay
Speculative	Ba	BB	BB	BB	Has speculative elements
Speculative	B	B	B	B	Lacks quality
Default	Caa	CCC	CCC	CCC	Poor standing
Default	Ca	CC	CC		Highly speculative
Default		C	C		Low quality, may never repay
Default		D	DDD[c] DD D	DD	In default

Moody = Moody's Investors Services, Inc.; S&P = Standard & Poor's, Inc.; Fitch = Fitch Investors Services, Inc.; DP = Duff and Phelps.
[a] Applies numerical modifiers 1, 2 and 3 to indicate relative position within rating category. For example, Baa will be Baa-1, Baa-2 or Baa-3.
[b] Uses + or − to indicate relative position within the rating category. For example, BBB will be either BBB+, BBB or BBB−.
[c] Different degrees of default, with D being worse than DD and DDD.

means bonds that stand behind senior bonds in the credit line in the event of default). Junk bonds are discussed in detail later in the chapter.

To enhance the credit quality of their bonds (to improve the rating and reduce the interest cost), firms agree to abide by certain restrictions and requirements that are spelled out in the **bond indenture** agreement. The bond indenture is a legal agreement between the bond issuer and the bondholders covering all the terms of the issue. It includes such stipulations as type of bond issued and amount of the issue, sinking fund provisions, restrictions on financial ratios, and call features.

Some bonds are secured with collateral and are thus called **secured bonds**. Mortgage bonds are an example of secured bonds. In the event of default, the bondholder takes possession of the underlying collateral (which may be in the form of land, buildings or even equipment). Unsecured bonds, known as **debentures**, are only backed by the 'full faith and credit' of the issuing firm.

A **sinking fund** is money put into a separate custodial account that is used to reduce the outstanding principal through repurchases. An independent third party manages the sinking fund. The effect of a sinking fund is to reduce the likelihood of default at the time of bond maturity.

Restrictions on financial ratios are established in an effort to ensure that the firm has the ability to meet its interest payments, as well as its sinking fund requirements. For example, there may be a restriction that requires the current ratio (the ratio of current assets divided by current liabilities) to be greater than 2. The purpose of this restriction is to ensure that the issuing firm has the liquidity necessary to make the bond's coupon payment. Indeed, financial analysts examine the financial ratios of some items taken from the firm's financial statements as indicators of the firm's financial strength.

Many firms like to have the option of calling their bonds back and refinancing them if interest rates fall. Typically, this call feature requires paying a bonus above the par value. The size of the bonus varies across bonds and even during the life of a bond, but it is typically about one year's interest. This call feature gives added flexibility to the issuing firm.

There is evidence that bond rating changes follow a pattern. Specifically, a bond that is downgraded once is much more likely to be downgraded a second time. Exhibit 7.6 presents some evidence of this phenomenon. Note that 64.4% of bond rating changes are downgrades. Of the bonds downgraded, a whopping 71.8% are downgraded a second time. For BBB bonds, the probability of a change in either direction is almost even after a first downgrade. After an upgrade, a bond's next ratings change is more likely to be another upgrade, but this is not significant (with the exception of AA bonds). The investment implication is that if a bond experiences a downgrade (except for the original rating of BBB), then you should consider selling the bond, because it is a good candidate for yet another downgrade which will induce a loss to the investors.

In an effort to provide timely information on bond ratings, S&P has developed a tool called CreditWatch.[7] When a firm is placed on CreditWatch, investors know that a potential rating change may be forthcoming. With this information, bond investors may reallocate their holdings of these bonds. For example, if a firm decides to increase its financial leverage, it may not be able to meet future debt obligations. Therefore, the risk of bankruptcy increases, and the firm may be moved to the CreditWatch list.

Rating agencies are used throughout the world. Rating agencies also evaluate the ability of governmental units, such as the Republic of Italy or Mexico, to meet their financial obligations.

Exhibit 7.6 Bond rating change experience, 1970 to 1985

Rating	First rating change		First rating change is down then next rating change is		First rating change is up, then next rating change is	
	Downgrade	Upgrade	Down	Up	Down	Up
AAA	100.0%	0.0%	78.6%	21.4%	N/A	N/A
AA	83.5	16.5	80.8	19.2	91.8%	8.2%
A	57.1	42.9	65.6	34.4	45.9	54.1
BBB	43.8	56.2	54.3	45.7	40.5	59.5
NIG[a]	50.0	50.0	72.0	28.0	42.9	57.1
Total	64.4	35.6	71.8	28.2	49.6	50.4

[a] NIG – not investment grade.

[7] CreditWatch is a service that alerts subscribers to the S&P bond rating agency that a particular security is being closely examined for a rating change.

7.5.2 Bond ratings and spreads over Treasuries

We have seen that bond ratings influence bond prices and, consequently, bond yields. The spread over Treasuries for similar bonds varies over time. For example, Exhibit 7.7 gives the yield to maturity for 10-year corporate bonds rated Baa by Moody's and for 10-year Treasury bonds from 1986 to 1996. The difference in yield between Baa bonds and Treasuries has changed over time.

For example, in 1989, the economy was strong, with the gross domestic product (GDP) growing at 7.7% per annum.[8] Yields on 10-year Treasury bonds were 8.49% and the spread was 0.79%; by 1995, the economy had slowed and the GDP was only 4.6% per annum. Treasury bond yields were at 6.57% and the spread was 1.97%. The increase in the spread reflects the market's demanding a premium for an increase in the risk of bankruptcy during a recessionary period. Thus, the health of the economy determines the chance of bankruptcy, hence the spread.

Another example corresponds to 1978–82 (not shown in Exhibit 7.7), when the interest rate rose sharply and bondholders incurred relatively large losses. An investment in 10-year Treasury bonds at $1,000 par in 1978 would have fallen to $824 in 1982 because of the increase in interest rates.[9] This is a 17.65% loss. Because the spread also widened, an investment in Baa bonds at a $1,000 par in 1978 would have fallen to $764, a 23.57% loss.[10] Thus, the widening of the spread from 1.08% in 1978 to 3.11% in 1982 resulted in an additional 5.92% loss.

The boxed *Financial Times* article opposite shows that the spreads widened due to the crisis in the equity markets, and the low-graded bonds were hit harder.

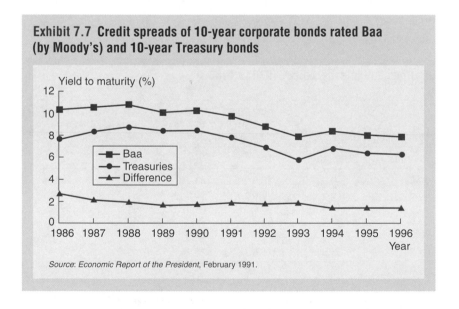

Exhibit 7.7 Credit spreads of 10-year corporate bonds rated Baa (by Moody's) and 10-year Treasury bonds

Source: Economic Report of the President, February 1991.

---

[8] The growth rate of the GDP is a measure of economic health. The higher the growth in the GDP, the healthier the economy (see Chapter 11).

[9] The value $824 was calculated using the standard bond pricing equation with the bond now being a six-year bond (four years have elapsed), and the yield to maturity has risen.

[10] These computations are based on semiannual bonds with 10 years to maturity initially (Treasury bonds with 8.41% coupon and Baa bonds with 9.49% coupon) and then six years to maturity left in 1982 to calculate the losses.

Secondary yield spreads widen

Yield spreads in the secondary market widened yesterday, in the first sign that the sharp declines in equity prices were feeding through to corporate bonds. The FTSE 100 index suffered its biggest one-day loss since October 1992 yesterday and the Dow Jones Industrial Average hit bear market territory. Traders said that there were no heavy selling of corporate bonds, but spreads were around 5 basis points wider. Bonds rated lower than Single A were hit harder.

Source: Financial Times, 23 March 2001, p. 28. Reprinted with permission.

PRACTICE BOX

Problem
After conducting extensive analysis, you believe the economy will continue to grow steadily, accompanied by very little change in Treasury yields. How could you profit from this belief (assuming it turns out to be correct)? Specifically, there is a BB bond with 30 years to maturity that is currently trading at par with a yield to maturity of 10%.

Solution
In a strengthening economy, the credit spread tends to decline, reflecting the lower default risk. Hence, you could invest in lower-rated bonds with the expectation that if the bond yields do decline, bond prices will rise. For example, if you invest in the BB bond and the credit spread narrows by 2%, then the price will appreciate by $225.16. (See Exhibit 7.3 for the 30-year bond: at 10% the bond trades at par of $1,000, and at 8% the bond trades for $1,225.16.)

■ Pre-tax and post-tax yields

The yield to maturity published in the financial media is the pretax yield. Because investors pay income tax on regular interest and capital gains tax on realized profit from the sale of the bonds, the published yields do not reflect the investor's after-tax rate of return. Municipal bonds (bonds issued by a state or local government) are exempt from income tax, whereas all other bonds are taxable. Hence, a comparison of the pretax yields on various types of bonds may be misleading.

Exhibit 7.8 provides the yields on utility bonds, long-term Treasury bonds and municipal bonds. It shows that the yield on municipal bonds is smaller than the yield on Treasury bonds. This phenomenon is quite common. For example, on 2 July 2001, the yield to maturity on Chicago Airport Financing was 5.561%, whereas the yield to maturity on US Treasury bonds (with the same 30 years to maturity) was 5.78%. Does this mean that municipals are less risky than government bonds? The reason municipals offer such low yields is that they are exempt from Federal income tax – not because their risk is lower than that of Treasury bonds.

From Chapter 2 recall that

$$R_{AT} = R_{BT}(1 - T)$$

where R_{AT} is the rate of return after taxes, R_{BT} is the rate of return before taxes, and T is the income tax rate.

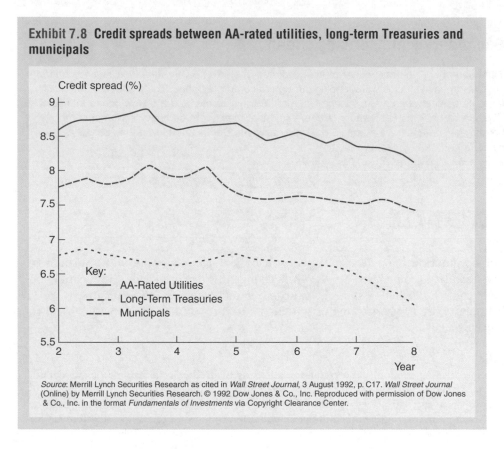

Exhibit 7.8 Credit spreads between AA-rated utilities, long-term Treasuries and municipals

Source: Merrill Lynch Securities Research as cited in *Wall Street Journal*, 3 August 1992, p. C17. *Wall Street Journal* (Online) by Merrill Lynch Securities Research. © 1992 Dow Jones & Co., Inc. Reproduced with permission of Dow Jones & Co., Inc. in the format *Fundamentals of Investments* via Copyright Clearance Center.

Thus, the implied before-tax rate of return when $T = 39.6\%$ and $R_{AT} = 6.06\%$ (Year 8 in Exhibit 7.8) is

$$R_{BT} = R_{AT}/(1 - T) = 6.06\%/(1 - 0.396\%) \cong 10.03\%$$

which exceeds both the Treasury bonds with eight years to maturity (at 7.48%) and the AA bonds (at 8.14%). Hence, we see that, as expected, municipals have significantly higher before-tax yields, which reflect the default risk premium.

7.5.3 Junk bonds

On 2 July 2001 the yield to maturity on Polaroid Bond was 40.4%. Did it become a very good investment? Not necessarily so, because it is a *junk bond*, on which the investor may lose the principal as well as the interest. What are junk bonds?

Junk bonds are lower-rated corporate bonds. About 25% of the junk bond market consists of bonds that were once investment grade but have had their credit rating downgraded below BBB (or Baa). These are known as **fallen angels**. Another 25% of the junk bond market consists of bonds issued by corporations that initially do not carry a high credit rating. Finally, about 50% of the junk bond market is composed of bonds issued in major restructurings, such as leveraged buyouts. This segment of the junk bond market was primarily composed of bonds issued in the period 1986 to 1989.[11]

---

[11] Edward I. Altman, 'Revisiting the high-yield bond market', *Financial Management*, Summer 1992, p. 78.

Exhibit 7.9 Historical default rates for junk bonds

Calendar year	Par value outstanding (billion $)	Par value in default (billion $)	Default rate (%)
1991	209	18.9	9.0
1990	210	18.4	8.7
1989	201	8.1	4.0
1988	159	3.9	2.5
1987	137	1.8	1.3
1986	93	3.2	3.4
1985	59	0.99	1.7
1984	41.7	0.034	0.83
1983	28	0.3	1.1
1982	18.5	0.58	3.1
1981	17.4	0.027	0.16
1980	15.1	0.2	1.48
1979	10.7	0.02	0.19
1978	9.4	0.12	1.27

Sources: Years 1978–88 from Edward I. Altman, *The High-Yield Debt Market: Investment Performance and Economic Impact* (Homewood, IL: Dow Jones-Irwin, 1990), p. 45; years 1989–91 from Edward I. Altman, 'Revising the high-yield bond market', *Financial Management*, Summer 1992, p. 82, Exhibit 4.

Exhibit 7.9 illustrates the growth of the junk bond market, as well as the subsequent growth of default rates. It was not until 1987 that the junk bond market exceeded $100 billion in par value. By 1989, however, it exceeded $200 billion. Notice that the default rates lagged behind this phenomenal growth by a few years. Clearly, the high default rates in the early 1990s were a result of excessive optimism in the late 1980s.

Although junk bonds have a considerable amount of default risk, they have one very attractive feature. Their yields are relatively high, which implies a high realized rate of return if bankruptcy does not occur. For example, the yield to maturity on 2 July 2001, was 6.84% on IBM and as high as 40.4% on Polaroid.[12] Because these bonds are so sensitive to the overall health of the issuing firm, each bond's price moves more with information related to the firm than with changes in overall interest rates. It turns out that a diversified portfolio of junk bonds with a relatively low correlation is many times less volatile than a diversified portfolio of US Treasury securities. Recall from our portfolio analysis that securities that have low correlations can be used to form portfolios with relatively low overall volatility.

7.5.4 Inflation-indexed bonds

Some countries that suffer from relatively high inflation issue bonds whose principal and interest are linked to the cost of living index (**indexed bonds**). For example, if a bond's face value is $1,000 and there was 10% inflation in the first year after the bond was issued and 20% inflation in the second year, then the bond's face value is adjusted to

$$\$1,000 \times 1.1 \times 1.2 = \$1,320$$

Similarly, the interest coupon payments are adjusted for inflation.

[12] See *Barron's*, 2 July 2001, p. MW47.

Recently, the US Treasury issued inflation-adjusted securities. The yield to maturity on such bonds is smaller than the yield to maturity on nonindexed bonds; however, these two yields are not comparable: one is real yield, whereas the other is nominal yield. For example, the yield to maturity in July 2001 was 3.375% on indexed bonds that mature in the year 2007, whereas the yield to maturity was about 5.16% on Treasury bonds with a similar maturity. The difference between these two yields reflects the expected annual inflation. The higher the inflation, the bigger is the expected difference between the nominal and real yields.

7.5.5 International bond markets

Recall from Chapter 3 (Exhibit 3.21) that US bonds account for nearly half of the global corporate bond market. As investors strive to achieve returns in excess of Treasuries, one popular strategy is a global bond portfolio. Although the potential returns are great, however, there are several risks.

The global bond market has its own terminology. For example, yankee bonds are issued by foreign corporations and foreign banks that pay in US dollars. Hence, yankee bonds are an efficient way to diversify default risk. If you allocate a portion of your bond portfolio to yankee bonds, when the United States goes into a severe recession you may not suffer as great a loss if these foreign corporations are not hit as hard.

As the financial markets become increasingly interrelated, corporations seeking the lowest funding costs are issuing bonds in different countries. These bonds, referred to as Eurobonds, are not related in any way to Europe. Eurobonds are sold to investors outside the issuing corporation's country. For example, Samurai bonds are yen-denominated Eurobonds offered by non-Japanese firms.

The primary benefits of international bonds, from the investor's point of view, are enhanced returns and diversification. Because of supply and demand imbalances, many international bonds have yields to maturity higher than comparable domestic securities even after adjusting for exchange risk. Also, international bonds are not perfectly correlated. Thus, it is possible to build an international bond portfolio that has a higher expected return and a lower volatility than a domestic bond portfolio.

The yields of a long-maturity bond in different countries reflect the expectation of a change in the foreign exchange rates of this currency. For example, in the US the yield is about 5.4%, in the UK about 4.25% and in Japan about 2%.

Why not issue bonds in Japan at 2% a year and lend in the United Kingdom at 4.25% a year and make a profit? This tempting transaction does not guarantee an arbitrage profit. The reason is that the difference in the yields represents different expected inflation rates in these two countries, which in turn reflects an expectation that the British pound will depreciate against the Japanese yen. When the investor converts the British pound back to Japanese yen (because the investor needs to pay back the loan), she may find that she loses money on what seems to be an arbitrage transaction.

7.6 THE IMPACT OF EMBEDDED OPTIONS

Issuers often add provisions to bonds to protect themselves from interest rate changes or to make the bonds more attractive to investors. Many features in corporate bond issues are essentially options. Recall from Chapter 2 that an option gives its holder the right, but not the obligation, to do something in the future. Both callable and convertible bonds contain option-like features. The option to call a bond and the option to convert a bond to stock dramatically change the fundamental price behaviour of bonds.

7.6.1 The call feature

In Section 7.3 we define the concept of yield to call. Here we elaborate on the features of **callable bonds**.

Most corporate bonds issued in the United States are callable by the issuing firm. That is, the issuer has the right to buy the bonds back at a stated redemption price. The bondholders face the risk that the bonds will be called at a time when they would prefer to hold them.

For example, in 1979, Duke Power Company issued a $10^1/_8$ coupon bond at $1,000 par that had a stated maturity of 1 March 2009.[13] The bonds were rated Aa by Moody's and thus contained little credit risk.

Suppose these bonds were purchased with the idea of holding them until 2009. As interest rates fell in the late 1980s and early 1990s, these bonds should have experienced a dramatic rise in price, except they were callable at 105.65% of par, or $1,056.50. Thus, even though yields on comparable bonds reached the mid-8% level, these bonds never rose much above $1,056.50. Thus, the call provision put a ceiling on the possible profit due to a fall in interest rates. No investor would be willing to pay more than $1,056.50 for such a bond knowing that the firm can redeem it at this price. On 23 December 1991, Duke Power Company called the bonds back and paid $1,056.50 (plus accrued interest).

The investor then had the problem of what to do with the $1,056.50 proceeds per bond. Unfortunately, the investor had to replace a $10^1/_8$ coupon bond with an $8^1/_2$ bond (the yield available at the time), resulting in an annual coupon loss of $1^5/_8$, or $16.25 − (0.01625 × $1,000), per bond per year.

Exhibit 7.10 illustrates the impact of the call feature on bond price behaviour with respect to yield to maturity, assuming everything else about the bonds is the same (maturity, coupon and so forth). If the callable and the noncallable bonds were priced the same, which bond would you rather own? You would prefer the noncallable bond, of course, because you could gain more if there were a large increase in price because of falling interest rates. Because every investor would prefer the noncallable bonds under these assumptions, their price must be high as shown in Exhibit 7.10. For example, for the same yield to maturity y_0, bond b (noncallable) is priced higher than bond a (callable). Thus, for similar bonds, a noncallable bond is always worth more. Indeed, Exhibit 7.10 demonstrates this property. The exhibit also shows that as yields to maturity get progressively higher, the difference in prices gradually declines. An investor would not expect too great a threat from a call feature at 105% of par when the bond is trading at, say, 70% of its par value. For example, if the two bonds issued at yield to maturity, y_0, and the yield goes up to y_1, the price of both bonds sharply declines. Thus, the market value of the call feature declines as yields to maturity rise.

Exhibit 7.10 also highlights the divergence in price when interest rates fall. Specifically, the callable bond usually does not trade much above the price at which the firm can call the bonds. Notice the left-hand side of Exhibit 7.10. As rates fall, the noncallable bond's

---

[13] From Moody's, *Corporate Bond Guide* (New York: Moody's Investor Service, 1991), p. 69.

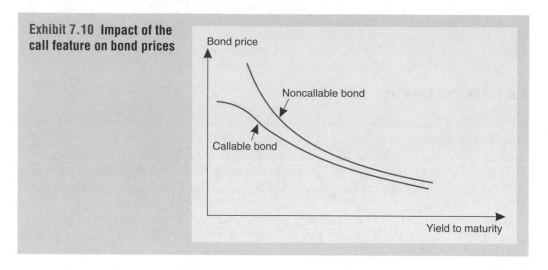

Exhibit 7.10 Impact of the call feature on bond prices

price continues to rise. However, the callable bond levels off at the value of the bond if it were called.

Why, then, do investors buy callable bonds? The reason is that issuing firms offer 'sweeteners' in the form of higher coupon rates in return for the call feature. The issuing firm of callable bonds offers the investor a higher yield to maturity. This means that with the high yield of the callable bond, we may have two bonds such as a and a', with the same market price, but the callable bond has a higher price. Once again, there is a trade-off between risk (the call feature) and return (the higher initial yield to maturity).

Why, then, do firms issue callable bonds? The call feature allows firms some flexibility in their financing policies. In particular, the firm is not locked into an expensive debt issue. When interest rates fall, the bonds can be refinanced at a lower rate.

7.6.2 The conversion feature

When firms want to reduce their required coupon rate, they sometimes offer to make their bonds convertible to common or preferred stock. One advantage from the issuing firm's viewpoint is that it will issue new common stock at a relatively high price when the conversion takes place in the future. Typically, the conversion price (which equals the par value of the bond divided by the conversion ratio) is set significantly above the current common stock price. If the firm raised capital through a new issue of common stock, it would have to offer the new issue at a price slightly less than the current stock price. Therefore, **convertible bonds** provide a way to achieve, albeit in the future, an equity issue at a higher price.

Consider the Cray Research Inc. (makers of supercomputers), coupon, semiannual convertible bonds, maturing on 1 February 2011, with a rating of Baa-2 by Moody's. The conversion ratio is 12.82, which means that for every bond converted, the firm will issue 12.82 shares of common stock. Thus, the conversion price is about $78 (par/conversion ratio = $1,000/12.82).

On 24 July 1992, the bonds closed at $73^1/_2\%$ of par, and the common stock closed at $29^3/_8$. These bonds offer a yield to maturity of approximately 9%. At the time, the Cray Research bonds offered a yield to maturity that was indistinguishable from comparable nonconvertible bonds. The conversion feature had very little value. The stock price must rise by 165.53% before the conversion price is reached [($78 − $29^3/_8)/$29^3/_8].

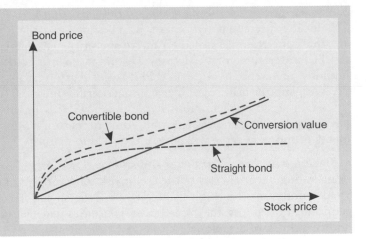

Exhibit 7.11 Impact of the conversion feature on bond prices

Thus, these bonds offer a strong 9% yield to maturity, and they also contain an 'equity kicker'. If the common stock price goes up considerably, then these bonds will likewise rise.

Convertible bond price behaviour is quite different from the price behaviour of regular bonds. The conversion value is the value of the bond if it is immediately converted into stock. Hence, as the stock price rises, so does the conversion value. Exhibit 7.11 illustrates the price behaviour of these bonds and compares them to the conversion value. Notice that the straight (nonconvertible) bond is almost insensitive to stock price changes except when the firm's stock price gets very low. For a very low stock price, a bankruptcy is possible, a case where the bonds lose value. When the stock price declines, the straight bond value is above the conversion value because it pays (if the firm does not go bankrupt) a fixed interest rate. The straight line represents the value of the bond if it is converted into stock. This value is known as the *conversion value*, which equals the conversion ratio times the current stock price. Clearly, as the stock price rises, so does the conversion value. Notice that the convertible bond price always exceeds the straight bond price, even for low stock prices, because the ability to convert the bonds to stock is always worth something (although it may not be worth very much at low stock prices). At a very high stock price, the convertible bond value converges to the conversion value because its value is very high and its lower value as a bond is irrelevant. Namely, the bond almost surely will be converted into stock. For example, if the stated price of Cray Research jumped to $200, the bond would be worth $200 \times 12.82 = \$2,564$, and the value of a bond of about $1000 is completely irrelevant.

SUMMARY

■ *The yield to maturity is the interest earned on a bond if held to its maturity.*
A yield curve is a relationship between a bond's time to maturity and its yield to maturity. The yield curve provides some clues regarding the future course of interest rates.

■ *Use the bond pricing equation to find bond prices and bond yields.*
When the bond's price is given, and given the coupons and par value, the yield to maturity can be computed. There is an inverse relationship between yield to maturity and bond prices.

■ *Summarize the theories that explain the shape and level of yield curves.*
The local expectations hypothesis (LEH) states that the holding period rates of return are the same regardless of the time to maturity. The unbiased expectations hypothesis (UEH) states that forward rates are unbiased predictors of future spot rates. The liquidity preference hypothesis (LPH) states that investors have a preference for securities with shorter maturities; hence, longer-term bonds will have a higher yield to maturity. The market segmentations hypothesis (MSH) is based on investors and borrowers having specific preferences regarding time to maturity. Supply and demand in these segments of the yield curve will govern the yield to maturity.

■ *Describe the behaviour of the spread over Treasuries.*
Bond rating agencies classify the credit risk inherent in bonds. Over time, the additional yield required for bearing this credit risk – the spread over Treasuries – varies. During economic downturns, the spread over Treasuries widens to compensate investors for the additional risk of default.

■ *Describe the impact of the call feature and the convertible feature on bond prices.*
The call feature causes bond prices not to rise as much as a comparable noncallable bond when interest rates (hence yields) fall. The option to call a bond held by the issuer becomes more valuable to the issuer of the bond when interest rates fall, because the bonds can be refinanced at a lower rate. The conversion feature causes bonds to behave like the underlying stock after the stock price has risen sufficiently.

KEY TERMS

Bond indenture
Callable bond
Convertible bond
Coupon yield
Credit quality
Credit risk
Current yield
Debenture
Fallen angel
Forward contract
Forward rate
 agreement (FRA)
High grade
Holding period rate
Indexed bond

Investment grade
Junk bond
Liquidity preference
 hypothesis (LPH)
Liquidity premium
Local expectations
 hypothesis (LEH)
Market segmentations
 hypothesis (MSH)
Nominal yield
Preferred habitat
 hypothesis
Price risk
Rating agency
Realized yield

Reinvestment risk
Secured bonds
Sinking fund
Speculative grade
 bond
Spot rate
Subordinated bond
Term structure of interest
 rates
Unbiased expectations
 hypothesis (UEH)
Wealth effect
Yield curve
Yield to call
Yield to maturity

QUESTIONS

7.1   What sparked the changes in bond management in the 1970s?

7.2   What determines the equilibrium level of interest rates?

7.3   If interest rates rise, will individuals save more or less? Explain your answer.

7.4 Describe some historical characteristics of the US Treasury yield curve.

7.5 Identify and discuss the various theories related to the behaviour of the yield curve.

7.6 Assuming a flat yield curve and a bond that is trading at par, why does the yield to call exceed the yield to maturity?

7.7 'The stock market seems risky these days. I am going to put my money in safe, 30-year US Treasury bonds.' Evaluate this statement.

7.8 Because of financial stress, the bonds of Intelo have been downgraded by Moody's from A to BBB. What is the predicted effect on the bonds' price? What is the predicted effect on the bonds' yield to maturity?

7.9 Suppose the only information you had regarding the current health of a country's economy was its credit spread between triple-B bonds and Treasury bonds. Specifically, the spread had recently widened considerably. What would you infer?

7.10 Suppose you are given the following information:

Maturities	Spot rates	Forward rates
1	8%	_a
2		7.8%
3	7.2	
4		6.0
5	5.0	

a Recall that forward rates involve an interest rate starting at some future point in time. Hence, most practitioners say the forward rate during the first period is just the one-period spot rate, which in this case is 8%.

(a) Complete the table assuming the rates are for annual, zero-coupon bonds.
(b) If the unbiased expectations hypothesis (UEH) is strictly true, what is the market forecast for the one-year spot rate in one year?

7.11 Describe the empirical evidence regarding patterns in bond rating changes. Is this evidence consistent with the efficient market hypothesis?

7.12 The maturity of a bond is one year ($n = 1$), the annual coupon is $C = \$100$, the par value is $\$1,000$, and the market value is $P = \$950$. Calculate the yield to maturity.

7.13 The yield on a one-year municipal bond is 6.4%, and the yield on a one-year Treasury bond is 7.5%. Ignoring default risk, if the tax rate is $T = 31\%$, which bond would you prefer? Why?

7.14 'If the yield to maturity is zero, no matter what the maturity is, the par value of the bond must be equal to its market value.' Evaluate this statement. Is there a specific type of bond for which this is true?

7.15 Suppose you are the chief financial officer of a large life insurance company. Looking at mortality tables, you estimate that you will have to pay the insured families $100 million in each of the next five years and $900 million in Year 6. What kind of bonds would you seek to make these payments? Would it make a difference whether the yield curve is flat or upward sloping?

7.16 Short-term bonds traded in the United States, like Treasury bills, are often referred to as the risk-free asset. In what respect are they risk-free?

7.17 Which asset would you consider to be riskier: three-month Treasury bills or a 30-year Treasury bond that matures in three months?

7.18 Looking at the international financial statistics, we find that the interest paid to US banks on loans to some Latin American countries is about 30% per year. The interest within the United States is only 10%.

(a) How can you explain the difference in interest rates if the loans are made in local currency?

(b) How can you explain the difference in interest rates when the loan in made in US dollars? After all, it is said, the government cannot go bankrupt. Why do US banks receive such a high interest rate on foreign loans?

SELECTED REFERENCES

Altman, Edward I. *The High-Yield Debt Market: Investment Performance and Economic Impact.* Homewood, IL: Dow Jones–Irwin, 1990.
This is an exhaustive book of readings related to the junk bond market.

Altman, Edward I., and Duen Li Kao. 'The implications of corporate bond ratings drift'. *Financial Analysts Journal*, May–June 1992, pp. 64–75.
This article examines in detail the corporate ratings drift.

Cottle, Sidney, Roger F. Murray, and Frank E. Block. *Graham and Dodd's Security Analysis*, 5th edn. New York: McGraw-Hill, 1988.
This reworking of a classic applies the basic principles of security analysis in determining security value.

Geanuracos, John, and Bill Millar. *The Power of Financial Innovation.* New York: Harper Business, 1991.
This book provides interesting insights into the global bond markets and has an emphasis on derivative securities.

Livingston, Miles. *Money and Capital Markets: Financial Instruments and Their Uses.* Englewood Cliffs, NJ: Prentice-Hall, 1990.
This book covers thoroughly many of the technical aspects of bond pricing and theories of term structure.

SUPPLEMENTARY REFERENCES

Altman, Edward I. 'Measuring corporate bond mortality and performance'. *Journal of Finance*, September 1989, pp. 909–22.

Altman, Edward I. 'Setting the record straight on junk bonds'. *Journal of Applied Corporate Finance*, Summer 1990, pp. 82–95.

Altman, Edward I. 'Revisiting the high-yield bond market'. *Financial Management*, Summer 1992, pp. 78–92.

Asquith, Paul, David W. Mullins, Jr., and Eric D. Wolff. 'Original issue high-yield bonds: aging analysis of defaults, exchanges and call'. *Journal of Finance*, September 1989, pp. 923–52.

Balduzzi, P., E.J. Elton, and T. Clifton Green. 'Economic news and bond prices: evidence from the U.S. Treasury market'. *JFQA*, forthcoming (2002).

Best, Peter, Alistair Byrne, and Antli Ilmanen. 'What really happened to U.S. bond yield'. *Financial Analysts Journal*, May–June 1998, pp. 41–9.

Blume, Marshall E., and Donald B. Keim. 'Realized returns and defaults on low-grade bonds: the cohort of 1977 and 1978'. *Financial Analysts Journal*, March–April 1991, pp. 63–72.

Blume, Marshall E., and Donald B. Keim. 'The risk and return of low-grade bonds: an update'. *Financial Analysts Journal*, September–October 1991, pp. 85–9.

Cornell, Bradfors. 'Liquidity and the pricing of low-grade bonds'. *Financial Analysts Journal*, January–February 1991, pp. 63–7, 74.

Fabozzi, Frank J. (ed.). *The New High-Yield Debt Market: A Handbook for Portfolio Managers and Analysts*. New York: HarperCollins, 1990.

Fama, Eugene F. 'Forward rates as predictors of future spot interest rates'. *Journal of Financial Economics*, October 1976, pp. 361–77.

Fama, Eugene F. 'The information in the term structure'. *Journal of Financial Economics*, December 1984, pp. 509–28.

Fons, Jerome S., and Andrew E. Kimball. 'Corporate bond defaults and default rates 1970–1990'. *Journal of Fixed Income*, June 1991, pp. 36–47.

Fridson, Martin S., Michael A. Cherry, Joseph A. Kim, and Stephen W. Weiss. 'What drives the flows of high-yield mutual funds?'. *Journal of Fixed Income*, December 1992, pp. 47–59.

Fridson, Martin S., and Christopher Garman. 'Determinants of spreads on new high yield bonds'. *Financial Analysts Journal*, March–April 1998, pp. 28–39.

Lederman, Jess, and Michael P. Sullivan (eds). *The New High-Yield Bond Market: Investment Opportunities, Strategies and Analysis*. Chicago: Probus Publishing, 1993.

Levy, Haim, and Robert Brooks. 'An empirical analysis of term premiums using stochastic dominance'. *Journal of Banking and Finance*, May 1989, pp. 245–60.

Lobo, B.J. 'Asymmetric effects of interest rate changes on stock prices'. *Financial Review*, 35(3), August 2000.

Ma, Christopher K., Ramesh Rao, and Richard L. Peterson. 'The resiliency of the high-yield bond market: the LTV default'. *Journal of Finance*, September 1989, pp. 1085–97.

Ryan, Patrick J. 'Junk bonds – opportunity knocks?' *Financial Analysts Journal*, May–June 1990, pp. 13–16.

Yan, Hong. 'Dynamic modeling of the term structure'. *Financial Analysts Journal*, July/August 2000.

Chapter 8

BONDS: ANALYSIS AND MANAGEMENT

Learning objectives

After studying this chapter you should be able to:

1 List the basic principles of bond pricing.

2 Explain how duration is used to minimize interest rate risk.

3 Explain how immunization techniques protect bond portfolios from interest rate risk.

4 Describe active bond management strategies.

INVESTMENT IN THE NEWS

Bond's duration is handy guide on rates

Suppose you buy a 10-year Treasury note today at a yield to maturity of 6%, and interest rates shoot up to 8%. What happens to your investment?

A. You lose money.
B. You make money.
C. Nothing happens.
D. All of the above.

The answer: D. All of the above.

How is that possible? The trick is how long you hold the investment.

In the short run, you lose money. Since interest rates and bond prices move inversely to one another, higher rates mean the value of your bond investment withers when rates go up. For a 10-year Treasury yielding 6%, a two percentage-point rise in rates would cause the value of your principal to sink by roughly 14%, according to Capital Management Sciences, a bond research company.

However, if you hold the note, rather than selling it, you'll get to reinvest the interest received from it at the new, higher 8% rate. Over time, this higher 'interest on interest' adds up, allowing you not only to offset your initial loss of principal but also to profit more than if rates had never moved at all.

Over 10 years, for instance, a Treasury note with an initial yield of 6% would produce a total return – price change plus interest – of 6.5% a year if you could reinvest the interest payments at 8%, according to Capital Management Sciences. That compares with an average return of 6% if rates remain unchanged. If rates dropped, so that the reinvestment rate declined to 4%, the 10-year return would average just 5.5% a year.

Perhaps the best way to judge a bond's interest-rate sensitivity is to get a handle on its 'duration'. Duration is one measure of a bond's life. It's that sweet spot, somewhere between the short term and the long term, where a bond's return remains practically unchanged, no matter what happens to interest rates.

Source: Barbara Donnelly Granito, 'Bond's duration is handy guide on rates', *Wall Street Journal*, 19 April 1993, p. C1. Reprinted by permission of *The Wall Street Journal* © 1993 Dow Jones & Co., Inc. All Rights Reserved Worldwide.

Affer reading Chapter 7, you might have answered 'A' to the question posed by Granito in this chapter's *Investment in the news*, yet she explains that the other answers are also possible. The goal of this chapter is to analyze the risk associated with changes in the interest rate and to find out how investors can develop strategies to minimize interest rate risk – the risk faced by a bond investor when market interest rates change. The investigation begins with a look at basic factors that influence bond prices. The fundamental properties of bond price behaviour are called bond pricing principles. The bond pricing principles are used to explain convexity and duration (more advanced tools in interest rate risk management) and to build efficient bond portfolios.

8.1 BOND PRICING PRINCIPLES

This chapter's investigation of bond pricing principles begins with the basic bond pricing equation. The price of a bond is the present value of all future coupon payments plus the par value discounted to the present at the required rate of return which is the yield to maturity. Therefore, the price of a bond can be expressed as follows:

$$P = \sum_{t=1}^{n} \frac{C}{(1 + y)^t} + \frac{\text{Par}}{(1 + y)^n} \tag{8.1}$$

where n is the number of coupon payments left, C is the coupon paid each period, and y is the *periodic* yield to maturity. Equation 8.1 can be used to identify specific relationships among the factors that determine bond prices. These bond pricing principles will be used to develop more advanced tools used in interest rate risk management. In the rest of the chapter we refer to y as the yield to maturity or the interest rate corresponding to this maturity. Thus, yield to maturity and interest rate are used interchangeably.

8.1.1 Rule 1: Bond prices change with the passage of time

The first bond pricing principle is that the price of a bond – not just its quoted price but also its value including accrued interest – changes with the passage of time. That is, bond prices change as the number (n) of years left to maturity changes. Exhibit 8.1 illustrates the change in bond price that occurs with three different assumed yields to maturity. All three bonds are characterized by a 10% semiannual coupon rate, i.e. $50 is paid every six months, $1,000 par value with 20 years to maturity. For simplicity, assume the yield to maturity does not change over the 20-year period.

These bonds differ in their yield to maturity; they have 8%, 10% and 12% yields to maturity. These various yields could be due to differences in risk. The 10% yield bond is the essentially flat line at the par value. This bond's price moves up because of the accruing of interest. At a coupon payment date, the price drops back to $1,000. When a bond has a coupon rate of 10% and a yield to maturity of only 8%, it trades at a premium above par, because the coupon rate is higher than the yield to maturity (see Equation 8.1). That is, the price is greater than the par value. As time to maturity becomes shorter, there are fewer coupon payments to be paid, and the premium declines. Indeed, this bond's price drifts downwards over time, and it is redeemed at the par value. Similarly, a bond trading at a discount (when coupon rate = 10% and y = 12%) drifts upwards over time. Hence, bond prices change with the passage of time. Of course, the 10% yield, 10% coupon-paying bond has a par value equal to the

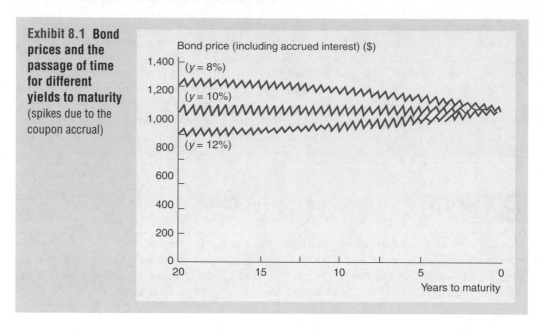

Exhibit 8.1 Bond prices and the passage of time for different yields to maturity (spikes due to the coupon accrual)

bond price; the price drifts neither upwards nor downwards, hence is flat, apart from the small spikes reflecting the accruing of interest.

8.1.2 Rule 2: Bond prices are inversely related to the yield to maturity

After a bond is issued, the interest rate in the economy may change (for example, because of a change in the rate of inflation), and thus the yield on bonds changes. As discussed in Chapter 7, for a given coupon rate, bond prices are inversely related to the yield to maturity. Exhibit 8.2 illustrates this relationship for a $1,000 par bond having a 20-year length to maturity and a 10% semiannual coupon rate. The resulting curve is convex – that is, it is curved away from the origin. As yields to maturity fall below 10%,

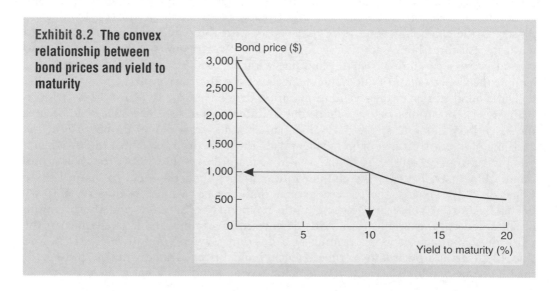

Exhibit 8.2 The convex relationship between bond prices and yield to maturity

the price rises at an increasing rate; as yields to maturity rise above 10%, the price falls at a decreasing rate.

The data in Exhibit 8.3 also show the convex relationship graphed in Exhibit 8.2. Consider the data for a bond with 20 years to maturity. Notice that the decline in the bond price becomes smaller for each 2.5% incremental increase in the yield. For example, when the yield rises from 5% to 7.5%, the price falls by $371 = $1,628 − $1,257. However, when the yield rises from 12.5% to 15%, the price falls by only $133 ($818 − $685). The explanation for this result is that the percentage change in interest rates from 5% to 7.5% (a 50% increase) is much greater than the percentage increase from 12.5% to 15% (a 20% increase). Thus, the price–yield relationship is convex – i.e. it has the kind of curve shown in Exhibit 8.2.

8.1.3 Rule 3: The longer the maturity, the more sensitive the bond's price to changes in the yield to maturity

The relationship between bond prices and changes in yield to maturity is different for various bond maturities. Specifically, for a given coupon at a given yield to maturity, the prices of longer-maturity bonds are more sensitive than the prices of short-maturity bonds to changes in the yield to maturity.[1] This property can be seen directly from Equation 8.1 as well as from Exhibit 8.3. The changes in the bond price for, say, 30 years are much larger than the changes for, say, five years to maturity.

The explanation for the relationship between bond price and maturity as shown in Exhibit 8.3 is straightforward: the longer an investor is locked in a contract (the bond's maturity) that pays, say, 10% a year when the market interest rate is only 8%, the larger the gain in present value terms (the price of the bond). Similarly, the longer the investor is locked in a contract that pays 10% when the market interest rate is 12%, the larger the loss. This explains the effect of the bond's maturity on its price as demonstrated in Exhibit 8.3.

Exhibit 8.3 Bond prices for different maturities and yields to maturity

Years to maturity	Yield to maturity				
	5%	7.5%	10%	12.5%	15%
1	$1,048	$1,024	$1,000	$977	$955
2	1,094	1,046	1,000	957	916
3	1,138	1,066	1,000	939	883
4	1,179	1,085	1,000	923	854
5	1,219	1,103	1,000	909	828
10	1,390	1,174	1,000	859	745
15	1,523	1,223	1,000	832	705
20	**1,628**	**1,257**	**1,000**	**818**	**685**
25	1,709	1,280	1,000	810	676
30	1,773	1,297	1,000	805	671
∞	2,000	1,333	1,000	800	667

---

[1] This is true as long as the coupon is unchanged. If two bonds have different coupons, their duration rather than their maturity measures the sensitivity of the bonds' price to changes in the interest rate. See the discussion later in the chapter.

PRACTICE BOX

Problem

Suppose you have a bond with $n = 10$ years to maturity that pays an annual coupon of $100 every year. The bond's price is $1,000, and the par value is $1,000. Determine the bond's price for the following yields to maturity: 2.5%, 5.0%, 7.5%, 12.5%, 15.0% and 17.5%. How would you change your answer if the bond is a zero-coupon bond with 10% yield to maturity?

Solution

Using Equation 8.1, the following bond prices can be determined when $n = 10$, Par = $1,000 and C = $100:

Yield to maturity	Price of coupon bond	Price of a zero coupon bond
2.5%	$1,656.40	781.20
5.0	1,386.09	613.91
7.5	1,171.60	485.19
10.0	1,000.00	385.54
12.5	861.59	307.95
15.0	749.06	247.18
17.5	656.87	199.35

We see from this example that the higher the yield to maturity, the less sensitive the bond price to the changes in the yield to maturity. This makes sense, because for a low coupon most of the bond's cash flows are far away in the future and hence more affected by the discounting process.

8.1.4 Rule 4: The sensitivity of the price of a bond to changes in the yield to maturity increases at a decreasing rate with the length to maturity

Although longer-term bonds are more sensitive to changes in yield to maturity, this sensitivity declines for longer maturities. To check the price difference of two bonds when the interest rates change, we refer back to Exhibit 8.3. Suppose that the yield to maturity increases from 10% to 15%. With such an event, the new price difference between a 5-year bond and a 10-year bond, with the new yield to maturity of 15%, is $83 = $828 − $745, whereas the price difference between a 25-year bond and a 30-year bond is only $5 = $676 − $671. Notice that when moving from a 30-year bond to a perpetuity, the price difference for a 5% yield to maturity is $227 = $2,000 − $1,773, whereas when moving from a one-year bond to a 10-year bond the price difference is $342 = $1,390 − $1,048. Thus, the price difference is much more sensitive to changes in yield to maturity for shorter-term bonds.

What can we learn from this pattern? Suppose that you are considering investing in either relatively short-term bonds (5 to 10 years to maturity) or long-term bonds (25 to 30 years to maturity). You expect changes in the interest rate, but you are uncertain of the direction of the changes. It is recommended that you devote more analysis to whether to invest in 5-year or 10-year bonds than to 25-year bonds or 30-year bonds. The reason is that any error in your decision has a greater impact for relatively short-term bonds.

8.2   DURATION AND CONVEXITY

The *Investment in the news* article mentions the duration as a crucial factor related to the risk of change in the interest rate. Most of this section is devoted to this important concept. Duration and convexity are useful tools in the process of managing interest rate risk. These advanced interest rate risk management tools are based on the various bond pricing principles discussed in the previous section.

A bond's risk stems mainly from possible changes in interest rates. Bond portfolio duration corresponds to the investment holding period at which the bond portfolio's interest risk is minimized. Is there a way to reduce or eliminate this interest-rate risk? To answer this question, let's look at the impact of a change in bond price when interest rates rise.

An increase in interest rates reduces the price of a bond, a phenomenon known as the **price effect**. However, when interest rates rise, investors can make more money on the new opportunities offering a higher interest rate. Investors who own a coupon bond can reinvest the coupon payments at a higher rate even though the bond's price falls. Thus, a rise in the interest rate results in a higher reinvestment rate for the coupon payments, a phenomenon known as the **reinvestment effect**. (This reinvestment effect does not exist for zero-coupon bonds.) In contrast, a fall in interest rates causes bond prices to rise. Reinvestment opportunities offer less attractive rates. In this case, the price and reinvestment effects have the opposite effect on bond investments than they do when market interest rates rise.

The holding period determines whether the price effect is greater than the reinvestment effect, regardless of the direction of the change in market interest rates. An investor who plans to hold the bond for only one day would be concerned exclusively with the price effect. For a one-day holding period, the investor does not reinvest any cash flow and therefore does not gain or lose from the reinvestment effect. However, if an investor plans to hold the bond until it matures, then only the reinvestment effect matters. The higher the coupon rate, the greater the reinvestment effect. (Because the investor will receive the par value of the bonds at maturity, assuming no default risk, there is no concern about the path the price takes to maturity, and the investor is concerned solely with the reinvestment of the coupons.) Finally, if an investor holds the bond until it matures and it pays no coupon, the investor is not concerned with either the price effect or the reinvestment effect. Thus, the planned holding period and the bond's dispersion of future cash flows are crucial in measuring the effect of changes in the interest rate.

It is important to stress here that we analyze below possible interest rate changes, but investors have no clue whether the interest will go up or down. If it is known to the investor that the interest rate is going to increase tomorrow, the best policy would be to sell the bond today before the price falls, then repurchase it at the lower market price. In such an unrealistic case when information on the interest rate is known, the investor can avoid the price effect and benefit from the reinvestment effect. In the rest of the chapter, we assume that there is no information about whether the interest rate will go up or down. Hence, the investor is exposed to both price effects and reinvestment effects. To illustrate how to evaluate price and reinvestment effects, suppose you purchase a four-year annual coupon bond that pays $100 each year, has a yield to maturity of 10%, and has a par value of $1,000. Because the coupon rate equals the yield to maturity, you know the bond is currently trading at $1,000. Suppose interest rates immediately jump to 12% after you purchase the bond. Are you glad or disappointed? If your holding period is only a day, you will be disappointed, because the price will fall to $939.25 – a loss of about 6.1%. If you hold the bond for two years (and rates do not change again), then your $1,000 investment will be worth $100 coupon payment at the end of Year 2 plus $100(1 + 0.12) = $112 for the coupon payment paid at the end of the first year (reinvested at 12% for one year) plus $966 (the price of a two-year, 10% coupon bond with a 12% yield). The total value of the bond holding at the end of the second year is thus $1,178 = $100 + $112 + $966, for an annualized rate of return of $8.5\% = \left[\left(\frac{\$1178}{\$1000} \right)^{\frac{1}{2}} - 1 \right]$. If you hold the bond for *four years*, at the end of the fourth year the bond holdings will be worth

$$\$1,000 + \$100 + \$100 \times (1 + 0.12) + \$100 \times (1 + 0.12)^2$$
$$+ \$100 \times (1 + 0.12)^3 = \$1,477.90$$

The annualized rate of return is $10.26\% = [(\$1,477.93/\$1,000)^{1/4} - 1]$, which exceeds the original 10% yield. Here we see the benefits of the additional interest with no loss due to the increase in interest rate.

Thus, for a one-day holding period, you are worse off. For a four-year holding period, you are better off. The opposite is true if interest rates decline rather than increase. You gain if you hold the bond for one day and lose if you hold it for four years. Because you do not know in advance the direction of the changes in the interest rate, you are exposed to interest rate risk. Can you eliminate this risk? Yes, you can. Somewhere between a holding period of one day and a holding period of the maturity of the bond, you would intuitively anticipate a holding period where the price effect and the reinvestment effect just offset one another. At this holding period, you should have little, if any, interest rate risk. When rates rise, you benefit enough from the reinvestment effect to just offset the cost encountered from the price effect, provided that indeed you hold the bonds for a predetermined period.

Let us examine the offsetting of price and investment effects with an example. Exhibit 8.4(a) lists information about three default-free bonds. The yield curve is upward sloping, because the yield of the shortest-maturity bond (Bond A) is less than the yield of the middle-maturity bond (Bond B), which is less than the yield of the lowest-maturity bond (Bond C): $Y_A < Y_B < Y_C$.

Suppose you have money to invest, and you definitely know that you will need the money back in exactly four years. What is relevant for you is the final change in your wealth at the end of four years. This is crucial in selecting your investment strategy. If you select Bond A, you incur considerable reinvestment risk; this bond matures in one year, and you will have to reinvest the cash available at the end of the first year in another bond at an unknown rate. (For simplicity, assume that you reinvest in one-year bonds three times.) If you select Bond C, which has a 10-year maturity, you incur considerable price risk, because you will have to sell the bond after four years. The price at the end of four years is greatly affected by the prevailing interest rates at that time (this bond will have six years left to maturity). What about Bond B? In four years, Bond B will have only one year left to maturity, so it will have some price risk. However, you have four years in which to incur reinvestment risk. Recall that these risks have offsetting effects.[2]

Exhibit 8.4(b) contains the annual holding period rates of return (compounded semi-annually) for these three bonds under three different scenarios. Assume that the yield curve either immediately shifts down by 3%, stays the same, or immediately shifts up by

---

[2] Exhibit 8.4 assumes that interest rates change only once – immediately after the bond is purchased. In practice, interest rates change every day. However, this type of analysis remains very helpful and is widely used.

Exhibit 8.4 Illustration of duration and its impact on a bond's volatility

(a) Parameters of three semiannual, default-free, $1,000 par bonds

Bond	Coupon rate	Yield to maturity	Years to maturity	Market price
A	9%	9%	1	$1,000
B	10.68	10.68	5	1,000
C	11	11	10	1,000

(b) Annualized holding period annual rates of return

			Holding period		
Yield to maturity	Bond	Years to maturity	1 Year	4 Years	7 Years
Decline of 3%	A	1	8.94%	6.73%	6.42%
	B	5	20.05	10.705	9.40
	C	10	28.22	12.88	10.77
No change	A	1	9.00	9.00	9.00
	B	5	10.68	10.68	10.68
	C	10	11.00	11.00	11.00
Rise of 3%	A	1	9.06	11.26	11.58
	B	5	2.02	10.704	11.97
	C	10	−3.74	9.42	11.37

(c) Mean and standard deviation of annual rate of return, assuming each scenario is equally likely

			Holding period		
	Bond	Years to maturity	1 Year	4 Years	7 Years
Mean	A	1	9.00%[a]	9.00%	9.00%
	B	5	10.92	10.70	10.69
	C	10	11.83	11.10	11.05
Standard deviation	A	1	0.05[b]	1.85	2.11
	B	5	7.36	0.01	1.05
	C	10	13.06	1.41	0.25

[a] The mean for Bond A with one-year holding period is $\frac{1}{3}(8.94\%) + \frac{1}{3}(9.00\%) + \frac{1}{3}(9.06\%) = 9.00\%$.

[b] The variance for Bond A with one-year holding period is $\frac{1}{3}(8.94\% - 9.00\%)^2 + \frac{1}{3}(9.00\% - 9.00\%)^2 + \frac{1}{3}(9.06\% - 9.00\%)^2 = 0.0024\%$; the standard deviation is $(0.0024)^{\frac{1}{2}} \cong 0.05\%$

3% (see column 1). A 3% shift down means that Bond A now has a yield to maturity of 6% (9% − 3%). Also examine three alternative holding periods: one year, four years, and seven years. The yield curve shift is assumed to be immediate and permanent. Also, assume that the coupons received are reinvested in the identical yield to maturity of the bond prevailing when the coupons are received. That is, coupons from the 10-year bond are reinvested in the same 10-year bond.[3]

Exhibit 8.5 gives the detailed calculations of one cell in Exhibit 8.4; it calculates the rate of return of about 10.7% for Bond B when rates fall by 3%. All other figures of Exhibit 8.4(b) are calculated in a similar way.

There are two parts to Exhibit 8.5. The first three columns are used to calculate the future value of the coupons received out to four years. A 10.68% coupon bond with a par value of $1,000 has a semiannual coupon payment of $53.4, or $0.1068 \times \frac{1}{2} \times \$1,000$. The second part of this table – the last three columns – is used to calculate the present value of the cash flows received after the fourth year. The value after four years is $1,517.60, or $489.2435 + \$1028.3564$. Hence, the semiannual rate of return is $(\$1,517.60/\$1,000)^{\frac{1}{8}} - 1 = 0.0535$ or 5.35%, or 10.7% on an annual basis ($5.35\% \times 2$), which is approximately 10.68%, the original coupon yield. Note that the precise annual yield is $(1.0535)^2 - 1 = 0.10986$, or about 10.986%. However, because practitioners commonly switch from semiannual yields to annual yields, ignoring the compounding effect, we adhere to their simple method of calculating the figure shown in Exhibit 8.4(b).

Notice that if there is no change in the yield to maturity, then the holding period rate of return exactly equals the initial yield to maturity. If yields fall by 3%, then for a one-year holding period the 10-year bond experiences a rate of return of 28.22% due to the large appreciation in price. (See the previous discussion on bond prices and maturity.) However, the one-year bond actually has a rate of return of 8.94% less than the original 9%, because the semiannual coupon had to be reinvested at 6% rather than 9%. If yields rise by 3%, exactly the opposite effect occurs for the one-year holding period.

Exhibit 8.5 Illustration of the rate-of-return calculation for the 10.68% coupon bond held for four years with a rate decline of 3%

Value of coupons due to first four years ($)			Value of coupon of fifth year and par value ($)		
Time to cash flow (years)	Semiannual coupon[a]	Future value[a] (end of fourth year) of coupon	Time to cash flow (years)	Cash flow	Present value[b] (end of fourth year) of coupon and par
0.5	53.40	69.5175	4.5	53.4	51.4253
1.0	53.40	66.9467	5.0	1053.4	976.9311
1.5	53.40	64.4710		Total	1028.3564
2.0	53.40	62.0869			
2.5	53.40	59.7909			
3.0	53.40	57.5799			
3.5	53.40	55.4506			
4.0	53.40	53.4000			
Total		489.2435			

[a] Coupon reinvested at $10.68\% - 3\% = 7.68\%$ and on a semiannual basis, at $7.68\%/2 = 3.84\%$. For example, $\$53.4 (1.0384) = \$55.4506$.
[b] Calculated at 3.84% on a semiannual basis. For example, $1,053.4/(1.0384)^2 \cong 976.9311$.

---

[3] For simplicity, ignore any potential changes that may occur as the bond's maturity shortens. That is, assume that the initial yield to maturity is earned over the life of the bond.

Exhibit 8.4(b) shows that for the seven-year holding period, the reinvestment effect is more prevalent. For example, if rates fall by 3%, then the one-year bond (Bond A) has to be reinvested at a lower rate. Hence, the rate of return is 6.42%.

Notice what happens at Year 4 for Bond B. The rates of return under all three scenarios are almost identical, at around 10.7%. Exhibit 8.4(c) presents the mean and standard deviation, assuming the yield curve shifts are equally probable. Notice that the standard deviation for only Bond B for a four-year holding period was almost 0. The reason for this result is that at a four year holding period, the price effect and reinvestment effect just offset each other for a five-year bond.

In summary, investors with a well-defined holding period should be able to invest in a bond or construct a bond portfolio that will have minimal overall interest rate risk. Investors accomplish this result by balancing the price effect against the reinvestment effect.

To find the investment strategy that minimizes the interest rate risk, we need to consider the bond's **duration**. The concept of duration takes into account the fact that the bond's par value is paid at maturity, whereas coupon payments are paid during the life of the bond. Duration is a weighted average of the timing of these various cash flows. The concept of duration and its definition was suggested first by Macaulay in 1938 (see the Selected References at the end of the chapter).

Duration of a bond or a portfolio of bonds is also the holding period that balances the price effect against the reinvestment effect. As we will see, the duration of a five-year bond is about four years. Recall that if an investor has a bond with a 10-year maturity, he does not wait 10 years to receive his money back (he may receive some of it earlier as coupon payments). Duration is similar to the average number of years investors have to wait to get their money back. It is not a simple average, because the farther away the cash inflow, the less weight investors give it, because it has a lower present value in comparison to the same amount of money received earlier.

The formal definition of duration is a present value-weighted average of the number of years investors wait to receive cash flows. The duration is calculated as follows:

$$D = \sum_{t=1}^{T} t w_t \tag{8.2}$$

where the weight w_t is given by $w_t = PV(CF_t)/P$ and $PV(CF_t)$ is the present value of the cash flows:

$$PV(CF_t) = \frac{CF_t}{(1 + y)^t}$$

and CF_t is the cash flow received (coupon payment or both coupon and Par) at time t, P is the current market price of the bond, y is the periodic yield to maturity, and T is the bond's time to maturity (i.e. the number of periods to maturity measured generally in years or half years – see next examples).

Because $P = \sum_{t=1}^{T} PV(CF_t)$, we see that duration is a weighted average of the time t when cash flows are received (where $PV(CF_t)/P$ serves as the weight). Note that for a zero-coupon bond there is only one future cash flow; hence, $P = PV(CF_t)$, and the duration is just the time to maturity. Moving from a zero-coupon bond to a coupon-paying bond, the duration declines.

The duration is calculated by employing Rule 5.

Rule 5: Calculate the PV of each cash flow as a proportion of the bond's price and multiply it by the year number at which this cash flow is obtained. Sum up all these terms to obtain the bond's duration.

Using the data of Exhibit 8.4 we show below how to calculate the duration of the five-year bond with 10 semiannual coupon payments (where $C = \$53.40$, or 10.68% on a semiannual bond, y is approximately equal to 0.1068/2, and Par = \$1,000):

$$D = \sum_{t=1}^{10} \left[\frac{tCF_t / \left(1 + \frac{0.1068}{2}\right)^t}{\$1,000} \right]$$

$$= \frac{1}{\$1,000} \sum_{t=1}^{10} \frac{t \times C}{1.0534^t} + \frac{1}{\$1,000} \times \frac{10 \times Par}{1.0534^{10}}$$

$$= 0.001 \left[\frac{1 \times 53.4}{1.0534^1} + \frac{2 \times 53.4}{1.0534^2} + \cdots + \frac{10 \times 53.4}{1.0534^{10}} \right]$$

$$+ \frac{1}{\$1,000} \times \frac{10 \times \$1,000}{1.0534^{10}}$$

$$\cong 0.001(\$2,057.588) + 5.944$$

$$\cong 8$$

It is not surprising that the duration for Bond B equals exactly eight *semiannual periods*, or the *four-year holding period*. Similar calculations reveal that the duration for the one-year bond is 0.98 of a year, and the duration for the 10-year bond is 6.3 years. Exhibit 8.6 shows the risk involved with five-year bonds for various holding periods. For holding periods shorter than four years, the price risk is more dominant than the reinvestment risk. This price risk declines for longer holding periods, as it is being offset by the benefits of reinvestment. For holding periods longer than four years, the reinvestment risk is more dominant. This reinvestment risk increases for longer holding periods because the benefits of the price effect are declining. For

Exhibit 8.6 Interest rate risk for a five-year bond with various assumed holding periods

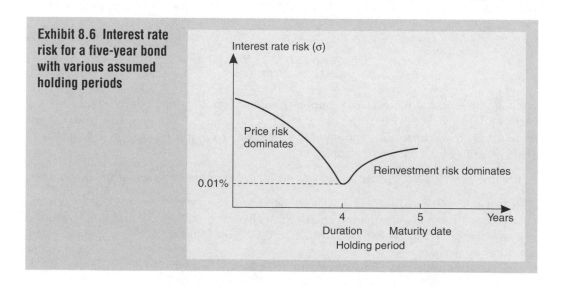

PRACTICE BOX

Problem

Calculate the duration of the following two bonds. Bond A is a two-year, zero-coupon bond trading at $850 (Par = $1,000). Bond B is a two-year, 5% annual coupon bond trading at par (Par = $1,000).

Solution

Equation 8.2 shows the following for Bond A:

$D = 2(\$850/\$850) = 2$ years

(Note that CF_t = Par and $PV(CF_t) = P$.) For Bond B, Equation 8.2 shows the following:

$$D = \sum_{t=1}^{2} t \times \left(\frac{CF_t/(1 + 0.05)^t}{\$1,000} \right) = \frac{1}{\$1,000}\left[1\left(\frac{\$50}{1 + 0.05} \right) + 2\left(\frac{\$1,050}{(1 + 0.05)^2} \right) \right]$$

$$\cong \frac{1}{\$1,000} (\$47.619 + \$1,904.762)$$

$$\cong 1.95 \text{ years}$$

Thus, the coupon payments are shown to reduce the value of duration.

a four-year holding period, the two risks almost offset each other; hence, σ is almost zero. Thus, finding a bond with a duration equal to the planned holding period minimizes the investor's risk.

Duration and maturity are widely used by investment analysts. Exhibit 8.7 provides an example of how Capital Gains, Inc. uses the duration as one of the tools to measure risk.

8.2.1 Duration principles

The following are well-known duration principles.

Rule 6: Duration normally declines over time, a pattern called the **duration drift**. Because duration declines over time, for a given investment period, the bonds portfolio should be rebalanced to minimize the risk.

However, duration does not decline at the same speed as time. For example, from the previous discussion, we know that the duration of a zero-coupon bond is equal to its time to maturity. Thus, duration will decline with the passage of time, requiring the portfolio to be periodically adjusted to keep the duration equal to the desired holding period. After four years, the five-year bond in Exhibit 8.4 will have a duration of almost one year; therefore, if the holding period remains four years, the bond portfolios employing duration-based strategies must be rebalanced periodically.

Rule 7: Normally, duration is inversely related to yield to maturity.

For higher yields, the present value of more distant cash flows will be discounted by a greater amount. Hence, those cash flows will receive less weight, resulting in a lower duration. Recall that duration is the present value-weighted average of the number of years investors wait to receive cash flows.

Exhibit 8.7

Duration – What does It Mean?
Published By Capital Gains Inc.

Professional Investment Managers are constantly measuring the "risk level" and the "potential return" of your bond portfolio, under a variety of different economic/interest rate scenarios. One of the best measurements of the risk/reward ratio is something called "**duration**". Duration is a term that you may have heard someone use before, but you may not know exactly what it means or how it relates to bonds.

A textbook definition is: the average percentage change in a bonds value (price plus accrued interest) under shifts in the U.S. Treasury curve +/− 100 bpi (1%). In other words, it calculates the percentage change in the value of your bond portfolio if interest rates move up or down in 1% increments. Duration is typically measured on a scale of 1 to 30. A portfolio consisting solely of 1 year U.S. Treasury STRIPS will have a duration of 1, and a portfolio consisting solely of 30 year U.S. Treasury STRIPS has a duration of 30.

Remember that there is an "**inverse**" relationship between bond **prices** and bond **yields**. When interest rates "fall" the market value of bonds increases and when interest rates "rise" the market value of bonds, decreases. The magnitude of these changes in the market value of your portfolio can be measured by the duration of your portfolio.

As an example, let's assume the current duration of your fixed income portfolio is 9.27. If interest rates move down 100 basis points (one percentage point), the value of your fixed income securities will increase 9.27%. Keep in mind that this 9.27% increase is tacked on to any interest received to date (the coupon rate of return of your portfolio). Therefore, if your coupon rate of return is 6.05% and interest rates fall 100 basis points, your total return is a positive 15.32% (6.05% coupon rate + 9.27% = 15.32%) increase in market value. Conversely if interest rates move up 100 basis points the total return in your fixed income portfolio will be a negative 3.22% (6.05% − 9.27% = −3.22%).

The chart below, "graphically illustrates" how the total return of a fixed income portfolio will change under a variety of interest rate scenarios.

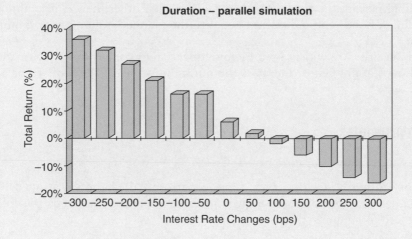

As fixed income managers, we will adjust the duration of your fixed income portfolio, based upon interest rate forecasts. If interest rates are expected to "fall", we will increase the duration of the portfolio (by selling shorter-term instruments and acquiring longer-term positions) to maximize the profit making potential of the portfolio. If on the other hand, interest rates are expected to rise, we will "shorten" the duration to minimize the loss in market value.

Successfully anticipating changes in interest rates is extremely difficult, but it can dramatically affect market value rates of return in your fixed income portfolio.

Calculating "duration" is one of the tools that we use to measure the risk/reward ratio before implementing an investment strategy designed to improve the rate of return in your fixed income portfolio.

Gary Karshna
Investment Manager

Source: Website at http://www.capitalgainsincorp.com/hottopic.htm, accessed 23 July 2001. 'Duration – What does it mean', 1 September 2000. © 2000, Capital Gains Incorporated. All rights reserved. This article is being distributed with the permission of Capital Gains Incorporated, www.capitalgainsincorp.com.

Rule 8: Normally, duration is directly related to the length to maturity.

Like zero-coupon bonds, most bonds exhibit the characteristic of having longer durations for longer maturities. This fact does not mean that longer-term bonds always have longer durations, because duration is affected by more than just maturity.

Rule 9: Normally, duration is inversely related to the level of coupon payments.

The higher the coupon level, the greater the weight given to the earlier cash flows (the coupon payments). Hence, the greater the coupon payments, the shorter the duration. Principles 3 and 4 are useful when an investor is altering the bond portfolio's duration. The investor who wishes to lengthen the duration should move to lower-coupon and longer-maturity bonds.

Rule 10: The duration of a bond portfolio is equal to the weighted average of the durations of the individual bonds, where the weights are determined by the market value of the bonds.[4]

Employing Rule 10, a bond portfolio duration, D, is given by

$$D = \sum_{i=1}^{n} w_i D_i \tag{8.3}$$

where $w_i = \text{MV}_i/\text{MV}$, MV_i is the market value of the portfolio holding of Bond i, MV is the market value of the total bond portfolio, D_i is the duration of Bond i, and n is the number of bonds in the portfolio.

PRACTICE BOX

Problem
Suppose the liabilities of a pension plan have a duration of five years. Also suppose there are two bond portfolios in which the pension manager could invest. Bond Fund A has a duration of 1 year, and Bond Fund B has a duration of 11 years. How can the money manager employ the duration matching strategy?

Solution
Recall from Equation 8.3 that

$$D = \sum_{i=1}^{n} w_i D_i$$

The manager has to determine what portion to place in Fund A and Fund B such that the pension assets have a duration of 5.0.

Specifically, $5 = w_1 + 11w_2 = w_1 + 11(1 - w_1)$. Thus, $5 = w_1 + 11 - 11w_1$. Solving for w_1 yields $w_1 = 0.6$, or 60%, and thus $w_2 = 40\%$. The manager should place 60% of the assets in Fund A and 40% in Fund B.

---

[4] To see that Equation 8.3 is appropriate, for simplicity we use zero-coupon bonds. Recall that the duration of a zero-coupon is its maturity. Denote by t_i the maturity of the ith bond. If we let each cash flow of a bond be represented as a zero-coupon bond, then the duration of a bond (a portfolio of zero-coupon bonds, and thus $\text{MV} = P$) can be represented as follows:

$$D = \sum_{i=1}^{n} w_i D_i = \sum_{i=1}^{n} \frac{\text{MV}_i}{\text{MV}} D_i = \sum_{i=1}^{n} \frac{\text{PV}(\text{CF}_i)}{P} t_i$$

where D_i is the duration of each cash flow, and thus $D_i = t_i$ for zero-coupon bonds, and n is the number of various bonds in the portfolio. We can treat a bond portfolio as one bond with numerous cash flows (each discounted at the individual bond's appropriate discount rate).

Therefore, an investor who wants a five-year duration (to manage the interest rate risk) can mix several bonds to achieve this goal. Thus, duration can be used to manage the interest rate sensitivity of bond portfolios.

Generally, duration increases with maturity. For zero-coupon bonds, duration increases linearly with maturity, because duration is equal to maturity. Curve 1 in Exhibit 8.8 describes this relationship for zero-coupon bonds.

Curve 2 describes a bond that pays an annual coupon. In such a case, the duration is shorter than the yield to maturity; hence, curve 2 is completely below curve 1.

According to Rule 8, it is tempting to believe that the duration always increases with the years to maturity. This idea is not necessarily true, because there is a coupon effect (Rule 9) that may offset the years to maturity effect. To clarify this idea, consider a 3% coupon bond whose yield is 15%. As the years to maturity increase, at the beginning the duration also increases. However, beyond some critical point, the weight of the par value drastically decreases (recall that it is discounted at 15%), and the weight of the coupons increases (in particular, the weight of the early coupons, which are not so heavily discounted). Hence, the duration may decrease. This type of relationship is described by curve 3.

In summary, the five principles state clearly the separate effect of each factor on duration. However, when more than one factor is changed simultaneously (for example, for a given yield, the coupon decreases and the maturity increases), the relationship between duration and years to maturity is more complex, as illustrated by curve 3 in Exhibit 8.8.

8.2.2 Convexity

Suppose that you have two bonds, A and B, with the same yield to maturity y_0 and the same price p_0: see Exhibit 8.9(a). Furthermore, assume that these two bonds also have the same duration. Should investors be indifferent with regard to investing in one of these bonds? Not really. The percentage gained or lost on the bond if the yield changes should also be taken into account. If duration is a perfect measure of risk of a bond, the answer is positive. However, duration is only one measure of risk and convexity complements.

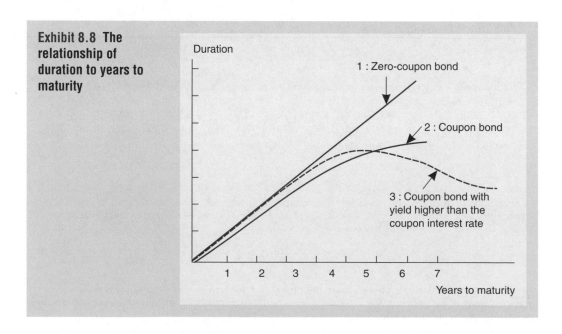

Exhibit 8.8 The relationship of duration to years to maturity

Convexity is a measure of the curvature of a bond's price–yield relationship. Exhibit 8.9(a) illustrates two bonds with different convexities. For simplicity, suppose that the yield to maturity of both bonds is y_0, and that the bonds have the same price, p_0. We do not make the assumption, however, that these bonds have the same maturity or the same coupon. The only assumption we make is that these two bonds have the same duration. Hence, all investors prefer Bond B, because no matter which direction yield to maturity goes, Bond B will always be worth more than Bond A. If the holding period is equal to the bond's duration, the risk of changes in interest rate is minimized. However, investors should not be concerned only about minimizing interest rate risk (or variance), but also they should strive to maximize convexity to capitalize on large changes in interest rates. The higher the convexity, the more curvature there is in the price–yield relationship. For example, in Exhibit 8.9(a), Bond B has a higher convexity than Bond A.

In general, we would not expect to find two bonds like Bond A and Bond B as in Exhibit 8.9(a). Investor demand for Bond B will drive its price up and therefore lower its yield to maturity. Investor preference for higher convexity results in higher prices for highly convex bonds, and thus they have lower yields to maturity.

Exhibit 8.9(b) presents the curves of two bonds corresponding to the following parameters:

	Coupon	Years to maturity	Yield	Duration
Bond A	15%	3	10%	3.3154
Bond B	13.78%	3.89	10%	3.3154

Thus, the two bonds have the same profitability yield of 10% and the same duration. The prices of the bonds given by the PV of all cash flows discounted at the 10% discount rate are $p_A = \$112.43$ and $p_B = \$103.29$. Is one bond more convex than the other? Exhibit 8.9(b) shows that this is not the case. If the yield goes up, the price of bond A falls less than bond B (in percent). However, if yields decline, the percentage of capital gain on bond B is larger. Thus, neither bond is more convex than the other. If investors believe that there is a high chance of an increase in yield, bond A should be purchased. If the investor believes there is a big chance of a decrease in yield, bond B should be preferred.

As with bond prices and duration, there are some basic principles related to convexity:

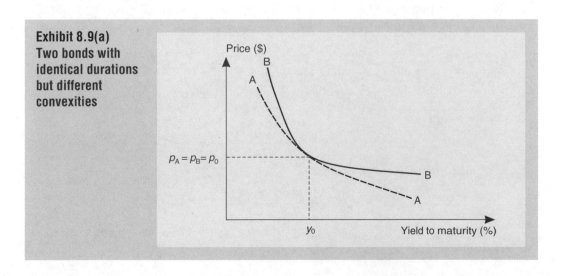

**Exhibit 8.9(a)
Two bonds with identical durations but different convexities**

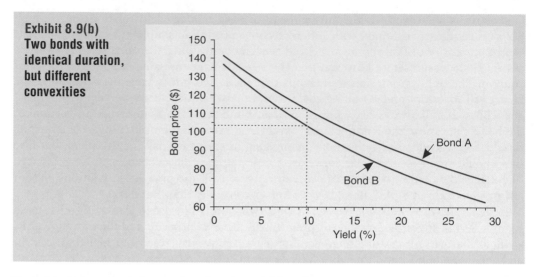

Exhibit 8.9(b)
Two bonds with identical duration, but different convexities

Rule 11: Convexity is inversely related to yield to maturity.

Recall from Exhibit 8.2 that the curvature was greater for lower yields than for higher yields.

Rule 12: Convexity is inversely related to the coupon. The curvature is flatter for higher-coupon bonds.

Rule 13: Convexity is positively related to duration.

PRACTICE BOX

Problem

Suppose you are considering an investment in two bonds. Bond A has a duration of eight years and a market price of $950, and Bond B has a duration of four years and a market price of $1,050. How should you invest $10,000 in these bonds if you have a desired holding period of seven years and wish to minimize interest rate risk?

Solution

We need to construct a portfolio with a duration of seven years. The duration of the bond portfolio can be found using Equation 8.3:

$$D = w_A D_A + w_B D_B = w_A D_A + (1 - w_A)D_B$$

Substituting for w_A yields

$$D = (MV_A/MV)D_A + (1 - MV_A/MV)D_B$$

Solving for MV_A yields

$$MV_A = \frac{MV(D - D_B)}{D_A - D_B}$$

Using the data given in the problem yields

$$MV_A = \frac{\$10,000(7.0 - 4.0)}{8.0 - 4.0} = \$7,500$$

Hence, $7,500 should be invested in Bond A, and $2,500 = $10,000 − $7,500 should be invested in Bond B.

These principles are useful for bond management. For example, if you wanted to lengthen duration and raise the convexity, you could move to lower coupon-bearing bonds. Recall from Rule 9 (duration) that duration is normally inversely related to the coupon level. Rule 12 (convexity) indicates that convexity is also inversely related to coupon. Hence, by selling high-coupon bonds and buying lower-coupon bonds of the same maturity, you can both lengthen the duration and increase the convexity.

The tools of duration and convexity can be used in bond portfolio management. Because these techniques are used primarily by institutional portfolio managers, we refer to *bond managers* rather than *bond investors*.

8.3 IMMUNIZATION

A bond manager who has a well-defined holding period can identify all the potential portfolios with the duration equal to the holding period and adopt the portfolio with the highest convexity. For example, a life insurance company may have a rather long holding period. Hence, it would seek a portfolio with a long duration. Strategies such as this are known as **immunization strategies**; they try to neutralize the adverse effects of changes in yield to maturity while still benefiting, if possible, from changes in interest rates. This section discusses two categories of immunization strategies: income immunization and price immunization.

8.3.1 Income immunization

Consider the problems facing a manager of a company's pension plan. Recall from the previous discussions that the smaller the coupon, the larger the percentage change in the bond's price in response to a given change in the bond's yield. The pension fund will need to pay out money to its clients based on their age; hence, the cash outflow can be accurately predicted. Having sufficient liquid assets in the portfolio to meet cash disbursements is critical to the pension manager's success. The manager can invest in bonds that minimize the probability that insufficient funds will occur in the future. The technique to achieve this goal is called *immunization*.

Income immunization strategies ensure that adequate resources are available to meet perceived cash disbursement needs. One appealing strategy is to invest in a bond portfolio that has coupon payments and principal payments that exactly meet the future cash needs. This approach is known as a **cash matching strategy**. A cash matching strategy is very restrictive and allows very little flexibility. Cash matching may eliminate many otherwise attractive bonds, e.g. with a relatively high yield and maybe with no coupons because they do not have the desirable cash flow properties.

An alternative approach is known as a **duration matching strategy**, which allows for a variety of potential portfolios so long as the duration of the liability stream equals the duration of the bond portfolio. However, this approach has a potential problem, too. To meet liquidity needs, bond managers may have to sell bonds at temporarily depressed prices. For example, one way to construct a portfolio with the needed payment stream would be to purchase only zero-coupon bonds that had a maturity exactly equal to the duration of the pension liability stream. Although this is a duration matching strategy (recall that the duration of a zero-coupon bond is its maturity), it will not prove useful for the pension manager, because next year's cash disbursements must be paid by selling bonds that may be depressed because of a temporary rise in interest rates. Of course, such a problem would be avoided in the unrealistic case where a pension fund would have only one payout to its pension holders at the maturity of the bond.

By combining the benefits of cash matching strategies with the benefits of duration matching strategies, the **horizon matching strategy** has been developed. In a horizon matching strategy, the manager designs a portfolio that is cash matched over the short horizon and duration matched over the long horizon. For example, the manager could cash match over the next four years to avoid having to sell in a bear market, and duration match the remaining liabilities. Thus, the horizon matching strategy provides the liquidity benefits of cash matching, as well as the flexibility of duration matching.

For example, suppose a pension plan must pay out $1 million in benefits in each of the next five years and then pay out $2 million a year for the next 20 years. The pension manager using the horizon matching strategy would invest in zero-coupon bonds with par values of $1 million that mature in each of the next five years (or any equivalent strategy that assures $1 million in cash each year) and then duration match the remaining liabilities.

All three income immunization strategies aim to provide sufficient resources to meet the future income needs of the pension plan. However, these strategies ignore the impact of changes in yield to maturity on the current market value of the portfolio. For example, the income immunization guarantees the needed income every year, but ignores possible reduction in the value of the bond portfolio. The current market value of the portfolio is a critical concern for bank portfolio managers who must maintain certain levels of capital for regulatory reasons. Also, the performance of fund managers is commonly judged by the market value of the assets managed. Managers who are concerned with the preservation of the original market value of the portfolio must consider the price immunization techniques discussed next.

8.3.2 Price immunization

Price immunization includes those strategies that ensure that the market value of assets always exceeds the market value of liabilities by a specified amount. For example, there is a push in the banking industry towards 'market value' or 'current value' accounting. Market value accounting seeks to restate the assets and liabilities to their current market value so that investors can assess the true worth of the equity. The goal is to have the market value of the assets, which is less vulnerable to changes in the interest rate than the market value of the liabilities.

Price immunization strategies use convexity. For example, the pension plan previously described seeks to develop a portfolio that is not only duration matched but also has the convexity of its assets exceeding the convexity of its liabilities. Exhibit 8.10 illustrates this bond portfolio strategy. It assumes that the pension fund was adequately funded such that the market value of the bond portfolio (assets) equalled the present value of the portfolio's future payments (liabilities). As long as the convexity of the assets exceeds the convexity of the liabilities, the market value of the difference will grow with changes in interest rates. Also, the greater the convexity, the greater will be the gains from changes in interest rates. Hence, in this case we say the pension fund is price immunized.

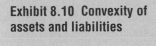

Exhibit 8.10 Convexity of assets and liabilities

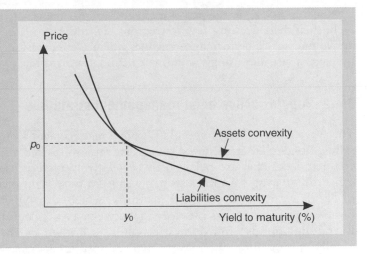

8.4 PASSIVE VERSUS ACTIVE BOND MANAGEMENT STRATEGIES

Up to this point in the discussion, the role of security selection to enhance the value of bond portfolios has been ignored. This section integrates security selection into bond management.

The immunization strategies already discussed can be passive or active. In a passively managed bond portfolio, the manager attempts to mimic a bond index. Recall that if the bond market is efficient, and thus all bonds are fairly priced, then the process of selecting bonds could be managed passively. Alternatively, active management implicitly assumes that the bond market is not efficient and, hence, that there are excess returns to be pursued.

Passive bond management requires few financial resources and uses little time. Passive bond managers can devote most of their energy to refining the immunization technique they adopt but not to bond selectivity, i.e. the selection of underpriced bonds.

8.4.1 Contingent immunization

Active bond managers are faced with a dilemma. How can they pursue active bond management strategies without exposing a bond fund to excessive interest rate risk? One solution is known as **contingent immunization**. This is an investment strategy designed to accommodate both the desire of bond managers to pursue active strategies and the desire to minimize the effect of adverse movements in interest rates. A bond manager using this approach pursues timing strategies or duration mismatches in an attempt to profit from forecast moves in interest rates. Alternatively, a bond manager may actively trade bonds that are believed to be mispriced by selling overpriced bonds and buying underpriced bonds.

The bond manager can act unimpeded as long as the performance is good. However, when she begins to experience relatively poor performance, she must move towards immunizing strategies. As performance continues to decline, the manager continues to move more quickly towards an immunized portfolio. Hence, the pension fund can establish a 'floor' on the active manager's performance. If the active manager performs well, then there are very few restrictions regarding exposure to interest rate risk. As the active manager's performance declines, there are increasing restrictions. Specifically, the manager must increasingly immunize the bond portfolio.

8.4.2 Popular active bond management strategies

There are many different speculative bond management strategies. One strategy involves selling bonds that are believed to be relatively overpriced and buying bonds with similar characteristics that are believed to be relatively underpriced. This strategy is called a **substitution swap**.[5] Another strategy, called a **pure yield pickup swap**, involves moving to bonds with a higher yield to maturity, which also typically implies longer-duration bonds. Speculating on the spread between two different bond markets, such as Eurodollar bonds[6] and domestic bonds, is known as an **intermarket spread swap**. Finally, a **rate anticipation swap** involves positioning a bond portfolio such that maximum gains are achieved if a perceived rate change occurs.

The overall objective of active bond management is to make superior selections of bonds. The selection of superior bonds can be achieved by superior foresight regarding the future of overall interest rates or by superior foresight regarding the credit quality of individual bonds. This chapter has discussed changes in a bond's price that are due to changes in the interest rate. Managers, therefore, try to predict the future market interest rate (see also Exhibit 8.7). Also, the price of specific bonds may decline because of firm-specific circumstances, such as financial distress. This condition may result in heavy losses. Unless they are buying only government bonds, managers should also analyze the risk of bankruptcy of a specific firm's bonds. For example, when Wang Laboratories filed for Chapter 11 bankruptcy, the price of its bonds fell 50%. Specifically, bond managers do not want to be caught holding bonds when a firm is declining in credit quality.

SUMMARY

■ *List the basic principles of bond pricing.*
The price of a bond is the present value of all future coupon payments plus the par value discounted to the present at the required rate of return (the yield to maturity). Bond prices change with just the passage of time. Bond prices are inversely related to the yield to maturity. Longer-term bonds are more sensitive to changes in yield to maturity. The sensitivity to changes in yield to maturity increases at a decreasing rate with maturity. Finally, higher-coupon bonds are less sensitive to changes in yield to maturity than lower-coupon bonds.

■ *Explain how duration is used to minimize interest rate risk.*
A bond portfolio's duration corresponds to the holding period at which the portfolio's interest-rate risk is minimized. Duration can also be used as a measure of relative bond price volatility. Convexity is a measure of the curvature of a bond's price–yield relationship. When everything else is the same, bond investors prefer higher convexity.

---

[5] The names given to these active strategies originated in Sidney Homer and Martin L. Leibowitz, *Inside the Yield Book: New Tools for Bond Market Strategy* (Englewood Cliffs, NJ: Prentice Hall, 1972).

[6] Recall that Eurodollar bonds are bonds that pay in US dollars but are issued outside the United States.

■ *Explain how immunization techniques protect bond portfolios from interest rate risk.* Immunization techniques protect both income streams and the current market value of the assets and liabilities from the effects of changing interest rates. Income immunization protects future income needs. Income immunization strategies include cash matching, duration matching and horizon matching. Price immunization uses convexity and seeks to protect current market values.

■ *Describe active bond management strategies.*
The overall objective of active bond management strategies is to make superior bond selections. Prudent bond trading strategies require the ability to forecast future events such as changing interest rates and overall economic activity. Default risk should always be of utmost concern. Contingent immunization is an investment strategy designed to accommodate both the desire of bond managers to trade actively and the desire of investors to minimize interest rate risk. Several bond trading strategies are designed to enhance returns, including substitution swaps, pure yield pickup swaps, intermarket swaps and rate anticipation swaps.

KEY TERMS

Cash matching strategy	Horizon matching strategy	Price immunization
Contingent immunization	Immunization strategy	Pure yield pickup swap
Convexity	Income immunization	Rate anticipation swap
Duration	strategy	Reinvestment effect
Duration drift	Intermarket spread swap	Substitution swap
Duration matching strategy	Price effect	

QUESTIONS

8.1 Suppose you have two similar bonds. Bond A is callable, and Bond B is not. However, Bond A offers a higher coupon such that both bonds are currently priced the same. Show graphically how these two bonds' prices will behave for different yields to maturity.

8.2 Several income immunization strategies were discussed in this chapter. Rank each immunization strategy from the least flexible to the most flexible. Explain your rankings.

8.3 'If the yield to maturity is zero, then the duration must be zero.' Evaluate this statement.

8.4 'Two bonds have the same market price, the same yield to maturity, the same par values and the same maturity. Thus, the two bonds must have the same duration.' Evaluate this statement. If you agree, then prove it. If you do not agree, then provide an example refuting this statement.

8.5 Which bond will have a shorter duration, a bond that is callable or the same bond that is not callable? Explain.

8.6 Suppose you have a bond with a yield to maturity of 5% and a duration of four years. Suddenly inflation escalates. How would this affect duration?

8.7 Suppose a new medicine has been invented that immunizes people against cancer. How should this invention influence the investment policy of the bond portfolio managers of life insurance companies? Explain your answer.

8.8 Suppose you invest in a 10-year, 8% semiannual coupon bond, $1,000 par, with a yield to maturity of 6%.

(a) What is the price of the bond?
(b) Show graphically the path of the bond's price over time if the yield to maturity remains the same.

8.9 The following table gives the bond prices for five-year and 30-year bonds for various yields to maturity. What inferences can be drawn from this information?

Years to maturity			Yield		
	5%	7.5%	10%	12.5%	15%
5	$1,219	$1,103	$1,000	$909	$828
30	1,773	1,297	1,000	805	671

8.10 Suppose you were given the following information on three semiannual Treasury bonds with the same maturity:

Bond	Coupon	Price
A	8%	$1,000
B	$7^5/_8$	?
C	7	975

What is the price of Bond B? (Hint: Arbitrage profits do not exist in equilibrium.)

8.11 Suppose you owned four different bonds with the following characteristics:

Bond	Market value of holdings	Duration
A	$14,327	1.27 years
B	$56,490	8.74 years
C	$19,467	5.66 years
D	$37,592	6.72 years

What is the duration of the bond portfolio?

8.12 Suppose you have an $n = 10$-year bond with a par value of $1,000 and an annual coupon of $50. The market price of the bond is $900.

(a) Calculate the bond's duration.
(b) How will the duration change if the coupon is paid at the beginning of each year rather than at the end of the year? (Assume that the yield to maturity remains the same.)

8.13 Suppose you owned a 10-year bond with a par value of $1,000 and a market value of $1,000 with a coupon of $50 paid at the end of each year.

(a) What is the yield to maturity?
(b) Calculate the market bond price for yields to maturity of 2.5%, 5%, 7.5%, 10%, 12.5%, 15%, 17.5% and 20%. Draw the market price of the bond as a function of the interest rate. Is there a convex relationship?

8.14 Suppose you have two bonds with the following characteristics: for Bond A, $P_A = $900 and $D_A = 8$ years; for Bond B, $P_B = $1,100 and $D_B = 15$ years. You have a holding period of 12 years. What bond portfolio mix will suit your holding period, assuming you wish to minimize interest rate risk? (Assume a $500,000 portfolio.)

8.15 There are five bonds, each of which has a duration of four years. Your holding period is two years. 'By diversifying between these four bonds, you can reduce the portfolio duration to two years.' Do you agree with this statement? Defend your answer.

SELECTED REFERENCES

Bierwag, G.O. *Duration Analysis: Managing Interest Rate Risk*. Cambridge, MA: Ballinger, 1987.
This book focuses on duration and how it is used to manage interest rate risk.

Fabozzi, Frank J. *Fixed Income Mathematics*. Chicago: Probus Publishing, 1988.
This book addresses the fundamentals of the relationship between bond prices and underlying variables. The specific focus is on duration and convexity.

Fabozzi, Frank J., and T. Dessa Fabozzi. *Bond Markets, Analysis and Strategies*. Englewood Cliffs, NJ: Prentice-Hall, 1989.
This book is similar to Fabozzi's Fixed Income Mathematics but also gives specific institutional details of the Treasury, corporate and municipal bond markets.

Homer, Sidney, and Martin L. Liebowitz. *Inside the Yield Book: New Tools for Bond Market Strategy*. Englewood Cliffs, NJ: Prentice-Hall, 1972.
This path-breaking book in the area of bond management developed the taxonomy of active trading strategies.

Macaulay, Frederick R. *Some Theoretical Problems Suggested by the Movements of Interest Rates, Bond Yields, and Stock Prices in the United States since 1856*. New York: National Bureau of Economic Research, 1938.
This monograph first developed the idea of duration.

SUPPLEMENTARY REFERENCES

Barber, Joel R., and Mark L. Copper. 'Is bond convexity a free lunch?' *Journal of Portfolio Management*, Fall 1997, pp. 113–19.

Bierwag, Gerald O., Iraj Fooladi, and Gordon S. Roberts. 'Designing an immunized portfolio: is m-squared the key?' *Journal of Banking and Finance*, 17(6), December 1993, pp. 1147–70.

Chapman, David A., and D. Neil Pearson. 'Recent advances in estimating term structure models'. *Financial Analysts Journal*, July/August 2001.

Christensen, Peter Ove, and Bjarne G. Sorensen. 'Duration, convexity, and time value'. *Journal of Portfolio Management*, 20(2), Winter 1994, pp. 51–60.

Dybrig, Philip H., and William Marshall. 'Pricing long bonds: pitfalls and opportunities'. *Financial Analysts Journal*, January–February 1996, pp. 32–9.

Hull, John, and Alan White. 'Interest rates – The essentials of the LMM', *Risk*, December 2000.

Kahn, Ronald N. 'Bond managers need to take more risk'. *Journal of Portfolio Management*, Spring 1998, pp. 70–6.

Kritzman, Mark. 'What practitioners need to know…about duration and convexity'. *Financial Analysts Journal*, 48(6), November–December 1992, pp. 17–20.

Leschhorn, H. 'Managing yield curve risk with combination hedges'. *Financial Analysts Journal*, May/June 2001.

Longstaff, Francis A., and Eduardo S. Schwartz. 'Interest rate volatility and bond prices'. *Financial Analysts Journal*, 49(4), July–August 1993, pp. 70–4.

Mehran, Jamshid, and Ghassem Homaifar. 'Analytics of duration and convexity for bonds with embedded options: the case of convertibles'. *Journal of Business, Finance and Accounting*, 20(1), January 1993, pp. 107–13.

Thomas, Lee, and Ram Willner. 'Measuring the duration of an internationally diversified bond portfolio'. *Journal of Portfolio Management*, Fall 1997, pp. 93–101.

Chapter 9

COMMON STOCKS: VALUATION

Learning objectives

After studying this chapter you should be able to:

1 Explain how investors use stock valuation models.

2 Describe the assumptions underlying the constant dividend growth model.

3 Value firms that are presently experiencing supergrowth.

4 Explain under what conditions the P/E ratio can be used safely.

5 Discuss the three main financial statements of the firm (Appendix 9A).

6 Warn that earnings can be manipulated.

INVESTMENT IN THE NEWS

Rating Your Broker's Stock Picks

Value investors learn new tricks: How they're adapting to the new economy

For years, two great armies of investors have done battle on Wall Street. In one camp stand the growth investors, willing to pay dearly for companies that they believe can generate big profits for years to come. In the other camp are the value investors. They're leery of the rosy forecasts. They'll buy only into companies with real assets and solid earnings in the here and now – and at bargain prices....

The new value investing relies more on forecasting – long a taboo for value investors. Benjamin Graham and David L. Dodd, who laid down the principles of value investing in the 1930s, frowned on earnings forecasts because they were too speculative. The new value investing looks more to another author of the same era, economist John Burr Williams. Williams' Theory of Investment Value taught that an investment was worth the present value of its future cash flows – which, of course, had to be estimated. 'People have been using static methods to think about a dynamic world', says Michael J. Mauboussin, an investment strategist at Credit Suisse First Boston. 'No wonder value investing hasn't worked well.'....

Source: Jeffrey M. Laderman, *Business Week*, 14 June 1999.

This chapter and Chapter 10 introduce methods investors use to value stocks. Most of the methods described are based on discounting future cash flows. In addition to valuation methods based on discounted cash flows, the price/earnings (P/E) ratio is also discussed. This widely used valuation measure, which is based on past performance, often appears in the financial press. Thus, investors should understand its predictive power and limitations.

Finally, although theoretically only future cash flows are relevant for stock valuation, in practice many other investment criteria are employed. As some of these investment criteria rely also on accounting data, we briefly discuss in Appendix 9A the firm's financial statements and the information contained in these statements.

As will be explained later in the chapter, in calculating the present value of future dividends we must assume some discount rate. The **discount rate** is the required rate of return by investors, given the riskiness of the stock. If investors hold only one stock in their portfolio, then the variability of future dividends determines the value of the discount rate (k). If investors hold many assets in their portfolios, then the variability of the asset's return, as well as the various correlations, determine the risk – hence determining the discount rate. Thus, the valuation method presented in this chapter does not contradict the portfolio analysis studied in Chapter 6 (see also Chapter 14).

For a given discount rate, valuation models are developed based on the future average cash flow. This chapter assesses whether investors should discount earnings, dividends or the future stock price. Also, it analyzes how retained earnings and the firm's reinvestment policy affect the stock price.

9.1 USES OF STOCK VALUATION MODELS

Why should stock valuation models be studied? Many investors rely on the stock values, obtained from the valuation models described in this chapter, to make investment decisions. This section looks at typical applications of model-generated stock values to demonstrate the use of stock valuation models in practice.

9.1.1 Assessing investment opportunities

The most important use of valuation models is in selecting stocks for investment. How can you tell if a share of British Airways stock traded at £302 is a good investment? Is the stock underpriced? Is it overpriced? The ability to correctly value securities is essential to successful investing. For example, if you value Amoco stock at £100 and the current market price is £85, this valuation suggests you should buy Amoco stock. Of course, you should actually buy the stock only after rigorously testing your model and gaining confidence in its valuation capabilities.

One group of investment theorists believe that changes in stock prices, particularly short-run changes in stock prices, cannot be predicted. They feel that no stock valuation model can locate underpriced or overpriced stock. Other groups of professional investors as well as investment theorists believe that underpriced stocks can be detected. We claim that even though you may not believe stock valuation models can locate mispriced stocks, you must include other people's opinions in your assessment of stock prices. After all, if a group of believers in a particular model of stock valuation predict that prices will move in a given direction, their actions could affect stock prices even though there is no economic foundation for this price change. For example, adherents of the 'Super Bowl indicator' will buy stocks after an NFL win and thus push stock prices higher (statistics reveal that after an NFL win, the stock market tends to rise significantly more than after an NFL loss). You may not agree with these investors, but you could benefit from knowing the direction the market will take based on their actions. If you weren't aware of their valuation model, you might miss a stock market rally. Indeed, the famous economist John Maynard Keynes describes the stock exchange as a place where successful investing is the art of what people think other people think about stock prices.[1]

9.1.2 Valuing a common stock issue: the case of IPO

When a firm goes public, it needs some method to estimate the value of its stock. Suppose you own a successful family firm that needs additional capital to expand internationally. You decide to issue stock to the public. (Recall from Chapter 3 that this is called an initial public offering, or IPO.) When you make this decision, there is no market price for your shares. To determine the selling price of your firm's stock, you need a way to value your equity. Even if you believe the market price of common stock equals the value of the stock, you need to employ a stock valuation model, because at the time of the first public offering there is no market price for the shares. By the same token, an underwriter who insures your issue needs some valuation model in order to decide the firm's economic value to be insured.

9.1.3 Estimating the appropriate discount rate

You studied the concept of a firm's cost of capital or discount rate in your course on the principles of finance. The evaluation of an investment project requires an estimate of the firm's cost of capital. The cost of equity is a major component in the cost of capital. Financial managers can use stock prices and stock valuation models to calculate the cost of equity.

9.1.4 Understanding the financial media

Articles and reports in the financial media use terms from stock valuation models: growth rate, supergrowth firms, price/earnings ratios, and so forth. By studying stock valuation models, you will know what these terms mean and how to apply them.

Many stock valuation models exist. The following sections explain how the different methods should be used and under what situations all these methods yield the same results.

---

[1] See John Maynard Keynes, *The General Theory of Employment and Money* (New York: Harcourt Brace, 1936), p. 156.

9.2 THE DISCOUNTED CASH FLOW PRINCIPLE

9.2.1 Buyers and sellers of a stock

Many stock valuation models have their roots in the discounted cash flow (DCF) principle, which states that the current value of any asset is the present value of all its future cash flows.

A stock is an asset whose future expected cash flows are $CF_1, CF_2, \ldots, CF_n$, where the subscript $i = 1, 2, \ldots, n$ denotes the year in which the cash flow is obtained. The value of the stock is simply the discounted value of all these cash flows. The cash flows to the investor are the received dividends and the cash flow from selling the stock. To illustrate how to value a given stock, suppose you forecast that Ford Motor Company will pay a £4 cash dividend per share at the end of the next year and a £5 cash dividend per share at the end of the second year. Furthermore, you estimate that you will be able to sell the shares of Ford two years from now for £130. Because these are only estimates, they are uncertain; and like any uncertain cash flow stream, you discount the cash flows at a discount rate (k), which is composed of the risk-free interest rate (time value of money) and a risk premium.[2] Suppose the discount rate is $k = 15\%$. The current stock price as published in the *Financial Times* is $P_0 = £100$. Should you buy the Ford stock? Like any other capital budgeting project, your decision is given by Rule 1 (where PV is the present value of the expected cash flows).

Rule 1: The decision is:
If $PV > P_0$, buy the stock (NPV > 0).
If $PV < P_0$, do not buy the stock (NPV < 0).
If $PV = P_0$, you are indifferent whether or not to buy the stock (NPV = 0).

These decision rules can be applied to all valuation models presented in this chapter.

To continue the example, the present value of Ford's £4 dividend paid at the first year is £3.48 (see Exhibit 9.1). At the end of the second year, £5 dividends are paid; however, the stock is also expected to be sold at £130, making the total expected cash flow £135, with a discounted value of £102.08. Therefore, the present value of all

---

Exhibit 9.1 Present value of £4 dividend in Year 1 and £5 dividend and £130 stock price in Year 2

	Beginning of first year (t_0)	End of first year (t_1)	End of second year (t_2)
Expected dividends		£4	£5
Expected price			£130
Total expected cash flow		£4	£135
Discount factor for each year		1/1.15	$1/1.15^2$
Contribution to present value		£4/1.15 ≅ £3.48	$£135/1.15^2 ≅ £102.08$
Present value of the total cash flows		£3.48 + £102.08 = £105.56	

---

[2] For simplicity, we ignore the effects of inflation.

expected cash flows is PV = £105.56. Because £105.56 is greater than the current price (P_0 = £100), the net present value (NPV = PV − P_0 = £105.56 − £100 = £5.56) is positive. If you expect these cash flows, you should buy the stock.

Who, then, sells Ford stock? Other investors in the market may have different predictions of the cash flows and hence a different future stock price. Suppose another investor believes, as you do, that the dividends will be £4 next year and £5 in two years, but unlike you, this investor believes that at the end of the second year the Ford stock will be selling only at £120. Even if this investor also uses a 15% discount rate, the present value of these cash flows is £98, as shown in Exhibit 9.2.

Suppose the second investor owns Ford stock. Because the present value is £98, which is less than the current stock price (P_0 = £100), this investor should sell the stock for £100. Indeed, every day investors trade Ford stock and almost all other stocks. Investors who believe a stock is undervalued buy the stock, and investors who believe a stock is overvalued sell their stock. Because investors have differing opinions, the stock of Ford, as well as the stocks of other firms, changes hands. However, note that in both cases, the stock valuation method employed is based on the discounted cash flow principle.

9.2.2 The investment holding period

The stockholder is entitled to an infinite stream of cash dividends. This infinite cash flow determines the stock's value. When the cash flow is cash dividends, stock valuation models based on the discounted cash flow principle are called **dividend discount models** (DDMs). However, in practice, investors do not hold the stock for an infinite period. How does this fact affect the valuation procedure? How does it affect the stock's price? In the examples in Exhibits 9.1 and 9.2, we assumed that investors hold the stock for two years, get two annual dividends, and then sell the stock. Now we will see that the valuation result does not change whether investors hold the stock for any number of years. We show below that the holding period does not affect the value of the stock.

To see this, suppose an investor invests for, say, one year and receives at the end of the first year a dividend of d_1. Then the investor sells the stock for P_1, where P_1 is the expected stock price at the end of the first year. The market is in equilibrium, namely, PV = P_0. How are P_0, P_1 and d_1 related? Because the current stock price is nothing but

Exhibit 9.2 Present value of £4 dividend in Year 1 and £5 dividend and £120 stock price in Year 2

Beginning of first year (t_0)	End of first year (t_1)	End of second year (t_2)
Expected dividends	£4	£5
Expected price		£120
Total expected cash flow	£4	£125
Discount factor for each year	1/1.15	1/1.15^2
Contribution to present value	£4/1.15 ≅ £3.48	£125/1.15^2 ≅ £94.52
Present value of the total cash flows	£3.48 + £94.52 = £98.00	

the discounted cash flows from future dividends and the stock sale, the stock price (P_0) is given by

$$P_0 = \frac{d_1}{1 + k} + \frac{P_1}{1 + k} \tag{9.1}$$

where k is the investor's required rate of return (given the stock's risk). For example, suppose that $d_1 = £5$ and $P_1 = £116$ and the discount rate is $k = 10\%$. Then, the current stock price which represents the PV of future cash flow will be:

$$P_0 = \frac{£5}{1.10} + \frac{£116}{1.10} = \frac{£121}{1.10} = £110$$

However, what if the investor considers holding the stock for two years and then selling it? We demonstrate below that the PV, i.e. the stock price, is not affected by the assumed length of time the investor plans to hold the stock. Let us show this claim. Assume that the investor invests for two years. The investor gets dividend d_1 at the end of the first year and d_2 at the end of the second year, and sells the stock for P_2 at the end of the second year, where P_2 is the expected stock price two years from now.

Suppose that the investor expects to get £5 in dividends in the first year and £6 at the second year. Because $P_1 = £116$ one can first estimate the stock price at the end of year 2. Given that $P_1 = £116$ (see above) is the PV of P_2 and d_2, P_2 should be the value which fulfils the following:

$$P_1 = £116 = \frac{£6}{1.1} + \frac{P_2}{1.1}$$

Therefore, $P_2 = £116 \times 1.1 - £6 = £127.6 - £6 = £121.6$.

If the investor holds the stock for two years rather than one year, the PV of all cash flows is

$$PV = \frac{£5}{1.1} + \frac{£6}{(1.1)^2} + \frac{£121.6}{(1.1)^2} \cong £4.54 + £4.96 + £100.50 = £110$$

Thus, $P_0 = PV = £110$, regardless of whether the stock is held for one year or two years.

One can continue the same logic and show that in general the stock price P_0 is given by

$$P_0 = \frac{d_1}{1 + k} + \frac{d_2}{(1 + k)^2} + \frac{d_3}{(1 + k)^2} + \cdots$$

$$= \sum_{t=1}^{\infty} \frac{d_t}{(1 + k)^t} = \sum_{t=1}^{n} \frac{d_t}{(1 + k)^t} + \frac{P_n}{(1 + k)^n} \tag{9.2}$$

where d_t is the dividend paid at the end of Year t, and n is the number of future dividend payments. Thus, if we discount all future dividends, or discount the n future dividends plus P_n, we get the same stock price, P_0.

Regardless of the assumed holding period, you will get the same value for the discounted cash flows (P_0). The intuitive explanation of this fact is that in Equation 9.1

PRACTICE BOX

Problem

Suppose you know that Zoom, Inc., is going to pay £5 in dividends at the end of next year and £6 in dividends at the end of Year 2, and you estimate a price of the stock at the end of Year 2 of £110. Suppose the required rate of return (k) is 12%.

1 What is the stock price today (P_0) based on Equation 9.2 when $n = 2$?
2 What is the price at the end of Year 1 (P_1)?
3 What is the price today (P_0) based on Equation 9.1 when the holding period is one year?

Solution

1. Based on Equation 9.2 and the data given in the problem,

$$P_0 = \frac{£5}{1 + 0.12} + \frac{£6 + £110}{(1 + 0.12)^2} \cong £96.94$$

2. The value P_1 is given by

$$P_1 = \frac{£6 + £110}{1 + 0.12} \cong £103.57$$

3. Based on Equation 9.1,

$$P_0 = \frac{£5}{1 + 0.12} + \frac{£103.57}{1 + 0.12} \cong £96.94$$

We see that the price today is independent of whether it is assumed that the investor holds the stock for one year or two years.

we discount the price P_1. However, P_1 is nothing but the discounted dividends paid in Year 2 plus the discounted value of the price, P_2. Continuing this process, we find that the stock price (P_0) is nothing but the discounted value of all future dividends plus the discounted value of the stock price at the end of the nth year, $P_n/(1 + k)^n$. As n approaches infinity, however, the present value of the stock approaches zero, and we can ignore the price of the stock for dividend-paying firms.[3] The discounted cash flow method is summarized in Rule 2.

Rule 2: To find the value of the stock, decide first on the holding period. Then estimate all cash flows, from dividends and from selling the stock. The current value of the stock is the present value of all these cash flows. Changing the planned holding period does not affect the current value of the stock.

Some investors may claim that they definitely will not hold the stock for an infinite number of years. Moreover, they may claim that they intend to hold the stock for a few years, and hence Equation 9.2, which discounts an infinite series of dividends, is irrelevant for them. As has just been demonstrated, if these investors employ an equation that assumes holding the stock for one year and then selling the stock, or

---

[3] Of course, we assume that the firm pays dividends such that the denominator $(1 + k)^n$ grows faster than the stock price. Otherwise, the stock price would be infinite.

holding the stock for two years and then selling it, or for that matter holding the stock for any finite number of years, the same result is obtained if the DCF principle (which relies on an infinite stream of dividends) is used. Thus, a stock valuation formula should be based on all future dividends. However, the same value is also obtained when the investment is assumed to be for n years only. In such a case, the current stock price is the present value of the n years' cash dividends plus the present value of the stock price that is sold after n years. Therefore, Equation 9.2 can safely be employed for stock valuation even if the stock will be held only for a short period. Therefore, from now on this chapter simply assumes that the stock price is nothing but the DCF of all future dividends. It also employs an equation that assumes an infinite holding period or, interchangeably, the DCF of any finite number of dividends plus the discounted value of the stock price when sold.

As will be shown, the DCF principle is the foundation on which several valuation models are built. The next section describes a dividend discount model that incorporates a simple growth rate of dividends into the investor's assessment of a given stock.

9.3   THE CONSTANT DIVIDEND GROWTH MODEL (CDGM)

When stock valuation is based on future dividends, it is called the *dividend discount model* because it discounts cash dividends. When the dividends grow at a constant rate every period, it is called the constant dividend growth model. The **constant dividend growth model (CDGM)** is the most common valuation model used to determine both stock values and the firm's cost of equity. This model determines the stock price by the first-year dividend (d_1), the discount rate (k) and the growth rate (g).

The model assumes that the firm pays a constant proportion of its earnings as dividends and the rest of the earnings are retained in the firm. It also assumes that the firm's earnings per share, dividends per share, and – as a result – the stock price are expected to grow every year by a constant growth rate denoted by g, where g is expressed as a percentage:[4]

$$P_1 = P_0(1 + g) \tag{9.3}$$

Substituting P_1 from Equation 9.3 into Equation 9.1 yields the following:

$$P_0 = \frac{d_1}{1 + k} + \frac{P_0(1 + g)}{1 + k} \tag{9.4}$$

Multiplying both sides of Equation 9.4 by $(1 + k)$ yields

$$P_0(1 + k) = d_1 + P_0(1 + g)$$

or

$$P_0(1 + k) - P_0(1 + g) = d_1$$

---

[4] Note that $P_0 = \dfrac{d_1}{1 + k} + \dfrac{d_1(1 + g)}{(1 + k)^2} + \dfrac{d_1(1 + g)^2}{(1 + k)^3} + \cdots$

and after a year,

$P_1 = \dfrac{d_1(1 + g)}{1 + k} + \dfrac{d_1(1 + g)^2}{(1 + k)^2} + \cdots$

because the dividend grows annually by g. As, after a year elapses, all terms in the numerators grow by g, the stock price also grows by g, and $P_1 = (1 + g)P_0$.

which can be further simplified as follows:

$$P_0(k - g) = d_1$$

The last equation can be written as the constant dividend growth model:[5]

$$P_0 = \frac{d_1}{k - g} \qquad (9.5)$$

The constant dividend growth model given by Equation 9.5 asserts that the value of the stock (P_0) is nothing but the first-year dividend per share (d_1), i.e. the dividend which will be paid one year hence, divided by the discount rate (k) minus the constant growth rate (g). Obviously, the greater the growth rate (g), other things being the same, the larger the discounted future dividends will be, resulting in a greater stock price (P_0). One nice feature of this model is that all future dividends do not have to be estimated directly. We need only estimate g. Rule 3 summarizes the CGDM.

Rule 3: To obtain the value of the stock today by the CDGM, you need to estimate the discount rate k and the growth rate g. The stock value is next year's dividend, d_1, divided by $k - g$.

Note that this formula holds only when the growth rate (g) is smaller than the discount factor (k). If $g > k$, dividends grow faster than the discount rate, and the DCF of an infinite stream of dividends yields an infinite price. Also, $g = k$ is not possible; it results in an infinite price. Because an infinite stock price does not exist in the market, we safely assume that $g < k$, or at least that $g > k$ cannot continue forever. The case where $g > k$ for a limited period of time is discussed later in the chapter.

9.4 SOURCES OF GROWTH

Very few firms fit neatly into the assumptions needed to derive the constant dividend growth model. This section examines the sources of growth and how to apply the constant dividend growth model effectively. It also explains when this basic valuation model is not appropriate.

Usually, the **earnings per share (EPS)** and **dividends per share (DPS)** grow simultaneously (for the definition of EPS, see Appendix 9A). However, if the dividend policy changes over time, the dividends and earnings may reveal a different growth rate. This discussion focuses on the cases where both the EPS and the DPS grow at the same rate. Suppose we observe in a given year a change in the growth rate of the DPS, say an increase from 5% to 9%. Does this increase imply that the stock's price should also increase? To answer the question, we need to have a closer look at the potential sources of growth in the firm and, in particular, the sources of possible changes in the firm's growth rate.

The DPS grows by (a) reinvestment of the retained earnings, even in normal-profit projects, and (b) undertaking projects with extraordinary profits even if all reclaimed earnings are paid as dividends. Of course, if both (a) and (b) occur, the growth rate is

---

[5] This model was originally developed by M.J. Gordon, 'Dividends, earnings and stock prices', *Review of Economics and Statistics*, 41, May 1959, pp. 99–105.

enhanced. Let us elaborate on these two sources of growth. They do not have the same impact on the stock price.

9.4.1 Source a: Reinvestment of earnings

Consider a firm with no extraordinarily profitable projects. Such firms are **normal-growth firms**. Given the riskiness of such firms, the stockholders require, say, $k\%$ return per year on their investment. Suppose the firm reinvests the retained earnings in projects yielding $k\%$, exactly as required by the stockholders. Thus, the net present value (NPV) of all accepted projects is zero. Can the firm's earnings and dividends grow in such a case? Yes, they can, because the firm pays only a portion of its earnings as dividends and has some cash left to reinvest in the firm. Moreover, paying less dividends and increasing the dollar amount invested in profitable projects leads to higher future earnings. A firm pursuing this dividend policy will achieve growth in earnings and dividends. In this case, the increase in investment is financed by internal sources, namely by cutting the current dividends. The lower the portion of earnings paid out as dividends, the greater the firm's future growth rate.

9.4.2 Source b: Opportunities for extraordinary profits

When firms have opportunities for extraordinary profits, they can increase the growth rate of the EPS and the DPS with no change in their dividend policy – that is, without reducing the current dividends. Firms with these opportunities are **supergrowth** firms. Such a firm reinvests the retained earnings in projects yielding more than $k\%$, which is the required rate of return by the stockholders, given the risk of the firm. Thus, the firm invests in projects with a positive NPV. Because the firm earns extra profits on these projects, it experiences increased growth in sales, earnings and dividends. It should be emphasized that the firm's profit increases with no change in risk; hence, the required rate of return by investors remains $k\%$.

It might seem as though supergrowth firms will always have a larger growth rate than normal-growth firms, but this is not always true. To illustrate, consider the following example. One firm may reinvest 90% of its profit at the required rate of return k and grow at $g = 10\%$, whereas another firm may reinvest only 20% of its profit in projects with extraordinary profits (those with a rate of return greater than k) and grow only at $g = 8\%$. The relatively low growth rate of the second firm results from the low proportion of the earnings retained. However, the firm with a 10% growth rate is classified as a normal-growth firm, whereas the firm with an 8% growth rate is classified as a supergrowth firm. In other words, the actual growth rate is determined by the rate of return on reinvested earnings, as well as the proportion of earnings reinvested in the firm. However, only the first factor – the profit on projects – determines whether the firm is classified as a normal-growth or a supergrowth firm.

Growth rates play a major role in stock valuation models based on the DCF principle. To examine whether an increase in g affects the stock price, the following sections analyze situations facing normal and supergrowth firms. They show that an increase in the growth rate caused by a cut in dividends changes the future dividends but does not lead to an increase in the current stock price, whereas an increase in the growth of dividends due to the availability of extraordinarily profitable projects does cause an increase in the current stock price.

9.4.3 Normal-growth firms

Let us look first at Exhibit 9.3(a). Year 0 stands for the current time, and P_0 is the current price. Similarly, Year 1 stands for the end of the first year. The normal-growth firm's earnings per share is £10, and the firm distributes £5 per share as dividends. The firm earns 10% on its investments, and the stockholder's required cost of equity is $k = 10\%$. Thus, all projects have zero NPV. The current stock price is P_0. In the second year the earnings grow to £10.5, because £5 per share earned in the first year is reinvested at 10%, yielding an additional £5 × 0.1 = £0.5 earnings per share. Because by assumption, the firm distributes 50% of its earnings as dividends, in the second year it pays dividends of £5.25, or $1/2$ × £10.5, per share. Thus, the earnings, dividends and hence the firm's stock price grow from the first year to the second year at a 5% growth rate.

By this process the earnings, dividends and stock price are expected to continue to grow at this rate in all other years. For example, the earnings of the second year are £10.5 × 1.05 = £11.025. Similarly, the dividend grows at 5%; hence, in the second year, the DPS is £5.25 × 1.05 = £5.5125.

Let us generalize these results. Denoting by b the proportion of the EPS retained in the firm (that is, not distributed as dividends) and by R the rate of return on the reinvested monies in the firm, called the **reinvestment rate**, then the growth rate is given by $g = b \times R$. Thus, if $b = 0.50$ and $R = 10\%$, the growth rate is $g = 0.5 \times 0.10 = 0.05$, or 5%, as the previous example reveals.

Exhibit 9.3 The growth rate in dividends, earnings and stock prices for normal-growth firms

(a) Growth rate of $g = 5\%$ with £5 first-year dividends

Year	EPS	DPS	Stock price
0			P_0
1	£10	£5	$P_0(1.05)$
2	£10.5	£5.25	$P_0(1.05)^2$
3	£11.025	£5.5125	$P_0(1.05)^3$
.	.	.	.
.	.	.	.
.	.	.	.

(b) Growth rate of $g = 9\%$ with £1 first-year dividends

Year	EPS	DPS	Stock price
0			P_0
1	£10	£1	$P_0(1.09)$
2	£10.9	£1.09	$P_0(1.09)^2$
3	£11.881	£1.1881	$P_0(1.09)^3$
.	.	.	.
.	.	.	.
.	.	.	.

Employing Equation 9.5, the stock price (P_0) corresponding to the example in Exhibit 9.3(a) is given by

$$P_0 = \frac{d_1}{k - g} = \frac{\$5}{0.10 - 0.05} = \frac{\$5}{0.05} = \$100$$

Note that although this firm earns 10% on its investment, the growth rate is only 5%, because only 50% of the EPS is retained. Exhibit 9.3(a) shows that a normal-growth firm will experience the same growth in EPS, DPS and its stock price.

Exhibit 9.3(b) still assumes a normal-growth firm – namely $k = 10\%$ and the firm reinvests 90% of its retained earnings in projects yielding 10%. The only difference between this case and the previous case is that the firm distributes only £1 (out of £10) as cash dividends and reinvests the retained earnings of £9 per share. The £9 per share is invested in projects yielding, as before, 10%; therefore, the dollar return on this reinvestment of the retained earnings is £0.90 (given by £9 × 0.1 = £0.90) per share.

Let us continue these computations for the second year: 10% of the EPS, or $0.1 \times 10.9 = £1.09$, is paid out as dividends in the second year. What is left is once again reinvested at 10%. Because the growth rate is 9% for all years, the EPS in the third year is £10.9 × 1.09 = £11.881, and the DPS is £1.09 × 1.09 = £1.1881; this growth rate continues forever. Note that in Exhibit 9.3(b), we have $b = 0.9$ and $R = k = 10\%$; hence, the growth rate is $g = bR = 0.9 \times 0.10 = 0.09$, or 9%. Comparing Exhibits 9.3(a) and 9.3(b), it is easy to see that by decreasing the dividends that are paid to the stockholders in the first year, more money is left to be reinvested. Hence, earnings and dividends grow at $g = 9\%$, in comparison with only $g = 5\%$ growth rate as in Exhibit 9.3(a). Therefore, when only 10% of earnings is paid out as dividends, the stock price at the end of the first year (P_1) should grow at 9% over the original price (P_0). Note that the increase in the stock price is not due to the availability of extraordinary projects. The firm reinvests, as before, in projects yielding 10%. However, by cutting the dividends from £5 per share to £1 per share, the dollar volume of the investment in projects increases, and hence the dividend growth increases.

Does the increase in the growth rate by moving from 5% to 9% affect the current stock price (P_0)? To answer this question, use Equation 9.5 in the case described in Exhibit 9.3(b) to obtain

$$P_0 = \frac{d_1}{k - g} = \frac{£1}{0.10 - 0.09} = \frac{£1}{0.01} = £100$$

From this result, you can see that an increase in the growth rate of the dividends *does not* increase the current stock price (P_0). It is true that in Exhibit 9.3(b) the future dividends grow at a faster rate than in Exhibit 9.3(a) (9% versus 5%). However, for the faster-growth case (9%), there is also a lower dividend base – a £1 first-year dividend versus a £5 first-year dividend. These two factors exactly cancel each other, and the stock price remains unchanged, at $P_0 = £100$. The price (P_1) at the end of the first period increases faster in Exhibit 9.3(b) than in Exhibit 9.3(a) because as less dividends are consumed, the money is kept in the firm. This higher stock price does not mean that the investor is better off, however. Although the investor gets more dividends and hence the price (P_1) is lower, the investor's total wealth is unaffected.

The intuitive economic explanation for this result is that stockholders require a $k = 10\%$ return on their investment. If the firm invests the retained earnings at 10%, then by investing more or less (that is, by changing the dividend level), the stockholders cannot be worse or better off. The reason is that the NPV of cash flows created by a 10% profit, discounted at 10%, is zero; therefore, no change in the current stock price occurs, and the stock price is unchanged at $P_0 = £100$.

To illustrate this argument, suppose you invest for two years in one of the two alternative firms given in Exhibit 9.3. If the firm pays out 50% of its earnings as dividends, at the end of two years you obtain $P_0 \times (1.05)^2 = £110.25$ plus the second-year dividend of £5.25 and the £5 dividend received in the first year. Assuming you can invest for a year at 10%, its value at the end of the first year is $5 \times 1.1 = £5.50$. You obtain £121 altogether $(110.25 + 5.25 + 5.50)$. Now suppose that the firm pays out only 10% of its earnings as dividends. At the end of two years you obtain $P_0 \times (1.09)^2 = £118.81$ plus £1.09 (the second-year dividend) plus the first-year dividends that you can invest at 10%, $£1(1.1) = £1.10$ – again, £121 altogether. As you see, the sum is the same in both cases; hence, the current price, P_0, will be the same.

PRACTICE BOX

Problem

The stock of BP Amoco, the gas company, trades at £25, will pay £1.50 in dividends next year (d_1), and has a required rate of return by the stockholders of 9.5%. BP Amoco is a normal-growth firm.

1 What is the implied growth rate of dividends?
2 If BP Amoco lowers its dividend by 10%, what is the percentage change in the growth rate of dividends?

Solution

1. From Equation 9.5, solve for g:

$$P_0(k - g) = d_1$$

$$(k - g) = \frac{d_1}{P_0}$$

$$g = k - \frac{d_1}{P_0}$$

Thus,

$$g = 0.095 - \frac{£1.50}{£25} = 3.5\%$$

2. A 10% decline in dividends will result in a dividend payment next year of $£1.50 \times 0.9 = £1.35$. For a normal-growth firm, the change does not affect the price, which remains at £25. Hence, because BP Amoco is a normal-growth firm,

$$g = 0.095 - \frac{£1.35}{£25} = 4.1\%$$

and the percentage change in the growth rate is 17.14%, or $(4.1\% - 3.5\%)/3.5\%$. Therefore, growth rates are very sensitive to dividend policy.

9.4.4 Supergrowth firms

In Exhibit 9.4, the change in the growth rate is due to the availability to the firm of extraordinarily profitable projects, i.e. projects with a positive NPV. Suppose the stockholders still require $k = 10\%$ (the risk of the firm does not change), but the firm can invest its retained earnings at 18% rather than 10%. To be more specific, suppose the firm pays £5 per share in the first year as a cash dividend, and £5 per share is reinvested at 18%. In this case, the second-year EPS will be £10 + (£5 × 0.18) = £10.90. The second-year dividend, assuming that 50% of earnings are paid as dividends, is $d_2 = \frac{1}{2} \times £10.9 = £5.45$. Similarly, the EPS and dividends grow at 9% in all other years.[6] Once again, the general formula can be applied to validate this 9% growth rate. In this example, $b = 0.5$, the reinvestment rate is $R = 18\%$, and hence $g = 0.5 \times 0.18 = 0.09$ or 9%.

Because dividends and earnings grow at $g = 9\%$ per year, the stock price should also grow at 9% per year. Equation 9.5 in this case yields:

$$P_0 = \frac{d_1}{k - g} = \frac{£5}{0.10 - 0.09} = \frac{£5}{0.01} = £500$$

Unlike the comparison of stock prices corresponding to Exhibits 9.3(a) and (b), a comparison of stock prices corresponding to Exhibits 9.3(a) and 9.4 (in both cases, 50% of earnings is paid as dividends) reveals a dramatic jump in the current stock price (P_0), from £100 to £500. How can we account for this large price increase? By shifting from Exhibit 9.3(a) to Exhibit 9.3(b), we see that the change in the growth rate (from 5% to 9%) is due to a change in the dividend policy. The firm reduces its dividend and reinvests more in projects (at 10%); hence, the growth rate increases from 5% to 9% at the expense of a reduction in the base dividend from £5 to £1. As a result, no gain in the stock price is achieved, and it remains $P_0 = £100$. However, in the comparison of Exhibits 9.3(a) and 9.4, the growth rate increases once again from 5% to 9%, not at the expense of a reduction in the base dividend, which is kept in the first year at $d_1 = £5$, but due to an increase in the project profitability (from 10% to 18%) with no change in the firm's risk. This is an economic gain, so the price increase from £100 to £500 is a reaction to the newly available profitable projects and is not due to an increase in the dollar volume invested.

Exhibit 9.4 The growth rate in dividends, earnings and stock prices for a supergrowth firm: 9% with £5 first-year dividends

Year	EPS	DPS	Stock price
0			P_0
1	£10	£5	$P_0(1.09)$
2	£10.90	£5.45	$P_0(1.09)^2$
3	£11.88	£5.94	$P_0(1.09)^3$
.	.	.	.
.	.	.	.
.	.	.	.

---

[6] Reinvestment at 18% of 50% of the EPS induces a growth rate of 18% × $\frac{1}{2}$ = 9%.

The key difference between normal-growth and supergrowth firms is that with the normal-growth firm, both the stockholders and the firm can reinvest at $k = 10\%$. The supergrowth firm, in contrast, can reinvest at 18%, whereas stockholders can reinvest the dividends at only 10%. The availability of projects with a positive NPV induces an increase in the stock price from £100 to £500.

In summary, Exhibit 9.3 shows normal-growth firms with different dividend policies. Exhibit 9.4 represents a supergrowth firm, which can reinvest money at a rate of return greater than the minimum rate required by the stockholders. A change in the growth rate of a firm that is due to a change in the proportion of earnings paid as dividends not accompanied by an increase in project profitability does not affect the stock price (see Exhibit 9.3). A change in the growth rate that is induced by the availability of more profitable projects, as expected, affects the stock valuation and thus the investors' view on whether a stock is overpriced or underpriced.

9.4.5 Supergrowth firms for a limited time period

The large increase in the stock price, from £100 to £500, should not come as a surprise. The price jump might seem to be very large and not justified by an increase in the projects' profitability from 10% to 18%. However, recall that this extra profit (18% rather than 10%) is assumed by the constant dividend growth model to continue forever on all earnings retained. Thus, the present value of the extra profit (18% − 10%) on all retained earnings is £400; hence, the stock price increases from £100 to £500.

Does it make sense to expect that the company can reinvest its earnings at 18% but investors require only 10% on their investment? The answer is absolutely yes. To see why, consider a firm that discovers a new drug (e.g. the recent Viagra pill) and is granted a patent on this new drug. The firm earns an 18% rate of return rather than the 10% it would make without this new drug. However, the firm's risk does not change, and the required rate of return by the stockholders remains 10%. Because the firm makes 18%, investors will buy the stock, so the price will go up until the rate of return on the stock is 10%.

Because the firm in this case invests at a rate of return higher than that required by the stockholders ($k < R$), it is a supergrowth firm. However, this supergrowth cannot continue forever, as Equation 9.5 assumes. Most firms face a limited number of years of supergrowth. Competition restricts the future growth of the firm. When one firm has an extraordinary profit, competitors will enter the market. Prices of the product, as well as its profitability, then go down. When Apple and IBM first entered the personal computer market, for example, prices were very high and these firms enjoyed extra profits. After a few years, many competitors were attracted to this profitable business, the prices of personal computers fell dramatically, and the extra profit disappeared. Firms such as IBM and Apple were supergrowth firms for a few years. When the accelerated growth levels off, they become normal-growth firms, with earnings and dividends growing at normal, rather than abnormal, rates.

Firms involved in the research and development of a new drug often achieve supergrowth for a limited period. If a firm's research is successful, the firm can obtain a patent on the drug for a limited number of years, during which supergrowth prevails. After the patent expires, competitors will be allowed to produce the drug, and the original firm becomes a normal-growth firm. The constant dividend growth model thus needs to be adjusted to reflect this nonconstant growth.

Let's consider the general method of evaluating a stock characterized by a supergrowth rate for only a limited period of time. Suppose that at the end of the first year, the dividend is $d_1 = £5$ per share, and the firm indeed can reinvest the retained earnings from the first year in a very profitable project with a positive NPV. This high rate of return is only for one year. (If it is for more than one year, a similar, but more complex, analysis applies.) The earnings retained from all subsequent years are invested at the firm's normal rate of 10%. In this case, the growth rate is not constant. Thus, Equation 9.5 cannot be employed to evaluate the stocks, because this equation is appropriate only for constant-growth cash flows. In this specific example the supergrowth lasts only one year, so we can apply Equation 9.5′. P_0 is thus given by

$$P_0 = \frac{d_1}{1 + k} + \frac{d_2}{(1 + k)^2} + \frac{P_2}{(1 + k)^2} \qquad (9.5')$$

Let us employ the data in Exhibit 9.5. In this example, the dividend for the first year is $d_1 = £5$. We assume that earnings and dividends grow for one year at 9% (the second year) and that beginning with the second year, dividends and earnings grow only at the normal growth of 5%. Therefore, for given dividends of $d_1 = £5$, $d_2 = £5 \times 1.09 = £5.45$, $d_3 = £5.45 \times 1.05 \cong £5.72$, and so on. (All future dividends after the second year grow at 5%.) Because $d_1 = £5$ (see Exhibit 9.5) and $k = 10\%$ (by assumption), if you know P_2, you can easily solve for P_0. However, P_2 can be found by using the constant dividend growth model, because after the second year the firm will grow at the normal and constant rate. According to Equation 9.5,

$$P_2 = \frac{d_3}{k - g} = \frac{£5.72}{0.10 - 0.05} = \frac{£5.72}{0.05} = £114.40$$

where $d_3 = £5.72$, which is $d_1 = £5$ growing at 9% in the second year and at 5% in all the years from the third year on (see Exhibit 9.5). Recall that P_2 is nothing but the present value of all dividends obtained in the third year and thereafter; hence, P_2 is the present value of $d_3, d_4, \ldots$. Because the growth rate after Year 2 is constant at 5% (normal growth), using Equation 9.5 to solve for P_2 is appropriate. Therefore, P_0 is given by:

$$P_0 = \frac{d_1}{1 + k} + \frac{d_2}{(1 + k)^2} + \frac{P_2}{(1 + k)^2} = \frac{£5}{1.1} + \frac{£5.45}{1.1^2} + \frac{£114.40}{1.1^2} = £103.60$$

Hence, because of the supergrowth of d_2 in comparison with d_1, the stock price increases from £100 to only £103.60. This result is quite different from the large jump

Exhibit 9.5 Supergrowth firm for one year and normal growth thereafter: growth rate of $g_1 = 9\%$ for the first year and $g_2 = 5\%$ after the first year with £5 first-year dividends

Year	EPS	DPS	Stock price
0			P_0
1	£10	£5	$P_0(1.09)$
2	£10.90	£5.45	$P_0(1.09)(1.05)$
3	£11.44	£5.72	$P_0(1.09)(1.05)^2$
.	.	.	.
.	.	.	.
.	.	.	.

of £400 in the stock price that occurred before, when the extra profit of 18%, and hence the supergrowth of 9%, were assumed to continue forever.

From this example it can safely be concluded that the longer the number of years a firm can enjoy extraordinary profits (or the slower the competitors are), the bigger the jump in the stock price due to the availability of these profitable projects.

This example assumed supergrowth for one year and normal growth thereafter. The valuation formula can be generalized for a stock with a supergrowth for n years and normal growth thereafter. For example, if a firm has a patent that protects it for $n = 7$ years, it has supergrowth for seven years. After seven years, competitors produce the protected product, and the growth rate is expected to go down. The firm steps into a second economic cycle characterized by a normal growth rate.

In summary, a firm's dividends can grow because of a current reduction in dividends paid, or by the firm's reinvesting funds in profitable projects. A firm that has extraordinarily profitable projects (projects with positive NPVs) is called a supergrowth firm. Otherwise, it is a normal-growth firm, regardless of the actual growth rate of EPS and DPS. Most supergrowth firms cannot enjoy this extraordinary investment opportunity forever; hence, a supergrowth firm model for a limited time period seems to be the most relevant stock valuation model to value the stock of supergrowth firms. With accurate valuation models that realize that supergrowth cannot continue forever, investors are better able to assess the reasonableness of current stock prices.

9.4.6 Supergrowth firms and risk

For supergrowth firms, the high stock price is based on the fact that the firm reinvests at $R > k$. But, if it is realized that R is smaller than what is expected, investors may revise their estimate of R (and hence of g) which may have a devastating effect on stock prices. For example, assume that $d_1 = £1$, $b = 0.5$, $k = 0.10$ and $R = 0.15$. Thus,

$$P_0 = \frac{£1}{0.1 - 0.5 \times 0.15} = £40$$

Suppose due to new information that R is revised to be, say, 12%. Thus,

$$P_0 = \frac{£1}{0.1 - 0.5 \times 0.12} = £25$$

i.e. even a relatively small drop in g would induce a 37.5% drop in the stock price ($£25/£40 - 1 = -0.375$ or -37.5%).

The high price of Internet stocks is an example of supergrowth expectation. If investors realize that the rosy future expectation is not that rosy, a sharper fall in the price of these stocks may occur. Indeed, this is what happened in 2001.

This may explain the difference in the 'growth investors' and 'value investors' mentioned in the *Investment in the news* article. It is possible that the value investors simply do not like to be involved in such risky investments. Thus, they probably realize the importance of future growth, but by the same token realize the risk involved with changes in the estimation of future growth. The possible changes of the earnings estimate of normal growth firms do not have such impact on stock price, because the firm has stable and well-known activities with a well-known market share for its products. Thus, the value investors prefer a solid 10% average return rather than, say, 25% average return with no strong swings.

9.5 CDGM VALUATION WHEN ALL THE EARNINGS ARE PAID AS CASH DIVIDENDS FOR NORMAL-GROWTH FIRMS

If a firm is a normal-growth firm and distributes all its earnings as cash dividends, the stock price (P_0) is nothing but the present value of an annuity discounted at k%. As an example, assume EPS = £10, and hence d_1 = £10. However, because all EPS is distributed as dividends, the firm does not grow, and next year's expected EPS, as well as dividends, will be constant at £10.[7] In this case,

$$P_0 = \frac{d}{1+k} + \frac{d}{(1+k)^2} + \frac{d}{(1+k)^3} + \cdots = \sum_{t=1}^{\infty} \frac{d}{(1+k)^t} = \frac{d}{k}$$

Using the data above yields the following:

$$P_0 = £10/0.1 = £100$$

This is exactly the value obtained before, when some of the profit was retained and reinvested in the firm, as long as these retained earnings were invested at k = 10% and not in extraordinarily profitable projects (k = 18%).

9.6 FINDING THE COST OF EQUITY CAPITAL WITH THE CDGM

Valuation models can be used for purposes other than finding overvalued and undervalued securities. Recall from your first finance course that the discount rate (k) is the required cost of equity capital by the stockholders, given the firm's risk. The constant dividend growth model can be used to estimate the cost of equity. In this case we assume the stock price to be the 'correct' or equilibrium market price and solve for the unknown value (k). According to the constant dividend growth model,

$$P_0 = \frac{d_1}{k-g} \text{ or } k = \frac{d_1}{P_0} + g$$

Because d_0 and P_0 are observed in the market and we can estimate the expected growth rate (g), then $d_1 = d_0(1+g)$ can be calculated, and we can solve for the required cost of equity by the stockholders, which is simply the expected rate of profit on equity. In the example that corresponds to the constant dividend growth model (with no super-growth) described by Exhibit 9.3(a), we get d_1 = £5, P_0 = £100, and g = 5%. Hence,

$$k = \frac{d_1}{P_0} + g = \frac{£5}{£100} + 0.05 = 0.05 + 0.05 = 0.10 \text{ or } 10\%$$

Therefore, investors who determine the stock price in the market are expecting (or requiring) to earn 10% on this investment. Given the risk of the stock, if an investor's required rate of return is greater than 10%, then the investor should avoid this investment. However, if the investor's required rate of return is lower than 10%, then this stock is an attractive investment.

---

[7] The firm reinvests the depreciation, which makes it possible to create the perpetuity of £10 per share.

PRACTICE BOX

Problem

A firm pays a £5 dividend per share and has a growth rate of 10% for four years. The growth rate is only 5% from then on. If the discount rate is a constant $k = 8\%$, what is the stock price today?

Solution

The value of this common stock in four years (P_4) will be based on the standard constant dividend discount model:

$$P_4 = \frac{d_5}{k - g_2} = \frac{d_4(1 + g_2)}{k - g_2}$$

$$= \frac{d_0(1 + g_1)^4 (1 + g_2)}{k - g_2} = \frac{£5(1 + 0.1)^4 \times (1 + 0.05)}{0.08 - 0.05} \cong \frac{£7.6865}{0.03}$$

$$\cong £256.2167$$

where $d_0(1 + g_1)^4 = d_4$, or the dividend paid at the fourth year, and g_2 is the growth rate from the fifth year and following. The present value of this stock price plus the present value of the dividends for the first four years is

$$P_0 = \frac{d_0(1 + g_1)^1}{(1 + k)^1} + \frac{d_0(1 + g_1)^2}{(1 + k)^2} + \frac{d_0(1 + g_1)^3}{(1 + k)^3} + \frac{d_0(1 + g_1)^4 + P_4}{(1 + k)^4}$$

$$= \frac{£5.5}{(1 + 0.08)^1} + \frac{£6.05}{(1 + 0.08)^2} + \frac{£6.655}{(1 + 0.08)^3} + \frac{£7.3205 + £256.2167}{(1 + 0.08)^4}$$

$$\cong £5.0926 + £5.1869 + £5.2830 + £193.7077 \cong £209.28$$

The firm's managers, in contrast, can use the market stock price as the market's equilibrium price and from this deduce the market's required rate of return (k). The firm can use this value to estimate the weighted average cost of capital, which is the appropriate discount rate used in project evaluation. Thus, the valuation formulas for stocks discussed in this chapter can be used by investors to estimate the price of a stock, as well as by a firm's management to estimate the firm's cost of equity capital. Chapter 10 discusses how historical data can be used to estimate the growth rate (g).

9.7 PICKING STOCKS USING THE P/E RATIO

Price/earnings (P/E) ratios for every firm (also known as P/E *multiple* or simply the 'multiple') are published by most economic media (for example, *Wall Street Journal* and *Barron's*). Although the P/E ratio is not based on the DCF principle, it is widely quoted and published. For example, *Barron's* of 2 July 2001 report a P/E of 16 for Hilton, 25 for Chase Manhattan and 91 for Peoplesoft Company. What does this ratio measure and how can we account for these differences in the P/E ratios?

This section discusses under what circumstances the P/E ratio conveys valuable information, discusses the factors which determine this ratio, and warns against potential misuse of the P/E ratio. Unlike the 'Super Bowl method', the P/E ratio does have some economic basis. This section covers the predictive power and limitations of the P/E ratio.

The P/E ratio published in the *Wall Street Journal, Barron's* and other financial media is the previous day's closing stock price divided by the *last* reported four quarters of EPS (denoted E). For example, if the closing stock price is $P = £100$ and annual EPS is £10, then P/E = £100/£10 = 10. This P/E ratio shows that an investor has to wait 10 years to recover the £100 initial investment in the stock. Similarly, a P/E ratio of 5 implies that an investor has to wait five years to recover an investment. Note that P is the current price (namely, P_0), but it is denoted as P and not P_0 in the P/E ratio.

Investment analysts, when recommending buying stock, talk about the relatively low **multiples**, a term they use synonymously with P/E ratios. They use either the P/E ratio expressed in years or its reciprocal, the E/P ratio, in a percentage figure to evaluate the investment profitability. The P/E rule says that if the P/E ratio is too low, the market will rise, and if the P/E ratio is too high, the market will fall.

Are analysts justified in using the P/E ratio? Is the P/E ratio consistent with the present value of dividends model (see Equation 9.5)? The following discussion explores when the P/E rule can safely be used.

It has been stated that what is relevant for investment valuation is the future cash flows. However, in the P/E calculation, E is the last (past) EPS, not the future EPS or the future dividends. When you buy a stock, though, you buy it for the future earnings, not for the past earnings. Also, earnings are also not cash flows to the investor. Therefore, using the E/P ratio (or the P/E ratio), which is based on past earnings, is conceptually wrong. However, in the following two cases, the E/P ratio yields a precise measure of profitability that is equal to the one implied by the constant dividend growth model, which probably accounts for its popularity:

- *Case 1*. Constant earnings, when all earnings are distributed as cash dividends. In this case all annual earnings (past and future) are constant and equal to the annual dividends.
- *Case 2*. Constant growth in earnings and dividends, as long as the firm has a normal growth rate (and not a supergrowth rate) and every year it pays out a fixed proportion of its earnings as dividends. In this case, however, P/E_1 is a relevant measure of profitability when E_1 is next year's EPS. The common P/E ratio based on last year's earnings is still misleading.

Let us elaborate.

■ Case 1: Constant EPS

Suppose the EPS and the DPS are constant at £10 (hence also $d_1 = £10$) and the stock price is $P = £100$. Therefore, E/P = d_1/P = £10/£100 = 10%. In this case, the E/P ratio is 10%, which is equal to $d_1/P + g$, because $g = 0$ and $d_1/P = 10\%$. This is a trivial case, because the past earnings are equal to the future earnings (and dividends); therefore, by looking at past earnings rather than future dividends, no harm is done. However, cases in which all earnings are distributed as dividends are rare; hence, the more realistic case is one in which some fixed portion of earnings is distributed as dividends.

■ Case 2: Normal-growth firm

Let us turn to more relevant cases by illustrating the two cases in Exhibit 9.3 which deal with normal-growth firms.

We will show that the expected rate of return measured by Equation 9.5 or by the P/E yield the same result. These two cases have the following cost of equity which is also the expected future rate of return.

(a) $k = \dfrac{d_1}{P_0} + g = \dfrac{£5}{£100} + 0.05 = 0.05 + 0.05 = 0.10$

(b) $k = \dfrac{d_1}{P_0} + g = \dfrac{£1}{£100} + 0.09 = 0.01 + 0.09 = 0.10$

Thus, the future profitability to the investor, using the constant dividend growth model, which is the correct method, is expected to be 10%. Indeed, when $E = £10$ is the next year's EPS, E/P = 0.10 in both cases, as £10/£100 = 0.10.

Hence, for normal growth firms the P/E ratio can be safely used. However, employing the P/E ratio (or the E/P ratio) for supergrowth firms is misleading. Comparing Exhibits 9.3(a) and 9.4 yields

For normal-growth firm: $\dfrac{E}{P_0} = \dfrac{£10}{£100} = 0.10$

For supergrowth firm: $\dfrac{E}{P_0} = \dfrac{£10}{£500} = 0.02$

Thus, using the P/E ratio (or its reciprocal E/P ratio), we get a precise figure for a normal-growth firm but a distorted figure for supergrowth firms. (Note that $k = 10\%$, not 2% – see Exhibit 9.4.)

Thus, although both firms – one with a normal growth rate and one with a supergrowth rate – yield the same rate of return of 10%, looking at the E/P ratio as an indicator of profitability leads to an error: 10% for the normal-growth firm and only 2% for the supergrowth firm. The reason for the bias is that for the supergrowth firm, the future earnings, which grow at an accelerated rate, are ignored in the E/P calculation, because that calculation is fully based on current (or past) earnings.

To stress the possible distortion of the P/E ratio, suppose the P/E of Microsoft is 63, namely E/P = 1/63 ≅ 1.59 %. Does that mean that the investor's required rate of return on equity is only 1.59%? No, it does not, because investors can earn a higher certain income by buying US Treasury bills. However, there are two possible interpretations of this low figure: (1) the firm is a supergrowth firm, so the P/E ratio is misleading as discussed above, or (2) the current EPS is low and does not represent the future average EPS. Thus, a random deviation in the EPS in a particular year leads to a biased P/E ratio. Which of these two interpretations is correct can be known only by carefully studying the firm's income statement. In the case of Microsoft, supergrowth is the explanation, and the last (or the next) year's EPS does not represent the future earnings. Finally, there is a technical disadvantage to the P/E ratio. When the EPS values are negative, they are undefined.

In an article which appears in the *Wall Street Journal*, there is a suggested formula on how to pick stocks by their P/E ratio and growth:

> Michael Culp, research director, says the firm's focus is 'mostly on growth stocks – companies that can deliver double-digit earnings gains the next couple of years.' To make the recommended list, the company should have a price/earnings ratio of less than the growth rate, Mr. Culp says. For example, a company whose earnings are expected to grow 15% a year should sell for a P/E ratio of less than 15.[8]

---

[8] *Source*: 'Rating your broker's stock picks', *Wall Street Journal*, 15 August 1997, p. C.23. Reprinted by permission of *The Wall Street Journal*. © 1997 Dow Jones & Co., Inc. All Rights Reserved Worldwide.

Now we have the tools to analyze this recommendation regarding stock selection. Suppose that you consider investing in stocks of two firms, both in the same industry. Hence, they have the same risk and the same discount rate of $k = 10\%$. Consider the following relevant data for these two firms:

	Firm A	Firm B
EPS	£10	£10
DPS	£1	£8
Price of stock	£70	£100
Rates of return on retained earnings (R)	9%	15%
Proportion of EPS retained in the firm (b)	0.9	0.2
Growth rate (g) = bR	8.1%	3%
P/E ratio	7	10

Which stock would you recommend to buy? An investor using the criterion for picking stocks as recommended above would prefer Stock A over Stock B, because Stock A has a lower P/E ratio and a higher growth rate. Moreover, according to the selection criterion, Stock A should be accepted (P/E $< g$) and Stock B should be rejected (P/E $> g$). Let us see if this recommendation is consistent with the dividend cash flow valuation formulas in this chapter.

Employing Equation 9.5, we find the following values of Stock A and Stock B:

$$\text{Value of Stock A: } d_1/(k - g) = £1/(0.1 - 0.081) = £1/0.019 \cong £52.63$$

$$\text{Value of Stock B: } d_1/(k - g) = £8/(0.1 - 0.03) = £8/0.07 \cong £114.29$$

Thus, the reverse is true: Stock A should be rejected because its price is higher than its discounted cash flows, and Stock B should be bought because the value of its discounted cash flows is higher than its market price. Thus, what is wrong with the recommendation given above? It simply ignores the source of growth in EPS: Firm A reinvests 90% of its earnings in the firm and thus has 8.1% growth. This growth is achieved in spite of the fact that the money is reinvested in projects with negative NPV whose rate of return (9%) is smaller than the cost of capital (10%). Firm B, in contrast, reinvests at 15%. It is a supergrowth firm, which explains its relatively high value of £114.29. However, because it reinvests only 20% of its earnings, its growth rate is relatively low. Thus, looking at the P/E ratio and g, as the article recommends, and ignoring the source of the growth rate (g) is simply misleading. This example illustrates the risk of using the P/E ratio for firms that are not normal-growth firms.

The financial media generally publish the P/E ratio in which P is the current price and E is the *last* published EPS. Exhibits 9.3(a) and (b) show that $d/p + g = E/p$; that is, for normal-growth firms, the constant dividend growth model and the reciprocal of the P/E ratio provide the same expected rate of return. However, it is important to note that even in this specific case the two methods provide the same result only when E is the *next year's* EPS, that is, the future EPS (see Exhibits 9.3(a) and (b)). Indeed, the financial media sometimes publish not only the P/E ratio with last year's earnings per share, E, but also the P/E ratio where E is next year's EPS.

In summary, investors should always rely on a stock valuation method that takes into account the discounted future dividends. However, the P/E ratio (or the E/P ratio) can be safely used for stock valuation (and for estimating the cost of equity) in the following two cases: (1) when all earnings are paid as cash dividends, and the dividends (and earnings) are constant across all years; and (2) when some constant percentage of the earnings is paid as cash dividends every year, and dividends grow over the years at a constant and normal growth rate – that is, the firm does not face an extraordinarily profitable project.

Although the P/E ratio is not based on the DCF principle, its ease of use has made it attractive for many investors. Appendix 10A and Appendix 10B at the end of the next chapter suggest two additional methods for valuing the stock of nondividend-paying firms: the free cash flow model and the economic value-added model.

9.8 A WORD OF CAUTION: THE QUALITY OF REPORTED EARNINGS

The EPS, which is the key factor for many valuation models and, in particular, for the P/E ratio discussed above, as well as for growth estimates discussed in the next chapter, are based on an accounting figure (see Appendix 9A), hence can be manipulated by management. Management can manipulate reported earnings in many ways. To boost short-term earnings, for example, they can aggressively push merchandise onto distributors. Similarly, they can depress earnings by adding to reserves for delinquent accounts. If such distortions occur, a valuation of stock or growth estimates of *g* which are based on earnings may be misleading. *The New York Times* of 1 July 1999 reports that Microsoft accounting was under scrutiny by the SEC. The SEC investigates the company's accounting practices involving the status of the reserves. It was claimed that in 1995 the chief financial officer of the company sent an e-mail to Bill Gates saying: 'I believe we should do all we can to smooth our earnings and keep a steady state earnings model' (see *The New York Times*, 1 July 1999, p. C6). In 2002, in the Enron scandal, the external auditor, Arthur Andersen, was blamed for not revealing manipulation of the reported earnings (see Exhibit 9.6 on p. 281).

While there are accounting rules asserting how a company should record revenue, there is a lot of flexibility given to the management to determine how to apply these rules. However, the purpose of the reserves is to reflect a company's true revenue – how much it will actually end up collecting in a given period if customers return merchandise or fail to pay their bills. But this flexibility opens up a door to smoothing earnings, if not done right. In the specific case of Microsoft, the company may have reserved too much, which would mean that it may have understated its profit. Indeed, financial analysts use *quality of earnings* systems which are based on the difference between the reported earnings and the actual earnings as estimated by them. Low quantity implies that the reported EPS differs greatly from the firm's actual EPS.

Along with measures of quality, analysts have devised checklists for review, or red flags to look for, when assessing the quality of earnings. The first item on the checklist is typically the audit report. Auditors write a letter – known as the *independent auditor's report* – to shareholders and the board of directors, giving an opinion on the fairness of management's financial statements, then the auditor will express them in this letter. The independent auditor's report is a part of the annual report to shareholders required by the Securities and Exchange Commission.

Finally, recall that analysts use the income statement and reported EPS as a means to estimate the future earnings ability of a firm. When trying to arrive at the actual earnings ability of a firm, the analysts must make several adjustments. For example, earnings attributable to nonrecurring items, such as the sale of a subsidiary, should not be expected to be repeated. Therefore, they should not be included in the EPS calculation.

SUMMARY

■ *Explain how investors use stock valuation models.*
A sound valuation method must rely on discounted future dividends. Whereas the current dividend is known, future dividends can only be estimated. Therefore, we say that the stock price is the present value of all expected dividends.

A valuation formula should be based on the discounted cash flow (DCF), hence it discounts all future dividends. However, the same value is also obtained when the investment is assumed to be for *n* years only. In such a case, the current stock price is the present value of the *n* years' cash dividends plus the present value of the stock price that is sold after *n* years.

■ *Describe the assumptions underlying the constant dividend growth model.*
The most popular valuation model is the constant dividend growth model, which assumes that every year the firm pays a constant percentage of its earnings as dividends, and the rest of the earnings are retained in the firm. Normal-growth firms invest the retained earnings at the required cost of equity, hence the percentage of profits retained in the firm does not affect the current stock price.

■ *Value firms that are presently experiencing supergrowth.*
Although the constant dividend growth model can be employed for normal-growth and supergrowth firms, economic logic and historical data tell us that constant supergrowth cannot continue forever. (IBM, for example, was a symbol of supergrowth, but faced a decline in profit, and even had negative earnings in 1992 and 1993.) Therefore, in the case of a supergrowth firm, a more reasonable assumption is that the supergrowth will last only for a given number of years. Then competitors will reduce the firm's growth, and after this supergrowth period, normal growth will characterize the firm. In any case, no matter whether the firm experiences normal growth or supergrowth after this initial period of supergrowth, the valuation formula changes, but the valuation is still based on the discounted value of future dividends. One task facing an analyst is how long the supergrowth will last.

■ *Explain when the P/E ratio can be used safely.*
The popular use of the P/E ratio as an investment criterion is not based on the principle of discounted future cash flows; hence, it is conceptually wrong. However, the use of the P/E ratio yields the same results as the use of the present value of future dividends for normal growth firms in two cases provided that the reported earnings are not manipulated by the management and that next year's EPS rather than the last year's EPS is used in the P/E calculation. The two cases are (a) all earnings are paid as cash dividends, and these dividends (and earnings) are constant across all years; and (b) some constant percentage of the earnings is paid as cash dividends every year, and dividends grow at a constant and normal growth rate. For supergrowth firms, the P/E ratio leads to misleading results and sometimes even to absurd results. Thus, the P/E ratio should be used with great care.

■ *Explain that reported earnings can be manipulated (see Enron).*

KEY TERMS

Balance sheet	Dividend discount model	Multiple
Constant dividend growth	(DDM)	Normal-growth firm
model (CDGM)	Dividends per share (DPS)	Price/earnings
Direct method (for cash	Earnings per share	(P/E) ratio
flows)	(EPS)	Reinvestment rate, R
Discount rate	Income statement	Statement of
Discounted cash flow	Indirect method (for cash	cash flows
(DCF) principle	flows)	Supergrowth firm

QUESTIONS

9.1 Suppose that the stock price is $P_0 = \$50$, and the dividend per share next year is $d_1 = \$2$. The discount rate is $k = 10\%$. What is the expected stock price (P_1) one year from now?

9.2 You expect to get a dividend per share of $d_1 = \$10$ next year and $d_2 = \$15$ two years from now. The stock price two years from now is expected to be $P_2 = \$120$, and the current stock price is $P_0 = \$100$. What is the equilibrium discount rate?

9.3 A stock, on average, pays $10 per share every year, and the stock price two years from now is $110. The risk-free interest rate is $r = 5\%$. Can you determine the maximum value of the stock? Explain.

9.4 In 1990, the stock of IBM traded for $P_0 = \$100$ with $d_1 = \$6$ per share, $k = 12\%$, and $g = 6\%$. Because of sharp competition in the computer industry and mismanagement, the market revised the estimate of the growth rate, making it only 4%. What should the effect be on the stock market?

9.5 Suppose the dividend at the end of the first year is $d_1 = \$10$. The growth rate will be $g_1 = 8\%$ for the next n years and then, from $n + 1$ forever, the growth rate will be $g_2 = 5\%$. The discount rate is $k = 10\%$.

(a) What is the stock price if $n = 1$?
(b) What is the stock price if $n = 10$?
(c) What is the stock price if $n = $ infinity?

9.6 A normal-growth firm has earnings of $10 per share and dividends of $5 per share. The discount rate is $k = 10\%$.

(a) What is the stock price?
(b) What is the multiplier, P/E?

9.7 One stock offers $10 a year from the next year to infinity. Another stock offers $5 next year and a growth rate of 10% a year.

(a) In what year will the dividends from both firms be equal?
(b) What stock will have a higher price if the discount rate for both is $k = 10\%$?

9.8 Suppose Firm A is a normal-growth firm. The firm's dividend policy is to maintain a dividend growth rate that is 50% of the firm's cost of equity (k). It is given that the stock price is $100, and $d_1 = \$10$. What is the firm's cost of equity (k)?

9.9 The P/E ratio of a normal-growth firm is P/E = 10. The dividend is d_1 = \$10, and the stock price is \$20. What is the growth rate (g)?

9.10 Suppose that the stockholder's required cost of capital is 23%. The dividend on the firm's stock was \$10 per share, which is estimated to grow in the future at 2% a year indefinitely. What is the present value of all future dividends?

9.11 In 1993, IBM cuts its quarterly dividends per share from more than 50 cents to 25 cents. Suppose the annual dividends next year will be \$1. IBM stock was trading for about \$40. Assuming a 10% cost of capital, what is the market's long-term estimate of the growth rate of dividends for IBM?

9.12 A firm's stock price is \$50, and its EPS is \$5. The firm changes its accounting procedures (for example, changes its method of valuing inventory). As a result, the EPS went up to \$7. How should this change affect the P/E ratio? How should it affect the present value of dividends? How should it affect the stock price?

9.13 Demonstrate that if a firm pays out a constant proportion of its earnings as dividends and reinvests its retained earnings at the cost of capital (k), then the dividend model and the P/E ratio (actually the inverse E/P ratio) yield the same value for the stock.

9.14 Suppose the average P/E ratio in the United States was about 20 in 2001. In Japan the average P/E ratio was about 50. Does this fact mean that the Japanese stock market should be considered expensive and the US market inexpensive?

9.15 'Any comparison of P/E ratios in a given country may be meaningful. However, an international comparison of P/E ratios may yield paradoxical results, because various countries have various accounting reporting standards.' Discuss this assertion.

SELECTED REFERENCES

Bower, Richard S. 'The n-stage discount model and required return: a comment'. *Financial Review*, 27(1), 1992, pp. 141–9.

Chollet, P., and E. Ginglinger. 'The pricing of French unit seasoned equity offerings'. *European Financial Management*, 2001, Vol. 7.

Danielson, Morris G. 'A simple valuation model and growth expectation'. *Financial Analysts Journal*, May–June 1998, pp. 50–7.

Diermeier, Jeff and Bruno Solnik, 'Global pricing of equity'. *Financial Analysts Journal*, July/August 2001.

Fouse, William L. 'Allocating assets across country markets'. *Journal of Portfolio Management*, 18(2), 1992, pp. 20–7.

Gehr, Adam K., Jr. 'A bias in dividend discount models'. *Financial Analysts Journal*, 48(1), 1992, pp. 75–80.

Good, Walker R. 'When are price/earnings ratios too high or too low?' *Financial Analysts Journal*, July–August 1991, pp. 9–12.

Gordon, M.J. 'Dividends, earnings and stock prices'. *Review of Economics and Statistics*, 41, May 1959, pp. 99–105.

Hayes-Yelken, S., Larry J. Merville, and Xu Yexiao. 'Identifying the factor structure of equity returns'. *Journal of Portfolio Management*, Summer 2001, Vol. 27, No. 4.

Leibowitz, Martin L., and Stanley Kogelman. 'The growth illustration: the P/E "cost" of earnings growth'. *Financial Analysts Journal*, March–April 1994, pp. 36–48.

Appendix 9A INFORMATION CONTAINED IN THE FINANCIAL STATEMENTS

Some stock evaluation methods or investment strategies are based on accounting data or on a mix of market and accounting data, e.g. book to market value, price earning ratio, etc. Therefore, in this section we briefly discuss the main financial statements provided by firms.

Analysts who evaluate a stock commonly use the financial statement analysis for the following purposes:

1 Investors can compare accounting earnings for firms in an industry to locate firms with below-average (or above-average) performance.
2 Investors can compare accounting earnings over time for a specific firm to detect future problems.
3 Accounting values can be used to predict future economic values.
4 Accounting values for earnings and dividends can be used as inputs to dividend discount models.
5 Bond investors can use financial statements to assess the risk that a firm will go bankrupt or be unable to make scheduled interest payments or repay principal.
6 Accounting values may predict future rates of return in the stock market.

Firms provide three major financial statements for investors:

1 *The income statement.* The **income statement** reports the firm's sales, cost of goods sold, other expenses, earnings and so forth during a given accounting period, quarter or year.
2 *The balance sheet.* Unlike the income statement, the **balance sheet** provides a 'snapshot' of the firm's assets and liabilities at a given moment, for example on 31 December 2001.
3 *The statement of cash flows.* The **statement of cash flows** is based on actual cash inflows and outflows rather than on accrual accounting. From this statement analysts can learn about the sources of a firm's cash flow and how these cash flows are used to pay for capital expenditures, dividends, interest expenses and so forth.

9A.1 Balance sheet

A balance sheet shows the assets, liabilities and equity of a firm on a specific date. The balance sheet is based on the following:

$$\text{Assets} = \text{liabilities} + \text{owners' equity}$$

The information contained in the balance sheet helps answer questions such as these: What is the size of the firm? Are most assets current or fixed? How is the capital being invested? What is the firm's capital structure?

When analyzing a balance sheet, investors look for patterns. Do any significant patterns emerge over time? Is a particular firm deviating significantly from others within its industry? Good financial statement analysis will always look beyond the numbers. However, the numbers often suggest which areas require further investigation.

Exhibit 9A.1 presents Microsoft's balance sheet, which contains data for two years. It reports the firm's assets and liabilities at the reported date, in our example the end of the year.

The current assets include mainly cash, short-term investment, e.g. Treasury Bills, and inventory. The fixed assets include long-term investment, mainly the plant equipment less the accumulated depreciation.

Exhibit 9A.1 Balance sheets

	(in millions)	
June 30	1997	1998
Assets		
Current assets:		
Cash and short-term investments	$8,966	$13,927
Accounts receivable	980	1,460
Other	427	502
Total current assets	10,373	15,889
Property and equipment	1,465	1,505
Equity investments	2,346	4,703
Other assets	203	260
Total assets	$14,387	$22,357
Liabilities and stockholders' equity		
Current liabilities:		
Accounts payable	$721	$759
Accrued compensation	336	359
Income taxes payable	466	915
Unearned revenue	1,418	2,888
Other	669	809
Total current liabilities	3,610	5,730
Commitments and contingencies		
Stockholders' equity:		
Convertible preferred stock – shares authorized 100; shares issued and outstanding 13	980	980
Common stock and paid-in capital – shares authorized 8,000; shares issued and outstanding 2,408 and 2,470	4,509	8,025
Retained earnings	5,288	7,622
Total stockholders' equity	10,777	16,627
Total liabilities and stockholders' equity	$14,387	$22,357

Source: Website at http://www.microsoft.com/MSFT/history.htm. © 2001 Microsoft Corporation, One Microsoft Way, Redmond, Washington 98052-6300 USA. All rights reserved.

The liabilities and equity are the other side of the balance sheet. It contains current liabilities (short-term debt, accounts payable, etc.), long-term debt and shareholders' equity. The firm's equity is composed of the par value of the stocks – the additional paid in capital less Treasury stocks and the employer benefit trust.

Financial analysts generally use this data to calculate the EPS and the book value per share, which are needed for stock valuation.

Financial analysts generally investigate the changes in the various items in the balance sheet. Are the changes in cash, and is this a signal that something is wrong (the firm has less project to invest) or are they due to a temporary change in cash? Why are accounts receivable increasing? To answer these questions, the analyst must look at the explanations to the balance sheet that are normally part of the financial statements. If satisfied by the explanations, the analyst can conclude that this is a firm with no *long-term* liabilities. Hence, it is mostly an equity firm with regard to its long-term financial policy. Thus, Microsoft has relatively little financial risk.

9A.2 Income statement

The income statement shows the flow of sales, expenses and earnings during a specified period. The income statement is also known as the profit and loss (P&L) statement. It provides a summary of the revenues, cost of goods sold and expenses of a firm for an accounting period.

The income statement helps investors assess the abilities of management. Specifically, the income statement demonstrates how profitably the firm operated over a period of time. Related to profitability is management's ability to control expenses.

The information contained in the income statement helps answer several questions that investors have. What were the primary sources of income, cost of goods sold, and expenses? What is the value of research and development? Does research and development produce income? What is the 'true' earning power of the firm, where 'true' implies actual benefits accruing to the firm? In particular, by comparing several years, what is the trend in revenues, market share and profits? Answers to these questions are found in part in the income statement.

Exhibit 9A.2 shows the income statement of Microsoft. The income statement reports the revenue and then the various costs which are needed to create these sales. The net

Exhibit 9A.2 Income statements

	(in millions, except earnings per share)		
Year ended June 30	1996	1997	1998
Revenue	$8,671	$11,358	$14,484
Operating expenses:			
Cost of revenue	1,188	1,085	1,197
Research and development	1,432	1,925	2,502
Acquired in-process technology	–	–	296
Sales and marketing	2,657	2,856	3,412
General and administrative	316	362	433
Other expenses	19	259	230
Total operating expenses	5,612	6,487	8,070
Operating income	3,059	4,871	6,414
Interest income	320	443	703
Income before income taxes	3,379	5,314	7,117
Provision for income taxes	1,184	1,860	2,627
Net income	2,195	3,454	4,490
Preferred stock dividends	–	15	28
Net income available for common shareholders	$2,195	$3,439	$4,462
Earnings per share:[1]			
Basic	$0.93	$1.44	$1.83
Diluted	$0.86	$1.32	$1.67

[1] Earnings per share have been restated to reflect a two-for-one stock split in February 1998. See accompanying notes.

Source: Website at http://www.microsoft.com/MSFT/history.htm. © 2001 Microsoft Corporation, One Microsoft Way, Redmond, Washington 98052-6300 USA. All rights reserved.

income is divided by the number of shares to yield the EPS figure. Of particular interest to financial analysts is the series of EPS and DPS for several years from which a trend can be detected and the growth rate can be estimated. As we can see, Microsoft is a supergrowth firm with EPS growing from $0.86 in 1996 to $1.67 in 1998.

9A.3 Statement of cash flows

Accounting principles are very different from valuation methods. By accounting principles a firm may be profitable, yet by valuation methods it could be near bankruptcy. Suppose Boeing sells 747 jumbo aircraft for $500 million each. The production costs, which are all paid in cash, are $470 million. Would Boeing be profitable? Your answer depends on the method you use to evaluate this firm. An accountant would report on the income statement $30 million in earnings for each plane sold. Suppose now that the planes are sold not for cash but on credit for one year. Does this affect accounting earnings? No, the earnings will be reported in the year of the transaction as $500 million in revenues, even though the $500 million has not yet been received. Thus, the $500 million will be on the balance sheet as accounts receivable. Now suppose that the appropriate annual discount rate is 10%. Clearly, $500 million received one year from now is worth only $500 million/(1 + 0.10) ≅ $454.5 million (recall the time value of money). Because it cost $470 million to produce the planes, Boeing actually loses in economic terms (or in market value), even though the accounting statement shows a profit.

Although the reported earnings can be adjusted to reflect the true economic earnings, such distortions can be identified in the statement of cash flow that is also reported by the firm. In our example, if there are accounts receivable of $500 million, this sum will not be written as cash flow this year but rather in the next year, when they are actually received.

The statement of cash flows tells us all the sources of cash for the firm (including borrowing or a new issue of stock) and how the firm uses this cash for expenses, investment, paying dividends and so forth. The statement of cash flows has three components: operating activities, investing activities and financing activities. Operating activities include almost all items in the income statement, as well as balance sheet items that directly relate to earnings activities. Investing activities include buying or selling securities or revenue-generating assets, as well as activities related to lending money. Financing activities include activities related to borrowing money, as well as transactions related to owners' equity. The statement of cash flows is beneficial in assessing the ability of the firm to pay future dividends, fund future growth and service its debts.

The statement of cash flows documents the flow of cash through the firm during an accounting period. There are two methods for reporting the cash flows. The **direct method** shows the cash receipts and payments from operations. This approach gives the analyst a better understanding of how cash moves through a firm. The most popular method of reporting the cash flows, however, is the **indirect method**, which takes net income and adjusts for non-cash items in order to convert it to cash from operations. The indirect method reconciles net income with cash from operations. For example, Exhibit 9A.3 presents Microsoft's statement of cash flows, which starts with net income and reconciles the change in the cash asset account on the balance sheet.

For example, the net income of Microsoft in 1998 was $4,490 million. However, this does not mean that the firm obtained $4,490 million in cash inflows. Cash inflows could be more or less. For example, the firm had depreciation of $1,024 million. This is not a cash outflow but an accounting allocation. Therefore, we add it to the $4,490 million, as cash flow to the firm.

Exhibit 9A.3 Cash flow statements

	(in millions)		
Year ended June 30	1996	1997	1998
Operations			
Net income	$2,195	$3,454	$4,490
Depreciation and amortization	480	557	1,024
Write-off of acquired in-process technology	–	–	296
Unearned revenue	983	1,601	3,268
Recognition of unearned revenue from prior periods	(477)	(743)	(1,798)
Other current liabilities	584	321	208
Accounts receivable	(71)	(336)	(520)
Other current assets	25	(165)	(88)
Net cash from operations	3,719	4,689	6,880
Financing			
Common stock issued	504	744	959
Common stock repurchased	(1,385)	(3,101)	(2,468)
Put warrant proceeds	124	95	538
Preferred stock issued	–	980	–
Preferred stock dividends	–	(15)	(28)
Stock option income tax benefits	352	796	1,553
Net cash from (used for) financing	(405)	(501)	554
Investments			
Additions to property and equipment	(494)	(499)	(656)
Cash portion of Web TV purchase price	–	–	(190)
Equity investments and other	(625)	(1,669)	(1,598)
Short-term investments	(1,551)	(921)	(4,828)
Net cash used for investments	(2,670)	(3,089)	(7,272)
Net change in cash and equivalents	644	1,099	162
Effect of exchange rates on cash and equivalents	(5)	6	(29)
Cash and equivalents, beginning of year	1,962	2,601	3,706
Cash and equivalents, end of year	2,601	3,706	3,839
Short-term investments	4,339	5,260	10,088
Cash and short-term investments	$6,940	$8,966	$13,927

See accompanying notes.

Source: Website at http://www.microsoft.com/MSFT/history.htm. © 2001 Microsoft Corporation, One Microsoft Way, Redmond, Washington 98052-6300 USA. All rights reserved.

In practice, we see from Exhibit 9A.3 that the cash flow calculations are more complex. The firm makes several adjustments to get a net cash inflow from operations in 1998 of $6,880 million. Similarly, there are cash flows from raising more capital, firm investing, etc. The end result is a cashflow of $13,927 million in 1998.

It is interesting to see from this analysis that the firm has a policy of repurchasing its stocks. Stock buybacks can be interpreted by investors in one of two ways. Either management has run out of projects with positive NPVs and seeks to give investors capital gains rather than taxable dividends, or management believes the stock is significantly underpriced. Instead of raising money by issuing more stock, Microsoft is using cash to repurchase its stocks. Because Microsoft policy has been consistent for the past few years, it probably reveals significant information. It is possible that management thinks that its stock is underpriced, and it is a good investment to repurchase the stock. Also, this repurchasing signals a strong cash balance, because the repurchase is financed not by borrowing but from the firm's past earnings. The repurchasing may also mean that the firm lacks other profitable (NPV > 0) investment opportunities. In the case of Microsoft it clearly indicates strong confidence in the stock by management and may be based on some positive information that management knows but investors do not.

9A.4 Earnings and Dividends Per Share (EPS and DPS)

The actual EPS generally is different from the reported EPS. Therefore, analysts employ various methods to measure these deviations. There are various reasons why management reports EPS which differ from the actual EPS. For example, in 1999 Microsoft was under scrutiny by the SEC, who claimed that Microsoft manipulated the EPS in order to 'smooth' the EPS time series. Many analysts have devised ranking systems that are referred to as quality of earnings. Low quality implies that the reported EPS number differs greatly from the firm's actual operating earnings. In the case of Enron, the analysts failed in their analysis and Wall Street was hit in early 2002 by the discovery that reported earnings had been distorted. This distortion cast doubt on the quality of earnings reporting by other companies, leading to a market decline during February 2002 (see Exhibit 9.6 below).

As investors analyze the financial statements, they seek information on the quality of earnings. They ask several questions about quality. For example, when managers can select among different accounting procedures, do they select conservative or liberal procedures? Can a firm actually pay out the reported EPS, or is it not yet fully realized? Recall the preceding example of Boeing, where the $500 million in sales are in accounts receivable, so they cannot be paid as dividends. Over time, does the firm have stable earnings, or are the earnings volatile? How hard is it to forecast future earnings? Analysts seek to establish their level of confidence in the reported EPS figure, generally measured by the standard deviation of the EPS.

Exhibit 9.6

Andersen chief shifts blame in Enron debacle

By Peter Spiegel in Washington

Joseph Berardino, Andersen's chief executive, on Tuesday blamed the structure of the accounting industry for contributing to the collapse of Enron, saying that audit rules barred Andersen accountants from warning the public about the energy giant's financial condition.

Mr Berardino urged lawmakers to change accounting regulations to allow auditors to grade the quality and risk of a company's financial statements. Currently, firms can only give a 'pass' or 'fail' to financial data submitted by the company.

'Some companies do the bare minimum to meet [accounting] requirements, while others are much more prudent in their accounting decisions and disclosures,' Mr Berardino told a congressional hearing. 'There are some companies that are pushing the envelope and investors don't know which one is which.'...

In his testimony before the same panel, Mr Berardino said his company repeatedly questioned Enron's accounting practices, pointing to a widely reported February 5 meeting of Andersen auditors in which some of Enron's practices were labelled 'intelligent gambling'.

But while accounting rules allowed auditors to raise their concerns with Enron's board, which Mr Berardino said they did regularly, they prevented any public disclosure unless there were clear-cut violations of accepted accounting principles.

'Our only option is to resign the engagement [but] resigning an engagement may destroy a company that is fundamentally sound,' he said. 'So those are our choices when faced with a client whose accounting treatments are risky: give it a pass or give it the death penalty.'...

Mr Berardino said Andersen was aware of Enron's now-infamous private partnerships, which enabled the company to take debts off its balance sheets, but insisted they were set up by Enron executives and investment bankers, with Andersen only giving passive judgments as to whether they passed accepted accounting principles.

He also said Andersen would set up a new ethics office which would investigate questionable audit reviews when concerns are raised about the integrity or independence of an accountant.

Source: Website at http://news.ft.com/ft/gx.cgi, 5 and 6 February 2002. Reprinted with permission.

Chapter 10

COMMON STOCKS: SELECTION

Learning objectives

After studying this chapter you should be able to:

1 Describe how to estimate the values of g and k of the discount dividend model with constant growth.

2 Explain why dividend discount models must be used with caution.

3 Explain the free cash flow model (FCFM) which is appropriate for normal-growth firms which do not pay dividends or which pay irregular dividends.

4 Identify some characteristics of a stock market winner.

5 Explain how an analyst views the stock valuation process.

6 Understand the possible manipulation of reported earnings and hence the importance of evaluating earnings by the cash dividends model.

INVESTMENT IN THE NEWS

Looking beyond the P/E

Pros don't rely on one valuation method. Neither should you

The price/earnings ratio is the most widely used method of valuing a stock, but it isn't foolproof: Companies can manipulate earnings in many ways. To boost short-term earnings, for example, they can be more aggressive about pushing merchandise onto distributors. Or they can depress earnings artificially by adding to reserves for delinquent accounts. Why make earnings look worse than they are? Because the following year's earnings will look that much better by comparison. 'Depending on how creative the CFO is, you can get some pretty flukey earnings numbers,' says David Walker, co-manager of Van Kampen Emerging Growth fund. Plus, the P/E is of no use in looking at young Internet or biotech companies that have no earnings.

What to do? To avoid being misled by the P/E, fund managers and other pros put stocks through several valuation tests before making a buy or sell decision. We'll take a look at five of those measures. They're not hard to calculate, and they give you a fuller picture of a stock – and the company that's behind it – than the P/E alone does...

INVESTMENT IN THE NEWS

Exhibit 10.1 There's more than one way to value a stock. . .

Valuation method S&P 500 average	How it's calculated	Why it matters
Dividend yield 1.4%	Current dividend divided by stock price	Increasing dividends signal a company that's in good shape
Price-to-cash-flow 14.7	Stock price/net income per share plus noncash costs	More telling than the P/E ratio after a merger or acquisition
Price-to-sales 1.9	Stock price/revenues per share	Revenues aren't as easy to manipulate as earnings
Price-to-book 4.4	Stock price/book value per share	Helpful in finding undervalued companies
Return on equity 18.0%	Income before extra-ordinary items/book value	Shows how efficiently shareholder money is used

Source: Sarah Rose, *Money*, February 1999, Vol. 28, No. 2. © Time Inc. All rights reserved.

As we see from the *Investment in the news* article, the professionals use several criteria for stock selection apart from the most common P/E criterion (which is identical to the constant DDM for most firms which are normal-growth firms). Enron's CEO and Andersen, the accounting firm auditing Enron, were very creative to 'get some pretty flukey earnings numbers' (see the article). Exhibit 10.1 lists the most important factors they employ. We will discuss in this chapter the main factors mentioned in Exhibit 10.1.

There are difficulties and inaccuracies in employing any single valuation model. Therefore, analysts do not rely on only one model: in the stock valuation process they are seeking many other factors, as mentioned in the above article. Thus, the cash flow discounting model, as well as the P/E ratio, are the main criteria employed, but practitioners are adding many other factors in security analysis and make investment decisions based on rather complicated and sometimes nonquantitative factors.

In this chapter we elaborate on the DDM and in particular on the way it is implemented in practice. We first show how the inputs of the constant DDM are estimated and discuss the problems with achieving these estimates. We also discuss other possible misleading factors which may occur in some cases with the DDM. We then discuss why the DDM should be employed, as any other valuation models, with great caution. We discuss the way investment professionals view the stock valuation process. However, even if a financial analyst has a valuation method that can identify winners in the stock market, this process is not risk-free, because it is based on averages, i.e. the analyst outperforms the market on average but not in every stock selected. In some cases, the analyst is wrong. Therefore, the analyst still needs to consider portfolio risk reduction and diversification even when the valuation method indicates that a given stock is a bargain.

10.1 ESTIMATING DIVIDEND DISCOUNT MODEL INPUTS

In Chapter 9, the constant DDM has been discussed and its use explained when it is assumed that g and k are known (see Equation 9.5). When investors use this model in practice to select stocks, however, they cannot simply work with assumed levels of g and k. They must estimate these values. This section illustrates how investors can do this. Actually applying the DDM requires estimating two critical parameters: the investor's required rate of return (k) on the firm's equity, and the growth rate of dividends (g).

10.1.1 Estimating the dividend growth rate (g)

There are several ways to estimate the **growth rate, g**. The simplest way is to estimate g by extrapolating the past dividend payments. If d_t represents the annual dividend payment at the end of year t, then g is represented by

$$d_t = d_0 (1 + g)^t$$

where d_0 represents the dividend paid t years ago and g is the growth rate in dividends. Solving for g yields the following:[1]

$$g = \left(\frac{d_t}{d_0} \right)^{1/t} - 1 \qquad (10.1)$$

This method for estimating g is known as the **point estimate method,** because only two dividend payments (two points in time) are used. The growth rate estimated by this method is very sensitive to the selected starting and ending year. Actually, it depends on only two observations, d_0 and d_t. For example, if CS, Inc. paid a £1.52 dividend per share in year 2001 and a £0.95 dividend per share in 1991, the growth rate for this 10-year period would be

$$g = \left(\frac{s1.52}{s0.95} \right)^{1/10} - 1 = (1.6)^{1/10} - 1 \cong 0.048$$

or about 4.8% annual growth rate. However, if we select a five-year period and suppose that the dividends per share paid in 1996 were £1.18 (see Exhibit 10.2 below), then the growth rate would be

$$g = \left(\frac{\$1.52}{\$1.18} \right)^{1/5} - 1 \cong (1.2881)^{1/5} - 1 \cong 0.052$$

or about 5.2%.

Although these growth rates may not appear to be very different, the impact on the respective stock prices is substantial. For example, if we assume that the discount rate

---

[1] By dividing by d_0 to get $d_t/d_0 = (1 + g)^t$, taking the tth root, and subtracting 1, we get Equation 10.1. When the firm changes its payout ratio, sometimes it is better to use the EPS series rather than the DPS series to estimate growth rates.

$k = 9\%$, then the estimated prices with growth rates of 4.8% and 5.2% respectively are (see Chapter 9, Equation 9.5):

$$P_0 = \frac{d_1}{k - g} = \frac{d_0(1 + g)}{k - g} = \frac{£1.52(1 + 0.048)}{0.09 - 0.048} \cong £37.93$$

$$P_0 = \frac{d_0(1 + g)}{k - g} = \frac{£1.52(1 + 0.052)}{0.09 - 0.052} \cong £42.08$$

Thus, a 0.4% (5.2% − 4.8%) difference in our estimate of g results in a £4.15 difference in the stock price. The estimation procedure is therefore very sensitive to the choice of the dividend growth estimation period. Selecting the estimation period is crucial to all other valuation models, but the point estimate method in particular is sensitive to this choice.

Another problem with the point estimate method is that it ignores the dividend payments made during the interim periods. For example, our future estimates for CS, Inc., would not be different if we knew that instead of gradually increasing dividends, as shown in Exhibit 10.2, there were no dividend payments between 1991 and 2001, which of course constitutes a major drawback. Thus, we would need to refine our analysis to incorporate the information contained in the interim periods. Appendix 10A elaborates on the following estimation equation, which relies on *all dividends* rather than only on the dividends of the first and the last years:

$$g = \exp\left\{\frac{\mathrm{Cov}(\ln(d), t)}{\sigma_t^2}\right\} - 1 \tag{10.2}$$

Exhibit 10.2 Hypothetical illustration for estimating g for CS, Inc.

Year	Dividend	t (years)[a]	$\ln(d)$[b]	$t \times \ln(d)$[c]	t^2
1991	£0.95	0	−0.05	0.00	0
1992	0.99	1	−0.01	−0.01	1
1993	1.04	2	0.04	0.08	4
1994	1.13	3	0.12	0.37	9
1995	1.16	4	0.15	0.59	16
1996	1.18	5	0.17	0.83	25
1997	1.24	6	0.22	1.29	36
1998	1.28	7	0.25	1.73	49
1999	1.40	8	0.34	2.69	64
2000	1.43	9	0.36	3.22	81
2001	1.52	10	0.42	4.19	100
Sum	£13.32	55.00	2.01	14.98	385
Average[d]	£1.21	5.00	0.18	1.36	35

[a] Starting t at zero is arbitrary. It is easier to compute the statistics with low numbers, however.

[b] The reported numbers are rounded. However, the product $t \times \ln(d)$ is calculated with the precise numbers of $\ln(d)$.

[c] The covariance between $\ln(d)$ and t and the variance of t are given by

$$\mathrm{Cov}[\ln(d), t] = 1.36 - (0.18 \times 5.0) = 0.46$$

$$\sigma_t^2 = 35 - 5^2 = 10$$

[d] The average is the sum divided by 11 (which is the number of years).

where ln(d) is the natural logarithm of dividend payments, t is a counter for time (years), σ_t^2 is the variance of the counter for time, Cov is the covariance of ln(d) and t, and exp stands for *exponential* (that is, 'e to the power of').

This method of estimating g is known as the **regression method**, because it is based on linear regression. Recall from our definition of covariance and variance (see Chapter 6) that:

$$\text{Cov(ln}(d),t) = \frac{1}{n}\sum_{i=1}^{n}[(\ln(d_i) - (\overline{\ln(d_i)})](t_i - \bar{t}) = \frac{1}{n}\sum_{i=1}^{n}\ln(d_i)t_i - \overline{\ln(d_i)t_i}$$

and

$$\sigma_t^2 = \frac{1}{n}\sum_{i=1}^{n}(t_i - \bar{t})^2 = \frac{1}{n}\sum_{i=1}^{n}t_i^2 - \bar{t}_i^2$$

where $\overline{\ln(d_i)}$ is the average of the ln(d_i), and $\bar{t}_i$ is the average of the t_i.

Exhibit 10.2 above illustrates the data required to estimate g using Equation 10.2:

$$g = \exp(0.46/10) - 1 = 4.7\%$$

(see footnote c to Exhibit 10.2).

Thus, the regression estimate of the growth rate of dividends over the past 10 years is 4.7%. In this particular case, the regression approach resulted in an estimate very close to the case with only two points, because in our hypothetical example of CS, Inc., CS has paid steadily increasing dividends over this 10-year period. In the hypothetical case of a steady increase in dividends with a sharp fall in the last year, the two methods yield quite different estimates.

An alternative method for estimating the dividend growth rate is to use the accounting figures. Recall that $g = bR$ (see Chapter 9) where b is the retention ratio and R is the rate of return on reinvested capital by the firm. Thus, one can use the accounting figures to estimate R. The retention ratio, b, is the proportion of EPS which is not distributed as cash dividends and reinvested in the firm. This figure can be easily calculated from the dividend per share (DPS) and EPS reported in the firm's financial statements. To obtain the growth rate, g, we need to estimate also R. The rate of return on the reinvested capital, R, in year t can be estimated by taking the return on equity ($\text{ROE}_t = \text{EPS}_t/\text{BVPS}_{t-1}$, where BVPS is the book value per share in year $t - 1$). Multiplying the return on equity by the retention ratio b provides an estimate for the growth rate, g:

$$g = b \times \text{ROE}_t = b \times (\text{EPS}_t/\text{BVPS}_{t-1})$$

This method of estimating g is known as the **accounting method**, because it is based on accounting data.

10.1.2 Estimating the investors' required rate of return (k)

We presented above several ways to estimate the growth rate, g. Another crucial factor needed for the DDM is the discount rate, k, or the required rate of return by the stockholders. There are various ways to estimate k. The analysts in practice employ more than one method; sometimes, having arrived at more than one objective estimate, they make their subjective estimate based on the objective estimates!

PRACTICE BOX

Problem

Calculate the growth rate of dividends (g) for CS from 1997 through 2001 using the data in Exhibit 10.2.

Solution

We need to construct a table similar to Exhibit 10.2 for the years 1997 through 2001:

Year	Dividend	t(years)	$\ln(d)^a$	$t \times \ln(d)^a$	t^2
1997	£1.24	0.00	0.22	0.00	0
1998	1.28	1.00	0.25	0.25	1
1999	1.40	2.00	0.34	0.67	4
2000	1.43	3.00	0.36	1.07	9
2001	1.52	4.00	0.42	1.67	16
Sum	£6.87	10.00	1.59	3.66	30
Average	£1.37	2.00	0.32	0.73	6

a See footnote b in Exhibit 10.2.

Thus, the covariance is

$$\text{Cov}[\ln(d),t] = 0.73 - (0.32 \times 2.00) = 0.09$$

and the variance of t is

$$\sigma_t^2 = 6 - 2^2 = 2$$

From Equation 10.2 we get the following (the exponential, e, is on most calculators):

$$g = e^{0.09/2} - 1 = e^{0.045} - 1 \cong 4.60\%$$

The first way to calculate the investors' required rate of return is to use the DDM itself to estimate k, as demonstrated in Chapter 9:

$$k = \frac{d_1}{P_0} + g \qquad (10.3)$$

where g is estimated by one of the methods suggested in the previous section, and d_1 and P_0 are observed (recall that $d_1 = d_0(1 + g)$ and d_0 is observed, hence d_1 can be estimated).

We also can use the capital asset pricing model (CAPM) discussed in Chapter 14 to estimate k. By the CAPM the risk of the stock (the stock's **beta**) is first estimated, then one adds to the riskless asset, r, the required risk premium as derived from the CAPM to estimate k.

A third method is to estimate the historical average rate of return on the common stock. This average rate of return is a proxy of what investors will require in the future. For example, suppose the average rate of return on CS common stock over the past 10 years is 15.6%. Thus, we could estimate the investor's required annual rate of return for the future as 15.6%.

Another method relies on the P/E ratio. Recall from Chapter 9 that there are circumstances when the E/P ratio (the reciprocal of the P/E ratio) is an appropriate estimate of k.

Notice that counting on the P/E ratio is true as long as earnings are not manipulated (see the Enron case). For this reason, it is better to use other methods, mentioned above, which rely on the future cash dividends and not on the earnings.

Finally, one can use the firm's bonds (if they exist) to estimate k. One can use the yield to maturity of a firm's long-term bonds to get a benchmark for k. Because common stocks are riskier than bonds, we must add a positive premium of, say, 4%. For example, assume CS has a $9^1/_2$% coupon bond that matures in 24 years. The bond's yield to maturity is presently 9%. Thus, we could estimate k as 13% (9% + 4%). This approach has the benefit of being forward looking, because the yield to maturity incorporates expectations about the market, as well as expectations about the firm's prospects. However, the addition of a risk premium is not precise, and does not rely on any quantitative model. The importance of this method, however, is that we have a lower bound on k: we know that it must be higher than 9%.

Although empirical studies provide support for DDMs as a successful investment criterion which enhances the portfolio return, they should be used in practice with caution because the DDMs rely on several strong assumptions. Moreover, in some cases the DDMs cannot be employed directly because dividends are not paid at all.

10.2 IMPLEMENTING DIVIDEND DISCOUNT MODELS

10.2.1 DDM assumptions[2]

If we use a DDM to identify undervalued (or overvalued) stocks, we are assuming that, although a stock is not now appropriately valued, someday soon its value will return to its appropriate level. If we apply the DDM to a stock, we might find that it is worth £120 when it is currently trading at £90. In this case, we would buy the stock, hoping that it would soon go to its DDM value of £120. That is, the DDM would be of no use if the stock did not revert back to its fair value soon, where fair value is based on the DDM.

A second assumption of the DDM is that the discount rate (k) is constant over time. In practice, this may not be the case. For example, many analysts believe that firms go through a life cycle as they move from infancy to maturity. Most firms have a rapid-growth phase, when they pay no dividends; then an expansion phase, when they begin to pay dividends; and finally a maturity phase, when they exhibit little or no growth. A DDM incorporates the changing dividends as the firm progresses through its life cycle. When discounting dividends through these different phases, why should we believe that the investor's required rate of return remains the same? After all, the risk of the firm also changes over the life cycle, so k should change with the firm's life cycle. Intuitively, we would anticipate that k would be lower when the firm is in maturation, because less risk is involved. Thus, to estimate stock value accurately, we need to allow for both changes in dividends and changes in the investor's required rate of return.

Finally, some firms, such as Microsoft, do not pay cash dividends at all, which make the DDM justifiable. We will show later in the chapter how one can circumvent this difficulty.

10.2.2 Proper inputs

The DDM is a forward-looking equation, yet most analysts rely on history to establish initial estimates. They combine history with current events to estimate future events.

---

[2] The following sections are based in part on John J. Nagorniak, 'Thoughts on using dividend discount models', *Financial Analysts' Journal*, November–December 1985, pp. 13–15.

One difficult job of an analyst is to make the appropriate alterations to historical estimates.

Clearly, such alterations require skills in evaluating things that are not quantifiable. For example, assessing the change in the quality of management and the impact it will have on the current stock price is difficult to quantify.

A final difficulty lies in establishing how long it will take for a firm to move from one phase to another. For example, how long can a firm remain in the supergrowth phase? How can this be estimated? Although not entirely impossible, it is a difficult task.

10.2.3 Interpreting the results of a DDM calculation

After the exercise of calculating stock values based on the DDM has been completed, what can you do with the results? For example, suppose you determine that a stock is 10% undervalued according to the DDM. What should you do? At first glance, you may say, 'Buy it, of course!' The answer, however, is not that clear-cut. For example, the factors that caused the price to be 10% undervalued may well drive it to be 20% undervalued before it begins to turn around. Thus, the timing decision is very tricky.

A second problem is determining whether the stock is really mispriced or whether you are just missing some crucial information. You must address why the stock is mispriced. Understanding the forces driving the mispricing (for example, institutional selling because of a legal constraint) will be helpful in assessing the appropriate action to take when mispricing actually occurs.

The final problem is determining how to assess the performance of the DDM. The DDM as an investment tool may lead to a successful result (or profit) on some stocks and to a failure (loss) on other stocks. The critical question is whether the predicted DDM performance leads, on average, to abnormal profit (or to a profit adjusted for risk). If so, it will be a valuable tool for the analyst.

All these deficiencies of the DDM, however, are not unique to this model. They characterize virtually all models which are employed to evaluate and select a stock. However, there are several problems unique to the DDM which we discuss next. These problems are often raised by students who try to implement the model to an actual data set, and we shall see that in most cases they are reasonably solved. We turn to this issue next.

10.3 HOW CAN ONE EMPLOY THE DDM TO FIRMS WHICH DO NOT PAY DIVIDENDS?

The student who tries to employ the DDM in practice may face a problem. Many firms, some of them very well known, like Microsoft, do not pay dividends at all, or if they do, they do not keep a constant payout ratio, which seems to imply that the DDM cannot be employed. To illustrate, suppose that a firm does not pay cash dividends but will pay dividends sometime in the future. In principle, the present value of these future dividends is the current value of the stock. Thus, regardless of whether dividends grow at a constant rate or not, and regardless of whether dividends are paid for some years or not, given a series of expected future dividends of $d_1, d_2, d_3, \ldots, d_n$, the present value of this dividend series can be calculated to obtain the value of the stock. To illustrate, suppose that a firm declares that it will not pay cash dividends, and that at the end of the tenth year it will liquidate all its assets and distribute the cash flow to the stockholders. From the investor's point of view, the cash flow obtained at the tenth year can be considered as a dividend, d_{10}. Therefore, in such a case, PV = $d_{10}/(1 + k)^{10}$, where d_{10} is the tenth-year expected liquidation value per share, k is the discount rate, and PV is the present value of d_{10}.

Conceptually, therefore, only future dividends or future cash flows to the stockholders are relevant for stock valuation. However, estimating these expected future cash flows is sometimes difficult. If the firm regularly pays a given portion of its earnings as cash dividends and the dividend per share grows at a constant rate, then dividends are generally expected to grow at a constant rate and can be reasonably estimated. In such a case, investors can apply the simple constant dividend growth model as a specific case of the present value of future dividends to evaluate the stock.

However, a look at the EPS, and the dividends per share, DPS, of the following example makes it obvious that this method is not applicable when the dividend payout ratio changes over time.

Year	EPS	DPS
2000	£10	£5
2001	£8	£8

From this example we see that dividends grow by 60% in 2001 but EPS drops by 20%. Can we employ the constant dividend model here to evaluate the stock? Apparently not, because the payout ratio increased from 50% to 100%. Here the constant dividend growth model is not intact, hence the P/E criterion, which is derived from the constant dividend growth model, also fails. Thus, what valuation model can be used in cases where future expected dividends change over time or are unknown? We next discuss the free cash flow method which comes to the rescue in this case.

10.4 THE FREE CASH FLOW MODEL (FCFM) FOR NORMAL-GROWTH FIRMS

The free cash flow model (FCFM) applies in such cases. The FCFM is a method of estimating the value of a stock even if dividends have not been paid in the past or if dividends are paid irregularly. In most cases, the FCFM provides the same value of the stock as the present value of unknown expected dividends. However, the FCFM does not require an estimate of the future dividends, which are hard to forecast. The value of the stock is calculated *as if* the future expected dividends were known, even though in fact they are not known. The important principle to remember is that even if the firm does not pay dividends, the free cash flow is what it *could* pay. The fact that the money is reinvested in the firm rather than paid as dividends does not change the value of the stock, because we deal with normal-growth firms. Thus, we can treat the free cash flow as dividends even if they are not paid at all.

Before defining free cash flow (FCF), a definition of the firm's cash flow (CF) from operations is in order. The firm's annual cash flow is the cash flow received from operations in a given year, after interest and taxes have been paid. For simplicity, assume that all the firm's expenses and revenues are for cash; then the cash flow from operations is simply the earnings plus the depreciation, denoted by D_p. We add the depreciation to the earnings, because depreciation is not a cash outflow. Thus,

$$CF = EPS + D_p$$

where CF, EPS and D_p are all per one share.

The CF has a clear-cut definition and is easy to measure, but the definition of the FCF, which we need for stock valuation, is more ambiguous. The most common definition of FCF is the cash flow the firm has after deducting the capital expenditure needed to maintain the ongoing operation of the firm *at its current level*. To illustrate, suppose the firm's CF is £50 million. It needs to invest £10 million to maintain its operation at the current level, but it invests £20 million because it wants to expand. After deducting the cash outlay on investment, the firm actually has only £30 million; however, according to the previous definition, its FCF is £40 million. It could distribute £40 million as dividends *without affecting its current level of operation*. If the firm needs to reinvest the depreciation to maintain the current level of operation (a reasonable assumption), then (once again assuming that all operations are for cash) the FCF equals the EPS, because

$$FCF = CF - D_p = EPS + D_p - D_p = EPS$$

To find the value of the stock, we need to discount the FCF (or EPS) per share.

Thus, if we adopt the FCFM as the model for stock valuation, the value of the stock is simply the present value of the EPS. In other words, the EPS is the maximum amount the firm *could* pay as dividends without affecting its current level of operation. Note that we assume that all free cash flow is distributed as cash dividends, even if in practice no dividend is paid. Hence, to be consistent in our methodology, the hypothetical EPS does not grow over time, even though in practice it does grow. The EPS should not grow in our calculation because all free cash flow is treated as dividends, hence the firm only invests the depreciation to maintain the EPS and its current level. Indeed, as is shown in the next practice box, next year's expected FCF (or EPS) is relevant for stock valuation, and any increase in the FCF in the future should be ignored; otherwise we will not get the correct value of the stock. Thus, the stream of hypothetical dividends (or FCF, which is actually not paid) is as follows:

Year	1	2	3	...
Hypothetical dividends	EPS	EPS	EPS	...

where EPS = FCF is the *next year's* earnings per share, and the present value of the FCF is EPS/k, where k is the appropriate discount rate.

Thus, EPS and FCF are based on next year's estimate of the EPS and should be kept constant in the discounting process, even though we know that in fact the EPS (and the FCF) grows over time (because the EPS is retained, and even if deposited in the bank will add income to the firm). The reason is that for a normal-growth firm, $k = R$, hence the fact that the EPS are not distributed as dividends does not change the value of the stock: the firm reinvests at $R = k$, hence the PV of all future dividends remains unchanged. Thus, without loss of generality, we can assume that the EPS is distributed as dividends even if actually no dividends are paid. This principle is illustrated in the next practice box.

The practice box illustrates that the dividend discount model implies that we can either discount all future dividends or simply discount the next year's EPS (i.e. £10 in our example) and ignore the future growth in EPS. (This is correct for normal-growth firms.) Both methods yield the same PV, because under our assumption that all operations are done for cash, and the depreciation is invested to maintain the firm's operation at the current level, the FCF can be estimated by the EPS. Therefore, we conclude that according to the FCFM, we should rely only on next year's EPS and ignore the future growth in EPS. Although the firm will have £11 free cash flow from Year 2 and thereafter, we look

PRACTICE BOX

Problem

Suppose that the EPS next year is £10. The firm invests the depreciation in such a way that it can maintain its operation at the current level forever. The discount rate is $k = 10\%$.

1 What is the value of the stock if the entire £10 per share is paid as cash dividends each year?
2 What is the value of the stock if the firm does not pay dividends in the first year and invests this £10 in a perpetuity at k? (Assume that from Year 2 and thereafter, all earnings are paid as dividends.) How does this relate to next year's EPS?
3 Assume that the characteristics of question 2 above apply, and we discount the future EPS rather than next year's EPS. What is the PV of all future earnings?

Solution

1 The value of the stock is given by the present value of the £10 annual dividends: £10/0.1 = £100.
2 If dividends are not paid in the first year, then the £10 is invested, yielding £10 × 0.1 = £1 in each of the following years. Thus, £11 will be paid from Year 2 onward, and the present value of future dividends is as follows:

$$\frac{0}{1.1} + \frac{£11}{(1.1)^2} + \frac{£11}{(1.1)^3} + \cdots = \frac{1}{1.1}\left(\frac{£11}{1.1} + \frac{£11}{(1.1)^2} + \cdots\right) = \frac{1}{1.1} \times \left(\frac{£11}{0.1}\right) = £100$$

We see that by the DDM, the value of the stock is £100 regardless of the dividend policy of the firm. Thus, even though earnings (and dividends) will be £11 per share in the future (from Year 2), the value of the stock can be obtained by dividing *the next year's earnings (£10) by the discount rate and ignoring the future growth in earnings*. Thus, only next year and not the future EPS are relevant for the PV calculation.

3 In this case, the PV of earnings is given by

$$\frac{£10}{1.1} + \frac{£11}{(1.1)^2} + \frac{£11}{(1.1)^3} + \cdots = \frac{£10}{1.1} + \$100 \cong £109.09$$

which is higher than the true value as obtained by the DDM.

at the next year's FCF of £10 and assume it will be at this level forever. Thus, using the FCFM, we discount the maximum dividends the firm *could pay* next year, not the dividends it actually will pay. The fact that stockholders did not get the £10 in the first year does not affect the value of the stock, because it is offset by the fact that the £10 is invested by the firm at the required rate of return, k, and therefore more will be paid to the stockholders in the future. Thus, assuming that the £10 was obtained in Year 1 (even though no cash was distributed to the stockholders) and ignoring the increase in future earnings (or FCF) that is due to the reinvestment of the retained earnings, the same present value as the present value of actual future dividends (see the practice box) is obtained.

In other words, the example just given reveals that the following two hypothetical cash flows have the same present value of £100:

1 £10, £10, £10,... ('next year's' FCF = EPS)
2 £0, £11, £11,... (future DPS)

Thus, although the second scenario represents the cash flows to the stockholder and the first scenario does not, we can switch from Scenario 2 to Scenario 1 without changing the present value. This is exactly what the FCFM does. It relies on next year's FCF (or EPS) (£10) and ignores the growth in next year's FCF (+£1). If we discount the future FCF (or EPS), rather than next year's FCF, we get an overvaluation, as in point 3 of the practice box.

Because we do not know the cash flow given by Scenario 2, or when the firm will stop reinvesting its earnings and start to pay cash dividends, we can use the FCF given by Scenario 1 to calculate the value of the stock. Thus, by using the FCFM, we can get the PV of future dividends without knowing what these dividends will actually be. This is true as long as the firm is a normal-growth firm, i.e. reinvests at k.

Finally, we assume that the EPS is cash obtained by the firm. This is not necessarily so, however, because firms sell on credit and take credit from their customers. Furthermore, there are some other differences between EPS and cash flow (CF) per share because of the accounting principles, which are not based on cash flow. If there are substantial differences between the EPS and the FCF per share, the FCF per share rather than the EPS is the relevant figure to discount. Also, the firm may need to invest more or less than its accounting depreciation to maintain its operation at the current level. An adjustment for this investment should also be considered, so the FCF may differ from the EPS. These adjustments to the cash flow are relatively easy to incorporate. Regardless of these adjustments, we discount the next year's expected cash flow and ignore its increase in the future – an increase that is due to the fact that retained earnings are reinvested in the firm. Thus, to get the correct value of the stock, we implicitly assume that all free cash flows are distributed as dividends, and therefore there is no growth in these cash flows.

Finally, supergrowth firms generally invest more than what is needed to maintain the current operation of the firm at the present level because they are able to project positive net prevent value. Thus, they invest at $R > k$, hence not distributing cash dividends may increase the value of the stock: each dollar is reinvested at R but discounted at a lower value k, hence a value is created. For these firms one has first to estimate the minimum investment needed to maintain the firm's operation at the present level, and then carefully analyze all additional investments. Because these additional investments create value, one has to add to the value of the stock an estimate of the net present value (per share) of all projects taken by the firm and financed by these additional investments. Unlike the normal-growth firms, for supergrowth firms the larger the investment, the larger the value of the firm.

10.5 HOW ANALYSTS VIEW THE STOCK VALUATION PROCESS

From the discussion of the DDM, the constant DDM and the FCFM as well as from the *Investment in the news* article, it is obvious that one cannot use one model and evaluate a stock without looking at other factors, e.g. the source of growth, competition and quality of management. We now discuss these factors, which are employed by the professionals. Still, the present value of all future cash flows is the only relevant model. However, the analysis of all the factors discussed below sheds light on these potential future cash flows and in particular on the reliability of the estimates for them.

10.5.1 The valuation process[3]

How do professionally trained security analysts evaluate common stocks? A survey of members of the Financial Analysts' Federation sheds some light on this question. This section examines how analysts value stocks in their pursuit of selecting winners.

The survey of the Financial Analysts' Federation overwhelmingly indicated that analysts examine the following economic factors: (1) expected changes in EPS, (2) expected return on equity, and (3) prospects of the relevant industry.

Arriving at the valuation of these factors, and in particular the valuation of changes in EPS, requires a detailed analysis of the firm. Based on their survey results, Chugh and Meador (see footnote 3) conclude the following:

> No single operating ratio from the company's financial statements, nor any single product or market event, captures for the analyst the long-term prospective value of the stock. Analysts appear to view a company in its entirety – its history, capabilities and position in the industry.... [Analysts] attached more importance to the regularity of new product introduction and product refinement, for example, than to anticipated introduction of a new product.... [Analysts also] look to qualitative factors such as quality and depth of management, market dominance and strategic credibility to validate quantitative financial and economic variables.

The analysts indicated that the quality and depth of a company's management was an important criterion in assessing a stock's value. Is the firm run by one superstar, or are there numerous highly qualified people managing the firm? How can analysts measure something like this? Analysts assess the quality and depth of management. The most relevant assessment media are (1) the performance record of management; (2) interviews, meetings and presentations of management to analysts; and (3) evidence of management's strategic planning and ability to meet stated objectives.

Exhibit 10.3 illustrates the stock valuation process as inferred from the results of the survey of the Financial Analysts' Federation. Standard information sources are combined with assessment media to develop predictors of financial performance. The predictors of financial performance are combined with the environment in which the firm operates to develop a systematic, or well-ordered, view of the company. From this systematic view, analysts develop long-term financial performance forecasts of EPS and return on equity (ROE, or net income/book value of equity). Finally, based on these long-term forecasts of EPS and ROE, analysts arrive at the value of the common stock.

Thus, we see from the discussion so far that the expected EPS and ROE are still the most important factors for stock valuation. In order to arrive at a solid estimate, one needs to analyze the management quality as well as the atmosphere in which the firm operates.

The *Investment in the news* article and in particular Exhibit 10.1 shed light on the important factors analysts consider. While it is true that (for normal-growth firms) the P/E ratio is widely employed, there is a risk that the EPS is manipulated (see the Enron case), hence the P/E ratio may be misleading. Therefore, some other criteria that are harder to manipulate are employed in the stock valuation process. Dividend yield and the change in dividend yield are important, and increasing dividend yield generally signals that the firm is in good shape. Then, the price-to-cash-flow substitutes (or complements) the P/E ratio, when cash flow is the earnings per share plus noncash costs such as depreciation. This is not the free cash flow approach discussed before, because here the investment needed to maintain the current operation of the firm is not deductible. An

---

[3] This section is based on Lal C. Chugh and Joseph W. Meador, 'The stock valuation process: The analysts' view', *Financial Analysts' Journal*, November–December 1984, pp. 41–8.

Exhibit 10.3 Stock valuation: a process model

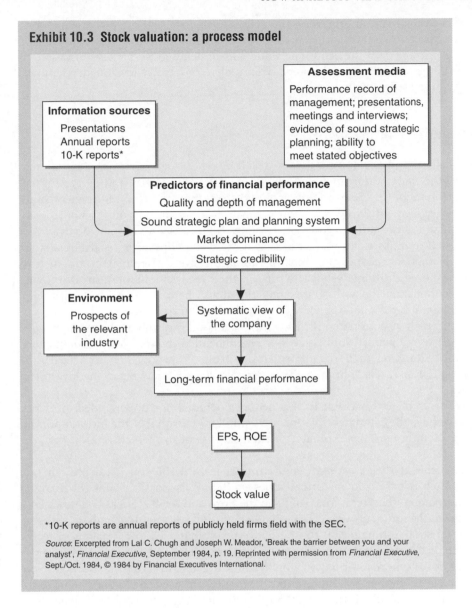

*10-K reports are annual reports of publicly held firms field with the SEC.

Source: Excerpted from Lal C. Chugh and Joseph W. Meador, 'Break the barrier between you and your analyst', *Financial Executive*, September 1984, p. 19. Reprinted with permission from *Financial Executive*, Sept./Oct. 1984, © 1984 by Financial Executives International.

important factor widely employed by practitioners is the price-to-book-value. If is a common belief that stock with low price-to-book ratio (i.e. stock price divided by the net book value of asset per share) are underpriced and will yield a high rate of return in the future, and the opposite holds regarding stock with a high price-to-book ratio (see next section).

From this discussion one thing is clear. The main factor which is important for stock valuation is the future cash flows, and knowing these cash flows one can employ the DDM to obtain the value of the stock. However, because dividends are sometimes hard to predict, the FCFM, the P/E ratio and other investment criteria are employed. The crucial issue the analyst faces is: How reliable is the EPS? Is it manipulated? What is the chance that the profitability will continue in the future? How strong is the quality of the management? To answer these questions, the analyst also uses other valuation criteria, including visits to the firm, interviewing the management, etc. All these complementary means are necessary to analyze the quality of the estimates of future earnings and dividends. In Appendix 10B the **economic value added**, denoted by EVA, is discussed as a tool for picking stocks by practitioners. This tool is relatively new but has enjoyed rapid growth among security analysts.

10.5.2 The analysts' forecast

Analysts use market and accounting data to reach buy–hold–sell decisions. Not all analysts agree on the information included in the financial statements and in the market data. The interpretation of the available data and the implication for future growth are generally not in agreement. Nowadays, with a click of a button on your computer, you can get an estimate of the future growth of earnings (g) as estimated by the analysts and the buy–hold–sell recommendation. Recall that if there is a consensus regarding a stock and all or most analysts recommend 'buy' or 'hold', the stock price may go up, at least in the short run, even if all analysts are wrong in their recommendation: investors who follow this recommendation will simply buy the stock, hence will push its price up. Exhibit 10.4 illustrates the analysts' view of IBM stock in mid-1999.

Firstly, all the analysts considered IBM stock to be a good investment: 13 recommended 'strong buy', 10 recommended 'buy' and four recommended 'hold'. None recommended selling the stock. Ranking their recommendations from 1 (strong buy) to 5 (sell), the consensus mean is 1.667, which implies a very strong optimistic view regarding investment in IBM's stock.

We also see from the exhibit that IBM is neither upgraded nor downgraded in its risk rating. Then we have the estimated EPS for 1999 and 2000. Probably the most important figure is the growth in earnings estimate for the next 3–5 years, which is 13% per year for IBM.

One can use this analyst's estimate and contrast it with the statistical growth rate estimate, g, which is based on historical series of EPS. It is possible that the analysts have more information (due to recent changes in the firm) and the historical EPS series does not represent well the future growth. Thus, a large deviation between the analysts' estimate of g and the 'statistical' estimate calls for more investigation and a future analysis of recent changes (e.g. change in management, spin off, merger, etc.) that have occurred in the firm.

Exhibit 10.4 reveals more information employed by investors in the stock selection. Note that apart from the common P/E ratio, also other ratios are used, including the price-to-book value. In the case of IBM, this is 12.665, i.e. the market price is 12.665 higher than the book value per share. The high price of IBM (as well as the high P/E ratio of 35.44) is due to the expected high future growth in EPS. The high growth rate affects the stock price (which is the PV of all future cash flows) but does not affect the reported EPS or the book value per share, hence the P/E and the market-to-book value are relatively high.

10.6 VALUATION OF STOCKS AND PORTFOLIO CONSIDERATION

If the market is perfectly efficient, all information on the company is already included in the stock price, therefore there are no bargains in the market. Thus, in an efficient market, all stocks are correctly priced, and no model can predict stocks that will have

Exhibit 10.4 Financial analyst forecast and recommendation for IBM stock

Analyst ratings

Strong buy	13
Buy	10
Hold	4
Underperform	0
Sell	0
Consensus (mean)	1.667[a]
Number of ratings upgraded last month	0
Number of ratings downgraded last month	0

Estimated quarterly EPS

Current (06/1999)	£0.88
Next (09/1999)	£0.88

Estimated yearly EPS

Current (1999)	£3.99
Next (2000)	£4.60

Upcoming earnings release dates

June 1999	21 July 1999
September 1999	20 October 1999

Long-term growth rate forecast

Expected annual increase in operating earnings over the next full business cycle (3–5 years)	13.00%
EPS	3.52
Price/earnings ratio	35.44 (Dec.)
Price-to-sales	2.77
Price-to-book	12.665
Annual dividend	0.48
Dividend yield	0.30

[a]1 = strong buy, 5 = sell.
Source: Website at http://www.Quicken.com

abnormal returns or be winners. In addition, if historical returns are perfectly representative of future returns, simply using the portfolio theory given in Chapter 6 to find the best portfolio combination would suffice.

However, some professional investors and academics claim that the market is inefficient and that there are some characteristics of some stocks (for example, small stocks) that to some extent predict future returns. Thus, these characteristics can be used to predict winners in the stock market. However, an investor who holds this view will not select stocks that will win with certainty. Although this investor's chances of picking a winner do increase, he or she may be wrong and lose money on some specific selected stock. Thus, due to the risk involved the investor will still diversify the investment in other assets to reduce the risk of a major loss. The investors will not put all their eggs in one basket.

For example, suppose there are two stocks, A and B, with mean returns of 10% and standard deviations of 10%. An analyst predicts that Stock A will be a winner. You then revise your estimate for Stock A – say, to a mean return of 15% and maybe even a standard deviation of 5% (but not a standard deviation of zero). The information that Stock A will be a winner will probably cause you to increase your investment proportion in Stock A (see Chapter 6), but you still diversify. The only case in which you ignore the benefits of diversification and invest only in Stock A is when its standard deviation is zero because you find a bargain with no error: the future excess cash flows are certain. However, no one, not even those who strongly believe they have the ability to locate winners, makes a claim that they can predict the return with certainty.

One practical way to insure an adequate level of diversification is not to diversify based solely on statistical parameters such as historical correlations. For example, an investor could make sure the portfolio is adequately diversified across various asset classes, such as stocks and bonds. Second, an investor could examine how the entire portfolio is diversified across sectors such as energy and construction. Investors who invest in several firms would not want to hold large amounts of, say, Exxon stocks and large amounts of Mobil Oil stock unless they were very bullish on energy. Finally, an investor should pay attention to how well diversified the portfolio is among different industries. Diversification can be qualitative as well as quantitative. That is, diversification can be achieved qualitatively by selecting stocks from various sectors, in addition to using such quantitative methods as calculating the efficient frontier (see Chapter 6). Obviously, investors use these quantitative and qualitative methods to increase their expected return and to reduce risk.

SUMMARY

■ *Explain how to employ the constant DDM in practice.*
To employ this model one needs to estimate the growth rate g and the discount rate k. Several ways to estimate these two values are presented.

■ *Explain how the free cash flow model is employed.*
Not paying dividends or paying irregular dividends induces a difficulty in applying the constant DDM. For most firms which are normal-growth firms, the free cash flow model (FCFM) can be employed even if the firm does not pay dividends at all. The FCFM provides exactly the same value as the DDM, but has the advantage that there is no need to estimate future dividends.

■ *Explain how an analyst views the stock valuation process.*
An analyst examines the long-run economic and financial outlook of the company, focusing on the expected change in EPS, the expected return on equity, the market to book value and many more other measures. Analysts also rely on the prospects of the relevant industry and consider the quality and depth of management based on its ability to develop sound strategic plans and implement them successfully. The analyst may be wrong with his valuation. Therefore, our investment risk remains, and investors should still diversify, because returns are uncertain and the stock selection process does not eliminate the need for diversification. However, when a winner is identified, its mean increases, and a higher investment proportion should be allocated to this stock.

■ *Identify the risks that are relevant in stock investment.*

Investment in common stock is risky because the future cash flows are uncertain. A change in the stockholder's required rate of return, k, is also a source of risk. Investors who understand a stock's risks are better able to select stocks that are appropriate for their portfolios.

■ *Describe how to estimate* g *and* k *of the constant dividend growth model in practice.*

Methods for estimating g include the point estimate method, the regression method, and the accounting method. Methods for estimating k include the DDM method, the CAPM method, using historical stock returns, the yield to maturity method, and using the inverse of the P/E ratio. No one method is always appropriate for estimating k and g. Part of the skill a security analyst acquires is knowing which method to use at what time.

■ *Explain why dividend discount models must be used with caution.*

Some empirical results indicate that dividend discount models can be used to build stock portfolios that outperform the market. However, analysts must be cautious when actually implementing DDMs. Using DDMs to identify mispriced stocks implicitly assumes that stocks are not correctly priced at present and that they will one day soon move towards the correct price. Also, DDMs assume that the discount rate is constant over time, which is not necessarily true. Combining the CAPM (a single-period model) with DDMs (infinite-period models) is difficult at best. Analysts doing so must modify historical parameter estimates in light of current conditions.

KEY TERMS

Accounting method (of estimating *g*)	Dividends per share (DPS)	Free cash flow model (FCFM)
Beta	Earnings per share (EPS)	Growth rate, *g*
Discounted dividend model (DDM)	Economic value added, EVA (see Appendix 10B)	Point estimate method
		Regression method

QUESTIONS

10.1 The following table gives the percentage growth rates in two firms' earnings per share over a recent five-year period:

Year	Firm A	Firm B
1	1.0	7
2	3.4	6.8
3	5.3	7.4
4	6.9	5.4
5	8.6	7.6

Which firm has experienced the phenomenon known as *accelerating earnings*? Explain your answer.

10.2 Describe the process of selecting stock.

10.3 'For a given cost of equity (k), the lower the growth rate of dividends (g), the lower the stock's duration.' Evaluate this statement, and defend your evaluations.

10.4 Suppose National Health Corporation will pay dividends in one year of $0.75 ($d_1 = \$0.75$), its required rate of return is $k = 11.5\%$, and its growth rate of dividends is $g = 5\%$. The stock follows the constant dividend growth model.

(a) What is the value of the common stock?
(b) Inflation is now thought to occur such that investors increase their required rate of return by 5%. What is the added growth rate in dividends because of this inflation if the stock price remains unchanged?

10.5 Suppose two assets, A and B, are uncorrelated and to the best of your knowledge have the following means and standard deviations:

Asset	Mean	Standard deviation
A	10%	10%
B	10	10

(a) Find the optimum mean–variance diversification. Draw the efficient frontier.
(b) Suppose now that a financial analyst predicts that Asset B is a winner. (Suppose it has a low price-to-book ratio.) As a result, you revise your estimate as follows:

Asset	Mean	Standard deviation
A	10%	10%
B	20	2

Would you still diversity? Assuming the risk-free rate of 5%, draw the efficient frontier. Explain.

10.6 The past rates of return on two stocks are the same, and therefore they have the same mean, standard deviation and beta (see Chapter 14). However, Stock A is a small firm with a low price-to-book ratio of 0.8, whereas Stock B is a large firm with a price-to-book ratio of 2.0. In which stock would you invest more? Why?

10.7 Suppose you are given the following historical data:

Year	EPS	DPS
1	$1	$0.5
2	2	1
3	1	0.5
4	2	1

The firm got a new contract that guarantees an EPS of $1.50 a year for the next 100 years. The DPS will not change during these 100 years. The cost of capital is $k = 10\%$. Use the constant dividend growth model to evaluate the stock.

10.8 Suppose you classify 10 stocks according to their price-to-book ratio and get the following rates of return:

Stock	Low price-to-book ratio	High price-to-book ratio
1	10%	7%
2	−5	0
3	20	5
4	10	17
5	10	−1

Analyze these data. In particular, calculate the mean and standard deviation across stocks of each group. If you had to choose one group, which group would you choose? Defend your choice.

SELECTED REFERENCES

Farrell, James L., Jr. 'The dividend discount model: a primer'. *Financial Analysts Journal*, November–December 1985, pp. 16–25.

Fouse, William L. 'Allocating assets across country markets'. *Journal of Portfolio Management*, Winter 1992, pp. 20–7.

Kahn, Sharon. 'What (global) dividend discount models say now'. *Global Finance*, March 1992, pp. 71–3.

Rohweder, Harold C. 'Implementing stock selection ideas: does tracking error optimization do any good?' *Journal of Portfolio Management*, Spring 1998, pp. 49–59.

Sorensen, Eric H., and David A. Williamson. 'Some evidence on the value of dividend discount models'. *Financial Analysts Journal*, November–December 1985, pp. 60–9.

SUPPLEMENTARY REFERENCES

Aragoné, José, Carlos Blanco, and Juan Mascarenas. 'Active management of equity investments portfolios'. *The Journal of Portfolio Management*, Spring 2001.

Diermeier, Jeff, and Bruno Solnik. 'Global pricing of equity'. *Financial Analysts Journal*, July/August 2001.

Ennis, Richard M. 'The case for whole stock portfolios'. *The Journal of Portfolio Management*, Spring 2001.

Taflin, E. 'Equity allocation and portfolio selection in insurance'. *International Journal of Theoretical and Applied Finance* (forthcoming, 2002).

Appendix 10A	ESTIMATING THE GROWTH RATE OF DIVIDENDS

This appendix uses the regression method for estimating the growth rate of dividends. It is given that

$$d_t = d_0(1 + g)^t$$

where d_t is the dividend paid in year t. Recall that linear regression analysis is based on many observations. However, the above relationship between dividend payments and time is not linear. We can make this relationship linear by taking the natural logarithm of both sides. Specifically,

$$\ln(d_t) = \ln(d_0) + t \times \ln(1 + g) \qquad (10A.1)$$

which resembles a standard linear regression equation ($y = \alpha + \beta x$), where $y = \ln(d_t)$, $\alpha = \ln(d_0)$, $\beta = \ln(1 + g)$ and $x = t$. The slope of the line β is given by

$$\hat{\beta} = \frac{\text{Cov}(y, x)}{\sigma_x^2} = \frac{\text{Cov}[\ln(d), t]}{\sigma_t^2} \qquad (10A.2)$$

Substituting Equation 10A.2 for $\ln(1 + g)$ yields

$$\hat{\beta} = \ln(1 + g) = \frac{\text{Cov}[\ln(d), t]}{\sigma_t^2}$$

Taking the exponential of both sides of the previous equation yields

$$1 + g = \exp\left\{ \frac{\text{Cov}[\ln(d), t]}{\sigma_t^2} \right\}$$

Finally, solving for g yields

$$g = \exp\left\{ \frac{\text{Cov}[\ln(d), t]}{\sigma_t^2} \right\} - 1 \qquad (10A.3)$$

Appendix 10B PICKING STOCKS WITH EVA

The economic value-added (EVA)® model is a relatively new tool for project evaluation, as well as for stock valuation (that is, for picking stocks). A brief description of this method is given in the advertisement shown in Exhibit 10B.1. Note that there is even The EVA Company, which provides consultations to firms on how to employ EVA.

The EVA is the economic value added to the investment, when the cost of capital on your investment is taken into account.

To illustrate, suppose that you consider buying a stock. For you, then, the investment is P, where P is the stock price. The earnings per share (EPS) is the profit that belongs to each share. Therefore, your EVA is

$$EVA = EPS - kP$$

where P is your investment, and k is the required discount rate by the stockholder, given the risk of the firm. By the EVA principle, again using the perpetuity formula, the net present value of all future earnings is given by

$$\frac{EPS}{k} - P \text{ or } PV - P$$

(we divide by k to obtain the PV of a perpetuity).

Exhibit 10B.1 EVA as an equity valuation tool

Use It Because It Works!

"EVA® – Economic Value Added – is a company's after-tax profit less the cost of the operation's *total* capital. Not just the cost of debt, but the cost of equity capital as well. At CS FIRST BOSTON, we use EVA as our primary equity valuation tool because it works.

"EVA helps us understand a company's financial strategies. EVA, as Stern Stewart calculates it, avoids the cash flow distortions you get using earnings per share. EVA makes our analysts account for investments in both fixed and working capital. With EVA, we ask better questions about sales, profit margins, cash tax rate and competitive advantage.

PICKING STOCKS WITH EVA

"Most important, EVA is a framework to quantify investor expectations. When you understand those expectations and put them in the appropriate relationship to stock price, you get better stock selection. Our analysts use EVA very effectively to pick stocks.

"Investors value a company in terms of cash flow, risk and duration. Only EVA captures all these elements. Statistically, EVA 'explains' half the movement in stock prices, which is a lot better than return on equity and far better than earnings per share. EPS doesn't help you predict stock prices. EVA does.

WHAT'S THE MARKET SAYING?

"As a CEO, you need a sense of whether the market's expectations about future performance and yours are in line. And if they're not, you need to identify the reasons and take steps. If you believe the market is undervaluing your stock, you can buy back shares, you can tell the story differently, you can spin off operations into IPOs, or you can divest the underperformers.

"When EVA is the framework for a total management system, it can help shape most corporate decisions – from a company acquisition to project financing or budgeting. Using EVA as the basis for incentive compensation, line managers are paid to bring greater value to the true bottom line.

"EVA, looked at as both an evaluation and management tool, can help you make the market assessment, then help you manage for increased value."

For more information, contact Al Ehrbar at Stern Stewart & Co. at (212) 261-0600. Stern Stewart developed EVA® and has helped more than 200 companies to implement its EVA framework for financial management and incentive compensation.

Stern Stewart & Co.
THE EVA COMPANY®

© All rights reserved for Stern Stewart & Co. EVA® is a registered trademark of Stern Stewart & Co.

Source: Fortune, 8 September 1997. Reprinted with permission of Stern Stewart & Co.

If the PV of all future EVAs is greater than the stock price (that is, $PV > P$), a value is created and the stock is undervalued and should be bought. Thus, the EVA, in principle, is no different from the simple stock evaluation methods discussed in Chapter 10. In cases where the EPS can be used to evaluate the cash flow (CF) attached to each share, then the present value of the earnings per share is EPS/k, and if it is greater than the stock price P, the stock should be purchased. If there are differences between the cash flow and the EPS, the EPS can be adjusted to obtain next year's estimate of the cash flow per share, and EVA yields the same results as the FCFM, as well as the PV of future dividends. Thus, if measured correctly, the present value of the EPS, the present value of free cash flow, EVA, and the present value of future dividends all provide the same results.

Chapter 11

MARKET AND INDUSTRY ANALYSIS

Learning objectives

After studying this chapter you should be able to:

1 Identify and describe the macro-economic variables that measure economic health.

2 Describe the impact of government fiscal and monetary policy on investment decisions.

3 Describe the measures used to value the stock market as a whole.

4 Evaluate market sectors and specific industries.

INVESTMENT IN THE NEWS

Three bears suggest fears of a recession are make believe FT

The downturn, like two before, has not lasted long enough for despair to set in, says Philip Coggan

Once upon a time, it was easy to spot bear markets, and to understand why they occurred. Back in 1973–74, the world suffered from stagflation, an oil price surge and banking collapses – it was hardly surprising that share prices plunged.

But it is much less easy to put your finger on why equity markets are in such a bad state now. Unemployment is low – in the UK, it fell below 1m in February for the first time since 1975 – and inflation is under control. Central banks are cutting interest rates. Currency markets are relatively calm. The developed world is at peace. As the English comic Stanley Holloway put it, there are "no wrecks and nobody drowned".

There were rumours yesterday of a Japanese banking collapse. But market falls are often accompanied by such rumours and the weakness of Japan's financial system is hardly a big surprise.

The downturn in the market bears a distinct resemblance to two other episodes in the last 25 years – the stock market crash of 1987 and the bond market collapse of 1994.

Economists are still not agreed on what prompted the crash of 1987, when the Dow Jones Industrial Average fell 22 per cent in one day. But in retrospect, it seems clear that the anomaly was not the crash but the first half of 1987, when a speculative surge carried markets sharply higher. Investors priced the market for perfection and disappointment became inevitable.

In 1994, bond prices plunged when the Federal Reserve raised interest rates, after a long period at 3 per cent. For the previous three years, speculators had enjoyed easy pickings by borrowing at the short-term rate and investing in the higher yields available on long-term bonds; they had become complacent.

Note that in neither case did the market falls prove to be a useful economic signal. The 1987 crash was not followed by a slump; economic growth surged in

▶

INVESTMENT IN THE NEWS

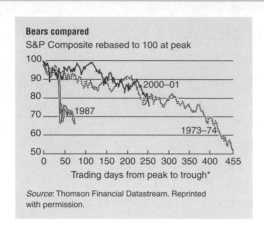

Bears compared
S&P Composite rebased to 100 at peak

2000–01

1987

1973–74

Trading days from peak to trough*

Source: Thomson Financial Datastream. Reprinted with permission.

question of "buying on the dips". In a bear market, investors sell on the rallies.

In late 1999 and early 2000, investors became too optimistic about the potential for profits growth in the technology, media and telecommunication sectors.

Over the last year the TMT bubble has been deflated. The state of the economy is, in a sense, irrelevant since markets paid little attention to fundamentals on the way up. The TMT bubble was all about momentum – investors bought the stocks that had already moved higher. That same momentum is working against the sector on the way down.

So while the S&P 500 and some markets in Europe have met the first requirement for a bear market – a fall of 20 per cent – the downturn has not yet lasted long enough or caused sufficient despair to meet all the criteria.

For that to happen, the US slowdown needs to develop into a fully-fledged recession and, probably, the European economies have to slow sharply as well.

Source: *Financial Times*, 15 March 2001, p. 17.

1988. And 1994's fall in bond prices was not followed by a surge in inflation.

In each case, the bear phase was short-lived. A true bear market requires not only the conventional definition of a 20 per cent fall in prices, but also time. Investors need to become depressed by day after day of declines so that there is no longer any

* The graph shows, for example, that in 1987 the crash lasted for about 70 days and the S&P fell by more than 30%. The 1973 crisis lasted for about 455 days and the index fell by 50%.

We see from the above *Investment in the news* article that spotting a trend in the stock market is very important but is a very difficult task. For example, the 1973–74 crises in the stock market had a macro-economic explanation (oil price crisis, stagflation, etc.). But how can we explain the one-day drop in the Dow Jones Industrial Average October 1987 crash? We see from this article that sometimes the health of the economy is directly related to stocks and bonds prices, but in other cases such a relationship is vague.

This chapter examines the major principles related to evaluating the overall health of a country's economy. It also looks at the role that government policy plays in economic health.

Why should investors analyze the whole economy, or even a given industry, when they are interested only in evaluating stocks or bonds? After all, investors are interested in the potential earnings of a specific firm, not the whole economy. Investors buy individual stocks, not industries or whole economies. Thus, it may seem that macro-economic analyses are not of much value to individual investors. However, as we see from the above article, this is not the case.

It is well known that the majority of the variation in a stock price can be explained by movements in the overall market.[1] Therefore, this chapter examines economic factors that influence the entire market, and hence also affect the prices of individual stocks. After accounting for market movements, the environment in which a firm operates – the

[1] See, for example, B. King, 'Market and industry factors in stock price behavior', *Journal of Business*, 39, January 1966, pp. 139–90.

firm's sector and industry – also explains a significant portion of a stock's price movement. For example, the expected low futures interest rate boosts stocks' price. The banking industry in particular benefits from low interest rates.

This chapter first reviews some basic economic principles and their influence on financial markets. It then establishes the necessary links between the economy and financial markets. Next it focuses on valuing the overall stock market, specifically by examining book value, dividends and earnings of broad stock market indexes. The chapter concludes with an overview of how to assess the relative value of market sectors and industries.

11.1   MACRO-ECONOMIC EVALUATION

A vibrant and growing economy needs a well-functioning capital market. In turn, when the economy is growing and firms are profitable, investors are willing to invest and thus provide the funds needed for capital expansion. All firms are influenced by the economic environment in which they operate. Therefore, the ability to forecast the overall economy is a key to being a successful portfolio manager.

However, the most important key is the ability to find economic factors that change *before* the stock market changes, not after the stock market changes. Identifying these economic factors enables the investor to buy stocks before stock prices rise or to sell them before they drop. Unfortunately, it is very difficult to identify such factors, because the stock market is a leading index (it reacts first) relative to most other economic indicators. Nevertheless, forecasting long-term economic trends and government policy and, in particular, the Central Bank policy regarding interest rate may be beneficial for long-run investors who consider investing in stocks or bonds.

11.1.1 Understanding gross domestic product

The most widely used measure of the health of the overall economy is the **gross domestic product (GDP)**. The GDP is typically measured both quarterly and annually, and the government issues preliminary estimates throughout the year. The GDP, or the **nominal GDP**, as it is sometimes called, is the value of all goods and services produced in an economy in a particular time period. The US GDP is measured in dollars. Because inflation changes the value of dollars, economists adjust GDP values to include the effects of inflation. This inflation-adjusted measure, called the **real GDP**, allows economists and investors to compare the GDP over time, ignoring the impact of inflation. In the United States, statistics on the GDP and related measures of economic health are produced by the Bureau of Economic Analysis of the US Department of Commerce.

Gross national product (GNP) counts goods and services produced by US nationals in a foreign country but does not include goods and services produced by foreigners in the domestic country. Thus, a factory built in Spain by US citizens would count in the US GNP but not in Spain's GNP. The GDP, on the other hand, counts goods and services produced within the country's borders, ignoring who produced them. Thus, the factory built in Spain by US citizens would count as part of Spain's GDP but not as part of the US GDP.

Several measures of economic activity provide clues on the magnitude and direction of the real GDP. Exhibit 11.1 lists some of these measures, what component of the GDP they influence, and when these measures are announced. For example, the number of

Exhibit 11.1 Measuring inflation and components of the GDP and when they are reported

Component	Percentage of GDP	Economic measures	When available[a]
Consumption	69%	Car sales	After 3 days (biweekly)
		Retail sales	11th–14th
		Personal income/expenditures	22nd–31st
Investment	13	Housing starts/building permits	16th–20th
		Durable goods orders	22nd–28th
		New home sales	28th–4th
		Construction spending	1st (2 months prior)
		Factory orders/business inventories	30th–6th (2 months prior)
Government spending	19	Public construction	1st (2 months prior)
Net exports	−0.5	Merchandise trade balance	15th–17th (2 months prior)
GDP[b]	100[c]	Purchasing managers' index	1st
		Employment	1st–7th
		Industrial production capacity	14th–17th
Inflation		Producers price index	9th–16th
		Consumers price index	15th–21st

[a] Unless otherwise stated, the dates refer to the following month. See page 15 of the source.
[b] A negative figure implies that exports are smaller than imports.
[c] The sum is not exactly 100% because of rounding.

Source: W. Stansbury Carnes and Stephen D. Slifer, *The Atlas of Economic Indicators* (New York: HarperCollins Publishers, 1991).

cars sold is announced every two weeks about three days following the end of the second week. Clearly, car sales represent consumption, and they help give early clues as to whether consumers are loosening their purse strings. Consumers tend to purchase cars when they have confidence in the overall economy.

The value of these published economic measures depends heavily on how soon they are available. Car sales, for example, are very valuable, because they are published after only three days (as well as biweekly). Factory orders are not as valuable, because they are published only several months after the order day.

11.1.2 The business cycle and economic indicators

A **business cycle** is a period of expansion and contraction of aggregate economic activity measured by the real GDP. When the economy expands, stock prices rise, because firms are relatively profitable. The opposite is true in periods of contraction. Thus, predicting the business cycle is relevant for investors in the security market. Exhibit 11.2 illustrates the stages of a business cycle. The black line moving up through time represents long-run growth. As economic activity contracts, the real GDP dips below this growth rate. It reaches a low point known as the **trough**. Eventually the economy expands until it reaches the high point of the business cycle, known as the **peak**. An economy is in an **expansion** phase between a trough and before a peak; it is in a **contraction** phase after a peak and before a trough. Because business cycles do not occur regularly or predictably,

**Exhibit 11.2
A business cycle**

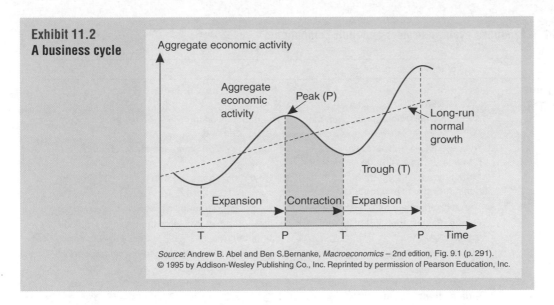

Source: Andrew B. Abel and Ben S. Bernanke, *Macroeconomics* – 2nd edition, Fig. 9.1 (p. 291).
© 1995 by Addison-Wesley Publishing Co., Inc. Reprinted by permission of Pearson Education, Inc.

they are difficult to forecast. Even harder is predicting how financial markets will react to changes in the business cycle.

Because financial markets and business cycles are generally related, investors can be hurt if they forecast a business cycle incorrectly. For example, if an investor bought stocks that tend to move with the business cycle, known as *cyclical stocks*, and the economy suddenly deteriorated, then these stocks probably would incur substantial losses for the investor.

The National Bureau of Economic Research has constructed measures of business activity known as *composite indexes*, which are made up of selected economic data that vary depending on the purpose of the composite index.

The three main indexes (also called indicators – a technical measurement used to forecast the market's direction) are the leading, coincident and lagging indexes. **Coincident indicators** are indicators that are supposed to move directly with the business cycle. **Leading indicators** and **lagging indicators** are indicators that are supposed to lead and lag behind the business cycle. For example, the composite index of 11 leading indicators is a weighted average of 11 economic statistics that are supposed to lead the business cycle. Exhibit 11.3 gives these 11 components. Each index is given a specific reference number that helps analysts keep track of how a particular index or a composite index is constructed. Thus, each index can be identified uniquely by its number. For example, the average weekly hours worked in manufacturing is Series 1.

From time to time, the composition of these composite indexes is changed. We see from Exhibit 11.3 that the 11 series making up the leading index are statistics that would be expected to change first with changes in the business cycle. For example, Series 1, the average weekly hours worked by manufacturing labour, would tend to rise as businesses perceived that the economy was entering an expansion phase and demand was rising. It is interesting to note that Series 19, the index of stock prices (which is actually the Standard & Poor's 500 index), is one of the best-performing leading indicators of the business cycle.

Exhibit 11.3 Business cycle indicators and their components

Series	Type of index component	Explanation
Leading index components		
1	Average weekly hours, manufacturing	Length of working week increases with perceived future demand
5	Average weekly initial claims on unemployment insurance	Claims decline as an economy rebounds
8	Manufacturers' new orders, consumer goods and materials	New orders increase with a stronger economy
32	Vendor performance, slower deliveries	A stronger demand will result in slower deliveries
20	Contracts and orders for plant and equipment	New orders increase as the business outlook brightens
29	Index of new private housing units	People build houses based on the forecast of future prospects
92	Change in manufacturers' unfilled orders, durable goods	Unfilled orders indicate future GNP growth
99	Change in sensitive materials prices	The demand for certain materials increases as an economy expands
19	Index of stock prices, 500 common stocks	Stock prices are based on forecast *future* performance
106	Money supply, M2 (M1, M2 and M3) are three measures of the money supply as defined by the Federal Reserve. M1 represents all money that can be converted to cash immediately; M2 includes M1 plus savings accounts and time deposits; M3 is M2 plus the M3 is M2 plus the money market funds held by institutions	Economies are sensitive to the quantity of money available
83	Index of consumer expectations, University of Michigan	Consumers with bright expectations will spend more
Coincident index components		
41	Employees on nonagricultural payrolls	The number of persons employed moves with the business cycle
51	Personal income less transfer payments	Employee pay moves directly with the business cycle
47	Index of industrial production	Production moves directly with the demand for goods
57	Manufacturing and trade sales	Sales move directly with the business cycle
Lagging index components		
91	Average duration of unemployment	Length of unemployment declines after an economy rebounds
77	Ratio of manufacturing and trade inventories to sales	After an economy rebounds, sales increase and inventories decline
62	Change in labour cost per unit of output	Labour costs rise after an economy rebounds
109	Average prime rate charged by banks	Interest rates rise in response to business demand for funds

▶

Exhibit 11.3 (continued)

Series	Type of index component	Explanation
101	Commercial and industrial loans outstanding	Borrowing increases after an economic rebound
95	Ratio of consumer instalment credit outstanding to personal income	People borrow a greater percentage of their income *after* an economic recovery
120	Change in Consumer Price Index for services	Price levels tend to rise only after an economy is expanding

11.1.3 Fiscal and monetary policy

The government uses **fiscal policy** and **monetary policy** to influence the level of real GDP in the economy and to promote GDP growth, relatively full employment and stable prices. The government can also intervene to avoid bankruptcy trends. For example, in November 1997, the fourth largest investment house in Japan declared bankruptcy. The Nikkei index dropped sharply, igniting fear of a bankruptcy chain reaction. The Japanese government immediately announced a reform plan to avoid the chain reaction, and the Nikkei index recovered in response to this plan. Thus, governments, in implementing their policies, can affect the business environment as well as the stock market.

■ The federal government and fiscal policy

Fiscal policy refers to the taxation and spending policies of the government designed to achieve GDP growth, relatively full employment and stable prices. Governments can stimulate growth in real GDP with tax incentives for investment. For example, a reduction in the corporate capital gains tax rates may motivate businesses to make capital expenditures. This increase in investment directly increases the GDP. Personal tax rates also affect the stock market. For example, if investors had been able to forecast that the Clinton administration would reduce the maximum capital gains tax from 28% to 20% (or even to 18% for a five-year holding period) in 1997, before this information was public or even before it was publicly discussed, they could have made money by purchasing stocks, because such an announcement usually induces an increase in stock market prices. Fiscal policy seeks to find the optimal strategy that maximizes GDP growth and employment and at the same time maintains stable prices.

The government can affect the unemployment rate in various ways. One method of stimulating a sluggish economy is for the government to hire unemployed persons to perform various tasks, such as building roads. Without tax increases, however, this government spending will produce **budget deficits**. Similar to a personal budget deficit, a governmental budget deficit occurs when a government spends more in a given period than it takes in as tax revenues. Budget deficits make prices unstable. If budget deficits are financed by printing money – something the United States has yet to do – the result is inflation. If budget deficits are financed by borrowing money, there is less capital for business investment.

Assessing the fiscal soundness of a country's government is a critical task for international portfolio analysis, as well as analysis of domestic portfolios. Even good companies have difficulty remaining profitable if they operate in a country whose government is irresponsible. Hence, one key assessment criterion for international investment is the integrity of the foreign government's fiscal policy.

■ The Federal Reserve Bank and monetary policy

In 1913, Congress created the Federal Reserve Bank (the Fed) to carry out monetary policy. Monetary policy refers to actions by a central bank to control the supply of money and interest rates that directly influence the financial markets. Like fiscal policy, monetary policy aims to achieve growth in the real GDP, relatively full employment and stable prices. The Fed's primary focus is on interest rates and money supply. Additionally, the Fed acts as a lender of last resort (when there is a cash drain on a bank) and guards against severe currency depreciation. The Fed will lend to banks, for example, when there are unusually large withdrawals. It will also try to support its currency in volatile foreign exchange markets. However, if the interest rate increase is moderate and expected and the Fed hints of more increases in the near future, the stock market may soar (see the *Investment in the news* article). Generally, when the Fed announces an interest rate increase, the stock market falls. Similarly, an interest rate decrease is accompanied by an increase in stock prices. Thus, analyzing the Fed's policy and being able to predict it ahead of time can turn out to be very profitable. To stimulate the economy the central bank decreases the interest rate. After the 11 September terrorist attack, in order to stimulate the economy, the Federal Reserve Bank cut interest rates several times and it was 1.75% as of February 2002. A relatively low interest rate makes consumers spend more money (even borrow money and spend it on goods), corporations enjoy an increase in demand, and more sales and more profit will generally push stock prices up. However, this is not always the case. The economy may be stuck in recession regardless of the low interest rate. In Japan, from 1999 the interest rates are very close to zero. Yet consumers refused to spend money and businesses declined to invest, a phenomenon known among economists as the 'liquidity trap'. This was the case in Japan in 1999 and it was feared that America would fall into the same trap. If this occurs, the central bank loses its power to steer the economy, i.e. a decrease in interest rate would not help either the economy or the stock prices. However, we would like to emphasize that the liquidity trap is the exception rather than the rule, and generally monetary policy is very powerful.

The Fed regulates the volume of bank reserves, affects the pace of money creation, and sets the percentage of funds that banks are required to hold as reserves. It rarely uses bank reserves as a policy tool in its efforts to manipulate the economy. **Bank reserves** are the percentage of deposits that banks must hold in noninterest-bearing assets (cash). Reserve requirements set by the Fed are one of the key tools in deciding how much money banks can lend. The higher the reserve requirement, the tighter the money, and therefore the slower the economic growth. In a **recession**, the Fed can decrease the reserve requirement to stimulate the economy. The tool used most often by the Fed to alter the money supply is its **open market operations** (these are activities by which the Federal Reserve Bank of New York carries out the instructions of the Federal Open Market Committee, which intends to regulate the money supply in the market). By buying and selling US Treasury securities directly in the bond market, the Fed can expand or contract the volume of bank reserves.

Exhibit 11.4 illustrates how the Federal Reserve system influences economic activity. Note that changes in bank reserves influence both the money supply and interest rates, which in turn influence both economic activity and inflation.

The Fed also establishes the **bank discount rate**, which is the rate the Fed charges banks when they borrow directly from it. Indirectly, the bank discount rate influences other interest rates. The **federal funds rate** is the rate charged for reserves borrowed between banks. The bank discount rate and the federal funds rate are highly correlated.

The ability of a central bank such as the Fed to maintain stable prices and stable interest rates is a key ingredient in providing an environment conducive to running business

Exhibit 11.4 The actions of the Federal Reserve Bank and its influence on the economy.
Open market operations occur when the Federal Reserve buys or sells US Treasuries to influence the reserves held by banks.

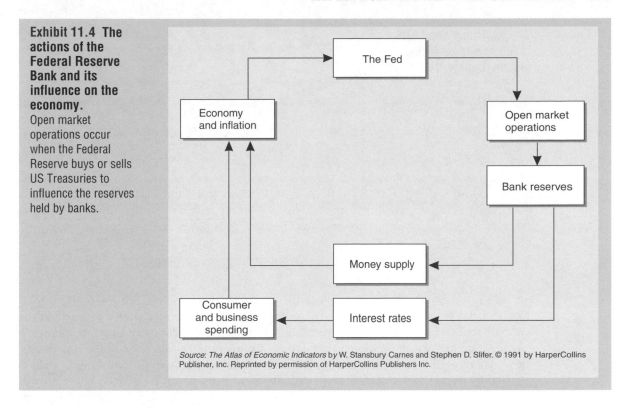

Source: *The Atlas of Economic Indicators* by W. Stansbury Carnes and Stephen D. Slifer. © 1991 by HarperCollins Publisher, Inc. Reprinted by permission of HarperCollins Publishers Inc.

profitably. Thus, investors need to assess the current abilities of Federal Reserve Bank authorities, as well as compare central bank operations across countries.

11.2   THE ECONOMY AND THE FINANCIAL MARKETS

This section examines the relationship between the overall economy and the bond and stock markets. An economy experiencing real growth in GDP will have a strong stock market. A strong economy implies that firms are working near capacity and profit margins are high. These higher earnings suggest higher stock prices. A productive country will also experience a strong demand for its currency as outside investors convert their currency and invest in the vibrant economy. A strong economy also implies a threat of some inflation, which is not favourable for the bond market. When firms are operating at capacity, the ability to raise prices (and to spark inflation) is always a consideration. Higher inflation translates into higher interest rates, which generally means falling bond prices.

Although we can make the intuitive link between the economy and the financial markets, what is the empirical evidence for such a link? Let's look at the actual experience of the United States.

11.2.1 Bond market

Exhibit 11.5 shows the relationship between changes in real GDP and the bond markets. Specifically, the exhibit compares changes in real GDP with the nominal yield to maturities

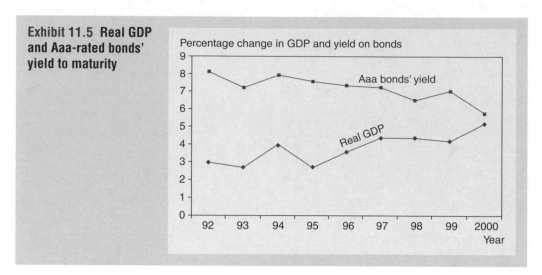

Exhibit 11.5 Real GDP and Aaa-rated bonds' yield to maturity

on Aaa-rated bonds. There is no general pattern in these trends. For example, during 1992–95 the percentage change in GDP and the yield on Aaa bonds tended to move in the same direction. However, in other years, and in particular in 2000, an opposite change is recorded: an increase in the change in GDP is accompanied by a decrease in the Aaa bonds' yield. There is no consistent pattern of these two curves, because the Aaa bonds' yield is affected by two factors: inflation and a probability of bankruptcy. A decrease in the growth rate of the GDP indicates a recession. Hence, the probability of firms going bankrupt increases, bond prices fall and the yield increases. Similarly, with an expansion of the economy, the increase in the change in the GDP decreases the probability of bankruptcy, bond prices increase and the yield decreases. Thus, in the absence of inflation, the two series given in Exhibit 11.5 should move in the opposite direction to that in 1999–2000. Inflation is another factor which affects yield. If the inflation rate is high, bond prices which guarantee a fixed interest will fall and the yield will go up to compensate investors for the inflation. The opposite occurs when the inflation rate decreases. However, inflation may go up or down. When inflation is up in a recession, the two forces of inflation and default risk join each other, and bond prices plummet. When the inflation and the economy are down (as in the early 1990s), there are conflicting forces and bond prices are relatively stable.

11.2.2 Stock market

The link between the stock market and real GDP growth is even less clear. However, there are several possible links between the business cycle and the stock market.

One link is based on earnings. In an expansion phase, firms typically have wider profit margins and hence are able to pay higher dividends or reinvest in projects with positive NPVs. Either way, investors are being well served, and stock prices tend to rise.

Another link, as already explained, is based on interest rates. Falling interest rates at the end of recessions tend to lift stocks. When the interest rate falls, the cost of capital (which is made up of the interest rate plus a risk premium – see Chapter 14) also falls. Recall from the constant dividend growth model that if the cost of capital (k) declines, then stock prices (P_0) rise.

Finally, as occurred in May 1999, the Fed increases the interest rate but due to innovation and improved productivity, many firms announce an increase in profit. The latter factor outweighs the first factor and the stock market soars.

Exhibit 11.6 Real GDP and the stock market as measured by the S&P 500 Stock Index

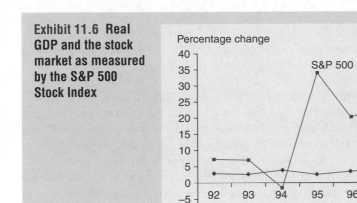

Source: Website at http://www.yahoo.com and the economic report to the President.

The stock market tends to move before the GDP, and although we would like to predict the stock market moves by looking at GDP changes in earlier periods, we cannot. The stock market is one of the best leading indicators of trends in real GDP, so tracking the GDP to get a preview of stock market trends is not of much use to an investor.

Exhibit 11.6 shows the relationship between real GDP and the US stock market for 1992–2000. There is a positive relationship between real GDP and the stock market; unfortunately, however, the stock market tends to lead the real change in GDP. If this is true, a sharp fall in the S&P 500 index in 2000 predicts a decrease in the GDP in 2001. Indeed, in August 2001 a slowdown in the US economy was reported. The annualized growth rates in the GDP were 1.3% and 0.2% in the first and second quarters of 2001, respectively. These changes in GDP are much lower than in the corresponding two quarters of 2000 (2.3% and 5.7%, respectively). In the third quarter of 2001, the GDP even became negative: −1.3%.

11.3   VALUING THE OVERALL STOCK MARKET

Once analysts have established an overall view of the future direction of the economy, they can assess how the overall stock market compares with this view. For example, if an analyst believes that an economy is headed for an extended expansionary period and overall valuation measures of the stock market indicate that the market is underpriced, then the analyst will have a bullish view of stocks in general. This section reviews three measures of the overall stock market's value: book value, dividends and earnings.

11.3.1 Book value

The ratio of a stock's price to its book value is sometimes used to predict up and down trends in the stock market. Book value is the accounting measure of the net worth of a firm. Indexes are constructed for book value in the same manner as for market value of stock. For example, a value-weighted index would sum up the book values of each firm rather than multiplying the number of shares times the stock price. An index of book value of some groups of stock, e.g. of the S&P 500 or S&P 400, is reported in the financial media. Thus, one can compare the index of market value to an index of book value.[2]

In the past, the difference between the market value and the book value has generally narrowed during recessions and widened during growth periods.

In general, when the market value is sufficiently higher than the book value, the stock market is considered to be overpriced and is predicted to fall. When the market value is sufficiently lower than the book value, the stock market is considered to be underpriced and is predicted to rise. Fama and French empirically found the relationship between price-to-book ratio and subsequent average returns to be statistically significant.[3] Hence, there is empirical support for monitoring book value in relation to market value to tell us when we might expect the overall market to rise or fall. For example, in the early 1990s the market value was much higher than the book value, hence by the above argument we would conclude that in the early 1990s the US stock market was overpriced. One counter-argument to this conclusion, however, is that accounting conventions, which in the United States do not adjust assets to inflation, severely understated the value of the assets on the books in the early 1990s, hence the gap between market and book values simply reflect the shortcomings of the accounting methods employed rather than an expected fall in stock prices.

11.3.2 Dividends

Dividends are a second tool used in appraising the overall stock market. Dividing the stock market index per share by the dollar dividend paid per share on an index such as the S&P 500 indicates how many years an investor has to wait until the investment is recovered by the paid dividends. The dividend divided by the price (the D/P ratio) is called the **dividend yield**. For example, in February 2002 the dividend yield was 1.4%. Normally, this value is compared with the interest rate to see which investment has higher cash flows. When the ratio of the price divided by the dividend is high, it generally indicates that the stock market is overpriced, and shifting to bonds is recommended. Exhibit 11.7 illustrates an overpriced stock market in the 1990s. Specifically, the graph plots the dividend yield (D/P) as well as the price/earnings (P/E) ratio, which is discussed in the next section. As the stock market of the 1990s rose (and dividends remained virtually constant), the dividend yield decreased. However, not everyone interpreted this as bad news for the stock market.

11.3.3 Earnings

Some experts claim that the P/E ratio is a good indicator of whether the stock market is overpriced or underpriced. Recall that a high P/E ratio means a low E/P ratio, or a low profit on investment. Exhibit 11.7 (see left vertical axis which corresponds to P/E ratio) gives the P/E ratio in the period 1975–2000 for the S&P 500. The P/E ratio climbed from about 10 in 1975 to about 23 in 1992 and then fell to a level of about 20 in 1996. In June 1997 the P/E was 24.35, and it continued to rise in 1998 to a level of 31.73 on 24 June 1998. The P/E ratio fell to a level of 26.2 on 7 June 1999. The decline in the P/E ratio continued also during 2000, to a level of 25.13 in February 2001 and rise to a level of 28.3 in February 2002.

---

[2] The S&P 400, an index of 400 industrial stocks, is one of the most widely used indexes for assessing the stock market as a whole. The S&P 500 includes the S&P 400, 40 financial stocks, 40 utility stocks, and 20 transportation stocks.

[3] See Eugene F. Fama and Kenneth R. French, 'The cross-section of expected stock returns', *Journal of Finance*, 47, June 1992, pp. 427–65.

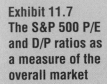

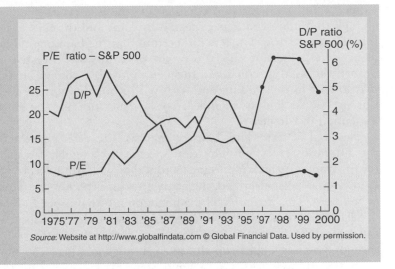

Exhibit 11.7 The S&P 500 P/E and D/P ratios as a measure of the overall market

Source: Website at http://www.globalfindata.com © Global Financial Data. Used by permission.

11.4 INDUSTRY ANALYSIS

There are periods when stocks of some industries flourish or drop significantly more than the whole market. The task of industry analysis is to forecast the activities of these specific industries. For example, when there is an oil crisis consumers spend less money on purchasing new cars, and the car industry is in a recession. Biotech stocks were very attractive with a high rate of return in 1991 and also in 1992, and then in the first quarter of 1998 most of the major Biotech stocks fell by 50–78%! Not approving some drugs by the FDA pushed the prices of the whole industry down. No matter if it is right or wrong, investors tend to shift from one industry to another, hence affecting the prices of stocks in various industries. When the Biotech stocks were hot, stock prices went up, which created optimization, which pushed the stocks further up. Not approving one or more new drugs by the FDA induces a decline in stock prices (due to shift to other stocks) which creates a momentum to further decline in the Biotech stocks. Thus, bad news affects the Biotech stocks which were always news driven. Also, when the whole stock market is down, and there is a chance of a rebound, investors tend to shift to cyclical stocks – those that tend to rebound fastest as the economy recovers. To buy the auto and manufacturing cyclical stocks, investors left the Biotech stocks which enhanced the fall in the stock prices of these firms.

The above analysis, as well as the *Investment in the news* article, indicate that not all industries react in the same way to changes in macro-economic phenomena, e.g. inflation, recession, economic recovery and change in the interest rate. The financial analyst's task is to analyze and forecast the forthcoming changes and to shift investment to those industries which will be most favoured due to the future changes. However, one should always recall portfolio theory asserting that diversification in various industries is important. For example, suppose that due to some change in the interest rates, one expects the banking industry to get the most enjoyment from the change. The financial analysts who forecast the change in the interest rate should shift some of the invested capital to the banking industry. However, we do not expect a full shift for two reasons: (a) the analyst is not certain that the Fed will change the interest rate as expected by him, and (b) even if the Fed does change the interest rate as forecast, it is not certain that the banking industry stocks will respond as expected. Thus, if say 10% of the portfolio was invested in the banking industry before the analyst considers the Fed's possible change in the investment rate, the investment in the banking industry will probably increase to 15–20%, but certainly not to 100%, due to possible errors in the forecast and portfolio consideration as explained in Chapter 6.

The goal of sector and industry analysis is to determine the relative attractiveness of the different sectors and industries. Specifically, an analyst wants to determine the risk – return trade-offs and important factors that will affect future performance. Once these factors have been identified, the analyst will seek to forecast future trends in each sector or industry. This exercise will shed light on future prospects.

Sector and industry analysis is an important element in successful investing. Although the overall market may be going up, a particular industry may decline. Thus even though you are bullish on the overall stock market, you must carefully assess the strengths and weaknesses of each industry.

11.4.1 The industrial life cycle

Many analysts believe that industries go through **life cycles**. A life cycle is a discernible pattern for an industry in which it is first born, then goes through an expansion phase of rapid growth, and finally reaches a period of maturation. Each industry is unique in how it progresses through each phase. Some industries, such as the biotechnology industry, develop rapidly; others, such as the natural gas industry, develop slowly. It is important for analysts to understand where in the industrial life cycle a particular industry is located, as future prospects depend on the remaining life of the industry.

External forces greatly influence a particular industry's progression through its life cycle. Political and regulatory changes influence the growth or decline of a given industry. For example, environmental legislation has spurred the growth of industries engaged in reducing pollution and cleaning toxic waste sites. Social and demographic forces also play an important role. For example, as the US population grows older with the ageing of the 'baby boomers', the pharmaceutical industry probably will experience stronger sales.

11.4.2 Demand and supply analysis

When analyzing a particular industry, it is helpful to break down the analysis based on factors that influence demand for the industry's products, as well as factors that influence the supply of the industry's raw materials. Analysts focus on real and nominal growth rates of the factors, as well as overall trends and cyclical variation.

On the demand side, analysts try to identify who the end users of products are and how they may change their behaviour in the future. Analysts are ever watchful for technological innovations that may have dramatic influences on demand for an industry's products. For example, a recent technological innovation is the ability to send interactive television signals via telephone wires. If this technology develops, the cable television industry will suddenly have as a competitor the telephone industry, which already has a direct connection to most homes.

On the supply side, analysts try to identify the degree of concentration within an industry. The **concentration ratio** is a measure of how much of the industry is dominated by the largest firms. How do these firms compete? Is the competition based on price, quality or warranties? For example, software firms and airline firms are both notorious for their price-cutting wars. Clearly, when a group of firms is willing to cut its prices drastically to gain market share, this could have an adverse impact on share prices.

11.4.3 Industry profitability

Industry analysts try to assess the future profitability of an industry. They use supply and demand analysis in an effort to understand how these different factors interact. Will any cost factors get out of control? Will price wars erupt that will seriously dampen profitability? What technological innovations are on the horizon that may redefine the entire industry? Will future governmental regulations dramatically alter how a particular industry functions? These are some of the important questions that analysts must address when examining an industry.

Analysts seek to forecast the future short-term and long-term profitability for an industry. Once they have estimated the future earnings potential, they can translate that estimate into an overall valuation of the industry. For example, analysts who believed that the outlook for the telephone systems industry was particularly bright relative to where stocks in this industry were trading would want to increase their holdings of telephone stocks.

A special case of industry effect has to do with the computer and Internet stocks. In July 1999, Microsoft, the largest corporation in the world, recorded a market value of more than $500 billion. The whole computer and Internet industry soared. Some pessimistic financial analysts predicted a crash in the Internet-computer industry. These gloomy forecasts became a reality in 2000 and 2001.

11.4.4 Selecting a stock from a given industry

Investors generally invest in a portfolio of securities composed from various industries. No matter what valuation model is employed, a comparison of stocks taken from various industries should be done with great caution. For example, it is meaningless to compare P/E ratios of two firms, one taken from the banking industry and one from the Internet industry. However, such a comparison is more meaningful within an industry characterized by similar risk, similar industry growth, etc.

Suppose that you would like to include one oil company in your portfolio. The data given in Exhibit 11.8 provide the relevant basis for comparing of firms which belong to the same industry.

From the P/E comparison it seems that Repsol is the less expensive stock with P/E = 18.4. Also, the price-to-book ratio of 2.8 is the lowest in the industry, indicating that this stock is a candidate to be included in the portfolio. The return on capital is 10.5%, the second highest in the industry. However, before making a final decision we need to analyze the growth rate of this firm (it may be the lowest in the industry, which explains the relatively low P/E ratio) as well as the quality of the management. However, we would like to emphasize that comparison of the various financial ratios needed for investment decision making is meaningful only when done within a given industry, because the industry risk and the industry prospect and probability along with the growth rate are very similar.

Exhibit 11.8 Drilling for value

Company	Country	Recent price (US$)	P/E	Est. 1999 EPS (US$)	Est. 2000 P/E	Price/ book	Price/ cash	Yield (%)	Return on capital (%)	Price change year to date (%)	Market value (US$m)
BP Amoco	UK	18.15	50.4	0.56	23.8	4.2	49.1	2.1	7.3	26.1	176,249
Chevron	US	92.75	34.5	3.08	23.8	3.6	14.9	2.6	9.2	11.8	60,619
Elf Aquitaine	France	146.39	31.6	5.17	22.4	3.3	8.0	2.4	8.1	42.6	40,309
ENI Group	Italy	6.31	20.8	0.34	15.5	3.4	9.3	2.6	NA	8.0	50,457
Exxon	US	79.81	35.3	2.67	25.9	4.4	17.6	2.1	13.2	9.1	193,768
Mobil	US	101.25	55.6	3.09	27.9	4.5	18.8	2.3	7.9	16.2	79,097
Repsol	Spain	18.68	18.4	1.07	15.1	2.8	8.4	2.5	10.5	18.2	16,816
Royal Dutch	Neth/UK	58.39	NM	1.62	29.2	3.6	21.9	2.6	9.0	32.0	125,202
Texaco	US	63.50	83.6	2.06	22.8	3.0	16.2	2.8	3.4	19.8	34,037
Total	France	125.64	33.3	4.83	21.5	3.1	14.1	2.5	6.7	39.7	44,019

As of 9 June 1999.
NA: Not available. NM: Not meaningful.

Source: John H. Christy, 'A bureaucrat with a head for oil', *Forbes*, 5 July 1999, pp. 54–6. Reprinted with permission of *Forbes* Global Magazine. © 2002 Forbes Global Inc.

SUMMARY

■ *Identify and describe the macro-economic variables that measure economic health.*
The key measure of economic health is the gross domestic product (GDP). The GDP is composed of consumption, investment, government spending and net trade. Real GDP (GDP adjusted to include the effects of inflation) is used, because inflation changes the value of dollars. Analysts attempting to establish relationships between macro-economic variables such as GDP and financial markets must incorporate a complex revision process into their analysis. Relationships that may appear based on final estimates of GDP may not appear based on advanced estimates of GDP.

■ *Describe the impact of government fiscal and monetary policy on investment decisions.*
Fiscal and monetary policy are key tools governments use to achieve GDP growth, relatively full employment and stable prices. Fiscal policy includes taxation and spending policies, whereas monetary policy includes actions taken by a central bank, such as controlling the money supply and manipulating interest rates. The effectiveness of a government is a key factor to consider when analyzing a country's financial market. Governments use both fiscal and monetary policies to stimulate economic growth, which directly affects financial markets.

■ *Describe the measures used to value the stock market as a whole.*
The three key measures of an overall stock market are book value, dividends and earnings. It is useful to compare the P/E ratio, dividend yield and book value over time to establish reasonable historical ranges. With these ranges established, investors can assess the relative value of the overall stock market.

■ *Evaluate market sectors and specific industries.*
A careful assessment of market sectors and specific industries helps investors allocate their portfolios effectively. A significant portion of a stock's volatility can be attributed to its industry. Thus, analysts seek to determine the future prospects within sectors and industries.

KEY TERMS

Bank discount rate	Federal funds rate	Monetary policy
Bank reserves	Fiscal policy	Nominal GDP
Budget deficit	Gross domestic product	Open market operations
Business cycle	(GDP)	Peak
Coincident indicator	Gross national product	Real GDP
Concentration ratio	(GNP)	Recession
Contraction	Lagging indicator	Trough
Dividend yield	Leading indicator	
Expansion	Life cycle	

QUESTIONS

11.1 Assume that Germany dramatically increased its interest rate. How should this increase affect the US stock market? How should it affect the US bond market?

11.2 Suppose the consumption in the United States increased by $10 billion, and this increase was in imported goods. How would this influence the GDP?

11.3 Suppose the Federal Reserve Board reduced the interest rate, and at the same time the price of bonds went down. Is this result what was predicted by macro-economic analysis? If not, how can you explain this result?

11.4 Suppose another oil crisis is predicted in the near future. How will this crisis affect car industry stocks? How will it affect food industry stocks? Explain your answer.

11.5 Some analysts claim that portfolio holdings of auto stocks, such as GM and Ford, as well as holdings of oil stocks, such as Exxon and Mobil, would be a good hedge against an oil crisis. Does this make any sense?

11.6 The price-to-book ratio is 40 in Japan and 25 in the United States. Do these ratios mean that there is a higher probability of a stock market crash in Japan? Explain your answer.

11.7 In some countries the book value of assets is adjusted every year to inflation. In the United States such an adjustment is not done. In your view, how would this adjustment affect the price-to-book ratio?

11.8 A financial analyst who analyzed CBM Corporation concludes that its earnings are expected to grow at 10% every year for the next 10 years. The analyst highly recommends buying this stock. After a week, the Federal Reserve increases the interest rate from 4% to $4\frac{1}{2}$%. The S&P 500 index drops by 8%. CBM drops by 4%. Explain these outcomes.

11.9 Suppose that for each $\frac{1}{4}$% increase in the interest rate, the stock market falls by 5%. In 2001 the Dow Jones Industrial Average is at 10,800 points, and the interest rate is at 4%. What would be the predicted value of the Dow if interest rates went up to 6%? What if interest rates went down to 2%?

11.10 A one-year bond is trading for $1,000, and the coupon is $50 paid annually. The face value is $1,000 and the maturity is one year. A stagflation (inflation along with a recession) erupts. The inflation was zero before and is now predicted to be 3%. The risk of bankruptcy increases from 0% to 10% on a yield-to-maturity basis. By how much will the bond price fall if investors demand the same average real rate of return as they had before? Do the calculations separately for inflation and recession, as well as for both.

11.11 Suppose you have the following two alternatives (A and B):

Year	Change in GDP		Rates of return	
	A	B	A	B
1	5%			20%
2	0	5%	20%	−10
3	1	0	−10	5
		1	5	

(a) Analyze the two sets of figures.

(b) What set, A or B, is typical in the market? What set would investors like to have?

11.12 Suppose the government taxes consumers by taking 4 cents from each dollar of gas sold. The total taxes raised is $10 billion, and consumers reduce their spending by $5 billion. The government spends all of this $10 billion on developing a space station. What is the net change in GDP?

11.13 A low-dividend yield is predicted by practitioners as a sign of a bear market. Analyze the following figures:

Year	Dividend yield	Interest rate
1	6%	12%
2	5	8
3	4	6
4	2.9	2.5

Do analysts necessarily expect a crash in the stock market in Year 4? Explain your answer.

11.14 Suppose a firm has total assets of $100 million and liabilities of $20 million. There are 40 million shares outstanding. The price-to-book ratio is 2.0. What is the current stock price?

11.15 How will your results in Question 11.14 be affected by a 2-for-1 split if the split results in a price-to-book ratio of 2.2?

SELECTED REFERENCES

Abel, Andrew B., and Ben S. Bernanke. *Macro-economics*. Reading, MA: Addison-Wesley, 1992.

Baker, H. Kent. *Improving the Investment Decision Process – Better Use of Economic Inputs in Security Analysis and Portfolio Management*. Charlottesville, VA: Association for Investment Management and Research, 1992.

Black, Fischer. 'The ABCs of business cycles'. *Financial Analysts Journal*, November–December 1981, pp. 75–80.

Carnes, W. Stansbury, and Stephen D. Slifer. *The Atlas of Economic Indicators*. New York: HarperCollins Publishers, 1991.

Council of Economic Advisers. *Economic Report of the President*. Washington, DC: US Government Printing Office, various issues.

Fama, Eugene F., and Kenneth R. French. 'The cross-section of expected stock returns'. *Journal of Finance*, 47, June 1992, pp. 427–65.

King, Benjamin F. 'Market and industry factors in stock price behavior'. *Journal of Business*, 39, January 1966, pp. 139–90.

McFall, R. Lamm, Jr. 'Asset allocation implication of inflation protected securities'. *Journal of Portfolio Management*, Summer 1998, pp. 93–101.

Petrie, Thomas A. (ed.). *Industry Analysis – the Oil and Gas Industries*. Charlottesville, VA: Association for Investment Management and Research, 1993.

Treynor, Jack. 'Bulls, bears, and market bubbles'. *Financial Analysts Journal*, March–April 1998, pp. 69–74.

US Bureau of the Census. *Statistical Abstract of the United States*. Washington, DC: US Government Printing Office, various issues.

SUPPLEMENTARY REFERENCES

Bursch-Supan, A., and A. Brugiavini. 'Savings: The policy debate in Europe'. *Oxford Review of Economic Policy*, Spring 2001, Vol. 17, Issue 1.

Cavagalia, S., D. Cho, and B. Singer. 'Risks of sector rotation strategies'. *The Journal of Portfolio Management*, 2001, Vol. 27, No. 4.

Lusardi, A., J. Skinner, and S. Venti 'Saving puzzles and saving policies in the United States'. *Oxford Review of Economic Policy*, Spring 2001, Vol. 17, Issue 1.

Part IV

DERIVATIVES

Chapter 12

FORWARD AND FUTURES CONTRACTS

Learning objectives

After studying this chapter you should be able to:

1 Explain the terminology of futures contracts.
2 Describe the process of buying and selling futures.
3 Explain margin and mark to market cash flows.
4 Describe the basic strategies involving futures contracts.
5 Discuss the relationship between the futures and spot prices.
6 Calculate equilibrium futures values using the fact that arbitrage profit also cannot exist in equilibrium.

INVESTMENT IN THE NEWS

Click here for index futures

Every morning, coffee cup in hand, Todd Brown parks himself in front of his computer 15 minutes before the futures markets open at 8:30 central standard time. He logs into his account at Zap Futures and prepares for action. His game is the Standard & Poor's 500-stock index futures contract, and his goal is to make $500 before 10 a.m. That's when he starts his real job selling software from his Houston home...

Before you set up an account, bear in mind that futures trading, particularly without a broker, is as risky a way to play the market as you can find.

Futures contracts are leveraged, with margin requirements as low as 5%. So they are far more volatile than index funds or stocks. They also have more downside risk than stocks, funds, or options. The most you can lose buying stocks or put and call options on the S&P 500 is your investment. With futures, you're obligated to honor a contract. If the market moves against you, you have to ante up more cash to maintain your position, making your downside unlimited.

Source: Business Week, 25 January 1999.

What are futures contracts? A gain of $500 every morning before 10 a.m. looks very good but, as the second part of the article asserts, the downside risk is much larger than simply buying the stocks themselves. This is true with future as well as other derivatives.

Derivatives are financial assets whose price is derived from the price of another asset, hence the name 'derivative'. The derivative market is very colourful. There are options, futures, forward contracts, options on futures, and many more complicated assets. The derivatives have one thing in common: their price is derived from another asset, called the *underlying asset*, which can be oil, wheat, euros, a stock index, and so on. The derivatives can be employed to reduce risk or as speculative investments that drastically enhance risk. If you gamble and are wrong in the position you take (for example, you predict the stock index will fall, but it actually rises), you may lose a good deal. To mention just one example, Barings Bank collapsed in 1995 after losing more than a billion dollars in the futures market.

The main categories of derivatives are futures and forward contracts and options contracts. Futures and forward contracts are distinctly different from options contracts. With an options contract the buyer has the *right* to buy some asset, such as common stock, in the future, whereas with futures and forward contracts the buyer is *obligated* to buy some asset in the future. Because futures and forward contracts are obligatory, they are often considered risky. Therefore, many state legislatures prohibit placing retirement money in futures and forward contracts.

This chapter introduces futures contracts and describes how traders can gain or lose from investments in futures. It surveys the different futures markets and their organizational structures. We begin with a discussion of forward contracts, which are the simplest contracts used to hedge (or increase) risk. A knowledge about forward contracts and their limitations is the basis for an understanding of more complicated contracts, such as futures and options. We focus in this chapter on the discussion of futures, whereas options are discussed in the next chapter.

12.1 FORWARD CONTRACTS

In conducting a cash transaction, a buyer pays cash when the seller delivers goods. In contrast, when engaging in a **forward contract**, the buyer and the seller agree to exchange goods for cash at some future date (say, 1 January of the next year), at a predetermined price. The short position means that the investor has to deliver the good while the long position means that the investor has a commitment to receive the good. Thus, the seller of the contract is in a **short position**, whereas the buyer is in a **long position**. Various forward contracts can be made, but the most common are foreign exchange forward contracts.

Exhibit 12.1 Spot and forward exchange rates against the dollar

	Closing	1 Month	3 Months	6 Months
Britain (pound)	1.4153	1.4138	1.4105	1.4054
Japan (yen)	0.008018	0.008044	0.008095	0.008175

Source: Barron's, 2 July 2001, p. MW52. Barron's Online by *Barron's*. © 2001 by Dow Jones & Co., Inc. Reproduced with permission of Dow Jones & Co., Inc. in the format *Fundamentals of Investments* via Copyright Clearance Center.

Exhibit 12.1 reports data on forward contracts. For example, on 2 July 2001, one British pound could be traded for 1.4153 US dollars. That was the **current exchange rate** for cash transactions, also called the **spot rate**. The **forward exchange rate** – or, simply, the **forward rate** – between these two currencies depended on the delivery date. If you wished to buy or sell dollars for delivery one month later, on 2 August 2001, you could close a deal for 1.4138 dollars per pound. If you wished a delivery date six months later (2 February 2002), the forward rate was 1.4054 dollars per pound. The following practice box demonstrates how forward contracts can be used to hedge foreign currency risk.

PRACTICE BOX

Problem

A US investor buys agricultural machinery in the United States for $1 million and sells it to a Japanese client. The US investor pays in cash but sells the machines to the Japanese client on six months' credit terms. The sale is for 120 million yen. Assume that the current exchange rate is 126.40 yen per dollar.

(a) The discount rate is 5% for the six-month period. What will be the Net Present Value (NPV) if the future exchange rate remains at 126.40 yen per dollar?
(b) What will be the NPV if the exchange rate six months from now is 80 yen per dollar? If it is 130 yen per dollar?
(c) Suppose also that the forward rate six months from now is 113.86 yen per dollar. Show how the US investor can guarantee a positive NPV by using a forward contract.

Solution

(a) The investor will receive 120 million yen six months from now at the exchange rate of 126.40 yen per dollar. The investor will receive about $0.949 million (120 million yen/126.40 yen per dollar).

If the investor invests $1 million today, the NPV of this transaction is as follows:

$$\frac{\$0.949 \text{ million}}{1.05} - \$1 \text{ million} \cong -\$96,190.48$$

(b) If the exchange rate six months from now is 80 yen per dollar, the investor will receive $1.5 million (120 million yen/80 yen per dollar = $1.5 million). The NPV is

$$\frac{\$1.5 \text{ million}}{1.05} - \$1 \text{ million} \cong \$428,571$$

If the exchange rate is 130 yen per dollar, the investor will receive about $0.923 million (120 million yen/130 yen per dollar). The NPV is

$$\frac{\$0.923 \text{ million}}{1.05} - \$1 \text{ million} \cong -\$120,879.12$$

With no hedging, the investor may profit ($428,571) or may lose ($120,879), if there are adverse changes in the foreign currency exchange rate as assumed above.
(c) The investor cannot know the future exchange rate. Moreover, the investor does not want macro-economic factors such as international trade or government monetary policy to interfere with her operation. Therefore, the investor can hedge the risk by buying a forward contract to sell yen at a predetermined price six months from now.

Practice Box (continued)

Suppose the investor buys a contract to sell 120 million yen at 113.86 yen per dollar six months from now. The investor will receive about $1,053,925.87 (120 million yen/113.86 yen per dollar). The NPV is

$$\frac{\$1,053,925.87}{1.05} - \$1 \text{ million} \cong \$3,738.93$$

If the investor uses a forward contract, she eliminates foreign currency risk. The transaction is riskless and has a positive NPV, hence should be accepted.

The preceding practice box demonstrates how an investor can completely eliminate foreign exchange risk by using forward contracts. Who is taking this risk? You buy a forward contract from your bank. Does this mean that the bank is exposed to the risk? No, it does not; the bank can operate as a mediator. It finds another customer (say, a Japanese investor who exports to the US on credit) who wishes to sell dollars six months from now. Both sides eliminate risk through the transaction. This risk reduction is in effect as long as neither of the parties defaults.

Forward contracts have a major deficiency. If prices fall sharply, one party has a strong incentive to default. For example, suppose Cone Mills has a forward contract to buy cotton from Cotton Corporation in July at 76.4 cents per pound. Suppose the current price of cotton is 75 cents per pound, but it falls in July to 40 cents per pound. Cone Mills can buy cotton in July at 40 cents in the market, but is committed to paying 76.4 cents per pound to Cotton Corporation. Because Cone Mills loses sharply on the transaction, it has a strong incentive to default – to walk away from this transaction. Firms and institutions that know and trust each other engage in forward transactions. When such trust does not exist, a firm needs a financial tool that minimizes the incentive to default. This is exactly what a futures contract does.

12.2 FUTURES CONTRACTS

Futures contracts exist on a wide variety of items: agricultural products (corn, oats, wheat, livestock and meat, coffee, orange juice, cotton and sugar), metals and petroleum (gold, silver and crude oil), and financial assets (various currencies, Treasury bonds and various stock indexes). Like a forward contract, a **futures contract** can be used to hedge risk. Both contracts commit buyer and seller to exchange goods for cash at some future date at a predetermined price. The futures contract, however, has the following differences: it is traded on a financial exchange, it offers more flexibility in its delivery date, and its cash flows differ.

12.2.1 Characteristics of futures contracts

Futures contracts are traded on organized exchanges, whereas forward contracts are not. Therefore, the prices of futures contracts are reported daily in the financial media. Because they have an organized market, futures contracts are more liquid than forward contracts; buyers of futures contracts can 'net out' their position by selling a similar futures contract. For example, a buyer who has a July contract to buy cotton and a July contract to sell cotton would not have to make a delivery of cotton.

The second difference between forward and futures contracts relates to delivery dates. Forward contracts specify precise delivery dates. With futures contracts, the seller can choose any delivery date during the specified *delivery month*. If the seller of a July cotton futures contract notifies the exchange clearinghouse that he will deliver the cotton on July 15, the clearinghouse notifies one of the contract buyers to be ready to receive the cotton in a few days. (The clearinghouse selects one of the many July buyers at random.) Choosing the delivery date at any day during the month gives the seller some flexibility.

The third difference between forward and futures contracts is in their cash flows. With forward contracts, one party delivers the product and the other pays cash for it on the delivery date. Futures contracts, in contrast, are marked to market on a daily basis. With a **mark-to-market** cash settlement, cash flows in and out (between buyer and seller) are on a daily basis whenever there are changes in the futures contract prices. As will be explained later, this mark-to-market daily cash settlement drastically reduces the risk of default. It was noted earlier that forward contracts should be conducted between 'friends' who trust each other. In contrast, futures contracts can be executed between strangers, because the incentive to default is relatively small. This feature makes futures contracts the better financial tool.

Exhibit 12.2 demonstrates the cash flows to the buyer and the seller of a futures contract. Suppose that on 24 November 2001, Cone Mills buys a July 2002 futures contract at 90.75 cents per pound. If it had been a forward contract, then on 16 July 2002 the buyer would pay $13,612.5 (90.75 cents per pound $\times$ 15,000 pounds) where each contract is for 15,000 pounds per contract. Instead, with a futures contract, cash

---

Exhibit 12.2 Cash flows to buyer and seller of cotton futures contracts: mark-to-market daily cash settlements

	Date and closing price (cents per pound)			
	November 24 90.75	March 1 93.75	May 1 90.25	July 16 80
Buyer	Buyer purchases cotton futures contracts at 90.75 cents per pound	Buyer receives 3 cents per pound from the clearing house within one business day	Buyer must pay the clearinghouse 3.50 cents per pound within one business day	Buyer pays 90.25 cents per pound and receives the cotton
Seller	Seller sells futures contracts at 90.75 cent per pound	Seller pays the clearinghouse 3 cents per pound within one business day	Seller receives from the clearing-house 3.50 cents per pound within one business day	Seller receives 90.25 cents per pound of cotton and delivers the cotton to the buyer within one business day
Buyer's cash flow per 15,000-pound contract	–	3 cents per pound $\times$ 15,000 pounds = $450	3.50 cents per pound $\times$ 15,000 pounds = –$525	–90.25 cents per pound $\times$ 15,000 pounds = –$13,537.5
Seller's cash flow per 15,000-pound contract	–	–$450	$525	$13,537.5

flows are involved each time the price changes. Actually, the daily profit (or loss) is transferred from one side to another. For simplicity, assume the price changes only three times. (In reality, the price is likely to change daily, and the same technique for determining the cash flow would be used on a daily basis.) Suppose that on 1 March the price rises to 93.75 cents. The seller, who loses from such an increase (because she is committed to sell at a lower price), must pay 3 cents per pound to a clearinghouse that, in turn, pays the sum to the buyer. Then, on 1 May, the price drops to 90.25 cents, and the buyer pays the clearinghouse 3.50 cents per pound, which is passed along to the seller. Although the price on 16 July falls to 80, as was decided in the contract the buyer pays the seller 90.25 cents per pound on 16 July, and the seller delivers the cotton. The total dollar amount paid by the buyer for all dates is $13,612.5 (+ $450 − $525 − $13,537.5). This amount is exactly what the buyer would have paid in a forward contract. Similarly, the seller receives $13,612.5, just as she would have received in a forward contract. Note that in both forward and futures contracts, 90.75 cents per pound are paid, but while in forward contracts there is one cash payment, in futures contracts there are daily cash payments.

Thus, there are two differences between the cash flows of forward and futures contracts. The first difference is that in futures contracts, the interim cash flows cannot be ignored, and the present value with interim cash flows in a futures contract may be different from the present value of cash flows in a forward contract. The more important difference is that the incentive to default is lower with futures contracts, because the daily losses are not very large. With forward contracts all losses are accumulated to one payment on the delivery date, producing a stronger incentive to default.

Exhibit 12.2 presents the mark-to-market cash flows between the buyer and the seller. However, on top of these cash flows, each trader establishes a margin account, typically of 5% to 10% of the contract value, that is paid to the clearinghouse. The margin is a security account consisting of near-cash securities to ensure that traders are able to satisfy their obligations under futures contracts. Because both parties are exposed to possible losses, both must post a margin. However, because the margin is in terms of interest-earnings securities, it does not impose a substantial cost on the traders.

Continuing the previous example, Cone Mills has hedged its risk against an increase in the price of cotton by buying a futures contract at 90.75 cents per pound. But what happens if the price of a pound of cotton falls to 40 cents? Cone Mills is locked into this transaction and must pay 90.75 cents per pound. Is there a way for Cone Mills to hedge possible increases in the cotton price while also enjoying the lower price of cotton if the price falls? As will be shown in Chapter 13, options can provide Cone Mills a hedge against price increases and a benefit if the price falls. However, because there are no free lunches in the market, these options cost money. We devote the next chapter to options.

12.2.2 Reading financial data on futures

The financial media provide data on futures contracts. Exhibit 12.3 shows trading information for various futures contracts. The major types of futures contracts are (1) fibres, (2) grains and feeds, (3) livestock and meat, (4) food, (5) currencies, (6) interest rates and (7) stock indexes.

Many financial institutions find interest rate futures useful in managing their exposure to changes in interest rates. Multinational corporations and international investors use currency futures to manage their exposure to changes in foreign exchange

Exhibit 12.3 Futures quotes from the financial press

Futures

Fibers

COTTON 2 (NYCE CT)
50,000 lbs.- cents per lb.

Season's High	Season's Low	Month	Week's High	Week's Low	Sett	Net Chg	Open Int.
71.10	37.50	Jul 01	43.50	39.20	42.75	+ 4.14	686
67.20	40.45	Oct 01	42.55	40.80	41.70	+ .89	3,975
67.70	42.30	Dec 01	43.60	42.31	42.81	+ .25	38,967
67.10	44.08	Mar 02	45.05	44.08	44.20	− .15	5,544
68.80	44.90	May 02	45.90	44.90	45.14	− .36	3,950
68.50	45.95	Jul 02	46.80	45.95	46.00	− .43	2,588
65.50	48.10	Oct 02	48.50	48.10	48.10	− .03	157
64.75	49.00	Dec 02	49.60	49.00	49.20	− .38	1,940
55.25	52.25	Mar 03	...	...	50.30	− .55	120

Grains and Feed

BARLEY (WCE WA)
20 metric tons- can $ per ton

Season's High	Season's Low	Month	Week's High	Week's Low	Sett	Net Chg	Open Int.
139.50	123.90	Jul 01	135.10	133.00	133.50	− 2.10	1,043
137.90	125.50	Oct 01	128.00	125.50	127.00	− .60	7,708
138.20	128.50	Dec 01	131.10	128.50	130.00	− .10	3,602
139.30	132.00	Mar 02	133.40	132.20	132.50	− .60	2,735

CANOLA (WCE RS)
20 metric tons- can $ per ton

Season's High	Season's Low	Month	Week's High	Week's Low	Sett	Net Chg	Open Int.
325.00	263.20	Jul 01	325.00	312.00	316.80	+ 3.10	17,450
320.50	278.30	Aug 01	320.50	312.00	311.50	− 1.80	140
310.10	272.50	Sep 01	...	...	309.10	− 3.20	1,267
315.50	271.10	Nov 01	315.50	308.00	308.80	− 1.00	53,377
316.00	277.00	Jan 02	316.00	310.10	310.70	− .20	3,236
316.30	290.00	Mar 02	316.30	310.30	310.30	− .50	5,810
316.00	304.50	May 02	316.00	311.60	311.60	+ 1.10	165

CORN (CBOT NC)
5,000 bu minimum- cents per bushel

Season's High	Season's Low	Month	Week's High	Week's Low	Sett	Net Chg	Open Int.
287.50	184	Jul 01	193.50	184	188.75	+ 1.50	55,773
276.50	192	Sep 01	202.50	192	197.25	+ 2	117,954
234	199	Nov 01	208.25	199	204.50	+ 2.25	194
275	202.25	Dec 01	213.25	202.25	208.25	+ 2.75	181,790
220.75	206.50	Jan 02	212	206.50	212	+ 2.75	359
270	**205**	**Mar 02**	**224.75**	**213.50**	**220**	+ 3	**26,099**
266.25	221	May 02	231	221	226.75	+ 3	7,723
279.50	227.25	Jul 02	237	227.25	233.50	+ 3.25	11,881
262.25	233	Sep 02	239	233	238.50	+ 3.25	911
272	239.75	Dec 02	250	239.75	246.75	+ 4.50	8,960
258.50	258.50	Jul 03	...	...	260	+	2
268.75	256.50	Dec 03	262.50	257	262.50	+ 4.50	598
Fri to Thu sales 530,778					Open Int		400,258

Livestock & Meat

CATTLE (CME LC)
40,000 lbs.- cents per lb.

Season's High	Season's Low	Month	Week's High	Week's Low	Sett	Net Chg	Open Int.
75.57	70.00	Aug 01	75.57	73.35	74.00	+ .13	52,342
76.50	71.95	Oct 01	76.20	74.42	75.05	+ .08	29,605
77.17	72.80	Dec 01	76.27	74.77	75.50	+ .08	18,944
77.50	73.32	Feb 02	76.65	75.50	75.97	− .03	9,104
78.30	75.00	Apr 02	77.45	76.60	76.92	− .18	4,369
74.50	72.35	Jun 02	74.00	73.20	73.50	− .20	292
Fri to Thu sales 78,699					Open Int		115,849

FEEDER CATTLE (CME FC)
50,000 lbs.- cents per lb.

Season's High	Season's Low	Month	Week's High	Week's Low	Sett	Net Chg	Open Int.
92.75	86.00	Aug 01	92.75	90.90	91.22	− .78	11,322
92.00	86.05	Sep 01	92.00	90.55	90.80	− .52	1,803
92.10	86.05	Oct 01	92.10	90.65	90.75	− .55	2,937
92.30	86.40	Nov 01	92.30	90.90	91.20	− .37	2,482
91.50	86.45	Jan 02	91.50	90.35	90.45	− .55	887
90.80	87.35	Mar 02	90.80	89.45	89.80	− .55	100
91.15	88.30	Apr 02	90.85	90.00	90.25	− .25	85
90.30	89.70	May 02	90.20	89.70	89.70	− .35	31
Fri to Thu sales 9,936			Spot 90.47		Open Int.		19,647

Food

COCOA (CSCE CO)
10 metric tons- $ per ton

Season's High	Season's Low	Month	Week's High	Week's Low	Sett	Net Chg	Open Int.
1245	753	Jul 01	974	893	974	+ 64	529
1246	776	Sep 01	966	882	964	+ 64	28,600
1237	805	Dec 01	960	889	959	+ 54	20,118
1257	835	Mar 02	960	900	959	+ 41	16,486
1267	835	May 02	976	960	974	+ 37	6,499

Season's High	Season's Low	Month	Week's High	Week's Low	Sett	Net Chg	Open Int.
1242	874	Jul 02	...	...	989	+ 35	6,361
1196	897	Sep 02	...	...	1007	+ 32	8,206
1264	926	Dec 02	1027	1010	1027	+ 28	11,254
1142	1003	Mar 03	1042	1038	1042	+ 24	9,000
1070	1070	May 03	...	...	1056	+ 19	1,950
Fri to Thu sales 35,779					Open Int		109,003

COFFEE C (CSCE KC)
37,500 lbs.- cents per lb.

Season's High	Season's Low	Month	Week's High	Week's Low	Sett	Net Chg	Open Int.
127.00	54.10	Jul 01	56.80	54.10	56.10	+ .20	288
127.75	57.10	Sep 01	59.70	57.10	58.50	− .75	39,474
129.25	61.10	Dec 01	63.55	61.10	62.25	− .90	8,140
110.00	64.70	Mar 02	67.25	64.70	65.75	− .90	4,474
90.50	67.50	May 02	69.80	67.50	68.15	− 1.10	1,736
84.50	70.00	Jul 02	72.25	70.00	70.55	− 1.10	1,749
86.00	72.10	Sep 02	74.50	72.10	72.90	− .85	216
Fri to Thu sales 26,616					Open Int		56,077

Financial & Money

10 YR. AGENCY NOTES (CBOT DN)
$100,000 prin-pts & 32nds & half 32nd.

Season's High	Season's Low	Month	Week's High	Week's Low	Sett	Net Chg	Open Int.
101–175	97–15	Sep 01	100–075	98–13	97–305	− 2–11	60,994
Fri to Thu sales 12,868					Open Int		61,267

10 YR. TREASURY (CBOT TY)
$100,000 prin-pts & 32nds & a half 32nd

Season's High	Season's Low	Month	Week's High	Week's Low	Sett	Net Chg	Open Int.
106–28	100–015	Sep 01	105–04	102–255	103–005	− 1–315	488,880
104–11	100–015	Dec 01	103–25	102–04	102–065	− 2–00	2,567
Fri to Thu sales 872,295					Open Int		493,271

2 YR. TREASURY NOTES (CBOT TU)
$200,000 prin-pts & 32nds & a quarter 32nd

Season's High	Season's Low	Month	Week's High	Week's Low	Sett	Net Chg	Open Int.
103–09	99–207	Sep 01	103–09	102–14	102–182	− 215	57,729
Fri to Thu sales 41,962					Open Int		53,556

Foreign Currencies

AUSTRAL. DOLLAR (CME AD)
100,000 dollars, $ per A $

Season's High	Season's Low	Month	Week's High	Week's Low	Sett	Net Chg	Open Int.
.5596	.4790	Sep 01	.5215	.5036	.5084	− .0062	15,779
.5641	.4790	Dec 01	.5200	.5040	.5070	− .0062	149
.5195	.5033	Mar 02	...	...	.5056	− .0062	295
.5166	.5166	Jun 02	...	...	.5042	− .0062	1
.5156	.5156	Sep 02	...	...	.5028	− .0062	...
.4988	.4988	Dec 02	...	...	.5014	−	...
Fri to Thu sales 9,256			Spot .5061		Open Int		16,224

BRITISH POUND (CME BP)
62,500 dollars, $ per pound

Season's High	Season's Low	Month	Week's High	Week's Low	Sett	Net Chg	Open Int.
1.4630	1.3636	Sep 01	1.4180	1.3990	1.4094	+ .0026	35,295
1.4676	1.3600	Dec 01	1.4080	1.3988	1.4038	+ .0026	45
1.4412	1.3774	Mar 02	...	...	1.3976	+ .0026	8
1.4066	1.4066	Jun 02	...	...	1.3914	+ .0026	...
1.4026	1.4026	Sep 02	...	...	1.3852	+ .0026	...
1.3740	1.3740	Dec 02	...	...	1.3790	−	...
Fri to Thu sales 29,910			Spot 1.4080		Open Int		35,348

Indexes

S&P COMP. INDEX (CME SP)
250 x index

Season's High	Season's Low	Month	Week's High	Week's Low	Sett	Net Chg	Open Int.
1685.00	1113.00	Sep 01	1245.50	1205.60	1236.50	+ 1.50	466,801
1666.00	1123.00	Dec 01	1253.00	1219.00	1250.50	+ 7.40	8,367
1638.30	1161.50	Mar 02	1260.30	1232.00	1260.30	+ 8.80	1,077
1675.00	1141.00	Jun 02	1270.20	1239.00	1270.00	+ 7.50	577
1632.60	1264.50	Sep 02	...	...	1268.20	− 1274.00	260
1465.00	1265.60	Dec 02	...	...	1281.40	− 1286.00	113
1343.70	1231.60	Mar 03	...	...	1296.40	− 1298.00	...
1299.60	1299.60	Jun 03	...	...	1311.40	− 1310.00	...
Fri to Thu sales 291,362			Spot 1226.23		Open Int		477,195

S&P MIDCAP 400 (CME MD)
500 x index

Season's High	Season's Low	Month	Week's High	Week's Low	Sett	Net Chg	Open Int.
564.90	501.00	Sep 01	524.25	501.00	522.00	+ 12.00	15,979
531.70	531.70	Dec 01	...	...	521.15	− 514.90	...
485.00	485.00	Mar 02	...	...	525.20	− 518.95	...
521.85	521.85	Jun 02	...	...	530.10	− 523.85	...
Fri to Thu sales 5,384			Spot 512.70		Open Int		15,979

S&P Mini INDEX (CME ES)
50 x index

Season's High	Season's Low	Month	Week's High	Week's Low	Sett	Net Chg	Open Int.
1335.00	1140.00	Sep 01	1245.50	1206.00	1227.00	− 8.00	81,010
1258.00	1213.00	Dec 01	1258.00	1213.00	1235.50	− 1243.00	6
Fri to Thu sales 675,754					Open Int		81,016

rates. Equity investors find stock index futures useful when managing the systematic risk of their portfolios. If investors have adverse exposures, they can invest in futures contracts to help offset these exposures.

The format for reporting futures trading information is to give the season's high and low prices followed by the high and low for the week (see the top of Exhibit 12.3). Next, the settle price and the change from the previous day are given. For example, March 2002 corn has a season's high of 270 and a low of 205 cents per bushel. This futures contract reached a high of 224.75 cents and a low of 213.50 cents during the week. March 2002 corn contracts settled at 220 cents, up 3 cents from the previous day. The **settle price** is an average of the trading prices that occur during the last few minutes of the day. Open interest on this contract is 26,099. **Open interest**, which is reported in the last column, is the number of contracts outstanding. It is half of the total number of positions both purchased and sold (which are the same).

A futures contract, as has been discussed, is mark to market. Profits and losses are taken daily. Because futures contracts are mark to market, large traders are tempted to drive prices up at the end of the day if they are long on futures contracts. The higher the price at the end of the day, the more profit futures buyers receive. Thus, settle prices were developed to avoid manipulation of futures prices at the end of the day. Using settle prices rather than the last trade of the day makes it much more difficult to move the price. Trading does not occur at the settle price; the settle price is an average of the trading prices occurring during the last few minutes of trading. However, typically, the settle price is close to the price of the last trade of the day.

Open interest is used as a measure of the liquidity of a futures contract. Higher open interest indicates that more buyers and sellers exist, which means a high volume of trading activity. The more trading activity there is, the easier and cheaper it will be to enter into a futures contract.

Most futures traders close their position rather than actually deliver or take delivery of the specified asset. A corn farmer in Iowa, for example, will find it more convenient to close his Chicago delivery futures contract than to actually deliver corn to Chicago! Most futures investors close or offset their positions rather than hold them to maturity. Futures traders offset their positions when they take an opposite position from the position held. For example, suppose an investor purchased 10 contracts of December 2001 (Dec 01) corn on the Chicago Board of Trade (CBOT). The investor can offset this position by selling 10 contracts of December 2001 corn on the CBOT. The 10 contracts sold will automatically negate the 10 contracts initially purchased. Thus, the investor now has no position at all in CBOT December 2001 corn futures contracts. This action will reduce open interest only if both buyers and sellers are offsetting.[1] If one seller sells to a new trader, the open interest remains the same.

When futures markets originally developed, physical delivery of the underlying commodity was required. For example, the investor who bought corn futures contracts actually purchased the required quantity of corn. Over time, however, market participants pressed for cash settlement instead. **Cash settlement** is the exchange of cash at the expiration of the futures contract based on the value of the spot asset rather than the

---

[1] Each futures contract is actually two contracts: a contract between the buyer and the clearinghouse and a contract between the seller and the clearinghouse. Hence, when both buyer and seller are offsetting a position, the clearinghouse has no position with either the buyer or seller, and the open interest declines.

actual exchange of the physical asset. For example, it is much easier to make a cash settlement for an S&P 500 futures contract than to actually deliver 500 different securities (with different quantities of each security). Thus, the S&P 500 futures contract is strictly a cash-settled futures contract.

12.3 BUYING AND SELLING FUTURES CONTRACTS

This section examines the process by which a futures trade is executed, the function of clearinghouses, and the margin requirements for an investment in futures.

12.3.1 Trading a futures contract

All trading on futures exchanges is conducted by **futures commission merchants (FCMs)**, who are equivalent to stockbrokers. The typical order follows the sequence given in Exhibit 12.4(a). First, the buyer and seller contact their brokers, who usually are futures commission merchants (Step 1 in Exhibit 12.4(a)). A broker who is not an FCM typically works through an FCM. The FCM contacts its floor brokers regarding the buy or sell orders (Step 2). A **floor broker** handles orders for several FCMs. Floor brokers are distinguished from **locals**, who trade solely for their own accounts. The floor brokers have the trade executed in the **pit**, the part of the futures exchange where all buying and selling of futures contracts take place (Step 3). If a buyer wants to acquire December corn futures at $2.21 per bushel and a seller wants to sell December corn futures at $2.22, then no transaction will take place. It is not until the buyer and seller reach a price acceptable to both that a transaction takes place.

Once the buyer and seller reach a mutually acceptable price, the trade can occur. The clearinghouse now enters the picture to effect the trade. Exhibit 12.4(b) shows the path of activity once the transaction has been made in the pit. The exact terms of the trade are sent back to the floor broker, who then contacts both the FCM and the clearinghouse.

12.3.2 The clearinghouse

The **clearinghouse** plays a key role in futures trading. As with an options contract (described in Chapter 13), the clearinghouse guarantees both sides of a futures contract. The clearinghouse not only helps eliminate default risk but also guarantees the quality of the goods delivered. Most commodity futures contracts have a specified quality level, and the clearinghouse makes sure that a commodity of the appropriate quality is delivered.

The clearinghouse also facilitates the exchange of daily cash flows between the winners and the losers. It makes sure that both the buyer and the seller of futures contracts provide adequate collateral.

The clearinghouse thus plays three vital roles:

1 *Banker.* The clearinghouse provides for the daily exchange of profits and losses of the investors.
2 *Inspector.* The clearinghouse insures good product delivery.
3 *Insurer.* The clearinghouse guarantees that each trader will honour the contract.

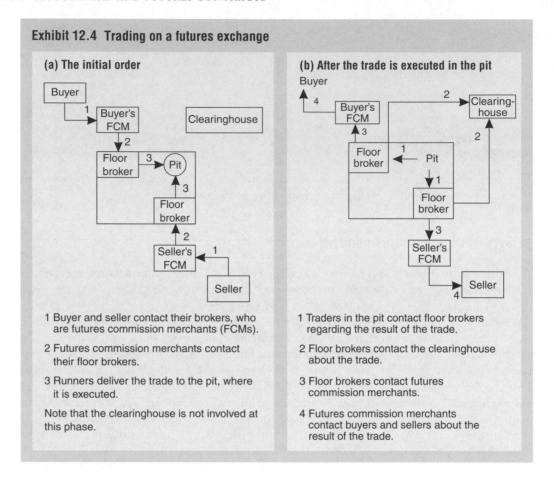

Exhibit 12.4 Trading on a futures exchange

(a) The initial order

1 Buyer and seller contact their brokers, who are futures commission merchants (FCMs).

2 Futures commission merchants contact their floor brokers.

3 Runners deliver the trade to the pit, where it is executed.

Note that the clearinghouse is not involved at this phase.

(b) After the trade is executed in the pit

1 Traders in the pit contact floor brokers regarding the result of the trade.

2 Floor brokers contact the clearinghouse about the trade.

3 Floor brokers contact futures commission merchants.

4 Futures commission merchants contact buyers and sellers about the result of the trade.

12.3.3 Margin requirements

Margin monies are required by the clearinghouse to reduce the default risks related to futures trading. Recall from Chapter 3 that initial and maintenance margins are required for investors who borrow money to purchase stock. In the same way, initial and maintenance margins are required for both buyers and sellers of futures contracts. The actual margin requirements change frequently, but they are usually significantly lower than margins for stocks and they are as low as 5%.

Exactly how do margin requirements work? The initial margin is the monies placed with the clearinghouse when the trade is initially executed. For example, investors who buy futures contracts must place the initial margin of 5% with the clearinghouse. If prices go up, then the gains are received daily by the contract buyer. However, if prices fall, the buyer does not have to post more margin until the maintenance margin level is reached.

Margin requirements for futures contracts are the subject of controversy. Stock traders have to post margin of at least 50%, whereas futures traders in the S&P 500 index have to post margin at only approximately 5% to 10%. Thus, investors can take a larger speculative position with futures contracts than with the stocks themselves. This ability to take more speculative positions with futures contracts concerns some people, because the high leverage in futures contracts increases the risk to the investor.

Margin requirements have a direct bearing on the rate of return realized by a futures trader. Because margin requirements on futures contracts are lower than they are for stocks, investors are allowed greater leverage than that allowed by margin trading on the underlying securities, which in turn affects the returns. Consider the following example. Suppose the S&P 500 index is at 1407.67, and the nearest-maturity S&P 500 futures contract is trading at 1407.20. Also suppose the futures margin is 5% of the contract, and the security margin is 50%. One unit of the S&P 500 futures contract would require a margin deposit of $70.36 (5% × 1407.20), and one unit of the S&P 500 index contract would require $703.835 (50% × 1407.67). Now suppose that *both* markets rise by 10%; hence, the futures contract is at $1,547.92 (1.1 × 1407.20), and the S&P 500 index is at 1,548.437 (1.1 × 1407.67). The rate of return on the futures contract's buyer is

$$R_{Futures} = \text{profit/investment} = (1,547.92 - 1407.20)/70.36 = 200\%$$

The rate of return on the S&P 500 is[2]

$$R_{S\&P\ 500} = \text{profit/investment} = (1,548.437 - 1,407.67)/703.835 = 20\%$$

Now suppose that *both* markets fall by 10%; hence, the futures contract is at 1266.48 (0.9 × 1407.20), and the S&P 500 index is at 1266.903 (0.9 × 1407.67). In this case, the rate of return on the futures contract's buyer is

$$R_{Futures} = (1266.48 - 1407.20)/70.36 = -200\%$$

and the rate of return on the S&P 500 is

$$R_{S\&P\ 500} = (1266.903 - 1407.67)/703.835 = -20\%$$

Clearly, the highly leveraged trading in futures contracts increases the volatility of returns. In the example above, the rates of return are magnified by a factor of 10.

12.4 INVESTMENT STRATEGIES WITH FUTURES CONTRACTS

Investors use futures contracts in four strategies: hedging, speculating, arbitrage and portfolio diversification. Hedgers use futures contracts to offset an existing long or short position, whereas speculators seek to profit by exposing themselves to more risk. Thus, hedging strategies use futures contracts to transfer price risk. In contrast, speculative strategies are based on some prior belief about the future course of asset prices. If investors believe that stocks will rise, then they buy index futures contracts. If they are wrong in their belief, as occurred with Nicholas Leeson of Barings bank, their loss can be devastating. (Mr Leeson traded on the derivatives for speculative reasons. He was wrong in guessing the market direction, inducing a loss of more than $1 billion to Barings bank.)

If we ignore the effects of mark to market, then the payoff diagrams for buying and selling futures contracts and holding them to maturity are represented by Exhibit 12.5.

---

[2] Investors can buy the S&P index. Securities based on the S&P 500 now trade on the American Stock Exchange and are known as *spiders*.

PRACTICE BOX

Problem

Suppose a futures contract on palladium (a platinum alloy used as a catalyst and in dental products) is trading at $90 per troy ounce, and each contract is for 100 troy ounces. The margin requirement is $675 per contract, and the spot market price is $95. Compute the rate of return both on buying one futures contract and on a cash purchase of 100 troy ounces if palladium rises to $108 per troy ounce or falls to $72 per troy ounce at the expiration of the futures contract.

Solution

Recall that the rate of return is profit divided by investment. For the futures contract, then,

$$R_{Futures} = 100(\$108 - \$90)/\$675 = 267\% \text{ if price goes up}$$

$$R_{Futures} = 100(\$72 - \$90)/\$675 = -267\% \text{ if price goes down}$$

Note that the price at the expiration of the futures contract must be equivalent to the price in the spot market. Therefore, for the cash purchase we have

$$R_{Cash} = 100(\$108 - \$95)/\$9,500 = 13.7\% \text{ if price goes up}$$

$$R_{Cash} = 100(\$72 - \$95)/\$9,500 = -24.2\% \text{ if price goes down}$$

where $\$9,500 = 100 \times 95$.

Thus, futures contracts are much more volatile than spot market purchases, because futures contracts allow for highly leveraged transactions.

Mark to market may have a minor influence on the value of a futures contract. When a futures contract matures, it will be worth the price of the underlying asset. A futures contract at expiration is the same as a spot contract at that date. Specifically, at maturity,

$$F_t = S_t$$

where F_t is the value of the futures contract at maturity, and S_t is the value of the underlying asset at time t.

Exhibit 12.5(a) shows that a trader profits or loses from buying futures when the underlying asset price changes. The gain equals the payoff of owning the underlying asset. The losses are limited by the underlying asset price, which at most can drop to zero. Suppose you buy a futures contract on corn for $F_0 = \$2.07$ per bushel. If at maturity the spot corn price (S_t) is exactly $2.07 per bushel, you will have no profit or loss on the trade. Suppose, however, that the spot price is $S_t = \$2.17$ per bushel at maturity. Then you can buy the corn for $F_0 = \$2.07$ per bushel with the futures contract and sell the corn for $S_t = \$2.17$ per bushel in the spot market, profiting $0.10 per bushel (or $500 per contract, because each corn futures contract is for 5,000 bushels). Hence, in this case, for every dollar increase in the spot price at maturity, there is an additional dollar profit per bushel on the futures contract. In the same way, if the spot price is $1.97 at maturity and you have an obligation to buy at $2.07, you buy it for $2.07, sell for $1.97, and lose $0.10 per bushel. Therefore, the line in Exhibit 12.5(a) is at a 45-degree angle, passing through point $F_0 = S_t$, where neither loss nor profit occurred. Because the most that can be lost is F_0, the line stops at the intersection with the vertical axis.

Exhibit 12.5 Payoff diagrams for futures contracts

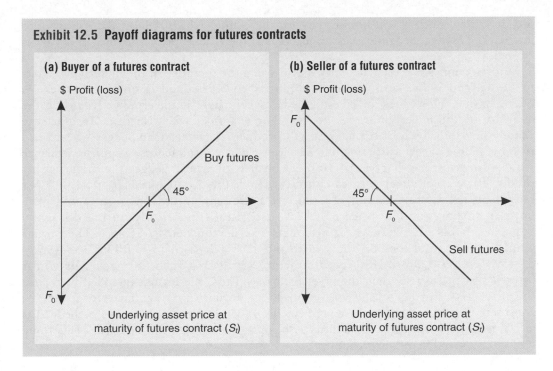

(a) Buyer of a futures contract

$ Profit (loss)

Buy futures

45°

F_0

F_0

Underlying asset price at maturity of futures contract (S_t)

(b) Seller of a futures contract

$ Profit (loss)

F_0

45°

F_0

Sell futures

Underlying asset price at maturity of futures contract (S_t)

A similar example illustrates the dollar profits and losses from selling a futures contract. The payoff diagram is similar to short selling stock (see Exhibit 12.5(b)). Suppose you sell a futures contract on corn for $F_0 = \$2.07$ per bushel; there will be no profit or loss on the trade. Now suppose that the spot price is $S_t = \$2.17$ per bushel at maturity. Then you must sell the corn for $F_0 = \$2.07$ per bushel with the futures contract and buy the corn for $S_t = \$2.17$ per bushel in the spot market, resulting in a loss of $0.10 per bushel. For every dollar increase in the spot price at maturity, there is an additional dollar loss. In the same way, if the spot price is $S_t = \$1.97$ at maturity and you sell at $F_0 = \$2.07$ with the futures contract and buy for $S_t = \$1.97$, you gain $0.10 per bushel, if the price of the underlying asset at maturity is $2.07 per bushel. Therefore, the line has a negative 45-degree angle, passing through the point $F_0 = S_t$.

Note that for a futures contract buyer the loss is limited: if the price drops to zero, at most F_0 can be lost exactly as for a stock buyer (see Exhibit 12.5(a)). However, for a future seller, the loss is unlimited: the higher the price at maturity, the higher the loss (see Exhibit 12.5(b)). This is the downside risk mentioned in the *Investment in the news* article opening this chapter.

12.4.1 Hedging

One reason for trading futures contracts is to transfer price risk from an entity that has the price risk to another party who is willing to take it. Price risk arises in many different settings.

Suppose that Cotton Mills agreed to sell products during the year at a predetermined price. It needs cotton to produce these textile products. If the price of cotton rises during the year, the firm loses. Cotton Mills can buy future cotton contracts, hence will know precisely how much it will need to pay for the cotton, which reduces the risk of price increases. This is a hedging transaction because the risk of price volatility of cotton is hedged.

Futures contracts are particularly useful when the quantity of the underlying assets to be hedged is known. When the quantity to be hedged is uncertain, there is quantity risk. How does an investor hedge when there is uncertainty regarding the quantity of the underlying asset at risk? For example, wheat farmers are not sure exactly how much wheat the harvest will produce. A farmer who hedges wheat price risk by selling wheat futures could face very bad consequences. Suppose a farmer anticipating a spring harvest of 100,000 bushels of wheat hedges the price risk by selling 20 March wheat futures contracts (each for 5,000 bushels) at $3.495 per bushel on the Chicago Board of Trade. If a drought occurs, the farmer will have nothing to harvest. The price of wheat also rises dramatically during droughts. Suppose in this case that wheat prices rise $2 per bushel, to $5.495. The farmer would take a total loss on the wheat and face a loss of [100,000 × ($3.495 − $5.495)] = $200,000 in futures contracts. (Recall that if an investor sells wheat futures and prices rise, then the investor loses.) Thus, the farmer intended to reduce the price risk but he or she was exposed to a quantity risk. Therefore, futures contracts should be used as hedging vehicles only when the quantity to be hedged is fairly certain. When there is quantity risk, option contracts can be used. (This topic will be discussed in the next chapter.)

12.4.2 Speculating

There are many ways to speculate with futures contracts. Central to speculation is some belief about future prices. For example, if you believe that Treasury bond prices are going to fall (because of a perceived increase in interest rates), then you can speculate by selling Treasury bond futures contracts.[3] If one is wrong in his or her belief, the loss from speculation could be very large.

12.4.3 Arbitrage

An arbitrage is a position which guarantees a positive cash flow in the future with zero investment today. Thus, arbitrage is different from speculation, because typically there is little or no price risk with arbitrage. An arbitrageur attempts to create an asset synthetically and trade the synthetic asset against the actual asset. The objective is to design a portfolio with no investment and positive cash flows in the future or positive cash flows today with no liabilities in the future.

12.4.4 Portfolio diversification

Recently, futures contracts have been used to gain additional portfolio diversification benefits. Many portfolio managers recognize the tremendous benefits available from finding securities that are not highly correlated. The correlation between futures and

---

[3] Alternatively, you could short sell US Treasury bonds, but this requires a considerable amount of capital. Recall that futures trading margin requirements are much lower than the securities market.

stocks is relatively low. Recall that the lower the correlation between assets, the greater the overall risk reduction potential. Hence, portfolio managers have found that a carefully crafted portfolio of futures contracts can provide decent returns, as well as diversification benefits.

12.5 PRICING FUTURES CONTRACTS

This section develops general pricing models for futures contracts. Futures prices rarely equal the current value of the spot asset. This section develops a method of valuing futures contracts. First, however, the concept of the basis must be introduced.

12.5.1 The basis

The difference between the current spot price and the current futures price is known as the **basis**. Specifically,

$$\text{Basis} = \text{spot price} - \text{futures price}$$

$$B_{0,t} = S_0 - F_{0,t}$$

where $B_{0,t}$ denotes the basis using a futures contract maturing at time t, S_0 is the current spot price, and $F_{0,t}$ is the current futures price of a futures contract maturing at t.

Arbitrage-based pricing uses existing assets to design zero-risk portfolios from which the equilibrium futures price can be determined. We turn now to determining the equilibrium futures price for stock index futures contracts, assuming a zero-risk portfolio is created.

12.5.2 Pricing stock index futures

Futures are financial assets one may consider including in the portfolio with bonds and stocks. What should the value of a futures contract be prior to maturity? Suppose that the price of the S&P 500 index is S_0. What should be the price of futures contract on the S&P 500 index? Let us look in detail at an S&P 500 index futures contract. For simplicity of the presentation, we call the S&P index 'the stock'.

Consider the following strategy: borrow $S_0 + m$, where m is the margin required on one futures contract, and S_0 is the current stock price. The borrowing is for a pre-determined period, e.g. one month. Hence, the future cash flow when the borrowing is paid back is $-(S_0 + m)(1 + r)$, where r is the interest rate for the relevant borrowing period. At the end of the period it is the expiration date of the contract at which the spot price, S_T, is equal to the futures price, F_T. Buy one stock for S_0; hence, the future cash flow is $S_T + D$, where S_T is the stock price at the end of the period, and D is the cash dividend paid at the end of this period. Sell one futures contract; hence, you pay today a margin of m, on which you earn interest and get in the future $m(1 + r)$. In addition, your cash flow on the futures is $F_0 - S_T$, where F_0 is the current price and $S_T = F_T$ at maturity date.

As Exhibit 12.6 reveals, the total cash flow today, by construction of the financial-strategy, is zero. To avoid an arbitrage profit, the future cash flow must be also zero,

Exhibit 12.6 Determining the equilibrium price of stock index futures

Strategy	Cash flow today ($)	Cash flow at the end of one period ($)
Borrow ($S_0 + m$)	$S_0 + m$	$-(S_0 + m)(1 + r)$
Buy stock for S_0	$-S_0$	$S_T + D$
Sell one futures contract	$-m$	$(F_0 - S_T) + m(1 + r)$
Net position	0	$F_0 - S_0(1 + r) + D$

namely,

$$F_0 - S_0(1 + r) + D = 0$$

or

$$F_0 = S_0(1 + r) - D$$

Because D/S_0 is the dividend yield, we obtain

$$F_0 = S_0(1 + r) - S_0 \frac{D}{S_0} = S_0(1 + r - d) \qquad (12.1)$$

or

$$F_0 = S_0 (1 + r - d)$$

where $D/S_0 \equiv d$ is the dividend yield.[4]

Thus, the futures price is a function of the current index value, the risk-free interest rate, the dividend yield and the time to maturity. Intuitively, the futures price is equal to the spot price times the cost of carrying the spot asset. That is, if the S&P 500 index (the 'stock' in the above example) is purchased by borrowing at the risk-free interest rate, the cost of financing for the relevant period is r. However, actually owning the securities in the S&P 500 gives investors a dividend flow that reduces these financing costs. For this reason, Equation 12.1 is often referred to as the **cost of carry model**. Thus, observing S_0 and r and estimating d, the price of the futures F_0 can be determined by Equation 12.1.

Notice that if $r > d$, then $r - d > 0$ and $F_0 > S_0$.[5] It is interesting to note that the expectation regarding future prices does not enter the equation for futures pricing except through S_0.

If Equation 12.1 does not hold, there will be arbitrage activity. The arbitrageur plays an important role in making the securities market efficient by trading on price discrepancies. However, the arbitrageur does take some risks, such as the risk of misestimating the dividend yield or the current interest rate.

---

[4] If we have annualized and continuing compounded dividend and interest, the equation can also be rewritten as $F_0 = S_0 e^{(r-d)t}$ where t is a fraction of year between the two periods, and $r - d$ is the total rate of return on the stock less the dividend rate of return components – that is, the rate of return that is due to capital gains only.

[5] The exact reverse is true if $r < d$.

12.5.3 Pricing of other assets futures

Currency futures are used by firms having exposure to foreign exchange risk. If a US company sells its goods in the United Kingdom, it receives British pounds in exchange for its products. Because exchange rates fluctuate, the value of the pound in dollars might vary from the time the goods are exchanged until payment is made. To minimize the effects of foreign exchange risk on the value of the products sold, the firm might want to sell British pound futures today to hedge adverse movement in the exchange rate between dollars and pounds.

In a similar way to Exhibit 12.6, it can be shown that futures on foreign currency price must be F_0, given by:

$$F_0 = \frac{S_0(1 + r_L)}{1 + r_f} \tag{12.2}$$

where S_0 and F_0 are the spot and futures prices of one asset of foreign currency in terms of a local currency, and r_L and r_f are the interest rates in local and foreign currency respectively for the relevant period until maturity.

In a similar way the price of commodity futures which avoid an arbitrage profit is given by Equation 12.3, where r is the interest rate and C is the storage costs of the commodity for the relevant period.

$$F_0 = S_0(1 + r) + C \tag{12.3}$$

Recall that the investor who owned the S&P 500 received dividends, so the financing cost was reduced by the benefit of the dividends. With commodities, storage costs are an additional cost to carrying the asset.

The ability to value futures contracts is useful in many ways. Investors are able to assess whether the current futures prices are reasonable. Also, even when futures are not being traded, futures prices contain useful information.

PRACTICE BOX

Problem

Suppose you are an arbitrage trader in the Swiss franc foreign exchange. After a major move in exchange rates, you observe the following information: $S_0 =$ \$0.65/SwF (the foreign exchange rate between US dollars and Swiss francs), $F_0 =$ \$0.64/SwF (foreign exchange futures price), $r_L = 3\%$ (the annual US risk-free rate), $r_f = 6\%$ (the annual Swiss risk-free rate), and $t = \frac{1}{2}$ year. Are these prices in equilibrium? How will you profit if they are not in equilibrium?

Solution

To see whether these prices are in equilibrium, calculate the theoretical future price, F_0, and compare it with the actual futures price. Thus,

$$F_0 = \frac{S_0(1 + r_L)^{1/2}}{(1 + r_f)^{1/2}} = (\$0.65/\text{SwF}) \times \left(\frac{1.03}{1.06}\right)^{1/2} = \$0.6407/\text{SwF}$$

which is a little greater than the current futures price of \$0.64/SwF. Thus, the futures price is too low relative to spot price, hence the future contracts are underpriced and should be purchased.

12.6   SWAPS

Swaps are a recent innovation in financial risk management. A **swap** is a contact between two **counterparties** (the two sides of a swap) who agree to exchange payments based on the value of one asset in exchange for a payment based on the value of another asset. A simplified example would be two bondholders – one holding a floating-rate bond and the other holding a fixed-rate bond – who agree to exchange coupon payments over the life of the bonds.

The three major types of swaps are interest rate swaps, currency swaps and commodity swaps. Most swaps are cash settled. For interest rate swaps, the exchange of cash payments is based on the level of interest rates. For currency swaps, the exchange of cash payments is based on the level of foreign exchange rates. For commodity swaps, the exchange of cash payments is based on the level of commodity prices.

12.6.1 Interest rate swaps

To explain how swaps work, we examine an interest rate swap in detail and then examine how to use interest rate swaps to manage interest rate risk. In an **interest rate swap**, the counterparties exchange interest payments based on specified interest rates. For example, in an interest rate swap, one counterparty typically exchanges fixed-rate interest payments for floating-rate interest payments. This particular swap is called a **fixed for floating swap** (or a **plain vanilla swap**). The two parties in a fixed for floating swap are the **receive fixed counterparty** and the **receive floating counterparty**. The receive fixed counterparty receives payments based on the fixed rate and makes payments based on the floating rate (pay floating). The receive floating counterparty receives payments based on the floating rate and makes payments based on the fixed rate (pay fixed).

For the receive fixed counterparty, the cash exchanged is computed as follows:[6]

$$\begin{array}{l} \text{Payment} \\ \text{(receipt)} \end{array} = \begin{bmatrix} \text{Payment based on} \\ \text{floating rate} \end{bmatrix} - \begin{bmatrix} \text{Payment based on} \\ \text{fixed rate} \end{bmatrix}$$

$$= r_{fl}(\text{NP})(t/360) - r_{fx}(\text{NP})(t/360)$$

where r_{fl} denotes the floating rate (which typically is the London Interbank Offer Rate, or LIBOR), r_{fx} denotes the fixed rate, t is the number of days during which interest accrues (for example, for a semiannual paying swap, $t = 180$), and NP is the **notional principal** (the amount on which the dollar interest calculation is made). For example, if you had a \$1,000 loan at 5%, your annual interest payment would be \$50, or 0.05 × \$1,000. With swap payments, the notional principal is equivalent to the loan amount. We can rearrange the above expression as

$$\text{Payment (receipt)} = (r_{fl} - r_{fx})(\text{NP})(t/360)$$

Hence, when the floating rate exceeds the fixed rate, the receive fixed counterparty has to pay. When the fixed rate exceeds the floating rate, the receive fixed counterparty receives a payment.

---

[6] LIBOR is based on a 360-day year and an actual day count, which we assume here is 180 days. For credit risk reasons, only the net cash flows are exchanged rather than the receive fixed counterparty's paying at 8% and the receive floating counterparty's paying at 7%.

For example, a three-year LIBOR-based swap will have six future payments (one at the end of each semiannual period). If the fixed rate is 7% and the notional principal is $1,000,000, then the future cash flows will depend on the difference between 7% and the current LIBOR rate. For example, if after six months the LIBOR rate is 8%, then the receive fixed counterparty must pay the receive floating counterparty $5,000 (0.08 − 0.07) $1,000,000 (180/360).

The next practice box discusses the motivation for using swaps, along with some of the issues surrounding them. For example, interest rate swaps, along with some of the issues surrounding them. For example, interest rate swaps can be used to realign risks so that all participants are better off or are unaffected. After the rate swap, the hamburger franchise has, in essence, the fixed-rate loan he desired; the Chicago commercial bank is unaffected; Exim Japan has, in essence, the floating-rate loan it desired; and the insurance company is unaffected.

Swaps, like futures contracts, are a derivative security, but there are three major differences. First, futures contracts involve only one future transaction, whereas swaps typically have several future transactions. Second, futures contracts are typically short term, whereas swaps tend to extend over several years. Hence, futures are used to hedge a single-risk exposure over a short time period, whereas swaps are used to hedge multiple exposures over a longer time period. Finally, unlike futures, swaps are typically not mark to market. This lack of marking to market results in swaps' having more credit risk than futures contracts.

12.6.2 Currency swaps

A **currency swap** requires the exchange of different currencies. The first currency swap occurred in August 1981, between IBM and the World Bank. The details of a currency swap are similar to those of an interest rate swap, except the future exchanges are different currencies.

For example, suppose British Petroleum (BP) expects to receive $900,000 from US sales each quarter for the next two years. BP would like to hedge this foreign exchange exposure, but exchange-traded futures contracts do not extend two years into the future. BP might find a company such as PepsiCo (PC) that has United Kingdom sales and is headquartered in the United States. PepsiCo would like to convert its UK pounds into US dollars. A currency swap could hedge the foreign exchange risk for both parties. Specifically, based on current foreign exchange market conditions, a currency swap could be developed in which BP agrees to swap with PC $900,000 for £600,000 each quarter for the next two years. Thus, both British Petroleum and PepsiCo have locked in an exchange rate of $1.5/£($900,000/£600,000).

12.6.3 Commodity swaps

A **commodity swap** requires the exchange of cash based on the value of a specific commodity at specified points in the future. For example, a three-year crude oil swap with quarterly payments would have 12 (4 quarters × 3 years) cash exchanges. If the contract price in the swap for crude oil was $20 per barrel, then the cash exchange would be the difference between the current price of crude oil and $20. If crude oil was selling for $25 per barrel at a quarterly payment, then one counterparty would receive $5 ($25 − $20) per barrel from the other counterparty.

PRACTICE BOX

Problem

Read the following article and illustrate graphically the suggested swap.

> A hamburger franchisee gets his capital from a commercial bank in Chicago, where he can borrow only at a floating rate (say, prime plus 1%) because the bank simply can't risk loading up its balance sheet with any assets of longer duration than 90 days. Why? Because the bank's liabilities – cheque accounts, for example – are of very short duration. A cheque customer does not want to be told that he has to wait five years for his pay cheque to clear.
>
> The restaurateur, meanwhile, would much prefer the safety of a fixed rate over the next five years, even though the longer-term loan will cost him plenty. Indeed, the yield curve is so steep these days that seven-year Treasury notes yield percentage points more than six-month T-bills. That steepness translates immediately into a similar yield curve for the restaurant owner: he's going to pay a certain spread over the relevant Treasury in any event. He's willing to pay the extra points of interest to avoid the risk that the prime will spike up to 15% and bankrupt him.
>
> Now add two more players to the drama: a bond issuer and an insurance company. The bond issuer might be the Export-Import Bank of Japan. Its size and prime credit quality give it access to a credit market the restaurant owner doesn't have, namely publicly traded seven-year notes. The notes are fixed-rate because that's what Exim Japan lenders – pension funds and insurance companies, for the most part – want. Exim, Japan's treasurer, however, is willing to take a chance on floating rates. After all, this company is not going to be bankrupted by a sudden jump in the prime, and the yield curve is so abnormally steep that borrowing at the short end is irresistible for borrowers who can stomach the risk.
>
> The solution is rate swaps mediated by banks or securities firms. In a rate swap, no principal changes hands, just exposures to the yield curve. The hamburger outlet, in effect, picks up Exim Japan's obligation to pay a fixed rate over seven years, while Exim Japan assumes the hamburger outlet's floating-rate exposure. No risk of principal is involved since the players are swapping only streams of interest.

Source: Based on Robert Lenzner and William Heuslein, 'The age of digital capitalism', *Forbes*, 19 March 1993, pp. 62–72. Reprinted by permission of *Forbes* magazine, © Forbes Inc., 1993.

Solution

The excerpt describes two borrowers: the hamburger franchise (HF) and the Export-Import Bank of Japan (EI). HF is borrowing at a floating rate and would rather have a fixed rate, whereas EI is borrowing at a fixed rate and would rather have a floating rate. The following diagram illustrates the interest payments of these two firms, where CB denotes the Chicago bank and IC denotes the insurance company.

Exhibit 12.7(a)

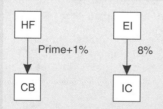

1 HF borrows from CB at a floating rate but wants to borrow at a fixed rate.
2 EI borrows from IC at a fixed rate but wants to borrow at a floating rate.

Practice Box (continued)

Now suppose an investment bank (IB) offers a receive floating and pay fixed swap to HF and a receive fixed and pay floating swap to EI. Of course, the investment bank would want to be compensated for its efforts. The resulting cash flows could look something like the following diagram, where IB denotes the investment bank:

Exhibit 12.7(b)

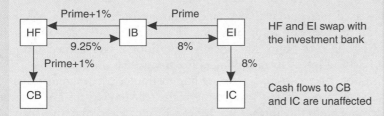

After the swap, HF is essentially paying the fixed rate, because the prime + 1% paid to the CB is received from IB. EI is essentially paying the floating rate, because the 8% paid to IC is received from IB. Finally, IB is making 25 basis points (0.25%), because it gains 1.25% (9.25% − 8%) on the fixed side and loses 1% on the floating side.

In this case the Chicago commercial bank may be losing out on an opportunity. Its client, the hamburger franchisee, desires, and thus is willing to pay a premium for, a fixed-rate loan. Thus, the bank could generate more profits by making a fixed-rate loan to the franchisee and using interest rate swaps to convert these assets to floating-rate assets.

Another example is the jet fuel price risk that airlines face. When jet fuel prices rise, there is a lag in the airline's ability to pass this higher cost on to passengers in the form of higher ticket prices. Hence airlines need a security that will be useful in managing future jet fuel purchases. Commodity swaps fulfil this need. Airlines may use jet fuels to lock in their future purchase price of fuel, thus providing stability to their costs. Jet fuel suppliers like commodity swaps because swaps allow them to lock in a fixed sales price.

12.7 RECENT FINANCIAL ENGINEERING INNOVATIONS

Innovations in managing financial risk have been introduced at a rapid pace. In the past, financial risk management depended on available financial opportunities. Today, financial institutions stand ready to offer almost any conceivable opportunity a client may find desirable. Thus, in the assessment of financial strategies to manage risk, the availability of specific financial vehicles is no longer a consideration. In the future, innovative strategies will determine available financial opportunities. This section briefly reviews some of these recent innovations in 'financial engineering'.

Many recently introduced innovative products are related to swaps. In **amortizing swaps**, the notional principal is amortized (reduced) over the life of the swap. Many loans are amortized. Alternatively, in **step-up swaps**, the notional principal is increased over the swap. This unusual variation is applicable to banks with interest rate risk that increases with longer maturities. There are many other variations on swap structures. The demand for exotic swap contracts produces the supply of exotic securities.

Other innovations included caps, floors and collars. A **cap** is an option-based instrument that sets a ceiling on the impact of a risk variable. For example, an interest rate cap will set a ceiling on the losses incurred if a firm issues a floating-rate loan. Specifically, the cap buyer receives money when rates are up (offsetting losses on a floating-rate loan).

A **floor** is an option-based instrument that sets a minimum on the impact of a risk variable. For example, an interest rate floor will set a floor on the interest paid for an investor who holds a floating-rate bond. Specifically, the floor buyer receives money when rates are down (offsetting losses from holding a floating-rate bond).

A **collar** is a combination of a cap and a floor. For example, a firm that issues a floating-rate loan could enter a collar and receive the benefit of having set a ceiling on rates at the cost of setting a floor on rates. One benefit of collars is that they can be designed to require no initial outlay. Caps and floors both require the payment of an initial premium in a similar way to option contracts.

As the innovation process continues, an increased array of financial vehicles will no doubt be offered. Therefore, it is essential for people involved in investments to have a solid understanding of these financial vehicles.

SUMMARY

■ *Explain the terminology of futures contracts.*
A futures contract is a marketable obligation to deliver a specified quantity of a particular asset on a given day (or during a given period). A forward contract is similar to a futures contract, except a forward contract is not marketable.

■ *Describe the process of buying and selling futures.*
All trading in futures contracts is handled by futures commission merchants (FCMs). The clearinghouse guarantees performance by both sides of the futures contract. It ensures that the futures contract buyer will deliver and the futures contract seller agrees to accept delivery.

■ *Explain margin and mark to market amounts.*
Margin is required by the clearinghouse to reduce the default risk related to futures trading. The initial margin amount is usually higher than the maintenance margin. With futures contracts, profits and losses are taken daily through a process known as mark to market. When a losing position reduces the margin account balance below the required maintenance margin, then a margin call is placed to replenish the margin account to its initial margin level.

■ *Describe the basic strategies involving futures contracts.*
Four strategies use futures contracts: hedging, speculating, arbitrage and portfolio diversification. Hedging strategies use futures contracts to offset an existing risk exposure, whereas speculating seeks to profit by taking more risk. Arbitrage strategies are based on equal pricing between various markets. Some investors now view a portfolio of futures contracts as a separate asset class that can be used to diversify an investment portfolio.

■ *Calculate futures values using the futures pricing equations.*
The difference between the current spot price and the current futures price is known as the basis. The basis can be explained for most futures contracts based on the ability to implement arbitrage trading strategies. The futures price depends on the current spot price, the risk-free interest rate, the time to expiration of the futures contract, and the cost of carrying the underlying asset (which includes dividends). The owner of the stock index portfolio receives the dividend yield, the owner of the currency receives the foreign interest rate, and the owner of the commodity has to pay the cost of storing it.

KEY TERMS

Amortizing swap	Fixed for floating swap	Notional principal
Basis	Floor	Open interest
Cap	Floor broker	Pit
Cash settlement	Forward contract	Plain vanilla swap
Clearinghouse	Forward (exchange) rate	Receive fixed counterparty
Collar	Futures commission	Receive floating
Commodity swap	merchant (FCM)	counterparty
Cost of carry model	Futures contract	Settle price
Counterparty	Interest rate swap	Short position
Currency swap	Local	Spot rate
Current exchange rate	Long position	Step-up swap
Financial engineering	Mark to market	Swap

QUESTIONS

12.1 If the open interest was 162,022 on the S&P 500 December contract, and the futures price fell by 2.45 points on a given day, what was the total gain or loss over all long positions? (Each contract is 500 times the index.)

12.2 'Because futures prices of different maturities all move together, it doesn't matter which maturity is used when hedging. They all work about the same.' Evaluate this statement using just the data given in Exhibit 12.3.

12.3 Suppose the initial margin is $12,000 for an S&P 500 index futures contract, and the maintenance margin is $10,000. Each S&P 500 index futures contract is for 500 times the index value. Suppose that on Day 0 you purchased one futures contract at 418 points. Describe the cash flow to and from your account, given the following 10 days of settle prices. Assume there is no withdrawal from the account, and the surplus remains in the new account.

Day	Settle price	Day	Settle price
0		6	$422
1	$420	7	417
2	425	8	410
3	418	9	415
4	415	10	420
5	419		

12.4 Suppose you have $12,000 to invest. You believe that the stocks in the S&P 500 index are going to appreciate by 20% over the next three months. However, they may also depreciate by 20%. Discuss the relative merits of the following three strategies:

(a) Invest $12,000 in SP DRS (pronounced 'spiders'), which are depository receipts for the S&P 500. These securities were designed to track the S&P 500. Assume that this investment perfectly tracks the value of the S&P 500 index.

(b) Borrow an additional $12,000 (assuming a 50% initial stock margin), and buy SP DRS for $24,000. (Assume, for simplicity, that the interest rate is zero.)

(c) Buy one S&P 500 index futures contract with three months to maturity with an initial futures margin of $12,000. Assume that the futures price and the spot price are the same, at 420.

Be sure to address the consequences of (1) the S&P 500's appreciating by 20%, as well as (2) the S&P 500's depreciating by 20%. (Assume that the initial futures price is the same as the SP DRS value on a per-unit basis.)

12.5 Assume that the spot price of gold is $340 per troy ounce. Suppose also you observe the following gold futures prices:

Time to maturity (in years)	Futures price (in troy ounces)
$1/4$	$344.28
$1/2$	348.61
$3/4$	353.00
1	357.43

(a) Calculate the basis for each futures contract.

(b) If the risk-free interest rate is 3%, what is the implied storage cost of gold (per cent) for one year?

12.6 If the current Canadian foreign exchange rate is $0.805/Can $ (that is, US dollars per Canadian dollar) and the six-month futures foreign exchange rate is $0.80/Can $, what is the implied difference in interest rate between the United States and Canada?

12.7 Suppose the NYSE Composite Index closed at 342.02. If the dividend yield is 2% for six months and the current six-month risk-free rate is 4%, what is the equilibrium value of a six-month futures contract on the NYSE Composite?

12.8 Suppose you are the Chief Financial Officer at Yummie Chocolate Company (YCC) and have just entered a contract to deliver a large amount of chocolate candy to McDonald's Corporation in six months. You know that your firm will be purchasing 1,000 metric tons of cocoa in five months. A five-month futures contract on cocoa is trading at $1,000 per metric ton, and each contract is for 10 metric tons. If the cost of cocoa is $1,000 per metric ton in five months, you anticipate a profit of $100,000.

(a) Map the profit and loss from this contract with the fast-food chain with respect to future cocoa prices.

(b) Graphically illustrate the profit and loss from purchasing one five-month cocoa futures contract.

(c) How could you completely hedge the cocoa price risk? Demonstrate your results graphically.

(d) Discuss the costs and benefits to YCC of hedging with futures contracts.

12.9 Suppose a fourth-generation cattle rancher in Texas has an amazing ability to forecast the future price of live cattle. This ranch usually has 8,000 cattle with an average weight of 500 pounds per head. The rancher has made considerable money from buying and selling cattle at the local auction.

(a) What alternative is available for the cattle rancher to speculate on live cattle?
(b) Suppose the current price of live cattle is $0.85 per pound. How is this rancher affected by changes in live cattle prices? Draw a diagram for the different hypothetical prices.
(c) Suppose the rancher believed that in six months, live cattle would be trading at $1.00 per pound. How could the rancher speculate with futures contracts?
(d) Discuss the consequences of the rancher's buying 100 six-month futures contracts on live cattle at $0.82 per pound. (Each live cattle futures contract is for 40,000 pounds.) Draw the profit and loss line on (1) the futures contracts, (2) the value of the cattle on the ranch, and (3) a combination of both (1) and (2).

SELECTED REFERENCES

Aurell, E., R. Baviera, O. Hammarlid, M. Serva, and A. Vulapiani. 'A general methodology to price and hedge derivatives in incomplete markets'. *International Journal of Theoretical and Applied Finance*, forthcoming.

Chance, Don M. *An Introduction to Options and Futures*, 2nd edn. New York: Dryden Press, 1991.

Duffie, Darrell. *Futures Markets*. Englewood Cliffs, NJ: Prentice-Hall, 1989.

Ehrhardt, M.C., J.V. Jordan, and R.A. Walking. 'An application of APT to futures markets: test of normal backwardation'. *Journal of Futures Markets*, 7(1), February 1987, pp. 21–34.

Green, J., and E. Saunderson. 'No room at the top'. *Risk*, February 1998.

Institute of Chartered Financial Analysts. *CFA Readings in Derivative Securities*. Charlottesville, VA: Institute of Chartered Financial Analysts, 1988.

Kaufman, P.J. *Handbook of Futures Markets: Commodity Financial, Stock Index, and Options*. New York: Wiley, 1984.

Miffre, J. 'Efficiency in the pricing of the FTSE 100 future contract'. *European Financial Management*, 7, 2001.

Robertson, Malcolm J. *Directory of World Futures and Options*. Englewood Cliffs, NJ: Prentice-Hall, 1990.

Tucker, Alan L. *Financial Futures, Options and Swaps*. New York: West, 1991.

Tyson-Quah, K. 'Clearing the way'. *Risk*, August 1997.

Chapter 13

OPTIONS: BASIC CONCEPTS AND STRATEGIES

Learning objectives

After studying this chapter you should be able to:

1 Name the benefits of modern option contracts.

2 Understand the process of buying and selling of put and call options.

3 Explain the risk of holding naked options.

4 Describe the role of the Options Clearing Corporation (OCC).

5 Use payoff diagrams to determine the value of an option upon expiration.

6 Identify profitable option strategies based on beliefs about future asset price movements.

7 Explain the option price boundaries and put–call parity.

8 Explain the Black–Scholes valuation model and how to use it.

INVESTMENT IN THE NEWS

Options

An option contract enables the holder to buy or sell a fixed quantity of a security at a set, or striking price, within a specified period. A call gives the holder the right to buy the security, while a put gives the right to sell the security within the specified time. A buyer of a call option hopes to profit from a rise in the price of the underlying stock. The seller of a put expects the price of the underlying stock to hold above the striking price, thus enabling him to profit from the premium obtained from the sale of the put without having to buy the stock.

Source: Barron's, 2 July 2001, p. MW49.

As we can see from *Barron's* definition, the profit or loss on a call and a put option is derived from the stock price on which these options are written. A **derivative security**, like the above options, is any asset that derives its value from another asset. A derivative security is also called a **contingent claim**, because its claim is contingent on the value of the underlying security.

The basic concepts of derivatives are very simple. Derivatives seem to be like a bet on a Super Bowl, soccer or football game. However, if derivatives are merely bets, why are they of interest to investors or firms? Derivatives are important because they can be employed by both investors and firms to hedge risk. In addition, derivatives can be used for speculative reasons. In both cases, the investors who wish to speculate or to hedge risk should know the implied future cash flow of such derivatives.

Although derivatives can be considered as a simple bet, putting a value on such bets is complicated. How can investors determine the worth of a 'ticket' to play such a bet? This chapter examines the basic cash flow of options and the role that derivatives play in reducing risk, as well as the pricing of derivatives.

An **option** is a legal contract that gives its holder the right to buy or sell a specified amount of an underlying asset at a fixed or predetermined price. There are two basic types of options: call options and put options. A **call option** gives its holder the right to buy a specified amount of the underlying asset during some period in the future at a predetermined price. If you hold a call option on British Airways (BA) common stock and the option expires in three months with a predetermined price of £100, then you have the right to buy BA stock for £100 on or before the expiration date, regardless of the current market price. Similarly, a **put option** gives its holder the right to sell a specified amount of the underlying asset during some period in the future at a predetermined price. Although puts and calls can be based on the same underlying asset, such as shares of BA, they are separate securities.

13.1   THE DEVELOPMENT OF MODERN OPTION TRADING

Option contracts began to appear in the United States in the 1790s, shortly after the Buttonwood Agreement – the agreement that established the New York Stock Exchange.

Although options have been around for a long time, organized option trading did not occur until the passage of the Investment Act of 1934, which legalized option trading. Option trading was regulated by the Securities and Exchange Commission (SEC), and the Put and Call Brokers and Dealers Association was established in the early 1940s to assist option traders in their efforts to develop a market.

The Chicago Board of Trade (CBOT) created the Chicago Board Options Exchange (CBOE). The CBOE began option trading on 26 April 1973, at 10:00 a.m. eastern standard time. Initially, 16 call options were traded on common stocks (that is, the underlying assets were common stocks). Since 1973, the growth of the option market has been explosive. Nowadays, options are traded on many exchanges in the US and abroad. There are options on stocks, on indexes of stocks, on Treasury bonds, on foreign currency and on futures. Thus, the option market is very colourful.

13.2 BUYING AND SELLING OPTIONS

This section shows how investors buy and sell options. In the explanations of the transactions, the vocabulary used by option traders to describe the process is introduced.

13.2.1 The option buyer

An **option buyer** is the purchaser of an option contract. Recall that a call option gives its holder the right to buy the **underlying asset** at a predetermined price. Thus, if you bought a call option on Compaq common stock, by **exercising** the option contract you would be purchasing Compaq common stock (which is the underlying asset) at a predetermined price. This predetermined price is the **strike price** or **exercise price**. Likewise, if you bought a put option on British Airways common stock, by exercising the option contract you would be selling British Airways stock at the strike or exercise price. The buyer who holds an option – whether a call or a put option – takes a long position in an option.

Options trading is involved also with a required margin. When investors purchase a put or call they pay the price of the option in full and no purchase on margin is allowed. At most, the buyer will lose the investment. If, however, the investor writes a call or a put option, the loss is unlimited, and margin as well as maintenance margin are required.

13.2.2 The option seller

To purchase call and put options, there must be people willing to sell the options. Option sellers are called **option writers**, and they can write both call and put options. The option writer is the person from whom the option buyer purchases the option contract. Options trade between individual investors – the option writer and the option buyer. The option writer is obligated to honour the terms of the option contract if the buyer decides to exercise the option. The option writer takes a **short position** in an option (thus the writer has agreed to sell the underlying asset, as defined by the option contract).

It is worthwhile to distinguish between an option writer and a short seller of stock. A short seller of a stock sells stock that is not owned but rather is borrowed from a broker. Therefore, the short seller has an obligation to eventually repurchase the actual shares of stock so that the borrowed stock can be returned to the broker. An option writer, in contrast, may or may not actually have to supply or acquire the underlying asset.

13.2.3 The option contract

Some actual figures and possible transactions in call and put options will demonstrate how an option contract works. The relevant information on option prices is reported in several sources, including online services, satellite communications, newspapers and television. This section briefly explains how to read option quotes in newspapers such as the *Financial Times, Barron's* and *The Wall Street Journal*.

Consider the example of Cisco in Exhibit 13.1. The first column has the option name in abbreviated form, along with the closing price of the underlying security, which in this case is a stock. Cisco stock closed at 19.35 on this date. The option prices listed under call and put last prices headings are the prices for the last trade of the day, which could have been hours before the closing time, 4:15 p.m. eastern standard time. The option prices are given on a per-share basis, although option contracts are written in multiples of 100 shares. The second column gives the strike price (or exercise price) for the options. This column also includes the expiration date. The third column presents the type of option. Call options are identified either by 'c' or by no symbol at all, and 'p' stands for put option. The fourth column gives the number of option contracts traded (sales volume) on 1 July 2001. To demonstrate how to read an option quote, look at the bold Jan 40 put option. The Jan 40 strike price of the put option for Cisco last traded at $21.20. Because each option contract is for 100 shares of the stock, the cost of one option contract is $100 \times \$21.20 = \$2,120$.

The expiration date (or **maturity date**) of an option contract is the date on which the option expires or ceases to exist if the option contract is not exercised. For most stock options, the expiration date is the Friday before the third Saturday of the expiration month. Options on underlying assets other than stocks, such as interest rate options, have unique expiration dates. Eurodollar futures options expire on the Monday preceding the third Wednesday of the contract month. If the third Wednesday of March is, for example, 16 March, then the March contract expires on Monday 14 March.

The cost of purchasing an option contract is called the **option premium**. Specifically, the option premium is the price that the option buyer pays to the writer of the option. For example, if an option buyer pays $3.50 for the call option (Cisco Jan 20; see Exhibit 13.1), the total premium would be $\$3.50 \times 100 = \$350$, because each option contract is for 100 shares. This $350 premium is not just a good faith

Exhibit 13.1 Option price quotes as reported in *Barron's*

Company Exch Close	Strike Price		Sales Vol	Open Int	Week's High	Low	Last Price	Net Chg
42.90	Aug	40.00	2776	7469	7.10	3.30	7.00	+3.50
42.90	Jul	45.00	2752	3235	2.50	0.55	2.25	+1.60
Brocade	Jul	40.00	3771	7058	6.10	2.45	5.60	+2.20
43.45	Jul	45.00	3232	11610	3.10	1.10	3.00	+1.20
43.45	Jul	50.00	5566	6481	1.30	0.60	0.90	−0.10
CVS Corp	Aug	40.00	3268	2926	2.30	1.20	1.85	−14.55
Cabltrn	Jul	17.50	2505	5500	5.00	2.25	4.90	+2.80
22.85	Jul	20.00	3494	5308	2.75	0.80	2.75	+1.95
22.85	Jan	20.00	2729	5223	5.50	3.40	5.30	+1.80
22.85	Jan	25.00	2662	2310	3.20	2.10	2.95	+1.55
Cadence	Nov	20.00	3794	4070	2.00	2.00	2.00	−3.10
Calpine	Jul	40.00	5630	5583	2.10	1.00	1.30	−0.25
37.80	Jul	45.00	4969	7426	0.65	0.20	0.30	−0.15
CardnlHl	Aug	70.00p	3099	2938	3.70	1.30	3.70	+2.75
CaremkRx	Jul	15.00	3731	3230	2.10	1.10	2.00	+0.70
Caterp	Jul	55.00p	2693	2633	5.90	2.60	4.70	+2.05
50.05	Aug	55.00p	4026	5329	6.50	3.40	6.50	+3.75
50.05	Jan	55.00p	7520	7634	7.60	6.20	7.60	+1.60

▶

Exhibit 13.1 (continued)

Company Exch Close	Strike Price	Sales Vol	Open Int	Week's High	Low	Last Price	Net Chg
AppleraBio	Aug 30.00	4021	4078	1.45	1.35	1.45	−0.10
Celestica	Sep 55.00	6846	7935	4.30	1.85	5.00	+2.95
Cendant	Aug 15.00	3338	17610	5.30	4.70	5.30	...
19.50	Jul 17.50	6358	4177	2.80	2.10	2.10	−0.60
19.50	Aug 17.50p	3750	30130	0.55	0.30	0.35	−0.10
19.50	Jul 20.00	4263	10607	0.85	0.45	0.50	−0.25
ChkPoint	Jul 45.00p	2503	3260	3.40	1.05	1.30	−1.60
50.99	Jul 50.00	2909	8543	6.70	2.70	4.30	+0.60
50.99	Jul 50.00p	2596	3858	5.80	2.25	3.00	−2.90
50.99	Jul 55.00	2533	3874	3.90	1.30	2.05	+0.15
Chevrn	Jul 95.00	2701	2220	2.25	0.20	0.40	−1.90
CienaCp	Jul 30.00p	2744	15694	1.55	0.55	0.95	+0.20
37.94	Jul 35.00p	4628	7571	3.40	1.10	2.20	+0.30
37.94	Jul 40.00	12452	10581	6.00	2.00	2.60	−2.50
37.94	Jul 40.00p	3247	7664	6.20	3.00	4.40	+0.70
37.94	Jul 45.00	14628	8522	3.90	0.90	1.35	−1.55
37.94	Aug 45.00	3175	1584	6.00	2.35	3.20	−1.60
37.94	Jul 50.00	5844	8646	2.30	0.45	0.65	−0.95
37.94	Jul 55.00	3478	8895	1.00	0.15	0.25	−0.50
37.94	Jul 70.00p	2717	3686	32.00	1.70	32.00	+3.10
37.94	Jul 80.00p	3768	1076	43.00	39.00	43.00	...
Cisco	Aug 12.50p	7292	12016	0.30	0.15	0.15	−0.10
19.35	Jul 15.00p	5244	39815	0.50	0.05	0.10	−0.35
19.35	Aug 15.00p	6550	6871	0.80	0.30	0.30	−0.50
19.35	Jan 15.00p	23758	35074	2.00	1.35	1.35	−0.65
19.35	Jul 17.50	38360	47986	2.70	1.35	1.75	+0.30
19.35	Jul 17.50p	14293	38638	1.25	0.35	0.65	−0.70
19.35	Aug 17.50p	12550	17155	1.75	0.90	1.20	−0.65
19.35	Oct 17.50	3945	18658	4.20	2.95	3.40	+0.60
19.35	Oct 17.50p	3181	34607	2.50	1.65	2.00	−0.55
19.35	Jul 20.00	50277	81710	1.05	0.45	0.45	−0.05
19.35	Jul 20.00p	6299	37153	3.00	1.00	2.00	−0.90
19.35	Aug 20.00	21676	39681	1.85	1.00	1.35	+0.25
19.35	Aug 20.00p	13712	10343	3.30	1.90	2.55	−0.55
19.35	Oct 20.00	5140	27502	2.80	1.85	2.55	+0.65
19.35	**Jan 20.00**	**3713**	**42542**	**3.70**	**2.65**	**3.50**	**+0.90**
19.35	Jul 22.50	13845	68760	0.30	0.10	0.20	...
19.35	Aug 22.50	10997	4566	0.90	0.45	0.55	...
19.35	Jan 22.50	3385	26834	2.80	1.85	2.55	+0.65
19.35	Jul 25.00	5183	81576	0.10	0.05	0.05	−0.05
19.35	Oct 25.00	5033	29385	1.15	0.55	0.85	+0.05
19.35	Jan 25.00	25064	59993	1.95	1.30	1.85	+0.50
19.35	Jul 30.00p	22361	14450	12.30	10.80	10.80	−1.70
19.35	Jul 35.00p	3514	1589	17.20	15.70	15.70	−1.80
19.35	Jul 40.00p	9500	1379	22.20	2.10	20.70	−1.80
19.35	**Jan 40.00p**	**5124**	**2223**	**22.30**	**20.80**	**21.20**	**−1.30**
19.35	Jan 45.00p	4801	1550	27.00	26.40	27.00	−1.50
19.35	Jan 55.00p	5950	437	37.00	35.70	35.70	−1.00
19.35	Jan 60.00p	11755	2844	42.20	40.70	40.70	−1.80
19.35	Jan 65.00p	7150	2106	47.20	45.70	45.70	−1.80
19.35	Jan 70.00p	6000	1725	52.20	50.70	50.70	+1.40

Source: Barron's, 2 July 2001, p. MW50. Barron's Online by *Barron's*. © 2001 by Dow Jones & Co., Inc. Reproduced with permission of Dow Jones & Co., Inc. in the format *Fundamentals of Investments* via Copyright Clearance Center.

deposit or a down payment but rather a nonrefundable fee. The option price refers to the current market price of the option. The option premium and the option price are the same at the time of the option transaction ($350 in the above example). However, after the time of purchase, the option premium is $350, whereas the option price can change with current market conditions. For example, if the stock price rallies, the option price may rise to $800 per contract, whereas the option premium is still $350. The option premium refers to the option price when first purchased, not the current market price.

A distinction is made between when an option contract is initiated and when the contract is closed. An **opening transaction** occurs when a new position is established. A **closing transaction** occurs when an already established position is eliminated. For example, suppose you purchased one Cisco Jan 20 call to open on 2 July for a premium of $3\frac{1}{2}$ per share. After two months you decide to sell one Cisco Jan 20 call for a market price that happens to be $6 per share. The opening transaction takes place when you purchase the Cisco Jan 20 call. When you sell the call option, the transaction will be closed. Hence, after selling the options, you have no option position, and you have $2\frac{1}{2}$ per-share profit ($6 - $3\frac{1}{2}$) before transaction costs. Therefore, after the sale of one Cisco Jan 20 call on 2 September you would have no outstanding position, because the sale of the previous purchase is offsetting.

Another distinction related to option contracts involves when the contract can be exercised: European-style versus American-style options. **European-style options** can be exercised only on specific dates. For example, contracts that can be exercised only on the last day of the contract, such as foreign exchange options, are traded on the Philadelphia Stock Exchange. **American-style options**, in contrast, can be exercised any time on or before the expiration date of the contract. The holder of an American option has the freedom to decide when, if ever, the option contract will be exercised. Note that these terms do not refer to, or even reflect, geographical location (that is, Europe or the United States). Most stock options are American-style options, and many index options and interest rate options are European-style options.

Exhibit 13.2 illustrates quotes on long-term options on individual stocks, as well as options on various financial products: options on various indexes (for example, Dow Jones or S&P 100 and S&P 500), foreign currency, etc. As an example of an option on an index, the quote of a DJIA index put option (December 2001) with a strike price of $100 is $2.70 (see the 'Last Price' column). As an example of a quote on options on foreign currency, the call option to buy a euro until Sept 2001 with a strike price of 86 American cents per euro costs 0.11 cents. (The current exchange rate is 84 cents per euro.)

13.2.4 Investing in options versus investing in stock

Suppose Bill Ups, an eternal optimist, believes the price of Compaq stock will rise sharply over the next three months. Compaq stock is currently trading at $63.6875 per share. How can Bill profit from his hunch? He could simply buy Compaq stock: one round lot (100 shares) would cost him $63.6875 \times 100 = $6,368.75. Alternatively, he could buy call options on Compaq stock at a much lower initial cost. He would profit more on options if his prediction was correct. For example, if a three-month call option was $5.25 with a strike price of $65, he would pay only $525 to take a **long position** in 100 call options on shares of Compaq at the expiration date. If Compaq rose to $75, then a 100 long position of call options in Compaq will result in a profit of

Exhibit 13.2 Various listed option quotations

Equity Options

Company Exch Close	Strike Price	Sales Vol	Open Int	Week's High	Low	Last Price	Net Chg
ADC Tel	Aug 5.00p	45255	638	0.25	0.10	0.10	-0.10
AES Cp	Aug 40.00p	4543	9641	2.60	2.00	2.35	-0.65
43.05	Aug 45.00	3988	1866	3.00	1.55	2.60	+0.90
A M R	Jul 35.00	2428	1405	1.75	0.55	1.55	+0.15
AmOnline	Jan 45.00p	3212	22464	3.30	2.75	2.75	-0.25
53.00	Jul 50.00	4509	36423	4.60	1.50	3.80	-0.60
53.00	Jul 50.00p	5738	21997	1.30	0.65	0.70	-0.30
53.00	Aug 50.00p	2734	3545	2.05	1.55	1.60	-0.15
53.00	Jul 55.00	16289	67047	1.50	0.60	0.85	-0.50
53.00	Jul 55.00p	3100	7406	3.80	2.55	2.70	-0.30
53.00	Aug 55.00	6665	8581	2.45	1.55	1.80	-0.30
53.00	Jul 60.00	4278	43058	0.30	0.05	0.10	-0.15
53.00	Oct 60.00	17632	39408	2.25	1.55	1.90	-0.15
ASML Hld	Aug 25.00	3631	1510	1.20	0.95	0.95	-0.05
ATT Wrls	Jul 17.50	3901	10421	0.60	0.15	0.40	+0.15
16.35	Jul 17.50p	4256	5723	2.30	1.30	1.45	-0.55
16.35	Oct 17.50	2757	3294	1.55	1.00	1.50	+0.25
AT&T	Jul 15.00	6011	10786	6.90	6.40	6.90	+1.10
22.00	Jul 15.00p	6000	8562	0.05	0.05	0.05	-0.30
22.00	Jul 20.00p	2917	15548	0.60	0.20	0.20	-0.25
22.00	Aug 20.00	3183	3931	2.45	1.70	2.45	+0.45
22.00	Aug 20.00p	15700	42132	1.05	0.50	0.50	-0.35
22.00	Jan 20.00	3120	20920	3.50	2.80	3.50	+0.50
22.00	Aug 22.50	3498	18791	0.45	0.15	0.40	+0.15
22.00	Aug 22.50	3411	6143	0.90	0.35	0.85	+0.10
AdvFibCm	Aug 15.00	2550	2000	7.60	7.30	7.50	...
A M D	Oct 17.50p	46554	15730	1.25	0.85	0.85	-0.50
28.90	Oct 20.00p	3165	4418	1.85	0.90	1.00	-0.15
28.90	Jul 25.00	7243	16005	5.50	2.05	4.40	+2.30
28.90	Jul 25.00p	5390	12271	2.15	0.40	0.60	-1.90
28.90	Oct 25.00	4807	10021	4.10	2.15	2.15	-1.95
28.90	Jul 27.50	4688	6878	3.40	1.00	2.75	+1.50
28.90	Jul 27.50p	11653	5321	3.80	0.90	1.20	-2.70
28.90	Jul 30.00	6755	18458	1.75	0.55	1.20	+0.65
28.90	Jul 30.00p	4067	16121	5.70	1.70	2.35	-3.75
28.90	Jul 32.50	2932	8180	0.80	0.25	0.50	+0.15
105.02	Jul 102.00p	2071	2000	1.20	0.45	0.50	-0.30
105.02	Aug 102.00p	556	1285	2.05	1.20	1.35	-0.20
105.02	Sep 102.00p	221	2652	2.85	1.80	2.20	...
105.02	Jul 103.00	1552	515	3.80	2.70	3.50	...
105.02	Jul 103.00p	401	432	1.55	0.65	0.65	...
105.02	Jul 104.00	853	757	3.30	2.10	2.40	-1.60
105.02	Jul 104.00p	5426	12519	2.00	0.80	0.95	-0.30
105.02	Aug 104.00	892	708	4.60	3.10	3.40	-0.90
105.02	Aug 104.00p	661	2524	2.80	1.75	1.75	-0.10
105.02	Sep 104.00p	2834	19082	3.60	2.35	2.60	-0.30
105.02	Dec 104.00p	190	4938	5.10	4.00	4.00	-0.30
105.02	Jul 105.00	1710	763	2.85	1.40	1.85	-0.80
105.02	Jul 105.00p	766	736	2.40	1.15	1.55	+0.15
105.02	Jul 106.00	3764	2820	2.25	1.15	1.25	-0.90
105.02	Jul 106.00p	1649	8437	3.00	1.50	2.10	+0.15
105.02	Aug 106.00	492	938	3.10	2.05	2.50	-0.80
105.02	Aug 106.00p	489	1166	3.50	2.45	2.60	-0.30
105.02	Sep 106.00	4324	12709	4.50	3.10	3.60	-0.80
105.02	Sep 106.00p	3187	11281	4.40	3.30	3.40	-0.20
105.02	Jul 107.00	4642	3314	1.60	0.85	1.10	-0.60
105.02	Jul 107.00p	11834	6896	3.60	1.90	2.35	-0.10
105.02	Jul 108.00	4060	5107	1.25	0.50	0.75	-0.45
105.02	Jul 108.00p	24695	14473	4.30	2.35	3.10	...
105.02	Aug 108.00	506	1185	2.40	1.50	1.50	-0.75
105.02	Aug 108.00p	1175	6705	4.90	3.30	3.90	-0.10
105.02	Sep 108.00p	250	8182	5.80	4.00	4.20	-0.30

Interest Rate Options

CBOE

Yields

Company Exch Close	Strike Price	Sales Vol	Open Int	Week's High	Low	Last Price	Net Chg
10yrTN	Aug 50.00	125	12518.24	15.07	15.07	...	570.00
10yrTN	Sep 45.00	450	22552.10	42.31	42.31	...	570.00
10yrTN	Mar 47.50 p	50	2511.10	11.10	11.10	...	570.00
10yrTN	Mar 55.00	3	10617.06	17.06	17.06	-10.05	570.00
Call Vol.		1,725	Open Int.				2,707
Put Vol.		204	Open Int.				1,963

Index Options

Company Exch Close	Strike Price	Sales Vol	Open Int	Week's High	Low	Last Price	Net Chg
Am BioT	Jul 770.00	400	339	0.25	0.05	0.10	-1.10
Bank Idx	Aug 900.00	300	1	31.10	31.10	31.10	...
909.97	Aug 900.00p	300	...	30.10	30.10	30.10	...
909.97	Jul 905.00	301	302	25.80	23.00	24.70	+8.70
DJ Inds	Sep 90.00p	161	13657	0.65	0.35	0.35	-0.05
105.02	Dec 90.00p	2490	15804	1.45	0.90	1.05	-0.10
105.02	Jul 92.00p	2396	1871	0.10	0.05	0.05	-0.20
105.02	Jun 92.00p	902	1628	2.80	2.50	2.50	-0.40
105.02	Sep 94.00p	350	832	1.05	0.75	0.75	-0.25
105.02	Jul 96.00p	1135	7589	0.30	0.20	0.20	-0.05
105.02	Sep 96.00p	3614	11893	1.30	0.95	0.80	-0.05
105.02	Dec 96.00p	1205	8782	2.40	2.10	2.00	-0.40
105.02	Jul 100.00p	1350	12675	0.80	0.30	0.30	-0.20
105.02	Aug 100.00p	788	3917	1.35	0.80	0.95	+0.10
105.02	Sep 100.00p	220	1588	8.70	6.80	8.00	-0.60
105.02	Sep 100.00p	1517	8290	2.25	1.45	1.50	-0.25
105.02	**Dec 100.00p**	**182**	**13180**	**3.70**	**2.70**	**2.70**	**20.25**
105.02	Jul 101.00p	342	434	0.95	0.40	0.45	-0.40

Foreign Currency Options

Philadelphia Exchange

50,000 Australian Dollars-cents per unit.

Company Exch Close	Strike Price	Sales Vol	Open Int	Week's High	Low	Last Price	Net Chg	
ADollr	Sep 52.00	4	18	0.08	0.08	0.08	...	54.26

31,250 Brit. Pound-cents per unit.

BPound	Sep 130.00 p	125	525	0.01	0.01	0.01	...	147.69

50,000 Canadian Dollars-cents per unit.

CDollr	Sep 65.00	4	4	0.12	0.12	0.12	...	66.48
CDollr	Dec 65.00	37	37	0.15	0.15	0.15	...	66.48
CDollr	Dec 66.00 p	84	109	0.13	0.13	0.13	...	66.48
CDollr	Mar 63.50	5	5	0.27	0.27	0.27	...	66.48
CDollr	Mar 65.00	2	4	0.17	0.17	0.17	...	66.48
CDollr	Mar 66.00 p	62	62	0.15	0.15	0.15	...	66.48

62,500 Euro-cents per unit.

Euro	Jul 82.00 p	4	51	0.01	0.00	0.01	-0.00	88.15
Euro	Jul 84.00 p	27	20	0.05	0.01	0.03	...	88.15
Euro	Jul 86.00	34	117	0.05	0.02	0.02	-0.06	88.15
Euro	Jul 86.00 p	8	28	0.07	0.07	0.07	...	88.15
Euro	Jul 86.00 p	11	25	0.17	0.09	0.17	+0.03	88.15
Euro	Jul 88.00	10	22	0.03	0.03	0.03	-0.04	88.15
Euro	Sep 80.00 p	33	50	0.03	0.03	0.03	-0.01	88.15
Euro	Sep 84.00 p	2	36	0.08	0.08	0.08	...	88.15
Euro	**Sep 86.00**	**2**	**10**	**0.11**	**0.11**	**0.11**	**20.30**	**88.15**
Euro	Sep 90.00	3	20	0.05	0.05	0.05	...	88.15
Euro	Sep 91.00	50	50	0.02	0.02	0.02	...	...
Euro	Sep 92.00	100	100	0.01	0.01	0.01	...	88.15
Euro	Sep 96.00	200	226	0.01	0.01	0.01	...	88.15
Euro	Sep 98.00 p	1	63	1.19	1.19	1.19	-0.09	88.15

6,250,000J. Yen-100ths of a cent per unit.

JYen	Jul 80.00 p	45	96	0.04	0.04	0.04	...	92.53
JYen	Jul 81.00 p	20	22	0.11	0.11	0.11	-0.01	92.53
JYen	Jul 82.00 p	20	46	0.15	0.15	0.15	...	92.53
JYen	Sep 80.00	15	15	0.20	0.20	0.20	...	92.53
JYen	Sep 80.00 p	5	330	0.12	0.12	0.12	+0.06	92.53
JYen	Sep 80.50 p	7	7	0.12	0.12	0.12	...	92.53
JYen	Sep 81.00	15	30	0.16	0.16	0.16	...	92.53
JYen	Sep 81.00 p	10	65	0.17	0.17	0.17	+0.10	92.53

Source: Barron's, 2 July 2001, pp. MW49–50. Barron's Online by *Barron's*. © 2001 by Dow Jones & Co., Inc. Reproduced with permission of Dow Jones & Co., Inc. in the format *Fundamentals of Investments* via Copyright Clearance Center.

($75 − $65) × 100 = $1,000. A $1,000 profit on a $525 investment results in a rate of return of ($1,000/$525) × 100 = 190%. The rate of return from merely buying the stock is only about ($7,500 − $6,368.75)/$6,368.75 = 17.8%. Clearly, Bill would rather have the 190% rate of return. Thus, call options provide a low-cost way of taking large positions in stock at a lower cost than buying the stock directly. The profit on options is taxable; the tax calculation is explained in Appendix 13A.

Now suppose Jane Downs, an eternal pessimist, believes Compaq's stock price will fall over the next six months. Short selling the stock is risky, requires margin money, and may not be allowable for regulatory reasons (depending on the nature of the invested funds). Rather than short sell stock, Jane could buy a put option. Recall that a put option gives its holder the right to sell the underlying asset at a predetermined price. Put options cost less than the margin required to short sell the stock, and the loss is limited to the purchase price of the put.

For example, assume the price of a six-month put option with a strike price of $60 is $2. Jane would pay only $200 to take a short position in 100 shares of Compaq. If, at the expiration date, Compaq fell to $50, then the put option would have a profit of ($60 − $50) × 100 = $1,000. A $1,000 profit on a $200 investment results in a rate of return of ($1,000/$200) × 100 = 500%. Clearly, investors bearish on Compaq's stock would be attracted to put options.

With such tremendous gains available to option buyers, why would anyone wish to write options? The primary benefit is that option writers receive the option premium. If the asset price moves against the option buyer, then there are no future costs to the option writer.

PRACTICE BOX

Problem
Consider the call option price for Genentec, Inc., of $2 with the strike price of $25. The stock price never goes above $20 before the maturity (the expiration date) of the option. What is the profit or loss to the call writer? What is the profit or loss to the call buyer? What is the call option worth at expiration? Why? What is the premium? (Recall that each option contract is for 100 shares, and the option price is quoted on a per-share basis.)

Solution
The premium of the option is $2. Because the stock price never exceeds the strike price, the call option expires worthless. (You would not wish to buy a stock at a price higher than it is currently trading in the market.) The call writer will keep the entire option premium of $2 × 100 = $200. The call buyer will lose the entire option premium of $200.

13.2.5 The underlying asset and the option

Options are categorized by the relationship that exists between the current market price of the underlying asset and the option's exercise price. Let S_0 represent the current market price of the underlying asset (for example, the stock price) and X represent the option exercise price. An **in-the-money option** is an option that would generate a positive cash flow if it were exercised *now*. That is, a call option is an in-the-money option if the market price of the underlying asset is greater than the strike price ($S_0 > X$) of the option contract. If the option is American style, an investor could exercise the call option, pay X dollars for the stock, and turn around and sell the stock for S_0, generating a positive cash flow of $S_0 - X$. For put options, an in-the-money option is an option in which the price received for exercising the option, X, is greater than the current price of the stock ($X > S_0$). An **out-of-the-money option** is the exact opposite of an in-the-money option. That is, for calls, $X > S_0$ (for puts, it is out-of-the-money if $X < S_0$). In the case of out-of-the-money options, there is no incentive to exercise the put or call. **At-the-money options** occur when the current price of the stock is exactly equal to the exercise price, $S_0 = X$.

Sometimes option traders refer to *deep in-the-money options* or *deep out-of-the-money options*. The word *deep* emphasizes that the distance between S_0 and X is relatively large. For example, for a deep in-the-money call option, S_0 is much higher than X. In the case of deep out-of-the-money call options, S_0 is much lower than X.

A call option written when the investor does not own the underlying asset is a **naked position**. A **covered position** is a call option written when the underlying asset is already owned. Writing a call option without owning the underlying asset is very risky and hence exposes the writer to great risk.

13.3 OVERVIEW OF OPTION MARKETS

Option trading occurs on exchanges, over the counter, and directly between buyers and sellers. There are many different exchanges on which options are traded. The most active option exchanges are the Chicago Board Options Exchange (CBOE), the American Stock Exchange (AMEX), the Chicago Board of Trade (CBOT), the Philadelphia Stock Exchange (PHLX), the Chicago Mercantile Exchange (CME) and the Pacific Stock Exchange (PSE). On the CBOE alone, the total volume of contracts traded increased over 600% in the years 1997 to 2001: see Exhibit 13.3.

Option transactions are similar to stock transactions. For example, if John Q decides to buy call options on Compaq, he would call his broker and state his desires. The broker would communicate this order to the appropriate option exchange, where the trade would occur either with an investor wanting to sell call options on Compaq or with the market maker (see Chapter 3).

The **Options Clearing Corporation** (OCC) maintains the records of option trades and is one of the major clearing corporations (organizations that facilitate the validation, delivery and settlement of security transactions). The OCC is owned and backed by several exchanges (such as the CBOE, AMEX, NYSE and PHLX). Hence, the OCC is a very creditworthy corporation. It issues all option contracts and guarantees both sides of

Exhibit 13.3 Option contract volume on the CBOE

Date	Call volume	Put volume	Total volume
1 December 1995	326,385	239,526	565,911
2 December 1996	375,228	200,637	575,865
1 December 1997	443,900	264,396	708,296
30 July 2001	3,136,695	1,926,657	5,063,352

the contracts. Thus, the option buyer does not have to evaluate the credit risk of the option writer. Also, all option contracts have standardized features that make them easier to resell, thus enhancing the option contract's liquidity. The OCC provides a prospectus for each contract, which details the regulations related to trading options and processes all transactions related to option trading.

Suppose that you purchase a call option with an exercise price of $50. The stock price subsequently increases to $200. Who guarantees that the call writer will pay you the difference (that is, $200 − $50 = $150)? The OCC requires that the call writer (as well as all other option writers) provide collateral, known as margin. The margin requirements, which are explained in detail in Appendix 13B, ensure that the option writer will pay the option buyer if the events indeed occur in the buyer's favour.

13.4 OPTION VALUES AT EXPIRATION

This section examines the value of options at expiration. In this examination, it is helpful to use graphs with lines that plot the future possible values of the underlying asset. These graphs, called *payoff diagrams*, are used in Section 13.4.2 to compare the objectives of different option-based trading strategies. This section first examines option values and then explains the mechanics of payoff diagrams.

13.4.1 Option prices: intrinsic and time value components

Option prices can be broken down into two components: intrinsic value and time value. The **intrinsic value** of an option is the value of the option if it is immediately exercised (assuming it is an American-style option) or zero. That is, the intrinsic value for calls (IV_c) is

$$IV_c = \max(0, S_0 - X) \tag{13.1}$$

The intrinsic value for puts (IV_p) is

$$IV_p = \max(0, X - S_0) \tag{13.2}$$

As the stock price changes, the intrinsic value of the option may change as well. It remains zero if the option remains out of the money. The **time value** of an option is whatever value an option currently has above its intrinsic value. Even if an option is out of the money, the chance that the stock price may change and the option may end up in the money gives the option time value. Most often, the term *time value* refers to discounting future cash flows. When related to options, time value has a different meaning. It is the value of the option related to the chance that the option may go in the money (or further in the money, if it is already in the money).

Let C_0 and P_0 represent the call and put premiums, respectively. Then the time value of a call (TV_c) is

$$TV_c = C_0 - IV_c \tag{13.3}$$

The time value of a put (TV_p) is

$$TV_p = P_0 - IV_p \tag{13.4}$$

Clearly, from the definition of *time value* and *intrinsic value*, we can represent option prices as follows:

$$C_0 = IV_c + TV_c = \max(0, S_0 - X) + TV_c$$

and

$$P_0 = IV_p + TV_p = \max(0, X_0 - S_0) + TV_p$$

For example, suppose the current price of GNE stock now is $28 ($S_0 = \$28$). If the current price of a GNE July 25 call, C_0, is $6^1/_2$ ($C_0 = \$6^1/_2$, $X = 25$), then the call's intrinsic value, IV_c, is $28 - \$25 = \$3$, and the time value, TV_c, is $6^1/_2 - \$3 = \$3^1/_2$. If the GNE July 25 put is trading at $3/_4$, then the put's intrinsic value, IV_p, is $\max(0, 25 - 28) = \$0$, and the time value, TV_p, is $3/_4 - \$0 = \$3/_4$.

PRACTICE BOX

Problem

Suppose you are given the following option quotes for United Airlines:

Stock price	Strike price	Calls			Puts		
		Oct.	Nov.	Dec.	Oct.	Nov.	Dec.
114	110	$4^1/_4$	$7^1/_2$	$8^1/_4$	$3/_8$	$2^1/_4$	3
114	115	$7/_8$	$3^7/_8$	5	$1^3/_4$	$4^1/_2$	$5^1/_4$
114	120	$1/_8$	2	$2^1/_2$	$6^1/_8$	$7^3/_4$	$8^1/_4$

Compute the intrinsic value and time value for each option.

Solution

The intrinsic value is the dollar amount of an in-the-money option. For calls only, the 114 strikes are $4 in the money. For puts, the 115 strikes are $1 in the money, and the 120 strikes are $6 in the money. Thus, we can construct the following table for intrinsic value:

Strike price	Calls			Puts		
	Oct.	Nov.	Dec.	Oct.	Nov.	Dec.
110	4	4[a]	4	0	0	0
115	0	0	0	1	1	1
120	0	0	0	6	6[b]	6

[a] $IV_c = \max(0, S_0 - X) = \max(0, \$114 - \$110) = \$4$.
[b] $IV_p = \max(0, X - S_0) = \max(0, \$120 - \$114) = \$6$.

The time value is nothing but the option value minus the intrinsic value. We can construct the following table of time value:

Strike price	Calls			Puts		
	Oct.	Nov.	Dec.	Oct.	Nov.	Dec.
110	$1/_4$	$3^1/_2$[a]	$4^1/_4$	$3/_8$	$2^1/_4$	3
115	$7/_8$	$3^7/_8$	5	$3/_4$	$3^1/_2$[b]	$4^1/_4$
120	$1/_8$	2	$2^1/_2$	$1/_8$	$1^3/_4$	$2^1/_4$

[a] $TV_c = C_0 - IV_c = \$7^1/_2 - \$4 = \$3^1/_2$.
[b] $TV_p = P_0 - IV_p = \$7^1/_4 - \$6 = \$1^1/_4$.

13.4.2 Payoff diagrams

A payoff diagram relates to various values at the expiration date of the options. It is a graph that illustrates (1) the relationship among the values of securities (the value line), (2) the dollar profit or loss (the P/L line), or (3) both the value line and the P/L line.

Let us illustrate these concepts with a call option on Apple with a strike price of $50 ($X = \$50$) and a call price of $5 ($C_0 = \$5$). The value line in Exhibit 13.4(a) illustrates the value of the call option at its expiration date. If the stock price falls below $50 at expiration, then the option is worthless. For example, if the stock price is selling for $30 at maturity, the call price is $0. If the stock price rises above $50 at expiration, the option is in the money and has a positive price. Specifically, for every dollar the stock is above $50, the option is worth an additional dollar. If the stock price rises to $70 at expiration, then the call option has a value of $70 - $50 = $20, because at expiration we receive the right to buy the stock for $50 when its market value is $70. Hence, we buy the stock via the option contract for $50 and sell the stock received for $70, with a profit of $20. Thus, the value line is zero on the horizontal axis up to the strike price. At the strike price it becomes a positive 45-degree line. From the value line we see clearly that a call option is very profitable when the underlying stock price goes up.

If an option expires in the money, then it has intrinsic value. The option investment is said to *break even* if the proceeds from the exercise of the option at expiration are just equal to the original option premium. For example, when the stock price at maturity date is $S_t = \$55$ and $X = \$50$, then we just break even because $C_0 = \$5$.

Exhibit 13.4(b) illustrates the P/L line for this $5 call, at a strike price of $50. If the stock price falls below $50 at expiration, then the option is worthless, and the investor who bought a call option loses the $5 option premium. For every dollar the stock rises above $50, the investor makes an additional dollar. With a $5 premium, the stock must rise to $55 in order to break even on the contract. For every additional dollar above $55, the option provides an additional dollar of profit. Hence, if the stock price reaches $70 at maturity, then the profit from this option is $70 - ($50 + $5) = $15.

We now examine the profit or loss of a call option at expiration from the call writer's point of view. Exhibit 13.5 illustrates the payoff diagram of writing a call option on Apple stock with a strike price of $50 and a call premium ($C_0$) of $5. Recall that when you short a call, you receive the cash flow C_0, which is the call premium. The P/L line is equal to +5 as long as the stock price at expiration is less than $50, and then it starts declining at −45 degrees, because for an $1 increase in price the call writer loses $1. For example, if the stock price falls to $30, then the call writer keeps the call premium of $5 and has no obligations at maturity, because the option buyer will not exercise the call option. However, if the stock price rises to $70 at maturity, then the writer loses $20 at expiration and has a dollar loss of −$20 + $5 = −$15. Clearly, call writers face large liabilities when the stock price rises sharply.

In a similar fashion, Exhibit 13.6 presents the P/L line for buying a put option for $5 at a strike price of $50. Recall that buying a put option, in the case of stocks, gives the buyer the right to sell a stock at the strike price. Hence, a put option is more valuable as the price of the stock declines. In contrast, the value of the put option at expiration is zero if the put option expires out of the money (when the stock price is above $50, in this case).

The dollar P/L line is −$5 for stock price above, $50, because the buyer of the put option in this example pays $5 for the put which expires worthless. For puts, the breakeven point is when the strike price less the stock price is equal to the purchase price, which in our case is $50 − $45 = $5, i.e. for a stock price of $45 the put buyer exactly breaks even. For example, if the stock price rises to $70 at maturity, the put option is worth $0, and the dollar loss is $5 (the put price). If the stock price falls to $30 at maturity, the put option is worth $50 − $30 = $20, and the dollar profit will be $20 − $5 = $15. Thus, buying a put option is similar to buying a call option, except money is earned when the stock price falls. The put P/L diagram can be viewed as the

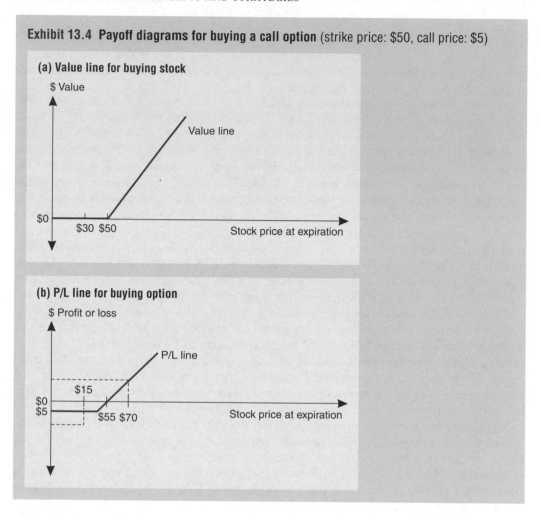

Exhibit 13.4 Payoff diagrams for buying a call option (strike price: $50, call price: $5)

(a) Value line for buying stock

(b) P/L line for buying option

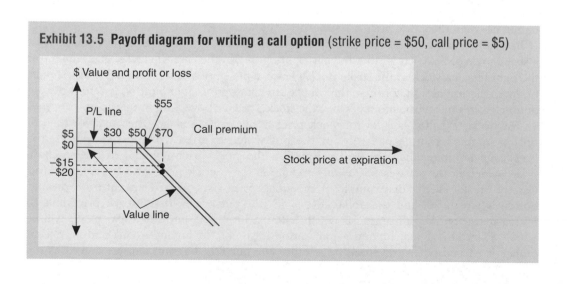

Exhibit 13.5 Payoff diagram for writing a call option (strike price = $50, call price = $5)

Exhibit 13.6 Payoff diagram for buying a put option (strike price = $50, put price = $5)

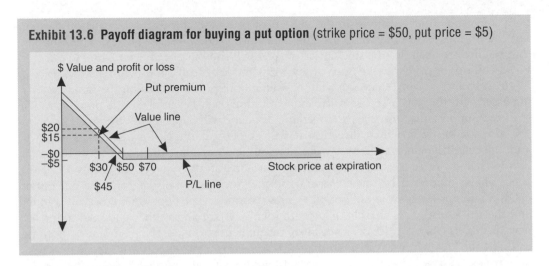

Exhibit 13.7 Payoff diagram for writing a put option (strike price = $50, put price = $5)

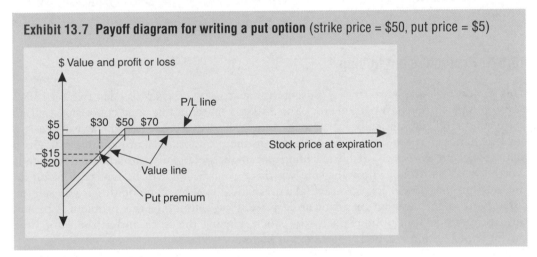

mirror image of the call P/L diagram, except the mirror is placed vertically on the strike price. (Note there is no requirement that the put price equal the call price. We adopted these values to simplify the discussion.)

Exhibit 13.7 presents the P/L lines for writing put options. Recall that put writing obligates an investor to buy a stock from the put buyer at a specified price. Hence, as the stock price falls, the put buyer will want to exercise the option and sell stock at X. Therefore, the put writer loses as the stock price declines. If the stock price falls to, say, $30 the put writer has to pay $50 - $30 = $20 but as he or she obtains a premium of $5 for selling this put option, the net loss is only $15. The lines in Exhibit 13.7 are the mirror image of those in Exhibit 13.6, where the mirror is placed on the horizontal axis.

13.5 INVESTMENT STRATEGIES USING OPTIONS

There are many possible investment strategies composed of various combinations of call and put options as well as the underlying asset. For example, a **spread** involves holding both long and short positions on the same type of option (for example, calls on Exxon), but the options have different expiration dates and exercise prices. For example, suppose that the investor believes the stock price of IBM will rise but not above $240. He can then buy a call option with a strike price of say $190 and sell a call option with a strike price of $240. A **straddle** involves either buying or selling both puts and calls on the same underlying asset with the same exercise price and expiration date. Let us elaborate on the straddle strategy. Suppose that you believe something dramatic will happen with the stock price but you do not know in which direction it will go. For example, an oil firm is going to announce shortly either a discovery of a new oil field or failure due to all wells becoming dry. In such a case, it is suggested to employ a straddle strategy composed of buy a call and a put at the money. If bad news occurs and the stock price falls sharply, the put option yields a large profit and the call option expires worthless. The opposite holds if oil is found and the stock price rises sharply. If you are totally wrong and neither good news nor bad news occurs, the stock price does not move much, hence you lose the premium on both the call and the put which expires worthless. This section first describes in detail two basic option-based strategies which are commonly used: protective put buying and covered call writing.

13.5.1 Protective put buying

This section reviews several strategies using the data for Exxon stock listed in Exhibit 13.8.

Suppose you purchase Exxon stock for $50 per share and become concerned that its price might fall dramatically in the near future. However, you also believe there is a strong chance that Exxon stock will double in the near future. (For example, there is a chance that an expensive offshore drilling site might yield gains and a chance the site is worthless.) You do not know for sure which of your beliefs will be realized. If you do not sell you may lose if Exxon stock falls dramatically. What can you do? If you sell the stock, you might miss out on a run up in price. One solution to this problem is to buy out-of-the-money put options on Exxon stock. Having the stock and at the same time buying a put option is called **protective put buying**.

Exhibit 13.9(a) shows the P/L line of buying the stock and the P/L line of buying a $45 strike, $1.50-per-share put option. Recall that a put option will benefit investors when the stock price falls. If the stock price remains at $50 per share, then the investor has no profit or loss on the stock and has a $1.5-per-share loss on the put option, because it expired out of the money. At a stock price of $45, the investor has a total

Exhibit 13.8 Exxon stock data

Strike price	Call price	Put price
$X_L = \$45$	$C_{0,L} = \$8$	$P_{0,L} = \$1^1/_2$
$X = \$50$	$C_0 = \$5$	$P_0 = \$3^1/_2$
$X_H = \$55$	$C_{0,H} = \$3$	$P_{0,H} = \$6^1/_2$

Current stock price is $S_0 = \$50$.
L stands for a lower strike price, and H stands for a higher strike price.

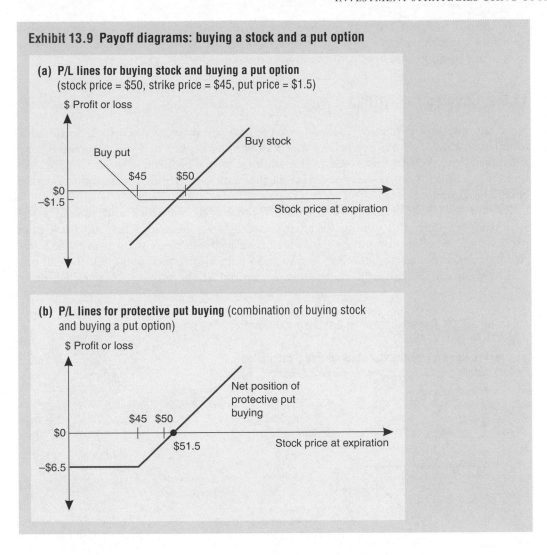

Exhibit 13.9 Payoff diagrams: buying a stock and a put option

(a) P/L lines for buying stock and buying a put option
(stock price = $50, strike price = $45, put price = $1.5)

(b) P/L lines for protective put buying (combination of buying stock and buying a put option)

loss of $6.5, because the stock position has a loss of $50 − $45 = $5 and the put position is still not in the money, resulting in a $1.5-per-share loss. The maximum loss is $6.5 because below a $45 stock price, for every additional dollar lost on the stock position, the put position gains a dollar, resulting in no overall change in the protective put buying portfolio. For any stock price above $45, for every additional dollar gained on the stock position, the put is worthless and adds a constant loss of $1.5 to the protective put buying position. Thus one dollar increase in the stock price above $45 results in one dollar gain for the protective put buying portfolio. Exhibit 13.9(b) illustrates the net position for protective put buying. Note that for a stock price of $51.5, the net profit is zero, as $1.5 is earned on the stock but the investor loses $1.5, which is the premium on the put option. Notice that the net position is very similar to the P/L line derived when simply buying a call option. The only actual difference between protective put buying and buying a call option relates to the timing of cash flows and the required discounting of these cash flows. Payoff diagrams ignore the time value of money.

It should be clear from the above discussion that by purchasing a put option, investors can dramatically alter the risk–return profile of their investments. With protective put options, investors can set a floor on their losses.

13.5.2 Covered call writing

Now suppose you purchased Exxon stock for $50 per share, wanted to generate additional cash flow, and did not believe that Exxon's stock price had much potential for a substantial rise. What could you do? One solution to this problem is to write out-of-the-money call options on Exxon stock. Having the stock and writing a call option is called **covered call writing**.

Exhibit 13.10 illustrates the P/L lines of both buying the stock and writing a $55 strike, $3-per-share call option. Recall that a call buyer benefits when the stock price rises; hence, a call writer suffers a loss in this case. If the stock price rises to $55 (the strike price), the investor has a $55 − $50 = $5 gain in the stock and a $3 (the call premium) gain on the call option, because it expired at the money. Notice in Exhibit

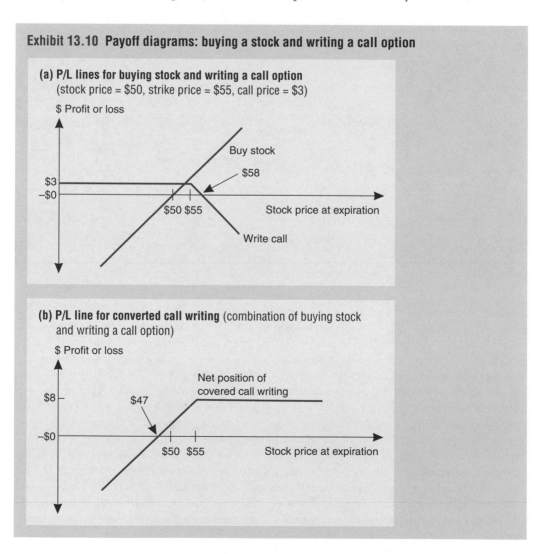

Exhibit 13.10 Payoff diagrams: buying a stock and writing a call option

(a) P/L lines for buying stock and writing a call option
(stock price = $50, strike price = $55, call price = $3)

(b) P/L line for converted call writing (combination of buying stock and writing a call option)

13.10(a) that above a $55 stock price, for every additional dollar gained on the stock position, the call option position loses a dollar. Hence, the profit is greatest at $8 ($5 from the stock and $3 from selling the option). Below a $55 stock price the call option is worthless; hence for every additional dollar reduction in the stock position, the call position's cash flow does not change and the net position loses a dollar.

Exhibit 13.10(b) illustrates the net position of covered call writing. Notice that the net position is very similar in its shape to the P/L line derived when just writing a put option. Again, the actual differences relate to the timing of the cash flows. Covered call writing dramatically alters the risk–return profile of a stock position; it sets a ceiling on the potential gain. Investors are willing to accept this ceiling in return for receiving the call premium.

13.6 OPTION VALUATION

At expiration date the value of the option is easy to determine: it is either zero if is out of the money, or the stock price less the strike price if it is in the money. The difficult problem is to determine the option price before the expiration date. Black and Scholes (B&S) provide such a valuation formula (see Section 13.8).

This section covers the pricing of options and how investors can detect whether an option is underpriced or overpriced. Option pricing heavily relies on the no-arbitrage argument – that is, in equilibrium, no arbitrage profit prevails.

Understanding the price behaviour of options requires a knowledge of **options arbitrage.** When there are arbitrage opportunities available, they do not last long. With the lightning-fast computer technology available today, investors need to be quick to exploit arbitrage opportunities. Arbitrage is basically a 'free lunch', which occurs rarely and does not last very long.

Although there are many possible definitions of arbitrage, this text focuses on two popular definitions. An arbitrage opportunity exists when either (1) a portfolio can be constructed at zero cost (by selling some securities short) that has future positive cash flows but absolutely zero probability of negative cash flows, or (2) a portfolio can be constructed for a negative cost (that is, the investor receives money today) that has no risk of future losses. In equilibrium, arbitrage opportunities do not exist. The existence of arbitrage profit thus represents disequilibrium. Option prices are determined for the most part by option traders eliminating arbitrage opportunities.

This section examines the pricing of European-style options (that is, options where early exercise is not allowed). First, we examine the option pricing boundaries that all option prices must satisfy. Option prices remain within the boundaries because of arbitrage forces in the market. Then we discuss the Black–Scholes pricing approach to determining the equilibrium price of an option. Finally, we examine a risk management strategy called *portfolio insurance*, which uses this approach.

Most of the illustrations in this section relate to pricing stock options. However, the same principles demonstrated in this chapter apply to pricing options on any underlying asset, such as stock index options, futures or foreign currency options.

13.6.1 Option boundaries

Option boundaries provide a helpful first step in the quest to understand option price behaviour. Option boundary conditions represent the range where we would anticipate

Exhibit 13.11 Closing price options based on Microsoft

(a) Closing price quotes

Stock price	Strike price	Calls			Puts		
		31 day	91 day	182 day	31 day	91 day	182 day
100	90	10.80	12.85	15.47	0.42	1.74	3.26
100	95	6.76	9.39	12.31	1.35	3.21	4.97
100	100	3.70	6.57	9.62	3.27	5.33	7.16
100	105	1.74	4.41	7.38	6.30	8.11	9.80
100	110	0.70	2.84	5.57	10.24	11.47	12.86

(b) Lower bounds

Stock price	Strike price	Calls			Puts		
		31 day	91 day	182 day	31 day	91 day	182 day
100	90	10.37	11.09	12.16	0.0	0.0	0.0
100	95	5.39	6.15	7.28	0.0	0.0	0.0
100	100	0.41	1.21	2.40	0.0	0.0	0.0
100	105	0.0	0.0	0.0	4.57	3.73	2.48
100	110	0.0	0.0	0.0	9.55	8.67	7.36

The closing price quotes are based on the Black–Scholes option pricing model discussed later in this chapter. They assume a 5% interest rate and a standard deviation of 30%.

finding option prices. Option prices must satisfy certain boundaries; otherwise, investors could make an infinite profit at no risk. (This arbitrage activity would push the option price inside these bounds.) The derivation of option prices is based on the assumption that there are sophisticated investors in the market. Whenever these investors see arbitrage opportunities, they exploit them. This trading activity causes prices to change until the arbitrage profits disappear and option prices lie within the designated boundaries.

Exhibit 13.11 is a hypothetical closed market quote sheet for a market maker in Microsoft options. How are we to make sense out of all these numbers? Are these reasonable prices? Are they overpriced? Are they underpriced? Finding option boundaries helps to answer these questions.

An arbitrageur would like to find option prices that are either too high or too low. The analysis in this section establishes ways of assessing the validity of option market prices. The section first examines call option boundaries and then put option boundaries.

13.6.2 Call option boundaries

For a call option, there is both an upper and a lower boundary for the current call price. If the call price is above the upper boundary or below the lower boundary, then an arbitrageur will be able to make money with no risk. This section first examines call option boundaries and then describes what happens when option prices get outside them.

Lower boundary

The prices of a European-style call option (c_0) must lie above the following boundary:

$$c_0 \geq \max\left[0, S_0 - \frac{X}{(1+r)^t}\right] \tag{13.5}$$

where S_0 is the price of a security or underlying asset today; X is the strike or exercise price; t is the time to maturity until the expiration date (in fraction of years); and r is the annual risk-free interest rate, which is assumed to be constant.

In Exhibit 13.12 we establish an investment strategy which will guarantee an arbitrage profit as long as Equation 13.5 does not hold. The trading strategy presented in Exhibit 13.12 will establish the lower boundary by examining cash flows at time 0 and maturity date t. (We assume that any trade opened at time 0 is closed at t.) Note that we separate the future into two possibilities: $S_t \geq X$ and $S_t < X$. More information on the exact value of S_t is not needed.

Column 1 of Exhibit 13.12 identifies the exact trading strategy to adopt at time 0 (today). As a cash flow table, columns 2, 3 and 4 contain dollar cash flows. Column 2 shows the dollar cash flows today from following the trading strategy in column 1. (Recall that when you short sell the stock, you receive money.) The net cash flow at the bottom of this column is found by summing the cash flows in the 'Today' column (the required investment). The question mark (?) indicates that we investigate whether the investment will be positive, zero or negative if arbitrage profits are absent. Columns 3 and 4 depict the cash flow when $S_t > X$ (column 3) and when $S_t \leq X$ (column 4).

According to Exhibit 13.12, if the cash flow today (0) is positive (that is, the question mark in the exhibit is positive), then an arbitrage profit opportunity (sometimes called a **money machine**) prevails. That is, we are able to generate a positive cash flow today with no risk of future loss (and possibly a positive future cash flow). The last column of this table is positive by assumption ($S_t \leq X$). Thus, to avoid this arbitrage or money machine, we must find the cash flow today to be negative. Therefore, we must have, in equilibrium,

$$-c_0 + S_0 - \frac{X}{(1+r)^t} \leq 0$$

Exhibit 13.12 The lower boundary for call options: a cash flow table

	Cash flows		
(1)	(2)	(3)	(4)
Trading strategy	Today (0)	At expiration	
		$S_t > X$	$S_t \leq X$
Buy one call option	$-c_0$	$S_t - X$	0
Sell short one share of stock	$+S_0$	$-S_t$	$-S_t$
Lend $X/(1+r)^t$	$-X/(1+r)^t$	X	X
Net cash flow	$-c_0 + S_0$	0	$X - S_t$ (zero or positive)
	$-X/(1+r)^t = ?$		

c_0 = the current call price, S_0 = the current stock price, S_t = the stock price at expiration, X = the strike price, r = the risk-free interest rate, and t = the time to maturity in fractions of a year.

which implies that

$$c_0 \geq S_0 - \frac{X}{(1+r)^t}$$

How do the actions of the arbitrageur influence market prices? If $-c_0 + S_0 - X/(1+r)^t$ is positive, everyone will want to buy call options, short sell the stock, and borrow to create this money machine. These actions will push the price of the call up and the price of the stock down until the cash flow is nonpositive (0). Also, because of limited liability of an option, the option price cannot be negative ($c_0 \geq 0$). Recall that the option buyer does not have to exercise the options. We can conclude that the inequality given in Equation 13.5 holds.

■ Upper boundary

Using similar arguments, we can demonstrate that the price of a European-style call option must lie below the underlying stock price:

$$c_0 \leq S_0 \qquad\qquad (13.6)$$

Intuitively, we would not pay more for an option to buy a security than we would pay for the underlying security if we purchased it directly. For example, why should we pay $100 for the right to buy the stock when we could buy it directly in the market for $S_t = \$90$? Thus, a call option is always worth less than the underlying security on which the option is written.

Exhibit 13.13 illustrates the boundaries for call options. Note that if we have an American-style call option and it is exercised, the value is $S_0 - X$. Because $c_0 > S_0 - [X/(1+r)^t] > S_0 - X$, it never pays to exercise the call option before maturity. (You are better off selling the option.) Thus, the boundaries of European-style call options also apply to American-style options.

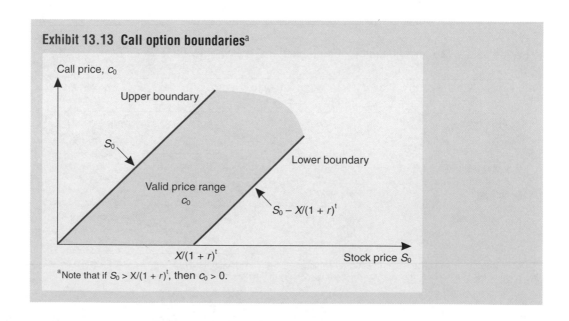

Exhibit 13.13 Call option boundaries[a]

Call price, c_0

Upper boundary

S_0

Valid price range
c_0

Lower boundary

$S_0 - X/(1+r)^t$

$X/(1+r)^t$

Stock price S_0

[a] Note that if $S_0 > X/(1+r)^t$, then $c_0 > 0$.

Exhibit 13.14 The lower boundary for put options: a cash flow table

	Cash flows		
(1)	(2)	(3)	(4)
Trading strategy	Today (0)	At expiration	
		$S_t \geq X$	$S_t < X$
Buy one put option	$-p_0$	0	$X - S_t$
Borrow $X/(1 + r)^t$	$+X/(1 + r)^t$	$-X$	$-X$
Buy one share of stock	$-S_0$	$+S_t$	$+S_t$
Net cash flow	$-p_0 + X(1 + r)^t - S_0 = ?$	$S_t - X$ (zero or positive)	0

p_0 = the current put price, S_0 = the current stock price, S_t = the stock price at expiration, X = the strike price, r = the risk-free interest rate, and t = the time to maturity in fractions of a year.

13.6.3 Put option boundaries

◼ Lower boundary

As with call options, European-style put options have pricing boundaries. The lower boundary for the put price (p_0) is

$$p_0 \geq \max\left[0, \frac{X}{(1+r)^t} - S_0\right] \tag{13.7}$$

The trading strategy employed to demonstrate the lower boundary of a put option consists of three parts: (1) borrowing the amount $X/(1 + r)^t$, (2) buying one share of stock, and (3) buying one put option. Exhibit 13.14 illustrates the cash flows. The next-to-last column of this table is nonnegative (0) by assumption ($S_t \geq X$). Therefore, if the cash flow today (0) is positive (? > 0), then this is an arbitrage opportunity. We are able to generate a positive cash flow today with no risk of future loss (and possibly a positive future cash flow). Thus, to avoid this arbitrage, we must find the cash flow today to be negative. We must have

$$-p_0 + X/(1 + r)^t - S_0 \leq 0$$

which implies

$$p_0 \geq X/(1 + r)^t - S_0$$

If we observe that $-p_0 + X/(1 + r)^t - S_0$ is positive, everyone will want to buy put options, buy the stock, and lend to create this money machine. Buying the stock and the put option will drive the stock price and the put price up, and eventually any arbitrage profits will vanish.

◼ Upper boundary

The most you can lose from writing a put option (or earn by buying a put option) is the strike price (see Equation 13.8). This occurs when the stock price falls to zero. Because this loss occurs at maturity and not on the day the put option is purchased, the put option price must be below the discounted value of the strike price:

$$p_0 \leq \frac{X}{(1 + r)^t} \tag{13.8}$$

Why would you pay more for an option than the present value of its maximum pay-off? The answer is that you would not. For example, a one-year put option ($t = 1$) with a strike price of $100 at a 5% risk-free rate has an upper boundary of $100/(1 + 0.05)^1$ = $95.24. Investors will not pay more than $95.24 for a put option that gives them the right to make at most $100 one year from now.

Exhibit 13.15 illustrates the boundaries for put options. Again, the valid range of prices is still wide. We must investigate option pricing further to find out whether we can make a more precise assertion regarding the option price. We turn now to examine the relationship between stock, put option and call option prices.

Unlike with the call options analysis, with put options there may be value associated with an early exercise. Thus, American-style put options may have a higher

---

PRACTICE BOX

Problem

Based on the following information from *Barron's*, verify that the closing prices of Borland's put and call options satisfy the boundary conditions. The time to maturity is one month ($t = \frac{1}{12}$), Borland's stock price is $41^7/_8$, and the annual risk-free interest rate is 3%. Are there any arbitrage opportunities?

Expiration date and strike price	Closing Price ($)
Borland Oct 40 call	$3^3/_4$
Borland Oct 40 put	$1^3/_4$
Borland Oct 45 call	$1^5/_8$
Borland Oct 45 put	$4^1/_4$
Borland Oct 50 call	$^1/_2$
Borland Oct 50 put	$8^1/_4$

Solution

Clearly, none of these prices approaches the upper bounds ($41^7/_8$ for calls and $40, $45 and $50 discounted for one month at the risk-free rate for puts). We now examine the lower bounds. The discount factor is $1/(1 + r)^t = 1/(1 + 0.03)^{1/12} = 0.9975$. Thus, for $X = $40 we have $40 \times 0.9975 = $39.9; for $X = $45 we have $45 \times 0.9975 = $44.8875; and for $X = $50 we have $50 \times 0.9975 = $49.875.

Let us consider calls first. When $X = $40, we have a lower boundary of $41.875 − $39.9 = $1.975, which is lower than the closing price of $3^3/_4$. When $X = $45, we note that $44.8875 > $41.875, and the lower boundary is zero. This is also true when $X = $50. In both cases, the lower boundary holds.

The boundaries for puts (using Equation 13.8) are as follows:

$$X = \$40: p_0 = 0$$
$$X = \$45: p_0 = \$44.8875 - \$41.875 = \$3.0125$$
$$X = \$50: p_0 = \$49.875 - \$41.875 = \$8.0$$

We see that each lower boundary is below the put option prices. Thus, based on these observations, there are no arbitrage opportunities.

Exhibit 13.15 Put option boundaries*

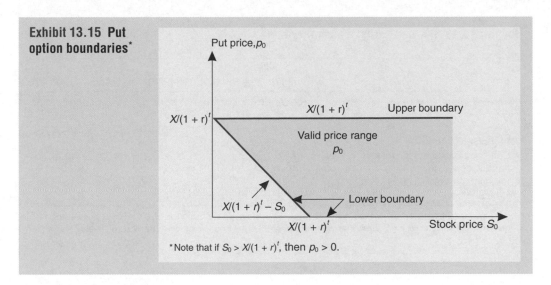

*Note that if $S_0 > X/(1 + r)^t$, then $p_0 > 0$.

value than European-style put options. To illustrate, suppose that you buy a put option on a firm that is under financial distress, and its stock price is, say, 1 cent. If the strike price is, say, $10, you had better exercise your right, get the cash flow (of $10 less 1 cent), and deposit the money in the bank to earn interest on this cash flow. The interest received may be more than the maximum additional profit from holding the put option (1 cent at most if the stock price drops to zero) until maturity. Thus, unlike with call options, with put options there is economic value for the possibility of an early exercise. We therefore expect the market value of American-style put options to be higher than the market value of similar European-style put options.

13.7 PUT–CALL PARITY

Put–call parity is very useful in establishing pricing relationships between securities such as calls and puts. The notion of **put–call parity (PCP)** was first published by Russell Sage in the late nineteenth century. Put–call parity establishes an exact relationship among the current stock price, the call price and the put price. In other words, put–call parity establishes the relationship among the underlying security, the risk-free interest rate, and call and put options that have the same strike price. Given any three of the following four securities – (1) the underlying security, (2) zero-coupon bonds (borrowing or lending), (3) a call option and (4) a put option – we can synthetically create the fourth. That is, by creating a portfolio of three assets, we can duplicate the cash flow of the fourth asset. Put–call parity can be written as follows:

$$c_0 = S_0 - \frac{X}{(1 + t)^t} + p_0 \tag{13.9}$$

Again, we assume that any trade opened at time 0 is closed at the option maturity date (t). Exhibit 13.16 establishes the validity of Equation 13.9.

As in Exhibit 13.14, the first column of Exhibit 13.16 identifies a trading strategy adopted at time 0 (today). The other three columns show the relevant cash flows. The

Exhibit 13.16 Put–call parity: a cash flow table

			Cash flows		
(1)		(2)		(3)	(4)
Trading strategy		Today (0)		At expiration	
				$S_t \geq X$	$S_t < X$
Buy one call option		$-c_0$		$S_t - X$	0
Sell short one share of stock		$+S_0$		$-S_t$	$-S_t$
Lend $X/(1 + r)^t$		$-X/(1 + r)^t$		X	X
Sell (write) one put option		$+p_0$		0	$-(X - S_t)$
Net cash flow		$-c_0 + S_0 - X/(1 + r)^t + p_0$		0	0

c_0 = the current call price, p_0 = the current put price, S_0 = the current stock price, S_t = the stock price at expiration, X = the strike price, r = the risk-free interest rate, and t = the time to maturity in fractions of a year.

net cash flows are simply the sum of all cash flows from the investment. For example, the net cash flow in column 2 represents the required investment today (if negative) or the cash inflow to the investor (if positive).

Exhibit 13.16 shows that the future net cash flow from this portfolio is zero regardless of the future stock price. (That is, the sums of columns 3 and 4 are zero.) Hence, from capital budgeting, we know that the discounted value of these payoffs (which are zero) is definitely zero (regardless of the discount rate used). Therefore, the cash flow today must be zero, or else there exists a 'money machine'. If the net cash flow today is positive, everyone would want such an investment; the demand for the call options would increase their price, selling short the stock would decrease the price of the stock, and selling the put would decrease the put price. This selling will continue until the cash flow at time 0 is zero and any arbitrage profit vanishes.

PRACTICE BOX

Problem
Using the information in the previous problem on Borland, evaluate whether the put–call parity holds when the strike price is $X = \$40$.

Solution
From Equation 13.9 we know that

$$c_0 - p_0 = S_0 - \frac{X}{(1 + r)^t}$$

and we have $c_0 = \$3^3/_4$, $p_0 = \$1^3/_4$, $S_0 = \$41^7/_8$, $X = \$40$, $r = 3\%$ and $t = {}^1/_{12}$. We need to evaluate whether the following equality exists:

$$\$3.75 - \$1.75 \cong \$41.875 - \$39.9$$

$$\$2 \neq \$1.975$$

Thus, put–call parity does not hold precisely. However, it would probably be impossible to profit from this discrepancy because of transaction costs. In practice, put–call parity holds very closely.

13.8 BLACK–SCHOLES OPTION PRICING MODEL (BSOPM)

The Black–Scholes option pricing model (BSOPM) was developed in a famous paper published by Fischer Black and Myron Scholes in 1973 in the *Journal of Political Economy*. The BSOPM was distinct from other, similar models proposed in the late 1960s and early 1970s in that the option price does not depend on the expected returns of the underlying stock. Moreover, the model is based on a creation of a fully hedged position; thus, the riskless asset is employed to discount the future cash flows.

To better understand the usefulness and limitations of the BSOPM, let us examine the primary assumptions required for the BSOPM to be developed:

1 The market is frictionless.
2 Investors are price takers.
3 Short selling is allowed, with full use of the proceeds.
4 Borrowing and lending occur at the risk-free rate, which is continuously compounded.
5 Stock price movements are such that past price movements cannot be used to forecast future price changes.

A **frictionless market** is a market where trading is costless; there are no taxes, bid–ask spreads, brokerage commissions, and so forth. The second assumption means that no single investor can significantly influence prices. As discussed in Chapter 3, short selling is selling stock that you do not own with the understanding that you will return stock to the lender in the future.

The assumption that the risk-free interest rate is compounded continuously is made for convenience and conforms with standard practice. The fifth assumption determines the stock price distribution. The assumption that the stock price movement in the future cannot be predicted from the past is used by Black and Scholes, when obtaining the BSOPM.

13.8.1 Call options

Black and Scholes used the assumptions to develop a model for pricing call options. At first glance, the BSOPM looks difficult. However, a familiarity with the symbols and steps required to systematically solve pricing problems, as well as software packages, makes the BSOPM easier to use.

The BSOPM for call options is as follows:

$$c = SN(d_1) - Xe^{-r_c t}N(d_2) \tag{13.10}$$

where

$$d_1 = \frac{\ln(S/X) + [r_c + (\sigma^2)/2]t}{\sigma\sqrt{t}}$$

$$d_2 = \frac{\ln(S/X) - [r_c + (\sigma^2/2)]t}{\sigma\sqrt{t}} = d_1 - \sigma\sqrt{t}$$

$N(d)$ is the cumulative area of the *standard normal distribution*. For example, if $d_1 = 1.645$, then using the normal distribution, the cumulative areas up to 1.645 (which is the intersection of 1.600 in the vertical column and 0.045 on the horizontal column of Exhibit 13.17) are 95%. Hence, $N(d_1) = 0.95$ (see Exhibit 13.17). Thus, the area under the normal curve right to d_1 is 0.05. Suppose that $\sigma = 24.5\%$, or 0.245, and

Exhibit 13.17 Values for N(d) given d

d	Second decimal of d																			
	0.0000	0.0050	0.0100	0.0150	0.0200	0.0250	0.0300	0.0350	0.0400	0.0450	0.0500	0.0550	0.0600	0.0650	0.0700	0.0750	0.0800	0.0850	0.0900	0.0950
−2.9000	0.0019	0.0018	0.0018	0.0018	0.0018	0.0017	0.0017	0.0017	0.0016	0.0016	0.0016	0.0016	0.0015	0.0015	0.0015	0.0015	0.0014	0.0014	0.0014	0.0014
−2.8000	0.0026	0.0025	0.0025	0.0024	0.0024	0.0024	0.0023	0.0023	0.0023	0.0022	0.0022	0.0022	0.0021	0.0021	0.0021	0.0020	0.0020	0.0020	0.0019	0.0019
−2.7000	0.0035	0.0034	0.0034	0.0033	0.0033	0.0032	0.0032	0.0031	0.0031	0.0030	0.0030	0.0029	0.0029	0.0028	0.0028	0.0028	0.0027	0.0027	0.0026	0.0026
−2.6000	0.0047	0.0046	0.0045	0.0045	0.0044	0.0043	0.0043	0.0042	0.0041	0.0041	0.0040	0.0040	0.0039	0.0038	0.0038	0.0037	0.0037	0.0036	0.0036	0.0035
−2.5000	0.0062	0.0061	0.0060	0.0060	0.0059	0.0058	0.0057	0.0056	0.0055	0.0055	0.0054	0.0053	0.0052	0.0052	0.0051	0.0050	0.0049	0.0049	0.0048	0.0047
−2.4000	0.0082	0.0081	0.0080	0.0079	0.0078	0.0077	0.0075	0.0074	0.0073	0.0072	0.0071	0.0070	0.0069	0.0069	0.0068	0.0067	0.0066	0.0065	0.0064	0.0063
−2.3000	0.0107	0.0106	0.0104	0.0103	0.0102	0.0100	0.0099	0.0098	0.0096	0.0095	0.0094	0.0093	0.0091	0.0090	0.0089	0.0088	0.0087	0.0085	0.0084	0.0083
−2.2000	0.0139	0.0137	0.0136	0.0134	0.0132	0.0130	0.0129	0.0127	0.0125	0.0124	0.0122	0.0121	0.0119	0.0118	0.0116	0.0115	0.0113	0.0112	0.0110	0.0109
−2.1000	0.0179	0.0176	0.0174	0.0172	0.0170	0.0168	0.0166	0.0164	0.0162	0.0160	0.0158	0.0156	0.0154	0.0152	0.0150	0.0148	0.0146	0.0144	0.0143	0.0141
−2.0000	0.0228	0.0225	0.0222	0.0220	0.0217	0.0214	0.0212	0.0209	0.0207	0.0204	0.0202	0.0199	0.0197	0.0195	0.0192	0.0190	0.0188	0.0185	0.0183	0.0181
−1.9000	0.0287	0.0284	0.0281	0.0277	0.0274	0.0271	0.0268	0.0265	0.0262	0.0259	0.0256	0.0253	0.0250	0.0247	0.0244	0.0241	0.0239	0.0236	0.0233	0.0230
−1.8000	0.0359	0.0355	0.0351	0.0348	0.0344	0.0340	0.0336	0.0333	0.0329	0.0325	0.0322	0.0318	0.0314	0.0311	0.0307	0.0304	0.0301	0.0297	0.0294	0.0290
−1.7000	0.0446	0.0441	0.0436	0.0432	0.0427	0.0423	0.0418	0.0414	0.0409	0.0405	0.0401	0.0396	0.0392	0.0388	0.0384	0.0379	0.0375	0.0371	0.0367	0.0363
−1.6000	0.0548	0.0542	0.0537	0.0532	0.0526	0.0521	0.0516	0.0510	0.0505	0.0500	0.0495	0.0490	0.0485	0.0480	0.0475	0.0470	0.0465	0.0460	0.0455	0.0450
−1.5000	0.0668	0.0662	0.0655	0.0649	0.0643	0.0636	0.0630	0.0624	0.0618	0.0612	0.0606	0.0600	0.0594	0.0588	0.0582	0.0576	0.0571	0.0565	0.0559	0.0554
−1.4000	0.0808	0.0800	0.0793	0.0785	0.0778	0.0771	0.0764	0.0756	0.0749	0.0742	0.0735	0.0728	0.0721	0.0715	0.0708	0.0701	0.0694	0.0688	0.0681	0.0675
−1.3000	0.0968	0.0959	0.0951	0.0943	0.0934	0.0926	0.0918	0.0909	0.0901	0.0893	0.0885	0.0877	0.0869	0.0861	0.0853	0.0846	0.0838	0.0830	0.0823	0.0815
−1.2000	0.1151	0.1141	0.1131	0.1122	0.1112	0.1103	0.1093	0.1084	0.1075	0.1066	0.1056	0.1047	0.1038	0.1029	0.1020	0.1012	0.1003	0.0994	0.0985	0.0977
−1.1000	0.1357	0.1346	0.1335	0.1324	0.1314	0.1303	0.1292	0.1282	0.1271	0.1261	0.1251	0.1240	0.1230	0.1220	0.1210	0.1200	0.1190	0.1180	0.1170	0.1160
−1.0000	0.1587	0.1574	0.1562	0.1551	0.1539	0.1527	0.1515	0.1503	0.1492	0.1480	0.1469	0.1457	0.1446	0.1434	0.1423	0.1412	0.1401	0.1390	0.1379	0.1368
−0.9000	0.1841	0.1827	0.1814	0.1801	0.1788	0.1775	0.1762	0.1749	0.1736	0.1723	0.1711	0.1698	0.1685	0.1673	0.1660	0.1648	0.1635	0.1623	0.1611	0.1599
−0.8000	0.2119	0.2104	0.2090	0.2075	0.2061	0.2047	0.2033	0.2019	0.2005	0.1991	0.1977	0.1963	0.1949	0.1935	0.1921	0.1908	0.1894	0.1881	0.1867	0.1854
−0.7000	0.2420	0.2404	0.2389	0.2373	0.2358	0.2342	0.2327	0.2312	0.2296	0.2281	0.2266	0.2251	0.2236	0.2221	0.2206	0.2192	0.2177	0.2162	0.2148	0.2133
−0.6000	0.2743	0.2726	0.2709	0.2693	0.2676	0.2660	0.2643	0.2627	0.2611	0.2595	0.2578	0.2562	0.2546	0.2530	0.2514	0.2498	0.2483	0.2467	0.2451	0.2435
−0.5000	0.3085	0.3068	0.3050	0.3033	0.3015	0.2998	0.2981	0.2963	0.2946	0.2929	0.2912	0.2894	0.2877	0.2860	0.2843	0.2826	0.2810	0.2793	0.2776	0.2759
−0.4000	0.3446	0.3427	0.3409	0.3391	0.3372	0.3354	0.3336	0.3318	0.3300	0.3282	0.3264	0.3246	0.3228	0.3210	0.3192	0.3174	0.3156	0.3138	0.3121	0.3103
−0.3000	0.3821	0.3802	0.3783	0.3764	0.3745	0.3726	0.3707	0.3688	0.3669	0.3650	0.3632	0.3613	0.3594	0.3576	0.3557	0.3538	0.3520	0.3501	0.3483	0.3464
−0.2000	0.4207	0.4188	0.4168	0.4149	0.4129	0.4110	0.4090	0.4071	0.4052	0.4032	0.4013	0.3994	0.3974	0.3955	0.3936	0.3917	0.3897	0.3878	0.3859	0.3840
−0.1000	0.4602	0.4582	0.4562	0.4542	0.4522	0.4503	0.4483	0.4463	0.4443	0.4424	0.4404	0.4384	0.4364	0.4345	0.4325	0.4305	0.4286	0.4266	0.4247	0.4227

Exhibit 13.17 (continued)

Second decimal of d

d	0.0000	0.0050	0.0100	0.0150	0.0200	0.0250	0.0300	0.0350	0.0400	0.0450	0.0500	0.0550	0.0600	0.0650	0.0700	0.0750	0.0800	0.0850	0.0900	0.0950
0.0000	0.5000	0.5020	0.5040	0.5060	0.5080	0.5100	0.5120	0.5140	0.5160	0.5179	0.5199	0.5219	0.5239	0.5259	0.5279	0.5299	0.5319	0.5339	0.5359	0.5378
0.1000	0.5398	0.5418	0.5438	0.5458	0.5478	0.5497	0.5517	0.5537	0.5557	0.5576	0.5596	0.5616	0.5636	0.5655	0.5675	0.5695	0.5714	0.5734	0.5753	0.5773
0.2000	0.5793	0.5812	0.5832	0.5851	0.5871	0.5890	0.5910	0.5929	0.5948	0.5968	0.5987	0.6006	0.6026	0.6045	0.6064	0.6083	0.6103	0.6122	0.6141	0.6160
0.3000	0.6179	0.6198	0.6217	0.6236	0.6255	0.6274	0.6293	0.6312	0.6331	0.6350	0.6368	0.6387	0.6406	0.6424	0.6443	0.6462	0.6480	0.6499	0.6517	0.6536
0.4000	0.6554	0.6573	0.6591	0.6609	0.6628	0.6646	0.6664	0.6682	0.6700	0.6718	0.6736	0.6754	0.6772	0.6790	0.6808	0.6826	0.6844	0.6862	0.6879	0.6897
0.5000	0.6915	0.6932	0.6950	0.6967	0.6985	0.7002	0.7019	0.7037	0.7054	0.7071	0.7088	0.7106	0.7123	0.7140	0.7157	0.7174	0.7190	0.7207	0.7224	0.7241
0.6000	0.7257	0.7274	0.7291	0.7307	0.7324	0.7340	0.7357	0.7373	0.7389	0.7405	0.7422	0.7438	0.7454	0.7470	0.7486	0.7502	0.7517	0.7533	0.7549	0.7565
0.7000	0.7580	0.7596	0.7611	0.7627	0.7642	0.7658	0.7673	0.7688	0.7703	0.7719	0.7734	0.7749	0.7764	0.7779	0.7793	0.7808	0.7823	0.7838	0.7852	0.7867
0.8000	0.7881	0.7896	0.7910	0.7925	0.7939	0.7953	0.7967	0.7981	0.7995	0.8009	0.8023	0.8037	0.8051	0.8065	0.8078	0.8092	0.8106	0.8119	0.8133	0.8146
0.9000	0.8159	0.8173	0.8186	0.8199	0.8212	0.8225	0.8238	0.8251	0.8264	0.8277	0.8289	0.8302	0.8315	0.8327	0.8340	0.8352	0.8356	0.8377	0.8389	0.8401
1.0000	0.8413	0.8426	0.8438	0.8449	0.8461	0.8473	0.8485	0.8497	0.8508	0.8520	0.8531	0.8543	0.8554	0.8566	0.8577	0.8588	0.8599	0.8610	0.8621	0.8632
1.1000	0.8643	0.8654	0.8665	0.8676	0.8686	0.8697	0.8708	0.8718	0.8729	0.8739	0.8749	0.8760	0.8770	0.8780	0.8790	0.8800	0.8810	0.8820	0.8830	0.8840
1.2000	0.8849	0.8859	0.8869	0.8878	0.8888	0.8897	0.8907	0.8916	0.8925	0.8934	0.8944	0.8953	0.8962	0.8971	0.8980	0.8988	0.8997	0.9006	0.9015	0.9023
1.3000	0.9032	0.9041	0.9049	0.9057	0.9066	0.9074	0.9082	0.9091	0.9099	0.9107	0.9115	0.9123	0.9131	0.9139	0.9147	0.9154	0.9162	0.9170	0.9177	0.9185
1.4000	0.9192	0.9200	0.9207	0.9215	0.9222	0.9229	0.9236	0.9244	0.9251	0.9258	0.9265	0.9272	0.9279	0.9285	0.9292	0.9299	0.9306	0.9312	0.9319	0.9325
1.5000	0.9332	0.9338	0.9345	0.9351	0.9357	0.9364	0.9370	0.9376	0.9382	0.9388	0.9394	0.9400	0.9406	0.9412	0.9418	0.9424	0.9429	0.9435	0.9441	0.9446
1.6000	0.9452	0.9458	0.9463	0.9468	0.9474	0.9479	0.9484	0.9490	0.9495	0.9500	0.9505	0.9510	0.9515	0.9520	0.9525	0.9530	0.9535	0.9540	0.9545	0.9550
1.7000	0.9554	0.9559	0.9564	0.9568	0.9573	0.9577	0.9582	0.9586	0.9591	0.9595	0.9599	0.9604	0.9608	0.9612	0.9616	0.9621	0.9625	0.9629	0.9633	0.9637
1.8000	0.9641	0.9645	0.9649	0.9652	0.9656	0.9660	0.9664	0.9667	0.9671	0.9675	0.9678	0.9682	0.9686	0.9689	0.9693	0.9696	0.9699	0.9703	0.9706	0.9710
1.9000	0.9713	0.9716	0.9719	0.9723	0.9726	0.9729	0.9732	0.9735	0.9738	0.9741	0.9744	0.9747	0.9750	0.9753	0.9756	0.9759	0.9761	0.9764	0.9767	0.9770
2.0000	0.9772	0.9775	0.9778	0.9780	0.9783	0.9786	0.9788	0.9791	0.9793	0.9796	0.9798	0.9801	0.9803	0.9805	0.9808	0.9810	0.9812	0.9815	0.9817	0.9819
2.1000	0.9821	0.9824	0.9826	0.9828	0.9830	0.9832	0.9834	0.9836	0.9838	0.9840	0.9842	0.9844	0.9846	0.9848	0.9850	0.9852	0.9854	0.9856	0.9857	0.9859
2.2000	0.9861	0.9863	0.9864	0.9866	0.9868	0.9870	0.9871	0.9873	0.9875	0.9876	0.9878	0.9879	0.9881	0.9882	0.9884	0.9885	0.9887	0.9888	0.9890	0.9891
2.3000	0.9893	0.9894	0.9896	0.9897	0.9898	0.9900	0.9901	0.9902	0.9904	0.9905	0.9906	0.9907	0.9909	0.9910	0.9911	0.9912	0.9913	0.9915	0.9916	0.9917
2.4000	0.9918	0.9919	0.9920	0.9921	0.9922	0.9923	0.9925	0.9926	0.9927	0.9928	0.9929	0.9930	0.9931	0.9931	0.9932	0.9933	0.9934	0.9935	0.9936	0.9937
2.5000	0.9938	0.9939	0.9940	0.9940	0.9941	0.9942	0.9943	0.9944	0.9945	0.9945	0.9946	0.9947	0.9948	0.9948	0.9949	0.9950	0.9951	0.9951	0.9952	0.9953
2.6000	0.9953	0.9954	0.9955	0.9955	0.9956	0.9957	0.9957	0.9958	0.9959	0.9959	0.9960	0.9960	0.9961	0.9962	0.9962	0.9963	0.9963	0.9964	0.9964	0.9965
2.7000	0.9965	0.9966	0.9966	0.9967	0.9967	0.9968	0.9968	0.9969	0.9969	0.9970	0.9970	0.9971	0.9971	0.9972	0.9972	0.9972	0.9973	0.9973	0.9974	0.9974
2.8000	0.9974	0.9975	0.9975	0.9976	0.9976	0.9976	0.9977	0.9977	0.9977	0.9978	0.9978	0.9978	0.9979	0.9979	0.9979	0.9980	0.9980	0.9980	0.9981	0.9981
2.9000	0.9981	0.9982	0.9982	0.9982	0.9982	0.9983	0.9983	0.9983	0.9984	0.9984	0.9984	0.9984	0.9985	0.9985	0.9985	0.9985	0.9986	0.9986	0.9986	0.9986

$t = 1$. Then $d_2 = d_1 - \sigma\sqrt{t} = 1.645 - 0.245 = 1.400$, and the cumulative area up to $d_2 = 1.400$ is about 92%. Hence, $N(d_2) \cong 0.92$, and the area right of d_2 is about 0.08. Thus, the area between d_2 and d_1 is about 3%, or 0.03.

The other parameters of Equation 13.10 are as follows: ln( ) is the natural logarithm; σ is the continuously compounded, annualized standard deviation of stock returns; r_c is the continuously compounded, annual risk-free interest rate; t is the time to maturity as a fraction of a year (with some software, we need to plug in t as the number of days to expiration); X is the strike price; S is the current stock price; and e is the base of natural logarithms and is equal to 2.7128. Thus, we need five variables (σ, r_c, t, X and S) to calculate the price of a call option using the BSOPM (for the calculation of r_c and σ on a continuous basis, see Appendix 13C and Appendix 13D, respectively).

Calculating the call option price is easy with the available software. All we have to do is to insert S, X, σ, r_c and t (in some software, t is given in days to expiration – for example, 182 days – rather than as a fraction of a year) and the call option price, c, then appears on the screen. However, tables with $N(d_1)$ and $N(d_2)$ are also available. We can use them along with a calculator to derive c. For example, suppose we are given the following parameters: $S = \$100.0$, $X = \$100.0$, $\sigma = 30\%$, $r_c = 7\%$ and $t = 182$ days (about $^1/_2$ year). The use of a software package reveals that $c = \$10.12$.

Using EXCEL and inserting d_1 and d_2, we obtain (without a need for tables) the values of $N(d_1)$ and $N(d_2)$. Then it is simple to obtain c by inserting these values in Equation 13.10.

13.8.2 Put options

The appropriate formula for put options can be found using the BSOPM for call options and put-call parity. Rearranging Equation 13.9 (with continuous compounding rather than discrete compounding) yields the following:

$$P = C - S + Xe^{-r_c t} \tag{13.11}$$

13.8.3 Estimating inputs to the BSOPM

There are five input parameters in the BSOPM: S, X, t, r_c and σ. The current stock price (S) is easily obtainable by calling a broker, by some Internet sites, or by contacting an information service, such as Reuters or Telerate. The strike price (X) is specified in the options contract and published in the financial media, such as the *Wall Street Journal* and *Barron's*.

Time to maturity (t) is the fraction of the year remaining until the option expires. There is some debate on whether the year should be measured in business days (days when the market is open, which is approximately 20 days per month) or calendar days. The consensus appears to be calendar days. Hence, if there are 73 calendar days before expiration, then $t = 73/365 = 0.20$ (assuming that the year is not a leap year).

The risk-free interest rate (r_c) is slightly more difficult to estimate. We know that we should use fixed-income securities that are default-free, such as US or UK Treasury bills. Thus, the appropriate rate to employ is the continuously compounded yield to maturity closest to the option maturity date. For example, if the option is for $t = ^1/_5$ of a year, then we want a Treasury bill that pays \$1 in $^1/_5$ of a year that is trading now for P_B (the price of the bill). Mathematically, we have the following relationship:

$$P_B = 1 \times e^{-r_c \times 1/5} = e^{-r_c/5}$$

or

$$\ln(p_B) = -r_c/5$$

and, solving for r_c,

$$r_c = -\frac{\ln(P_B)}{t} = -\frac{\ln(P_B)}{1/5}$$

Thus, for the observed price P_B, we can solve for r_c. Appendix 13D elaborates on the relationship between the discrete and continuous interest rates.

The last and most difficult parameter to estimate is the volatility of stock returns, which is measured by σ. There are several methods to estimate volatility, including the use of historical return data. Recall that the standard deviation of returns is calculated based on the following equation:

$$\sigma = \sqrt{\frac{1}{n}\sum_{t=1}^{n}(R_t - \overline{R})^2}$$

where R_t is the continuously compounded rate of return.

An alternative method is estimating the implied volatility of stock returns by basically turning the BSOPM around and finding the volatility that gives the current option price. However, this procedure assumes that the call price is given as observed in the market. Calculating manually the **implied volatility** is difficult, but software that computes these values swiftly is available.

The B&S formula has its problems too, as asserted by Kyle Rosen, a portfolio manager:

> 'Black–Scholes works great when the markets are quiet, but when turmoil hits, it gets thrown out the window.' Prices explode too fast, as they did Monday, for anyone to sit patiently plugging numbers into a model. And the quickest reflexes in the world can't change things, particularly if accurate quotes aren't available, as was the case during the fast-moving markets, and if it takes more than an hour to open trading in an option, such as it did on the Philadelphia Stock Exchange on Tuesday and Thursday in Dell Computer.'

> *Source*: Sandra Ward, *Barron's*, 3 November 1997, p. MW17. Reprinted by permission of *Barron's*, © 1997 Dow Jones & Co., Inc. All Rights Reserved Worldwide.

13.8.4 Valuing portfolio insurance using the BSOPM

One benefit of the BSOPM is the ability to estimate the cost of engaging in various risk management strategies. Recall that protective put buying is the strategy of buying puts on the underlying portfolio and is one form of portfolio insurance. **Portfolio insurance** is any strategy in which the maximum loss is set or determined in advance.

Suppose you are a portfolio manager responsible for a $100 million stock portfolio that closely resembles the Standard & Poor's 500 (S&P 500) stock index. Because of an unprecedented rise in stock prices, you are concerned that recent gains will be lost in another 'crash' like the ones that occurred in October 1987, October 1997, August 1998 and November 2001. Of course, if you wanted to guarantee no loss at all, you would have to pay a high price for the insurance. For example, you might buy a put option on your portfolio with a strike price of $100 million. Then, no matter what the value of your portfolio became, you would be guaranteed to have a value no less than your original $100 million minus the cost of the put option.

More realistically, suppose you allow for some loss – say, not more than 10%. Suppose it is now August, and you are considering 'insuring' your portfolio risk for

182 days. How much should such a put option cost? If current interest rates are around 7% and the S&P 500 index has a volatility of 20%, how much should the insurance cost? Without option pricing analysis, this would be a difficult problem to solve.

Because this type of portfolio insurance is nothing more than buying a put option, you can employ the BSOPM for puts. The inputs are $S = \$100$ million, $X = \$90$ million (or 10% loss), $r_c = 7\%$, $\sigma = 20\%$ and $t = 182$ days (or about $^1/_2$ year).

Using a software package, you find that according to the BSOPM, the insurance policy should cost $1,127,709.50. Hence, the fair value for this insurance policy is $1,127,709.50, or about only 1.1% of the portfolio value. Thus, if there is a crash in the market and the market value of your portfolio goes down to $70 million, you sell the put option for $20 million (which is the strike, $90 million less $70 million). After the cost of the put option, you have $90,000,000 − $1,127,709.50 = $88,872,290.50. If, in contrast, the value of the portfolio goes up to $110 million the option expires worthless. What is left in this case is $110,000,000 − $1,127,709.50 = $108,872,290.50. Thus, you have established a floor on your losses at the cost of some of the gains if prices rise.

SUMMARY

■ *Name the benefits of modern option contracts.*
Although options have been around for a long time, they were not actively traded until 1973. In that year the Chicago Board Options Exchange introduced an option contract that was standardized, was transferable, and provided insurance against defaults of option writers. Since 1973, the growth of option trading has been phenomenal.

■ *Understand the process of buying and selling of put and call options.*
An option buyer has the right, but not the obligation, to exercise the option in the future. A call option buyer has the right to buy stock in the future at a stated price, whereas a put option buyer has the right to sell stock in the future at a stated price. An active secondary market allows option investors to get out of an option trade if they so desire and accept the current market price.

■ *Explain the risk of holding naked options.*
Writing a call option without owning the underlying asset is very risky and hence exposes the writer to great risk.

■ *Describe the role of option clearing corporations.*
Clearing corporations protect option buyers from the consequences of a default by an option writer. They also issue option contracts, maintain appropriate records, and process all the necessary financial transactions.

■ *Explain how margin requirements on option writers protect buyers from default.*
Option clearing corporations require option writers to post and maintain adequate collateral to cover potential losses. The OCC issues all options contracts and guarantees both sides of the contracts. The OCC is owned by several exchanges, such as the CBOE, AMEX and NYSE.

■ *Use payoff diagrams to determine the value of an option upon expiration.*
The value of an option at expiration is its intrinsic value. With this observation, investors can examine a wide array of alternative risk–return trade-offs using payoff diagrams. A payoff diagram is a graphical means of illustrating the relationship among the dollar profit or loss (the P/L line), when the price of the underlying asset changes.

■ *Identify profitable option strategies based on beliefs about future asset price movements.* Protective put buying sets a floor on potential losses, whereas covered call writing sets a ceiling on potential gains.

QUESTIONS

13.1 Why was option trading thin between 1934 and 1973?

13.2 Why was 1973 such a pivotal year in option trading history?

13.3 What is the difference between an opening option transaction and a closing option transaction?

13.4 What is the difference between European-style options and American-style options?

13.5 If $S_0 = \$100$ and $X = \$90$, are puts in the money or out of the money? What about calls?

13.6 Can option prices be negative? Explain your answer.

13.7 If $S_0 = \$120$ and $X = \$130$, what is the intrinsic value of puts and calls? Given that the call price is c_0 and the put price is p_0, write the time value of the put and call in terms of p_0 and c_0.

13.8 Is it possible that a put and a call option on the same stock with the same strike price would have the same time value? Could they have the same intrinsic value?

13.9 Using payoff diagrams, describe the difference between being long a call at the money and being short a put at the money.

13.10 'A call buyer who buys a call for $c = \$10$ does not need to deposit any initial margin.' Do you agree with this assertion? Explain.

13.11 Describe in nonfinance terms (to your non-business major friend) what could be the motivation behind selling naked positions in options.

Questions 13.12 through 13.16 are based on the information about Microsoft in the following table:

Microsoft's option data

Option and NY close	Strike price	Calls–settle			Puts–settle		
		June	July	October	June	July	October
$100^3/_4$	$95	$5^7/_8$	$8^3/_4$	$12^3/_8$	$1/_{16}$	$2^3/_8$	$5^1/_2$
$100^3/_4$	100	$1^5/_8$	$5^1/_2$	$10^3/_8$	$3/_4$	4	$7^5/_8$
$100^3/_4$	105	$1/_8$	$3^1/_4$	$8^5/_8$	$4^1/_2$	$6^3/_4$	$11^1/_8$

13.12 Draw the payoff diagram (profit and loss line only) for long July calls for all strike prices ($95, $100 and $105) on one graph. Be sure to identify the exact breakeven point. Describe the relative costs and benefits of each strategy.

13.13 Draw the payoff diagram (profit and loss line only) for long July puts for all three strike prices ($95, $100 and $105) on one graph. Be sure to identify the exact breakeven point. Describe the relative costs and benefits of each strategy.

13.14 Create two tables similar to the one given for Microsoft, except that one table has the time value, and the other table has the intrinsic value. What general inferences can you draw about time value from your table?

13.15 Suppose the stock price is $100 and the call price is $5 with a strike price of $105. What is the profit or loss on the following two strategies when the stock price goes up to $110 *and* when the stock goes down to $90?

(a) Write a call option.
(b) Write a covered call option; that is, write a call and buy a stock.

13.16 Suppose the call price is c_0 = $10, the stock price is $100, and the strike price is X = $95.

(a) Calculate the initial margin for selling a call option.
(b) Suppose now that the stock price goes up to $120, and the call price falls to $1. What is the maintenance margin required?

13.17 Refer to the following table. Suppose you buy a call option for $6^3/_4$ that matures in June with a strike price of $65.

Pfizer stock price	Strike price	Calls–settle June
$69^1/_2$	65	$6^3/_4$
$69^1/_2$	70	$3^1/_2$
$69^1/_2$	75	$1^3/_4$

(a) What is your dollar profit if the stock price in June is $70? What if it is $50?
(b) Calculate the rate of return.

13.18 Referring to the following table, suppose you buy a put option for that matures in June with a strike price of $65.

Pfizer stock price	Strike price	Puts–settle June
$69^1/_2$	65	$1^5/_8$
$69^1/_2$	70	$3^1/_2$
$69^1/_2$	75	$6^3/_4$

(a) What is your dollar profit if the stock price in June is $70? What if it is $50?
(b) Calculate the rate of return.

13.19 Referring to the data in Question 13.18, suppose that in June the stock price falls to $60. Calculate your dollar profit and rate of return for the following strategies:

(a) Buy one stock for $69^1/_2$ and one put option with a June maturity and a strike price of $65.

(b) Buy one stock and two put options with a June maturity and a strike price of $65.

13.20 Repeat Question 13.19, but this time in June the stock price jumps to $75. Compare and analyse the results of Questions 13.18 and 13.19.

13.21 Prove that $c_0 \leq S_0$ is the call price's upper boundary, using an arbitrage table.

13.22 Prove that $p_0 \geq$ max $[0, X/(1 + r)^t - S_0]$ is the put price's lower boundary, using an arbitrage table.

13.23 Prove that $p_0 \leq X/(1 + r)^t$, the put price's lower boundary, using an arbitrage table.

13.24 Is the value of $N(d_1)$ always greater than the value of $N(d_2)$? Explain.

13.25 Suppose you work for an express mail service that will purchase 10 million gallons of gasoline in three months. Assume that a gallon of gas costs $1.00 wholesale, and you wish to guarantee a maximum price of $1.10. Also, you feel that gasoline price volatility is about 25%, and the six-month interest rate is 7% (annualized). Assuming that the BSOPM is valid, how much would it cost to hedge 10 million gallons of gas with options? What is the appropriate option strategy? (Assume that a gas option contract exists on an exchange.)

13.26 What is the price of a call option if $S_0 = \$25$, $X = \$20$, $r = 10\%$, $t = {}^1/_2$, and the put option value is $p = \$1.50$? (Make whatever assumptions are necessary.)

13.27 Suppose the interest rate decreases from 5% to 1%. How should this affect the lower boundary of a call option when $S_0 = \$100$, $X = \$80$, and $t = {}^1/_2$? How will this affect the lower boundary for a put option?

13.28 Based on the following information from *Barron's*, verify that the closing prices of Coke's put and call options satisfy the boundary conditions. The time to maturity is five months ($t = {}^5/_{12}$), Coke's stock price is $41, and the annual risk-free interest rate is 3%.

Expiration date and strike price	Closing price
Coke May 40 call	$3^3/_4$
Coke May 40 put	$1^1/_2$
Coke May 45 call	1
Coke May 45 put	$4^1/_4$

13.29 Suppose there are puts and calls on IBM stock with the same strike price and the same maturity. You observe that $c_0 = p_0$, and the interest rate for the period remaining until expiration is 5%. Is the call option in the money, at the money or out of the money? Is the put option in the money or out of the money? Explain.

13.30 Suppose $\sigma = 35\%$, $S_0 = \$100$, $X = \$100$, $r_c = 5\%$ and $t = {}^1/_2$. Calculate the Black–Scholes call and put option prices.

13.31 Suppose the standard deviation is $\sigma = 35\%$, $S_0 = \$58$, $X = \$55$, $r_c = 4\%$ and $t = {}^1/_2$. Calculate the Black–Scholes call and put option prices.

13.32 Suppose the standard deviation is $\sigma = 30\%$, $S_0 = \$100$, $X = \$100$, $r_c = 5\%$ and $t = {}^1/_2$. Calculate the Black–Scholes call and put option prices.

13.33 Suppose you manage a portfolio of $100 million. You estimate that there is a probability of 20% that the portfolio value will go to $80 million next year and a probability of 80% that it will go to $120 million. If the value is less than $90 million, you will be fired. How can you protect yourself with put options?

SELECTED REFERENCES

Chance, Don M. *An Introduction to Options and Futures*. 2nd edn. New York: Dryden Press, 1991.
This text provides a good introduction to options and other derivative securities.

Danielsen, Barley R., and Sorin M. Sorescu. 'Why do option introductions depress stock prices? A study of diminishing short-sale constraints'. *Journal of Financial and Quantitative Analysis*, forthcoming.

Hull, John, C. *Options, Futures and Other Derivative Securities*. 2nd edn. Englewood Cliffs, NJ: Prentice-Hall, 1993.
This text presents a more advanced introduction to options and other derivative securities.

Isakov, D. and B. Morard. 'Improving portfolio performance with option strategies: evidence from Switzerland'. *European Financial Management*, Vol. 7, 2001.

Peoa, I., G. Rubio, and G. Serna. 'Smiles, bid-ask spreads and option pricing,' *European Financial Management*, Vol. 7, Issue 3, 2001.

Yang, H.L., and T.K. Siu. 'Coherent risk measures for derivatives under Black-Scholes economy'. *European Financial Management*, Vol. 7, Issue 3, 2001.

SUPPLEMENTARY REFERENCES

Black, Fischer, and Myron Scholes. 'The pricing of options and corporate liabilities'. *Journal of Political Economy*, 81, May–June 1973, pp. 637–54.

Bookstaber, Richard M. *Option Pricing and Investment Strategy*. 3rd edn. Chicago: Probus Publishing, 1991.

Cox, John C., Stephen A. Ross, and Mark Rubinstein. 'Option pricing: a simplified approach'. *Journal of Financial Economics*, 7, September 1979, pp. 229–63.

Cox, John C. and Mark Rubinstein. *Options Markets*. Englewood Cliffs, NJ: Prentice-Hall, 1985.

Fabozzi, Frank J. (ed.) *The Handbook of Fixed-Income Options Pricing, Strategies & Applications*. Chicago: Probus Publishing, 1989.

Foglewski, Stephen, William L. Silber, and Marti G. Subrahmanyam (eds). *Financial Options from Theory to Practice*. Homewood, IL: Business One Irwin, 1990.

Gibson, Rajna, *Option Valuation Analyzing and Pricing Standardized Option Contracts*. New York: McGraw-Hill, 1991.

Konishi, Atsuo, and Ravi E. Dattatreva (eds.). *The Handbook of Derivative Instruments*. Chicago: Probus Publishing, 1991.

McLean, Stuart K. (ed.). *The European Options and Futures Markets*. Chicago: Probus Publishing, 1991.

Merton, Robert. 'Theory of rational option pricing'. *Bell Journal of Economics and Management Science*, 4, Spring 1973, pp. 141–83.

Options Institute (ed.). *Options: Essential Concepts and Trading Strategies*. Homewood, IL: Business One Irwin, 1990.

Robertson, Malcolm J. *Directory of World Futures and Options*. Englewood Cliffs, NJ: Prentice-Hall, 1990.

Smith, Clifford W., Jr., and Charles W. Smithson. *The Handbook of Financial Engineering*. New York: Harper Business, 1990.

Smith, Clifford W., Jr., Charles W. Smithson, and D. Wilford Sykes. *Managing Financial Risk*. New York: Harper & Row, 1990.

Tsiveriotis, K., and N. Chriss. 'Pricing with a difference'. *Risk*, February 1998.

Appendix 13A	TAXES

The tax consequences of option trading depend on a number of factors, such as the tax status of the investor, the underlying interest involved, whether the option is exercised or not, whether the position is a covered or an uncovered position, and whether the position is subject to a closing transaction. Taxes are usually paid in the year in which the position is closed. As with all tax laws, however, there are exceptions. For example, index options are mark to market (gains and losses are taxed even if the position is still held) at year-end for tax purposes. As a result, the paper profits and losses are taxed in each year (as opposed to waiting until an offsetting position is taken, as is true with options on individual stocks, such as IBM, AT&T, and so forth).

Suppose you purchased an index option for $500 in June of Year 1 that matures in June of Year 2 (see Exhibit 13A.1). On 31 December the index option is worth $1,100; thus, you have taxable income of $600 ($1,100 − $500) even if you do not sell it. Now further suppose that in Year 2 the option expires worthless. In this case, you have a tax loss of $1,100 ($500 purchase price + $600 gain in Year 1) in Year 2.

Exhibit 13A.1 Example of tax liabilities from option trading with 28% tax bracket

(a) Index options

Date	Action	Option value	Cash flow
June, Year 1	Buy 1 index option	$500	−$500
December, Year 1	Mark to market for tax purposes	1,100	−168[a]
June, Year 2	Option matures out of the money	0	308[b]

[a] −$168 = 0.28($1,100 − $500). Tax on paper gain at year end.
[b] $308 = 0.28 × $1,100. Tax credit on loss of the $1,100.

(b) Stock cost basis via call option

Action	Cost per share
Buy call option ABC 120	$8 + commission
Exercise option	$120
Cost basis for future tax calculation	**$128 + commission**

As Exhibit 13A.1 shows, with options on individual stocks, taxes are paid when the options are sold. However, when options on individual stocks are exercised, the option premium is used to adjust the cost basis, and no taxes are paid until the underlying asset is sold. For example, suppose you paid $8 per share for an option on ABC with a strike price of $120. At the expiration date you exercise your option and purchase ABC at $120. Your cost basis is $128 + commission (see Exhibit 13A.1(b)). Hence, taxable gains will occur only if ABC is subsequently sold for a price above $128 plus commissions.

Appendix 13B   MARGIN REQUIREMENTS

Suppose an investor purchased 100 call option contracts for $5 per share (the total cost would be $50,000 = $5 × 100 shares per contract × 100 contracts), and the stock was in the money $20 on the expiration date (that is $S_0 - X = \$20$). Then the 100 option contracts would be worth $200,000 ($20 × 100 shares per contract × 100 contracts). Will the call writer pay cash to the OCC as a result of the price increase? Yes!

Clearing corporations such as the OCC protect themselves against option writers' defaulting by requiring Clearing Members to provide collateral known as *margin*. These Members in turn require margin from their customers. Margin requirements reduce the incentive of the option writers to default on their obligations. If the writer has posted a substantial amount of collateral, then the writer is less likely to default. The risk of default is intimately related to the volatility of the underlying asset. The more volatile the asset, the higher the risk of default by option writers. For example, in the crashes of October 1987, 1989 and 1997, there were several defaults by option writers. (However, do not forget that option buyers were protected by the guarantees provided by option clearinghouses such as the OCC.)

The risk of default is limited to option writers. The Federal Reserve Board (the regulatory body for US option transactions) allows options to be purchased on margin (by borrowing money). The Federal Reserve Board regulates margin requirements through Regulation T, which covers the extension of credit to customers by security brokers, dealers and members of the national securities exchanges. Regulation T establishes initial margin requirements and defines which securities are eligible to be traded on margin. The brokerage firms have the discretion to require higher margins if they wish. Option buyers must pay for the option in full; this totally eliminates the possibility of default by the option buyer. Thus, option buyers could never default on the contract, because option contracts give the option buyers the right but not the obligation, to do something in the future. Specifically, an option buyer at most could lose the option premium, but the buyer had to pay that up front.

The *initial margin* is money that option writers send to the OCC when they initially sell the specific options. The *maintenance margin* is the dollar amount that must be kept at the OCC throughout the life of the contract. The maintenance margin changes as asset prices change.

Exhibit 13B.1 compares the initial and maintenance requirements for margin accounts for different types of contracts traded on the CBOE. Recall that margin accounts are required to keep securities (or cash) on deposit with the broker as collateral. In the options market, margin implies the money deposited by the option writer as collateral for the potential future liability. As Exhibit 13B.1 illustrates, margin requirements are complex and differ across different types of securities and purposes (long, short and spreads). Margin requirements change with market conditions.

As an illustration, consider writing one call option on the S&P 100 stock index. The option contract is actually for 100 times the index. Index options are *cash settled*, which means that cash, rather than securities in the amount of the intrinsic value of the options, is exchanged at expiration. For example, if the index rises to 470 and the strike price is 370, the index call writer must pay $10,000 [100($470 − $370)].

The formula for finding the margin requirement of the option writer based on Exhibit 13B.1 (see 'Short puts – Index' row and 'Initial margin' column) is as follows:

$$\text{Margin} = \max(A, B)$$

where

Exhibit 13B.1 Initial and maintenance margin requirements

	Option Type	Cash Account Initial Requirement	Margin Account Initial (Maintenance) Requirement
Long Put or Long Call *9 months or less until expiration*	Equity, Broad and Narrow Based Indexes, Interest Rate Options, Long CAPS.	Pay for option in full.	Pay for option in full.
Long Put or Long Call *More than 9 months until expiration*	Equity, Broad and Narrow Based Indexes only [For all other options types, the requirement is the same as for 9 months or less option (above).]	Pay for option in full.	Listed 75% of the total cost (market value) of the option.
Short Put or Short Call	Equity, Broad and Narrow Based Indexes, Interest Rate Composite, Currency and Cross Rate.	Deposit cash or cash equivalents equal to the exercise price or put option deposit letter for short put. Deposit appropriate escrow agreement for short call. Sales proceeds not released until deposit is made. Short Calls are not permitted for Interest Rate options.	100% of the option proceeds plus • 20% of the underlying stock value. • 15% of the underlying broad-based index value. • 20% of the underlying narrow-based index value. • 10% of the underlying aggregate interest rate composite value. • 4% of the underlying currency value (also applies to Cross Rate options). Less out-of-the-money amount, if any, to a minimum for puts (calls) at option proceeds plus • 10% of the exercise price (underlying stock value). • 10% of the exercise price (underlying broad-based index value). • 10% of the exercise price (underlying narrow-based index value). • 5% of the exercise price (underlying aggregate interest rate composite value). • 75% of the exercise price (underlying currency value) (also applies to Cross Rate options). Currency or Cross Rate option requirement may be satisfied with a letter of credit from an approved bank. Cross Rate margin is calculated in the base currency of the contract.
	Capped Index.	Deposit cash, cash equivalents or appropriate escrow receipt equal to the cap interval times the index multiplier.	The lesser of: A: The cap interval times the index multiplier, or B: 100% of the option proceeds plus 15% of the underlying index value less the out-of-the-money amount, if any, to a minimum for puts (calls) of the premium plus 10% of the exercise price (underlying index value).
Short Put and Short Call (Short Capped Index and Short Index permitted)	Equity, Broad and Narrow Based Indexes, Capped Index, Interest Rate Composite, Currency and Rate.	Deposit an escrow agreement for each option. See requirement for appropriate short put/call. Not permitted for Interest Rate options.	For the same underlying • Equity • Capped Index • Currency • Index • Interest Rate Composite • Cross Rate With the same multiplier, short put or short call requirement, whichever is greater, plus the option proceeds of the other side.
Put Spread or Call Spread (long side expires with or after short side, long Capped index vs. short options cannot receive spread treatment	Equity, Broad and Narrow Based Indexes, Capped Index, Interest Rate Composite, Currency and Cross Rate.	Not permitted for American Style options.	For the same underlying • Equity • Capped Index • Currency • Index • Interest Rate Composite • Cross Rate With the same multiplier, the amount by which long put (short call) aggregate exercise price is below short put (long call) aggregate exercise price; long side must be paid for in full.
	Broad and Narrow Based Indexes.	All options must be cash settled European Style options, and all must expire at the same time. Deposit and maintain cash or cash equivalents equal to the amount by which the long put (short call) aggregate exercise price is below the short put (long call) aggregate exercise price. Long side must be paid in full.	See above.
Short Call and Long Underlying (not permitted for CAPS or Interest Rate Composite options)	Equity, Currency and Cross Rate.	Pay for the underlying position in full.	No requirement on short call. 50% requirement on long stock position. 100% requirement on currency position.
	Broad and Narrow Based Indexes.	Not permitted.	No requirement on short call 50% requirement on long underlying stock basket; or unit investment trust or open and mutual fund approved by the Exchanges.
Short Put and Short Underlying (not permitted for CAPS, Interest Rate Composite, Currency or Cross Rate options)	Equity, Broad and Narrow Based Indexes.	Not permitted	No requirement on short put. Short sale proceeds plus 50% requirement on short stock position.

Source: *Pocket Options Margin Guide.* Reprinted with permission of The Options Clearing Corporation.

$$A = c_0 + (0.15 \times 100 \times \text{index}_0) - [100 \times \max(0, X - \text{index}_0)]$$

$$B = c_0 + (0.10 \times 100 \times \text{index}_0)$$

where c_0 is the call price (per 100 units), and $100 \times \max(0, X - \text{index}_0)$ is the out-of-the-money amount. For example, suppose we observe the S&P index at 365, along with a call option with a strike price of $370 and a call price of $900. In this example,

$$A = \$900 + (0.15 \times 100 \times \$365) - \max[0, 100 \times (\$370 - \$365)]$$

$$= \$900 + \$5,475 - \$500 = \$5,875$$

$$B = \$900 + (0.10 \times 100 \times \$365) = \$900 + \$3,650 = \$4,550$$

Hence, the margin is

$$\text{Margin} = \max(\$5,875, \$4,550) = \$5,875$$

To write one call option contract on the S&P index, we are required to post margin of $5,875. This margin is quite a bit more than the possible proceeds of $900. The reason is that if stock prices rise, the option writer must pay the option buyer the difference between the index value and the exercise price. Exhibit 13B.1 shows that for the above specific short positions in options, the maintenance margin is the same as the initial margin. The equations for both A and B above are directly influenced by the value of the index. As the index rises, so does the margin required. For example, if the index rises to 375 and the call price rises to $1,500, then the required maintenance margin is

$$A = \$1,500 + (0.15 \times 100 \times \$375) - \max[0, 100 \times (\$370 - \$375)]$$

$$= \$1,500 + \$5,625 - 0 = \$7,125$$

$$B = \$1,500 + (0.10 \times 100 \times \$375) = \$1,500 + \$3,750 = \$5,250$$

Hence, the margin required is

$$\text{Margin} = \max(\$7,125, \$5,250) = \$7,125$$

Thus, the option writer must place additional monies as margin. Specifically, $7,125 − $5,875 = $1,250 more must be placed as margin.

Appendix 13C CONTINUOUSLY COMPOUNDED INTEREST RATES

This appendix compares annually compounded interest rates with continuously compounded interest rates. The Black–Scholes option pricing model (BSOPM) uses continuously compounded interest rates. *Annual compounding* implicitly assumes that interest is paid annually. *Continuous compounding assumes* that interest is paid continuously – that is, more frequently than every second. If we let PV denote present value and FV denote future value, then Equations 13C.1 and 13C.2 express the relationship between PV and FV via annual compounding (r) and continuous compounding (r_c), respectively:

$$FV = PV(1 + r)^t \qquad \text{(annual)} \qquad \text{(13C.1)}$$

$$FV = PVe^{r_c t} \qquad \text{(continuous)} \qquad \text{(13C.2)}$$

where e stands for the exponential. Solving for the compound rate, r and r_c, we have

$$r = \left(\frac{FV}{PV} \right)^{1/t} - 1 \qquad \text{(13C.3)}$$

$$r_c = \frac{\ln\left(\dfrac{FV}{PV} \right)}{t} \qquad \text{(13C.4)}$$

where ln() is the natural logarithm.

For example, suppose that $t = \frac{1}{2}$ year (hence, $1/t = 2$), FV = \$105 and PV = \$100. What is the relationship between r_c and r?

$$r = \left(\frac{105.0}{100.0} \right)^2 - 1$$

$$= 0.1025 \text{ or } 10.25\%$$

$$r_c = \frac{\ln\left(\dfrac{105.0}{100.0} \right)}{\frac{1}{2}}$$

$$= \ln(1.05)/(0.5) = 0.04879/0.5$$

$$\cong 0.09758 \text{ or } 9.758\%$$

Hence, continuous compounding is another method of accounting for the time value of money. Continuous compounding is used in calculating option prices, because it most closely relates to the underlying assumptions of the BSOPM, which assumes a continuous change in the hedge ratio (as illustrated in the binomial option pricing model).

Appendix 13D CALCULATING CONTINUOUSLY COMPOUNDED STANDARD DEVIATIONS

Recall from Chapter 6 that the standard deviation of stock rates of return is calculated by the following equation:

$$\sigma = \sqrt{\frac{1}{n}\sum_{t=1}^{n}(R_{i,t} - \overline{R}_i)^2} \qquad (13D.1)$$

where $R_{i,t}$ is the rate of return on stock i during period t, $\overline{R}_i$ is the average rate of return on stock i, and n is the number of historical observations. Chapter 5 presented the interim rate of return (modified for stocks) as follows:

$$R_{i,t} = \frac{P_{i,t} - P_{i,t-1} + D_{i,t}}{P_{i,t-1}} \qquad (13D.2)$$

where $P_{i,t}$ is the price of stock i at t, $P_{i,t-1}$ is the price of stock i at $t-1$, and $D_{i,t}$ is the dividend of stock i, if any, paid at t. The only difference in calculating the standard deviation with continuous compounding is the equation to calculate $R_{i,t}$. With continuous compounding, the proper equation for calculating rates of return is

$$R_{i,t} = \ln\left(\frac{P_{i,t} + D_{i,t}}{P_{i,t-1}}\right) \qquad (13D.3)$$

where ln( ) is the natural logarithm.

Exhibit 13D.1 Illustration of continuously compounded rates of return compared with annually compounded rates of return

Year	Index	Continuously compounded rates of return[a]	Annually compounded rates of return[b]
1	100.0		
2	138.8	0.328	0.388
3	216.6	0.445	0.561
4	556.9	0.944	1.571
5	332.7	−0.515	−0.403
6	136.0	−0.895	−0.591
7	274.1	0.701	1.015
8	373.0	−0.308	0.361
9	317.6	−0.161	−0.149
10	360.9	0.128	0.136
11	634.4	0.564	0.758
Mean		0.185	0.365
Standard deviation		0.536	0.624

[a] Based on $R_{i,t} = \ln\left(\dfrac{P_{i,t} + D_{i,t}}{P_{i,t}}\right)$

[b] Based on $R_{i,t} = \dfrac{P_{i,t} - P_{i,t-1} + D_{i,t}}{P_{i,t-1}}$

Note that this index is without dividends included, so $D_{i,t}$ is always zero.

It can be shown that for sufficiently short time periods (or small changes in the stock price), the rates of return given by Equations 13D.2 and 13D.3 are about the same. However, for long holding periods (greater than one week), the differences are more substantial.

To illustrate the magnitude of the differences in the two methods of estimating the standard deviation, let us consider the annual price information of a stock index. The second column in Exhibit 13D.1 gives the index values for a recent decade. The third column gives the continuously compounded rates of return, and the fourth column gives the annually compounded rates of return. As the exhibit shows, the differences between the standard deviations can be sizable. This case was based on data from Hong Kong stocks, which are very volatile. The holding period was assumed to be one year, which is fairly long. The less volatile the assets in question and the shorter the holding period, the smaller the differences will be between these methods.

Part V

RISK REDUCTION AND DIVERSIFICATION

Chapter 14

RISK AND RETURN: THE LINEAR RELATIONSHIPS AND THE CAPITAL ASSET PRICING MODEL

Learning objectives

After studying this chapter you should be able to:

1 Define and explain how to measure beta.

2 Understand why beta is the appropriate measure of risk.

3 Understand why the security market line (SML) and the capital asset pricing model (CAPM) describe the equilibrium relationship between risk and expected rate of return.

4 Understand how practitioners who believe in market inefficiency use alpha and beta to select underpriced stocks.

5 Understand the single index model (SIM) and the multifactor model.

6 Understand the arbitrage pricing theory (APT).

INVESTMENT IN THE NEWS

Hollywood or bust

Dana Giacchetto at Cassandra shoots to profit for his A-list clients

NEW YORK. On a sunny midsummer morning, Sandra Bullock is shooting *28 Days on Broadway* outside Dana Giacchetto's SoHo loft. It could be a perfect time for Giacchetto – money manager to the stars and Leonardo DiCaprio's lad about town when he comes to the Big Apple – to troll for clients.

But he's blasé about the bustle on his doorstep. Giacchetto is holed up in the eighth floor office of his investment boutique. The Cassandra Group Inc., flitting from phone to laptop, keeping tabs on his trades and the stock market...To pick stocks, he looks at three things – technical charts of the stock's historical movement, the company's record on hitting earnings projections and the 'beta,' which measures how volatile a stock is.

Source: Alex Frew McMillan, CNNfn, 17 July 1999.

Three things are taken into account in stock selection by the professional investor, Dana Giacchetto: technical charts (that will be covered in Chapter 18), earnings projections (covered in Chapters 9 and 10) and beta, which measures how volatile the stock is. This chapter is devoted mainly to beta as a measure of risk, to the risk–return relationship called the Capital Asset Pricing Model (CAPM), developed by William Sharpe and John Lintner for which Sharpe won the 1990 Nobel Prize in economics, and to the arbitrage pricing theory (APT).

In Chapter 6 we saw that investors will choose a portfolio taken from the **capital market line (CML)** regardless of their risk preferences (see Equation 6.4). It has also been shown that the risk of an **efficient portfolio** is measured by its standard deviation or variance. In this chapter, it will be shown that beta is the correct measure for risk for individual assets and portfolios alike, regardless of whether or not these portfolios are efficient. However, for efficient portfolios, the investor can use either the standard deviation or beta (which will be defined below) to size up risk without affecting the ranking of the portfolios by their risk. Because beta corresponds to individual securities as well as portfolios, this chapter uses the word *asset* where it refers to both individual assets and portfolios. When the discussion refers to individual assets only, it explicitly states this.

14.1 BETA AS A MEASURE OF RISK

How can we size up risk of an individual asset, e.g. Marks and Spencer stock, or even an inefficient portfolio, e.g. a mutual fund which may be located below the CML (for the CML definition, see Chapter 6)? As asserted in the *Investment in the news* article opening this chapter, beta (denoted by the Greek letter β) measures risk. Actually it measures the risk of individual assets, an inefficient portfolio as well as an efficient portfolio.

14.1.1 How to calculate beta

First, let us define beta and demonstrate how to calculate it. The **beta** of Asset i, denoted by β_i, is defined as

$$\beta_i = \frac{\text{Cov}(R_i, R_\text{m})}{\sigma_\text{m}^2} \tag{14.1}$$

where R_i is the rate of return on the ith asset, R_m is the rate of return on the **market portfolio** (portfolio m, see Chapter 6) and Cov is the covariance as defined in Chapter 6. Thus, beta measures the co-movement of the return on Asset i and the return on the market portfolio. In practice, the market portfolio is not observable and it is common to take as a proxy to it some broad index, e.g. the FTSE 100, the S&P 500, the Dow Jones, etc.

With historical data when equal probability is assigned to each period, beta can be calculated as follows:[1]

$$\beta_i = \frac{\frac{1}{N}\left(\sum_{t=1}^{N} R_{i,t} \times R_{m,t}\right) - \overline{R}_i\overline{R}_m}{\frac{1}{N}\left(\sum_{t=1}^{N} R_{m,t}^2\right) - \overline{R}_m^2} \tag{14.2}$$

where N denotes the number of observations and t denotes historical periods (for example, years, months and so forth). Obviously, beta also can be calculated for portfolios (efficient and inefficient alike) and mutual funds.

14.1.2 The meaning of beta – characteristic lines

Why does beta measure risk? We provide here an intuitive explanation and in Section 14.4 we prove that beta sizes up risk. Note that β (or β_i, where i stands for Asset i) is nothing but the slope of the regression line given by[2]

$$R_{i_t} = \alpha_i + \beta_i R_{m_t} + e_{i_t} \tag{14.3}$$

where R_{i_t} is the rate of return on the ith stock in period t, α_i is the intercept of the line, R_{m_t} is the rate of return on the market portfolio for the same period t, and e_{i_t} is the deviation from the regression line of the observation corresponding to period t, called the **error term**. In practice, the error term is not directly observable. However, it can be calculated from Equation 14.3, because R_{i_t} and R_{m_t} are directly observable, and α_i and β_i

---

[1] Recall from Chapter 6 that

$$\text{Cov}(R_i, R_m) = E[(R_i - \overline{R}_i)(R_m - \overline{R}_m)] = \frac{1}{N}\sum_{t=1}^{N}(R_{i,t} - \overline{R}_i)(R_{m,t} - \overline{R}_m)$$

which can be rewritten as

$$\text{Cov}(R_i, R_m) = \frac{1}{N}\sum_{t=1}^{N}(R_{i,t} \times R_{m,t}) - \overline{R}_i\overline{R}_m$$

Similarly, the denominator of Equation 14.2 is the variance because

$$\text{Variance}(R_m) = \frac{1}{N}\sum_{t=1}^{N}(R_{m,t} - \overline{R}_m)^2 = \frac{1}{N}\sum_{t=1}^{N} R_{m,t}^2 - \overline{R}_m^2$$

[2] In running the following kind of regression:

$$y = \alpha + \beta x + e$$

the slope of the regression line is β, given by

$$\beta = \frac{\text{Cov}(x, y)}{\sigma_x^2}$$

Thus, for $y = R_i$ and $x = R_m$, we get

$$\beta_i = \frac{\text{Cov}(R_i, R_m)}{\sigma_m^2}$$

Also, a well-known statistical result is

$$\alpha = \overline{y} - \beta\overline{x}$$

and in our specific case we have

$$\alpha_i = \overline{R}_i - \beta\overline{R}_m$$

PRACTICE BOX

Problem

The rate of return for three years on the market portfolio (market return) and on Exxon stock is as follows:

Year	Exxon stock	Market return
1	0.12	0.10
2	0.20	0.15
3	0.10	0.08

Calculate the beta of Exxon where the probability of each annual outcome is $1/3$.

Solution

Let Exxon's rates of return be denoted by R_i and the market's rate of return be denoted by R_m. Construct the following table:

Year	R_i	R_m	$R_i \times R_m$	R_m^2
1	0.12	0.10	0.012	0.0100
2	0.20	0.15	0.030	0.0225
3	0.10	0.08	0.008	0.0064
Sum	0.42	0.33	0.050	0.0389
Average	0.14	0.11	0.0167	0.0130

Using Equation 14.2 we get

$$\beta_i = \frac{0.0167 - 0.14 \times 0.11}{0.013 - 0.11^2} = \frac{0.0013}{0.0009} \cong 1.44$$

are estimated.[3] The regression line describing the relationship between R_i and R_m is called the **characteristic line**.[4] The slope of the regression line is equal to β_i and it measures the risk of the ith asset. The following discussion sheds more light on this risk measure.

If you hold a well-diversified portfolio, you can eliminate a large portion of the risk by diversification; however, the risk of the fluctuations in the whole market as measured by the fluctuations in the market portfolio cannot be eliminated. Exhibit 14.1 shows the 10 biggest one-day percentage declines of the Dow Jones Industrial Average (until the year 2000). Even if you hold the market portfolio (e.g. the S&P 500 index), you cannot avoid the fluctuations of the whole market. For example, on 19 October 1987, the whole

---

[3] We will show later on in the chapter that when the regressions are conducted in terms of excess return, **alpha** (α) has an economic meaning; it measures the return in excess of the risk-adjusted return as implied by the CAPM and therefore is called the *abnormal return* (see Section 14.5).

[4] The characteristic line measures the expected rate of return on the ith asset for a given R_m. A point on the line is given by $R_{i_t} = \alpha_i + \beta_i R_{m_t}$ (i.e. the error term is assumed to be zero). For example, if $R_{m_t} = 10\%$, and $\beta = 2$ and $\alpha = 5\%$, we have $R_{i_t} = 5\% + (2 \times 10\%) = 25\%$. However, if R_{m_t} changed from 10% to 14%, the average rate of return on the stock would be $R_{i_t} = 5\% + (2 \times 14\%) = 33\%$, and the *change* in the expected rate of return would be 8%, as a beta of 2 would predict.

Exhibit 14.1 Biggest one-day declines in the DJIA

Days with greatest percentage loss in index points

Rank	Date	Close	Net change	% change
1	19 October 1987	1738.74	−508.00	−22.61
2	28 October 1929	260.64	−38.33	−12.82
3	29 October 1929	230.07	−30.57	−11.73
4	6 November 1929	232.13	−25.55	−9.92
5	18 December 1929	58.27	−5.57	−8.72
6	12 August 1932	63.11	−5.79*	−8.40
7	14 March 1907	76.23	−6.89	−8.29
8	26 October 1987	1793.93	−156.83	−8.04
9	21 July 1933	88.71	−7.55	−7.84
10	18 October 1937	125.73	−10.57	−7.75

Source: Website at http://www.dowjones.com. Wall Street Journal Online (Staff produced copy only). © 2001 by Dow Jones & Co., Inc. Reproduced with permission of Dow Jones & Co., Inc. in the format *Fundamentals of Investments* via the Copyright Clearance Center.

stock market went down by more than 20%. No matter how well diversified your portfolio was on 19 October 1987, or any of the other days shown in Exhibit 14.1, you could not have avoided this loss.

Similarly, no amount of diversification can avoid the risk of economic recession. Thus, macro-economic factors such as unemployment, the trade balance, budget deficits, changes in interest rates (see Chapter 11) or events such as war can significantly affect the market rate of return. This risk cannot be diversified away, because it affects the whole market. Beta of an asset captures this macro-economic risk, and therefore it is also called **market risk**.

To illustrate, suppose that the Central Bank suddenly increases sharply the interest rate. The whole market falls by, say, 10%. If beta of a stock is 2, the stock price is expected to fall by 20%. Suppose that on the same day the firm announces its research and development failure to discover a new drug. The stock price falls by an additional 5%. Thus, the 5% in our example corresponds to the error term e_i, in Exhibit 14.2 and it is the **firm's specific risk** or the firm's specific variability. The firm's specific factor could be due to the discovery of new oil fields, firing the CEO, etc. (see also Section 14.3).

Beta measures the slope of the line given by Equation 14.3; it measures the sensitivity of the ith stock to market fluctuations which cannot be diversified away. For example, if $\beta_i = 2$, when the market rate of return increases by 1%, this stock's rate of return is expected to go up by 2% on average. However, when the market rate of return goes down by 1%, the stock's rate of return is expected to fall by 2%. Thus, this stock is considered to be an **aggressive stock**, or a stock that is more risky than the market portfolio. This stock, on average, fluctuates twice as much as the market portfolio. Similarly, if $\beta_i = \frac{1}{2}$, the stock fluctuates half as much as the market and is considered to be not very risky; it is called a **defensive stock**. A defensive stock 'defends' the investor from large losses but also denies the investor large gains. Finally, if $\beta_i = 1$, the stock moves exactly with the market on average. It is called a **neutral stock**.

Exhibit 14.2(a) presents pairs of rates of return on the market portfolio and on the ith stock, where each pair of points corresponds to a given period (e.g. year, month), along with the regression line that best fits this 'cloud' of points, that is, the corresponding characteristic line. The intercept of the line is α_i, the slope is β_i and the vertical

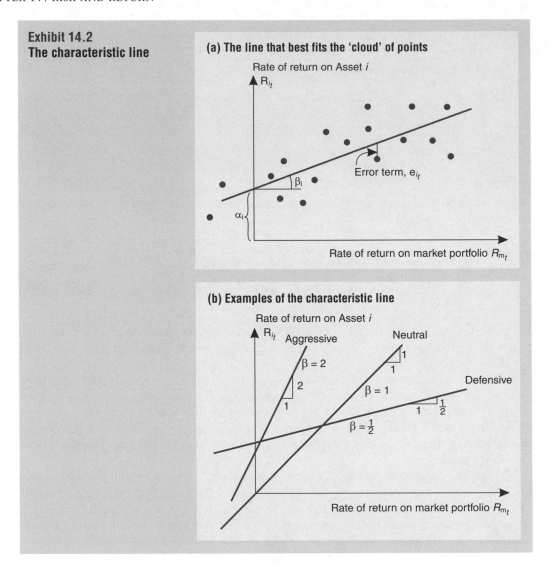

**Exhibit 14.2
The characteristic line**

(a) The line that best fits the 'cloud' of points

Rate of return on Asset i

R_{i_t}

Error term, e_{i_t}

β_i

α_i

Rate of return on market portfolio R_{m_t}

(b) Examples of the characteristic line

Rate of return on Asset i

R_{i_t} Aggressive   Neutral

$\beta = 2$

Defensive

$\beta = 1$

$\beta = \frac{1}{2}$

Rate of return on market portfolio R_{m_t}

deviations of the points from the line are the error terms, e_{i_t}. The closer the points are to the line, the better the fit of the regression line to the various points.

Exhibit 14.2(b) describes characteristic lines corresponding to aggressive, defensive and neutral stocks. Hi-tech firms, such as Apple Computer and Microsoft, are considered to be aggressive stocks. When the market is up by $x\%$, they usually go up by more than $x\%$; when the market is down by $x\%$, they usually go down by more than $x\%$. The stocks of utilities such as Florida Gas or British Petrolium are considered to be defensive. When the market is up by $x\%$, the demand for gas or electricity increases, but by less than $x\%$. When the market is down by $x\%$, the demand for gas and electricity goes down less sharply than the overall demand for other products; hence, the stock of these firms decreases by less than $x\%$. Thus, beta measures the sensitivity of the ith stock (or the portfolio) rate of return to changes in the market portfolio rates of return.

Note that apart from beta, other risk factors are reported, e.g. the financial strength. Thus, although beta is the theoretical measure of risk (as we see from Exhibit 14.3 in the following pages), practitioners complement it by another measure of risk called financial strength.

There are several important rules corresponding to beta.

Rule 1: Beta of the market portfolio, m, is equal to 1.
To see this, recall that a covariance of one variable with itself is the variance. Thus, $\text{Cov}(R_m, R_m) = \sigma_m^2$, hence

$$\beta_m = \frac{\text{Cov}(R_m, R_m)}{\sigma_m^2} = \frac{\sigma_m^2}{\sigma_m^2} = 1$$

Rule 2: Beta of the riskless asset is zero.
To see this, recall that the riskless interest rate is constant and a covariance of a constant with other variables is always equal to zero.[5]

Rule 3: $\beta_p = \Sigma w_i \beta_i$ where β_p is the portfolio beta, w_i is the weight of the ith asset in the portfolio and β_i is the ith asset beta.

Let us elaborate. The portfolio rate of return is given by $R_p = \sum_{i=1}^{n} w_i R_i$,

where R_p is the rate of return on the portfolio and w_i the investment weight in the portfolio of the ith asset whose return is R_i.

Therefore, the portfolio beta, β_p, is given by:[6]

$$\beta_p = \frac{\text{Cov}(R_p, R_m)}{\sigma_m^2} = \frac{\text{Cov}\left(\sum w_i R_i, R_m\right)}{\sigma_m^2} = \frac{\sum w_i \text{Cov}(R_i, R_m)}{\sigma_m^2} = \sum w_i \beta_i$$

Rule 4: The percentage contribution of the ith asset to the market portfolio risk is $w_i \beta_i$.
To see this, recall, by Rule 1, that for the market portfolio $\beta_m = 1$. Also, by Rule 3, for the market portfolio we have $\beta_m = \Sigma w_i \beta_i = 1$. Hence, $w_i \beta_i$ is the percentage contribution of the ith asset to the market portfolio risk which is equal to 1.

Rule 5: Beta of an efficient portfolio (see Chapter 6) located on the CML is given by

$$\beta_p = 1 - w$$

where w is the investment proportion in the riskless asset and $(1 - w)$ is the investment proportion in the market portfolio, m.
To see this, recall from Chapter 6 that all efficient portfolios are combinations of portfolio m and the riskless asset. Namely,

$$R_p = wr + (1 - w) R_m$$

And because r is constant, wr has zero covariance with R_m. Therefore, we have

$$\beta_p = \frac{\text{Cov}(R_p, R_m)}{\sigma_m^2} = \frac{(1 - w)\text{Cov}(R_m, R_m)}{\sigma_m^2} = (1 - w)\frac{\sigma_m^2}{\sigma_m^2} = 1 - w$$

We will use some of these rules in the rest of the chapter.

---

[5] $\text{Cov}(r, R_m) = E[(r - Er)(R_m - ER_m)]$, but because $Er = r$ the covariance is equal to zero (see Chapter 6).
[6] We employ the statistical rule asserting that $\text{Cov}(ax + by, R_m) = a\,\text{Cov}(x, R_m) + b\,\text{Cov}(y, R_m)$.

Exhibit 14.3 Using beta as a measure of risk in practice

Page	Ticker	Company	Recent price	P/E	Yield (%)	Beta	Financial strength
1682	AZO	AutoZone Inc.	29	20.1	Nil	1.10	B ++
		Industry sector: Retail (Special Lines)					
2198	BMCS	BMC Software	66	29.9	Nil	1.30	B ++
		Industry sector: Computer Software & Svcs					
904	ETH	Ethan Allen Interiors	39	20.0	0.3	1.30	B +
		Industry sector: Furn./Home Furnishings					
681	HBOC	HBO & Co.	48	45.7	0.2	1.30	B ++
		Industry sector: Healthcare Information					
1881	HAL	Halliburton Co.	49	24.9	1.0	0.90	B ++
		Industry sector: Oilfield Services/Equip.					
317	LDRY	Landry's Seafood	24	20.7	Nil	1.35	B +
		Industry sector: Restaurant					
1064	LLTC	Linear Technology	57	26.5	0.4	1.40	A
		Industry sector: Semiconductor					
2153	KRB	MBNA Corp.	27	20.8	1.2	1.55	B ++
		Industry sector: Financial Services					

Source: The Value Line Investment Survey, 9 January 1998, p. 6424. Reprinted with permission.

14.1.3 The use of beta in practice

Beta is commonly used in many publications as a measure of the risk of an investment (or as an index for safety). Beta is a risk index for portfolios (mutual funds), as well as for individual securities. The larger the beta, the more risky the corresponding asset or portfolio. Exhibit 14.3 illustrates how beta is used as a risk measure by Value Line.

14.1.4 US market portfolio and the world market portfolio

At this stage, one should ask, what is the composition of the market portfolio m? Conceptually, it should include all available risky assets. Should international securities markets be included in Portfolio m? In other words, can we get a steeper CML by diversifying internationally? In principle, the answer is yes, we can gain from international diversification. In the age of electronic communications, the world market has become one large market, and it is easy to invest in the securities of foreign countries. However, most macro-economic shocks affect all markets. For example, the 1987 crash or the 2000 crisis was not just a US or UK phenomenon but a world phenomenon. Still, as long as correlations between markets are not perfect, the investor can benefit from international diversification.

International diversification achieves two objectives: (1) it increases the number of assets available, and (2) it decreases, but does not eliminate, the market portfolio risk. It is possible to reduce the market portfolio fluctuations by investing in the world market portfolio, but certainly these fluctuations cannot be completely eliminated. Thus, in principle, when calculating beta, portfolio m should be taken as the world market, not just the US market. However, for practical reasons, in calculating beta, only the US market is used (or at best, the US market plus the UK market and other markets in

Western Europe and Japan, which have accessible databases on rates of return). We will elaborate on the gain from international diversification in Chapter 15.

14.2 THE SECURITY MARKET LINE (SML)

In Chapter 6, we describe the CML, which provides the linear relationship between expected return and risk (standard deviation) that holds only for efficient portfolios. Here we show the existence of a linear relationship, called the security market line (SML), between expected return and risk (beta) of individual assets as well as portfolios, regardless of whether they are efficient or not. For an *efficient portfolio*, both beta and sigma measure risk and indeed the SML and CML coincide.

So far, we explain intuitively that beta is the risk of an individual asset. However, how is the expected return on an individual asset related to beta? Answering such a question requires the introduction of a new concept, the *security market line* (SML). Each asset has its own risk–return profile. If the expected return exactly compensates investors for the risk exposure, we say that the market is in equilibrium. There is no incentive to sell or buy stocks, and no investors will wish to change their portfolio compositions. When the market is in equilibrium, all assets are correctly priced, and there are no 'bargains' in the market.

The asset pricing model that determines the equilibrium relationship between the expected return and risk of individual assets, as well as portfolios, is called the **capital asset pricing model (CAPM)**. The induced linear relationship between expected return and beta that follows from the CAPM is called the **security market line (SML)**. Although we use the terms SML and CAPM interchangeably for the linear risk–return relationship, keep in mind that the CAPM is an equilibrium pricing model, whereas the SML is the end result of this model. We first describe the SML and then discuss the CAPM.

The main results of the CAPM are summarized in the SML linear relationship, which describes the risk–return relationship of individual assets as well as portfolios, whether they are efficient or not. The SML is summarized by Rule 6.

Rule 6: To find the expected return on the ith asset, first calculate its beta. Multiply it by the market risk premium $[E(R_m) - r]$, and add to it the riskless interest rate. Thus, the following linear risk–return relationship should hold in equilibrium:[7]

$$E(R_i) = r + [E(R_m) - r]\beta_i \qquad (14.4)$$

expected rate of return = risk-free rate + risk premium

where $E(R_i)$ = the expected rate of return on the ith asset, $E(R_m)$ = the expected rate of return of the market portfolio, r = the risk-free interest rate, and β_i = the risk of the ith asset (or its beta). The SML asserts that the expected rate of return on asset i is equal to the risk-free rate plus a risk premium. This risk premium is equal to the market risk premium $[E(R_m) - r]$ multiplied by the asset's beta.

---

[7] The linear relationship between $E(R_i)$ and β_i holds for any security or portfolio as long as portfolio m is mean–variance efficient. However, to develop the equilibrium model, we must assume that all investors are risk averse and that they select their portfolios according to the mean–variance rule. In addition, we must assume homogeneous expectations among investors, the absence of transaction costs, and the availability of the risk-free asset. Under these assumptions, all investors hold portfolio m (the separation property), from which the CAPM follows.

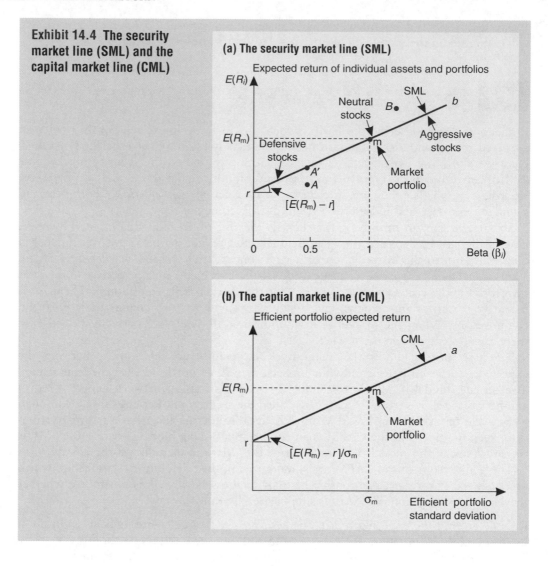

Exhibit 14.4 The security market line (SML) and the capital market line (CML)

(a) The security market line (SML)

Expected return of individual assets and portfolios

(b) The captial market line (CML)

Efficient portfolio expected return

Exhibit 14.4(a) demonstrates the SML. Note first that if $\beta_i = 0$, the *i*th asset is similar to the risk-free asset. Indeed, if we substitute zero for β_i in Equation 14.4, we obtain $E(R_i) = r$. Thus, as expected, the return on a risk-free asset is r. Second, if $\beta_i = 1$ then $E(R_i) = E(R_m)$. In this case, the asset's price fluctuates, on average, in tandem with the market, therefore the asset has the same risk as the market and hence yields, on average, the same rate of return as the market portfolio, $E(R_m)$. If the stock is a defensive stock ($\beta_i < 1$), the expected return will be smaller than $E(R_m)$. When $\beta_i > 1$, the stock is aggressive – that is, more risky than the market portfolio. Therefore, in equilibrium, the aggressive stock will be characterized by a higher expected return than the market.

Because $E(R_m) - r$, the slope of line *rb* in Exhibit 14.4(a), is the same for all stocks, we conclude that the higher β_i is, the greater the risk and thus the higher the required risk premium. Therefore, for a high β_i, the corresponding $E(R_i)$ will also be relatively large.

Why is the risk–return linear relationship called a pricing model, although no prices appear in Equation 14.4? Suppose that according to Equation 14.4, $E(R_i) = 15\%$, and

Problem

Suppose the mean rate of return on the market is 10% and the risk-free interest rate is 5%. Given that beta is 2.48 for Hilton Stock, what is the expected rate of return on Hilton stock?

Solution

Based on Equation 14.4, the expected rate of return is

$$E(R_i) = 5\% + [(10\% - 5\%) \times 2.48] \cong 17.4\%$$

the stock's expected price at the end of the investment period is $E(P_1) = \$115$. Assuming no dividends, what is the current stock price? It must be $P_0 = \$100$, because $15\% = (\$115 - \$100)/\$100$. Suppose now that for some reason, the stock's beta increases so that $E(R_i)$ as implied by the CAPM (or by SML, which is a result of the CAPM) increases to $E(R_i) = 20\%$. Assume that there is no change in the expected price at the end of the period; hence, $E(P_1)$ remains $115. (One can also relax this assumption without affecting the analysis.) The current price (P_0) must now decrease until

$$E(R_i) = 20\% = (\$115 - P_0)/P_0$$

or

$$(0.2 \times P_0) + P_0 = \$115$$

or

$$P_0 \times (0.2 + 1) = \$115$$

Therefore $P_0 = \$115/1.2 \cong \$95.83$. Thus, according to the CAPM, a change in $E(R_i)$ causes a change in the current price of the asset – hence the name capital asset *pricing* model. The expected return $E(R_i)$ as implied by the CAPM is also called the *required* rate of return, because it is the return that investors require in equilibrium as compensation for the risk exposure. In Section 14.4 below we show that under certain assumptions the CAPM and the SML hold, which justify beta as a risk index.

14.3 SYSTEMATIC AND UNSYSTEMATIC RISK

When a portfolio composed of a large number of assets is held, the firm's variance has almost no role in determining the asset's risk premium. To elaborate, let us recall Equation 14.3:

$$R_{i_t} = \alpha_i + \beta_i R_{m_t} + e_{i_t}$$

The variance of R_i is as follows:[8]

$$\sigma_i^2 = \beta_i^2 \sigma_m^2 + \sigma_{e_i}^2 \tag{14.5}$$

[8] Because α_i and β_i are constant (α_i is the intercept of the line), their variances are zero. We take the variance of both sides to obtain Equation 14.5. Note that we also employ the rule, Variance $(ax) = a^2 \times$ variance (x), where a is constant, and use the fact that in regression analysis by construction, $\text{Cov}(e_i, R_m) = 0$. Hence, we have only two terms appearing in Equation 14.5, where $\sigma_{e_i}^2$ is the variance of e_i.

Thus, the variance σ_i^2 can be broken down into two terms. The first term, $\beta_i^2 \sigma_m^2$, is the firm's **systematic risk** component, which represents the part of the stock's variance that is attributable to overall market volatility. The second term, $\sigma_{e_i}^2$, is the firm's **unsystematic risk** component, which represents the part of the stock's variance that is *not* attributable to overall market volatility. The component $\sigma_{e_i}^2$ is the variance of the error term e_i, and σ_{e_i} is its standard deviation. The unsystematic risk component is related to the firm's specific volatility. If all points fall exactly on the regression line (the error term e_i is zero for all points; see Exhibit 14.2), then $\sigma_{e_i}^2 = 0$. The farther the points are from the regression line, the larger is $\sigma_{e_i}^2$, which measures the dispersion of the points around the regression line (see Exhibit 14.2).

Note that β_i appears only in the systematic risk component. Therefore, we can conclude that only the systematic part of the firm's variance is relevant in determining expected rates of return and, hence, the required risk premium. The CAPM does not account for the component, $\sigma_{e_i}^2$, which implies that this risk is irrelevant. It is irrelevant because it can be eliminated by holding a well-diversified portfolio. Obviously, $\sigma_{e_i}^2$ is irrelevant for asset pricing only if a well-diversified portfolio is held. If an investor holds only one stock in his portfolio, β is irrelevant and σ_i^2 (which includes $\sigma_{e_i}^2$ as one component) is the correct measure of risk.

If we divide both sides of Equation 14.5 by σ_i^2, we have the following:

$$1 = \frac{\beta_i^2 \sigma_m^2}{\sigma_i^2} + \frac{\sigma_{e_i}^2}{\sigma_i^2}$$

where the first term is the *proportion* of the total risk of a security that is systematic, and the second term is the proportion that is unsystematic.

14.4   THE CAPITAL ASSET PRICING MODEL (CAPM)[9]

So far we have provided an intuitive explanation why beta measures the risk. Namely, beta measures the volatility of a given asset relative to the volatility of the market portfolio. In Chapter 6, we show that at the optimum, all investors should hold the market portfolio whose risk is measured by its standard deviation. Therefore, the market portfolio's standard deviation is the risk exposure. We will show here that beta of an individual asset is its contribution to the market portfolio risk held, and therefore is identified as the individual's asset risk: the higher the beta, the higher the required rate of return from the asset.

The SML describes the relationship between the expected return and beta of assets. Suppose that there is an asset which is not on the SML: is it overpriced? Underpriced? We show in this section that all assets in equilibrium must fall on the SML. Any deviation from the SML will be corrected in equilibrium. This implies that beta is the risk index, because by the SML the higher the beta, the higher the expected return, $E(R_i)$. However, to achieve this result we must make some assumptions. Under these assumptions the CAPM holds, and the SML is the resulting equilibrium as determined by the CAPM.

[9] For a detailed proof of the CAPM, see William F. Sharpe, 'Capital asset prices: a theory of market equilibrium', *Journal of Finance*, September 1964, pp. 425–42, and John Lintner, 'Security prices and maximal gains from diversification', *Journal of Finance*, December 1965, pp. 587–615. Sharpe won the 1990 Nobel Prize in economics in part because of this paper.

To derive the CAPM, we must make the following assumptions: (1) investors make their investment decisions according to the mean–variance rule; (2) investors incur no transaction costs that would prevent sufficient diversification to achieve Portfolio m; (3) investors can borrow and lend at the riskless rate, r; and (4) there are no taxes. Given these assumptions, the CAPM would place all risky individual assets and portfolios on line rb in Exhibit 14.4(a), that is, on the SML. However, these assumptions are needed to derive the CML given in Exhibit 14.4(b) from which the CAPM of Exhibit 14.4(b) is taken. Indeed, if we show that all assets lie on the SML, Equation 14.4 holds, and so does the CAPM. The CAPM can be proven in the following two steps.

■ Step 1: Efficient portfolios

Relying on the assumption that investors make their own decisions by the mean–variance rule, we showed in Chapter 6 that the investors will mix portfolio m and the riskless asset. The fact that there are no transaction costs allows us to diversify among many assets, i.e. to hold the market portfolio or an efficient portfolio located on the CML (see Chapter 6 and Exhibit 14.4(b)). We show first that for *efficient portfolios* the SML and CML coincide. Thus, the SML holds for efficient portfolios. In the second step we show that the SML holds also for individual assets or inefficient portfolios.

In the first step, we prove that the SML holds for all efficient portfolios whose returns are R_p. Thus, we claim that all points on line rb (see Exhibit 14.4(a)) are attainable by mixing portfolio m, whose beta is equal to 1, and the risk-free asset. Thus, all efficient portfolios (combinations of portfolio m and the riskless asset (see Chapter 6)) are located on the SML given by line rb in Exhibit 14.4(a).

To see this, construct an efficient portfolio, R_p:

$$R_p = wr + (1 - w)R_m$$

where w is the investment weight in the risk-free asset and $(1 - w)$ is the investment weight in the market portfolio. The expected return on this efficient portfolio is

$$E(R_p) = wr + (1 - w)E(R_m)$$

and its beta is (see Rule 5):

$$\beta_p = 1 - w$$

Substituting $w = 1 - \beta_p$ and $1 - w = \beta_p$ in the above equation for $E(R_p)$, we obtain the following:

$$E(R_p) = (1 - \beta_p)r + \beta_p E(R_m)$$

or

$$E(R_p) = r + [E(R_m) - r]\beta_p$$

Because r and $[E(R_m) - r]$ are the intercept and slope of the SML, the pair $[E(R_p), \beta_p]$ lies on the SML. By altering the investment proportion w, we can select any point $[E(R_p), \beta_p]$ lying on the SML (line rb in Exhibit 14.4(a)). Thus any point on line rb is a feasible investment: it can be achieved by mixing the market portfolio of the CML, m, and the riskless asset.

■ Step 2: Individual assets

From Step 1 we can conclude that all points on line rb of Exhibit 14.4(a) can be achieved by mixing portfolio m with the riskless asset. Now we show that in equilibrium all assets, efficient or inefficient, must also lie on the line rb.

To see why this claim holds, consider Asset A, whose beta is $\beta_A = 0.5$, which is located below the SML (see Exhibit 14.4(a)). No investor would be willing to hold Asset A, because by mixing portfolio m and the risk-free asset, investors could achieve point A′ (see Step 1 above). In the specific example with $\beta = 0.5$, the mix would be achieved by investing 50% in m and 50% in r (we obtain a portfolio whose beta is 0.5 because $\beta_p = \frac{1}{2} \times 1 = \frac{1}{2}$: see Rule 5 above). Because Asset A′ has the same risk as Asset A ($\beta_{A'} = \beta_A = 0.5$) but a higher expected return, investors who held Asset A would prefer to sell Asset A and buy Asset A′. As a result, the price of Asset A will go down and its expected rate of return will go up until, in equilibrium, point A shifts upward to line *rb*. Only when point A is located on line *rb* will equilibrium be restored and there will be no further incentive to sell Asset A and buy Asset A′.

By the same argument, no asset, such as Asset B, can be above line *rb*, because in this case all investors would sell Portfolio m and hold this superior asset (see Exhibit 14.4(a)). The price of Portfolio m (or of the securities making up Portfolio m) will fall, and the price of Asset B will increase until equilibrium is restored, with all assets located on line *rb*. When all assets are on line *rb*, Equation 14.4 holds. This proves that in equilibrium, the linear relationship between expected return and risk (the SML) holds also for individual assets or inefficient portfolios.

Note that in the above proof of the CAPM and the resulting SML, we do not assume that beta is a measure of risk; it emerges as a result. We assume only the CAPM assumptions, from which we can conclude that all investors will select a portfolio located on the CML (see Chapter 6). Then we show that all efficient portfolios are located also on the SML, hence we can switch (for efficient portfolio) from sigma to beta as an index for risk. Thus, we prove that for an efficient portfolio beta (as well as sigma) can serve as the risk index. Finally, we show that in equilibrium all assets (efficient or inefficient) must be located on the SML, hence beta (but not sigma) is a risk index for individual assets as well as for inefficient portfolios.

Finally, once beta is accepted as a measure of risk, it follows from the CAPM that for any two assets *i* and *j*, the following must hold in equilibrium:

$$\frac{ER_i - r}{\beta_i} = \frac{ER_j - r}{\beta_j}$$

or the risk premium for a unit of risk must be the same across all assets. To see this recall that, by the SML,

$$ER_i = r + (ER_m - r)\beta_i$$

or

$$\frac{ER_i - r}{\beta_i} = ER_m - r$$

and for stock *j* the same holds:

$$\frac{ER_j - r}{\beta_j} = ER_m - r$$

hence

$$\frac{ER_i - r}{\beta_i} = \frac{ER_i - r}{\beta_j} = ER_m - r$$

This CAPM relationship is summarized in Rule 7.

Rule 7: In the CAPM equilibrium, the asset's risk premium divided by its beta must be equal across all assets.

14.5 USING THE CAPM FOR STOCK SELECTION

14.5.1 The abnormal return

How are alpha of Equation 14.3 and the CAPM employed in securities selection? If Equation 14.4 holds for all assets, it implies that all assets are located on the SML. In such a case, we say that the market is in equilibrium or that there are no inefficiencies in the market. The expected return on such stocks is exactly determined by their risk.

For example, if $E(R_m) = 15\%$, $r = 5\%$ and $\beta_i = 1.5$, then according to the CAPM, the expected return on the ith stock is (see Equation 14.4)

$$E(R_i) = 5\% + [(15\% - 5\%) \times 1.5] = 20\%$$

Thus, this stock lies on the SML. It is a good investment, although certainly not a bargain. The investor is fully compensated for the risk exposure. However, what if we expect to have $E(R_i) = 25\%$, with no change in β_i? We say that this stock has a 5% **excess return** or **abnormal return** above and beyond the compensation for the risk involved in investing in such a stock (the return on the stock is more than expected by the CAPM, thus it has an abnormal return). If the market is not in equilibrium, and if this excess return persists for a long time, we say that the market is *inefficient* (see Chapter 16). Of course, investors should grab such a stock.

This strategy is exactly the strategy employed by many practitioners for picking stocks. Let us elaborate. According to the CAPM, in equilibrium all assets are located on the SML: there are no deviations, hence there is no abnormal return and the following should hold (see Equation 14.4):

$$E(R_i) - r = [E(R_m) - r]\beta_i$$

However, if there are excess returns in the market, there is a deviation from the line, and the equation becomes

$$E(R_i) - r = \alpha_i + [E(R_m) - r]\beta_i$$

where α_i is the deviation of the ith stock from the SML which is exactly the 'excess return'. Thus, α_i measures the abnormal return of the ith stock. In the previous example, α_i is 5%. Of course, in practice the expected return, $E(R_i)$, as well as β_i, is unknown and is estimated from historical data.[10]

Of course, if the CAPM is an accurate model and the market is efficient, this excess return will instantly disappear. The trick is to be the first one to discover the high-alpha stocks (see Exhibit 14.5 for reported α and β) and buy them before everyone else does, thus forcing the stock prices up (recall the $100 bill found on the pavement – see the Preface).

---

[10] In Equation 14.3, α_i can be estimated by running the regression of R_i, on R_m. One can also run the regression of $R_i - r_t$ on $R_m - r_t$ and estimate alpha where these two variables are stated in terms of excess return in comparison with the risk-free interest rate. Generally we refer to alpha when excess returns are employed. Therefore, if $\alpha_i > 0$ a positive abnormal return is observed, and if $\alpha_i < 0$ a negative abnormal return is observed.

Exhibit 14.5 The use of alpha and beta in practice

Risk and rating statistics	High	Low	Average
CDA rating	94	4	52
Beta (vs. S&P)	2.41	0.01	0.84
Beta (vs. category)	2.82	0.01	1.00
Standard deviation	10.06	0.12	3.52
Alpha	7.2	−3.6	−0.5
R^2	100	2	88

Source: Thomson Financial.

It is also interesting to note that the suggested strategy does not rely solely on the CAPM. Once the high-alpha stocks are selected, fundamental analysis is used in choosing stocks from this group. Thus, practitioners feel that the CAPM is useful but has its shortcomings. They do not rely solely on the CAPM in making portfolio investment decisions. Indeed, we can see in Exhibit 14.5 that apart from alpha and beta, many other variables are reported which are probably employed in stock picking.

14.5.2 Using alpha and beta in practice

Exhibit 14.5 shows that practitioners use beta, as well as alpha, and consider these two parameters very informative. Thus, practitioners consider beta (and the CAPM) to be a useful risk index. Exhibit 14.5 shows the α, β, σ and R^2 of mutual funds. The table also provides risk-rating statistics. The 'highs' and 'lows' refer to funds with abnormal results. The CDA rating is a composite percentile rating from 1 to 99 based on a fund's performance over past market cycles.

In Exhibit 14.5, two calculations of beta are presented. The first uses the regression line of the fund calculated using the S&P index as the market portfolio. The other uses a category portfolio as a proxy for the market portfolio; a category portfolio is the average return on all funds (in the long-term growth class).

Alpha appears next; alpha is estimated by running a regression of $R_{i_t} - r_t$ on $R_{m_t} - r_t$ (see footnote 10). Funds with a positive alpha outperformed the market, or revealed an abnormal return.

14.6 SHORTCOMINGS OF THE CAPM

We can test the CAPM by estimating Equation 14.4 with past data, substituting historical values for $E(R_i)$ and β_i. Of course, we do not expect to get an exact relationship, and we anticipate deviations from the line. Thus, it is possible to test the CAPM using the following equation:

$$\overline{R}_i = \gamma_0 + \gamma_1 \hat{\beta}_i + e_i$$

where $\overline{R}_i$ is the historical average return on the ith asset, γ_0 is the historical intercept, $\hat{\beta}_i$ is the historical estimate of the stock's beta, and e_i is the deviation from the line. The 'hat' emphasizes that this is an estimate of the true beta. γ_0 and γ_1 are the regression coefficients (if the CAPM is true, we should have that $\gamma_0 = r_f$ and $\gamma_1 = [E(R_m) - r_f]$: see Equation 14.4).

Many empirical studies have tested the CAPM. Most of them show that γ_1 is positive and significant (that is, there is a positive association between average return and risk). However, the fit is not as good as would be expected from the CAPM. (With individual stocks, R^2, which describes how well the model fits, was approximately 20%, which means that only 20% of this association could be explained by beta.) Recently, a study by Fama and French (see footnote 11) claimed that γ_1 is not significantly different from zero, which means that a positive association between beta and average return could not be found. In other words, Fama and French claim that beta is not the appropriate risk index, which casts doubt on the validity of the CAPM. Other researchers disagree with this conclusion and show a positive relationship between average return and beta.[11] In particular, Amihud, Christensen and Mendelson use an advanced econometric technique to show that expected return and beta are positively associated even when the same data set used by Fama and French is used. In their words, 'beta is still alive and well'.[12]

Roll showed that it is very difficult, if not impossible, to empirically test the CAPM.[13] Roll also showed that if beta is calculated with an efficient portfolio (a portfolio taken from the efficient frontier), then there is always a perfect positive association between average return and beta ($R^2 = 1$). Thus, the fact that empirical studies show a less than perfect linear association indicates only that an inefficient portfolio (a portfolio interior to the efficient frontier, i.e. a portfolio located below the CML – see Exhibit 14.4(b)) has been selected as a proxy to the market portfolio. According to Roll, the only testable question is whether the market portfolio is mean–variance efficient – that is, whether the market portfolio lies on the frontier or not. However, such a test is technically impossible with existing computers, because it involves using thousands of securities to solve for the efficient frontier.

Roll and Ross claim that the empirical findings regarding the CAPM are very sensitive to the proxy of the market portfolio that is employed to calculate the beta of each individual security.[14] They claim:

> This implies that an index proxy can conceivably be substantially inefficient and still produce a strong cross-sectional regression between expected returns and betas or it can conceivably be close to the efficient frontier and yet produce zero cross-section relation.[15]

They conclude:

> The empirical findings are not by themselves sufficient cause for rejection of the theory.[16]

---

[11] For more details on studies showing a positive association between mean return and beta, see M. Miller and M. Scholes, 'Rate of return in relation to risk: a reexamination of some recent findings', in M. Jensen (ed.), *Studies in the Theory of Capital Markets* (New York: Praeger, 1972); H. Levy, 'Equilibrium in an imperfect market: a constraint on the number of securities', *American Economic Review*, 68, September 1978, pp. 643–58; and Y. Amihud, B.J. Christensen and H. Mendelson, 'Further evidence on the risk–return relationship', working paper, Stanford University, 1992. An example of a study showing no association between risk and return is E. Fama and F. French, 'The cross-section of expected stocks returns', *Journal of Finance*, 47, 1992, pp. 427–66.

[12] Amihud, Christensen and Mendelson, p. 1.

[13] R. Roll, 'A critique of the asset pricing theory's test, Part I: On past and potential testability of theory', *Journal of Financial Economics*, 4, 1977, pp. 129–76.

[14] R. Roll and S. Ross, 'On the cross-section relation between expected return and betas', *Journal of Finance*, 49, March 1994, pp. 101–122.

[15] *Ibid*, p. 109.

[16] *Ibid*, p. 115.

Thus, some claim that beta is dead, and some claim that beta is alive and well. It seems that this controversy is not going to end soon. However, as have seen, practitioners employ beta as a measure of risk, hence they think that beta is alive but not well. Because it is not well, they employ additional investment criteria and do not rely solely on the CAPM.

It is obvious that some of the assumptions of the CAPM do not hold. For example, there are transaction costs, and in general the larger the number of shares bought, the lower the percentage paid in transaction costs. Investors, and in particular small investors, hold only a relatively small number of stocks in their portfolios; hence, they do not invest in portfolio m. Therefore, some extensions of the CAPM which relax these unrealistic assumptions are called for.

For the case in which there is only a limited number of stocks in the optimum portfolio, Levy, Markowitz, Merton and Sharpe himself suggest an alternative model that is similar to the CAPM but that allows investors to hold a relatively small number of assets in their portfolios.[17] This model is called the General Capital Asset Pricing Model (GCAPM); it is general in the sense that once the transaction costs are eliminated from the model, the CAPM is obtained as a specific case of the GCAPM. Under this model, each investor holds a different portfolio; therefore, each portfolio has a different beta (which is measured against the portfolio held). The beta of the ith asset is obtained as a weighted average of all these betas.

In summary, the CAPM provides insight into the risk–return relationship, but it has its shortcomings.[18] An investor cannot rely solely on the CAPM, and practitioners realize this. Therefore, despite the wide use of the CAPM, as well as the use of beta as a measure of risk and alpha as a measure of excess return, practitioners require additional tools in choosing their investment portfolios. Indeed, practitioners use the CAPM as a screening tool to divide all stocks into high-alpha and low-alpha groups. Their final investment decisions, however, rely on the analysis of dividends, price-to-book ratios, growth, earnings surprises and so forth.

14.7   THE SINGLE INDEX MODEL (SIM)

The **single index model (SIM)** suggested by Sharpe[19] has two important roles. First, it facilitates the derivation of the mean–variance frontier, and secondly, it paves the way to the arbitrage pricing theory (APT) developed by Ross (see Section 14.8).[20] The APT is an equilibrium model similar to the CAPM, but relies on another set of assumptions.

---

[17] For more details on the GCAPM, see H. Levy, 'Equilibrium in an imperfect market: a constraint on the number of securities in a portfolio', *American Economic Review*, 68, 1978, pp. 613–58; Harry M. Markowitz, 'Risk adjustment', *Journal of Accounting, Auditing and Finance*, Winter/Spring 1990; Robert C. Merton, 'A simple model of capital market equilibrium with incomplete information', *Journal of Finance*, 42, 1987, pp. 483–510; and W.F. Sharpe, 'Capital asset prices with and without negative holdings', *Journal of Finance*, 46, June 1991, pp. 489–510.

[18] See H. Levy, 'Risk and return: an experimental analysis', *International Economic Review*, February 1997. This paper uses an investment experiment to show that both the CAPM and the GCAPM are not 'dead' and can be used in risk–return equilibrium model analysis.

[19] See W.F. Sharpe, 'A simplified model for portfolio analysis', *Management Science*, January 1963, pp. 277–93.

[20] See S. Ross, 'Mutual fund separation in financial theory – the separating distributions', *Journal of Economic Theory*, April 1978; S. Ross, 'The arbitrage theory of capital asset pricing', *Economica*, 1976.

14.7.1 Common-factor and firm-specific rates of returns

The SIM has some basic assumptions about the way rates of return are generated. According to the SIM, two factors are responsible for a given stock's rate of return: the percentage change in some index (or the **common factor**) and changes related to firm-specific events. The index could be any variable that is correlated with security rates of return, such as the inflation rate, gross domestic product (GDP), or even the S&P 500 or FTSE 100 index.

The SIM assumes that the rate of return on Asset i is given by

$$R_i = \alpha_i + \beta_i I + e_i \tag{14.6}$$

where R_i is the rate of return on Asset i, I is the *percentage change* in some index that is common to all stocks, and e_i is the change in Asset i's rate of return related to firm-specific events. In the CAPM, beta is related to the market portfolio, and hence I is chosen to be the market portfolio. Like beta in the CAPM, in the SIM β_i measures the sensitivity of the ith asset's return to changes in the index (I).

For example, if $\beta_i = 2$ and I is the GDP, it means that if the GDP goes up by 1%, R_i, on average, will go up by 2%. The term α_i is the intercept that measures the anticipated return when $I = 0$.

The term e_i is the random deviation from the straight line given by $R_i = \alpha_i + \beta_i I$. It can be either above the line (positive) or below the line (negative), and it is zero on average.[21] The straight line in Exhibit 14.6 has an intercept of α_i and a slope of β_i. If all points (R_i) are exactly on the line, then all deviations (e_i) are zero. However, in general, some points are located above the line and some below it. Hence, there are positive as well as negative deviations.

The index (I) and the sensitivity factor (β_i) determine the expected rate of return on Asset i.

For example, suppose the common index determining stock prices is the rate of return on the FTSE 100 index, and the stock under consideration is British Airways (BA).

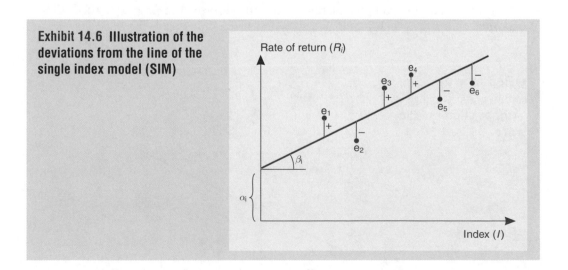

Exhibit 14.6 Illustration of the deviations from the line of the single index model (SIM)

---

[21] If the mean of e_i is not zero, we can always add the mean of e_i to α_i, then the mean of the deviations left is, by construction, zero. Also when we run a regression to estimate β_i, the sample mean $\bar{e}_i$ is zero.

Moreover, suppose $\alpha_{BA} = 1\%$ and $\beta_{BA} = 2$. Then the following relationship holds for BA:

$$R_{BA} = 1\% + 2I + e_{BA}$$

Suppose that in a given year, $I = 10\%$ (namely, the FTSE index goes up by 10%). If no information regarding e_{BA} is available, the best estimate is that $e_{BA} = 0$. Then the rate of return on BA in this specific year is expected to be

$$R_{BA} = 1\% + (2 \times 10\%) + 0 = 21\%$$

Now suppose that I goes up by 12%. Would we predict the rate of return on BA to go up? Absolutely:

$$R_{BA} = 1\% + (2 \times 12\%) + 0 = 25\%$$

This is our best prediction when nothing is known about the firm-specific component (e_{BA}). The *realized return* (in contrast to the expected return) on BA, however, can be larger or smaller than 25%, depending on the sign of the actual deviation of e_{BA} from the straight line. For example, suppose that when the FTSE index goes up by 12%, BA also announces that it failed to develop a new personal computer model. This **firm-specific news** (news that relates to the firm specifically and not to the whole market) will make e_i negative; hence, BA stock will show an actual return lower than 25%. For example, if $e_{BA} = -10\%$, we get

$$R_{BA} = 1\% + (2 \times 12\%) - 10\% = 15\%$$

Thus, what determines the *actual* or realized future return on each asset is the common index change (I), beta, and the firm-specific factor e_i. On average, we expect the firm-specific factor to be zero. In any given period, however, it can be either negative or positive, depending on whether the news is good or bad.

If an investor can predict the common index as well as the firm-specific news, the investor can predict the rate of return on the stock. Unfortunately, these types of predictions are hard to make.

Exhibit 14.7 demonstrates graphically the component of the return that is due to the common index and the component that is due to the firm-specific risk (e_i) for AT&T. We assume that $\alpha_{AT\&T} = 1\%$ and $\beta_{AT\&T} = 0.5$. If the index (say, the S&P 500) shows

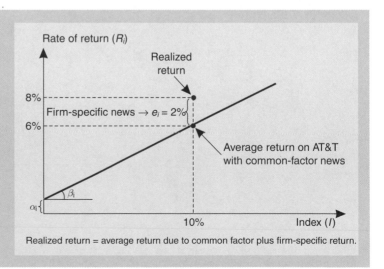

Exhibit 14.7 The return components: common factor and firm-specific factor

Realized return = average return due to common factor plus firm-specific return.

in a given year a return of 10%, then we expect *on average* that the return on AT&T in this year will be 6%:

$$R_{AT\&T} = 1\% + (^1/_2 \times 10\%) = 6\%$$

However, suppose that AT&T announces some positive information – for example, a new service that will greatly increase its profit. This firm-specific event will cause a deviation from our prediction that is based on the index only. For example, the deviation (e_i) would be positive, say 2% (see Exhibit 14.7). Therefore, the *realized rate of return*, given the information on the index as well as AT&T specific news, is

$$R_{AT\&T} = 1\% + (^1/_2 \times 10\%) + 2\% = 8\%$$

which can be rewritten in more general terms as follows:

$$R_i = \alpha_i \quad + \quad \beta_i \times I \quad + \quad e_i$$
$$\text{constant} + \text{common factor news} + \text{Firm-specific news}$$

One of the main benefits of the SIM in solving for mean–variance efficient portfolios located on the efficient frontier is the reduction in the number of inputs that must be estimated. Chapter 6 showed that in order to solve for the mean–variance efficient set, we have to minimize the portfolio's variance for a given mean return. The portfolio's variance, in turn, is a function of all possible covariances. If we have 100 stocks, for example, we first have to calculate the covariance of all possible pairs of the 100 assets. In this case, the number is $100!/(98! \times 2!) = 4{,}950$, which is quite a large number to handle.[22] The SIM is a simplified model that drastically decreases the necessary number of calculations of covariances. Using Equation 14.6, the covariance of Assets i and j is

$$\text{Cov}(R_i, R_j) = \text{Cov}(\alpha_i + \beta_i I + e_i, \alpha_j + \beta_j I + e_j)$$

The SIM assumes that Firm i's specific news is independent of Firm j's specific news. This means that if some success or failure occurs at BA, it does not affect the chance of success or failure at Marks & Spencer. In statistical terms, this assumption implies that $\text{Cov}(e_i, e_j) = 0$. Also, the deviation from the lines for e_i is assumed to be independent of the common factor, namely $\text{Cov}(I, e_i) = 0$. With these assumptions, the covariance of these two stocks is reduced to the following:[23]

$$\text{Cov}(R_i, R_j) = \beta_i \beta_j \sigma_i^2 \tag{14.7}$$

Thus, if we have 100 stocks and we estimate 100 values of β_i and σ_i^2 we get all possible covariances. Therefore, with the SIM we have to estimate only 100 betas (and σ_i^2) to get all 4,950 covariances needed without the assumptions of the SIM.[24]

---

[22] All combinations of selecting two assets out of 100 assets are given by the following formula:

$$C_2^{100} = \frac{100!}{(100 - 2)!2!}$$

where C_2^{100} denotes the combination of two taken from a population of 100, and ! denotes a factorial. For example. $4! = 4 \times 3 \times 2 \times 1 = 24$. If we know the weights, then there is no problem calculating the variance of the portfolio, because we simply calculate the variance of the given portfolio corresponding to the known weights. However, when we are trying to determine the optimal weights to select, we need all of these covariances.

[23] Recall that α_i, α_j and β_i, β_j are constants, and that the deviation from the line e_i is assumed to be independent of the index level I. That is, $\text{Cov}(I, e_i) = 0$ and $\text{Cov}(I, I) = \sigma_i^2$. Because α_i and α_j are constants, and e_i and e_j are independent, we have $\text{Cov}(R_i, R_j) = \text{Cov}(\alpha_i + \beta_i I + e_i, \alpha_j + \beta_j I + e_j) = \text{Cov}(\beta_i I, \beta_j I)$, namely, $\text{Cov}(R_i, R_j) = \beta_i \beta_j \sigma_i^2$.

[24] See Footnote 22.

Thus, the assumptions of the SIM, and in particular the assumption that $Cov(e_i, e_j) = 0$, greatly reduce the number of estimates needed for the derivation of the efficient frontier.

The SIM is similar in its structure to the arbitrage pricing model we discuss next. To see this, recall that the expected value of the firm's specific term is zero: $E(e_i) = 0$. Taking the expected value from both sides of Equation 14.6 yields

$$E(R_i) = \alpha_i + \beta_i \times E(I)$$

or

$$\alpha_i = E(R_i) - \beta_i \times E(I)$$

Substituting this expression for α_i in Equation 14.6, we get

$$R_i = \{E(R_i) - \beta_i \times E(I)\} + (\beta_i \times I) + e_i$$

which can be rewritten as

$$R_i = E(R_i) + \beta_i[I - E(I)] + e_i$$

This form of the SIM is exactly how the arbitrage pricing theory advocates that rates of return be generated. However, to derive equilibrium prices by the APT, some additional assumptions are needed. We now turn to the arbitrage pricing theory.

14.8 THE ARBITRAGE PRICING THEORY (APT)

The **arbitrage pricing theory (APT)**, like the CAPM, is an equilibrium pricing model. The APT, developed by Stephen Ross, reaches conclusions similar to those of the CAPM. However, the APT is based on a different set of assumptions. Recall that in deriving the CAPM, we assume that all investors make their investment decisions by a mean–variance rule. With this assumption, investors maximize the slope of the capital market line (CML), seeking the highest expected return for a given level of standard deviation. In deriving the APT risk–return relationship, Ross does not assume risk aversion or rely on the mean–variance rule. Rather, he explains the linear relationship between expected return and risk as arising because in equilibrium there are no arbitrage opportunities in security markets. If investors can find a portfolio that earns with certainty a positive return with a zero net initial investment, all investors will seek this attractive investment. As a result, the price of this investment will change until, in equilibrium, the positive return drops to zero, and such attractive investments vanish from the market. Indeed, the prices of all such bargains increase until no arbitrage profit opportunities are available. When this occurs, the linear risk–return relationship, which is very similar to the SML, holds.

14.8.1 Examples of arbitrage

Consider first the simplest case of arbitrage, where you can borrow $100 at Bank A at 5%, and you can deposit the money in a second fully insured Bank B to earn 6%. In this simple example, you have a zero out-of-pocket investment at t_0 and a profit of $1 at the end of the year (t_1). If such a financial situation existed, it would be an arbitrage opportunity. If you could borrow an unlimited amount of money at 5% and lend it at 6%, the potential profit would be infinite. Such a case is called a money machine; one has a machine, so to speak, to create money.

Although in general such situations do not exist in the market, the simple example illustrates the concept of an arbitrage opportunity. You create a financial transaction such that with zero net investment, you earn a positive return. If such a situation exists, arbitrage profit is available, and the financial transaction by which this profit is achieved is called an **arbitrage** transaction.

An essential property needed for the derivation of the APT is the allowance of short selling of securities. Recall that when investors sell a security short, they sell shares they do not own. The process of short selling is as follows. The investor borrows the shares from a broker and then sells the shares in the market to receive the proceeds from the sale. At some future date, the investor must buy the stocks in the market to replace the shares borrowed.

To illustrate how an investor can create an arbitrage profit using short-selling transactions, suppose you have three securities, A, B and C, with returns as given in Exhibit 14.8. For simplicity, assume that each share is trading at $100, so the profit or loss in dollars is also the percentage return on your investment. For example, making $10 on a $100 investment means a 10% rate of return. It is obvious from Exhibit 14.8 that Stock B does not always earn a better return than Stock A – Stock B yields a lower return in a recession and in a stable economy than does Stock A. In addition, Stock C does not always earn a better return than Stock A. Stock C yields a lower return than Stock A when the economy booms.

Although neither Stock B nor Stock C is always better than Stock A, you can create a portfolio of B and C such that arbitrage opportunities are available. Recall that when an investor short sells an asset, the dollar profit to the short-seller is reversed. If the profit is −$2 (see Stock A in a recession), this means the stock dropped by 2%. However, because the short-seller sells it today and returns the stock to the broker after buying it back at a lower price, the short-seller's profit is +$2. Suppose you borrow a share from the broker and sell it for $100. (The broker just lends you a share and hence you do not pay any money.) After a month, the stock drops to $98 (a +2% rate of return). You buy it back for $98, return the stock to the broker, and make a profit of +$2.

We will show below that holding a portfolio of Stocks B and C and selling short Stock A produces an arbitrage profit. Suppose you sell short two shares of Stock A for $200, take the $200 proceeds from the short sale, and buy one share of Stock C for $100 and one share of Stock B for $100. The return from the transaction in dollars is given in Exhibit 14.9. If a recession occurs, then stock A will lose −$2. However, you were short two shares of Stock A, and you have a gain of 2 × 2 = $4, as illustrated in the second column of Exhibit 14.9. Buying one share of Stocks B and C in a recession will result in a $4 loss on Stock B and no profit or loss on Stock C, as illustrated in the third column of Exhibit 14.9. A similar calculation shows a profit of $14 on Stocks B and C in a stable economy and a profit of $22 if the economy booms. Hence, the total net return from the arbitrage transaction is +$4 − $4 = $0 if recession

Exhibit 14.8 Profit and loss on an investment

State of the economy	Securities		
	A	B	C
Recession	−$2	−$4	$0
Stable	6	4	10
Boom	10	16	6

Exhibit 14.9 Arbitrage profit with short sales

Cash flow from transaction

State of the economy	Short sale of two shares of Stock A	Portfolio of one share of Stock B and one share of Stock C	Total net return from the arbitrage transaction
Recession	2 × ($2) = $4	(1 × −$4) + (1 × −$0) = $4	+$4 − $4 = 0
Stable	2 × (−$6) = −$12	(1 × $4) + (1 × $10) = $14	−$12 + $14 = $2
Boom	2 × (−$10) = −$20	(1 × $16) + (1 × $6) = $22	−$20 + $22 = $2

occurs. Following similar logic, you have a $2 gain if either a stable or a boom economy exists.

The initial investment on the transaction described in Exhibit 14.9 is zero (ignoring any trading costs), because the investor sells short two shares of stock A, gets the $200 proceeds, and invests $100 in Stock B and $100 in Stock C. The investor's future net return is always nonnegative regardless of the state of the economy. The investor gains either nothing (in a recession) or $2 (in a stable or boom economy). This is clearly an arbitrage opportunity. Why not double the transaction to $400 and make a potential profit of $4 (or $0), or invest $2,000 in Stocks B and C to make a profit of $20 (or $0), or even invest $1 million in Stocks B and C to make an arbitrage profit of $10,000 (or $0). The investor will continue to sell Stock A short and buy Stocks B and C to earn arbitrage profits. With these three stocks we have a money machine. However, by the APT this is impossible to hold in equilibrium.

With many such transactions in large amounts, there will be selling pressure on Stock A and buying pressure on Stocks B and C. Therefore, the price of Stock A will fall (hence the investor will get less from the short sale), and the price of Stocks B and C will go up (hence the investor will pay more for Stocks A and B) until eventually no arbitrage opportunities are available. The arbitrage will disappear because with these new prices the investor has to pay out-of-pocket money to create the transaction suggested above. For example, if the investor pays $1 for the suggested position (e.g. the price of A falls to $99.75 and the price of B and C increases to $100.25) and a recession occurs, the income is zero (see Exhibit 14.8), and the investor loses because he could earn a riskless interest on the investment of $1. Obviously, the larger the investment, the larger the loss. Thus, with these new prices of the three stocks, arbitrage profit vanishes.

14.8.2 The APT: assumptions and risk–return relationship

Recall that by the definition of an arbitrage opportunity, with a zero investment, the future return on the portfolio must be nonnegative. Ross employs this argument to derive the APT. Because prices change when arbitrage exists, he explores which asset prices should be in equilibrium in order to eliminate arbitrage opportunities. The mean return and risk of each asset also change until arbitrage opportunities disappear. In short, when arbitrage transactions are available, the economy is not in equilibrium. This is why the APT is an equilibrium pricing model. Thus, the APT investigates the market equilibrium prices when all arbitrage transactions are eliminated. This section examines the assumptions and resulting asset pricing of the APT.

The assumptions underlying the APT follow:

1 Rates of return depend on some common factors and some 'noise', which is firm specific. This return dependency is called a return-generating process.
2 A very large number of assets exist in the economy.
3 Short sales are allowed, and the proceeds are available to the short-sellers.
4 There are no transaction costs.
5 Investors prefer more wealth to less.

Note that unlike the CAPM, there is no need to assume that investors choose the investment by the mean–variance rule.

According to the APT, the rates of return on Security i, R_i, in a given period (say, a month) are generated by the following process:

$$R_i = E(R_i) + \beta_i[I - E(I)] + e_i \tag{14.8}$$

where R_i is the rate of return on Security i ($i = 1, 2, \ldots, n$), I is the value of the factor (or index) generating the return R_i (that is, the percentage change in some index, as in the SIM), and $E(I)$ is the mean of this factor. Because only one factor is involved, this model is called the *one-factor model*. The coefficient β_i measures the sensitivity of changes in R_i as a result of changes in I. The term e_i is the 'noise', or the deviation from the line that is the firm specific factor; that is, whereas all firms have the same common factor I, each has a different e_i.

The assumed return-generating process is identical to the return process predicted by the SIM (see Section 14.7). However, whereas the SIM's main purpose is to provide an easy way to calculate all possible pairs of correlations, the return-generating process given by Equation 14.8 is constructed for the purpose of deriving the risk–return linear relationship (similar to the CAPM); hence, further assumptions beyond the return-generating process are needed to derive the APT results.

The most important characteristic of this return-generating process is that I is a common factor to all risky assets, just as it is in the SIM. Because this factor is common to all assets, its fluctuations cannot be diversified away. The common factor could be the inflation rate in the economy, the unemployment rate, the interest rate on government bonds, the gross national product (GNP), or even, as in the CAPM, the rate of return on the market portfolio R_m. Note that the APT uses $I - E(I)$ instead of simply I. This is called the 'surprise' factor. For example, if we expect the inflation rate to increase on average by, say, $E(I) = 10\%$, and it actually increases by $I = 12\%$, we have a 2% surprise, or unexpected, factor. Thus, the APT measures the difference between expectations and actual outcome rather than simply actual outcome.

The larger an asset's beta, the larger the effect of the surprise on the asset's return. Another possible surprise is firm specific and is given by e_i, which is predicted to be zero before the firm-specific news is declared. As with the SIM, this firm-specific news could be the resignation of the chairman of General Motors, an increase in the dividends of AT&T, or a new drug discovery by Johnson & Johnson. Thus, like the SIM we have a common factor's surprise, $I - E(I)$, and a firm's specific surprise, e_i.

14.8.3 The linear APT relationship

To examine the relationship between risk and expected return implied by the APT, we first examine a unique portfolio that has a zero beta and requires no investment due to short selling. Thus, the determination of asset prices by the APT relies on the following rule.

Rule 8: Zero beta, zero investment portfolios must yield zero return.

The main result of the APT is the implied linear risk–return relationship similar to the SML. The proof of this relationship relies on Rule 1. Suppose we invest a proportion of our wealth (w_i) in the ith asset. Then, by multiplying all terms in Equation 14.8 by w_i and summing up for all n assets held in the portfolio, we get

$$\sum_{i=1}^{n} w_i R_i = \sum_{i=1}^{n} w_i E(R_i) + [I - E(I)]\sum_{i=1}^{n} w_i \beta_i + \sum_{i=1}^{n} w_i e_i$$

Because $\sum_{i=1}^{n} w_i R_i = R_p$ is the return on the created portfolio whose mean return is $\sum_{i=1}^{n} w_i E(R_i) = E(R_p)$, the above equation can be rewritten as follows:

$$R_p = E(R_p) + [I - E(I)]\sum_{i=1}^{n} w_i \beta_i + \sum_{i=1}^{n} w_i e_i$$

For *a very large portfolio* composed of many securities (that is, n is very large), the noise factors tend to cancel each other, so we can safely assume that $\sum_{i=1}^{n} w_i e_i \cong 0$. Therefore, for a very large portfolio, R_p is given by

$$R_p = E(R_p) + [I - E(I)]\sum_{i=1}^{n} w_i \beta_i$$

where $\sum_{i=1}^{n} w_i \beta_i$ is the portfolio beta, which is actually the average of all the assets' betas weighted by their proportion (w_i) in the portfolio. Thus, the rate of return on a portfolio by the APT is equal to the expected return plus an adjustment for unanticipated changes in the common factor. Deviation of the portfolio return from what was expected is a function of the portfolio beta and the magnitude of the unanticipated change in the common factor.

Now suppose you can create a portfolio with *zero investment* and with *zero risk*, namely, $\sum_{i=1}^{n} w_i = 0$ and $\sum_{i=1}^{n} w_i \beta_i = 0$. Such a portfolio is called a zero beta portfolio. What should the return be on such a portfolio? According to the above equation, the return must be $R_p = E(R_p)$, because the second term on the right-hand side is zero. Note that the rate of return on such a portfolio is equal to its mean $[E(R_p)]$, and because $E(R_p)$ is constant the return R_p has *no variability*. Because by assumption this is a zero investment portfolio, the expected return must be equal to zero (see Rule 8); otherwise, we have an arbitrage opportunity. For example, if the zero beta, zero investment portfolio had positive dollar returns, then this would be a money machine because you can earn positive return with no risk. Alternatively, if this portfolio had negative dollar returns, then an investor could construct another portfolio with exactly opposite weights (i.e. short this portfolio) that would result in positive dollar returns.

With no arbitrage opportunities and using the zero beta and zero investment portfolio, Ross demonstrated that the mean return on the ith asset, $E(R_i)$, is related to β_i in a linear fashion as follows:

$$E(R_i) = \alpha_0 + \alpha_1 \beta_i \tag{14.9}$$

where α_0 and α_1 are constant across securities. This result is very similar to the CAPM. Indeed, when we use the market portfolio as the index, we get $\alpha_0 = r$, and $\alpha_1 = E(R_m) - r$, with the APT and CAPM yielding identical results.

But how can one construct zero beta portfolio with zero investment? For simplicity, we demonstrate how to do this with three stocks; however, recall that in order for the ATP to hold, we need many assets to be included in the portfolio. To show that Equation 14.9 is intact, let us look at the following three stocks. (For simplicity, assume each stock has the same market price.)

	Stock		
	A	B	C
Mean return, $E(R_i)$	8%	13%	?
Beta, β_i	1	2	3

Our goal is to select a mean rate of return on Stock C such that we can construct a zero investment, zero risk portfolio of Stocks A, B and C with no arbitrage opportunities. Suppose we plot A and B and connect them by a straight line. What mean rate of return should hold such that also Stock C will place it on line AB? We will show that when the mean rate of return of Stock C is determined such that no arbitrage exists, point C will be on the straight line connecting points B and A. Namely, all points are located on a straight line, which illustrates that the APT linear relationship given by Equation 14.9 is intact.

If we select investment proportions $w_A = 1$, $w_B = -2$ and $w_C = 1$, then[25]

$$\sum_{i=1}^{n} w_i = 1 - 2 + 1 = 0$$

and

$$\sum_{i=1}^{n} w_i \times \beta_i = (1 \times 1) + (2 \times (-2)) + 3 \times 1 = 0$$

Thus, we have constructed a zero investment and zero risk portfolio.

According to Rule 8 the portfolio with zero beta and zero investment should not provide arbitrage profit, so we must have[26]

$$1 \times 8\% - 2 \times 13\% + 1 \times E(R_{\hat{C}}) = 0$$

Therefore, $E(R_{\hat{C}}) = 26\% - 8\% = 18\%$. If $E(R_{\hat{C}}) = 18\%$, there is no arbitrage profit. Let us elaborate. Suppose that $E(R_{\hat{C}}) = 20\%$. Then we can earn the following on a portfolio with a zero risk and zero investment:

$$R_p = E(R_p) = 1 \times 8\% - 2 \times 13\% + 1 \times 20\% = 2\%$$

---

[25] To obtain the weights, we solve two equations with two unknowns (w_1 and w_2):

$$w_1 + w_2 + (1 - w_1 - w_2) = 0$$

and

$$(w_1 \times 1) + (w_2 \times 2) + ((1 - w_1 - w_2) \times 3) = 0$$

Note that a negative weight implies short selling.

[26] The equation claiming that $R_p = E(R_p) = 0$ is generally not true for only three stocks, because for three stocks, we would not expect that the sum of the error terms would actually be zero. We really need a large number of stocks to demonstrate the APT. Thus, here we assume that the sum of the error terms is zero (as if we had an infinite number of assets) but demonstrate the linear relationship by focusing on only three points. This greatly simplifies the demonstration.

Hence, there are arbitrage opportunities. Holding such a portfolio creates a positive certain profit with no investment. This is impossible in equilibrium, because it constitutes a 'money machine'. Similarly, if $E(R_{\hat{C}})$ is lower than 18%, say 15%, with zero investment and risk, we get a negative return of

$$R_p = E(R_p) = 1 \times 8\% - 2 \times 13\% + 1 \times 15\% = -3\%$$

Then, by short selling such a portfolio with zero investment, we get a positive return, which is again a money machine.[27] To sum up, in equilibrium with no arbitrage possibilities, we must have $E(R_{\hat{C}}) = 18\%$. We will use this result later in the APT linear relationship demonstration.

Now what is left to show is that the point given by $E(R_C) = 18\%$ and $\beta_C = 3$, which characterizes Stock C when there are no arbitrage opportunities, indeed lies on the same straight line as Stocks A and B, as asserted by the APT. Exhibit 14.10 demonstrates the straight line connecting points A and B with the relevant parameters taken from the example. The slope of the line is $(13\% - 8\%)/(2 - 1) = 5\%$, which is the line KB (the rise) divided by the line KA (the run). The intercept of this line can be found by inserting the parameters of point A (or point B) and employing the straight-line formula with a slope of 5%:

$$E(R_i) = \alpha_0 + (5\% \times \beta_i)$$

Because for Stock A we have $E(R_A) = 8\%$ and $\beta_A = 1$, we get $8\% = \alpha_0 + (5\% \times 1)$; thus, $\alpha_0 = 3\%$. Therefore, the straight line connecting Stocks A and B is given by $E(R_i) = 3\% + (5\% \times \beta_i)$, where $\alpha_0 = 3\%$ and $\alpha_1 = 5\%$. Because one can pass a straight line between any two points, these findings so far neither support nor refute the APT. The crucial test of the APT is whether Stock C with $E(R_C) = 18\%$ and $\beta_C = 3$, which are the necessary parameters to eliminate an arbitrage profit, also lies on the same line. To test this, we substitute 18% for $E(R_C)$ and 3 for β_C, and check whether there is an identity with this straight-line parameter:

$$18\% = \alpha_0 + \alpha_1 \times 3$$

Indeed, with $\alpha_0 = 3\%$ and $\alpha_1 = 5\%$, we have

$$3\% + (5\% \times 3) = 18\%$$

which implies that the third point, corresponding to Stock C, also lies on the same straight line. If $E(R_C)$ is greater than 18% (say, 23%), the point is above the line (see point C_1 in Exhibit 14.10). If $E(R_C)$ is lower than 18% (say, 13%), the point is below the line (see point C_2 in Exhibit 14.10).

Because a mean return of exactly 18% for Stock C eliminates an arbitrage possibility, and all three stocks lie on the same straight line, we conclude that when arbitrage opportunities are eliminated, we get the following linear relationship for the three stocks under consideration:

$$E(R_i) = \alpha_0 + \alpha_1 \beta_i$$

where α_0 and α_1 are the intercept and the slope of the APT line, respectively. This is similar to the CAPM risk–return relationship. When arbitrage opportunities are

---

[27] Recall that when you short sell a portfolio with zero initial investment, you get no proceeds from the short sale. If you hold a portfolio of two assets (say, $w_1 = +1$, $w_2 = -1$ and $\Sigma w_i = 0$), then by short selling it you get $w_1 = -1$, $w_2 = +1$, and again $\Sigma w_i = 0$. Thus, selling a zero investment portfolio remains a zero investment strategy.

Exhibit 14.10 Illustration of no arbitrage under the APT

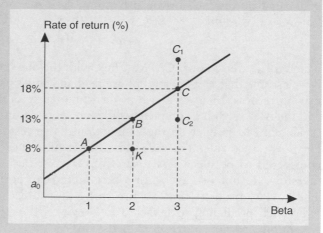

available, not all stocks will lie on this line; hence, it will not describe the relationship between $E(R_i)$ and β_i. When all arbitrage opportunities vanish, all assets must lie on this straight line.

The APT linear relationship has been illustrated with three stocks, but the same principle holds with a portfolio having any number of stocks. As long as one of the stocks is not on the straight line, an arbitrage profit can be made. To eliminate such an arbitrage profit, all $[E(R_i),\beta_i]$ points must lie on the one straight line. We assumed a zero investment, zero beta portfolio to derive the APT, but the linear relationship derived holds for any individual asset, no matter what the beta is and, of course, for nonzero investments. For example, if $\alpha_0 = 5\%$ and $\alpha_1 = 10\%$, and the beta of Xerox is 2, we expect to earn on an investment in Xerox $5\% + (10\% \times 2) = 25\%$. Thus, every \$1 investment in Xerox is expected to grow to \$1.25. Similarly, if beta is zero, every dollar invested is expected to grow to \$1.05.

Let us now turn to the intuitive explanation of the linear risk–return relationship and to the meaning of the coefficients α_0 and α_1. First, because the APT assumes that a large portfolio is held, the variance of the unsystematic risk of each asset is not important.[28] This by no means implies that unsystematic risk does not exist. However, investors will not change the required risk premium from the asset due to the 'noise', because this part of the risk is eliminated in a large portfolio. If two stocks have the same beta, but one has a large unsystematic risk and the other has zero unsystematic risk, both will be priced the same and hence have the same average return.

14.9 THE APT AND THE CAPM

When the common factor in the APT model is the market portfolio – for example, the S&P 500 index – then $\alpha_1 = E(R_m) - r$, the risk premium of the market portfolio. In this instance, the APT and the CAPM yield the same results. To see this, select the market portfolio as the common factor, where the beta of the market portfolio is $+1$; it would

---

[28] Unsystematic and systematic risk have the same interpretation with the APT as with the SIM.

be located on the line shown in Exhibit 14.10 (see point A). The line can be found as follows: $\alpha_0 = r$ and $\alpha_1 = [E(R_m) - r]/1$ (the slope of the line). From Equation 14.9,

$$E(R_i) = r + [E(R_m) - r]\beta_i$$

which is the well-known CAPM. Thus, with the market portfolio as the common factor, if we assume that large portfolios are held and some specific return-generating process is driving returns, then we arrive at the same result as the CAPM. However, the CAPM and the APT rely on a completely different set of assumptions.

The CAPM is built on the assumption that investors are risk averse and follow the mean–variance rule. The APT does not require these assumptions. Thus, the APT is considered to be much less restrictive. That is, the APT can apply to markets where investors are not risk averse or where more than portfolio mean and variance matter. The CAPM predicts that all investors will hold the same market portfolio; there is no such prediction with the APT. However, the APT assumes some specific return-generating process not required by the CAPM.

The APT also can be extended to include more than one common factor in the return-generating process. The major disadvantage of the APT is that it fails to tell us exactly what the common factors are. Many researchers have attempted to establish the appropriate number of factors, as well as exactly which variables are the best to use as the factors. Similarly, if there is only one factor, the APT fails to tell what that factor is.

14.10 MULTIFACTOR APT MODEL

So far, we have assumed that only one factor, I, generates the return on the various assets. It is possible, however, that several macro-economic factors generate the return on the assets, such as the inflation rate and the unemployment rate. Denoting the jth factor by I_j whose mean is $E(I_j)$, the multifactor model assumes that rates of return on the ith asset are generated by the following process:

$$R_i = E(R_i) + \beta_{i1}[I_1 - E(I_1)] + \beta_{i2}[I_2 - E(I_2)] + \ldots + \beta_{iK}[I_K - E(I_K)] + e_i$$

where there are K factors, and β_{ij} is the sensitivity of the return of the ith stock to the I_j factor ($j = 1, 2,\ldots, K$). The same no-arbitrage-opportunity approach can be used where we have zero investment ($\Sigma w_i = 0$) with zero betas for each of the above factors. Thus, $\Sigma w_i \beta_{i1} = 0$, $\Sigma w_i \beta_{i2} = 0$, and so forth, and there is no arbitrage opportunity. Following this procedure, we get a linear relationship similar to the one-factor APT of the following form:

$$E(R_i) = \alpha_0 + \alpha_1\beta_1 + \alpha_2\beta_2 + \ldots + \alpha_K \beta_K$$

which is a generalization of the APT when K factors, rather than one factor, are generating the returns. α_0 is the rate of return expected if all betas are zero (the risk-free rate), α_i is the market price of the risk related to factor i on a per-unit basis, and β_i is the sensitivity of the security to factor i.

In practice, the relevant risk factors are selected based on their historical influence on returns. For example, Berry, Burmeister and McElroy suggest the following factors:

1 Unanticipated changes in bond default premiums (government bonds versus corporate bonds).
2 Unanticipated changes in the term structure (20-year government bonds versus one-month Treasury bills).
3 Unanticipated changes in inflation.

4 Unanticipated changes in the growth rate of corporate profits.
5 Unanticipated changes in residual market risk (the part of the S&P 500 return not explained by the previous four factors).[29]

The remaining task in applying this five-factor model is to estimate the market price of risk for each factor. Although the market price of risk is difficult to estimate, this task is not impossible. Clearly, the multifactor APT model is much more flexible than the CAPM.

SUMMARY

■ *Understand why beta is the appropriate measure of risk.*
Beta – the slope of the characteristic line – is a risk measure that takes into account the variance of the asset under consideration, as well as the covariances with all other assets included in the portfolio. Beta is the correct risk measure of individual assets as well as portfolios.

■ *Understand why the security market line (SML) and the capital asset pricing model (CAPM) describe the equilibrium relationship between risk and expected rate of return.*
In equilibrium, all assets, individual stocks and portfolios lie on a straight line called the security market line (SML). According to the CAPM, the higher asset risk (beta) is, the higher the expected rate of return will be. In equilibrium, all assets are correctly priced, and one cannot find 'bargains'. Any deviation from the SML implies that the market is not in the CAPM equilibrium.

■ *Understand that if a well-diversified portfolio is held, only the systematic risk which cannot be washed out by diversification determines the risk premium.*
The nonsystematic risk is irrelevant. Show that for efficient portfolios the CML (of Chapter 6) coincides with the SML. Hence, for efficient portfolios, sigma as well as beta can serve as measured risk.

■ *Show that all assets must be located on the SML including individual assets and inefficient portfolios.*
Hence, beta is a measure of risk of all assets.

■ *Understand how practitioners who believe in market inefficiency use alpha and beta to select underpriced stocks.*
Practitioners use the CAPM's beta (systematic risk) as a measure of risk but believe that the market is not always in equilibrium. Therefore, they try to find underpriced stocks (that is, stocks that are located above the SML). These stocks are characterized by a relatively large alpha.

■ *Explain the single index model (SIM) and why it reduces the efficient frontier computations.*

■ *Explain the arbitrage pricing theory (APT), its assumptions and the resulting linear relationship.*
The primary assumption of the APT is that security returns are generated by a linear factor model. The APT is based on a no-arbitrage condition. That is, an investor should

---

[29] See Michael A. Berry, Edwin Burmeister and Marjorie B. McElroy, 'Sorting out risks using known APT factors', *Financial Analysts Journal*, March–April 1988, pp. 29–42.

not be able to build a zero risk, zero investment portfolio that has positive returns. However, the APT assumes that there are many assets in the economy and that there is some specific return-generating process:

$$E(R_i) = \alpha_0 + \alpha_1\beta_1 + \alpha_2\beta_2 + \ldots + \alpha_K\beta_K$$

■ *Compare and contrast the relationship between the CAPM and the APT.*
The APT is an alternative equilibrium pricing model that is built on different assumptions from the CAPM. Specifically, the APT does not assume that investors make decisions according to the mean–variance rule; also, investors do not have to be risk averse.

KEY TERMS

Abnormal return	Characteristic line	Market portfolio
Aggressive stock	Common factor	Market risk
Alpha	Defensive stock	Neutral stock
Arbitrage	Efficient portfolio	Security market line
Arbitrage pricing theory	Error term	(SML)
(APT)	Excess return	Single index model (SIM)
Beta	Firm-specific news	Systematic risk
Capital asset pricing	Firm's specific risk	Unsystematic risk
model (CAPM)	General capital asset	Zero beta portfolio
Capital market line (CML)	pricing model (GCAPM)	

QUESTIONS

14.1 The rates of return on GM and on the market portfolio (R_m) for the last four years follow:

Year	GM	R_m
1	−5%	+10%
2	20	15
3	−2	−6
4	+30	+25

(a) Calculate the beta.
(b) Calculate the systematic and unsystematic risk, as well as the proportion of each in the variance of GM stock.

14.2 It is given that $E(R_m) = 10\%$, $\sigma_m = 10\%$ and $r = 5\%$. Draw the CML.

14.3 According to the CML, we have

$$E(R_p) = r + \frac{E(R_m) - r}{\sigma_m}\sigma_p$$

which holds for efficient portfolios (p). According to the SML, we have

$$E(R_p) = r + [E(R_m) - r]\beta_p$$

which holds for efficient portfolios as well as inefficient portfolios and individual assets. Show that for efficient portfolios, these two formulas are equivalent (hence, no contradiction arises).

14.4 Suppose there are two portfolios on the CML denoted by x and y. Calculate the correlation of x with y.

14.5 You have the following information: the stock is an aggressive stock, the systematic risk is 0.016, and the market portfolio has the following rates of return:

Year	Rate of return
1	5%
2	20%
3	10%

Calculate the stock's beta.

14.6 Suppose you receive the following rates of return on Assets X and Y:

Probability	X	Y
$1/2$	5%	3%
$1/2$	5%	20%

Calculate the expected rate of return and variance of each asset, as well as the covariance of X and Y. Explain your results.

14.7 (a) Suppose there are only two stocks in the market. The portfolio is composed of $1/2$ of Asset A and $1/2$ of Asset B. The standard deviations are $\sigma_A = 10\%$ and $\sigma_B = 20\%$. The covariance is $Cov(R_A, R_B) = 0.02$. What is the percentage contribution of each asset to the portfolio variance?

(b) Suppose that the means are $E(R_A) = 10\%$ and $E(R_B) = 10\%$, and the risk-free interest rate is 5%. Is the market in equilibrium? Does the CAPM hold with these parameters?

14.8 (a) Prove that the beta of the market portfolio is equal to 1.

(b) Calculate the beta of the market portfolio with the following data:

Year	Rate of return on the market portfolio
1	5%
2	10
3	20

14.9 Suppose that in the regression line

$$R_{i_t} = \alpha_i + \beta_i R_{m_t} + e_{i_t}$$

all residuals are $e_{i_t} = 0$. 'The beta, then, must be equal to 1.' Evaluate this statement. Demonstrate your answer graphically.

14.10 (a) Suppose there are two stocks, A and B, with $\beta_B = \beta_A$. 'Then, if the CAPM holds, it must be true that $E(R_B) = 2E(R_A)$.' Do you agree? Demonstrate your answer with $\beta_A = 1$, $\beta_B = 2$, $E(R_m) = 10\%$ and $r = 5\%$.

(b) How would you change your answer to (a) if $r = 0$?

14.11 Suppose that the CAPM holds and $\beta_i = 0.9$, $E(R_i) = 10\%$ and $E(R_m) = 10.5\%$. Calculate the risk-free interest rate (r).

14.12 Suppose you have the following data for Stock A and the market portfolio:

Year	Rate of return on Stock A	Rate of return on the market
1	5%	8%
2	3	-2
3	20	30

(a) Calculate β_A.

(b) Calculate σ_A^2.

(c) Calculate the systematic and nonsystematic risk component. Discuss these rules in proportional terms.

14.13 Suppose you have the following figures:

Year	Stock A return	Market portfolio return
1	10%	5%
2	5	2.5
3	20	10

(a) Calculate the unsystematic risk component.

(b) Calculate the correlation between R_A and R_m.

(c) Prove that when the unsystematic risk is zero and the beta is positive, then the correlation coefficient is +1.

SELECTED REFERENCES

Bansal, Ravi, David A. Hsieh, and S. Viswanathan. 'A new approach to international arbitrage pricing'. *Journal of Finance*, 48, December 1993, pp. 1719–47.

Berry, Michael A., Edwin Burmeister, and Marjorie B. McElroy. 'Sorting out risks using known APT factors'. *Financial Analysts Journal*, March–April 1988, pp. 29–42.

Grundy, Kevin, and Burton Malkiel. 'Reports of beta's death have been greatly exaggerated'. *Journal of Portfolio Management*, Spring 1996, pp. 36–45.

Lintner, John. 'Security prices and maximal gains from diversification'. *Journal of Finance*, December 1965, pp. 587–615.

Merton, Robert. 'An intertemporal capital asset pricing model'. *Economica*, 41, September 1973, pp. 867–80.

Roll, R. 'A critique of the asset pricing theory's tests, Part I: On past and potential testability of the theory'. *Journal of Financial Economics*, 4, March 1977, pp. 129–76.

Ross, S.A. 'The arbitrage theory of capital pricing'. *Journal of Economic Theory*, December 1976, pp. 341–60.

Sharpe, William F. 'A simplied model for portfolio analysis'. *Management Science*, January 1963, pp. 277–93.

Sharpe, William F. 'Capital asset prices: a theory of market equilibrium'. *Journal of Finance*, September 1964, pp. 425–42.

Shleifer, Andrei, and Robert W. Vishry. 'The Limits of Arbitrage'. *Journal of Finance*, March 1997, pp. 35–55.

SUPPLEMENTARY REFERENCES

Beliossi, G. 'Take the long and short route'. *Risk*, November 2000, Vol. 13, No. 11.

Lundin, M., and Satchell, S. 'The long and the short of it'. *Risk*, August 2000, Vol. 13, No. 8.

Miller, Edward M. 'Why the low returns to beta and other forms of risk?' *The Journal of Portfolio Management*, Winter, 2001.

Chapter 15

INTERNATIONAL INVESTMENT

Learning objectives

After studying this chapter you should be able to:

1 Identify the risks and returns in international investment.

2 Explain how an investor can benefit from international diversification.

3 Understand purchasing power parity.

4 Understand interest rate parity.

5 Describe the techniques used to predict exchange rates.

INVESTMENT IN THE NEWS

Missing out on international diversification

By Andrew West, CFA

Huge companies like J.P. Morgan and Merrill Lynch can't see beyond the tech and telecom giants dominating global indexes, but the wise investor may well benefit from considering smaller international stocks that are off the beaten path.

...Back in 1990, it was easy to demonstrate the importance of global investing. A twenty-year history of global indexes showed that international equities had generated higher returns than US stocks, while international stocks' low correlations with the US created diversification benefits. So international stocks had a history of boosting returns while reducing portfolio risk.

The next ten years changed this perspective, as the US stock market soared and the Japanese and other foreign markets lagged. Further, emerging markets were hit hard between 1995 and 1996, with crises in Latin America, Asia and Eastern Europe. Thanks to all of this, a superficial review of the data indeed suggested that investing overseas is no longer compelling.

According to the *New York Times* article, Merrill Lynch recently reduced its recommended foreign stock allocation for wealthy clients from 35%

to 5%. J.P. Morgan Chase recently lowered its allocation guideline to 10% to 15%. Both downgrades were based on an increase in correlation between the returns of US and international stock indexes...

One thing to understand about correlation is that **some industries are correlated across countries and some industries are not**. For example, iron or gold mining stocks are highly correlated, regardless of origin, because the main factors affecting them are pretty much the same – the price of iron or gold. Giant multinational corporations, no matter where their home, also tend to be correlated, as they depend on the same **global economy**. The price of a computer memory chip is pretty much equal around the world, so chipmakers are similarly affected and correlated to changes in the industry. On the other hand, many industries are affected primarily by **local conditions**, and their stocks tend to have little correlation across borders. For example, retailers, restaurants, real estate, and local banks have few common factors across borders, particularly if small size limits their geographic spread...

▶

INVESTMENT IN THE NEWS

Why have Finland's stock market and the Nasdaq index become highly correlated? Because Nokia happens to represent over 60% of Finland's market, the company is affected by global telecommunications sales, and among its largest holders are US based technology fund groups like Janus...

Given this, if you want more benefits from international diversification, then consider buying small-cap stocks that are owned mostly by local (foreign) investors and are affected by mostly *local* business conditions. Perhaps huge companies like J.P. Morgan and Merrill Lynch can't see beyond the tech and telecom giants dominating global indexes, but the wise investor may well benefit from considering smaller international stocks that are off the beaten path.

Andrew West is a Contributing Economics Editor for Capitalism Magazine. He is Senior Portfolio Manager and Senior Vice President at Global Assets Advisors Inc., a subsidiary of International Assets Holding Corp. He is currently working at the firm's New York City branch.

Source: Website at http://www.capitalismmagazine.com/2001/february/aw_int_diversify.htm. *Capitalism Magazine*, 14 February 2001. © *Capitalism Magazine* 2001.

Dow Jones Global Indexes

Region/ Country	DJ Global Indexes, Local Curr. Latest Fri.	Wkly % Chg.	DJ Global Indexes, U.S. $ Latest Fri.	Wkly % Chg.	DJ Global Indexes, U.S. $ on 12/29/00	Point Chg. From 12/29/00	% Chg From 12/29/00
Americas			**270.82**	**−0.26**	**299.12**	**−28.30**	**−9.46**
Brazil	1519800.45	−0.27	244.28	−0.54	331.64	−87.36	−26.34
Canada	247.92	+0.52	187.02	+1.30	225.44	−38.43	−17.04
Chile	251.94	+1.17	141.28	+0.31	143.39	−2.11	−1.47
Mexico	486.21	+2.35	162.82	+2.35	132.23	+30.59	+23.13
U.S.	278.77	−0.33	278.77	−0.33	306.88	−28.11	−9.16
Venezuela	500.69	−0.41	42.62	−0.62	39.07	+3.54	+9.06
Latin America			**160.67**	**+0.67**	**173.23**	**−12.56**	**−7.25**
Europe			**193.69**	**+0.53**	**241.06**	**−47.37**	**−19.65**
Austria	135.34	−0.83	92.52	−0.08	86.11	+6.41	+7.44
Belgium	254.51	−1.53	174.07	−0.79	196.67	−22.60	−11.49
Denmark	295.92	−0.40	206.25	+0.31	243.91	−37.66	−15.44
Finland	1299.44	+5.14	794.47	+5.93	1536.01	−741.54	−48.28
France	292.45	+1.49	202.63	+2.25	252.58	−49.94	−19.77
Germany	262.37	−0.12	178.80	+0.63	218.82	−40.02	−18.29
Greece	248.76	+9.26	125.52	+10.09	169.28	−43.76	−25.85
Ireland	476.50	−3.28	318.22	−2.55	311.95	+6.27	+2.01
Italy	267.85	+1.35	150.44	+2.11	191.99	−41.55	−21.64
Netherlands	403.81	+0.58	275.33	+1.34	335.33	−60.00	−17.89
Norway	208.14	−0.02	136.59	+0.93	167.45	−30.86	−18.43
Portugal	237.13	+0.71	140.73	+1.46	184.28	−43.54	−23.63
Spain	316.49	−1.24	162.62	−0.50	193.29	−30.68	−15.87
Sweden	409.96	+1.42	228.96	+2.38	338.88	−109.92	−32.44
Switzerland	379.94	−2.41	299.61	−2.08	415.49	−115.87	−27.89
United Kingdom	219.87	+0.07	167.46	−0.24	199.82	−32.36	−16.20
South Africa			**91.28**	**−1.95**	**93.89**	**−2.61**	**−2.78**
Pacific Region			**81.64**	**−1.02**	**93.05**	**−11.40**	**−12.26**
Australia	221.03	−2.89	147.87	−2.35	156.17	−8.30	−5.31
Hong Kong	211.03	−1.46	210.42	−1.47	245.57	−35.15	−14.32
Indonesia	162.38	−3.37	32.19	+7.11	31.25	+0.94	+3.01
Japan	75.19	−0.87	75.97	−1.29	88.30	−12.32	−13.96
Malaysia	118.83	+0.00	85.09	+0.00	88.50	−3.41	−3.86
New Zealand	131.23	+0.92	99.99	+1.70	96.68	+3.31	+3.43

INVESTMENT IN THE NEWS

Region/ Country	DJ Global Indexes, Local Curr. Latest Fri.	Wkly % Chg.	DJ Global Indexes, U.S. $ Latest Fri.	Wkly % Chg.	DJ Global Indexes, U.S. $ on 12/29/00	Point Chg. From 12/29/00	% Chg From 12/29/00
Philippines	129.41	−1.29	62.89	−1.75	73.52	−10.63	−14.46
Singapore	121.49	−0.11	109.71	+1.53	135.32	−25.61	−18.93
South Korea	99.06	+1.47	57.99	+1.86	53.14	+4.85	+9.13
Taiwan	113.37	+2.02	84.16	+2.69	95.88	−11.72	−12.23
Thailand	52.80	−5.71	27.28	−5.37	27.19	+0.09	+0.34
Euro Zone			195.41	+1.45	246.62	−51.21	−20.77
Europe (ex.U.K.)			206.31	+0.99	263.06	−56.75	−21.57
Nordic Region			273.60	+3.20	425.85	−152.25	−35.75
Pacific Region (ex. Japan)			127.11	−0.36	138.35	−11.24	−8.12
World (ex. U.S.)			130.53	+0.05	156.88	−26.35	−16.79
DOW JONES WORLD STOCK INDEX			184.31	−0.17	210.90	−26.59	−12.61

Indexes based on 12/31/91 = 100.

Source: *Barron's*, 20 July, 2001, p. MW6. Barron's Online by *Barron's*. Copyright 2001 by Dow Jones & Co., Inc. Reproduced with permission of Dow Jones & Co., Inc. in the format *Fundamentals of Investments* via Copyright Clearance Center.

The above *Investment in the News* article reveals that the benefit from international diversification depends on the correlation between rates of return in various countries. Although J.P. Morgan Chase recently recommended a reduction in the proportion of the portfolio allocated to foreign countries (due to the alleged increase in correlations), the author of this article argues that the benefit from international diversification still exists, mainly by buying Small Cap stocks that are owned mostly by local (foreign) investors.

This chapter expands investment opportunities to the international markets. It is true that international diversification has always been available, but the fast communication between markets and the expanding Internet trading today literally makes our world almost a single financial marketplace. Thus, it is easier nowadays to take advantage of the available opportunities that exist abroad. Some investors still do not exploit this opportunity, however. No matter how effective the lines of communication between countries, many investors consider investing internationally too risky. Part of the perceived risk results from a simple lack of information. Investors are more comfortable investing in domestic firms with which they are familiar, namely, firms from which they buy products on a daily basis. Yet, in constructing the internationally diversified portfolio, a special focus should be on the changes in correlations due to the operation of multinational firms. Hence, to benefit from international diversification one should select industries located in various countries with a relatively low correlation.

Investing in foreign securities, however, has two significant risks which do not exist in the US market: foreign exchange risk and political risk. Rates of return on international investments are influenced by movements in foreign exchange. This risk, called **foreign exchange risk**, is discussed in detail in this chapter. **Political risk** refers to the possibility that a country will take over a publicly held firm or disallow foreign investors to withdraw their profit (and principal investment) from the country. This sometimes occurs when a country is at war or in severe economic crisis.

These risks are offset by important benefits. Three benefits of international investments are:

1 *Portfolio risk reduction.* Investing in the international equity and bond markets enhances the gain from diversification. Because the correlations between some of these markets are not very high, the portfolio risk can be reduced with international investments.

2 *Enhancement of portfolio expected return.* Some of these economies are growing faster than others, which may offer the investor a higher potential return. For example, looking in *Barron's* on 4 February 2002 (p. MW9), we can see that the stock's rate of return in US dollars was −0.2%, while it was 4.3% in Turkey and 3.7% in Peru.

3 *Exploiting riskless investment opportunities.* At times investors can find attractive international investment opportunities that are essentially riskless. For example, suppose an investor can borrow in the US at 4% and lend (buy government bonds) in the UK at 6%. It is sometimes possible to hedge the foreign currency risk in such a way that a portion of the difference in interest rates can be captured at no risk. (In most international markets and for most investors, these investment opportunities do not exist, because astute investors will exploit such opportunities so quickly that for the unsophisticated, average investor it will be too late.)

This chapter first shows the gains from international diversification in the stock and bond markets. It then analyses some relationships among interest rates, inflation rates and forward rates in the various markets – concepts that are helpful in identifying the investment opportunities just discussed.

15.1 RISKS AND RETURNS IN INTERNATIONAL INVESTMENTS

15.1.1 The relative size of the various markets

The US stock market is by far the largest stock market, with about 62% of the total world capital market (see Exhibit 15.1). For both 1997 and 1998, its market share in the world market capitalization remained almost the same. In the past, Japan had a much larger share of the world capital market (the Nikkei index reached almost 40,000, and then fell to below 9,500 points in February 2002!), but nowadays its share has shrunk to about 10%.

Despite the dominance of the US market, still about 40% of market capitalization is abroad. This does not necessarily imply that the American investor should invest 40% of her equity abroad, but given the high returns in some of these countries, one should certainly try to gain from these international investment opportunities.

15.1.2 Correlations of international markets

Diversification is one of the driving forces behind global investment. By diversifying internationally, investors gain the opportunity for higher returns and the potential to reduce risk further than if they invested only domestically. This section begins by looking at risk reduction. It illustrates the gain from international diversification from the US investor's viewpoint – namely, all local returns are translated into US dollars. It also discusses the precise calculations involved.

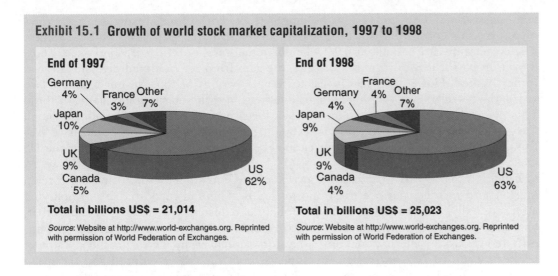

Exhibit 15.1 Growth of world stock market capitalization, 1997 to 1998

End of 1997

Germany 4%
France 3%
Other 7%
Japan 10%
UK 9%
Canada 5%
US 62%

Total in billions US$ = 21,014

Source: Website at http://www.world-exchanges.org. Reprinted with permission of World Federation of Exchanges.

End of 1998

France 4%
Germany 4%
Other 7%
Japan 9%
UK 9%
Canada 4%
US 63%

Total in billions US$ = 25,023

Source: Website at http://www.world-exchanges.org. Reprinted with permission of World Federation of Exchanges.

Because international markets are not perfectly correlated with each other or with the US market, investors can achieve reductions in risk beyond those achieved by investing in a variety of US industries. Exhibit 15.2 illustrates the correlation of US markets with large international companies (Large Cap) and with small international

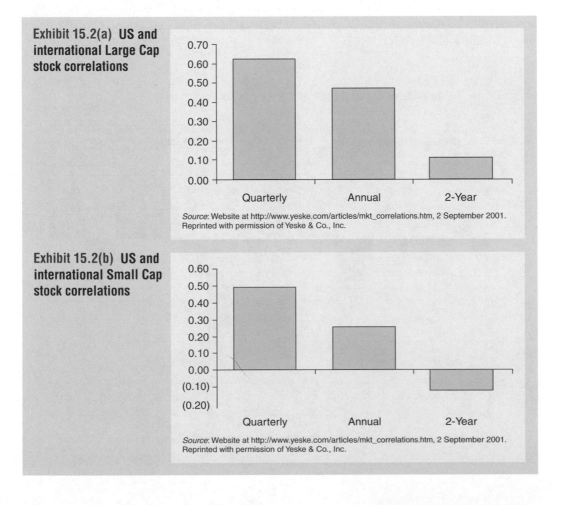

Exhibit 15.2(a) US and international Large Cap stock correlations

Source: Website at http://www.yeske.com/articles/mkt_correlations.htm, 2 September 2001. Reprinted with permission of Yeske & Co., Inc.

Exhibit 15.2(b) US and international Small Cap stock correlations

Source: Website at http://www.yeske.com/articles/mkt_correlations.htm, 2 September 2001. Reprinted with permission of Yeske & Co., Inc.

companies (Small Cap) for various holding periods. For example, using quarterly rates of return, this correlation is a little above 0.60 with Large Cap (see Exhibit 15.2(a)). The correlation drops to about 0.10 when biannual rates of return are employed. Thus, if you invest for the short period of time, the gain from international diversification is rather limited. However, if you invest for longer periods of time, in our example two years, the correlation is very low, enhancing the gain from international diversification. This phenomenon is even pronounced when the American investor diversifies in Small Cap international firms. For this investment period the correlation is negative (see Exhibit 15.2(b)), which presumably cannot be achieved by diversification in the US itself.

Exhibit 15.3 reveals that in some periods the US market outperforms the foreign market and in other periods the opposite holds. This indicates that by diversifying internationally, one can stabilize the portfolio, i.e. reduce risk. Exhibit 15.4 shows that, based on the period from January 1969 to February 1996, the investor could dramatically reduce risk by international diversification. Moreover, by increasing the investment proportion up to 70% in foreign investments, both the risk is reduced and the mean return is increasing. Of course, these results are based on historical rates of return which dictate historical means, variances and correlations. If one wishes to change these parameters, e.g. think that the correlations in the future will be higher than the observed *ex-post* correlations, one can simply change them, find the new efficient frontier and obtain the gain from international diversification with the new parameters.

So far, we have demonstrated the gain from international diversification in foreign stocks from the American point of view, where we have only two assets: US equity and foreign equity (see Exhibit 15.4).

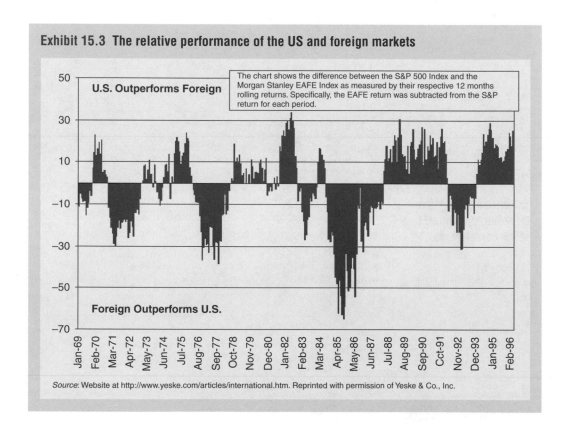

Exhibit 15.3 The relative performance of the US and foreign markets

Source: Website at http://www.yeske.com/articles/international.htm. Reprinted with permission of Yeske & Co., Inc.

Exhibit 15.4 The efficient frontier with international diversification

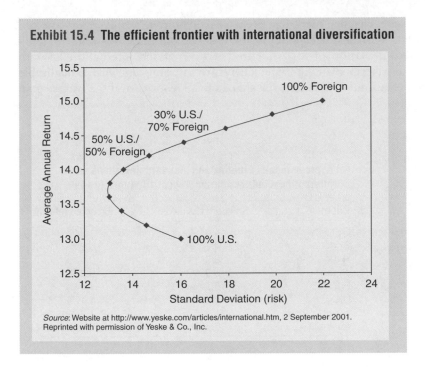

Source: Website at http://www.yeske.com/articles/international.htm, 2 September 2001.
Reprinted with permission of Yeske & Co., Inc.

We turn now to a more detailed analysis when some specific foreign countries are considered and not 'foreign equity' combined as one asset. Before we present the detailed discussion, a word of warning is called for. Any such international diversification analysis depends on the selected time period. The magnitude of the gain from international diversification varies, but the conclusion that in most cases international diversification is beneficial to the investors remains intact.

Exhibit 15.5 reveals the efficient frontier and the basic data employed to derive it for the period August 1994 to July 1999. In this period, the US market was one of the best, with the second highest mean return and with a relatively low standard deviation.

Indeed, we see that the US dot falls on the frontier, which seems to indicate that there is no gain from international diversification. This is not the case, because even in this period, adding the riskless asset (say $r = 0.3\%$ per month) the investor may gain from international investment because the line raising them is not necessarily tangential to the efficient frontier at the US dot. Secondly, with short sales, the efficient frontier is located left of the US dot, hence there is a clear gain from international diversification. It is interesting to note that in this period the correlations were relatively large which restricts the gain from international diversification. As indicated above, measuring the historical gain from international diversification depends on the period selected. In Exhibit 15.4 we have seen that for the period 1969–96 the US market was inferior to the foreign markets, hence a large gain from international diversification is revealed. In the period from August 1994 to July 1999, the US market was superior and the gain from diversification to the American investor was relatively small.

Exhibit 15.6 demonstrates the gain from international diversification for other selected time periods, for other groups of countries, for bonds, stocks, and bonds and stocks combined. Exhibit 15.6(a) illustrates the improved efficient frontiers for bond portfolios with international investing. For example, a portfolio of US bonds had a standard deviation of 5.5% and an average return of 4.3%. By adding international bonds and choosing a portfolio with weights such that point *m* is achieved, the average expected return increases to 9% with a corresponding increase in standard deviation of only 0.2% (or to a standard deviation of 5.7%). Thus, by diversifying internationally with bonds, a dramatic increase in average expected return is achieved with a negligible increase in standard deviation.[1] Obviously, the shape of the frontier and the precise gain

Exhibit 15.5 Efficient stock portfolio for US investor diversifying across eight countries

(a) Average monthly returns and standard deviations on international indexes during August 1994 to July 1999

Country	Standard deviation	Expected return
US	4.01%	1.84%
Canada	4.66%	0.94%
Hong Kong	9.54%	0.94%
Japan	5.95%	−0.07%
France	5.70%	1.44%
UK	3.50%	1.17%
Brazil	11.93%	1.91%
Australia	3.70%	0.67%

(b) Correlation matrix

	US	Canada	Hong Kong	Japan	France	UK	Brazil	Australia
US	1							
Canada	0.804	1						
Hong Kong	0.613	0.616	1					
Japan	0.430	0.321	0.267	1				
France	0.559	0.512	0.364	0.430	1			
UK	0.639	0.654	0.566	0.384	0.660	1		
Brazil	0.526	0.470	0.420	0.556	0.465	0.505	1	
Australia	0.629	0.608	0.587	0.485	0.434	0.689	0.608	1

(c) The efficient frontier with and without short sells

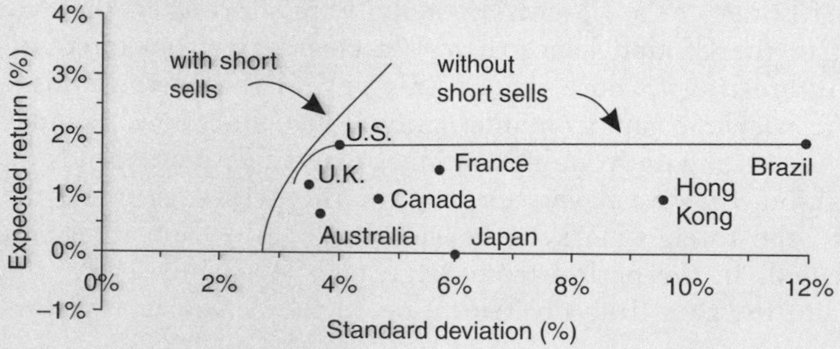

[1] Based on Haim Levy and Zvi Lerman, 'The benefits of international diversification in bonds', *Financial Analysts Journal*, September–October 1988, pp. 56–64.

PRACTICE BOX

Problem

Suppose that a US investor is considering diversifying internationally. This investor currently holds a widely diversified portfolio of US stocks. Given the data in the following table (all returns have been converted to US dollars), what is the expected rate of return and standard deviation of a portfolio that is equally weighted between the United States, Europe and the Far East? What is the investor's gain from diversifying globally?

	Expected return	Standard deviation	Correlation		
			United States	Europe	Far East
United States	9.6%	14.1%	1		
Europe	7.5%	12.7%	0.54	1	
Far East	11.2%	15.4%	0.32	0.21	1

Solution

The expected return of the portfolio is

$$E(R_p) = \sum_{i=1}^{n} w_i E(R_i)$$

$$= \frac{1}{3}(0.096) + \frac{1}{3}(0.075) + \frac{1}{3}(0.112)$$

$$= 0.094 \text{ or } 9.4\%$$

and the portfolio variance is

$$\sigma_p^2 = (\tfrac{1}{3})^2(0.141)^2 + (\tfrac{1}{3})^2(0.127)^2 + (\tfrac{1}{3})^2(0.154)^2$$

$$+ 2(\tfrac{1}{3})^2(0.127)(0.141)(0.54)$$

$$+ 2(\tfrac{1}{3})^2(0.141)(0.154)(0.32)$$

$$+ 2(\tfrac{1}{3})^2(0.127)(0.154)(0.21)$$

$$\cong 0.0021 + 0.00179 + 0.00264 + 0.00215 + 0.00154 + 0.00091$$

$$\cong 0.01124$$

Note that $w_i = w_j$ for all i and j. Thus, the portfolio standard deviation is

$$\sigma_p = \sqrt{0.01124} \cong 0.106 \text{ or } 10.6\%$$

The gain from diversifying is $(14.1\% - 10.6\%)/14.1\% = 24.8\%$ due to reduction in the standard deviation, with only $(9.6\% - 9.4\%)/9.6\% = 2.1\%$ reduction in the expected return.

from diversification depend on the historical period employed to derive the frontier. Yet, for a long enough period (what is necessary for future prediction of the frontier), the principle remains intact: adding international securities to the portfolio increases the US investor's welfare, sometimes substantially.

Exhibit 15.6 Various efficient frontiers

(a) Efficient bond portfolio for a US investor diversifying across 13 countries

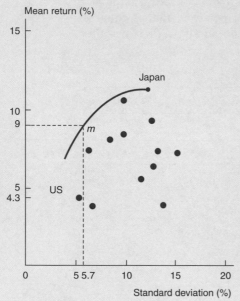

Source: Adapted with permission from Haim Levy and Zvi Lerman. 'The benefits of international diversification in bonds', *Financial Analysts Journal*, September–October 1988, pp. 56–64. © 1988, Association for Investment Management and Research. Reproduced and republished from *Financial Analysts Journal* with permission from the Association for Investment Management and Research. All rights reserved.

(b) Efficient stock portfolio for a US investor diversifying across 28 countries (riskless rate r = 5%)

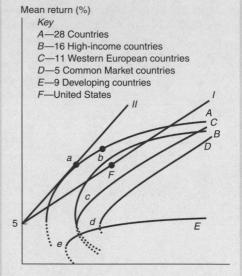

Source: Haim Levy and Marshall Sarnat, 'International diversification of investment portfolios', *Amercian Economic Review*, September 1970. p. 673. Reprinted with permission of the American Economic Association.

(c) Efficient bond and stock portfolio for a US investor diversifying across 13 countries

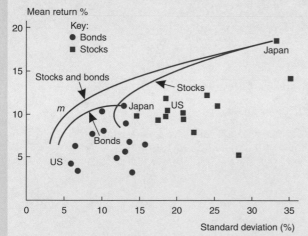

The dots denote bond portfolios from different countries and the squares denote stock portfolios from different countries.

Source: Adapted from Haim Levy and Zvi Lerman 'The benefits of international diversification in bonds,' *Financial Analysts Journal*, September–October 1988, pp. 56–64. © 1988, Association for Investment Management and Research. Reproduced and republished from *Financial Analysts Journal* with permission from the Association for Investment Management and Research. All rights reserved.

Exhibit 15.6(b) focuses on international diversification in the equity market and illustrates several efficient frontiers derived from various combinations of country portfolios. Point *F* is a portfolio of US equity securities, and the benefit to US investors from international diversification is clear. Notice the significant gains in risk reduction and return enhancement by considering 28 countries (curve *aA*). As in the bond market, the analysis of the equity market shows that considerable gains are achieved by diversifying internationally. To calculate the required rate of return, given the risk involved in international investment, one can use the international CAPM model. In this model one can use the world index (published in the financial press) as the market portfolio.

Exhibit 15.6(c) illustrates efficient frontiers for an international bond portfolio, a stock portfolio, and a combined stock and bond portfolio. A global portfolio of both bonds and stocks results in an efficient frontier that is superior to the portfolios of either just bonds or just stocks. Overall, this is a strong case for global diversification across both bonds and stocks.

Exhibit 15.7 illustrates risk reduction via international diversification in a slightly different manner. Recall that Chapter 6 illustrated the reduction in a portfolio's variance as the number of securities increased. The same principle can be applied to international portfolios. Exhibit 15.7 illustrates the gain from diversifying both domestically and internationally. However, rather than measuring risk by the variance of the portfolio, Exhibit 15.7 illustrates the risk reduction in percentage terms. That is, if we denote by 100% the average risk of an undiversified portfolio (i.e. the average standard deviation of all stocks included in the portfolio), then with about 20 stocks the portfolio risk is reduced to about 30% with only US stocks, and to about 15% with international stocks.[2]

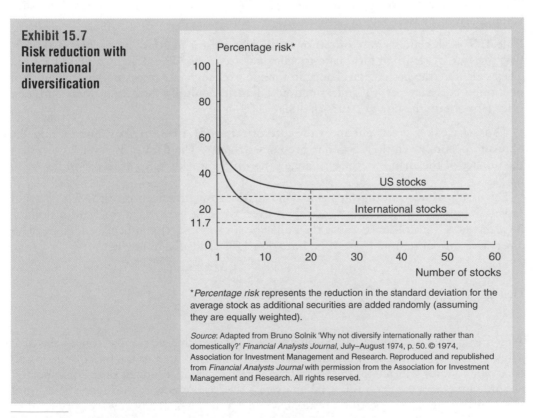

Exhibit 15.7
Risk reduction with international diversification

Percentage risk represents the reduction in the standard deviation for the average stock as additional securities are added randomly (assuming they are equally weighted).

Source: Adapted from Bruno Solnik 'Why not diversify internationally rather than domestically?' *Financial Analysts Journal*, July–August 1974, p. 50. © 1974, Association for Investment Management and Research. Reproduced and republished from *Financial Analysts Journal* with permission from the Association for Investment Management and Research. All rights reserved.

---

[2] These results are based on a series of randomly diversified portfolios.

15.1.3 Currency risk

So far, this chapter has illustrated the gain to US investors from international diversification. However, the text has not explained the role that exchange risk plays in such calculations. The rate of return in foreign investments is influenced also by changes in the exchange rate (see also the *Investment in the news* article). It is therefore important to factor those changes into rate-of-return calculations.

The rate of return on a foreign investment expressed in the domestic currency (R_D) is calculated as follows:

$$R_D = \frac{fx_1(DC/FC)}{fx_0(DC/FC)}(1 + R_L) - 1 = (1 + R_{fx})(1 + R_L) - 1 \qquad (15.1)$$

where $fx_1(DC/FC)$ is the exchange rate in domestic currency per foreign currency at time 1, $fx_0(DC/FC)$ is the exchange rate in domestic currency per foreign currency at time 0, R_L is the rate of return in the stock market in the local currency, and R_{fx} is the rate of return on the foreign exchange. For example, suppose the rate of return on stocks in Canada was 11.5%, and the Canadian dollar becomes stronger. The percentage change in the foreign exchange rate between the United States and Canada is +3.5% in US dollars per Canadian dollars. Namely, each Canadian dollar is worth, after the change in the exchange rate, 3.5% more in terms of US dollars. Based on Equation 15.1, the rate of return to the US investor in Canada – that is, in US dollars – is,

$$R_D = [(1 + 0.035)(1 + 0.115)] - 1 \cong 0.154 \text{ or } 15.4\%$$

The relationship between exchange rates and rates of return in foreign and local currency is summarized by Rule 1.

Rule 1: To calculate the rate of return to the US investor in a foreign country, calculate first the rate of return in local country currency (e.g. Canadian dollars) and add 1 to it. Then calculate the percentage change in foreign exchange rate (measured by the amount of foreign currency per US dollar) and add 1 to it. Multiply these two terms and subtract 1 to obtain the rate of return in dollars.

Thus, a weaker dollar enhances the rate of return of a US investor abroad, and the opposite occurs when the US dollar becomes stronger. The data in Exhibit 15.8 reflect the impact of the change in the exchange rates on the weekly rates of return in the bond markets.

Let us illustrate with the Japanese bond market. An American investor who bought Japanese bonds earned 4.71% in yen. However, when he exchanged the yen for dollars, he received fewer dollars (because the dollar became stronger) and hence ended up with a negative rate of return of −0.61%. Equation 15.1 yields the following:

$$-0.0061 = (1 + R_{fx})(1.0471) - 1$$

Hence,

$$R_{fx} \cong -0.051$$

This means that the dollar gained about 5.1% of its value in comparison to the yen. Thus, the foreign exchange fluctuations should be incorporated to the rate of return calculation, a factor which does not exist if the investor decides to invest only domestically.

Some investors are good financial analysts – they know how to evaluate stocks – but have only vague ideas regarding future exchange rates, which anyway are very hard to predict. They wish to diversity internationally, but to eliminate, at least partially, the

Exhibit 15.8 Total rates of return on international bonds

	In local currency	In US dollars
Japan	4.71%	−0.61%
UK	−2.20	0.62
Germany	0.33	0.24
France	−0.11	0.29
Canada	−0.97	0.54
Netherlands	0.19	0.24
Non-US	0.93	0.03
World[a]	0.44	0.29

[a] Includes 17 international government bond markets.
Source: *Wall Street Journal*, 7 July 1999, p. MW72. Wall Street Journal (Online) by *Wall Street Journal*. © 1999 by Dow Jones & Co., Inc. Reproduced with permission of Dow Jones & Co., Inc. in the format *Fundamentals of Investments* via the Copyright Clearance Center.

foreign exchange risk. A way to achieve this goal is to hedge the currency risk by conducting a forward transaction (see Chapter 12). For example, an American investor who invests 1 million euros in Germany for six months knows that he will need to convert euros to dollars in six months. She can enter a forward contract to sell euros and buy dollars at a fixed rate which is determined today, hence eliminating the foreign exchange risk. However, with investing in the stock market, one cannot totally eliminate this risk, because the investor does not know how many euros will be received six months hence. If the stock market in Germany is up and the value of the 1 million euros jumps to 1.5 million euros, the 1.5 million euros have to be converted. If the market is down and the value drops to 0.5 million euros, less euros have to be converted. Because the number is unknown in advance (unlike the case where the money is simply deposited in the bank in Germany) by investing in the stock market and conducting a forward contract, most, but certainty not all, foreign exchange risks can be eliminated.

PRACTICE BOX

Problem

Suppose that last year a US investor bought a portfolio of UK stocks when the exchange rate was $2/£. There has been a gain of 20% on the stock portfolio measured in pounds, and the investor is considering selling her portfolio. If the current exchange rate is $1.5/£, what was the rate of return measured in US dollars?

Solution

From Equation 15.1, in the problem (where $fx_1(\$/£) = 1.5$, $fx_0(\$/£) = 2$, and $R_L = 0.2$) we have

$$R_D = \frac{1.5}{2}(1 + 0.2) - 1 = -0.1 \text{ or } -10\%$$

or a loss of 10%. Hence, although the investor experienced a gain of 20% on the UK investment, that did not translate into a gain in US dollars because the British pound weakened against the US dollar. Namely, the investor paid $2 for each pound bought and received only $1.50 for each pound when the portfolio was sold.

Another way to partially eliminate the foreign exchange risk is by buying put options to sell euros and receive dollars (see Chapter 13). Here, again, the investor does not know in advance how many put options should be bought, because the amount of euros needed to be sold is unknown in advance.

15.1.4 International diversification: various points of view

As we have seen, the rate of return on international investments depends on both the securities' prices and foreign exchange fluctuations. Suppose that the rate of return on Japanese stocks, in yen, is +10%. An American investor and a UK investor invest in Japan and earn this 10% in Japanese yen. Will the investors each receive the same rate of return of 10% in their own currencies? They will not; the 10% rate of return will be translated differently into dollars or pounds, because the dollar–yen and pound–yen fluctuations are generally different. Thus, an American investor and a UK investor who face the same available international investment opportunities in local currencies will face different investment options once these returns are translated into their own domestic currencies – in our example, dollars and pounds, respectively. Therefore, even if all experts agree on rate-of-return distributions in local currencies, the efficient frontier and the optimal international diversification depend on the investors' currency. What constitutes the optimal investment for the UK investor may be a non-optimal investment for the American investor, and vice versa.

To illustrate, take the monthly rates of return for the period October 1992 to October 1997 for Japan, the United States, the United Kingdom and Germany from Morgan Stanley Capital International. Exhibit 15.9(a) shows the mean rate of return and the standard deviation when returns are calculated in German marks and US dollars. Exhibit 15.9(b) shows the correlation between rates of return calculated in dollars (the American point of view) and in marks (the German point of view).

First, note that if there were no foreign exchange fluctuations, there would be no difference between the German investor's point of view and the American investor's point of view in Exhibit 15.9(a). The differences are due to foreign exchange fluctuations. For example, the dollar mean rate of return on US stocks is 1.37%. However, for the German investor who invests in the United States, the mean rate of return is 1.56%. This implies that the dollar becomes stronger on average relative to the German Mark, and the German investor earns in the US stock market as well as gains from the foreign exchange fluctuations which were, on average, in the German investor's favour for this specific period.

By the same token, the standard deviations and correlations are also affected by the currency used by the investor. For example, investing in the United States is riskier for a German investor than for an American investor due to the added risk of currency fluctuations. Because all historical parameters needed to derive the efficient frontier are dependent on the investor's point of view (that is, the currency used), the mean–variance efficient frontier also will depend on the investor's point of view.

Exhibits 15.10 and 15.11 illustrate the efficient frontier with and without short sales when German marks and US dollars are the currencies used by the investor. Curves with similar shapes are obtained in both currencies, as well as very similar locations of the various countries (in terms of mean and standard deviations). However, the optimum investment portfolio is not the same from both investors' points of view. For example,

Exhibit 15.9 Market data based on the investor's point of view (currency used)

(a) Monthly means and standard deviations

	German investor's point of view		American investor's point of view	
	Mean	Standard deviation	Mean	Standard deviation
Germany	1.43%	4.90%	1.27%	4.29%
Japan	0.46	6.73	0.31	6.45
UK	1.38	4.20	1.23	3.55
US	1.56	4.76	1.37	3.10

Source: Data from Morgan Stanley Capital International website at http://www.ms.com/mscidata

(b) Correlations

	German investor's point of view				American investor's point of view			
	Germany	Japan	UK	US	Germany	Japan	UK	US
Germany	1	0.279	0.645	0.632	1	0.161	0.515	0.410
Japan	0.279	1	0.437	0.385	0.161	1	0.351	0.209
UK	0.645	0.437	1	0.722	0.510	0.351	1	0.498
US	0.632	0.385	0.722	1	0.410	0.209	0.498	1

Source: Data from Morgan Stanley Capital International website at http://www.ms.com/mscidata

see Exhibit 15.12, which shows the composition of the minimum variance portfolio (without short sales), denoted by MVP in Exhibits 15.10 and 15.11, in German marks and US dollars. The investment proportions depend on the investor's point of view. The biggest difference is in the investment in the United States. The German investor would

Exhibit 15.10 Mean–variance frontier in US dollars

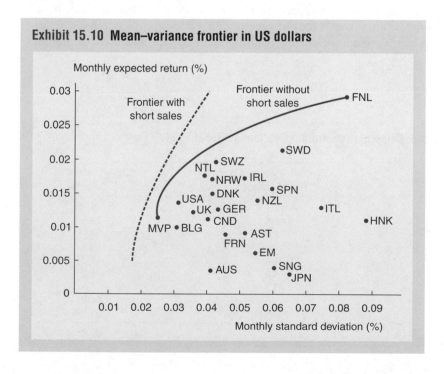

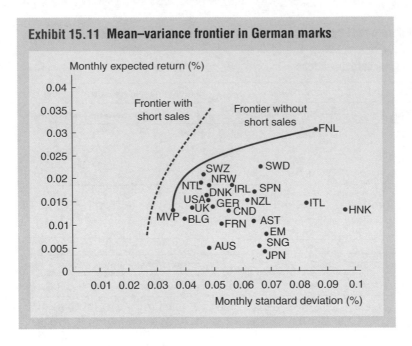

Exhibit 15.11 Mean–variance frontier in German marks

invest zero in the US market, whereas the American investor would invest about 34% in the US market.

The minimum variance portfolio also demonstrates how the portfolio composition is affected by the foreign exchange fluctuations (see point MVP in Exhibits 15.10 and 15.11). The same phenomenon holds with respect to the other portfolios on the frontier, regardless of whether short sales are allowed or not. This finding strongly implies that in considering the optimal international diversification, it is crucial that the investor take into account the foreign exchange fluctuations: what is good for the American investor is not necessarily good for the German or Japanese investor.

Exhibit 15.12 Composition of the minimum variance portfolio, MVP (without short sales)

Asset included on the portfolio	German investor's point of view	US investor's point of view
Austria	13.7%	15.9%
Belgium	41.5	33.6
Denmark	8.6	4.9
Ireland	—	0.1
Italy	—	1.6
Japan	4.3	1.6
United Kingdom	9.1	—
United States	—	34.0
Total	100%	100%

15.2 INTERNATIONAL PARITY RELATIONSHIPS[3]

Exchange rates are a key variable in determining returns from international investments. Investors rely on four parity relationships when they attempt to predict future exchange rates. A parity relationship is an expression that illustrates a hypothesized relationship between financial variables. This section covers purchasing power parity, foreign exchange expectations and interest rate parity.

15.2.1 Purchasing power parity

Suppose that there is high inflation in one country (Country A) and no inflation in another country (Country B). Under these circumstances, the inhabitants of Country A will buy their products from Country B. To do so, they will buy foreign currency, so the foreign exchange rate will be affected. Thus, differential inflation in two countries affects the foreign exchange rate.

Purchasing power parity is the relationship between two countries' inflation rates and their foreign exchange rates. This parity relationship is used to estimate exchange rates based on expected inflation rates. To clarify the appropriate relationship between inflation rates and exchange rates, suppose we have an internationally traded good (say, aluminium) with no trading restrictions. That is, suppose we can trade aluminium internationally with no transportation or other costs. As before, let DC denote domestic currency ($ in the following example) and FC denote foreign currency (£ in the following example). Thus, $P_{0,DC}$ denotes the price of aluminium in the domestic currency today, and $P_{0,FC}$ denotes its price in the foreign currency today.

If we can trade internationally and costlessly, then we would expect aluminium to cost the same in either the local market or the foreign market, adjusted for the foreign exchange rate. That is,

$$P_{0,DC} = (\text{foreign exchange rate today}) \times P_{0,FC} \qquad (15.2)$$

where the foreign exchange rate today is in terms of domestic currency per foreign currency. For example, if aluminium was selling for £0.65 and the foreign exchange rate today was \$1.5385/£, then the price of aluminium in the United States should be

$$(\$1.5385/£)(£0.65) \cong \$1.00$$

If the cost of aluminium in the United States is any value other than $1, arbitrage profits can be made. For example, if the actual price in the United States is $1.01 (still assuming that transactions are costless), then we can buy aluminium in the United Kingdom for £0.65 (with dollars exchanged at \$1.5385/£) and sell it for $1.01, making a penny profit for each pound of aluminium; with a large volume of such transactions, an investor has a 'money machine' and he can be rich at no risk.

Now suppose that over the next year, the United States experiences 3% inflation, and the United Kingdom experiences 5% inflation. If inflation were the only influence on aluminium prices, we would expect the following prices for aluminium:

---

[3] This section is based on Chapter 1 of Bruno Solnik, *International Investments*, 2nd edn. (Reading, MA: Addison-Wesley, 1991).

$$P_{1,DC} = (1 + \text{domestic inflation rate}) \times P_{0,DC}$$
$$= (1 + 0.03)\$1 = \$1.03$$

$$P_{1,FC} = (1 + \text{foreign inflation rate}) \times P_{0,FC}$$
$$= (1 + 0.05)£0.65 = £0.6825$$

To maintain equilibrium in the international markets with no possible arbitrage transaction, we know (according to Equation 15.2 but related to Period 1) that at the end of the year, we must have

$$P_{1,DC} = (\text{foreign exchange rate in a year}) \times P_{1,FC}$$

In our case with aluminium, we must have

$$\$1.03 = (\text{foreign exchange rate in a year})(£0.6825)$$

Solving for the foreign exchange rate, we have

$$\text{Foreign exchange rate in a year} = \$1.03/£0.6825 \cong \$1.5092/£$$

Thus, we see that the higher inflation rate in the United Kingdom has the effect of lowering the foreign exchange rate (the pound is said to depreciate).

Note that the percentage difference in the foreign exchange per dollar is approximately equal to the difference in the inflation rate in the two countries, i.e.

$$(£0.6626/\$)/(£0.65/\$) - 1 \cong 0.05 - 0.03$$

$$1.0194 - 1 \cong 0.02$$

$$0.0194 \cong 0.02$$

The precise figure is 2%, and the figure obtained by the approximation is 1.94%; hence, the approximation is very reasonable.

In principle, then, we should be able to look at the differences in expected inflation rates and get an estimate of future foreign exchange rates. In practice, however, there are two factors to consider. First, international trade is not costless, and there are actually significant trade barriers (such as tariffs). Second, purchasing power parity requires knowing the future inflation differential, but the actual inflation that will occur is unknown. Nevertheless, although far from perfect, purchasing power parity establishes a link between the foreign exchange market and the inflation differential that can be useful.

15.2.2 Foreign exchange expectations

Foreign exchange expectations are estimated by the relationship between the current forward foreign exchange rate and the expected future foreign exchange rate. The **forward foreign exchange rate** is the exchange rate available today to exchange currency at some specified date in the future. The ability to convert one currency into another is critical for the successful management of international portfolios, because investors often know that they will have to exchange currencies at some future date.

For example, suppose a US investor has a yen-denominated certificate of deposit (CD) maturing in six months in Tokyo. In response to demand by investors to minimize the impact of currency swings on their portfolios, a forward market in foreign exchange has developed. As explained in Chapter 12, a **forward foreign exchange contract** is a contract that obligates an investor to deliver a specified quantity of one currency in return for a specified amount of another currency. For example, if the US investor has a 10-million-yen CD maturing in six months, the investor may enter into a forward foreign exchange contract to deliver 10 million yen in return for, say, $100,000. With a forward foreign exchange contract, the investor has eliminated any future risk related to changes in exchange rate.

Because the forward foreign exchange rate reflects investors' expectations regarding the future exchange rate, it is commonly asserted that the forward rate is an unbiased estimate of the future spot foreign exchange rate. That is,

$$E[fx_1(DC/FC)] = F[fx_1(DC/FC)] \tag{15.3}$$

where $F[fx_1(DC/FC)]$ denotes the forward foreign exchange rate today for foreign exchange at time 1, and $E[fx_1(DC/FC)]$ denotes the expected spot rate for foreign exchange at time 1.

If this assertion is true, then there is no benefit from bearing foreign exchange risk. On average, the return that is due to foreign exchange charges above or below the forward rate is zero. Thus, the expected return is zero for bearing foreign currency risk. Therefore, some argue that a risk offering no positive expected return should be hedged.

15.2.3 Interest rate parity

Assume that the interest rate is about 3% in Germany and less than 1% in Japan (the actual rates in February 2002). It seems that an investor can take advantage of this situation and make a profit by borrowing money in Japan and investing it in Germany. Although such a transaction is default-free (because the investor buys German government bonds), it is not free from foreign exchange risk. The Japanese investor may earn the interest difference but may lose money when the euros are converted to yen when the loan has to be paid back. To avoid such a risk, the investor can lock in a transaction in the forward market that essentially allows the exchange of euros for Japanese yen at the end of the period at an exchange rate that is determined today. If such a transaction with a forward risk protection yields a positive rate of return, it is an arbitrage position. The demand for such transactions will affect interest rates and forward exchange rates until the arbitrage profit vanishes, because in equilibrium arbitrage profit cannot exist.

To further illustrate this point, suppose that a Japanese investor borrows 1 million yen and invests them in Germany. The Japanese investor will invest 1 million yen $\times$ $fx_0(FC/DC)$ euros, and at the end of the year will obtain the following:

$$1 \text{ million yen} \times fx_0(FC/DC) \times (1 + R_{n,FC}) \text{ euros}$$

When this amount is sold in the forward market, the amount of yen obtained will be

$$1 \text{ million yen} \times fx_0(FC/DC) (1 + R_{FC})/F[fx_1(FC/DC)]$$

where R_{FC} is the interest rate in the foreign country, i.e. Germany in our example.

PRACTICE BOX

Problem
Suppose you observe today that the Swiss forward foreign exchange rate in one year is SwF 1.58/$ when the current spot rate is SwF 1.53/$. What inferences can you draw regarding future (one year hence) expected foreign exchange rates between the United States and Switzerland?

Solution
Based on the foreign exchange expectations approach to forward foreign exchange rates, you would conclude that the US dollar will strengthen against the Swiss franc. Specifically, the foreign exchange rate is expected to rise to SwF 1.58/$ in one year. Note that this is what is expected to happen, not what will necessarily happen.

In equilibrium, when no arbitrage profit prevails, this must be equal to the amount of yen the borrower has to return to the lender in Japan, namely 1 million yen $\times$ (1 + R_{DC}) where R_{DC} is the interest in the domestic country, Japan in our specific example. Thus, in equilibrium, the following must hold:

$$fx_0(FC/DC)(1 + R_{FC}) = F[fx_1(FC/DC) \times (1 + R_{DC})$$

or

$$\frac{F[fx_1(FC/DC)]}{fx_0(FC/DC)} - 1 \cong \frac{1 + R_{n,FC}}{1 + R_{n,DC}} - 1 \cong R_{FC} - R_{DC}$$

Thus, no-arbitrage equilibrium is called interest rate parity.

Interest rate parity establishes a link between the forward foreign exchange rates and nominal interest rates where arbitrage profit does not exist. Specifically, interest rate parity can be expressed as follows:

$$F_{fx} \equiv \frac{F[fx_1(FC/DC)]}{fx_0(FC/DC)} - 1 \cong R_{FC} - R_{DC}$$

where F_{fx} denotes the percentage difference in the forward foreign exchange rate relative to the prevailing current spot exchange rate. Thus, the percentage difference of the forward foreign exchange rate and the current exchange rate should be approximately equal to the prevailing difference between the nominal interest rates in the foreign and domestic countries. For example, if the British pound exchange rate with the US dollar is currently at £0.67/$, and the one-year forward rate is at £0.7/$, then we would expect the interest rate differential between the United Kingdom and the United States to be

$$(£0.7/\$)/(£0.67 /\$) - 1 \cong 0.0448 \text{ or } 4.48\%$$

Specifically, we would anticipate that the British pound would weaken compared with the US dollar by about 4.48%, according to interest rate parity.

This important relationship between exchange rates and interest rates is summarized in Rule 2.

Rule 2: To avoid arbitrage in the foreign exchange market, the foreign exchange rate divided by the current exchange rate must be equal to the foreign interest rate less the local interest rate for the corresponding period. If this does not hold, an arbitrage profit prevails.

Let us check this rule with data taken from *Barron's*, 4 February 2002. For example, on that day the following interest rates prevailed in the US and UK for 180 days (the interest is, however, on an annual basis).

UK	4.10875%
US	1.3400%

The spot exchange rate was 1.5765 dollars per UK pound, and the forward rate (for 180 days) was published in *Barron's*, 4 February 2002, as 1.4035 dollars per pound. Can one exploit the interest rate difference in the two countries? For example, an American investor can borrow £100 from a bank in the UK and invest this in an American bank. He/she will first exchange the pounds for dollars, receiving £100 $\times$ $1.4178/£ = $141.78. Then with interest at the end of 180 days, the investor will have

$$\$141.78 \times 1.019400 = \$144.53$$

The investor has to pay the bank in the UK £100 $\times$ 1.0410875 = £104.10875. Buying these pounds in the forward market, he/she will pay in dollar terms

$$£104.10875 \times 1.4035\$/£ = \$146.11$$

Thus, it seems that this transaction yields an arbitrage profit of $1.58. However, in practice, even this little profit is washed out due to the fact that the interest rate published in the newspapers is the interest rate for *lending* (or what one can get on deposit). Once you try to *borrow* (in our case in the UK), an institution such as a bank pays a slightly higher interest rate which will wash out the above small arbitrage profit. Individual borrowers will pay much higher interest on borrowing, hence for the individual borrower there is no question that there is no arbitrage profit in the market.

SUMMARY

■ *Identify the risks and returns in international investment.*
International diversification has several benefits. An international portfolio can actually be less risky than a domestic portfolio, with no loss in the mean rate of return. International securities are not as highly correlated as domestic securities. This lack of high correlation affords substantial diversification benefits. Moreover, because some economies are growing faster than others, international markets offer higher potential returns. At times investors can even find attractive international investments that are essentially riskless. However, there is always an element of risk when investing internationally.

■ *Explain how an investor can benefit from international diversification.*
Although international investments involve foreign exchange risk (because rate of return in foreign investment is influenced by changes in exchange rate), a potential for risk reduction exists because of the relatively low correlation between assets of different countries. Thus, an investor can actually invest in riskier international securities and end up with a portfolio that is less risky than a domestic portfolio. Also, an investor can hedge the foreign exchange risk by engaging in forward transactions.

■ *Explain that foreign exchange risk can be partially eliminated by forward transactions or by purchasing options on foreign currency.*

■ *Describe the techniques used to predict exchange rates.*

Three important parity relationships that influence the international financial markets are purchasing power parity, foreign exchange expectations and interest rate parity. Their key goal is predicting future exchange rates.

KEY TERMS

Foreign exchange
  expectations
Foreign exchange
  risk

Forward foreign exchange
  contract
Forward foreign exchange
  rate

Interest rate
  parity
Political risk
Purchasing power parity

QUESTIONS

15.1 'An investment in a security that is not in the investor's country will always have a higher standard deviation than the same investment made by a person in the country where the security is located.' Evaluate this statement.

15.2 Suppose a US investor places 80% in the US market and 20% in the Japanese market. The investor also spends 80% of her money on US products and 20% on imported goods from Japan. Which portfolio mean and variance is relevant for her – the one that is adjusted for the exchange rate changes or the one that is unadjusted? Why?

15.3 The nominal rates of return in local currency in the Canadian and US markets are as follows:

Year	Canada	United States
1	10%	3%
2	8	7
3	−1	−2

Assume that international diversification is not allowed. Can we safely assert that the Canadian investors are better off?

15.4 Suppose you are considering investing in bonds and have the following information:

			Correlation	
	Mean	Standard deviation	DBF	IBF
DBF	7.1%	8.35	1	0.15
IBF	9.2%	10.4%	0.15	1

DBF denotes the Domestic Bond Fund, and IBF denotes the International Bond Fund. Assume that the risk-free rate is 4%. Graph the efficient frontiers in domestic currency for the following:

(a) The Domestic Bond Fund with the risk-free rate.
(b) The International Bond Fund with the risk-free rate.
(c) The Domestic Bond Fund and the International Bond Fund with no risk-free rate.

(d) All three – the Domestic Bond Fund, the International Bond Fund and the risk-free rate. Assess the gain from diversification. What conclusions can you draw from these frontiers?

15.5 Suppose a US investor earned 14.3% in the United Kingdom (before adjusting for exchange rate movements). If the US investor earned 12.7% on this investment in US dollars, what was the percentage change in the foreign exchange rate?

15.6 Suppose a US investor earned 10.7% in the Swiss stock market when measured in Swiss francs. The exchange rate at the beginning of the investment was SwF 1.57/$. If the rate of return on this investment in US dollars was −3.7%, what was the foreign exchange rate at the end of the investment period?

15.7 Suppose we observe that the expected inflation rate in France is 3% and the expected inflation rate in the United States is 9% over the next year. If the current foreign exchange rate is Fr 5.7/$, what is the expected foreign exchange rate next year?

15.8 Suppose there is a total of only 10,000 financial securities in the world. Further assume that each security has a standard deviation of σ_0^2, and all securities are uncorrelated. What is the percentage reduction in variance from diversifying globally if only 2,000 securities are located in the domestic country? Assume that the investments are equally weighted.

15.9 Suppose the rates of return in local currency on a portfolio of Japanese stocks and a portfolio of US stocks are as follows:

Year	US portfolio (%)	Japanese portfolio (%)	Exchange rate ($/yen)
0			0.008503
1	10	0	0.008613
2	−5	20	0.008594
3	20	−1	0.008724

(a) Calculate the annual rates of return to a US investor who buys the Japanese portfolio.
(b) Calculate the annual rates of return to a Japanese investor who buys the US portfolio.
(c) Calculate the variance and covariance in US dollars and Japanese yen.
(d) Suppose the Japanese investor diversifies by placing 50% of the investment in the Japanese portfolio. Also suppose the US investor does the same. Calculate the mean and variance of these portfolios. Who gains more from this type of diversification? Analyze your results.

15.10 (a) Referring to Question 15.9, assume that the exchange rate is fixed. The US investor and the Japanese investor now have the same efficient frontier. Do you agree? Explain your answer.

(b) Now suppose the risk-free rates in Japan and the United States are the same. Would the two investors have the same diversification policy? Explain.

15.11 Suppose you can borrow in US dollars at 6% a year, and you can invest in the bank in Germany and earn 10% in euros. Both positions are riskless. Assume that the current exchange rate is 1.62 euros per dollar. The one-year forward rate is 1.61.

(a) Are there arbitrage possibilities? If yes, show in detail what arbitrage you would conduct.
(b) What should be the forward exchange rate such that there would be no arbitrage possibilities?

15.12 Suppose a US investor can invest in US Treasury bills and receive 4% a year and can also invest in Swiss francs and get 8% a year. The current exchange rate is SWF1.62 per dollar. Suppose now the foreign exchange rate will be 1.58 one year from now with a probability of $1/2$ and 1.80 with a probability of $1/2$.

(a) Calculate the mean and variance on the two alternative investments from a US investor's viewpoint.

(b) Calculate the mean and variance on the two alternative investments from a Swiss investor's viewpoint.

(c) What would be the exchange rate instead of 1.80 (but still with a probability of $1/2$) such that the US investor definitely would choose to invest in the Swiss market?

15.13 Suppose Japan and the United States have the following estimated parameters of the stock market indices in local currency. The foreign exchange is fixed and the correlation is 1.0.

	Mean	Standard deviation
Japan	15%	10%
United States	10	10

(a) Who will gain from international diversification – the Japanese investor or the US investor?

(b) Who gains from international diversification if the correlation is $-1/2$?

(c) Now suppose the foreign exchange rates are not fixed. Who will gain more?

15.14 Suppose there are three portfolios: Japan, United States and United Kingdom. All have the same mean return (μ_0) and standard deviation (σ_0) in local currency. All correlation coefficients are zero.

(a) What is the optimal diversification if the foreign exchange rate is fixed?

(b) What is the optimal diversification, knowing that with foreign exchange fluctuations we still have the same mean ($\mu_1 = \mu_0$) across all portfolios, but the standard deviations are doubled ($\sigma_1 = 2\sigma_0$)?

15.15 The following data regarding a US portfolio and a German portfolio, stated in local currency, are estimated:

Probability	United States	Germany
$1/2$	10%	7%
$1/2$	20	12

As an American, you decide to own only one portfolio, either the US or the German portfolio.

(a) Which portfolio will you choose, knowing that the exchange rate is fixed at 1.62 euros per dollar?

(b) Which portfolio will you choose when you are also allowed to borrow and lend at 4% in the United States?

(c) How would your answer change if the exchange rate were 1.58 euros per dollar with a probability of $1/2$ and 1.70 euros per dollar with a probability of $1/2$? (Assume that the returns and exchange rates are uncorrelated.)

15.16 Suppose that a Japanese investor holds $1,000 in cash, and an American investor holds 120,000 yen in cash. The current exchange rate is 120 yen per dollar. At the end of the year, the yen is depreciated by 10%. Both investors convert their holdings to the local currencies. What is the rate of return to each investor? Is the average rate of return of the two investors zero? Explain.

SELECTED REFERENCES

Black, Fischer, and Robert Litterman. 'Global portfolio optimization'. *Financial Analysts Journal* 48, September–October 1992, pp. 28–43.

Christie, E., and A. Marshall. 'The impact of the introduction of the Euro on foreign exchange risk management in UK multinational companies', *European Financial Management*, Vol. 7(2), 2001.

Eichholtz, Piet M.A. 'Does international diversification work better for real estate than for stocks and bonds?'. *Financial Analysts Journal*, January–February 1996, pp. 56–62.

Fisher, Irving. *The Theory of Interest*. New York: Macmillan, 1930.

Hauser, Shmuel, Miron Rozenkranz, Uri Bn-Zion, and Uzi Yaari. 'International hedge of fixed income contracts'. *The Journal of Portfolio Management*, Winter 2001.

International Monetary Fund. *International Financial Statistics Yearbook*, various editions.

Investing Worldwide. Charlottesville, VA: Association for Investment Management, various years.

Levy, Haim, and Zvi Lerman. 'The benefits of international diversification in bonds'. *Financial Analysts Journal*, September–October 1988, pp. 56–64.

Levy, Haim, and Marshall Sarnat. 'International diversification of investment portfolios'. *American Economic Review*, September 1970, pp. 668–75.

Lofthouse, Stephen. 'International diversification'. *Journal of Portfolio Management*, Fall 1997, pp. 53–6.

Longin, Francois, M., and Bruno Solnik. 'Extreme correlation of international equity markets'. *Journal of Finance*, 56, 2001.

Peavy, John W. III. *Managing Emerging Market Portfolios*. Charlottesville, VA: Association of Investment Management and Research, 1994.

Persaud, A. 'Will G-7 integration mark the Euro's turn?'. *Risk*, October 2000.

Solnick, Bruno. 'Why not diversify internationally rather than domestically?' *Financial Analysts Journal*, July–August 1974.

Solnik, Bruno. *International Investments*. 2nd edn. Reading MA: Addison-Wesley, 1991.

Solnik, Bruno. *International Investment*. 3rd edn. Reading, MA.: Addison-Wesley Publishing Company, 1996.

Speidell, Lawrence S., and Vinod B. Bavishi. 'GAAP arbitrage: valuation opportunities in international accounting standards'. *Financial Analysts Journal*, November–December 1992, pp. 58–66.

Speidell, Lawrence S., and Ross Sappenfield. 'Global diversification in a shrinking world'. *Journal of Portfolio Management*, 19, Fall 1992, pp. 57–67.

Part VI

MARKET EFFICIENCY, MUTUAL FUNDS AND TECHNICAL ANALYSIS

Chapter 16

EFFICIENT MARKETS: THEORY AND EVIDENCE

Learning objectives

After studying this chapter you should be able to:

1 Define an efficient market.
2 Identify the types of information related to each form of the efficient market hypothesis.
3 Compare the investment strategies in efficient markets with investment strategies in inefficient markets.
4 Describe the findings of researchers who tested each form of the efficient market theory.
5 Define anomaly, and identify the common types of anomalies.

INVESTMENT IN THE NEWS

The Efficient Market

What is Efficient Market Theory?
Evidence to support the Efficient Market Theory
Ways to beat market averages
Why people try to beat the market

What is the Efficient Market Theory?

Assumptions

- The market is full of intelligent investors
- Information useful for determining prices is available to everyone nearly simultaneously

Under these conditions it is very difficult to beat the market averages

Another way to look at it,

Everyone thinks they can beat the market averages.

But by definition, not everyone can beat the market averages
- Half do better
- Half do worse

▶

INVESTMENT IN THE NEWS

Evidence to support the Efficient Market Theory

There are about 100,000 full-time investment professionals who follow perhaps 3,000 stocks

Since each follows about 30 stocks, there are 1,000 professionals following each stock.

A fund that blindly invests in an index that matches the Standard & Poors 500 has outperformed about 75 percent of all actively managed stock mutual funds. The low fees charged by the index fund are a key factor in this superior performance

Ways to beat market averages

Dumb luck:

Forbes dartboard portfolio roundly beats market averages and most professionals

By accepting more risk:

Peter Lynch has a great record of beating the averages. But in the 1987 crash, when most stock funds lost 16 percent of their value, Lynch's Magellan fund lost 32 percent of its value

Why people try to beat the market?

Because of compounding, beating the market by a little over time can dramatically increase your wealth

It's fun!

Source: Numen Lumen website, www.numen-lumen.com, 23 August 1999; body text © 1997 by David Luhman.

This chapter's *Investment in the news* claims that if the market is efficient (and there is evidence that it is efficient), then the 100,000 full-time professionals are probably wasting time and money: the index fund is doing better than most of the managed funds. The only way to beat the average, apart from luck, is to take more risk.

In studying the impact of information on stock prices, we refer to the efficient market theory (EMT).[1] Basically, the theory claims that stock prices reflect all available information that is relevant for the stock, and that no investor can earn an abnormal return (or an excess return after adjusting for risk) by trying to find buying or selling opportunities in the market. For example, if an investor could analyze the historical prices of IBM stock and develop a buy–sell rule that will yield a positive, risk-adjusted return, this would contradict the EMT. This chapter explores the various ways to interpret the EMT.

In general, academics support the EMT, whereas practitioners do not. Indeed, practitioners on Wall Street use investment strategies that rely on market *inefficiency*. Recently, however, some academics who preached for decades in support of the EMT have found empirical evidence favouring market inefficiency.[2] Chapter 18 describes some widely used valuation methods that assume market inefficiency, at least to a certain degree.

---

[1] The EMT is also widely referred to as the *efficient market hypothesis* (EMH).
[2] See Eugene F. Fama and Kenneth R. French, 'The cross-section of expected stock returns', *Journal of Finance*, 47, June 1992, pp. 427–66.

Your own perception of the EMT will govern, in large part, the particular investment philosophy you adopt. The objective of this book is not to persuade you to adopt one school of thought over another but rather to give you the analytical tools needed to reach your own conclusions. This chapter examines the investment implications and appropriate investment strategies to use if markets are efficient or, alternatively, inefficient. It also surveys the available empirical evidence regarding market efficiency.

16.1 EFFICIENT MARKET DEFINED

How efficiently do markets process information? An investigation of the effect of information on security prices must begin with a definition of an efficient market. A well-functioning financial market in which prices reflect all relevant information is said to be an **efficient market**. Another way to state this is that the EMT claims that security prices reflect all relevant information; that is, the current market price of a security incorporates all relevant information. If a financial market is efficient, then the best estimate of the true worth of a security is given by its current market price.

A large number of analysts are assessing the true value of stocks. The analysts try to find stocks whose market prices are substantially different from their true values. If the analysts find such 'mispriced' securities, they buy or sell them, driving the market price instantaneously towards the true value of the security. Hence, in an efficient market competition in the stock market pushes prices to their 'true' value. Thus, stock prices change every day, every hour, even every second as new information flows into the marketplace.

Is the market efficient? Are there 'bargains' in the market? Actually, it is almost impossible to test purely whether the market is efficient, which explains why there are no clear winners in the market efficiency dispute. Most of the tests of market efficiency are joint tests – that is, one is testing jointly whether the model measuring risk-adjusted returns is appropriate and whether markets are efficient. Thus, one of the reasons for the market efficiency dispute is that tests of market efficiency are *joint tests* of the assumed model *and* of market efficiency.

To illustrate, suppose that an analyst claims he observes the historical price movement of IBM stock, and based on these historical figures, he reaches the conclusion that IBM stock is a bargain (that is, it is underpriced). Suppose he buys IBM stock, and his annual realized rate of return on the stock is 12%. Can we then conclude that the market is inefficient? Did the analyst succeed in exploiting the information on historical prices to make an extraordinary return? To reach such a conclusion, we first need to find out the risk involved with the investment in IBM stock and figure out whether there is an abnormal return adjusted for this risk. For example, suppose that we use the CAPM (see Chapter 14) and IBM's beta to estimate the expected rate of return on IBM to be 11%. In such a case, the analyst has an *extraordinary profit* of 1%. This extraordinary profit is also called an **abnormal rate of return**. It seems that based on this result, we might claim that the market is inefficient. However, what if the CAPM is an incorrect model, and therefore the 11% estimate of the required expected return was wrong? Then we may come to the wrong conclusion regarding market efficiency, because we employed an incorrect model to measure the **'normal' rate of return**.

Thus, in testing for market efficiency, first we should estimate what should be the normal rate of return on an asset, which is also called the **risk-adjusted rate of return**. For that purpose, we need a model asserting what the risk is and what the corresponding risk premium should be. Then we compare the realized return by the analyst's investment policy to this normal return. If the realized return is significantly higher than the normal return, researchers generally assert that the market is inefficient, because the analyst made abnormal or **excess returns**.

However, by this procedure, we see that we have a **joint hypothesis** and therefore should conduct a joint test of the model and of market efficiency. To illustrate, suppose that the CAPM is wrong, and the variance of the rate of return, rather than beta, is the correct measure of risk. We may conclude that with this risk measure, the required rate of return is 12% in the IBM example. Now the analyst does not make any profit after adjusting for risk. Thus, testing market efficiency is based on a normal return as a benchmark. Because this normal return is deduced from some model, empirical tests are joint tests of the model and of market efficiency. Therefore, we cannot claim unequivocally that the market is efficient, even if empirical tests seem to reveal market efficiency (that is, that there are no abnormal returns).

16.2 WHAT CONSTITUTES THE APPROPRIATE INFORMATION SET?

A great deal of information is available in the stock market: historical stock prices, earnings and dividends, macro-economic data, private information known only to insiders, and other information that seems irrelevant for stock valuation (for example, the age and eye colour of a firm's chief executive officer). At one extreme, it might be argued that all information is useful in earning an abnormal return. An investor can use all available information and make an extraordinary profit. In other words, it pays to analyze available information in making a security selection.

At the other extreme, it might be argued that the observed prices reflect all information that exists. That is, everything that can be known about a security is already incorporated in its price. For example, even the poor health of an important member of upper management would be reflected in the stock price. From this point of view, any data collection or economic analysis is a waste of time.

Clearly, these two extremes are irrational and probably irrelevant in price determination. However, somewhere between these two extremes lies a reasonable set of the information employed in determining stock prices. Along the journey across the continuum from 'no information' to 'all information' lie three milestones or information sets: historical, public and private information. The efficient market theory, which describes the impact of information on the market prices of securities, can be analyzed in terms of these specific information sets and their impact on price determination. These three sets of information correspond to weak, semistrong and strong EMT. Let us elaborate.

16.2.1 Weak form of the EMT

The first form of the efficient market theory is the **weak form of the EMT**.[3] According to the weak form of the EMT, today's stock prices reflect all information about the historical prices of the stock, so **historical prices** are not useful for investment decisions.

---

[3] See Roberts (1967), as quoted in Burton Malkiel, 'Efficient market hypothesis', in John Eatwell, Murray Milgate and Peter Newman (eds), *The New Palgrave: Finance* (New York: Macmillan Press, 1989). In 1991 Fama suggested broadening this category to include other variables used in determining return predictability.

Thus, trading technique based on historical prices, well known as **technical analysis** (see Chapter 18), is not useful according to the weak form efficiency. However, other information – for example, historical earnings – may be useful in earning an abnormal profit. If this is true, then an investor could not use historical stock price information to find mispriced stocks and thus profit from buying or selling these stocks. The stock prices already would have adjusted for this information. Technical analysts try to use historical price information to locate mispriced stocks. Therefore, under the weak form of the EMT, we would not expect them to find opportunities that generate abnormal returns using these techniques. Investors would just earn the normal profit for the risk taken.

If the weak form of the EMT holds, and thus prices are independent of the pattern of historical stock prices, we say that price *changes* will appear to follow a random walk.[4] A **random walk** is a statistical concept that predicts that the next outcome in a series does not depend on its prior outcomes. A simple way that illustrates the random walk notion is with a flipping of a coin. For example, although the first three tosses may be heads, these outcomes do not affect the probability of head or tail in the next toss. The result in the next toss has no memory; it does not depend on previous results.

Because risky securities offer positive expected returns, we would anticipate stock prices to rise over time. Despite this trend, price changes may still follow a random walk. For example, suppose we have a security presently trading at $100. We know that in each period, the price will rise by 12% with a 75% probability, or fall by 10% with a 25% probability. In this case, on average, three out of four times (75%) the return will be 12%, whereas only one out of four times (25%) the return will be −10%. The expected return in this case is $E(R)$:

$$E(R) = 0.75(12\%) + 0.25(-10\%) = 6.5\%$$

Although the expected return is 6.5%, the particular outcome observed in a given year is random. Hence, even in this case, we say that the security follows a random walk.

Going back to the coin-tossing example, suppose you flip a biased coin with a probability of heads of $^3/_4$ and a probability of tails of $^1/_4$.[5] Do the results of the first three tosses affect the result of the next toss? Absolutely not. This process has no memory, and the probabilities are still $^3/_4$ for heads and $^1/_4$ for tails.

16.2.2 Semistrong form of the EMT

The second form of the efficient market theory is the **semistrong form of the EMT**. According to the semistrong form of the EMT, prices reflect all relevant publicly available information. In addition to historical stock prices, publicly available information includes financial statements, notes to the financial statements, and supplementary information required by accounting regulations. Publicly available information also includes other external financial and regulatory filings such as property taxes paid, as well as market-related data such as the level of interest rates and the stock's beta.

According to the semistrong form of the EMT, an investor could not earn abnormal returns on trading strategies built on publicly available information. Thus, if the market

---

[4] Technically, stocks, on average, will move up by the stock's expected return. Hence, the random walk concept is applied after adjusting for the expected return.
[5] A biased coin is typically heavier on one side. Hence, tossing it results in outcomes different from 50–50.

is semistrong efficient, a diligent study of financial statements is of no economic value. The idea behind this view is that, once this information becomes public, all investors react instantaneously and push the price to reflect all public information. For example, hearing on CNN that Enron manipulated its reported earnings is too late, because the stock price will already have dropped and so you cannot then sell the stock at the relatively high price that prevailed before the news became public. Thus, when you read the *Wall Street Journal* with your morning coffee and see some public information, such as a new drug discovery or a financial crisis in Asia, it is too late for you to earn an abnormal profit. The price at which you can buy or sell the stock already reflects this information.

In contrast to proponents of the semistrong form of the EMT, there are investors who think they can profit from a careful study of publicly available data – particularly accounting data. These investors practice **fundamental analysis** and use the information in financial statements and other public sources to identify mispriced stock. The two factors commonly employed to identify underpriced stock in a fundamental analysis are the **price/earnings (P/E) ratio** and the **market-to-book-value (M/B) ratio**, where M is the market value (stock price) and B is the book value per share.

16.2.3 Strong form of the EMT

The third form of the efficient market theory is the **strong form of the EMT**. The strong form states that current prices already reflect all publicly and privately available information. Thus, the strong form includes all relevant historical price information and all relevant publicly available information, as well as information known only to a select few such as management, the board of directors and private bankers. For example, suppose a member of the board of directors of Intel knows that the firm has decided to take over another firm. The board member's spouse then buys shares of Intel stock before the takeover becomes public information. This would be considered trading on inside information, and is illegal. If the strong EMT form were true, then insiders would not profit from trading on their information. There is much evidence that the market is not strong-form efficient, because there is money to be gained from trading on inside information (although such trading is illegal). Insiders who know about future takeovers or acquisitions can earn large profits. However, it is illegal to trade on private information, and many inside traders have received prison sentences for doing so.

Because semistrong form information is a subset of strong form information, and weak form information is a subset of semistrong information, it is clear that if the market is weak form inefficient, it is also semistrong and strong form inefficient; if it is semistrong form inefficient it is also strong form inefficient. Exhibit 16.1 summarizes the discussion thus far from the viewpoint of an analyst. If an analyst believed that the weak form of the EMT was not true, then the analyst should be able to earn abnormal returns based on historical price data, as well as public and private data. If an analyst believed that the market was weak form inefficient, but not the semistrong form of the EMT, then the analyst should be able to earn excess returns based on public and private data but not based on historical prices. If an analyst believed that the semistrong form, but not the strong form, of the EMT was true, then the analyst should be able to earn excess returns only based on private information (which is illegal to trade upon). Finally, if an analyst believed that the strong form of the EMT was true, then no excess returns would be possible, no matter what information the analyst could access. Clearly, investment strategy is directly linked to the analyst's view of the EMT.

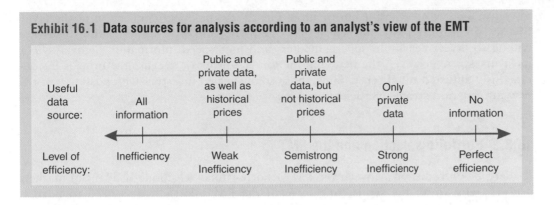

Exhibit 16.1 Data sources for analysis according to an analyst's view of the EMT

16.3 INVESTMENT STRATEGY IN AN EFFICIENT MARKET

It seems reasonable that markets do process historical and public data with relative efficiency, and this is the view of many academic investment theorists as well as practitioners who sell index funds which are unmanaged funds. Thus, this section examines how to structure a successful investment strategy in the semistrong form of the EMT. It first examines how resources are allocated in this market. Next, it examines portfolio selection and the usefulness of employing the expected risk–return trade-off when markets are efficient. It also distinguishes between passive and active portfolio management strategies.

16.3.1 Resource allocation and the EMT

If relatively more money is allocated to firms that have profitable capital budgeting projects and relatively less money is allocated to firms with poor projects, we say that money is allocated in the market in an effective manner. In efficient markets, resources are allocated to the various firms in an effective manner, because those firms with good prospects will be able to raise additional capital in the primary market on relatively good terms. That is, in constructing their portfolios, investors will allocate more money to those firms they deem a relatively good investment. For example, suppose IBM has a good new computer or Pfizer develops a new drug (such as Viagra). When this information becomes public, investors will allocate more of their money to IBM or Pfizer, and its stock price will instantaneously go up.

Thus, a firm with good projects will have a higher stock price and can issue stocks on better terms in the market. In contrast, a firm with poor projects (one that is expected to go bankrupt) would be unable to raise money through either a stock issue or a bond issue. Thus, the information on the firm's projects is reflected in the stock prices; the rosier the estimated future is, the higher the stock price.

This observation regarding the link between resource allocation and the EMT illustrates a seeming paradox. In order for markets to be efficient, new firm information should affect the stock price. Hence, some investors have to be paying attention to firm information. However, the EMT suggests there is no benefit to monitoring firm information. This paradox is solved once we understand that in practice, those investors with the least costly access to information capitalize on minor mispricing, which drives prices to reflect swiftly all relevant information. Hence, the practical application of the EMT focuses on trading costs and speed. This helps explain why some trading firms are willing to invest heavily in supercomputers and high-speed information highways. For most investors, however, the new information is worthless, because the price is instantaneously adjusted to reflect it. Thus, those sophisticated investors who possess first the new information create an efficient market.

16.3.2 Portfolio selection and the EMT

Is there a contradiction between the EMT and portfolio selection? If financial markets are efficient under the semistrong form of the EMT, is there any need to burden ourselves with portfolio diversification? Under the semistrong form of the EMT, the analysis conducted by technicians (who do technical analysis) and fundamentalists (who do fundamental analysis) will not generate excess returns. There are no 'bargains' in the market, and stock selection techniques are worthless. What is left for portfolio managers is portfolio diversification, which pays off even in efficient markets.

To demonstrate this idea, suppose that two stocks, 1 and 2, each trade for $10. You flip two coins, one corresponding to each stock. If a head comes up, the stock price increases to $13; if a tail appears, the stock price falls to $9. Of course, these stock price changes conform to semistrong-form market efficiency, because the price changes are dependent on a random coin toss and do not depend on historical or public information. If you do not diversify between the two stocks, the future mean and variance of each stock, for your $10 investment, are as follows:

$$\text{Mean: } (1/2 \times \$13) + (1/2 \times \$9) = \$11$$

$$\text{Variance: } \sigma^2 = 1/2 \, (13 - 11)^2 + 1/2 \, (9 - 11)^2 = 4$$

$$\sigma = \$2$$

Can you gain from diversification in such a market that obeys the EMT? The answer is yes. To see why, assume you invest $5 in Stock 1 and $5 in Stock 2. Because the two stocks are independent (you toss two coins, separately, one for each stock), you get the following returns:

Stock 1		Stock 2	Portfolio
$1/2 \times \$13$	+	$1/2 \times \$13 =$	$13 (with a probability of $1/4$)
$1/2 \times \$13$	+	$1/2 \times \$9 =$	$11 (with a probability of $1/4$)
$1/2 \times \$9$	+	$1/2 \times \$13 =$	$11 (with a probability of $1/4$)
$1/2 \times \$9$	+	$1/2 \times \$9 =$	$9 (with a probability of $1/4$)

where $1/2$ represents the proportion of investment in each stock ($5/$10 = $1/2$). The portfolio mean return is

$$(1/4 \times 13) + (1/4 \times 11) + (1/4 \times 11) + (1/4 \times 9) = \$11$$

which is exactly the same as investing in just Stock 1 or Stock 2 alone. Note, however, that the variance of the portfolio is lower:

$$\sigma^2 = 1/4 \, (13 - 11)^2 + 1/4 \, (11 - 11)^2 + 1/4 \, (11 - 11)^2 + 1/4 \, (9 - 11)^2 = 2$$

$$\sigma \cong \$1.41$$

Thus, you reduce the risk by diversifying.

Some believe that the semistrong form of the EMT implies that all stocks are correctly priced, and therefore you can select stocks at random – for example, by throwing a dart at a list of stocks obtained from the financial pages. This is not correct. Although you cannot predict which stock will go up and which will go down in the future, by diversification you can reduce your risk. If you ignore this diversification, you are exposing yourself to higher risk with no compensation in the form of a higher expected return. Note that in the previous example, your variance decreased through diversification, but your expected return remained the same, at $11.

The previous example can be extended to many assets with positive and negative correlations. For example, suppose you have a stock with a high variance but a low beta (for example, $\beta_i = 0.5$). According to the CAPM, the mean rate of return on the stock will be relatively low, because this stock has a low correlation with other securities, and hence portfolio risk is reduced. If you do not diversify and thus hold only one stock (or only a few stocks), you pay a relatively high price for the stock; you expose yourself to high risk (variance) and do not enjoy the benefits of the risk reduction possibilities that are due to the negative correlation, i.e. the low beta is irrelevant in the lack of diversification.

In summary, if the semistrong form of the EMT holds, technical and fundamental analysis are economically worthless. However, portfolio analysis remains important; in fact, more effort should be allocated to portfolio analysis. If the market is inefficient, then both security analysis (to find 'bargains' in the market) and portfolio analysis (to reduce risk) are economically important.

16.3.3 Passive versus active portfolio management

Portfolio managers face two main tasks:

1 *How to diversify among the various assets.* Finding the desired investment proportions and adhering to them or changing them as the S&P index changes weights, i.e. by computer rather than by human judgement, is called **passive investment strategy**.
2 *When to change the investment proportions in the various assets.* Managers try to predict whether the stock market or the bond market will be stronger, say, next month, and actively change the investment proportions according to their predictions. Such a management strategy is called **active investment strategy**. Managers may increase the proportion of stocks from 40% to 60% today, and reverse this proportion next month, reducing the stock proportion to 40% or even less.

If the market is efficient, only the passive management strategy is relevant, because according to the semistrong form of the EMT, publicly available information (for example, the budget deficit, the amount of money in the market, reported earnings by firms or unemployment) is not useful in predicting whether stocks or bonds will be better in the future. In such a case, portfolio managers do not have **'timing ability'**, or the ability to predict when is the best time to move from heavy bond investment to more stock investment or vice versa. Nearly all investors know that when interest rates go down more than expected, the stock market typically rallies. However, can they predict what the interest rate will be next month? If you believe in the semistrong form of the EMT, you cannot predict the interest rate changes; hence you cannot benefit from active investment strategies. The best investment strategy is simply to find some investment proportions and adopt a passive investment strategy; a portfolio manager should not try to outsmart the market.

Funds known as **index funds** do not engage in active rebalancing strategies. For example, the Vanguard Index 500 Portfolio holds stocks in the same proportions as the Standard & Poor's 500 stock price index. Thus, if you buy this fund, you really buy the index, and the manager does not make any attempt to outperform the S&P 500 index. Because index funds do not have a large turnover and do not need to spend money on economic analyses, they incur expenses of about 0.2%; for managed funds (funds that invest not just in indexes but in stocks, bonds, options, futures, currencies, etc., thus offering the investor the advantage of professional management), these fees are much larger (usually around 1.3%).

The *Investment in the news* article asserts that index funds outperform 75% of the mutual funds, indicating that active management on average is useless and even reduces returns.

16.4 INVESTMENT STRATEGY IN AN INEFFICIENT MARKET

In an inefficient market, the appropriate investment strategy is different than when the market is efficient. The particular strategy to pursue depends on the level of efficiency (or inefficiency). Investors who believe in the weak form of the EMT but not the semistrong form might locate mispriced securities using fundamental analysis. Hence, the investors who are the best at analyzing the data will earn an abnormal return.

Similarly, investors who do not believe in the weak form of the EMT would even benefit from some technical trading rules based on past historical prices, as well as fundamental analysis. Finally, investors who believe in the strong form of the EMT believe they cannot benefit even if they are insiders. Those insiders who do not believe in the strong form of the EMT can earn abnormal profits. However, they have to consider the risk–return profile, where they risk being sent to prison!

16.5 EMPIRICAL EVIDENCE RELATED TO THE EMT

Does actual price behaviour support the EMT? The existing evidence is vast; this text will survey just a few studies to answer this question.

However, before we look at the empirical tests of the various forms of market efficiency, it is worth noting another set of classifications that has been suggested by Fama.[6] His classifications are derived from the empirical tests conducted to figure out whether the market is efficient. The first category includes *tests for return predictability*, which includes historical prices and other variables such as dividends, interest rates, firm size, and so on. If one can use these variables to predict stock price or to make an abnormal return, we say that the market is inefficient. The second category includes **event studies**, which test whether an abnormal rate of return exists because of an announcement of an event such as an increase in dividends, or a merger. Once again, if one can make an abnormal return using this information, the market is inefficient. The third category includes *tests for private information*, which are similar to the tests for insider information discussed earlier.

---

[6] See Eugene F. Fama, 'Efficient capital markets: 2', *Journal of Finance*, 46, December 1991, pp. 1575–617.

This chapter will adhere to the original classifications of market efficiency. Nevertheless, keep in mind that these classifications are arbitrary and can be changed without changing the empirical tests for market efficiency. The names change, but not the content of the tests.

The objective of this section is to assess how efficient the market actually is in practice. To organize our investigation, we categorize the evidence according to how it is related to the three forms of the EMT (weak, semistrong and strong).

16.5.1 Evidence related to the weak form of the EMT

A large number of empirical studies have tested the weak form of the EMT; some are summarized in Exhibit 16.2. In general, the early research provides strong evidence in favour of markets' being weak-form efficient. More recent evidence has uncovered many **anomalies**, which are events that are not anticipated and that offer investors a chance to earn abnormal profits. (Researchers were so convinced that the EMT was true that they felt any contrary evidence must be an anomaly; some of these findings were referred to as *enigmas*.)

Two primary techniques are used to test the validity of the weak-form proposition: analysis of technical trading rules for abnormal rates of return, and statistical tests on historical data to locate significant patterns.

■ Analysis of technical trading rules for abnormal rates of return

To measure whether a given strategy or a technical rule is beneficial, we need first to define more precisely abnormal return. **Abnormal rates of return**, as defined earlier, are the rates of return that are above what we would expect to earn given the level of risk taken.

To calculate abnormal returns, we must first determine normal returns. We can use the CAPM, the SIM or the APT (see Chapter 14) to find normal returns. Let us demonstrate with the CAPM. By the CAPM, the expected return on Asset i (a security or a portfolio) is

$$E(R_i) = r + [E(R_m) - r]\beta_i \tag{16.1}$$

where r is the risk-free interest rate, $E(R_m)$ is the expected rate of return on the market portfolio, and β_i is the beta coefficient (defined as $\dfrac{\text{Cov}(R_i, R_m)}{\sigma_m^2}$). Thus, the normal expected rate of return is given by $E(R_i)$. The abnormal rate of return (AR_i) is defined as

$$AR_i = R_i - E(R_i) = R_i - \{r + [E(R_m) - r]\beta_i\} \tag{16.2}$$

or, in words,

Abnormal rate of return = Actual rate of return − Normal rate of return

where R_i is the realized or actual return on the ith stock. Because $E(R_m)$ and β_i are unknown parameters, they are usually estimated by using historical data. Hence, the normal return is estimated first, and then the abnormal return is estimated. This technique is commonly employed in the event studies explained next.

Many research studies of market efficiency examine the behaviour of these abnormal rates of return over time and in particular, the cumulative effect. Researchers measure this using the **cumulative abnormal rate of return** (CAR_i), the sum of all abnormal rates

Exhibit 16.2 Summary of evidence related to the weak form of the efficient market theory

Authors	Year	Assets studied	Weak form efficient?	Comments
Bachelier	1900	French securities	Yes	Tried to test whether the French government securities options and futures market was efficient
Roberts	1959	US stocks	Yes	Found that stock prices resemble random patterns
Osborne	1959	US stocks	Yes	Found that stock prices are similar to random movement of physical particles in water (Brownian motion)
Granger, Morgenstern	1963	US stocks	Yes	Employed spectral analysis (a powerful statistical tool that identifies patterns), but still found no significant patterns
Fama	1965	US stocks	Yes	Examined serial correlations and other statistical tools to check for patterns, and found no significant patterns
Fama, Blume	1966	US stocks	Yes	Examined technical trading rules and found no abnormal profits
Solnik	1973	Stocks in 9 countries	Yes	Used serial correlations and found no profitable investment strategies
Merton	1980	US stocks	No	Found that changes in variance are somewhat predicable from past data
French	1980	US stocks	No	Identified a weekend effect
Keim	1983	US stocks	No	Identified a January effect
Gultekin, Gultekin	1983	International markets	No	Identified seasonal patterns
Jaffe, Westerfield	1984	International markets	No	Identified seasonal patterns
Lehmann	1990	US stocks	No	Identified reversal effects
Serletis, Sondergard	1995	Canadian stocks	Yes	Using tests of the 1980s, it was found that efficiency holds for Canadian stocks
Masih, Masih	1996	Daily spot exchange rates	No	Tested spot rates and found that they suggest violation of market efficiency
Yu	1996	East Asian exchanges	No	Found that exchange rates contain predictive power about stock movements in Hong Kong
McQueen, Thorley	1997	Gold	No	Found that prior returns on an equally weighted portfolio of gold stocks predict gold returns

of return for the whole investment period, which is calculated for a particular trading strategy as follows:

$$\mathrm{CAR}_i = \sum_{t=1}^{m} \mathrm{AR}_{i,t} \qquad (16.3)$$

where m is the number of periods (which are usually days). If the cumulative abnormal rates of return are significantly positive, then we conclude that abnormal returns are possible following some strategy, and the EMT is wrong. An alternative conclusion would be that the risk of the portfolio was not appropriately estimated by its beta. Therefore, as discussed before, we face a joint hypothesis regarding EMT and the model used to measure the normal rate of return.

The CAR method is commonly employed in event studies. An **event study** is a technique to measure the impact of a particular event on a firm's stock price. It measures the response of the stock price to the event – for example, an announcement of an increase in cash dividends. Suppose that a firm announces an increase in cash dividends, and the stock price on the same day goes up by 2%. Is this an abnormal profit? The answer is not clear, because many other economic phenomena that may affect the stock price may occur on the same day – an announcement of a decrease in the interest rate, a new peace treaty, and so on. The aim of event study methodology is to measure the increase in price that is due solely to the event itself. Therefore, we measure the average abnormal return of many firms which increased their dividends on various dates, hence the name *event study*: in our example we test the event of an increase in dividends.

Because β_i is unknown, we cannot directly employ Equation 16.2 to measure AR_i. Therefore, in an event study, we commonly employ the single index model when the factor is some stock index (for example, the S&P 500 index). The event date is denoted by t. Then the abnormal rate of return on day t (see Equation 16.2) is estimated by e_t, given by the equation

$$R_t = a + bR_{m,t} + e_t$$

Namely, the abnormal return is estimated by e_t, given by

$$e_t = R_t - a - bR_{m,t}$$

where R_t and $R_{m,t}$ are the rates of return on the announcement date of the firm's stock and on the market portfolio (for example, the S&P 500 index), respectively, and a and b are the intercept and the slope, respectively, of the regression line of R_t regressed against $R_{m,t}$. In order not to contaminate the estimates of a and b by the event itself, generally some period before the announcement date is taken – for example, 60 months (starting 65 months before the announcement date) – and a regression of R_t on $R_{m,t}$ is conducted in this period to estimate a and b. Also, because there may be leaks of information before the event and a continuing effect after the event, it is common to measure the abnormal return corresponding to a few days surrounding the event date as well.

As mentioned above, to make sure that e_t measures the abnormal rate of return and not another economic factor occurring on the same date, many firms that increase the cash dividends from different dates in the past are included in the study. Thus, by having various periods, the effects of other economic factors tend to cancel each other. Thus, $\bar{e}_t$ which is the average of e_t across many firms, is the estimate of the abnormal return, AR_i across all firms on the various announcement dates (t). Having the average abnormal return ($\bar{e}_t$) of all the firms included in the study on the announcement date (which differs across firms but is still denoted by t) allows us to employ Equation 16.3 to calculate the average cumulative abnormal rate of return.

If the average abnormal return ($\bar{e}_t$) or the average cumulative abnormal rate of return is significantly different from zero, we say that the announcement itself provides an abnormal return, and the market is semistrong inefficient. If the average abnormal return is significant before the announcement date as well, we conclude that information was leaked before the announcement date. Finally, if the average abnormal return is significant after the event, we conclude that investors can earn an abnormal rate of return after the information is in the public domain for a few days, which strongly contradicts the market semistrong efficiency. However, do not forget that the event study has a joint test, and the commonly strong conclusion may be misleading, because the model employed to measure the normal return may be wrong!

The empirical evidence generally rejects the notion that abnormal returns are generated from simple trading rules which are based on historical prices. However, there are many trading rules, some of which are privately held; hence, not all rules have been tested and we cannot definitely assert that the market is weak form efficient.

▣ Statistical tests of historical data for significant patterns

A second way to test the validity of the weak form of the EMT is to conduct statistical tests on historical data to locate significant patterns. For example, autocorrelations or serial correlations can be examined to assess whether past returns had predictive power in determining future returns.[7] Alternatively, nonparametric tests can be employed to assess whether negative returns are followed by positive returns or vice versa.[8] Although some evidence suggests that weak patterns do exist, they are not strong enough to profit when transaction costs are taken into consideration.

Looking again at Exhibit 16.2, one pattern is clear. Early evidence appears to support the weak form of the EMT, but more recent evidence appears to reject it. Numerous patterns have been identified that suggest that markets do not even adhere to the weak form of the EMT.

16.5.2 Evidence related to the semistrong form of the EMT

When investigating whether the semistrong form of the EMT is true, researchers try to determine whether investors using fundamental analysis could earn abnormal returns. If these investors cannot earn abnormal returns consistently, then the semistrong form is true. Exhibit 16.3 lists some studies of the semistrong form of the EMT and their conclusions.

The evidence related to the semistrong form of the EMT investigates information obtained through fundamental analysis. Fundamental analysis focuses on the analysis of a firm's specific information and its stock prices. The most common information analyzed is the reported earnings per share (EPS). Thus, fundamental analysis seeks to determine whether there is a link between basic information about a company (such as earnings per share) and its stock price.

The key to understanding the relationship between earnings per share and stock prices lies in what was expected by the market. That is, we should ask, how different are the earnings from what was expected? Rendleman, Jones and Latané used this measure to analyze the validity of the semistrong form of the EMT, examining the cumulative abnormal rates of return for 10 groups of stocks.[9] The stock groups were constructed by rankings based on the following equation:

$$SUE = \frac{EPS - E(EPS)}{SEE} \tag{16.4}$$

[7] Autocorrelations or serial correlations look at how correlated past changes are with current changes. If past changes are highly correlated (positive or negative), they can be used to predict future changes.
[8] Nonparametric tests are statistical techniques that seek to determine whether patterns exist in a given set of data.
[9] Richard J. Rendleman, Charles P. Jones and Henry A. Latané, 'Empirical anomalies based on unexpected earnings and the importance of risk adjustments', *Journal of Financial Economics*, 10, 1982, pp. 269–87.

PRACTICE BOX

Problem

Suppose you know that the expected daily rate of return of Morgan, Inc., common stock is 0.0453%. You also observe the following daily rates of return around Day 3. Assume that the firm announced an increase in dividends on Day 3.

Date	Rate of return
1	−0.5%
2	0.3
3	5.0
4	3.0
5	0.05

Calculate the cumulative abnormal rates of return.

Solution

Given that $E(R_i) = 0.0453\%$, construct the following table:

Date	Rate of return	$AR_{i,t}$	$CAR_{i,t}$
1	−0.5%	−0.5453 %	−0.5453%
2	0.3	0.2547[a]	−0.2906[b]
3	5.0	4.9547	4.6641
4	3.0	2.9547	7.6188
5	0.05	0.0047	7.6235

[a] $0.2547 = 0.3 − 0.0453$.
[b] $−0.2906 = −0.5453 + 0.2547$.

The main implication of these results is not that there was a 5% return on Day 3 when the dividends announcement is made. The main implication is that there was a 3.0% return the day after, which could have resulted in abnormal profits. Thus, investors can buy the stock at Day 3 and still make money at Day 4. This example illustrates the concept of abnormal returns. However, five observations of one security are not enough to draw any conclusions.

where SUE = standardized unexpected earnings, EPS = earnings per share, E(EPS) = expected earnings per share, and SEE = the standard error of the estimate. The denominator helps adjust for some industries' having more or less volatility than other industries. For example, utility firms have a fairly predictable EPS, whereas software firms have a very unpredictable EPS. Thus, a 5% difference in the actual EPS from the expected EPS may be interpreted as dramatic by investors in a utility firm's stock but interpreted as insignificant by investors in software companies. The SEE would be greater for the software firm, reducing the SUE. After adjusting for this difference in earnings volatility, 10 groups of stocks were formed, where Group 1 represents firms with the lowest SUE, Group 2 represents firms with the next-to-lowest SUE, and so forth. Thus, Group 10 represents stocks with the highest SUE.

Exhibit 16.4 illustrates the results. Clearly, market prices react to unexpected earnings announcements as cumulative average excess returns move up or down due to the announcements. In contradiction to the EMT, however, the best (Group 10) and worst

Exhibit 16.3 Summary of evidence related to the semistrong form of the efficient market theory

Authors	Year	Assets studied	Semistrong form efficient?	Comments
Fama, Fisher, Jensen, Roll	1969	US stocks	Yes	Stock splits – no gains after announcements
Scholes	1972	US stocks	Yes	Large secondary offerings – price decline is permanent when insiders are selling
Jaffe	1974	US stocks	No	Insiders can profit from public information about insider trading
Ball	1978	US stocks	No	Earnings announcement reactions take considerable time
Watts	1978	US stocks	No	Reproduced work of Ball (1978) with better techniques and found same results
Dodd	1981	US stocks	Yes	No abnormal profits after merger announcement
Rendleman, Jones, Latané	1982	US stocks	No	Similar results to Ball (1978)
Roll	1984	Orange juice futures	Yes/No	Inefficient due to exchange limits; otherwise efficient
Seyhun	1986	US stocks	Yes	Insiders cannot profit from public information about insider trading
Fama, French	1992	US stocks	No	Investors can profit from information on the firm's size and the market-to-book-value ratio
Peterson	1995	US stocks	Yes	Abnormal returns associated with 'stock highlights' published by Value Line found consistent with EMT
Bernard, Seyhun	1997	US stocks	No	Using a stochastic dominance approach to test market efficiency following earnings announcements showed the market is inefficient
Blose, Shieh	1997	US stocks	No	Positive correlation found between Tobin's Q and stock price reaction to capital investment announcements, where Tobin's Q is defined as the ratio of the market value of the firm's assets to its replacement value

(Group 1) continue to move up and down, respectively, after the announcement. Thus, the information on the surprise in the past can be employed to make profits in the future. This is good evidence against the semistrong form of the EMT.

In response to this research, as well as other studies, the *Wall Street Journal* has now begun to publish 'Quarterly earnings surprises'. Investors may benefit from this information as Exhibit 16.4 reveals.

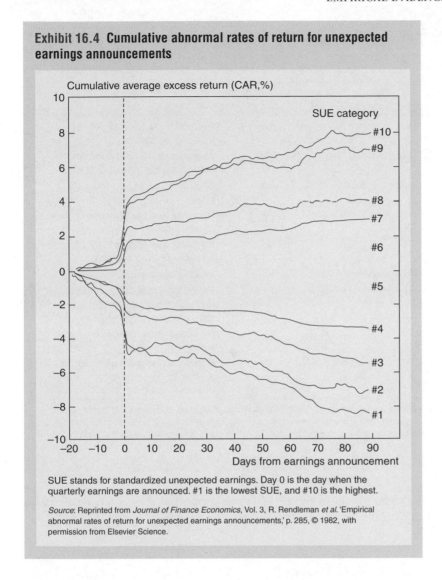

Exhibit 16.4 Cumulative abnormal rates of return for unexpected earnings announcements

SUE stands for standardized unexpected earnings. Day 0 is the day when the quarterly earnings are announced. #1 is the lowest SUE, and #10 is the highest.

Source: Reprinted from *Journal of Finance Economics*, Vol. 3, R. Rendleman *et al.* 'Empirical abnormal rates of return for unexpected earnings announcements,' p. 285, © 1982, with permission from Elsevier Science.

16.5.3 Evidence related to the strong form of the EMT

The evidence against the strong form of the EMT is irrefutable; some of this research is summarized in Exhibit 16.5. Several studies have found that insiders can profit significantly from the valuable information they possess. Exactly where you draw the line between private information and public information may influence your position on the strong form of the EMT. For example, Liu, Smith and Syed (1990) found significant price changes on stocks discussed in the 'Heard on the Street' column in the *Wall Street Journal*. When reporters find this information, is it private or public at that point? Clearly, after publication it is public information. However, reporters know this information before it is published, yet they are not insiders. Technically, however, it is inside information prior to publication.

If the strong form of the EMT is correct, then insiders should not be able to generate abnormal returns from their trading decisions. The evidence presented in this section is very convincing: insiders (but not mutual funds managers) can generate abnormal

Exhibit 16.5 Summary of evidence related to the strong form of the efficient market theory

Authors	Year	Assets studied	Strong form efficient?	Comments
Cowles	1933	Money managers[a]	Yes	Professionals do no better than the market as a whole
Friend, Brown, Herman, Vickers	1962	Mutual funds[a]	Yes	Average mutual fund does not outperform the market as a whole
Neiderhoffer, Osborn	1966	NYSE specialist	No	Specialists generate significant profits
Jensen	1968 1969	Mutual funds[a]	Yes	Risk-adjusted performance of mutual funds is no better
Scholes	1972	Insiders	No	Insiders have access to information not reflected in prices
Jaffe	1974	Insiders	No	Insiders can profit
Henriksson	1984	Mutual funds[a]	Yes	Before load fees but after expenses, mutual funds do about average
Seyhun	1986	Insiders	No	Before load fees but after other expenses, mutual funds do slightly better than average
Liu, Smith, Syed	1990	US stocks	No	Prices change with publication of articles in the 'Heard on the Street' column in the *Wall Street Journal*

[a] Many assumed that money and mutual fund managers were in possession of inside information. Hence, examining the performance of mutual fund managers was a test of strong-form efficiency. The evidence suggests that mutual fund managers are not in possession of material inside information (or at least they cannot profit from it if they have it).

profits, and hence the strong form of the EMT is not supported. However, recall again that it is illegal to trade on insider information.

16.6 MARKET ANOMALIES

The EMT has some widely known and well-documented violations. Recall that a market anomaly is any event that can be exploited to produce abnormal profits. Anomalies exist in any form of the EMT but in most cases relate to the semistrong form of the EMT.

Market anomalies imply market inefficiency. However, because all market efficiency tests are joint tests, it is possible that these anomalies are actually not anomalies but rather that we do not have a powerful model to explain them. This explanation is convincing, particularly in cases where anomalies persist for a long time. Why don't they disappear, as investors are well familiar with them? Exhibit 16.6 identifies four categories of anomalies: seasonal, event, firm and accounting anomalies.

Firm anomalies are anomalies that result from firm-specific characteristics. For example, small firms tend to outperform large ones on a risk-adjusted basis, an anomaly called the **size effect**. A similar anomaly is the **neglected firm effect**: the fewer analysts tracking a particular security, the larger the average return. This anomaly may be an instance of the size effect, because neglected firms tend to be small.

Exhibit 16.6 Summary of market anomalies

Anomaly	Description/implication
Firm anomalies	
Size	Returns on small firms tend to be higher, even on a risk-adjusted basis
Closed-end mutual funds	Returns on closed-end funds that trade at a discount tend to be higher
Neglect	Firms that are not followed by many analysts tend to yield higher returns
Institutional holdings	Firms that are owned by few institutions tend to have higher returns
Seasonal anomalies	
January	Security prices tend to be up in January, especially the first few days (as well as the last days of December)
Weekend	Securities tend to be up on Fridays and down on Mondays
Time of day	Securities tend to be up in the first 45 minutes and the last 15 minutes of the day
End of month	Last trading day of the month tends to be up
Seasonal	Firms with highly seasonal sales tend to be up during high sales periods
Holidays	Returns tend to be positive on the last trading day before a holiday
Event anomalies	
Analysts' recommendations	The more analysts recommending purchase of a stock, the more likely it will go down
Insider trading	The more insiders buying a stock, the more likely it is to go up
Listings	Security prices rise after it is announced that a firm will be listed on an exchange
Value Line rating changes	Security prices continue to rise after Value Line places a security in its #1 category
Accounting anomalies	
P/E ratio	Stocks with low P/E ratios tend to have higher returns
Earnings surprises	Stocks with larger-than-anticipated earnings announcements tend to continue to rise even after the announcement
Price/sales ratio	If the price-to-sales ratio is low, then the stock tends to outperform
Price/book ratio	If the price-to-book value is low, then the stock tends to outperform
Dividend yield	If the dividend yield is high, then the stock tends to outperform
Earnings momentum	Stocks of firms whose growth rate of earnings is rising tend to outperform

Fama and French analyze the market-to-book-value (M/B) ratio of stocks as a predictor of returns across securities.[10] The terms *book value* and *market value* relate to the book value and market value of the firm's equity. Fama and French classified all the

---

[10] Eugene F. Fama and Kenneth R. French, 'The cross section of expected returns', *Journal of Finance*, 47, 1992, pp. 427–65.

stocks included in their sample into 10 deciles, according to the M/B ratio. They found that the decile with the lowest M/B ratio had an average monthly rate of return of 1.65%, whereas the decile with the highest M/B ratio had a return of only 0.72% per month. Exhibit 16.7 shows their findings regarding the M/B anomaly.

A **seasonal anomaly** is an anomaly that depends solely on time. For example, the January anomaly (or January effect) is the tendency for stock prices to be abnormally up in January (and late December).

Exhibit 16.8 demonstrates the January effect for various assets for the periods 1926 to 1996 and 1987 to 1996. For the long period 1926 to 1996 (Exhibit 16.8(a)), the January effect is striking for small stocks, which had an average monthly rate of return of about 7% in January and less than 2% in most other months. For the S&P 500 index there is no January effect; a larger rate of return is recorded in July and August, and a similar rate of return is recorded in December. For the other assets categories (Treasury bills, long-term corporate bonds, long-term government bonds and intermediate-term government bonds), there is no January effect.

Exhibit 16.8(b) is the same as Exhibit 16.8(a) except that the averages of the rates of return are for only 10 years, 1987 to 1996. Although the rate of return on small stocks in January is higher than in any other month, the January effect was dramatically reduced. The January effect does not exist for the other assets. It is possible that investors, being more aware of the January effect in the recent period, bought the stocks earlier in the year (in December) in an attempt to gain in January. This possibility provides only a partial explanation for the reduction in the January effect in the last

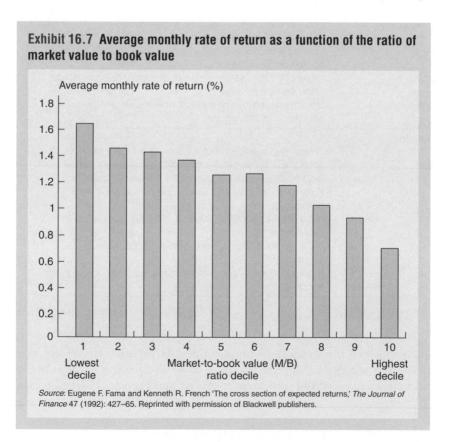

Exhibit 16.7 Average monthly rate of return as a function of the ratio of market value to book value

Source: Eugene F. Fama and Kenneth R. French 'The cross section of expected returns,' *The Journal of Finance* 47 (1992): 427–65. Reprinted with permission of Blackwell publishers.

Exhibit 16.8 The January anomaly

(a) Average monthly returns, 1926 to 1996

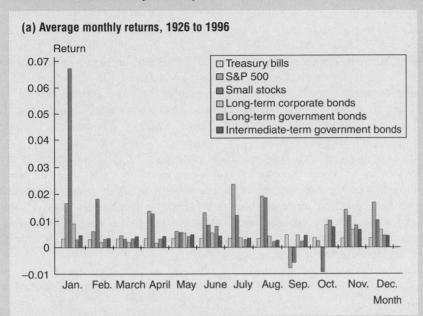

(b) Average monthly returns, 1987 to 1996

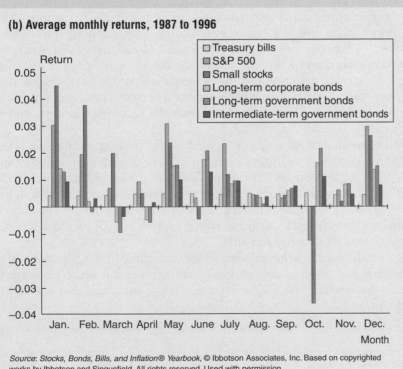

decade, because in February, May and December there is also a relatively high rate of return on the S&P index and on small stocks, which is not explained by this argument. Looking at the data for 1997–2001 (see Ibbotson, 2000), it seems that the January effect is still a puzzle. For example, in January 2000, the average return on the S&P 500 was −5.02%, while it was 9.78% in March 2000 and 6.21% in August 2000. In January 2001 it was 3.55%, but it was higher in April 2001 (7.77%) and higher relative to other months in 2001. Thus, it seems that the effect may be reduced for larger company stocks. For smaller company stocks, the average return in January 2001 was 13.8%, higher than for other months in 2001, but in January 2000 it was 5.95%, significantly lower than for February 2000 (23.58%) or June 2000 (13.68%). Whether the January effect disappears or not remains to be seen.

Several reasons have been offered for this stock price pattern. The size effect is the phenomenon that smaller firms tend to outperform larger firms on a risk-adjusted basis. Several studies have linked the January effect to the size effect. Although it is unclear why, smaller firms have a much more pronounced January effect. There also is some empirical support for the January effect's being related to tax-loss selling in December. By selling in December stocks that have fallen during the year, an investor is able to realize losses that are deductible for income taxes.

Another anomaly is the weekend anomaly, the observation that securities tend to be up on Fridays and down on Mondays. This anomaly is even more pronounced at holiday weekends.

Event anomalies are price changes that occur after some easily identified event, such as a listing announcement. Security prices of firms rise after it is announced that the firm's stock will be listed on the NYSE. Another event anomaly is analysts' recommendations. The more analysts there are recommending a particular security, the more likely it is that the security's price will fall in the near future. This puzzling result can be explained as follows. When one or two analysts discover an undervalued stock they recommend it to their clients, and when the clients buy the stock the price is driven up. This price increase attracts the attention of other analysts who subsequently recommend it, pushing the price even higher. This upward price pressure continues until some analysts start changing their buy recommendations to sell recommendations, and the price subsequently falls.

Finally, **accounting anomalies** are changes in stock prices that occur after the release of accounting information. For example, after an announcement of unusually high earnings, a firm's stock price continues to rise, as discussed earlier. Another accounting anomaly is the P/E ratio anomaly. Stocks with low price-to-earnings ratios tend to have higher returns. An anomaly that has attracted a lot of attention lately is the earnings momentum anomaly, in which stocks of firms whose growth rate of earnings has been rising tend to outperform other similar securities.

What can we conclude about market efficiency? As was stated at the beginning of the chapter, the purpose is not to place one position over another but rather to leave the final conclusion to the reader. The following are a few quotations that show what others have concluded:

> In general, the empirical evidence in favor of the efficient market hypothesis is extremely strong.[11]

> It's very hard to support the popular academic theory that the market is irrational [that is, that the EMT is true] when you know somebody who just made a twentyfold profit in Kentucky

---

[11] Burton Malkiel, 'Efficient market hypothesis', in John Eatwell, Murray Milgate and Peter Newman (eds), *The New Palgrave: Finance* (New York: Macmillan Press, 1989), p. 131.

Fried Chicken, and furthermore, who explained in advance why the stock was going to rise. My distrust of theorizers and prognosticators continues to the present day.[12]

Event studies are the cleanest evidence we have on efficiency....With few exceptions, the evidence is supportive.[13]

They [market inefficiencies] exist because we [practitioners] do not root out their basic causes. These causes are easy enough to identify, if one looks with enough dispassion and rigor. If the academics point to them, the rest of us can respond and...walk by.[14]

As you can see, disagreement regarding market efficiency still exists.

SUMMARY

■ *Define an efficient market.*
A well-functioning financial market in which prices reflect all relevant information is said to be efficient.

■ *Identify the types of information related to security prices in each form of the efficient market hypothesis.*
The efficient market theory (EMT) has three forms: the weak, the semistrong and the strong forms. The weak form of the EMT states that stock prices reflect information revealed by the historical price sequence. The semistrong form of the EMT states that stock prices reflect all relevant publicly available information. The strong form of the EMT states that prices reflect all publicly and privately available information.

■ *Compare investment strategies in efficient markets with investment strategies in inefficient markets.*
The existence of efficient capital markets has several important implications. Most important is that scarce resources are allocated in an efficient manner. Also, technical analysis is useless if at least the weak form of the EMT is true, and fundamental analysis is useless if at least the semistrong form of the EMT is true. Finally, no matter what form of the EMT an investor adheres to, portfolio selection benefits still hold. Thus, even under the EMT, portfolio selection is still important.

■ *Describe the findings of researchers who tested each form of the efficient market theory.*
Researchers have gathered empirical evidence related to the weak, semistrong and strong forms of the EMT. The evidence against the strong form is the most conclusive; some insiders are clearly able to make abnormal returns. The evidence related to the weak and semistrong forms is mixed; some technical trading strategies and some fundamental trading strategies have generated abnormal returns in the past.

■ *Define anomaly, and identify the common types of anomalies.*
An anomaly offers investors a chance to earn abnormal profits. Most of the anomalies that have been documented can be categorized in one of the following groups: firm, seasonal, event or accounting anomalies.

---

[12] Peter Lynch, *One Up on Wall Street* (New York: Penguin Books, 1989), p. 35.
[13] Eugene F. Fama, 'Efficient capital markets: 2', *Journal of Finance*, 46, December 1991, p. 1602.
[14] Dean LeBaron, 'Reflections on market inefficiency', *Financial Analysts Journal*, 39, May–June 1983, pp. 16–17, 23. Reprinted in Charles D. Ellis (ed.), *Classics 2: Another Investor's Anthology* (Homewood, IL: AIMR and Business One Irwin, 1991), p. 239.

KEY TERMS

Abnormal rate of return	Firm anomaly	Random walk
Accounting anomaly	Fundamental analysis	Risk-adjusted rate of
Active investment strategy	Historical prices	return
Anomaly	Index fund	Seasonal anomaly
Cumulative abnormal rate	Joint hypothesis	Semistrong form of the
of return (CAR)	Market-to-book-value	EMT
Efficient market	(M/B) ratio	Size effect
Efficient market theory	Neglected firm effect	Strong form of the EMT
(EMT)	Normal rate of return	Technical analysis
Event anomaly	Passive investment	Timing ability
Event study	strategy	Weak form of the EMT
Excess returns	Price/earnings (P/E) ratio	

QUESTIONS

16.1 Explain why it is important to determine how efficient the markets are.

16.2 Suppose you flip a coin. Whenever a head shows up, the stock price goes up by 10%. Whenever a tail shows up, the stock market drops by 5%. Are the stock rates of return following a random walk? Explain.

16.3 The rates of return on two stocks have the following values:

Day	Stock A	Stock B
1	+10%	+10%
2	−5	+10
3	+10	−5
4	−5	−5
5	+10	+10
6	−5	−5
7	+10	+10

16.4 (a) The rates of return of a given stock are serially correlated. Does this conform with the EMT?

(b) The rates of return on two stocks are correlated. Does this conform with the EMT?

16.5 IBM reported $7 EPS for the second quarter – lower than expected. The stock price on the publication date (t_0) was $P_0 = \$90$. In the five days after the announcement, the prices were $P_1 = \$89$, $P_2 = \$88$, $P_3 = \$85$, $P_4 = \$84$ and $P_5 = \$83$. In this period the market went up. Does this evidence tend to support or refute semistrong efficiency? Why?

16.6 The market-to-book value (M/B) ratio of a given stock is as follows:

Quarter	M/B	Stock price
1	1.2	$100
2	0.9	90
3	1.3	95
4	1.0	80

What can be learned from this regarding market efficiency?

16.7 A firm's beta is 0.5, the riskless interest rate is 10% and the mean annual rate of return on the market portfolio is 0.2. The annual rates of return on the firm's stock for five observations are $R_1 = 6\%$, $R_2 = 10\%$, $R_3 = 15\%$, $R_4 = 20\%$ and $R_5 = 10\%$. Calculate AR and CAR over this five-year period.

16.8 Five firms announce an increase in dividends. On the announcement date the daily rate of return on these five stocks was $R_1 = 1\%$, $R_2 = 0\%$, $R_3 = 10\%$, $R_4 = 5\%$ and $R_5 = 3\%$, where the index $i = 1, 2, 3, 4$ and 5 denotes the different firms. We are given the following additional information:

		Daily rates of return on the announcement date	
Firm	Beta	Market portfolio	Risk-free rate
1	1	1%	0.013%
2	0.5	0.5	0.014
3	2	0.02	0.012
4	0.8	−1	0.009
5	1	2	0.010

Are there any abnormal returns on the dividend announcement date? Explain.

16.9 Four firms announce major stock repurchases. On the announcement date the daily rate of return on these four stocks was as follows: $R_1 = -3\%$, $R_2 = 2\%$, $R_3 = 12\%$ and $R_4 = -5\%$, where the index $i = 1, 2, 3$ and 4 denotes the different firms. We are given the additional following information:

		Daily rates of return on the announcement date	
Firm	Beta	Market portfolio	Risk-free rate
1	1.2	1.5%	0.01%
2	0.4	0.5	0.014
3	2	0.02	0.009
4	0.8	3	0.015

Are there an abnormal returns on the stock repurchase announcement date? Explain.

16.10 IBM announced a loss of more than $2 billion in the third quarter of 1992. On the announcement date, IBM's stock price fell by 10%. Suppose that after the announcement date, the rate of return on IBM was as follows:

Days after announcement	+1	+2	+3	+4	+5	+6
Rate of return adjusted for risk	−1%	−0.5%	−2%	−1%	−3%	−6%

Does this result support the notion of the efficient market theory?

16.11 Suppose five firms announce they are going to split their stocks. On the announcement date you have the following *abnormal* returns:

Firm	Abnormal return
1	−1%
2	2
3	3
4	0.5
5	4

(a) Calculate the average abnormal return.
(b) 'Because Firm 1 has a negative return, we cannot conclude that a stock split announcement positively affects a particular stock's price.' Evaluate this statement.

16.12 You observe the following abnormal returns on McDonnell Douglas, Inc., stock:

	Day	Abnormal return
	1	0%
	2	0.02
	3	3
	4	4
Announcement date →	5	6
	6	0.1
	7	−0.1
	8	0.5
	9	−0.5
	10	0

On Day 5 the firm announces that a big contract has been signed with the Department of Defense.

(a) Calculate the cumulative abnormal return for Days 1 through 10.
(b) What can we conclude from this price behaviour?

16.13 Many investment analysts expect Xerox, Inc., to have earnings of $10 per share. The firm announced $12 earnings per share. What is the standardized unexpected earnings if the standard error of the estimate was 0.05?

16.14 Firm A announces an EPS of $10, whereas Firm B announces an EPS of $8 per share. The stock price of Firm A fell by 2%, and the stock price of Firm B went up by 4% on the announcement date. From this fact it is concluded that the lower the profit, the more positive is the market reaction. Do you agree?

16.15 There are two groups of firms. The first group consists of 100 small firms with an average size of $100 million, and the second group consists of 100 large firms with an average size of $1 billion. The average rate of return and beta of these groups are as follows:

	Small firms	Large firms
Average annual return	18%	12%
Beta	1.3	0.9

The average rate of return on the market portfolio is $\overline{R}_m = 13\%$, and the risk-free interest rate is 3%. Are there abnormal returns to the small firms? Are there abnormal returns to the large firms? Discuss.

16.16 Using cumulative abnormal rates of return over time, describe the expected behaviour of a stock before a major takeover when the following was true:

(a) There was no insider trading, nor was any insider trading anticipated.
(b) There was insider trading.
(c) Some astute investors rightly viewed the company as being underpriced.

SELECTED REFERENCES

Freund, W.C., and M.S. Pagano. 'Market efficiency in specialist markets before and after automation', *The Financial Review*, Vol. 35, No. 3, August 2000.

Kaiser, Kevin Stouraitis. 'Agency costs and strategic considerations behind sell-offs: The UK evidence', *European Financial Management*, Vol. 7, No. 3, 2001.

Ibbotson Associates, *Stocks, Bonds, Bills, and Inflation 2000 Yearbook*, Ibbotson Associates, Inc, Chicago.

Liu, Pu, Stanley D. Smith, and Azmat A. Syed. 'Stock price reactions to the *Wall Street Journal's* securities recommendations'. *Journal of Financial and Quantitative Analysis*, 25, September 1990, pp. 399–410.

Majnoni, G., and M. Messa. 'Stock exchange reforms and market efficiency: The Italian experience', *European Financial Management*, Vol. 7, 2001.

Malkiel, Burton. 'Efficient market hypothesis', in John Eatwell, Murray Milgate, and Peter Newman (eds.), *The New Palgrave: Finance*. New York: Macmillan Press, 1989.
This book is a concise review of the efficient market hypothesis.

Moy, Ronald L., and Ahyee Lee. 'A bibliography of stock market anomalies'. *Journal of Financial Education*, November 1991, pp. 41–51.
This article is a good place to begin examining the empirical evidence related to market anomalies.

Rendleman, Richard, J., Jr., Charles P. Jones, and Henry A. Latané. 'Empirical anomalies based on unexpected earnings and the importance of risk adjustments'. *Journal of Financial Economics*, 3, 1982, pp. 269–87.
This paper is one of many that address the quarterly earnings surprise anomaly.

Rubinstein, M. 'Rational markets: Yes or no? The affirmative case', *Financial Analysts Journal*, May/June 2001.

Tumarkin, R., and R.F. White Law. 'News or noise? Internet postings and stock prices', *Financial Analysts Journal*, May/June 2001.

SUPPLEMENTARY REFERENCES

Ariel, Robert A. 'A monthly effect in stock returns'. *Journal of Financial Economics*, 18, March 1987, pp. 161–74.

Bachelier, L. *Theorie de la speculation: Annales de l'Ecole Normale Superieure*, translated by A.J. Boness in P.H. Cootner (ed.), *The Random Character of Stock Market Prices*. Cambridge, MA: MIT Press, 1967.

Ball, R. 'Anomalies in relationships between securities' yields and yield-surrogates'. *Journal of Financial Economics*, 6, June–September 1978, pp. 103–26.

Bernard, Victor L. and Jacob K. Thomas. 'Evidence that stock prices do not fully reflect the implications of current warnings for future earnings'. *Journal of Accounting and Economics*, 13, December 1990, pp. 305–40.

Bhardwaj, R.K., and Brooks, L.D. 'The January anomaly: Effects of low share price, transaction costs and bid-ask bias', *Journal of Finance*, 47, January 1992, pp. 553–75.

Chan, K.C., and Nai-fu Chen. 'Structural and return characteristics of small and large firms'. *Journal of Finance*, 46, September 1991, pp. 1467–84.

Cochrane, John H. 'Volatility tests and efficient markets: A review essay'. *Journal of Monetary Economics*, 27, June 1991, pp. 463–85.

Connolly, Robert A. 'An examination of the robustness of the weekend effect'. *Journal of Financial and Quantitative Analysis*, 24, June 1989, pp. 133–69.

Cowles, A., and H.E. Jones. 'Some posteriori probabilities in stock market action', *Econometrica*, 5, No. 3, 1937, pp. 280–94.

Fama, E. 'The behavior of stock market prices'. *Journal of Business*, 38, No. 1, 1956, pp. 34–105.

Fama, Eugene F. 'Efficient capital markets: 2'. *Journal of Finance*, December 1991, pp. 1575–617.

Fama, Eugene F., and Kenneth R. French. 'The cross-section of expected stock returns'. *Journal of Finance*, 47, June 1992, pp. 427–65.

Fama, E., L. Fisher, M. Jensen, and R. Roll. 'The adjustment of stock prices to new information'. *International Economic Review*, 10, No. 1, 1969, pp. 1–21.

Granger, D., and O. Morgenstern. 'Spectral analysis of New York stock market prices'. *Kyklos*, 16, 1963, pp. 1–27.

Haugen, Robert A., and Jorion Philippe. 'The January effect: Still there after all these years'. *Financial Analysts Journal*, January–February 1996, pp. 27–31.

Huberman, Gur, and Shmuel Kandal. 'Market efficiency and Value Line's record'. *Journal of Business*, 63, April 1990, pp. 187–216.

Jegadeesh, Narashimham. 'Evidence of predictable behavior of security returns'. *Journal of Finance*, 45, July 1990, pp. 881–98.

Jersen, Gerald, Robert R. Johnson, and Jeffrey M. Mercer. 'New evidence on size and price to book effects'. *Financial Analysts Journal*, November–December 1997, pp. 37–42.

Kendall, M. 'The analysis of economic time series, 1: Prices'. *Journal of Royal Statistical Society*, 96, No. 1, 1953, pp. 11–25.

Lakonishok, Josef, and Edwin Maberly. 'The weekend effect: Trading patterns of individual and institutional investors'. *Journal of Finance*, 45, March 1990, pp. 231–43.

Merton, R. 'On estimating the expected return on the market: An exploratory investigation'. *Journal of Financial Economics*, 8, No. 4, 1980, pp. 323–61.

Ogden, J.P. 'Turn-of-month evaluations of liquid profits and stock returns: A common explanation for the monthly and January effects'. *Journal of Finance*, 45, September 1990, pp. 1259–72.

Roll, R. 'Orange juice and weather'. *American Economic Review*, 74, No. 5, 1974, pp. 861–80.

Seyhun, H.N. 'Can omitted risk factors explain the January effect? A stochastic dominance approach'. *Journal of Financial and Quantitative Analysis*, 28, June 1993, pp. 195–212.

Chapter 17

INVESTMENT COMPANIES AND MUTUAL FUNDS

Learning objectives

After studying this chapter you should be able to:

1 Compare and contrast hedge funds, closed-end and open-end funds.

2 Contrast the benefits and costs of investing in mutual funds.

3 Understand how to evaluate the performance of mutual funds based on risk and return.

4 Understand why small investors may buy mutual funds and index funds in spite of the fact that they do not outperform the market.

INVESTMENT IN THE NEWS

Funds of the future

Could hedge funds become the mutual funds of tomorrow, a routine part of every investor's portfolio? Given their secrecy, perceived volatility and the bad press they have received over the past two years, that might seem unlikely. In fact, it is already starting to happen.

The huge rise in Western stock markets this decade has left investors with a problem, albeit a nice one: where to put their money. In the US alone there are more than 2m high net worth individuals – the principal investors in hedge funds, who have the required $1m in investable assets. Together, they have more than $5 trillion of financial assets. Institutions, including pension funds and insurance companies, are in charge of another $10 trillion.

These investors are becoming more sophisticated and thus increasingly willing to put money into "alternative investments" such as hedge funds in their search for market-beating returns.

Because hedge funds can sell short, use leverage and take concentrated positions, they can produce those superior returns. Admittedly, they bear higher risks. But demographics is on their side as wealth passes from the conservative post-war generation to more risk-friendly Baby Boomers.

These factors have fuelled growth in hedge fund assets from $20bn in 1990 to more than $170bn by 1996, according to a study by KPMG and RR Capital Management, a New York hedge fund. It predicts a further ten fold rise to $1,700bn by 2006. Meanwhile, the number of funds has risen from fewer than 500 to more than 2,500 in five years.

But this has done little to modernise the industry. As private investment vehicles, hedge funds are exempt from many basic regulatory requirements, giving their managers broad discretion and little incentive to inform investors, whose money can be locked up for several years.

▶

INVESTMENT IN THE NEWS

While the top 15 per cent of funds, including George Soros' Quantum group and Julian Robertson's Tiger Management, control 80 per cent of managed assets, many are closed to new investment. Most funds are local, niche players with assets of less than $100m. Yet all carry their own marketing and support structures.

This will change, according to Rama Rao, chief executive of RR Capital Management and co-author of the report. He predicts that sophisticated investors will put pressure on hedge funds to transform themselves into a global, institutionalised industry.

"Hedge funds are now where mutual funds were in 1980, just before growth and consolidation took off," Dr Rao says.

Promisingly, the US Securities and Exchange Commission now allows hedge funds to update investors on their performance over their web sites, more or less in real time, replacing outdated quarterly reports. It has also relaxed its rules to allow 499 investors in a limited partnership, the most common hedge fund structure, up from 99 two years ago. As transparency and accountability increase, however, so will competition, making it harder for small funds to justify their administrative overheads.

Dr Rao predicts this will lead to the evolution of "families of hedge funds", where a group of funds with complementary strategies is run by one central operation. These families will look very similar to the big mutual fund houses.

A number of caveats spring to mind. The near-collapse of Long-Term Capital Management will have put many people off hedge funds for good and has sparked talk of stricter regulation. It is also questionable how well these funds, many with short track records would perform in a bear market.

Having said that, research by Matthias Becker at St Gallen University in Switzerland suggests long-term performance of hedge funds averages between 17 and 20 per cent – comparable with recent gains by the US stock market but above long-range nominal equity returns of about 10 per cent.

The quid pro quo is higher risk of course, though they can actually help diversify an investor's portfolio, thus reducing overall volatility. You may not be comfortable investing in hedge funds, but your children probably will. *www.rrcm.com*

Source: Daniel Bögler, *Financial Times*, 9 August 1999, p. 13. Reprinted with permission.

Probably everyone heard of the financial crises and the near collapse of the hedge fund called Long-Term Capital. Hedge funds are less regulated than mutual funds; they may sell short, use leverage and take a concentrated position in one asset. Therefore, they provide a relatively high average return, but if the hedge fund's management is wrong in their prediction of the market, the concentrated position may induce a big loss, as occurred with Long-Term Capital, and the hedge fund may collapse. Thus, a relatively high risk of return governs the operation of the hedge fund. Other mutual funds are less risky than hedge funds because they are regulated and not allowed to hold a concentrated position on one asset.

Mutual funds or trusts are a popular investment vehicle because they provide an easy way for small investors to profit in the financial markets. Small investors are aware of the benefits of diversification, and the variety of mutual funds currently available offers something for everyone. Furthermore, the returns on more traditional securities, such as bank certificates of deposit, are relatively low, so investors seeking higher returns may choose to invest in mutual funds.

An **investment company** or **trust company** is an organization that takes a pool of investors' money and invests it in securities according to a stated set of objectives. Like other publicly held companies, investment companies start by selling shares to a group of investors. These investment companies invest in securities and do not invest in plant and equipment. Thus, investment company managers manage a portfolio of securities on behalf of their shareholders. The primary benefits that these portfolio managers provide, especially for small investors, are diversification and professional management. Of course, there are no 'free lunches' in the capital market, and investors pay for these service fees in the form of management fee and load, which will be elaborated on in the rest of the chapter.

This chapter discusses hedge funds, closed-end funds and open-end funds (also known as mutual funds). The text examines the different types of mutual funds, as well as the costs and benefits of investing in these types of securities.

17.1 TYPES OF FUNDS

Hedge funds are a private investment partnership, which we will discuss later in the chapter. Investment companies (rather than partnerships) run two basic types of funds: open-end and closed-end. **Mutual funds** (also known as **open-end funds**) are able to issue new shares on a daily basis. Specifically, supply and demand for mutual fund shares governs how many shares are outstanding at any point in time. When an investor buys shares of a mutual fund, the purchase is made directly from the mutual fund that issues new shares. When an investor sells shares of a mutual fund, the sale is made directly with the mutual fund, which redeems the old shares. **Closed-end funds** (also known as **investment trusts**) are not able to issue new shares daily.[1] The investor who wishes to purchase shares of a closed-end fund must find a willing seller, whereas an investor can purchase shares of an open-end fund directly from the investment company. Most closed-end company shares trade on an exchange such as the NYSE or the AMEX. Thus, shares are traded with other investors. From time to time, closed-end investment companies do issue new shares in the same manner as other corporations. A new type of closed-end fund is the **term trust**, which has a termination date at which the fund liquidates its assets (generally bonds) and distributes the cash to the shareholders.

In the recent past, closed-end funds have been very popular with investors. For example, between 1969 and 1984 only 37 closed-end funds were issued. However, between 1985 and 1996 over 500 funds were issued.[2]

Mutual funds have experienced similar growth. Exhibit 17.1 shows that the total net assets and the total number of funds have grown dramatically since 1940. (Note that Exhibit 17.1 includes only funds that are members of the Investment Company Institute; it excludes money market mutual funds.)

Exhibit 17.2 shows data on the largest 10 mutual funds operating in the US. Fidelity Magellan is the biggest with $86.007 billion of assets, followed by the Vanguard 500 Index with $78.611 billion of assets. For the three-year period Amer Funds Growth shows the highest rate of return, while for 2001 (up to 30 July 2001), PIMCO has the highest rate of return (YTD return).

---

[1] This terminology is particularly confusing in international markets. For example, in Great Britain, mutual funds are called **unit trusts**. Also, it is common practice to refer loosely to both closed-end and open-end companies as *mutual funds*. This book holds to the strict definition and uses *mutual fund* to refer only to open-end companies.
[2] See CDA/Weisenberger Investment Companies Services, *Investment Companies Yearbook* (Rockville, MD, CDA/Weisenberger, 1997), p. 14.

Exhibit 17.1 **The growth of mutual funds (1940 to 1996)**

Year	Total net assets (million $)	Number of funds	Growth in net assets	Growth in funds
2001 (June)	$4,279	12,749	20%	103%
1996	$3,540	6,270	523%	165%
1990	568	2,362	879	331
1980	58	548	22	54
1970	47.6	356	180	121
1960	17	161	580	64
1950	2.5	98	525	44
1940	0.4	68		

Source: Data derived from CDA/Weissenberger Investment Companies Service: *Investment Companies Yearbook* (Rockville, MD: CDA/Weissenberger, 1997), p. 14. Data for 2001 is taken from www.morningstar.com.

Exhibit 17.2 **The largest 10 mutual funds**

Fund	Net Assets (billions)	Investment Objective	3-Year* Return	1-Week Return	YTD Return
Fidelity Magellan Fund	$86.007	Large Cap Core	4.90%	−0.55%	−8.30%
Vanguard 500 Index;Inv	78.611	S&P 500 Funds	3.11	−1.02	−8.35
Amer Funds Inv Co Am;A	55.818	Large Cap Value	8.55	−0.20	−2.14
Amer Funds Wash Mut;A	48.536	Large Cap Value	6.53	−0.90	3.23
Amer Funds Growth;A	37.051	Multi Cap Core	16.81	0.20	−9.45
Fidelity Gro & Inc	36.661	Large Cap Core	3.12	−1.17	−7.37
Fidelity Contrafund	34.664	Multi Cap Core	3.96	−0.93	−11.33
Janus Fund	33.170	Large Cap Growth	4.70	0.26	−18.38
PIMCO:Total Return;Inst	31.919	IID	7.24	0.29	5.29
SPDR Trust;1	30.033	S&P 500 Funds	3.01	−0.99	−8.25

*Annualized. Through Thursday.

Source: Lipper

Source: *Barron's*, 30 July 2001, p. F3. Barron's Online by *Barron's*. © 2001 by Dow Jones & Co., Inc. Reproduced with permission of Dow Jones & Co., Inc. in the format *Fundamentals of Investments* via Copyright Clearance Center.

■ Avoiding triple taxation

Generally, investing involves double taxation; a firm pays corporate tax, and then stockholders pay personal income tax on dividends received or capital gains tax on capital appreciation. Theoretically, investment in a mutual fund could involve triple taxation. Recall that a corporation normally pays corporate income tax, and shareholders pay income tax on dividends and capital gains tax on any stock appreciation (see Chapter 2, Appendix 2A). If investment companies bought stock of corporations and paid taxes, the shareholder would have triple taxation: the corporate tax, the investment company tax and the shareholder's tax. The Internal Revenue Service (IRS) makes sure this does not happen. The IRS allows an investment company to be classified under Regulation M of the IRS as a **regulated investment company**; such a designation allows the company to avoid taxation on the capital gains, dividends and interest income it receives. The investment company is acting as a conduit through which the investor's money flows, so capital gains and ordinary income should not be triple taxed (the **conduit theory**). Thus, there is no major tax disadvantage to buying mutual fund shares. (Note, however, that investors do pay tax on income once they receive it.)

Investment companies must meet specific requirements of the IRS to avoid such triple taxation. An investment company must pass almost all of its capital gains and ordinary income on to its shareholders; that income is taxed according to each individual share-holder's tax bracket. To be classified as a regulated investment company, 'the fund must meet such requirements as 98% minimum distribution of interest and dividends received on investment and 90% distribution of capital gains net income. Shareholders must pay taxes even if they reinvest their distributions.'[3]

17.1.1 Closed-end funds (investment trusts)

Closed-end funds were first developed in Europe in the 1820s and became very popular in Great Britain in the nineteenth century. They were the most popular form of invest-ment company in the United States until the stock market crash of 1929. Only recently have closed-end funds once again become popular.

Closed-end funds issue a specified number of shares, after which no additional shares are issued, unless a special public issue is conducted. Therefore, the behaviour of closed-end funds is much like that of common stock. As a particular fund becomes popular, demand rises and so does the market value of the closed-end fund shares. Investors do not trade the closed-end fund shares directly with the investment company; they trade in the secondary market.

Closed-end funds are easier to manage than open-end funds. After the initial issue, the portfolio manager does not have to be concerned with day-to-day liquidity needs of the shareholders. Unlike open-end funds, which allow investors to redeem their shares at any time and which consequently must have funds available to provide for possible redemption, closed-end funds do not need to have a large amount of liquid funds available. Closed-end funds are typically diversified portfolios of publicly traded securities that meet specific investment objectives.

Exhibit 17.3 summarizes the different categories of closed-end funds. It is clear from this exhibit that closed-end funds have many investment objectives. For example, some closed-end funds are portfolios of securities issued in a single country.

Barron's lists information on closed-end funds gathered by Lipper Analytical Services, Inc., a mutual fund data and analysis company. (The *Wall Street Journal* also carries this information.) As Exhibit 17.4 shows, this listing includes the fund's name and the stock exchange on which it is traded: N denotes the NYSE, A denotes the AMEX, O denotes the Nasdaq, C denotes the Chicago Stock Exchange, and T denotes the Toronto Stock Exchange. The vast majority of the closed-end funds trade on the NYSE.

The pricing of closed-end funds differs from the pricing of individual securities in that there are quotes for both a market price and an estimate of the current value of all securities within the fund. This estimate of current value, called the **net asset value (NAV)**, is listed in the third column of Exhibit 17.4. Specifically, NAV is the current market value of all securities held by the fund less any net liabilities divided by the total number of shares outstanding.

---

[3] John Downes and Jordan Elliott Goodman, *Dictionary of Finance and Investment Terms*, 2nd edn (New York: Barron's Educational Series, 1987), p. 334.

Exhibit 17.3 Categories of closed-end funds as classified by Lipper Analytical Services, Inc.

Category	Description
General equity	Invests primarily in domestic equities
Specialized equity	Limits investments to a specific industry
World equity	Invests in equities worldwide
Convertible securities	Invests primarily in convertible bonds and convertible preferred stock
Dual purpose	Two funds based on one portfolio; one fund receives the capital gains, the other receives any income
Loan participations	Invests primarily in commercial loans
Bond	Invests primarily in corporate and government bonds
World income	Invests in bonds worldwide, seeking high cash flow
National municipal	Invests in tax-free bonds nationally
Single state municipal	Invests in tax-free bonds issued in only one state to get state and local tax benefits

Net asset value is adjusted for liabilities to better represent the true value of a share in a closed-end fund, just as the book value of equity for a normal corporation is assets minus liabilities. One liability is securities purchased but not yet paid. (On most security exchanges there is a three-day settlement period between the time securities are purchased and their payment date.) Other liabilities include accrued fees, options that have been written, dividends payable and other accrued expenses.

The fourth column in Exhibit 17.4 shows the current market prices for the closed-end funds, which may differ from the NAV. The fifth column gives the premium or discount. The **premium** is the percentage difference between the current market price (P) and the NAV (dividing by the NAV) if the difference is positive. If the difference is negative, it is called the **discount**.

The premium or discount calculation is given in Rule 1.

Rule 1: To obtain the premium or discount, substract the NAV from the current price and divide by the NAV. Multiply by 100 to obtain a percentage figure.

For example, the Adams Express Fund was trading on Friday 27 July 2001 for $17.25; hence, the discount was

$$\text{Discount} = \frac{P - \text{NAV}}{\text{NAV}} = \frac{\$17.25 - \$19.34}{\$19.34} = -0.108$$

or a 10.8% discount.

The final column in Exhibit 17.4 shows the 52-week rate of return from investing in the closed-end equity fund.

Closed-end funds trading at large premiums are very risky. Consider, for example, a closed-end mutual fund investing in Chinese stocks that is traded at premium. If China's emerging stock market fell, for example, you could lose on the closed-end funds in two ways. First, the market value of the portfolio would fall; second, the premium over net asset value probably would also fall. Hence, closed-end funds have their own unique risks.

**Exhibit 17.4
A sample of
closed-end
funds as
reported in
*Barron's***

CLOSED-END FUNDS

Closed-end funds sell a limited number of shares and invest in securities. Unlike open-end funds, closed-ends generally do not buy their shares back from investors who wish to sell. Instead, shares trade on a stock exchange. The following list, provided by Lipper, shows the ticker symbol and exchange where a fund trades (A: American; C: Chicago; N: NYSE; O: Nasdaq; T: Toronto; z: does not trade on an exchange). The data also include the fund's most recent net asset value (NAV), share prices and the percentage difference between the market price and the NAV (the premium or discount), unless indicated by a footnote otherwise. For equity funds, the final column provides 52-week returns based on market prices plus dividends; for bond funds, the past 12 months' income distributions as a percentage of the market price at last month's end. Footnotes: a: the Net Asset Value and the market price are ex dividend. b: the NAV is fully diluted. c: NAV is as of Thursday's close. d: NAV as of Wednesday's close. e: NAV assumes rights offering is fully subscribed. v: NAV is converted at the commercial Rand rate. y: NAV and market price are in Canadian dollars. NA: Information is not available or not applicable. NS: Fund not in existence for whole period. ♣ Free annual or semi-annual reports are available by phoning 1-800-965-2929 or faxing 1-800-747-9384. Daily closed-end listings are available in The Wall Street Journal Interactive Edition at http://wsj.com on the Internet's World Wide Web.

Fund Name (Symbol)	Stock Exch	NAV	Market Price	Prem /Disc	52 Week Market Return
Friday, July 27, 2001					
General Equity Funds					
Adams Express (ADX)	♣N	19.34	17.25	−10.8	−24.7
Alliance All-Mkt (AMO)	N	23.18	23.65	+2.0	−28.2
Avalon Capital (MIST)	O	16.23	16.21	−0.1	5.3
Bergstrom Cap (BEM)	A	172.73	166.50	−3.6	−29.3
Blue Chip Value Fd (BLU)	♣N	7.66	7.88	+2.9	13.4
Boulder Tot Rtn (BTF)	N	17.92	15.81	−11.8	47.6
Brantley Cap Corp (BBDC)	O	NA	9.35	NA	−2.2
Central Secs (CET)	A	32.19	28.58	−11.2	−6.6
Cornerstone Strat Rtn (CRF)	N	10.43	8.35	−19.9	−18.9
Cornerstone Str Val (CLM)	N	9.60	8.00	−16.7	−34.3
Engex (EGX)	A	NA	14.03	NA	−55.4
Equus II (EQS)	♣N	14.67	9.25	−36.9	−6.3
Gabelli Equity Tr (GAB)-h	N	9.83	10.89	+10.8	8.4
General American (GAM)	♣N	37.24	36.07	−3.1	12.2
Librty AllStr Eq (USA)	♣N	11.62	12.60	+8.4	12.3
Librty AllStr Gr (ASG)	♣N	8.96	9.59	+7.0	−7.7
MFS Special Value (MFV)	N	9.80	15.81	+61.3	25.4
Morgan FunShares (MFUN)-c	O	7.77	7.20	−7.3	2.8
NAIC Growth (GRF)-c	C	11.79	11.50	−2.5	14.0
ProgressiveReturn (PGF)	N	11.31	9.55	−15.6	−19.5
Royce Focus Trust (FUND)	O	7.30	6.30	−13.7	24.1
Royce Micro-Cap Tr (OTCM)	O	12.05	10.62	−11.9	20.1
Royce Value Trust (RVT)	N	17.78	15.99	−10.1	25.9
Salomon Brothers (SBF)-j	N	14.65	13.84	−5.5	−13.1
SMALLCap (MGC)	♣N	12.88	11.70	−9.2	16.5
Source Capital (SOR)	N	54.65	59.01	+8.0	37.5
Tri-Continental (TY)	♣N	24.05	21.30	−11.4	−4.1
Zweig (ZF)	♣N	8.54	9.64	+12.9	8.5

Source: Barron's, 30 July 2001, p. F23. Barron's Online by Barron's. © 2001 by Dow Jones & Co., Inc. Reproduced with permission of Dow Jones & Co., Inc. in the format Fundamentals of Investments via Copyright Clearance Center.

17.1.2 Open-end funds (mutual funds)

Unlike closed-end funds, mutual funds (or open-end funds) can issue additional shares and buy shares when investors wish to sell. Thus, a mutual fund trades directly with investors. The share price is directly related to the net asset value. Mutual funds can be broadly classified as either no-load or load. The **load** is a sales commission paid by the investor. **No-load mutual funds** do not add any sales commissions to the fund price. Other funds carry a sales commission (load), and hence the offer price is higher than the NAV.

Each mutual fund is required by law to provide a prospectus to investors. The prospectus contains information regarding the fund's objectives, fund expenses, historical performance, risks, who should invest and who is managing the fund.

The Investment Company Act of 1940 requires every mutual fund to state its specific investment objectives in the prospectus. For example, the Fidelity Puritan Fund (FPURX) prospectus contains the following statement regarding its investment principles and risk:

> Puritan seeks as much income as possible, consistent with preservation of capital, by investing in a broadly diversified portfolio of high-yielding securities, such as common stocks, preferred stocks, and bonds. The fund also considers the potential for growth of capital.
>
> FMR manages the fund to maintain a balance between stocks and bonds. When FMR's outlook is neutral, it will invest approximately 60% of the fund's assets in stocks and other equity securities and the remainder in bonds and other fixed-income securities. FMR may vary from this target if it believes stocks or bonds offer more favorable opportunities, but will always invest at least 25% of the fund's total assets in fixed-income senior securities (including debt securities and preferred stock).
>
> The fund has the flexibility to pursue its objective through any type or quality of domestic or foreign security. FMR varies the proportions invested in each type of security based on its interpretation of economic conditions and underlying security values.[4]

By reading a mutual fund's prospectus, an investor can easily determine its objective – in other words, which type of fund it is. Exhibit 17.5 illustrates how Lipper Analytical Services, Inc. (LAS) categorizes the different mutual funds as they are reported in the *Wall Street Journal*.

LAS maintains performance averages for each category. These averages can be used to compare how a particular fund is doing relative to other funds of the same group. Exhibit 17.6 illustrates how these averages are reported as well as data for a sample of mutual stock funds.

At the top of Exhibit 17.6 we see the various funds categories by objective as well as the average returns. It is interesting that for the 1, 3, 5 and 10-year returns no category beats the S&P 500 index funds (see last line). The bottom part of the table provides the individual fund's data for a sample of funds. It is interesting that some funds charge a high local fee of 5.5% as well as a high management fee (expense ratio) of 1.36%. This is in contrast to other funds, in particular the Vanguard family which charges no load fee and a small management fee of about 0.20%.

Most mutual funds are members of a group of mutual funds known as a **family of funds**. For example, the SelValu Fund (Select Value) is one of several investment companies operated by the Vanguard Group of Investment Companies. Exhibit 17.7 lists the Vanguard family of funds. The Vanguard Group offers a range of funds, from

---

[4] From *The Fidelity Puritan Fund*, prospectus dated 26 September 1997, p. 9.

Exhibit 17.5 Mutual funds – classification

MUTUAL FUND OBJECTIVES

Categories compiled by The Wall Street Journal, based on classifications by Lipper Analytical Services Inc.

Stock Funds

Capital Appreciation (CP): Seeks rapid capital growth, often through high portfolio turnover.
Growth (GR): Invests in companies expecting higher than average revenue and earnings growth.
Growth & Income (GI): Pursues both price and dividend growth. Category Includes S&P 500 Index funds.
Equity Income (EI): Tends to favor stock with the highest dividends.
Small Cap (SC): Stocks of lesser-known, small companies.
MidCap (MC): Shares of middle-sized companies.
Sector (SE): Environmental; Financial Services; Real Estate; Specialty & Miscellaneous.
Global Stock (GL): Includes small cap global. Can invest in U.S.
International Stock (IL) (non-U.S.): Canadian; International; International Small Cap.
European Region (EU): European markets or operations concentrated in Europe.
Latin America (LT): Markets or operations concentrated in Latin America.
Pacific Region (PR): Japanese; Pacific Ex-Japan; Pacific Region; China Region.
Emerging Markets (EM): Emerging market equity securities (based on economic measures such as a country's GNP per capita).
Science & Technology (TK): Science, technology and telecommunications stocks.
Health & Biotechnology (HB): Health care, medicine and biotechnology.
Natural Resources (NR): Natural resources stocks.
Gold (AU): Gold mines, gold-oriented mining finance houses, gold coins or bullion.
Utility (UT): Utility stocks.

Taxable Bond Funds

Short-Term (SB): Ultrashort obligation and short, short-intermediate investment grade corporate debt.
Short-Term U.S. (SG): Short-term U.S. Treasury; Short, short-intermediate U.S. government funds.
Intermediate (IB): Investment grade corporate debt of up to 10-year maturity.
Intermediate U.S. (IG): U.S. Treasury and government agency debt.
Long-Term (AB): Corporate A-rated; Corporate BBB-rated.
Long-Term U.S. (LG): U.S. Treasury; U.S. government; zero coupon.
General U.S. Taxable (GT): Can invest in different types of bonds.
High Yield Taxable (HC): High yield high-risk bonds.
Mortgage (MG): Ginnie Mae and general mortgage; Adjustable-Rate Mortgage.
World (WB): Short world multi-market; short world single-market; global income; international income; Emerging-Markets debt.

Municipal Bond Funds

Short-Term Muni (SM): Short, short-intermediate municipal debt; Short-intermediate term California; Single states short-intermediate municipal debt.
Intermediate Muni (IM): Intermediate-term municipal debt including single-state funds.
General Muni (GM): A variety of municipal debt.
Single-State Municipal (SS): Funds that invest in debt of individual states.
High Yield Municipal (HM): High yield low credit quality.
Insured (NM): California insured, New York insured, Florida insured, all other insured.

Stock & Bond Funds

Balanced (BL): A balanced portfolio of both stocks and bonds with the primary objective of conserving principal.
Stock/Bond Blend (MP): Multi-purpose funds such as balanced target; convertible; flexible income; flexible portfolio; global flexible and income funds that invest in both stocks and bonds.

Source: *Wall Street Journal*, 2 January 1998, p. 34. Wall Street Journal (Online) by *Wall Street Journal*. © 1998 by Dow Jones & Co., Inc. Reproduced with permission of Dow Jones & Co., Inc. in the format *Fundamentals of Investments* via Copyright Clearance Center.

Exhibit 17.6 Fund's performance: *Barron's* Lipper Fund listings

BENCHMARKS

Objective	2nd Quarter	Annualized Return			
		1 Year	3 Years	5 Years	10 Years
Growth & Income	9.04%	14.48%	21.59%	21.72%	15.13%
Growth	7.07	18.87	22.76	22.64	16.16
Small-Cap	15.56	1.93	10.45	16.52	14.39
Gold	2.06	−5.17	−22.22	−12.12	−4.21
International	5.61	4.83	9.53	8.89	9.39
Emerging Markets	24.86	16.02	−3.10	−1.46	–
S & P 500 Funds	6.85	22.18	28.50	27.31	18.19

STOCK FUNDS

Name	OBJ	Assets ($ mil) 5/3/99	NAV ($/SHR) 6/30/99	Return Through 6/30 (Annualized)					Latest Week's Data		% Return		Phone Number	Fees			Manager	Since
				QTR	IYR	3YRS	5YRS	10YRS	Close NAV	WK'S CHG	1-WK	YTD		Load	Exp. Ratio	Redemption		
AAL BALANCED; A■	B	165.9	12.19	2.70	12.64	☆	☆	☆	12.25	+0.31	3.2	6.6	800-553-6319	4.00	N/A	None	Hilt/Plautz	'97/'98
AAL BALANCED; B■	B	12.5	12.15	2.41	11.67	☆	☆	☆	12.21	+0.33	3.2	6.1	800-553-6319	None	N/A	5.00	Hilt/Plautz	'97/'98
AAL CAP GR; A■	G	3546.7	37.06	6.49	23.43	29.53	26.67	17.66	37.43	+1.93	5.5	14.4	800-553-6319	4.00	0.98	None	Fred Plautz	'95
AAL CAP GR; B■	G	108.3	36.42	6.21	22.19	☆	☆	☆	36.79	+1.92	5.5	13.9	800-553-6319	None	1.91	5.00	Fred Plautz	'97
AAL EQTY INC; A■	EI	261.9	14.91	7.76	11.42	15.93	14.66	☆	14.98	+0.40	3.0	8.5	800-553-6319	4.00	1.11	None	Bo Bohannon	'95
ADVANTUS ENTERPRISE; A✱	SG	39.4	15.28	10.32	−2.80	3.60	☆	☆	15.24	+0.73	5.0	4.3	800-665-6005	5.50	1.27	None	Jim Tatera	'94
ADVANTUS ENTERPRISE; B	SG	6.6	14.60	10.11	−3.63	2.71	☆	☆	14.56	+0.69	5.0	3.9	800-665-6005	None	2.14	5.00	Jim Tatera	'94
ADVANTUS HORIZON; A	G	56.0	27.91	4.03	19.91	24.99	24.24	16.39	28.10	+1.55	5.8	7.5	800-665-6005	5.50	1.36	None	Gunderson/Erickson	'96/96
ADVANTUS HORIZON; B	G	22.2	26.57	3.83	19.09	24.16	☆	☆	26.75	+1.47	5.8	7.1	800-665-6005	None	2.07	5.00	Gunderson/Erickson	'96/96
ADVANTUS INDEX 500; A✱	SP	24.7	18.32	6.84	21.50	☆	☆	☆	18.44	+0.86	4.9	12.4	800-665-6005	5.50	0.74	None	Kevin Zwart	'98
ADVANTUS INDEX 500;	SP	22.5	18.22	6.61	20.45	☆	☆	☆	18.34	+0.85	4.9	11.8	800-665-6005	None	1.60	5.00	Kevin Zwart	'98

Exhibit 17.6 (continued)

Name	OBJ	Assets ($ mil) 5/3/99	NAV ($/SHR) 6/30/99	Return Through 6/30 (Annualized)					Latest Week's Data				Phone Number	Fees			Manager	Since
				QTR	1YR	3YRS	5YRS	10YRS	Close NAV	WK'S CHG	% Return 1-WK	YTD		Load	Exp. Ratio	Redemption		
ADVANTUS INTL BAL; A✱	GX	50.3	11.92	6.92	2.70	8.51	☆	☆	11.94	+0.10	0.8	6.9	800-665-6005	5.50	1.58	None	Demirors/ Clemons	'99/'98
ADVANTUS INTL BAL; B	GX	5.2	11.77	6.70	2.01	☆	☆	☆	11.79	+0.10	0.9	6.5	800-665-6005	None	2.77	5.00	Demirors/ Clemons	'97/'98
ADVANTUS SPECTRUM; A	FX	74.8	18.41	2.67	13.43	16.69	16.66	12.43	18.48	+0.70	3.9	4.1	800-665-6005	5.50	1.19	None	Thomas Gunderson	'89
ADVANTUS SPECTRUM; B	FX	23.5	18.32	2.49	12.63	16.00	☆	☆	18.39	+0.70	4.0	3.7	800-665-6005	None	1.84	5.00	Thomas Gunderson	'94
ADVANTUS VENTURE; A✱	SG	31.0	11.35	16.23	−9.17	☆	☆	☆	11.35	+0.38	3.5	1.6	800-665-6005	5.50	1.38	None	Mark Henneman	'98

◪ means the funds availability is limited. AHA Investment Funds, for example, are open only to participants in the American Hospital Associations Investment Program.
✱ means the fund has waived some fees.

Free financial information and prospectus available by calling 1-888-201-8508 or fax to 1-888-202-8187, or to download immediately, visit barrons.fundclub.net. Information is applicable to U.S. addresses only and will be sent the next business day subject to availability

Queries about the data in these pages should be directed to:
Lipper Client Services
Lipper Inc.
1380 Lawrence St., Suite 950
Denver, Colo. 80204
(303) 534-3472

Exhibit 17.7 An illustration of a family of funds

MUTUAL FUNDS

52 Week High	52 Week Low	Fund Name	Close NAV	Wk's Chg	YTD	− % Return − 3-Yrs
		VANGUARD FDS:				
24.38	20.54	♣ AssetA n	22.40	+0.01	−4.1	+14.9
11.19	10.71	♣ CAInsIT n	11.05	+0.02	+3.1	+17.9
11.87	11.17	♣ CAInsLT n	11.61	+0.04	+2.2	+18.5
33.34	22.77	♣ CapOp rn	25.21	+0.17	−3.9	+156.7
15.63	11.61	♣ Convrt n	12.38	+0.04	−2.6	+28.3
31.55	24.98	♣ Energy rn	27.32	+1.02	−2.7	+40.1
25.19	21.96	♣ EqInc n	23.70	−0.15	−2.0	+19.8
84.13	50.24	♣ Explr n	58.88	−0.29	−2.0	+54.5
11.60	10.92	♣ FLInsLT n	11.51	+0.03	+3.8	+18.8
14.38	11.74	♣ GlbEq n	12.52	−0.12	−0.8	+26.0
10.40	9.91	♣ GNMA n	10.40	+0.02	+5.4	+21.8
37.79	26.75	♣ GroInc n	29.28	−0.14	−8.2	+10.7
20.29	9.06	♣ GrowthEq n	10.41	+0.06	−21.6	+4.5
138.38	108.39	♣ HlthCare rn	120.48	−1.11	−7.9	+82.0
7.21	6.47	♣ HYCor rn	6.53	+0.04	+2.7	+4.5
10.95	10.11	♣ InflaPro n	10.83	+0.00	+7.3	NS
22.69	15.40	♣ IntlGr n	15.59	−0.06	−17.4	−3.8
28.24	21.62	♣ IntlVal n	22.92	−0.19	−11.9	+1.7
9.78	9.16	♣ ITCorp n	9.75	+0.02	+6.7	+20.8
11.14	10.29	♣ ITTsry n	10.99	+0.02	+4.7	+22.1
15.60	13.67	♣ LifeCon n	14.34	+0.01	−0.3	+17.3
22.09	16.86	♣ LifeGro n	18.06	−0.03	−6.7	+10.2
13.32	12.57	♣ LifeInc n	13.04	+0.03	+2.8	+20.3
18.82	15.49	♣ LifeMod n	16.37	−0.01	−3.5	+14.0
8.79	8.11	♣ LTCorp n	8.71	+0.02	+7.0	+16.9
11.18	10.22	♣ LTTsry n	10.85	+0.02	+2.8	+20.4
10.03	9.45	♣ MATxEx n	10.01	+0.03	+4.2	NS
24.36	13.65	♣ Morg n	15.32	+0.03	−10.0	+11.7
10.71	10.23	♣ MuHY n	10.71	+0.03	+5.2	+16.2
12.76	12.03	♣ MuInIg n	12.64	+0.04	+3.7	+18.5
13.49	12.98	♣ MuInt n	13.46	+0.03	+4.2	+17.1
11.27	10.63	♣ MuLong n	11.22	+0.04	+4.3	+17.8
10.91	10.61	♣ MuLtd n	10.91	+0.02	+4.2	+15.5
15.70	15.48	♣ MuSht n	15.68	+0.00	+3.1	+13.2
12.00	11.38	♣ NJInsLT n	11.94	+0.05	+4.0	+18.3
11.29	10.67	♣ NYInsLT n	11.22	+0.03	+3.8	+18.0
12.04	11.35	♣ OHLTte n	11.95	+0.04	+3.8	+17.6
11.43	10.82	♣ PAInsLT n	11.35	+0.04	+3.8	+17.9
9.12	6.49	♣ PrecMtls rn	7.68	−0.16	+2.8	+28.4
9.04	8.43	Prefd xn	8.58	−0.05	+0.0	+0.2
75.63	50.60	Primcp rn	54.59	+0.28	−8.9	+51.2
12.43	10.67	♣ REIT rn	12.21	−0.08	+8.4	+20.6
13.67	10.44	♣ SelValu n	13.50	+0.07	+18.1	+26.5
18.74	15.98	♣ STAR n	16.81	+0.01	+0.9	+23.9
10.85	10.48	♣ STCor n	10.85	+0.02	+5.7	+21.5
10.38	9.90	♣ STFed n	10.38	+0.01	.+5.4	+21.6
18.52	13.45	♣ StratgcEq n	15.26	−0.14	+4.7	+32.8
10.45	10.03	♣ STTsry n	10.45	+0.02	+4.9	+20.6

▶

Exhibit 17.7 (continued)

20.13	16.67	♣ TxMBal rn	17.63	+0.00	−2.6	+19.1
37.50	24.45	♣ TxMCap rn	27.26	−0.12	−10.9	+16.0
33.04	23.95	♣ TxMGl rn	26.21	−0.11	−8.1	+9.3
11.33	8.25	♣ TxMIn rn	8.36	−0.01	−17.6	NS
15.19	12.44	♣ TxMSC rn	14.69	+0.04	+3.2	NS
49.55	17.54	♣ USGro n	19.65	+0.04	−28.9	−23.3
11.92	9.89	♣ USValue n	11.74	−0.08	+4.4	NS
16.08	12.32	♣ Utility n	12.81	−0.22	−14.5	+11.8
21.03	19.10	♣ Wellsl n	20.77	+0.00	+5.3	+23.9
29.84	27.29	♣ Welltn n	28.80	−0.06	+3.8	+24.0
16.78	14.22	♣ Wndsr n	15.88	−0.17	+4.6	+28.0
29.31	25.00	♣ WndsrII n	27.31	+0.06	+1.4	+14.3
		VANGUARD INDEX FDS:				
140.62	101.83	♣ 500 n	111.39	−0.46	−8.1	+9.2
21.04	17.21	♣ Balanced n	18.38	−0.02	−2.1	+15.8
11.15	7.26	♣ CalSoc n	8.11	−0.02	−10.8	NS
10.21	7.38	♣ DevMkt n	7.47	−0.02	−17.6	NS
11.09	7.74	♣ EmerMkt rn	8.13	+0.06	−7.9	+3.7
28.02	20.46	♣ Europe n	21.08	+0.08	−18.9	−13.7
39.61	20.04	♣ Extnd n	23.51	−0.06	−8.3	+8.3
40.88	23.76	♣ Growth n	26.78	−0.28	−12.2	−0.9
10.33	9.54	♣ ITBond n	10.29	+0.03	+6.5	+22.8
11.03	10.09	♣ LTBond n	10.88	+0.03	+5.9	+20.9
13.93	10.07	♣ MidCp n	11.91	+0.02	−0.5	+51.7
11.20	7.56	♣ Pacific n	7.65	−0.12	−14.5	+11.8
25.42	17.18	♣ SmCap n	19.81	−0.12	+1.9	+19.8
13.16	8.91	♣ SmGth n	10.70	+0.06	−2.5	+20.9
10.70	8.59	♣ SmVal n	10.19	+0.01	+10.7	+34.0
10.21	9.75	♣ STBond n	10.21	+0.03	+6.0	+22.3
10.20	9.64	♣ TotBd n	10.18	+0.02	+6.0	+22.1
13.47	9.74	♣ TotIntl n	9.86	−0.01	−16.7	−6.8
34.60	24.21	♣ TotSt n	26.88	−0.11	−7.7	+9.1
23.95	19.55	♣ Value n	20.86	+0.05	−4.2	+17.4
		VANGUARD INSTL FDS:				
19.84	17.21	Ballnst	18.38	−0.02	−2.0	NS
10.14	7.33	DevMktInst n	7.42	−0.02	−17.6	NS
11.09	7.75	EmMkInst r	8.14	+0.06	−7.8	NS
28.02	20.46	EuroInst	21.09	+0.08	−18.8	NS
39.66	20.05	ExtndInst	23.54	−0.06	−8.2	+8.8
40.90	23.76	GrwthInst	26.79	−0.28	−12.1	−0.6
139.28	100.86	InstIdx	110.36	−0.45	−8.1	+9.6
139.29	100.87	InstPlus	110.36	−0.45	−8.0	+9.7
13.95	10.09	MidCpInst	11.94	+0.02	−0.4	+52.4
11.21	7.57	PacInst	7.66	−0.12	−14.4	NS
25.45	17.19	SmCapInst	19.83	−0.12	+2.0	+20.3
13.16	8.91	SmGthInst	10.71	+0.06	−2.4	+20.7
10.70	8.60	SmValInst	10.20	+0.01	+10.8	+32.7
10.85	10.48	STCorInst	10.85	+0.02	+5.8	+21.9
10.20	9.64	TotBdInst	10.18	+0.02	+6.0	+22.5
34.61	24.22	TotStInst	26.88	−0.11	−7.6	+9.4
37.53	24.46	TxMCaInst r	27.28	−0.12	−10.8	NS
33.04	23.95	TxMGlInst r	26.21	−0.11	−8.0	NS
11.15	8.26	TxMInst r	8.36	−0.02	−17.6	NS
23.96	19.55	ValueInst	20.86	+0.05	−4.1	+17.4

index funds (funds with names starting with Idx or Indx) to a fund that invests in junk bonds (HYCorp).

One benefit of a family of funds is the ease with which investors can reallocate their investment dollars among funds in a family. *Barron's* publishes data on each fund's income and dividend payments (see also www.Barrons.com/data).

A final category of mutual funds is money market mutual funds. These funds invest in debt securities of very short maturities. Most money market funds allow investors to write cheques on the balance invested in the fund. Hence, these funds are highly liquid. Money market funds typically invest in US government debt, commercial paper, bank certificates of deposit, repurchase agreements, banker's acceptances and other short-term securities. Money market funds have very little risk and have many restrictions on how they can invest shareholders' money. For example, the SEC requires money market funds to invest solely in commercial paper in the top two grades as evaluated by Moody's or Standard & Poor's.

17.1.3 Index funds

Index funds are funds that simply replicate a given index. For example, S&P index funds simply invest in the stocks and weights that compare with the S&P 500 index. Thus, these funds, so to speak, sell the S&P 500 index to their customers with relatively very low management fees; for example, the Vanguard Group of funds, a leading index fund, charges only 0.2% annually as a management fee. However, index funds hold no cash (because they replicate the S&P 500 index); hence, stocks held by the fund must be sold whenever investors redeem shares. This characteristic can cause difficulties for the fund's management and place some annoying obstacles in the way of nervous investors seeking quick redemptions. For example, index funds do not allow investors to sell shares by a telephone call, and they may charge a redemption fee for shares held for less than a given period, say six months. For instance, T. Rowe Price Associates charges 0.5% for shares held for less than six months, Fidelity Investment charges 0.5% for shares held for less than 90 days, and Dreyfus Corporation, a $1.2 billion S&P 500 index fund, charges a 1% redemption fee for shares held for less than six months.[5]

17.1.4 Hedge funds

Hedge funds are private investments of general partnership in which the partner has made a substantial personal investment. The fund can take a short or long position, invest in derivatives, etc. Because hedge funds use a high leverage position and move billions of dollars in and out of the market quickly, they can have a significant impact on day-to-day trading developments in the various assets. Only individuals with at least $1 million and a relatively high income can invest in a hedge fund. The minimum investment ranges from $250,000 to $10 million. Thus, it is limited to a certain group of investors. Because a hedge fund may take a concentrated speculative position, it is very risky. For example, suppose that you take a short position in government bonds and a long position in junk bonds, hoping that the spread between these two types of bonds

---

[5] For more details on index funds, see Jeff Benjamin, 'Index funds may not be so easy to exit', *Wall Street Journal*, 21 July 1997, p. C23.

will decrease. If it increases, this means that the price of junk bonds fall and thus incurs a loss. Having such a speculative position with a large volume of money may cause bankruptcy. Indeed, this is what happened to Long-Term Capital Management (LTCM) hedge funds which almost collapsed.

The LTCM was managed by John Meriwether, who had made a name for himself trading bonds at Solomon Brothers. The early successful trades of LTCM were its purchase of \$2 billion $29^{1}/_{2}$-year US Treasury Bonds and short sale of \$2 billion 30-year Treasury Bonds to exploit what it concluded was an unwarranted spread between the prices of these two securities. LTCM did not care whether interest rates went up, forcing all bond prices down, or interest rates went down, forcing all bond prices up. It was 'market neutral', or 'hedged' against such uniform price moves in the bond market. It sought merely to take advantage of the historically wide spread between the prices of these two securities. Indeed, the fund made a \$25 million profit on this transaction, in a very short period of time.

Next, in 1998, LTCM took a large position in Russian bonds and a large short position in US Treasuries when the spread between these two bonds was considered by LTCM to be very wide. It assumed that the spread could only narrow. The opposite occurred; the spread widened still further, inducing a massive loss to LTCM on 21 August 1998. By late 1998, LTCM's investors had lost over 90% of their capital. Thus, we see that despite its name, 'hedge fund', it is a very speculative fund which takes very risky positions.

17.2 BENEFITS AND COSTS OF INVESTING IN MUTUAL FUNDS

Mutual funds hold securities that, in principle, the individual investor can buy directly. Then why do investors buy mutual funds rather than owning the individual assets directly? There are obviously some benefits from buying funds rather than individual assets. This section examines the benefits and costs of investing in mutual funds.

17.2.1 Benefits of investing in mutual funds

The use of mutual funds provides several benefits, from increasing a society's supply of capital to free chequing accounts. The following are the main benefits:

1 *Diversification.* Mutual funds offer investors an easy way to diversify. Because of the large pool of money that a mutual fund is able to attract, it is not difficult for fund managers to diversify widely among a range of different securities.
2 *Professional management.* Many individual investors do not wish to devote the time that is necessary to learn how to participate in financial markets. Some investors do not have the necessary skills, particularly in analyzing international stocks. Hence, they would rather entrust their savings to someone who has been professionally trained. Using mutual funds is one way to obtain a professional money manager to make asset allocation and security selection decisions on your behalf, and without your consultation. Can you imagine the complexity involved in evaluating all the different securities? Most small investors would not wish to conduct such an enormous amount of research.

3 *Reduced trading costs.* Because of their sheer size, mutual funds enjoy a considerable reduction in the cost of trading securities.

4 *Portfolio risk reduction.* Small investors cannot diversify in many stocks. Hence, investing in mutual funds can achieve a risk reduction not otherwise achieved. To see this, consider the transaction costs facing a small investor with just enough resources to buy two securities, A and B, in round lots. Exhibit 17.8 illustrates the optimum portfolio for this investor (point O). Although the market portfolio lies on the more steeply sloped capital market line, this portfolio is not achievable by the individual because of trading costs. To diversify widely would require investing in odd lots, which is very expensive; the trading costs alone would wipe out any benefits from diversification. If a fund can position itself on a higher opportunity line, then the investor would prefer the fund over individual portfolio management. Mutual funds allow investors to achieve a better risk–return trade-off than they could otherwise have obtained. Investors should buy the mutual fund as long as it provides a higher line, after all costs are considered, than one that goes through point O (see Exhibit 17.8).

5 *Systematic accumulation and withdrawal plans.* Many mutual funds offer the advantage of either directly withdrawing funds from, or regularly depositing funds into, the investor's personal bank chequing account. (Many investors make monthly deposits, but some use other time periods.) These plans are beneficial for those who lack the financial discipline to save voluntarily or for retired individuals who need the monthly income. For example, a retired couple travelling around the world could have money deposited directly from the mutual fund to their bank account each month.

6 *Chequing accounts.* Many mutual funds offer investors the ability to write cheques and deposit monies into the mutual fund just as they would into a bank chequing account. However, because of the physical location of the mutual fund office, deposits are usually made by mail. Typically, there are dollar limits on the cheque withdrawals. The idea is to limit the volume of cheques written (and hence the cost of processing them).

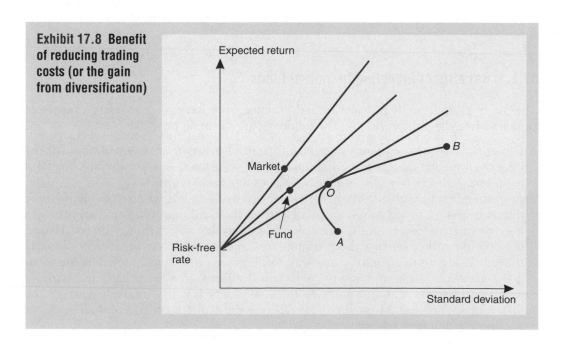

Exhibit 17.8 Benefit of reducing trading costs (or the gain from diversification)

7 *Switching services*. Most families of funds allow investors to switch between individual funds by telephone. Hence, if an investor's money is invested in a stock fund and she believes it would be better for the money to be in a bond fund, she can reallocate her wealth with one phone call. This affords a high level of flexibility to the individual investor. Typically, these switching services are free or available at a very reasonable cost. An investor holding individual securities would not have this flexibility.

8 *Security custody and bookkeeping*. Mutual funds eliminate the need to store the physical securities to keep track of an investor's trading activities. Most mutual funds also keep detailed records of investors' trading activities and related tax consequences. Hence, each year at tax time the mutual fund will determine the specific tax liabilities, ordinary income and capital gains.

9 *Increasing an economy's capital supply*. One of the often overlooked benefits of mutual funds is that by providing an attractive investment vehicle to the small investor, mutual funds are increasing the amount of capital available to firms. Without an efficient means to participate in the financial markets, individuals and families might decide to consume their income rather than save it in a poor-yielding bank savings account. Mutual funds provide a reasonable method for small investors to participate and hence increase an economy's savings rate.

With all of these benefits, one may wonder why everyone doesn't invest in mutual funds. Mutual fund investments also have costs, and investors must weigh them against the benefits when making investment decisions.

17.2.2 Costs of investing in mutual funds

Investors incur several costs when they use mutual funds:

1 *Load*. Open-end funds are classified as either load or no-load funds. Load funds are sold in the over-the-counter market by broker–dealers who do not receive an up-front sales commission. Instead, a load is added to the net value of the asset at the time of the purchase. A load is a fee paid to the seller of mutual funds. Recall, for example, that Fidelity Investment's OTC Fund carried a 3% load. A 3% load means that for every dollar invested in the OTC Fund, 3 cents goes to the salesperson (the broker–dealer) and only 97 cents is actually invested in the fund. If an investor bought a mutual fund for only one year and it earned 10%, the load would take about 30% of the earnings, resulting in a gain of only 7%. However, over a long period of time, this cost would decline on a percentage basis.[6] For many years the typical load was $8\frac{1}{2}\%$, but it is currently about $4\frac{1}{2}\%$ to 5%. Many load funds do not have an up-front load but rather impose a back-end load, which customers pay if they sell the fund shares within a stated period of time (for example, five years). The shares of a no-load fund, in contrast, are bought directly from the funds, thus saving the load payment. Note that dealers of closed-end funds obtain their income from commission fees, just as they do in any other stock transaction.

---

[6] However, a load is still costly over time in absolute dollar terms. For example, for 25 years a $10,000 investment in the load fund would be worth $(\$10,000 \times 0.97)(1 + 0.1)^{25} = \$105,096.65$, which is a 9.866% annual rate of return $[\$105,096.65/\$10,000)^{1/25} - 1]$. The no-load fund, with the same 10% annual rate of return, would be worth $\$10,000(1 + 0.1)^{25} = \$108,347.06$, or $3,250.41 more. Thus, this load would result in the investor's losing $3,250.41, but only 0.134% on an annual percentage basis.

2 *Management fees.* Whether or not a mutual fund has a load, every mutual fund incurs costs in its day-to-day management. These costs are passed directly on to mutual fund shareholders. The management fee is the fund's expense (not including transaction costs, which are a function of the volume of trade) usually given as a percentage of assets. In 1998 the stock funds fee reached 1.44% on average for all stock funds, up from 1.35% in 1993. For the long-run investor, these fees are very important and a search for funds with a lower expense may be worthwhile. Exhibit 17.9 demonstrates the effect of these fees on the total value of the investment.

We see from the bar chart that for the largest 25 funds the fund's expense ranges from a little more than 0.2% to more than 1.2%. The graph shows that investing $10,000 in 1989 in Vanguard 500 with an expense rate of 0.18% (not shown in the exhibit) would yield $20,742.02 more than if Vanguard charged the average fee of 1.44%. Similarly, by 2009 (20 years of investment) the difference would be $144,643.66. Thus, the expense fee, which seems to be very small, is on an annual basis and has a substantial accumulated effect. Of course, if a large management fee is for financial analysts who conduct research to improve performance, it might be justified. But in most cases this is not the case. Vanguard 500 has one of the highest returns over the years and it outperformed most other funds which charge a relatively high management fee.

3 *12b-1 fees.* On 28 October 1980, the SEC adopted Rule 12b-1, allowing mutual funds to pay selling expenses directly rather than charging investors a load. At issue is whether selling expenses are part of the ongoing expenses of the fund or are a one-time expense that is charged at the purchase date. By law, fund managers have to decide whether to invest in securities or to pay a sales force. From the time of the passage of Rule 12b-1, many funds have opted to use 12b-1 fees to pay selling and advertising costs. Typically, 12b-1 fees are less than 0.70%. By March 1996, 5,168 funds had adopted 12b-1 fees. Fund managers in favour of 12b-1 fees argue that these fees provide a more efficient mechanism for paying selling expenses.

4 *Transaction costs.* Mutual fund investors must pay for the trading costs incurred by the fund's management. Even though the trading costs may be lower for each share traded, mutual funds can still incur substantial costs from active trading. These costs are typically reported as part of the management fee. If the mutual fund manager is an active trader, then the fund will have higher transaction costs. Because of the obvious link between the volume of trading and transaction costs, these costs are usually measured by the fund's turnover. Turnover is usually defined as the value of securities purchased (or sold, whichever is less) divided by the average NAV for a given period. A related measure is the *expense ratio*. The expense ratio is the cost (including operating expenses and management fees) as a percentage of the NAV incurred by the mutual fund. For example, the Mid. Cap. Growth which belongs to the Lutheran family had a turnover ratio of 436% in 1998, whereas the municipal bond fund which belongs to the same family had only a 14% turnover in 1998. It is not surprising to find that the Mid. Cap. Income fund had an expense ratio of 1.95%. Over time, high turnover has two negative effects. First, capital gains will be realized, subjecting the investor to capital gains tax. Second, higher turnover will result in higher expenses, thus lowering returns.

5 *Higher income tax rate.* According to the 1997 US tax laws, the capital gains tax rate is 20% if a security is held for at least 18 months. Otherwise, the ordinary income tax rates apply. In a mutual fund with a relatively high turnover, assets are held for less than 18 months, so investors may be subjected to an income tax rate as high as 39.6% (versus 20%). This is a big disadvantage for some funds and always compares negatively with direct investment in stocks.

**Exhibit 17.9
The effect of the expense ratio on the terminal value of the investment**

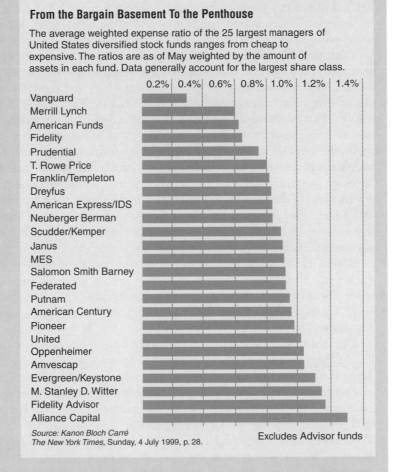

From the Bargain Basement To the Penthouse

The average weighted expense ratio of the 25 largest managers of United States diversified stock funds ranges from cheap to expensive. The ratios are as of May weighted by the amount of assets in each fund. Data generally account for the largest share class.

Vanguard
Merrill Lynch
American Funds
Fidelity
Prudential
T. Rowe Price
Franklin/Templeton
Dreyfus
American Express/IDS
Neuberger Berman
Scudder/Kemper
Janus
MES
Salomon Smith Barney
Federated
Putnam
American Century
Pioneer
United
Oppenheimer
Amvescap
Evergreen/Keystone
M. Stanley D. Witter
Fidelity Advisor
Alliance Capital

Source: Kanon Bloch Carré
The New York Times, Sunday, 4 July 1999, p. 28.

Excludes Advisor funds

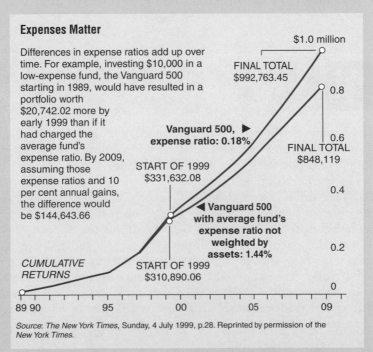

Expenses Matter

Differences in expense ratios add up over time. For example, investing $10,000 in a low-expense fund, the Vanguard 500 starting in 1989, would have resulted in a portfolio worth $20,742.02 more by early 1999 than if it had charged the average fund's expense ratio. By 2009, assuming those expense ratios and 10 per cent annual gains, the difference would be $144,643.66

$1.0 million

FINAL TOTAL
$992,763.45

**Vanguard 500, ▶
expense ratio: 0.18%**

START OF 1999
$331,632.08

FINAL TOTAL
$848,119

**◀ Vanguard 500
with average fund's
expense ratio not
weighted by
assets: 1.44%**

*CUMULATIVE
RETURNS*

START OF 1999
$310,890.06

89 90   95   00   05   09

Source: The New York Times, Sunday, 4 July 1999, p.28. Reprinted by permission of the New York Times.

6 *Accounting, distribution and other miscellaneous costs.* Each mutual fund incurs costs related to the day-to-day affairs of running a business. The mutual fund must conform to acceptable accounting procedures and must be audited. Most funds issue monthly statements to shareholders in order to report trading activities of the account, as well as price performance of the fund. Numerous other minor expenses are incurred, such as in fulfilling staffing requirements and obtaining office space. Recently, the SmCap Fund reported miscellaneous expenses of 0.04%, and the OTC Fund reported 0.33%. Again, the actively managed portfolio is incurring higher expenses.

7 *Suboptimal investment.* An often overlooked cost of investing in mutual funds is the fact that the asset allocation strategy may not be optimal for a particular investor. For example, consider a fund that allocates a significant portion of its assets in the retail industry. If an investor is an employee of a retail firm, such as WalMart, then the investor probably owns WalMart stock through an employee benefits programme. By purchasing a fund that has a large portion of its assets in retail stocks such as WalMart, the investor will be overallocated in the retail industry. Optimally, the investor would want a fund that invests less in the retail industry. (However, other investors may want just the opposite.)

It is difficult to find a mutual fund that has the appropriate asset allocation for each individual. This is especially true because a fund's management may alter the asset allocation of the fund at any time. Hence, even if an investor finds the ideal fund, the asset allocation may change tomorrow, resulting in a suboptimal allocation for that investor.

One solution to the problem of suboptimal investment is to invest in specialized funds. Many families of funds offer industry-specific mutual funds. For example, Vanguard offers specialized funds in energy, gold, health care, services, technology and utilities. With specialized funds, the mutual fund investor can control the asset allocation decision directly. Thus, investors can diversify across speciality funds to achieve their desired level of diversification.

8 *The disadvantage of being too big.* Sometimes being too big forces a mutual fund either to pick stocks it does not want or to hold too much cash. Both factors reduce the fund's return. Indeed, some funds declare that they are not open to new investment; they are simply too big.

17.3 MEASURING THE PERFORMANCE OF MUTUAL FUNDS

To examine performance, one can compare the returns in a given year or a given period of a mutual fund to the returns of other mutual funds as well as to the return on unmanaged portfolios, e.g. the S&P 500 index.

However, relying on one year is insufficient and cannot distinguish between 'good' and 'bad' funds. To see this claim, suppose that one fund invests in high-beta stocks and the other in low-beta stocks. In a year when the market is up, the high beta fund will probably outperform the low beta fund and the opposite holds when the market is down. Thus, we need to examine the return and risk for a relatively long period, reflecting years when the market is up as well as years when the market is down.

Portfolio managers could earn abnormal returns if they were able to select under-priced assets and to time movements into and out of the market. Managers face a risk–return trade-off in selecting assets. On the one hand, managers seek to maximize their expected return on the portfolio, and on the other hand, they seek to reduce the risk. Typically, pursuing higher expected returns requires taking a higher risk. Any analysis of a manager's ability must evaluate the manager's asset selection skills and ability to successfully time when to buy and sell, and then weigh these characteristics against the risk of the portfolio.

The two main customers of performance information are the funds' managers and potential investors:

1 *Managers*. The compensation committee of the portfolio manager needs performance information. If a portfolio manager consistently outperforms an unmanaged portfolio of equivalent risk, the manager should receive a bonus. If the manager consistently underperforms an unmanaged portfolio of equivalent risk, then the manager probably should be replaced.
2 *Investors*. Investors seeking an appropriate mutual fund can use performance information to help them make a selection. If the market is inefficient, then the best manager of the past may also turn out to be a successful performer in the future. If the market is efficient, past performance cannot be used to predict future performance, on average. However, investors may find a few good managers who have consistently outperformed the market and who will continue to do so in the future. Finding these superior managers is not easy, however.

17.3.1 How to measure risk

Exhibit 17.10 reports the top 10 and the bottom 10 mutual funds based on their weekly and annual (July 2000–July 2001) returns. As we can see, the weekly top 10 invested heavily in energy and the weekly bottom 10 invested heavily in different objectives, where the worst performing category was the S&P index funds (see the text below the heading of Exhibit 17.10). Thus, macro-economic factors (i.e. energy prices went up and S&P went down) dictate performance, rather than the quality of the management. Next week or next year the tables may turn around: the S&P index may go up and energy prices may go down. Investors who invest for one or two years pick at random returns, in our case from the rate of return distributions of gold or oil companies or the S&P 500. It is not known in advance whether the energy market will rally or fall or whether the price of gold will rise or decline. Therefore, we need measure the long-run average return relative to the risk involved and not rely on one-year returns.

To develop a measure of performance quality, we must quantify risk and return. Specifically, we need to find the risk and return of a portfolio – in this case, a mutual fund. Return is easy to quantify; it can be estimated with the rate-of-return methods described in Chapter 4. However, the appropriate measure of risk of mutual funds is not that obvious.

Chapter 6 introduced the capital market line, which gives the trade-off between expected return and standard deviation when there is a risk-free asset. In this case, the appropriate risk measure is the standard deviation of the portfolio, because the implicit assumption is that no other assets are held apart from this portfolio, so risk is the *total risk* of the portfolio (as opposed to the systematic risk).

Suppose an investor's financial holdings are well diversified, and apart from the mutual fund under consideration whose performance is being measured, the investor holds many other assets. In this case, the appropriate measure of risk is no longer the standard deviation. The investor's concern should be how the fund investment will influence the overall performance of the holdings, so the appropriate measure of risk is beta.

Exhibit 17.10 The weeks top 10 and bottom 10 mutual funds

SCOREBOARD

No Respite Yet

The dire earnings news kept flowing from major companies, but investors were largely unshaken, using a mid-week downdraft as an opportunity to reaffirm their faith in an economic recovery. The average domestic diversified equity fund was generally unscathed, dipping by 0.66% in the week ended Thursday. The worst-performing major category was S&P 500 index funds, which fell 1.02%, an indication that active stockpickers are retreating from the market. Natural-resources funds led with a gain of 2.63% on upbeat oil-company earnings. Utility funds lost 2.44% as the sell-off in that sector persisted. Domestic long-term fixed-income portfolios held firm with a rise of 0.19%. Among the largest 25 funds, **American Century Ultra** lost 1.28%, while **Janus** eked out an advance of 0.26%. Pimco Total Return, king of bond funds, gained 0.29%.

	One Week	Year-to-Date
U.S. STOCK FUNDS	−0.66	−8.79
U.S. BOND FUNDS	0.19	3.95
TOP SECTOR/Natural Resources Funds	2.63	−7.38
BOTTOM SECTOR/Gold Oriented Funds	−3.31	8.08

THE WEEK'S TOP 10

Fund	Investment Objective	One Week	Year-to-Date
Rydex:Energy Svcs;Inv	Natural Resources	8.61%	−23.61%
Fidelity Sel Enrgy Ser	Natural Resources	6.84	−21.58
AMIDEX:35 Mutual Fd;NL	International	6.05	−36.48
SS Research:Gl Res;A	Natural Resources	5.57	1.05
ICON:Energy	Natural Resources	5.41	−10.15
Strong Energy Fund	Natural Resources	5.33	−8.09
INVESCO Energy;Inv	Natural Resources	5.28	−13.12
Vanguard Energy	Natural Resources	5.25	−3.67
Westcore:Small-Cap Gro	Small Cap Growth	4.57	−23.31
Merrill Natl Res;D	Natural Resources	4.27	−8.23

THE WEEK'S BOTTOM 10

Fund	Investment Objective	One Week	Year-to-Date
American Heritage Fund	Specialty Diversified Equity	−12.50%	−6.67%
HSBC Fds:Intl Eq;Inst	International	−8.07	−14.48
ProFunds:Utilities;Inv	Utility	−6.37	−25.77
New Alternatives Fund	Specialty & Miscellaneous	−5.37	−10.39
Marketocracy:Tech Plus	Technology	−5.36	−10.00
Navellier:Top 20;A	Mid Cap Growth	−5.13	−16.72
AXP:Precious Metals;A	Gold Oriented	−4.75	2.56
ProFunds:UltraEurope;Inv	European Region	−4.73	−40.49
Thurlow Growth	Mid Cap Growth	−4.61	−23.54

However, investors who put their money in mutual funds generally trust that a fund will provide some level of diversification and hence do not buy numerous mutual funds. Therefore, it is very common to use the mutual fund standard deviation as a measure of risk. Thus, the most commonly used performance index of mutual funds is Sharpe's performance index, discussed below, which relies on the standard deviation as a risk index. Rule 2 summarizes the previous discussion.

Rule 2: If an investor holds only a mix of the mutual fund and the riskless asset, the standard deviation is the risk index. If the investor holds a mutual fund, the riskless asset and many other assets, beta is the risk index.

17.4 PERFORMANCE INDEXES

Analysts use four main performance measures or indexes. Each **performance index** is based on a different set of assumptions about portfolio risk.

17.4.1 Sharpe's performance index (PI$_S$)

For portfolios, as for mutual funds, **Sharpe's performance index** is a performance index that uses standard deviation as the appropriate risk measure.[7] Recall that Chapter 6 developed the capital market line (CML), which is a linear relationship between the expected return, $E(R_i)$, and standard deviation, σ_{R_i}:

$$E(R_i) = r + \frac{[E(R_m) - r]}{\sigma_m} \sigma_{R_i}$$

where r is the risk-free interest rate, $E(R_m)$ is the expected return on the market portfolio, and σ_m is the standard deviation of the market portfolio. By mixing a fund with a riskless asset a similar line is obtained.

Of course, we do not know the values of the parameters $E(R_i)$ and σ_{R_i}, and we estimate them by using the *ex-post* data. We denote these estimates by $\overline{R}$ and $\hat{\sigma}_{R_i}$ (rather than $E(R_i)$ and σ_{R_i}).[8] We normally assume that $\overline{R}$ and $\hat{\sigma}$ are the best estimates of $E(R_i)$ and $\hat{\sigma}_{R_i}$.

Exhibit 17.11(a) illustrates a historical CML. The average short-term interest rate over this period was approximately 5%. Note that both Fund A and Fund B lie below the historical CML. On the line denoted A in Exhibit 17.11(a) are all possible combinations of Fund A with borrowing or lending of the risk-free asset. Line B similarly denotes all possible combinations of Fund B with borrowing and lending. The line denoted CML represents all possible combinations of the market portfolio (approximated by Vanguard) and the risk-free asset.

Recall from the previous analysis that the steeper the line is, the higher the average return for a given level of risk (see Chapter 6). Hence, the Vanguard fund outperformed both Fund A and Fund B. That is, the set of all borrowing or lending combinations of the risk-free asset and the Vanguard fund produces a line that is steeper than the line that would be produced by either Fund A or Fund B and the risk-free asset.

An investor would prefer the fund that produces a line with the steepest slope. Hence, Sharpe suggests that when portfolios rather than individual securities are held, and only one portfolio is owned, the slope of the lines given in Exhibit 17.11(a) is an appropriate performance index. Specifically, Sharpe's index (PI$_{S,i}$) for each Portfolio i is given by Rule 3.

---

[7] See William F. Sharpe, 'Mutual fund performance', *Journal of Business*, January 1966, pp. 119–38.

[8] The symbol $\overline{R}$ is used when estimating the average return based on history, and $E(R_i)$ denotes the population parameters which are unobservable. $\hat{\sigma}$ denotes the historical standard deviation estimate, whereas σ is a population parameter, which is unobservable.

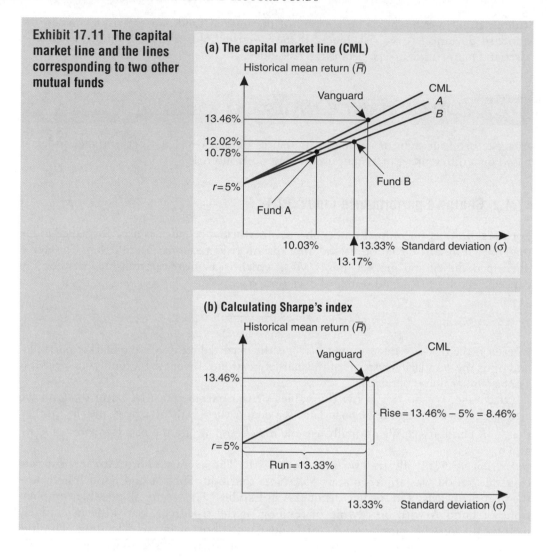

Exhibit 17.11 The capital market line and the lines corresponding to two other mutual funds

Rule 3: To obtain Sharpe's index, substract the riskless interest rate from the average historical rate of return on the fund and divide by the historical standard deviation. Namely,

$$PI_{S,i} = \frac{\overline{R}_i - r}{\hat{\sigma}_{R_i}} \tag{17.1}$$

where $\overline{R}_i$ is the average historical rate of return on Portfolio i, $\hat{\sigma}_{R_i}$ is the standard deviation of returns on Portfolio i, and the risk-free rate for this period is given by $r = 5\%$. As the numerator and the denominator are given in percentages, Sharpe's index is a pure number.

Exhibit 17.11(b) illustrates graphically Equation 17.1 for the Vanguard fund. Specifically, Sharpe's index is the 'rise over the run', or slope, of the line where the denominator of Equation 17.1 (the run) is $\hat{\sigma}_{R_i} = 13.33\%$, and the rise is $E(R_{\text{Vanguard}}) - r = 13.46\% - 5\% = 8.46\%$. The rise measures the additional return expected for taking the risk related to the Vanguard fund. The risk-free rate is compensation for the time value of money. Hence, Sharpe's index for the Vanguard fund is calculated as follows:

$$PI_{S,Vanguard} = \frac{13.46\% - 5.0\%}{13.33\%} \cong 0.635$$

In a similar manner, we can calculate Sharpe's performance indexes for the other two funds:

$$PI_{S,Fund\ A} = \frac{10.78\% - 5.0\%}{10.03\%} \cong 0.576$$

$$PI_{S,Fund\ B} = \frac{12.02\% - 5.0\%}{13.17\%} \cong 0.533$$

Assuming that standard deviation is the appropriate risk measure, we can conclude by Sharpe's performance index that the best-performing fund for this period is Vanguard, followed by Fund A. Fund B came in last, with the lowest Sharpe's index value.

17.4.2 Treynor's performance index (PI$_T$)

In 1965, Treynor evaluated portfolio performance based on the security market line (SML).[9] Treynor's performance index is the appropriate index to use in order to measure the performance of one specific portfolio while many other assets are also held in another portfolio. Recall from Chapter 14 that the security market line is the linear relationship between the expected return of a specific asset and its beta. Specifically, the SML was defined as follows:

$$E(R_i) = r + [E(R_m) - r]\ \beta_i$$

where $E(R_i)$ is the expected return on the specific asset (or portfolio), and β_i is the beta of the asset.

As with the CML, investors prefer the SML (rather than the CML) to be steeper. Of course, when the market is in equilibrium, all assets should lie on the SML. In actuality, however, some funds will be above the line and some below. Investors seek to achieve the highest return for a given beta or the lowest beta for a given return. Exhibit 17.12(a) illustrates the three mutual funds plotted using some values from Exhibit 17.11. Fund A is located above the SML and hence 'beat the market'; that is, Fund A outperformed the market on a risk-adjusted basis when beta measures the risk.

Treynor suggested using the slope of the SML as a benchmark to assess performance. Treynor's performance index for a given portfolio i (PI$_{T,i}$) is given by Rule 4.

Rule 4: To obtain Treynor's index, subtract the riskless interest rate from the fund's historical mean return and divide by the historical beta. Namely,

$$PI_{T,i} = \frac{\overline{R_i} - r}{\hat{\beta}_i} \tag{17.12}$$

[9] Jack Traynor, 'How to rate management of investment funds', *Harvard Business Review*, January–February 1965, pp. 63–75.

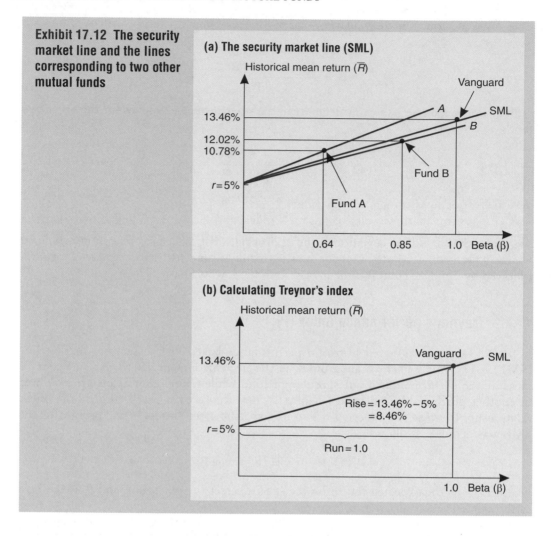

Exhibit 17.12 The security market line and the lines corresponding to two other mutual funds

where $\hat{\beta}_i$ is the historical beta, calculated with historical rates of return, that is the best estimate of the beta.

Exhibit 17.12(b) illustrates the calculations required for the Vanguard fund. This fund has a beta of 1.0, because we use this fund as a proxy for the market portfolio. Treynor's index compares the slope of the Vanguard fund with the slopes of other lines measuring other portfolios. Again, because this is a slope, we calculate the 'rise over the run'. Mathematically, we calculate the following for Vanguard:

$$\text{PI}_{\text{T,Vanguard}} = \frac{13.46\% - 5.0\%}{1.0} = 8.46\%$$

Note that because the terms in the numerator are percentages and beta is a pure number, Treynor's index is a percentage.

Using Equation 17.2, we can calculate Treynor's performance indexes for the other two funds:

$$PI_{T,\text{Fund A}} = \frac{10.78\% - 5.0\%}{0.64\%} \cong 9.03\%$$

$$PI_{T,\text{Fund B}} = \frac{12.02\% - 5.0\%}{0.85} \cong 8.26\%$$

If a fund neither outperforms nor underperforms the market, we expect it to lie on the SML – just as the Vanguard fund does – and to have a slope of 8.46%. If a fund has a line with a higher slope, it outperformed the market or unmanaged portfolio. The opposite is true for a line with a lower slope than the SML. Thus, under the assumption that beta is the appropriate risk measure, we conclude that the best-performing fund for this period was Fund A, followed by Vanguard. Fund B came in last again, with the lowest Treynor's performance index value.

A comparison of the results of Sharpe's index and Treynor's index shows that the choice of risk measure, standard deviation or beta affects the rankings. With Sharpe's index, we concluded that Vanguard is the best, whereas with Treynor's index, we concluded that Fund A is the best. This finding is not a contradiction, because different results could be appropriate for different investors. Sharpe's index is more relevant for investors who do not hold any other assets apart from the fund, whereas Treynor's index is more relevant for investors who hold many other assets apart from the mutual fund.

The Treynor and Sharpe indexes rank portfolios but do not indicate in terms of percentage return by how much a fund outperformed or underperformed the unmanaged portfolio. Thus, it is hard to understand intuitively the meaning of a PI_T of, for example, 8.26% per unit of risk. However, there is an alternative performance index based on beta that allows us to answer the question, 'How much better did the fund do in terms of percentage return on a risk-adjusted basis?' This method is *Jensen's performance index* that we discuss next.

17.4.3 Jensen's performance index (PIJ)

In 1968, Jensen suggested a performance measure based on the capital asset pricing model that could assess, on a risk-adjusted, percentage basis, how well a mutual fund performed.[10] Once again, recall from Chapter 14 that the CAPM equilibrium relationship between risk and return is as follows:

$$E(R_i) = r + [E(R_m) - r]\beta_i$$

Jensen's performance index examines the difference between the returns actually earned during the evaluation period and the returns expected using the CAPM. We can use historical rates of return to estimate $E(R_i)$, $E(R_m)$ and β_i by $\overline{R}_i$, $\overline{R}_m$ and the *ex-post* $\hat{\beta}_i$. We then substitute the estimates for the parameters in the CAPM. With *ex-post* data, we may not have a precise straight line; hence, we write

$$\overline{R}_i = r + (\overline{R}_m - r)\,\hat{\beta}_i + \alpha_i$$

---

[10] C. Michael Jensen, 'The performance of mutual funds in the period 1945–1964', *Journal of Finance*, May 1968, pp. 389–415.

where α_i is the deviation from the line. Indeed α_i is Jensen's performance index, which we denote by PI_j.[11] If $\alpha_i > 0$, we say that the fund earns more than is expected given its risk; the opposite holds for $\alpha_i < 0$. Thus, Jensen's performance index, α_i, is given in Rule 5.

Rule 5: First calculate the average rate of return on the fund, $\overline{R}_m$, and beta. Calculate $\overline{R}_m - r$, multiply it by beta and add to it r. Substract the result from $\overline{R}_i$ to obtain Jensen's index. Namely,

$$PI_{J,i} = \overline{R}_i - [r + (\overline{R}_m - r)\,\beta_i] \tag{17.3}$$

We find the following performance measures using Jensen's index on the three funds we have been tracking:

$$PI_{J,\,Fund\,A} = 10.78\% - [5\% + (13.46\% - 5\%)\,0.64] \cong 0.366\%$$

$$PI_{J,\,Fund\,B} = 12.02\% - [5\% + (13.46\% - 5\%)\,0.85] = -0.171\%$$

$$PI_{J,\,Vanguard} = 13.46\% - [5\% + (13.46\% - 5\%)\,1.0] = 0.0\%$$

These performance measures are expressed as percentages. Fund A earns an excess return of 0.366% compared with what it should earn given its beta. Notice that Jensen's performance index is zero for Vanguard. This is not a coincidence. We chose Vanguard as our market portfolio, hence $\beta = 1$ and $\overline{R}_m - [r + (\overline{R}_m - r) \times 1] = 0$. We find that the results using Jensen's measure are similar in some respects to the results using Treynor's measure. This, too, is no coincidence: both Treynor's and Jensen's indexes use beta as their risk measure. As such, they both yield the same 'beat-the-market' assessment. That is, if Treynor's index for a fund indicates that it outperformed the market portfolio, then we know that Jensen's index must yield the same result.[12] This does not mean that Treynor's and Jensen's indexes give the same fund rankings. In fact, the rankings generally will differ. That is, if, for example, we evaluate 100 funds, both measures may show that 26 funds outperformed the market portfolio and 74 underperformed the market portfolio. However, Jensen's measure may show that Fund 5 was the best, whereas Treynor's measure may rank Fund 18 as the best.

A benefit of Jensen's index is its intuitive interpretation. We can conclude that Fund A outperformed the Vanguard fund by 36.6 basis points (or 0.366%) and that Fund B underperformed the Vanguard fund by 17.1 basis points (or 0.171%). Jensen's measure allows an investor to determine by how much one fund outperformed or underperformed another fund. Statistical tests can also be run to determine the significance of these results.

---

[11] Formally, Jensen suggested running the following regression:
$$R_{i,t} - r_t = \hat{\alpha}_i + \hat{\beta}_i (R_{m,t} - r_t) + e_{i,t}$$
Taking the average for both sides, we get
$$\overline{R}_i - \overline{r} = \hat{\alpha}_i + \hat{\beta}_i (\overline{R}_m - \overline{r}) + \overline{e}_i$$
where the last term $\overline{e}_i$ is zero. Therefore, Jensen's performance index is α_i, given by
$$\hat{\alpha}_i = \overline{R}_i - \overline{r} - \hat{\beta}_i (\overline{R}_m - \overline{r})$$

[12] We ignore here the technical difficulties encountered with negative beta portfolios. Negative beta portfolios are very rare.

17.4.4 Summary of performance indexes

Three different methods can be used to assess the relative performance of a portfolio: Sharpe's index, Treynor's index and Jensen's index. Sharpe's index uses the standard deviation as a risk measure and the slope of the lines that are similar to the CML. Sharpe's index is relevant only when the standard deviation of the portfolio is the appropriate risk measure – that is, when there are no other assets held apart from the portfolio under consideration. Treynor's and Jensen's indexes use beta as a risk measure. Both indexes assume that only the market portfolio affects risk, but unlike Sharpe's index, they assume that other assets are held in the portfolio as well as the assets under consideration. For investors who are interested only in whether they 'beat the market', Treynor's index as well as Jenson's index are relevant. For investors who want to compare their performance with that of other fund managers, Jensen's index is relevant.

Of the three mutual funds just examined, none is clearly superior. If standard deviation is the appropriate risk measure, then the Vanguard fund is superior by Sharpe's index. If beta is the appropriate risk measure, then Fund A is superior by Treynor's and Jensen's indexes.

17.5 EMPIRICAL EVIDENCE OF THE PERFORMANCE OF MUTUAL FUNDS

Most research on the performance of mutual funds shows that they fall behind the market as a whole. That is, mutual funds on average consistently underperform the market.

Sharpe examined the performance of 34 open-end mutual funds from 1954 through 1963. He found that the major differences in their returns resulted from the expenses incurred by each mutual fund. Furthermore, as measured by Sharpe's index, the majority of these funds failed to outperform the Dow Jones Industrial Average based on Sharpe's index. This led Sharpe to conclude the following:

> The burden of proof may reasonably be placed on those who argue the traditional view – that the search for securities whose prices diverge from their intrinsic values is worth the expense required.[13]

Jensen examined the performance of 115 mutual funds for the 10-year period 1955 through 1964. Applying Jensen's index, he concludes:

> The evidence on mutual fund performance...indicates not only that these 115 mutual funds were on average not able to predict security prices well enough to outperform the buy-the-market-and-hold policy, but also that there is little evidence that any individual fund was able to do significantly better than that which we expected from mere random chance.[14]

More recently, Cumby and Glen examined a sample of 15 US-based international mutual funds from 1982 through 1988.[15] Using Jensen's index, they found no evidence

---

[13] See William F. Sharpe, 'Mutual fund performance', *Journal of Business*, January 1966, p. 138.

[14] See C. Michael Jensen, 'The performance of mutual funds in the period 1945–1964', *Journal of Finance*, May 1968, p. 415.

[15] Robert E. Cumby and Jack D. Glen, 'Evaluating the performance of international mutual funds', Journal of Finance, June 1990, pp. 497–521.

that these funds outperformed a broad, international equity index. That is, the market portfolio selected was an internationally diversified portfolio. It is interesting to note that they did find some evidence that the funds outperformed when a US-based market portfolio is used. That is, international mutual funds tend to do better when the risk is calculated with a domestic portfolio. The excess performance using a US-based index is easily attributable to the gains in diversification with international securities. The international portfolio is less correlated with the domestic portfolio, resulting in considerable gains from diversification.

Eun, Kolodny and Resnick also examined the performance of international mutual funds.[16] Their results are very interesting:

> According to the Sharpe performance measure, the majority of international funds outperformed the S&P 500 Index during the ten-year period of 1977–1986. Most of them, however, failed to outperform the MSCI [Morgan Stanley Capital International] World Index.[17]

Thus, international mutual funds tend to outperform the S&P 500. However, if the market portfolio is a global one, such as the Morgan Stanley Capital International World Index, the mutual funds did not outperform this index. This result supports earlier work by Lehman and Modest,[18] who demonstrate that the choice of a market portfolio is critical to the inferences drawn. Hence, the choice of a market portfolio is critical to analyzing a fund's historical performance. These findings also imply that there is a benefit from international diversification.

Exhibit 17.13 shows the percentage of pension funds outperformed by the passive S&P 500 index during the 1970s and 1980s using rate of return as the performance benchmark. The majority of pension plans are consistently outperformed by the S&P 500. For example, in 1991, almost 60% of pension funds were outperformed by the S&P 500 index. Thus, the argument in favour of following an investment strategy that passively mimics the S&P 500 appears strong.[19] This is the main motivation for the creation of the indexed funds that will be discussed below.

17.6 TIMING THE MARKET

Another portfolio management strategy that is employed by money managers is an attempt to time the market, that is, to decide when to move into and out of different asset categories. In recent years, newsletters advising investors when to move into and out of stocks have proliferated. Exhibit 17.14 provides some interesting insights into the quantity and quality of this advice. In 1980 there were only 14 mutual fund market-timing newsletters, and by the early 1990s there were over 100.[20] How have these newsletters performed their stated task? Exhibit 17.14 shows clearly that they have failed miserably.

---

[16] Cheol S. Eun, Richard Kolodny and Bruce G. Resnick, 'U.S.-based international mutual funds: a performance evaluation', *Journal of Portfolio Management*, Spring 1991, pp. 88–94.

[17] *Ibid.*, p. 93.

[18] Bruce N. Lehman and David M. Modest, 'Mutual fund performance evaluations: a comparison of benchmarks and benchmark comparisons', *Journal of Finance*, 42 (June 1987): 233–65.

[19] An alternative explanation would appear to be that most funds take less risk than the S&P 500.

[20] Exhibit 17.14 shows that there were 14 newsletters in 1980 and 85 at the start of 1989. However, the source cited in the exhibit goes on to state that there were over 100 newsletters in the early 1990s.

Exhibit 17.13 Percentage of pension funds outperformed by the S&P 500 index, 1971–1991

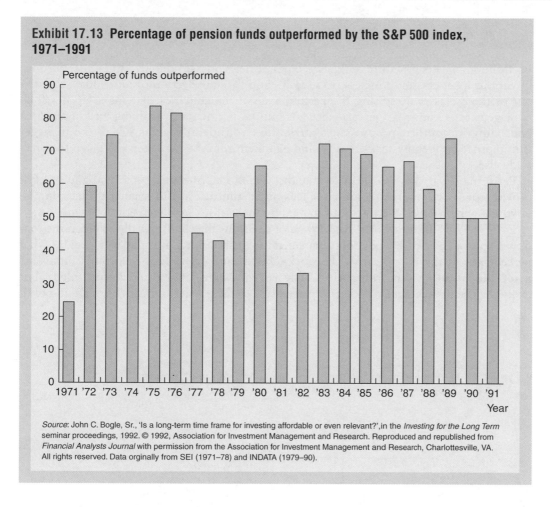

Source: John C. Bogle, Sr., 'Is a long-term time frame for investing affordable or even relevant?',in the *Investing for the Long Term* seminar proceedings, 1992. © 1992, Association for Investment Management and Research. Reproduced and republished from *Financial Analysts Journal* with permission from the Association for Investment Management and Research, Charlottesville, VA. All rights reserved. Data orginally from SEI (1971–78) and INDATA (1979–90).

To sum up, the performance of mutual funds does not reveal that the funds' managers have special knowledge in security selection. However, some have argued that the miserable performance of mutual funds can be attributed to problems with the performance indexes, not with the performance of the funds. We next look at some of the common problems with performance indexes.

Exhibit 17.14 Performance of mutual fund timing newsletters

Period	Number of newsletters	Advisors outpacing market	Advisors falling short	Median timing return	Market return
30 June 1980 to 30 June 1990	14	4	10	+271.5	+336.9
1 January 1989 to 30 June 1990	85	8	77	+17.1	+31.5

Source: John C. Bogle, Sr., 'Is a long-term frame for investing affordable or even relevant?', in the *Investing for the Long Term* seminar proceedings, 1992. © 1992, Association for Investment Management and Research. Reproduced and republished from *Financial Analysts Journal* with permission from the Association for Investment Management and Research, Charlottesville, VA. All rights reserved. Data from M. Hulbert, *The Hulbert Financial Digest* (New York: Institute of Finance, 1991).

17.7 PERFORMANCE ATTRIBUTION

Portfolio managers generally make two types of decisions: (a) the investment proportions in various asset classes (bonds, stocks, cash), and (b) the selection of individual securities out of these classes. Assessing the performance of the activities that make up portfolio management is known as **performance attribution**. If a manager is doing well in one area and badly in another, performance attribution will identify areas where the manager can improve or identify tasks that should be taken from the manager and given to somebody else.

Performance attribution seeks to take the overall rate of return on a fund and break it down into its component parts, such as asset allocation and security selection. To attribute performance, we just need to analyze the various management decisions.

Exhibit 17.15 illustrates the four layers of decisions that are typically made in the **top-down approach** used by portfolio managers. First, the portfolio manager decides what percentages of the portfolio will be stocks, bonds and cash. This decision is known as **asset allocation**. (Other categories, such as real estate, also could be included.) For example, the manager may decide to place 40% of the portfolio in stocks, 30% in bonds

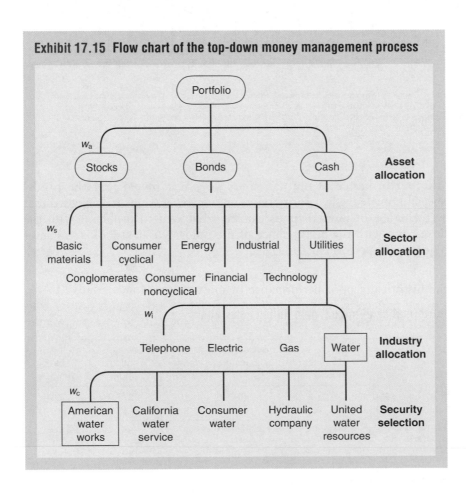

Exhibit 17.15 Flow chart of the top-down money management process

and 30% in cash. Using the notation w_a, the asset allocation proportion (or weight), we have $w_{a,Stocks} = 0.40$, $w_{a,Bonds} = 0.30$ and $w_{a,Cash} = 0.30$.

Next, the manager must decide how to allocate the 40% portion of stocks into various sectors, such as basic materials, conglomerates, and so forth. The sectors shown in Exhibit 17.15 are based on sector definitions provided in the *Wall Street Journal*. The decision to place 10% of the stock portion in utilities (denoted $w_{S,Utilities} = 0.10$), for example, is known as a **sector allocation** decision (how much of an asset to place in a specific sector). The sum of all the sector weights (w_s) will equal 100%. Hence, sector weights denote the portion of the stocks held given to a certain sector category.

The next decision managers make is how to allocate each of the sector portions into various industries. For example, the utilities sector can be broken down into four basic industries: telephone, electricity, gas and water. The **industry allocation** is the allotment of investment dollars given to a sector's industry components. For example, the manager may decide to allocate 30% of the utilities sector to the water industry (denoted $w_{i,Water} = 0.30$, where i denotes industry).

At this point, the manager is ready to select individual securities. For example, of the allocation given to the water industry, what portion should be invested in American Water Works (AWW)? This decision is known as **security selection**. The manager may decide to place 15% of the water industry allocation into American Water Works (denoted $w_{c,AWW} = 0.15$, where c denotes *company*).

To attribute performance among the various management decisions, an index portfolio is needed for comparison. This index portfolio plays the role of a benchmark portfolio. The fund manager knows that the fund's performance will be compared with this benchmark portfolio. For example, suppose the fund outperformed the index portfolio by 250 basis points. Senior management wants to be able to determine which decisions generated the excess returns. Was it the asset allocation decision to have less in stocks? Was it the sector allocation decision, the industry allocation decision and/or the security selections? The answer can be determined through the process of performance attribution.

17.8 INDEXING AND INTERNATIONAL DIVERSIFICATION

In response to the historically poor performance of most mutual funds relative to the index of stocks, many managers and investors are turning to indexing. Investors who follow an indexing strategy invest in a passively managed mutual fund that mirrors the market and incurs minimal expenses. If you are a manager or an individual investor who concludes that you have no ability to pick stocks or to time the market, you should consider diversifying according to an index.

If you desire to expand globally, you should diversify in various countries. Obviously, you cannot diversify directly in all stocks available in the world. However, you can buy most of them indirectly by buying existing index funds in these countries.

Vanguard Total International Fund offers a simple indexing strategy for investing in these international markets, providing broad diversification at the lowest costs. The allocation strategy of Vanguard is as shown in Exhibit 17.16.

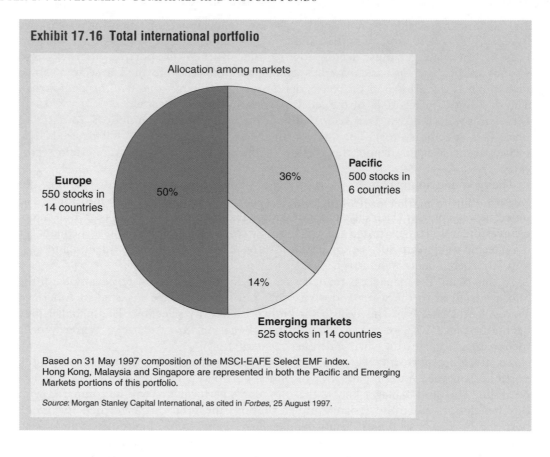

Exhibit 17.16 Total international portfolio

Allocation among markets

Europe
550 stocks in
14 countries

Pacific
500 stocks in
6 countries

Emerging markets
525 stocks in 14 countries

Based on 31 May 1997 composition of the MSCI-EAFE Select EMF index.
Hong Kong, Malaysia and Singapore are represented in both the Pacific and Emerging
Markets portions of this portfolio.

Source: Morgan Stanley Capital International, as cited in *Forbes*, 25 August 1997.

SUMMARY

■ *Compare and contrast hedge funds with closed-end and open-end funds.*
A closed-end fund rarely issues more shares after the original issue; open-end (mutual) funds continue to issue more shares, as well as redeem outstanding shares at the request of investors. Closed-end funds can trade at either a premium or a discount from the net asset value (NAV). One benefit of buying closed-end funds is the ability to purchase them at a discount from the funds' intrinsic net asset value. Mutual funds can be purchased at net asset value plus a load, if there is one. Mutual funds are sold at net asset value and can expand or contract according to investors' demands. Hedge funds are a partnership which is less regulated than mutual funds. It may take a speculative position, hence is very risky. There is a minimum investment constraint to be an investor in a hedge fund.

■ *Contrast the benefits and costs of investing in mutual funds.*
The benefits of mutual funds include diversification, professional management, reduced trading costs, systematic accumulation and withdrawal plans, chequing accounts, switching services, security custody and bookkeeping, and increasing an economy's capital supply. Costs of investing in mutual funds include the load; management fees; 12b-1 fees; transaction costs; higher tax burdens if a mutual fund has a relatively high turnover that forces shareholders to pay regular income tax rather than capital gains; accounting, distribution, and other miscellaneous costs; and suboptimal investment

costs. Each investor must weigh these benefits and costs before deciding whether to use mutual funds.

■ *Calculate portfolio performance using three performance indexes.*
Performance indexes provide a method of comparing funds with different risk–return characteristics. Three performance indexes used to rank portfolio performance are Sharpe's index, Treynor's index and Jensen's index. Sharpe's performance index compares fund performance where the standard deviation measures the risk, whereas Treynor's performance index compares fund performance where beta serves as the measure of risk. Sharpe's index is appropriate for portfolios in isolation, and Treynor's index is appropriate for portfolios in the context of the entire market portfolio. Jensen's performance index is also based on beta as a risk index, hence assumes that the investor holds the entire market portfolio. Jensen's performance index gives performance in terms of rates of return. Because Treynor's and Jensen's indexes are based on the CAPM framework, they both give the same assessment of overperformance or underperformance in relation to the market, but these two indexes can give different rankings within the two groups based on performance.

■ *Summarize the empirical evidence regarding portfolio managers' performance.*
The empirical evidence consistently finds that professional portfolio managers lag behind the market as a whole in performance. Even after adjusting for risk, which is measured in a variety of ways, managers are underperforming the market.

■ *Evaluate performance attribution as a means of identifying the sources of performance.*
Performance attribution breaks down a fund's excess return into component parts. The component parts correspond with the four layers of decisions that are typically made through a top-down portfolio management approach. The layers are the asset allocation decision, the sector allocation decision, the industry allocation decision and security selection.

KEY TERMS

Asset allocation	Load	Sector allocation
Closed-end fund	Mutual fund	Security selection
Conduit theory	Net asset value (NAV)	Sharpe's performance
Discount	No-load mutual fund	index
Family of funds	Open-end fund	Top-down approach
Industry allocation	Performance attribution	Treynor's performance
Investment company	Performance index	index
Investment trust	Premium	Trust company
Jensen's performance	Regulated investment	Unit trust
index	company	

QUESTIONS

17.1   Compare and contrast open-end and closed-end funds.

17.2   What is the conduit theory?

17.3   Suppose mutual funds have to pay taxes, and shareholders also must pay taxes. Is this double or triple taxation? Explain.

17.4 Can mutual funds be sold at a discount? At a premium? Explain.

17.5 What are the main advantages of investing in mutual funds versus direct investments? What are the main disadvantages?

17.6 Suppose a mutual fund charges a load of 4%. You would like to invest for six months. Would you buy this fund? What if you would like to invest for 10 years? Why does the length of the investment holding period influence this decision?

17.7 Suppose a mutual fund has the following assets and liabilities:

Stocks	$100,000
Bonds	200,000
Accounts payable	20,000

There are 1,000 shares outstanding.

(a) What is the NAV?

(b) Suppose the firm sells another 100 shares. It has a 3% load. What is the selling price?

17.8 Ford Motor Company has $100 billion in assets, and a closed-end fund has $100 million in assets. Which of these two firms will sell for the largest discount or premium? Why?

17.9 Suppose Dave wants to invest for one year, and Jane wants to invest for 10 years. Both purchase a mutual fund that earns 10% a year and charges a 3% load. What is the annualized rate of return for Dave and Jane? Who is hurt more by the load? Why? (Assume each has a $1,000 investment.)

17.10 Suppose the return on the S&P 500 index is 12%. A mutual fund has a group of experts who can earn 15%. The load is 2%, and the management fee is 1.5%. Suppose you can buy the S&P 500 index. Which of these two instruments would you prefer?

17.11 Suppose a mutual fund has the following rates of return:

Year	Rate of return	Rate of return on S&P 500
1	-2%	12%
2	0	8
3	30	10
4	20	20
5	15	15

(a) Calculate the mean and variance of the rates of return on the mutual fund and the S&P 500.

(b) Assume that the load is zero and the risk-free interest rate is 3%. Which portfolio would you prefer? (Hint: Draw the opportunity lines.)

(c) Repeat (b), but this time the fund charges a 3% load, and you are investing for one year only.

17.12 Suppose the rates of return on two stocks and one mutual fund you are considering buying are as follows:

Year	Stock A	Stock B	Mutual fund
1	10%	15%	25%
2	0	10	15
3	20	-20	-1
4	10	60	20

If you decide to buy stocks, then you will diversify equally between the two stocks. If the risk-free rate is 3%, would you buy the mutual fund or the stocks? Explain.

17.13 Suppose a closed-end fund is sold at a 10% premium. The value of the shares held is $100 million, and there are 1 million shares outstanding. Also, net liabilities are $100,000. What is the current market price of this closed-end fund?

17.14 Suppose the NAV is $10, and there are 10,000 shares traded. The fund has net liabilities of $20,000. What is the market value of all the assets the mutual fund holds?

17.15 Suppose a mutual fund holds 100,000 shares of National Health, Inc., which is trading at $48 per share, and 200,000 shares of Ford Motor, which is trading at $54 per share. There are 70,000 shares outstanding. The firm's NAV is $200. What is the fund's net liabilities?

17.16 A mutual fund invests in the exact composition of the market index (say it is the S&P 500 index). However, the fund is much smaller than the market value of the index. Will the fund have the same beta as the index? Explain how the different size influences the calculation of beta.

17.17 Closed-end Fund A holds only money market securities, and closed-end Fund B holds stocks. For which fund would a higher deviation be expected between NAV and the share's actual market price? Why?

17.18 An open-end fund is charging you a 5% load and is making, on average, 10% on its investment. What is your net annual rate of return if you invest for n years, where $n = 1$, 2, 5, 10, 50 and 100? Draw a graph, and explain your results.

17.19 Suppose an open-end fund offers you either a 5% load and a $1/2$% 12b-1 fee or a zero load and a 2% maintenance fee. Also, assume the fund is earning 10% on its investments. Which alternative would you choose? What is the critical number of years you would wish to invest such that you would be indifferent between these two alternatives?

17.20 Suppose an open-end fund holds a lot of Intel stock. In a recent year, Intel split its stock 2-for-1. How does this split affect the NAV?

SELECTED REFERENCES

Allen, Gregory C. 'Performance attribution for global equity portfolios'. *Journal of Portfolio Management*, Fall 1991, pp. 59–65.

American Association of Individual Investors. *The Individual Investor's Guide to No-Load Mutual Funds*. Chicago: International Publishing, various issues.

Anderson, Seth C., and Jeffery A. Born. *Closed-End Investment Companies: Issues and Answers*. Boston: Kluwer Academic Publishers, 1992.

Ankrim, Ernest M., and Chris R. Hensel. 'Multi-currency performance attribution'. *Financial Analysts Journal*, March–April 1994, pp. 29–35.

Blake, Christopher R., Edwin J. Elton, and Martin J. Gruber. 'The performance of bond mutual funds'. *Journal of Business*, 66(3), July 1993, pp. 371–403.

Bogle, John C. 'Selecting equity mutual funds'. *Journal of Portfolio Management*, Winter 1992, pp. 94–100.

Cappiello, Frank, W. Douglas Dent, and Peter W. Madlem. *The Complete Guide to Closed-End Funds*. Chicago: International Publishing, 1990.

CDA/Weisenberger Investment Companies Service. *Mutual Funds Panorama*. Boston: Warren Gorham & Lamont, various issues.

Cumby, Robert E., and Jack D. Glen. 'Evaluating the performance of international mutual funds'. *Journal of Finance*, June 1990, pp. 497–521.

Gastineau, Gary L. 'Exchange traded funds: an introduction'. *Journal of Portfolio Management*, Spring 2001.

Grinblatt, Mark, and Sheridan Titman. 'Performance measurement without benchmarks: an examination of mutual fund returns'. *Journal of Business*, 66, January 1993, pp. 47–68.

Halpern, Philip. 'Investing abroad: a review of capital market integration and manager performance'. *Journal of Portfolio Management*, 19, Winter 1993, pp. 47–57.

Hendricks, Darryll, Jayendu Patel, and Richard Zeckhauser. 'Hot hands in mutual funds: short-run persistence of relative performance, 1974–1988'. *Journal of Finance*, 48(1), March 1993, pp. 93–130.

Hodgos, Charles W., Walton R.L. Taylor, and James A. Yoder. 'Stocks, bonds, the Sharpe ratio, and the investment horizon'. *Financial Analysts Journal*, November–December 1997, pp. 74–80.

Investment Company Institute. *Mutual Fund Fact Book*. Washington, DC: Investment Company Institute, various issues.

Jensen, C. Michael. 'The performance of mutual funds in the period 1945–1964'. *Journal of Finance*, May 1968, pp. 389–415.

Lee, Charles C., Andrei Shleifer, and Richard H. Thaler. 'Closed-end mutual funds'. *Journal of Economic Perspectives*, 4(4), 1990, pp. 153–64.

Lee, Charles C., Andrei Shleifer, and Richard H. Thaler. 'Investor sentiment and the closed-end fund puzzle'. *Journal of Finance*, 46, March 1991, pp. 75–109.

Lehman, Bruce N., and David M. Modest. 'Mutual fund performance evaluations: a comparison of benchmarks and benchmark comparisons'. *Journal of Finance*, 42, June 1987, pp. 233–65.

Malkiel, Burton G., and Aleksander Radisich. 'The growth of index funds and the pricing of equity securities'. *Journal of Portfolio Management*, Winter 2001.

Morningstar's Mutual Fund Sourcebook. Chicago: Mutual Fund Sourcebook, various issues.

O'Neil, Edward S. 'Industry momentum and sector mutual funds'. *Financial Analysts Journal*, July/August 2000.

Roll, Richard. 'Ambiguity when performance is measured by the security market line'. *Journal of Finance*, September 1978, pp. 1051–69.

Roll, Richard. 'Performance evaluation and benchmark errors, 1'. *Journal of Portfolio Management*, Summer 1980, pp. 5–12.

Roll, Richard. 'Performance evaluation and benchmark errors, 2'. *Journal of Portfolio Management*, Winter 1981, pp. 17–22.

Sharpe, William F. 'Mutual fund performance'. *Journal of Business*, January 1966, pp. 119–38.

Sharpe, William F. 'Asset allocation: management style and performance measurement'. *Journal of Portfolio Management*, Winter 1992, pp. 7–19.

Standard & Poor's/Lipper. *Mutual Fund Profiles*. New York: Standard & Poor's, various issues.

Treynor, Jack. 'How to rate management of investment funds'. *Harvard Business Review*, January–February 1965, pp. 63–75.

Chapter 18

TECHNICAL ANALYSIS

Learning objectives

After studying this chapter you should be able to:

1 Describe a technical analyst's view of the market.
2 Explain how technical analysts use charts to make inferences about future prices.
3 Identify the basic tools used by technical analysts.
4 Describe some popular technical investment indicators.

INVESTMENT IN THE NEWS

Trading techniques

Combining technical and fundamental analyses

By Mark C. Snead, PhD

The two forms of analysis approach forecasting in radically different styles. Can they be combined?

Few topics generate as much heated discussion as the time-honored debate of technical vs. fundamental analysis. The two schools do, in fact, offer radically different approaches to market forecasting; fundamental analysis is concerned with identifying the relevant variables underlying price action, while technical analysis attempts to extract tradable information from price action itself...What is most interesting about this is the tendency for forecasters to rely solely on either fundamental or technical analysis. Many are merely following the conventional wisdom that each technique is logically more compatible with a given trading horizon. Because long-run movements in a market are ultimately steered by the underlying fundamentals, fundamental analysis is considered more suitable for long-term investors. Conversely, since short-term market movements are dominated by volatile price adjustments, technical analysis is the method of choice for most short-term traders...

Source: CPS (Stocks & Commodities), September 1999, http://www.traders.com/Documentation/Feedbk_docs/Abstracts_new/snead/snead09.html

Technical analysis is commonly employed by short-term investors while fundamental analysis is commonly employed by long-term investors.

What is technical analysis and in what respect is it different from fundamental analysis?

Technical analysis employed in stock selection is based on graphs and charts rather than on fundamental values such as dividends, sales and earnings. Although many analysts dispute the value of this method of analysis, it is widely used on Wall Street. Therefore, no matter how investors view the effectiveness of technical analysis, they should know how it works. Moreover, because many Wall Street traders follow the rules of technical analysis, this method may actually push prices up or down, at least in the short run. Thus, investors unfamiliar with technical analysis might miss a rally in the stock market even if it is economically unjustified.

Investors who practise fundamental analysis make investment decisions based on such economic factors as the firm's earnings, the firm's growth rate of dividends, the cash available for distribution, the P/E ratio and the strength of the firm's balance sheet. Investors using **technical analysis**, in contrast, rely on short-term historical technical figures related to the firm or the whole economy. For example, a technical analyst would evaluate factors such as the amount of short selling, the volume of trading or the past price behaviour of a stock.

If we assume that markets are perfectly efficient, all this historical information (regardless of whether it is macro-economic data, accounting data or market data) should already be reflected in the stock price. Adherents of the EMT would argue that these data cannot be used to improve the investment performance. Nevertheless, there are many market professionals whose sole task is to examine short-term historical market data to predict future price behaviour. Technical analysts believe that their analysis enables them to beat the market consistently and that their activities help move prices back into equilibrium. The existence of technical analysts suggests one of the following:

1 The market is inefficient, or at least there are many investors who believe it is not efficient.
2 Even if the market is efficient and thus, on average, technical analysts cannot earn abnormal profits, it is possible that some consistently earn abnormal profits.

This chapter introduces some of the key concepts used by technical analysts. First, it discusses the main justification for using technical analysis and provides reasons why technical analysis may be useful. Next, the main tools used by technical analysts, such as charts and technical indicators, are discussed and illustrated. Although the focus is on stocks, many of these tools are applied to bonds, currencies, commodities and other financial assets.

18.1 IN DEFENCE OF TECHNICAL ANALYSIS

The underlying premise of technical analysis is that financial prices are determined by investors' attitudes. Investors' attitudes are influenced by many factors, some rational and some irrational. Hence, formal rational models of financial prices will never fully reflect or explain the behaviour of financial prices. However, technical analysts assume that human nature is fairly static; that is, when current investors face situations similar to those faced by investors in the past, they will behave in a similar fashion. Therefore, technical analysts believe that the study of historical price patterns and relationships of prices with other variables provides clues as to how the market will behave in the future.

Martin J. Pring, president of the International Institute for Economic Research and a well-respected technical analyst, defines technical analysis this way:

> The technical approach to investment is essentially a reflection of the idea that prices move in trends which are determined by the changing attitudes of investors toward a variety of economic, monetary, political, and psychological forces. The art of technical analysis – for it is an art – is to identify trend changes at an early stage and to maintain an investment posture until the weight of the evidence indicates that the trend has reversed . . . .
>
> Since the technical approach is based on the theory that the price is a reflection of mass psychology ('the crowd') in action, it attempts to forecast future price movements on the assumption that crowd psychology moves between panic, fear, and pessimism on one hand and confidence, excessive optimism, and greed on the other . . . . [T]he art of technical analysis is concerned with identifying these changes at an early phase, since these swings in emotion take time to accomplish. Studying these market trends enables technically oriented investors to buy or sell with a degree of confidence, on the principle that once a trend is set in motion it will perpetuate itself.[1]

Pring thus views technical analysis as the art of being able to identify trends early.

In their popular book on technical analysis, Robert D. Edwards and John Magee define technical analysis as:

> The study of the action of the market itself as opposed to the study of the goods in which the market deals. Technical analysis is the science of recording, usually in graphic form, the actual history of trading (price changes, volume of transactions, etc.) in a certain stock or in 'the averages' and then deducing from that pictured history the probable future trend.[2]

Whether technical analysis is an art (as Pring believes) or a science (as Edwards and Magee suggest), it is clear that it deals with making inferences about future price trends based on historical price information and other related data.

Technical analysis is a direct challenge to the traditional view that markets are efficient and technical analysis is useless. Earlier research by Eugene F. Fama found evidence that markets *are* efficient.[3] Alternatively, more recent research identifies patterns in historical stock prices.[4] This more recent empirical evidence gives merit to the use of technical analysis.

18.2   CHARTING

To the technical analyst, the chart is the place to find clues regarding the future price direction of an asset. Technical analysis uses various charts. All these charts are based

---

[1] See Martin J. Pring, *Technical Analysis Explained* (New York: McGraw-Hill, 1991), pp. 2–3.

[2] See Robert D. Edwards and John Magee, *Technical Analysis of Stock Trends*, 6th edn (New York: New York Institute of Finance, 1992), p. 4.

[3] See Eugene F. Fama, 'Efficient capital markets: a review of theory and empirical work', *Journal of Finance*, 25, 1970, pp. 383–417.

[4] See, for example, Eugene F. Fama and Kenneth R. French, 'Permanent and temporary components of stock prices', *Journal of Political Economy*, 98, 1988, pp. 247–73; Kenneth R. French and Richard Roll, 'Stock return variances: the arrival of information and reaction of traders', *Journal of Financial Economics*, 17, 1986, pp. 5–26; and Andrew W. Lo and A. Craig MacKinlay, 'Stock market prices do not follow random walks: evidence from a simple specification test', *Review of Financial Studies*, 1, 1988, pp. 41–66.

on historical prices. Thus, the users of these charts obviously do not believe in weak-form market efficiency.

18.2.1 Bar charts

Bar charts are charts that illustrate each day's (or week's or month's) high, low and closing price movements for a specified time period. Exhibit 18.1 shows a bar chart of Coca-Cola Company stock price for one week. For example, on Tuesday the high for Coke was $68.8125; the low was $68, which was also that day's closing price. In Exhibit 18.1, the straight lines give the distance between the high and low prices, and the protruding horizontal nubs designate the closing prices.

Technical analysts use bar charts to determine trends and to observe when these trends will reverse themselves. The **trendline** is a line drawn on a bar chart to identify a trend where the angle of this line will indicate whether it is an up or a down trendline. For example, Exhibit 18.2 shows both an up trendline and a down trendline. In Exhibit 18.2(a), an up trendline is drawn to touch the lowest prices over several days. Exhibit 18.2(b) shows a down trendline drawn to touch the highest prices over several days.

Historical price data are used to draw trendlines. However, the precise manner in which technical analysts draw up and down trendlines is an art. That is, there is no widespread agreement about what criteria to use to establish when a trend has begun or about exactly how to draw the trendlines. Also, the number of days to check in order to select from the two lowest points is arbitrary.

Once analysts have drawn a trendline, they follow stock prices to identify changes in the trend. Exhibit 18.2(a) examines historical prices over the last n days and uses the lowest two points to draw the up trendline. Of course, other criteria could have been used. Exhibit 18.2(b) is similar to Exhibit 18.2(a) with the exception that it is a down trend.

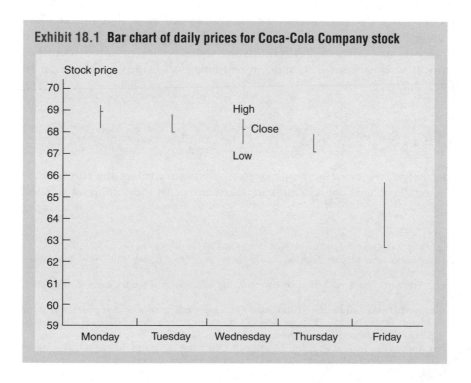

Exhibit 18.1 Bar chart of daily prices for Coca-Cola Company stock

Exhibit 18.2 Trendlines in technical analysis

(a) Penetration of an up trendline

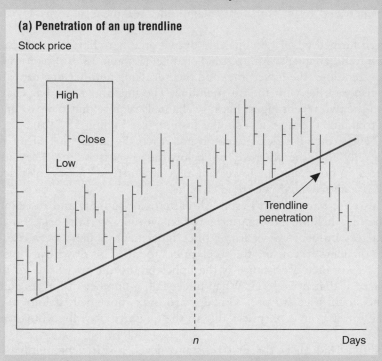

(b) Penetration of a down trendline

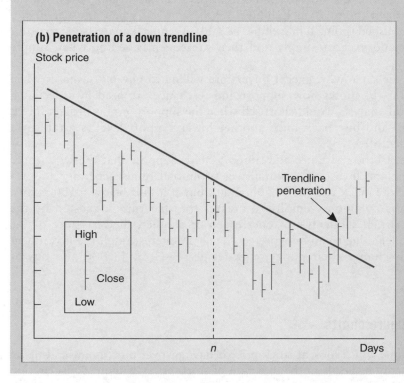

Source: Thomas A. Meyers, *The Technical Analysis Course* (Chicago: Probus Publishing, 1989), pp. 102, 103. Reprinted with permission of The McGraw-Hill Companies.

A trendline is said to be penetrated when market prices move across it. This penetration is viewed as a sell signal for an up trendline and a buy signal for a down trendline. When a trendline is penetrated by a 'sufficient' magnitude, technical analysts say the trend has changed.

A **channel** is a pattern formed when two lines are drawn on a bar chart. Exhibit 18.3 illustrates up and down trend channels. An up trend channel (Exhibit 18.3(a)) is formed by first drawing the up trendline (the lower line) and then drawing another line near the two recent highs but also parallel with the up trendline. The line above the bar chart, generally, cannot touch the two recent highs, because channels require that the two lines be parallel. The down trendline is drawn in a similar fashion (see Exhibit 18.3(b)).

Technical analysts believe that if stock prices do not reach the upper line of an up trend channel during a rally, then the price will fall below the lower trendline. They also assert that if stock prices do not reach the lower line of a down trend channel as prices fall, then the price will rise above the down trend channel.

Technical analysts also use bar charts to establish patterns of support and resistance (see Exhibit 18.4). The idea behind these patterns is that within a certain price range, demand and supply factors influence a security's price movement. When prices rise, a number of sellers enter the market, causing the stock prices to fall. This downward price movement is known as **resistance**. Resistance is the upper bound on prices due to the quantity of willing sellers at that price level. When prices fall, a number of buyers enter the market, causing the stock prices to rise. This upward price movement is known as **support**. Support is the lower bound on prices due to the quantity of willing buyers at that price level.

For example, in Exhibit 18.4(a), at the first resistance level, a sufficient number of shareholders are willing to sell, which keeps the price from rising above this resistance level. Once the resistance level is broken, the price moves up until supply exceeds demand and the rising price is hindered. Some technical analysts would buy when the resistance level is broken (point A in Exhibit 18.4(a)) and sell when another higher resistance level is established (point B in Exhibit 18.4(a)). Technical analysts try to profit by buying when demand exceeds supply and then subsequently selling when supply exceeds demand.

Support works in the same way, except buyers are willing to buy more shares when prices fall. Exhibit 18.4(b) shows how support and resistance are used in a declining market. Some technical analysts would short sell when the support level is broken (point A in Exhibit 18.4(b)) and buy back once another lower support level is established (point B in Exhibit 18.4(b)).

There is some logic to the resistance and support chart. Suppose that the Dow Jones index is at 10,000 points. Investment committees of mutual funds generally adopt a policy to sell stocks if the index rises to 10,500 and to buy if it falls below 9,500 points. This strategy which is commonly employed creates the structure suggested by the resistance–support chart. If suddenly, for one reason or another, the resistance or the support is penetrated (e.g. due to an unexpected change in interest rate), the investment committees generally change their policy, e.g. decide to sell at 11,000 and buy at 10,500.

18.2.2 Point-and-figure charts

In contrast to bar charts, which look at stock price behaviour over time, **point-and-figure charts** attempt to identify reversals in the direction of stock prices without consideration

Exhibit 18.3 Channels in technical analysis

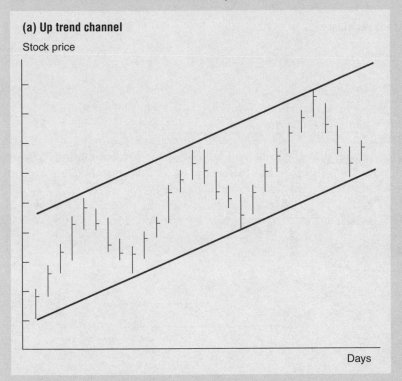

(a) Up trend channel

Stock price

Days

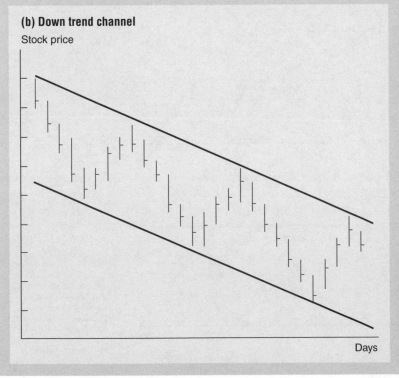

(b) Down trend channel

Stock price

Days

Source: Thomas A. Meyers, *The Technical Analysis Course* (Chicago: Probus Publishing, 1989), pp. 109–10. Reprinted with permission of The McGraw-Hill Companies.

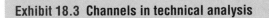

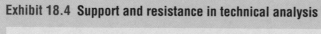

Exhibit 18.4 Support and resistance in technical analysis

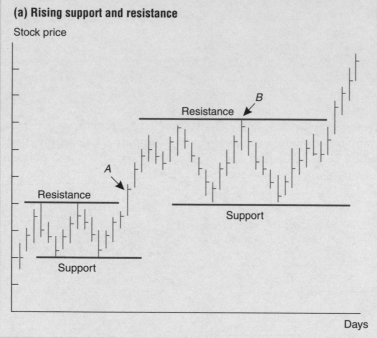

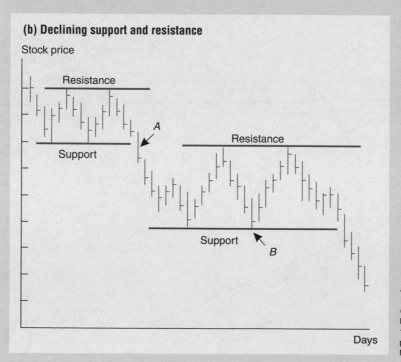

Source: Thomas A. Meyers, *The Technical Analysis Course* (Chicago: Probus Publishing, 1989), pp. 120, 121. Reprinted with permission of The McGraw-Hill Companies.

of time. Exhibit 18.5 is a point-and-figure chart constructed with daily closing prices. Notice that the chart is a series of Xs and Os positioned on a grid (see Exhibit 18.5(a)). The Xs represent price increases of, say, $2 or more, and the Os represent price decreases of, say, $2 or more. For example, in Exhibit 18.5(b), the stock price initially was at $18, and its first $2 move was up. Therefore, an X was placed in the first column by $20. Over the next few days the stock finally surpassed the $22 mark (without first falling below $18), so another X was placed in the first column at $22. Once again the stock rose to $24, so yet another X was added in the first column. After the price reached $24, the stock price fell more than $2. To show this, an O was placed in the second column on the row at $22. In this case, the price continued to fall to $16.

All of the trendline analysis, channels, and support and resistance information used in bar charts also can be applied to point-and-figure charts. Compare the general pattern in Exhibit 18.5 with Exhibits 18.1, 18.2, 18.3 and 18.4. Clearly, bar charts and point-and-figure charts look generally similar. Thus, technical rules developed for bar charts are also applied to point-and-figure charts. For example, some technical analysts would draw a down trendline, as illustrated in Exhibit 18.5(a). Point A shows a trendline penetration, and the technical analyst might view this as a bullish sign for this stock. In this example, the analyst would recommend buying this stock (see point A in Exhibit 18.5).

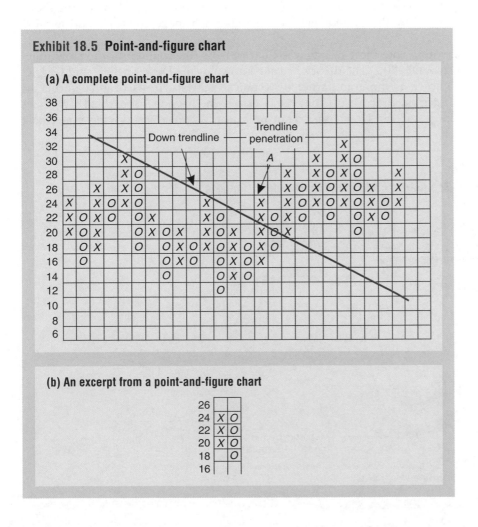

Exhibit 18.5 Point-and-figure chart

(a) A complete point-and-figure chart

(b) An excerpt from a point-and-figure chart

18.3 THEORETICAL BASIS OF TECHNICAL ANALYSIS

Technical analysts use certain tools with their charts to discern the future path of asset prices. Most interpretation of charts finds its roots in the Dow Theory. This section examines the basic tenets of the Dow Theory, as well as some of the other tools used by technical analysts.

18.3.1 Dow Theory

Most approaches to technical analysis assume that financial prices follow some sort of market cycle model. That is, overall prices tend to move through long trends of either rising or falling prices. Exhibit 18.6 illustrates a model of a market cycle. In theory, every 4 to $4^1/_2$ years, the market moves through a complete cycle. The broad double line, known as the **primary trend** cycle, represents this 4-to-$4^1/_2$-year cycle. Technical analysts assert that such broad trends appear in currencies, stocks, bonds, commodities and other financial assets. The solid black line that has more wave is known as the **intermediate trend,** which has a much shorter duration (from 3 weeks to 6 months). Finally, the **short-term trend,** denoted by the dotted line, documents much more volatility and is more erratic.

The first person to note these trends was Charles Dow (the founder of the Dow Jones news service), around 1900. The theory became known as the **Dow Theory,** and Charles Dow became known as the grandfather of technical analysis. In its original form, the Dow Theory asserted that a bull market is established when both the Dow Jones Industrial Average and the Dow Jones Transportation Average are moving up. A bear

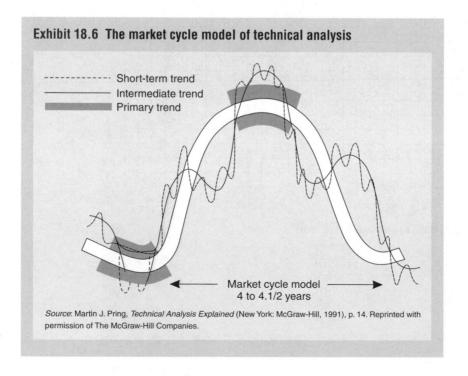

Exhibit 18.6 The market cycle model of technical analysis

- - - - - - - - Short-term trend
———— Intermediate trend
▬▬▬▬ Primary trend

Market cycle model
4 to 4.1/2 years

Source: Martin J. Pring, *Technical Analysis Explained* (New York: McGraw-Hill, 1991), p. 14. Reprinted with permission of The McGraw-Hill Companies.

market is established when the two indexes are moving down. The basic tenets of the Dow Theory can be summarized as follows:

1 No additional information is needed for the stock market apart from data on stock indexes.
2 The financial market has three distinct types of movements: the primary trend, the intermediate trend and short-term trends.
3 There is usually a positive relationship between a trend and the volume of shares traded.

The Dow Theory has been extended and reworked in many different ways, and most technical analysis theories originate from it.

Probably the most popular tool derived from the Dow Theory is moving averages to identify trends in stock prices, to which we turn next.

18.3.2 Moving averages

One of the most popular tools of technical analysis is the **moving average**. A simple moving average is built by taking the arithmetic average of a stock price over the past predetermined number of days and graphing these results over a period of time. For example, Exhibit 18.7 gives the closing prices of a stock for 20 days. The five-day moving average is found by taking closing prices for the past five days, adding them up, and dividing by 5. For example, on 8 January the five-day moving average can be calculated as

$$(68.9375 + 68 + 68.125 + 66.5625 + 62.6875)/5 = 66.8625$$

Exhibit 18.7 Calculating a five-day simple moving average for the Coca-Cola Company

Date (January 2002)	Closing price	Five-day total (A)	Five-day simple moving average (A/5)
4	$68.9375		
5	68		
6	68.125		
7	66.5625		
8	66.6875	$334.3125	$66.8625
11	63.75	329.125	$66.8625
12	60.9375	322.0625	64.4125
13	60.4375	314.375	62.875
14	60.125	307.9375	61.5875
15	58.75	304	60.8
18	60.375	300.625	60.125
19	60.8125	300.5	60.1
20	61.5	301.5625	60.3125
21	60.5625	302	60.4
22	60.6875	303.9375	60.7875
25	59.6875	303.25	60.65
26	59	301.4375	60.2875
27	58.625	298.5625	59.7125
28	58.25	296.25	59.25
29	57.3125	292.875	58.575

and on 11 January the earliest day (4 January) is dropped and the most recent one (11 January) is added. This process continues across the entire data set.

Investors compare the stock price to the moving average to identify trends. For example, one popular approach is that if the Dow Jones Industrial Index is above its 200-day moving average, then security prices should rise, and if it is below its 200-day moving average, then security prices should fall. Many technical analysts use moving averages in an attempt to identify the primary, intermediate and short-term trends.

Moving averages can also be used with individual stocks. For example, if a particular stock's price has been falling, then the moving average will typically be above the bar chart. If the stock's price subsequently rallies, breaking through the moving average line from below, technical analysts view this as a bullish sign. Alternatively, if a particular stock's price has been rising, then the moving average will typically be below the bar chart. If the stock's price subsequently falls, breaking through the moving average line from above, technical analysts view this as a bearish sign. As with other technical analysts' tools, there are many possible interpretations of moving averages.

18.4 TECHNICAL INDICATORS

At the very heart of technical analysis are charts that use technical indicators to interpret trends. Technical indicators typically draw from additional historical market-related data, such as volume of trading. Several technical indicators are believed to be leading indicators of future security price movements. These indicators can be classified as **breadth indicators**, which highlight overall market strength or weakness, and **sentiment indicators**, which highlight traders' opinions about the market. Because technical analyses rely on historical prices as well as other information (for example, volume), these methods are based on the semistrong inefficiency model of the market.

18.4.1 Breadth indicators

Breadth indicators include the advance–decline line, volume and new high/new low indicators. The **advance–decline line** is the number of advancing issues (stocks whose prices have gone up from the previous day) minus the number of declining issues (stocks whose prices have gone down from the previous day) on a particular day plus the cumulative total from the previous day (so trends can be monitored). Exhibit 18.8 provides some stock data from the NYSE Composite Index, a value-weighted index of all stocks traded on the NYSE. On 31 January 2002, advances (1,776) were higher than declines (823) by 953. Hence, the advance–decline line would be increased by 953 on 31 January. The advance–decline line on Day t (ADL_t) is the number of advancing issues on Day t (A_t) minus the number of declining issues on Day t (D_t) plus the cumulative total from the previous day ($\mathrm{ADL}_{t-1} - 1$). That is,

$$\mathrm{ADL}_t = A_t - D_t + \mathrm{ADL}_{t-1} - 1$$

In this case, if $\mathrm{ADL}_{30\,\mathrm{January}} = 1,500$, we have

$$\mathrm{ADL}_{31\,\mathrm{January}} = 1,776 - 823 + 1,500 = 2,453$$

Exhibit 18.8 NYSE composite index daily breadth

Daily	Jan 28	Jan 29	Jan 30	Jan 31
Issues Traded	3,354	3,324	3,326	3,349
Advances	**1,672**	**964**	**1,891**	**2,108**
Declines	**1,486**	**2,160**	**1,232**	**1,006**
Unchanged	196	200	203	235
New Highs	120	88	83	152
New Lows	24	48	70	22
Blocks	22,240	35,669	39,966	29,360
Total (000)	1,433,273	2,167,188	2,405,247	1,844,212

Source: *Barron's*, 4 February 2002, p. MW43. Barron's Online by Barron's. © 2002 by Dow Jones & Co., Inc. Reproduced with permission of Dow Jones & Co., Inc. in the format *Fundamentals of Investments* via Copyright Clearance Center.

Most technical analysts view a falling advance–decline line in a rising market as bearish and a rising advance–decline line in a falling market as bullish.

Many breadth indicators are based on trading volume, because technical analysts interpret changes in trading volume as indicators of the size of future price changes in securities. Most financial media report the volume of trading in individual securities. For example, a sharp rise in volume of a stock whose price has been rising is interpreted as a signal of even more dramatic price increases in the future. Alternatively, a sharp rise in volume of a stock whose price has been falling is interpreted to signal even more dramatic price declines in the future.

18.4.2 Sentiment indicators

Sentiment indicators attempt to gauge the overall mood, or sentiments, of investors. One measure of sentiment is a comparison of the number of stock market newsletters that are bullish with the number of those that are bearish. Technical analysts typically believe that on average, stock market newsletters are wrong. Hence, when the majority of newsletters are bearish, analysts interpret this as a bullish sign.

Another sentiment indicator is based on the quantity of **odd-lot trading**. Recall that an odd lot is any transaction involving fewer than 100 shares (trading in multiples of 100 is known as a *round lot*). Odd-lot trading is typically done by small investors, who, technical analysts believe, are usually wrong. Hence, technical analysts see odd-lot buying that exceeds odd-lot selling as a bearish signal, because they believe that small investors typically buy at the wrong time. One source for the amount of odd-lot trading is the market laboratory section related to stocks in the financial weekly *Barron's*.

Another sentiment indicator is the **put/call ratio**, which is found by dividing the volume of put option trading by the volume of call option trading. Technical analysts view excessive put buying as a bearish signal and excessive call buying as a bullish signal. Investors buy put options, which give them the right to sell stocks in the future, when they believe that stock prices will fall. Alternatively, investors buy call options, which give them the right to buy stocks in the future, when they believe that stock prices will rise. Therefore, when the volume of put buying exceeds the volume of call buying, it indicates that option buyers in the aggregate are bearish.

Finally, technical analysts also monitor the amount of short selling done by specialists. Recall that the specialist is the market maker on the NYSE. Specialists typically have superior information regarding a stock (they have the limit book – see Chapter 3) and are perceived as particularly good speculators. Hence, when specialists are selling short, it is a signal that the stock may decline. Specialists are also perceived as insiders, and investors want to mimic specialists' trading activities. Specialist short selling indicates a bearish view on a stock; hence, technical analysts would view increases in specialist short positions as bearish.

SUMMARY

■ *Describe a technical analyst's view of the market.*
Technical analysts believe that prices reflect investors' short-term attitudes, which may not be entirely rational. Thus, technical analysts believe that by studying short-term historical market data they can find clues regarding the future direction of security prices.

■ *Explain how technical analysts use charts to make inferences about future prices.*
Technical analysts plot market data on charts, such as bar charts and point-and-figure charts. The charts display historical information that enables technical analysts to extrapolate trends into the future.

■ *Identify the basic tools used by technical analysts.*
Most technical analysis procedures originate from the Dow Theory, which is based on the idea that prices tend to move in primary, intermediate and short-term trends. These trends are assessed mainly by using techniques of moving averages. Moving averages are obtained by averaging the most recent past price data.

■ *Describe some popular technical indicators.*
Two popular technical indicators are the breadth and sentiment indicators. The breadth indicators include the advance–decline line, volume and new high/new low indicators. The advance–decline line measures the number of stocks that rose compared with the number of stocks that fell. Sentiment indicators include stock market newsletters, odd-lot trading, the put/call ratio (a measure based on the volume of put and call option trading), and specialist short selling.

KEY TERMS

Advance–decline line	Moving average	Sentiment indicator
Bar chart	Odd-lot trading	Short-term trend
Breadth indicator	Point-and-figure chart	Support
Channel	Primary trend	Technical analysis
Dow Theory	Put/call ratio	Trendline
Intermediate trend	Resistance	

QUESTIONS

18.1 Given the following price data, draw a bar chart.

Day	High price	Low price	Closing price
0	$53\frac{1}{8}$	$50\frac{1}{2}$	$51\frac{3}{8}$
1	52	$48\frac{1}{8}$	$49\frac{3}{4}$
2	$53\frac{7}{8}$	$51\frac{1}{4}$	$53\frac{1}{8}$
3	54	$52\frac{1}{8}$	54
4	$55\frac{3}{8}$	$54\frac{3}{8}$	$54\frac{7}{8}$
5	$54\frac{3}{8}$	$52\frac{1}{8}$	$52\frac{1}{4}$
6	$56\frac{7}{8}$	55	$56\frac{3}{4}$
7	$58\frac{1}{2}$	57	$57\frac{1}{8}$
8	$59\frac{3}{8}$	$57\frac{1}{2}$	$58\frac{1}{2}$
9	$60\frac{1}{8}$	$59\frac{3}{8}$	60
10	61	$60\frac{1}{2}$	61

18.2 Given the data in Question 18.1, draw a point-and-figure chart using $1 gains and losses to determine when Xs and Os occur.

18.3 Given the following data for the past 10 days, calculate the five-day moving average for Days 5 through 10.

Day	High price	Low price	Closing price
1	$14\frac{7}{8}$	$13\frac{3}{4}$	$14\frac{1}{4}$
2	$15\frac{1}{2}$	$14\frac{7}{8}$	15
3	$17\frac{1}{2}$	$16\frac{1}{8}$	$16\frac{7}{8}$
4	19	$16\frac{1}{8}$	$18\frac{5}{8}$
5	$20\frac{1}{2}$	$17\frac{3}{8}$	$18\frac{3}{8}$
6	$18\frac{7}{8}$	$17\frac{3}{4}$	$18\frac{5}{8}$
7	$22\frac{1}{2}$	$19\frac{1}{2}$	21
8	22	$20\frac{7}{8}$	$21\frac{7}{8}$
9	$25\frac{1}{2}$	$20\frac{3}{8}$	$24\frac{3}{8}$
10	$22\frac{3}{4}$	$19\frac{7}{8}$	$22\frac{1}{2}$

18.4 Assuming that the advance–decline line for stocks in the NYSE Composite had a value of 1,237 on Day 0, calculate the advance–decline line for each of the following days. (Complete the table, and discuss your results.)

Day	Index value	Advancing issues	Declining issues
0			
1	250.13	1,055	1,199
2	248.37	1,757	580
3	251.87	1,143	1,194
4	252.11	757	1,410
5	253.98	969	1,197
6	254.54	722	1,418
7	255.01	938	1,193
8	254.39	906	1,260
9	257.72	645	1,460
10	260.18	862	1,230

18.5 Suppose the beta of a stock is 1.0, and the average rate of return over the past 20 years on the market portfolio was 12%. A technical analyst claims to have a method that signals buy and sell decisions. Over 10 years, she has made on average a return of 15% by trading in this stock.

(a) In your view, does the technical analyst have a method with which to buy and sell successfully?

(b) How would you change your answer if the beta of the stock were 2.0 and the risk-free interest rate were 4%?

18.6 A stock price is at $100. Suppose it goes up every day by $1/8 (lowest point = highest point = closing price). You want to draw a trendline.

(a) Does it make a difference whether you take the lowest two points in the first five days or the lowest two points in the first 20 days?

(b) How would you change your answer if the stock price went up every day by $1/8$%?

18.7 Suppose you have the following prices.

Day	High price	Low price	Closing price
1	$102	$98	$99
2	100	95	98
3	102	95	$97^{1}/_{2}$
4	101	100	$100^{3}/_{8}$

(a) Make a freehand drawing of the resistance and support lines.

(b) Suppose that on Days 5, 6 and 7 the prices have a high of $95 and a low of $90. Would you buy or sell the stock?

18.8 Suppose you have the following prices of a given stock:

Day	Price
1	$100
2	99
3	97
4	96
5	93
6	96
7	99

Draw the point-and-figure chart for price moves of the stock.

SELECTED REFERENCES

Clarke, Roger G., and Statman Meir. 'Bullish or bearish'. *Financial Analysts Journal*, May–June 1998, pp. 63–72.

Edwards, Robert D., and John Magee. *Technical Analysis of Stock Trends*, 6th edn. Boston: New York Institute of Finance, 1992.

Fama, Eugene F. 'Efficient capital markets: a review of theory and empirical work'. *Journal of Finance*, 25, 1970, pp. 383–417.

Fama, Eugene F., and Kenneth R. French. 'Permanent and temporary components of stock prices'. *Journal of Political Economy*, 98, 1988, pp. 247–73.

French, Kenneth R., and Richard Roll. 'Stock return variances: the arrival of information and reaction of traders'. *Journal of Financial Economics*, 17, 1986, pp. 5–26.

Jegadeesh, Narasimhan. 'Evidence of predictable behavior of security returns'. *Journal of Finance*, 45, July 1990, pp. 881–98.

Meyers, Thomas A. *The Technical Analysis Course*. Chicago: Probus Publishing, 1989.

Morris, Gregory L. *Candle Power: Advanced Candlestick Pattern Recognition and Filtering Techniques for Trading Stocks and Futures*. Chicago: Probus Publishing, 1992.

Pring, Martin J. *Technical Analysis Explained*. New York: McGraw-Hill, 1991.

SUPPLEMENTARY REFERENCES

Beckers, S., and G. Vaughn. 'Small is beautiful'. *The Journal of Portfolio Management*, Summer 2001, Vol. 27, No. 4.

Blitz, David, C., and A. Hottinga. 'Tracking error allocation'. *The Journal of Portfolio Management*, Summer 2001, Vol. 27, No. 4.

Chance, Don M., and Don Rich. 'The false teachings of the unbiased expectations hypothesis'. *The Journal of Portfolio Management*, Summer 2001, Vol. 27, No. 4.

Darrat, E.F., and M. Zhong. 'On testing the random walk hypothesis: A model-comparison approach'. *The Financial Review*, August 2000, Vol. 35, No. 3.

Appendix A
REVIEW OF TIME VALUE CONCEPTS

This appendix reviews a selection of corporate finance topics that are directly related to investments. Understanding the time value of money is crucial to making prudent investments. When you make investments, you reallocate cash flows over time. Specifically, you pay out money now with the expectation of receiving more in the future. Here, we review the concepts of future value, present value, uneven cash flows, net present value and internal rate of return.

Future value represents the value of a set of expected cash flows at a specific point in the future if compounded at a given interest rate. For a single cash flow today, CF_0, with an interest rate i for a period of a certain length n, we have the future value (FV_n) as follows:

$$FV_n = CF_0(1 + i)^n \qquad (A1)$$

For example, a $100 investment today ($CF_0 =$ $100) at 10% ($i = 0.10$) for five years ($n = 5$) will be worth

$$FV_5 = \$100(1 + 0.10)^5$$
$$= \$100(1.6105) \cong \$161.05$$

in five years.

The future value of a $1 annuity (which is $1 cash flow each period starting next period and denoted $FVIFA_{i,n}$, or future value interest factor for an annuity) can be found using the following equation:

$$FVIFA_{i,n} = \frac{(1 + i)^n - 1}{i} \qquad (A2)$$

This type of annuity is known as an *ordinary annuity*, because the first cash flow occurs one period from today, and we are determining the value when the final cash flow occurs. Another type of annuity occurs when the cash flows start today. The value one period is after the last pay-ment occurs. This type of annuity is known as an *annuity due*. All references in this appendix are to ordinary annuities. The future value of an annuity (FVA) with a given payment stream (denoted PMT) is therefore

$$FVA_n = PMT(FVIFA_{i,n})$$
$$= PMT\,\frac{(1 + i)^n - 1}{i} \qquad (A3)$$

For example, a $100 annuity (PMT = $100) at 10% for five years will be worth $610.50 at the end of five years:

$$FVA_5 = \$100\,\frac{(1 + 0.1)^5 - 1}{0.1}$$
$$\cong \$100\,\frac{1.6105 - 1}{0.1}$$
$$= \$100(6.105) = \$610.50$$

Present value represents the value today of future cash flows discounted at a specified interest rate. For a single cash flow n periods from now (CF_n) with a specified interest rate i, the present value is represented as follows:

$$PV = \frac{CF_n}{(1 + i)^n} \qquad (A4)$$

Note that because CF_n is the future value, we can write $CF_n = FV_n$. If we let $CF_n = \$161.05$, $i = 0.10$ and $n = 5$, we have the following:

$$PV = \frac{\$161.05}{(1 + 0.10)^5} \cong \$100$$

The present value interest factor of a $1 annuity (denoted $PVIFA_{i,n}$) can be found using the following equation:

$$PVIFA_{i,n} = \frac{1 - \left[\dfrac{1}{(1 + i)^n}\right]}{i} \qquad (A5)$$

For a given periodic payment amount (PMT), we have the present value of an annuity as

$$PVA_n = PMT(PVIFA_{i,n})$$

$$= PMT \frac{1 - \left[\dfrac{1}{(1 + i)^n}\right]}{i} \qquad (A6)$$

For example, a $100 annuity discounted at 10% for five years is worth $379.10 today:

$$PVA_5 = \$100 \frac{1 - \dfrac{1}{(1 + 0.1)^5}}{0.1}$$

$$\cong \$100 \frac{0.37908}{0.1} = \$379.08$$

In many cases, the series of cash flows are not the same amount each period (that is, the cash flows do not represent an annuity). Dividends, for example, are not necessarily the same each period. In this case, each cash flow must be discounted separately. Specifically, the present value of a set of future cash flows is as follows:[1]

$$PV = \sum_{t=1}^{n} (1 + i)^t \qquad (A7)$$

where CF_t represents the cash flow occurring at time t (e.g. CF_1 is the cash flow at the first period). For example, a three-year bond that pays $100 coupon at the end of each year, returns the original investment of $1,000 at the end of three years, and is discounted at 8%, is worth the following:

$$PV = \frac{\$100}{(1 + 0.08)^1} + \frac{\$100}{(1 + 0.08)^2}$$

$$+ \frac{\$100 + \$1,000}{(1 + 0.08)^3}$$

$$\cong \$92.59 + \$85.73 + \$873.22$$

$$= \$1,051.54$$

Net present value (NPV) is simply the present value of future cash flows minus any initial investment or cash outlay. Specifically, if the investment is represented as a negative cash flow, then NPV is as follows:

$$NPV = \sum_{t=0}^{n} \frac{CF_t}{(1 + i)^t} \qquad (A8)$$

where for $t = 0$ (rather than $t = 1$), we have the cash outflow CF_0, which is negative. For example, suppose we purchased the bond just described for $1,020. The NPV would be as follows:

$$NPV = \frac{-\$1,020}{(1 + 0.08)^0} + \frac{\$100}{(1 + 0.08)^1}$$

$$+ \frac{\$100}{(1 + 0.08)^2} + \frac{\$100 + \$1,000}{(1 + 0.08)^3}$$

Because $(1 + 0.08)^0 = 1$, we have

$$NPV \cong \$31.54$$

The internal rate of return (IRR) calculation finds the interest rate, i, that will result in a zero NPV. Specifically, let IRR denote the interest rate that solves the following:

$$\sum_{t=0}^{n} \frac{CF_t}{(1 + IRR)^t} = 0 \qquad (A9)$$

Unfortunately, solving for IRR is complicated and requires a calculator or trial-and-error techniques. For example, the IRR that solves the previous bond illustration was found, using a financial calculator, to be 9.207%. Thus, we observe the following:

$$\frac{-\$1,020}{(1 + 0.09207)^0} + \frac{\$100}{(1 + 0.09207)^1}$$

$$+ \frac{\$100}{(1 + 0.09027)^2} + \frac{\$100 + \$1,000}{(1 + 0.09207)^3}$$

$$\cong -\$1,020 + \$91.57 + \$83.85 + \$844.58$$

$$= 0$$

The IRR on future cash flows of a bond is called the yield to maturity (see Chapter 7).

---

1 Recall that

$$\sum_{i=1}^{n} x_i = x_1 + x_2 + \ldots + x_n$$

For example, if $x_1 = 11$, $x_2 = 19$ and $x_3 = 5$, we have

$$\sum_{i=1}^{3} x_i = x_1 + x_2 + x_3 = 11 + 19 + 5 = 35$$

Appendix B
INTERNATIONAL WEBSITES

advfn.com
A largely UK stock-market oriented site which provides live online share prices, news, charts, up-to-the-minute updates on indices, portfolio management tools and email alerts.

alumni.adweb.co.uk
Offers links to over 120 English language newspapers, and their resources including archives from across the world.

americanexpress.com
Features online stockbroking, a mutual funds super-market, foreign exchange rates, travel-related money and insurance as well as hotels and tickets.

bagfs.com
British Airways Global Financial Services – offshore banking, performance and information on offshore investments.

bankofengland.co.uk
The official site for the Bank of England, the UK central bank. It offers full, downloadable, versions of published reports such as the Bank of England Quarterly and details of interest rate decisions.

bigcharts.com
Provides charts of US stocks, mutual funds and market indices with a large degree of user choice on presenta-tion. There is a link to livecharts.com for investors who want charts 'streaming'.

bloomberg.com
Online version of one of the best known news and prices services used by professional investors. It fea-tures stock price quotes, historic performance of com-panies, and press coverage of chosen firms.

businesswire.com
A mix of specific news on selected industries, forth-coming IPOs, management changes, mergers and acquisitions, and current headlines and company news. Links to many other sites.

cantorindexcfd.com
Deals in contracts for difference, a method of low-cost buying and selling which avoids UK stamp duty. The site offers prices in top US and European companies plus the 350 biggest quoted firms in the UK.

carol.co.uk
Offers links to sites operated by over 3,000 leading companies in the US, Europe and the UK – mainly used by those looking for online company reports.

cbs.marketwatch.com
US based headline stories, market data, mutual funds, analyst ratings and discussion groups.

cityindex.co.uk
Spread betting company making a market in exchange traded futures and options, indices, bonds, currencies, interest rates, commodities, as well as the 250 biggest US stocks and the 500 biggest UK shares.

citywire.co.uk
News leads including directors' dealings and legal 'inside' information, listings and links to mutual funds, share prices with a 20-minute delay, technology news and regular e-mail alerts.

companiesonline.com
Information including addresses, directors, sales and profitability on over 100,000 quoted and unquoted US companies.

corporateinformation.com
A portal leading to worldwide industry and company information via links to other sites.

daytrader.co.uk
Finance headlines, company performance analysis and details of forthcoming IPOs in the US and UK.

digitallook.com
Equity research including brokers' forecasts, news, directors and their dealings plus institutional buying and selling in selected stocks.

dowjones.com
From the creators of the index series – information on constituents plus updates on index levels.

earningswhispers.com
Many US investors now relegate published broker research to second place, preferring unofficial 'chat'

or 'whispers' from traders and other market participants.

easdaq.be
The site for Europe's high-tech market modelled after the US Nasdaq. Has information on forthcoming IPOs, regulatory issues, listed stocks.

economist.com
The online version of the weekly news magazine whose influence – and opinionated editorials – stretch far beyond its UK base.

efinancialnews.com
Regular news service based on London's Financial News magazine aimed at fund management professionals and advanced investors.

eye4money.com
Investor education and personalised portfolio information.

federalreserve.gov
The US central bank site which features general information, articles and speeches on US monetary policy.

financialweb.com
Global e-finance marketplace with news, company profiles, small capitalisation stocks speciality, mutual funds, market buzz and due diligence reviews.

finance.news.com.au
News on Australian companies and markets from Interactive News.

fool.com and fool.co.uk
American and British versions of The Motley Fool website. This is a mix of investor information and education with the Fool philosophy, which demystifies investment by preaching how private investors can often outperform professionals.

fsa.gov.uk
Information, warnings, regulatory updates, and access to lists of approved brokers from UK investment watchdog the Financial Services Authority.

ft.com
Offers headlines and articles from the Financial Times with extra material from the site's own journalists. Aimed at smaller investors and those with money management needs.

funds-sp.com
Standard & Poors' performance statistics and details of 38,000 mutual funds across the globe.

gilt.co.uk
Despite its name, this is not operated by the UK government but by a broker specialising in UK government

stocks. It is a mine of information including regularly updated prices and yields.

globefund.com
News and commentary site focused on the Canadian mutual fund industry.

gni.co.uk
Has low-cost 24-hour dealing on futures quoted on the Liffe and Eurex markets.

gnitouch.com
For investors in contracts for differences, a low-cost method of accessing equities. It features real-time prices, charts, news and research on the Standard & Poor's 500, the Nasdaq 100 and the UK's biggest 350 companies.

growthcompany.co.uk
Linked to a magazine, this provides g stock prices, company history, statements and news releases from smaller UK companies including links to company sites.

hemscott.co.uk
Delayed share prices, information on UK quoted companies including recent news releases, directors, addresses and charts.

hoovers.co.uk
Global business news plus information on over 50,000 companies worldwide including sales, profits, top personnel, products and details of competitors.

icreditreport.com
Enables individuals to discover US company and individual credit ratings. Aimed at businesses and the plain curious.

iii.co.uk
UK stock market quotes, company information, discussion groups, and links to mutual funds and other packaged investments.

intermoney.com
Up-to-date bulletins on the international money markets including interbank rates, forward and spot rates. Aimed at serious investors and professionals.

investmentfunds.org.uk
Facts, news and statistics from the Association of Unit Trusts and Investment Funds, the UK trade body for open ended mutual funds.

investorama.com
A 'personal finance learning community' specialising in US mutual funds and investor education.

investorwords.com
Online lexicon specialising in financial, business and economic terms.

itruffle.com

UK site specialising in 'sniffing' out information on small quoted companies. It offers real-time interviews with selected CEOs as well as more general share price and index updates.

itulip.com

Named after the 17th-century Dutch tulip bulb price bubble, this site is the antidote for investors who fear being carried away on the next market mania. It features the '90 per cent club' – stocks which have fallen by 90 or more per cent since their peak.

londonstockexchange.com

The LSE's site contains share prices with a 20-minute delay, information on listed companies, press releases and research material.

marketeye.com also marketeye.co.uk

Internet version of the screen service used by market professionals. It features news, delayed share prices, and recent company information.

mlhsbc.com

Access to up-to-date investment research from 1,100 analysts worldwide. Also, investor education, charts and market data – as well as online investing and banking.

moneycentral.msn.com

Personal finance site aimed at US citizens with links to Reuters, American Express, Merrill Lynch and Charles Schwab.

moneyextra.com

UK personal money site offering loans and tax free savings.

moneynet-offshore.com

Aimed at the first-time offshore investor who needs basic information on jurisdictions as well as specific product information.

moreover.com

Daily headline round-up from 1,500 sources. They can be sorted by industry or country headings.

nasdaq.com

News and prices from the US high-tech company exchange. It has details of forthcoming IPOs, share graphs, company information and links to individual firms. And investors can even buy Nasdaq souvenirs such as mugs, t-shirts and baseball caps online.

ny.frb.org

From the New York branch of the Federal Reserve Board. It has decisions, speeches and articles from the Federal Open Market Committee, details of US government bonds, economic education, economic research and links to the US Treasury.

offshore.net

A guide to offshore bank accounts plus free access to portfolio and fund performance figures. There is up to date financial and share price information and an investment-oriented discussion board.

prnewswire.com

Source of US company releases covering results, major acquisitions and disposals, mergers and acquisitions, and initial public offerings. Aimed primarily at journalists, substantial parts of the site are free for the general public.

rate.net

Interest and other rates from over 11,000 US financial institutions in some 175 international markets. There are also links to bank and other money sites.

reuters.com

World political news as well as industrial, business and financial bulletins. It features interest rates, foreign exchange and has a 'global stock look-up' facility that provides information on a wide ranges of companies. The site also has a 'risk grading' tool.

riskgrades.com

Measures stocks for volatility against cash holdings taking interest rates, currency and markets into account. One useful tool tells if an asset's volatility is increasing or decreasing.

sec.gov

The US Securities and Exchanges Commission's site with statements on enforcement, rulemaking and settlements. It also has sections devoted to small business and investor protection plus links to professional organisations, federal agencies, the Library of Congress, Department of Justice and the Office of Foreign Asset Controls.

sec.gov/edaux/wedgar

Edgar stands for Electronic Data Gathering Analysis and Retrieval. It is an online database of US corporate information.

spreadexfinancials.com

Tax and commission-free trading via spread betting in the world's major stockmarkets and in the top 350 UK shares. Online investors can also take positions in bonds, currencies, and interest rates.

trustnet.com

UK site specialising in closed and open ended funds. Investors can regularly update portfolio valuations.

uksif.org

Information and opinions on socially responsible investment in the UK.

virtualtrader.co.uk

Investors can create virtual portfolios to try out investment concepts.

wallstreetcity.com

Features stock prices, international markets, financial planning and portfolio techniques.

worldbank.org

Information on the bank's activities, copies of reports and speeches.

wsj.com

The online version of the Wall Street Journal complete with archive access.

xe.net/map/

A simple currency conversion site aimed at travellers rather than foreign exchange dealers.

Source: First printed in British Airways *High Life* magazine, May 2001. © Tony Levine 2001. Reprinted with permission.

GLOSSARY

Abnormal rate of return Returns that are above what we would expect to earn, given the level of risk taken.

Accelerated earnings When the growth rate of earnings is increasing.

Accounting anomalies Trading strategies that generate abnormal returns based on observed accounting numbers.

Active investment strategy An investment strategy in which the portfolio manager actively manages investments by altering the proportions of assets in the portfolio.

Actual margin Initial investment as a percentage of the current market value.

Adjusted rate of return The simple rate of return adjusted for the effects of dividends.

Advance–decline line A measure that compares the number of stocks that rose with the number of stocks that fell.

Advanced estimates The first estimate of GDP released about one month after the measurement period.

Agency risk The risk that managers do not act in the owner's best interest.

Aggressive stock A stock with a beta greater than 1.

Alpha The intercept of a regression line.

American depository receipts (ADRs) Receipts for foreign shares held in a US bank.

American-style option An option that can be exercised early.

Amortizing swaps An interest rate swap where the notional principal declines based on an amortization schedule.

Anomalies Unanticipated events that can offer investors the opportunity of earning abnormal returns.

APT performance index Performance index based on the APT.

Arbitrage A zero investment portfolio that yields positive future returns.

Arbitrage pricing theory (APT) A linear relationship between expected return and risk derived by assuming that there is no arbitrage profit in the market.

Arithmetic average Figure obtained by adding up the returns of n observations and dividing this sum by n.

Arithmetic method Adds the rates of return and divides by the number of observations.

Asked price Price at which investors can buy securities.

Asked rate The discount rate at which Treasury bills can be purchased.

Asset Something owned by a business, institution, partnership, or individual that has monetary value.

Asset allocation The proportioning of an investment portfolio among asset classes.

At-the-money An option that would generate no cash flow if exercised now and liquidated.

Balance sheet An accounting statement showing the assets, liabilities and equity of a firm on a specific date.

Bank discount rate The interest rate charged to banks when they borrow directly from the central bank, for example the Bank of England, the Federal Reserve.

Bank reserves The percentage of deposits that banks must hold in non-interest bearing assets.

Bankers' acceptance Money market security that facilitates international trade.

Bar chart A graph showing price movements over time with high, low, and closing prices.

Basis The difference between the current spot price and the futures price.

Benchmark revisions Revisions to GDP made for estimates covering the past three years.

Beta The risk index of an individual's assets and portfolios alike; it is a measure of systematic risk.

Bid price Price at which investors can sell securities.

Bid-ask spread Asked price minus the bid price.

Bid rate The discount rate at which Treasury bills can be sold.

Blue chip stock Stock of a large, financially sound corporation.

Bond A financial contract that typically has a stated maturity and periodic interest payments.

Bond indenture A document detailing the terms of a bond issue.

Breadth Volume of orders above and below current price.

Breadth indicators Measures of overall market strength or weakness.

Broker A person who acts as an intermediary between a buyer or seller and the market.

Broker loan rate *See* Call loan rate.

Budget deficit When a government spends more in a given period than its tax revenues.

Bull spread An option strategy designed to allow investors to profit if prices rise, but limit their losses if prices fall.

Business cycle A period expansion and contraction of aggregate economic activity as measured by real GDP.

Business risk The risk that the firm cannot operate profitably.

Buyback share Purchase of identical share to cover a short sale or where a company buys back some of its shares from shareholders.

Callable bonds Bonds that can be repurchased by the issuing corporation at a stated price.

Call loan rate Interest rate charged on margin traders.

Call market Trading only occurs at specified times.

Call option A contract giving the right to buy a specified amount of an underlying asset during some period in the future at a predetermined price; gives an investor the right to buy a specified stock at a specified price on or before a specified date.

Candlestick chart A bar chart that includes the opening price as well as the high, low, and closing prices.

Candlestick line A graphical representation of the open, high, low, and closing prices.

Cap An option-based instrument that sets a ceiling on the impact of a risk variable.

Capital asset pricing model (CAPM) A model describing the relationship between beta and expected return.

Capital gains Profits earned when assets are sold at a higher price than purchased.

Capital market A market for bonds with maturities greater than one year and stocks.

Capital market line (CML) The highest sloped line achievable on the expected return and standard deviation graph.

Capital market security Long-term bonds and stocks.

Cash basis Calculated bond rates of return that ignore the accrued interest.

Cash dividend Payments to common stockholders from the firm that issued the stock.

Cash matching strategy An income immunization strategy that assures future cash needs are supplied.

Cash settled The option buyer receives the intrinsic value of the option at expiration automatically.

Cash settlement The exchange of cash rather than the physical asset in a futures contract.

Certainty When the value of an asset is known with probability 1.

Channel A pattern formed when two parallel lines are drawn on a bar chart, showing the up and down prices.

Characteristic line The linear relationship between an asset and the market portfolio.

Churning Excessive trading for the purpose of generating commissions.

Civilian unemployment rate The number of unemployed persons as a percentage of civilians working or actively seeking work.

Closed-end funds A mutual fund that cannot issue more shares.

Closing transaction A transaction that offsets an asset already held.

Coincident indicators Economic statistics that are supposed to move with the business cycle.

Collar An option-based instrument that sets both a ceiling and a floor on the impact of a risk variable.

Commercial paper Unsecured Notes of corporations, usually issued at a discount.

Commission broker A broker who is paid a fee for each trade that is conducted.

Commodity swap A contract to exchange payments based on a specific commodity price.

Common factor A factor that affects all asset prices, not necessarily at the same magnitude, e.g. interest rate, inflation rate, unemployment rate and rate of return on the market portfolio.

Common-factor news News that affects all stocks.

Common stock A security representing part ownership of a firm.

Concentration ratio A measure of how much of the industry is dominated by the largest firms.

Conduit Firms that sell pooled mortgages.

Conduit theory Capital gains and ordinary income should not be double taxed with investment companies.

Contingent claim *See* Derivative security.

Contingent immunization An investment strategy designed to accommodate both the desire of bond managers to trade actively and the desire of investors to minimize interest rate risk.

Constant dividend growth model The stock valuation model that assumes that dividends grow at a constant rate.

Continuous market Trading can occur any time the exchange is open.

Contraction The phase of the business cycle after a peak and before a trough.

Conversion premium The value of the option to convert in a bond.

Conversion price Par value divided by the conversion ratio.

Conversion ratio The number of stocks per bond issued when the bond is converted.

Conversion value Intrinsic value of a bond if immediately converted.

Convertible bond Contains an option to convert the bond into some stock.

Convexity A measure of the curvature of the bond's price-yield relationship, used in price immunization strategies.

Corporate bond Debt securities issued by corporations to finance investment in new plant and equipment.

Corporate governance Method of controlling the corporation.

Correlation A unitless measure of the degree of dependency between two assets.

Cost of carry model A futures pricing model based on the implied cost of owning the underlying asset.

Counterparties The two entities participating in a swap.

Coupon-bearing bond A bond that pays periodic interest payments.

Coupon payment The fixed periodic interest payment on bonds.

Coupon yield The promised annual coupon rate.

Covariance A measure of the degree of dependency between two assets.

Covered call writing An option strategy composed of buying a stock and writing a call option. The profit/loss from this strategy corresponds to that in put writing.

Covered position Using options when the underlying asset is already owned.

Credit quality A measure of the likelihood of default; letters are assigned such as AAA, AA, and so forth.

Credit risk The risk that the bond issue's interest or principal will not be paid.

Crossborder bonds Bonds that firms issue in the international market.

Cumulative abnormal rate of return (CAR) The amount of abnormal return accumulated over time.

Cumulative preferred stock Dividends accumulate if they are not paid.

Currency swaps A contract to exchange different currencies on specified dates.

Current yield The stated annual coupon payment divided by the current bond price.

Cyclical stock Stock moves with the business cycle.

Date of record The date ownership is assessed for dividends.

Day order Order that expires at the end of the day.

Debentures Unsecured bonds.

Declaration date Date dividend is announced.

Defensive stock A stock with a beta less than 1; moves opposite the business cycle.

Depth When traders are willing to trade at prices above and below the current price.

Derivative security An asset that derives its value from another asset.

Direct method A method of reporting the statement of cash flow that gives the cash receipts and payments.

Discount A closed-end fund trading below NAV, as a percentage of NAV.

Discount rate The method of quoting Treasury bill interest rates; the required rate of return, given the riskiness of the stock.

Display rule Requires that limit orders placed by customers and priced better than a specialist's or market maker's quote must be displayed.

Dividend discount model (DDM) Valuation Model based on the present value of cash dividends.

Divisible Assets of which you are able to buy small portions.

Divisor A number used in price-weighted indexes that is adjusted for security changes such as stock splits.

Dow theory A technical theory that is based on primary, intermediate, and short-term trends.

Dual listing Security listed on more than one exchange.

Duration The holding period that balances the price effect against the reinvestment effect.

Duration drift The change in duration due to the passage of time.

Duration matching strategy An income immunization strategy that matches asset duration with the duration of the liabilities.

Efficient frontier The set of all investment strategies with the highest mean for a given variance.

Efficient market A market in which prices reflect all relevant information about the stock.

Efficient portfolio A portfolio that is not dominated by the m-v rule by any other portfolio.

EMT The theory that all assets are correctly priced and that there are no 'bargains' in the market.

Eurodollars A deposit denominated in US dollars held in a bank outside the United States.

European-style option An option that cannot be exercised early.

Event anomalies Trading strategies that generate abnormal returns based on specific events.

Ex-ante value Forecasted rate of return used in estimating statistics.

Excess return or abnormal return Deviation from the return predicted by the CAPM.

Ex-dividend date First day when stockholders no longer receive dividends if stock is purchased.

Execution costs The cost of setting prices.

Exercise Make use of a right available in a contract (e.g. in a put option or a call option).

Exercise price *See* strike price.

Exercising Buying or selling assets through an option contract.

Expansion The phase of the business cycle after a trough and before a peak.

Expected return A measure of the average return anticipated on an asset.

Expiration date The date on which the option contract expires.

Ex-post average The historical average rate of return on an asset.

Ex-post rate of return Historical rate of return used in estimating statistics.

Face value *See* Par value.

Fallen angels Investment grade bonds that have subsequently been downgraded to a speculative grade.

Family of funds Several different mutual funds offered by the same investment company.

Federal agency bond US government agency bond, such as FNMA.

Federal funds US money market securities facilitating interbank borrowing.

Federal funds rate The interest rate charged to US banks when they borrow other banks' excess reserves.

Fiduciary Must act for the benefit of another party.

Financial assets Intangible assets, such as stocks and bonds.

Financial engineering The design, development, and implementation of innovative financial instruments and processes, and the formulation of creative solutions in finance.

Financial risk The risk related to debt.

Financial statement A report that contains basic accounting data which help investors to understand the firm's financial history.

Financial statement analysis Analysis of a firm's financial statements to assess the worth of its securities as well as its ability to meet its financial obligations.

Firm anomalies Trading strategies that generate abnormal returns based on firm-specific characteristics.

Firm-specific news News that only affects a specific firm.

First market Exchange-traded securities traded on the exchange.

Fiscal policy Taxation and spending policies by a government designed to achieve GDP growth, relatively full employment and stable prices.

Fixed for floating swap An interest rate swap where the payments are based on a fixed rate and a floating rate.

Floor An option-based instrument that sets a floor on the impact of a risk variable.

Floor broker A person who handles buying and selling futures contracts for others; brokers who are willing to work for other member firms to assist in the trading process.

Foreign exchange expectations The relationship between the current forward foreign exchange rate and the expected future spot exchange rate.

Forward contract A contract to do something in the future, for example borrow or lend money.

Forward foreign exchange contract Obligates an investor to deliver a specified quantity of one currency in return for a specified amount of another currency.

Forward foreign exchange rate The exchange rate available today to exchange currency at some specified date in the future.

Forward rate The yield covering a period of time starting in the future.

Fourth market Exchange-traded issues traded directly between buyer and seller.

Frictionless market A market where trading is costless to conduct.

Fundamental analysis Assesses the intrinsic value of a firm; trading strategies are based on the asset's publicly-available information.

Futures Commission Merchants (FCMs) People qualified to trade futures contracts.

Futures contract An agreement to make or take delivery of an asset at a later date at a given price; the trading price of a futures contract.

GCAPM General capital asset pricing model that allows investors to hold a small number of assets in the portfolio.

General obligation bond (USA) Backed only by the municipality.

Geometric average Figure obtained by the product of n observations and years (1 + rates of return), taking the $1/n$ root and subtracting 1.

Geometric compounding Used when assuming any cash payments are reinvested.

Geometric method Compound rate of return that mimics an investor's actual performance.

Good-till-cancelled order (GTC) An order to trade that is *effective* until cancelled.

Gross Domestic Product (GDP) The total of goods and services produced in an economy.

Gross spread Difference between the firm commitment price and the issue price.

Growth stock Stocks from smaller firms having sales and earnings growth in excess of the industry average.

Hedge A technique used to limit loss potential.

Hedge ratio The number of stocks to buy or sell with options such that the future portfolio value is risk-free.

High grade Bonds with credit quality of AAA or AA.

Holding period rate The rate of return earned on a bond by holding it for the next period.

Horizon matching strategy An income immunization strategy that cash matches over the next few years and duration matches the rest.

Immunization strategies Strategies that seek to neutralize the adverse effects of changes in yield to maturity.

Income immunization strategies Those strategies that ensure adequate future cash flow.

Income statement An accounting statement showing the flow of sales, expenses and earnings during a specified period.

Income stock High-dividend-paying stock.

Index funds Passively managed funds that try to mimic a specified index.

Index method Method for calculating rates of return that is based on initial and terminal values.

Indifference curve A curve representing points of indifference for assets having different expected returns and standard deviations.

Indirect method A method of reporting the statement of cash flow that takes net income and, through a series of adjustments, reconciles it to cash from operations.

Industry allocation The decision as to what proportion to invest in each industry.

Inefficient frontier The set of all investment strategies with the lowest variance (below the minimum variance portfolio).

Inefficient portfolio A portfolio that is dominated by the m-v rule by at least one other portfolio.

Inflation risk The risk related to the purchasing power of an investment.

Information asymmetry Differences in information available to different participants.

Initial margin Initial investment in a margin trade, in per cent; money the option writer sends to the OCC to sell the specific options.

Initial public offerings (IPOs) Securities traded in the primary market for the first time.

Interest-rate parity The relationship between the forward foreign exchange rate and nominal interest rates.

Interest rate risk The risk faced by bond investors when market interest rates change.

Interest rate swap A contract to exchange payments based on interest rates.

Interim rate of return The rate of return earned between cash flows.

Intermarket spread swap Speculating on bonds in different markets.

Intermediate trend A trend lasting from 3 weeks to 6 months in price data.

In-the-money An option that would generate positive cash flow if exercised now and liquidated.

Intrinsic value The value of the option if immediately exercised, or zero, whichever is greater.

Investment Financial capital used in an effort to create more money.

Investment bankers These help firms issue IPOs.

Investment company An organization that pools investors' money and invests it in securities.

Investment grade Bonds rated BBB (or Baa) or above.

Investment policy A written document detailing the objectives and constraints for the investment.

Investment trust A closed-end fund.

Jensen's performance index A performance measure based on the SML.

Junk bonds Very risky, higher coupon bonds; *see also* speculative grade.

Lagging indicators Economic statistics that are supposed to move behind the business cycle.

Leading indicators Economic statistics that are supposed to move ahead of the business cycle.

Levered portfolio A portfolio partially financed by borrowing.

Life cycle A discernible pattern over the life of an industry.

Limit order Trade only at a specified price.

Linking method Method for calculating rates of return that multiplies 1 plus the interim rate of return.

Liquidity preference hypothesis (LPH) A hypothesis stating that longer-term bonds should have a higher yield due to investors' preferences for liquidity.

Liquidity premium The difference between the yield based on the unbiased expectations hypothesis and the actual yield.

Load The fee paid as a sales commission to vendors of mutual funds.

Local A person who trades for his own account in a futures pit.

Local expectations hypothesis (LEH) A hypothesis stating that all similar bonds, except maturity, will have the same holding period rate of return.

Long position An agreement to *take* delivery in the futures market.

Long position in an option Refers to extended buying options.

Maintenance margin The dollar amount that must be kept at the OCC throughout the life of the contract; percentage of the amount of securities that must always be set aside as margin.

Margin call A broker calls for more collateral to be posted.

Margin trading Buying securities in part with borrowed money.

Mark to market Taking profits and losses daily on futures contracts.

Market A means by which products are bought and sold.

Market capitalization Market value of all shares outstanding.

Market maker Traders who post the bid and asked prices.

Market microstructure The functional setup of a market.

Market order Trade at the best existing price.

Market portfolio The optimum portfolio with riskless borrowing and lending.

Market segmentations hypothesis (MSH) A hypothesis stating that different maturity bonds trade in separate segmented markets.

Marketable security Securities that are easily bought and sold.

Maturity date *See* Expiration date.

Maximum expected return criterion (MERC) Choosing the asset with the highest expected return.

Maximum return criterion (MRC) Choosing the asset with the highest return.

Mean *See* Expected return.

Mean-variance criterion (MVC) Prefer a higher mean and/or a lower variance.

Mean-variance frontier The set of investment strategies with the lowest variance for all possible means.

Mean-variance set *See* Mean-variance frontier.

Mid-market The price around which the market maker derives the bid and asked prices.

Minimum variance portfolio (MVP) The portfolio with the smallest variance from the mean variance set.

Monetary policy Actions by a central bank to control the supply of money and interest rates that directly influence the financial markets.

Money market A market for bonds with maturities of less than one year.

Money market security Short-term bonds, usually less than one year.

Mortgage Collateralized bonds, usually for property or land.

Mortgage-backed securities Securities whose value depends on a set of mortgages.

Moving average A method of averaging the most recent past price data.

Multiplier A term used when referring to the P/E ratio as a payback measure.

Municipal bond State and local government securities.

Mutual fund A managed pool of money invested in securities.

Naked position Using options without holding to any underlying security.

Negotiable certificates of deposit Large denomination certificates of deposit that can be traded.

Net asset value (NAV) Current market value of securities in a fund, less liabilities on a per share basis; intrinsic value of a mutual fund.

Neutral stock A stock with a beta of 1.

No-load fund Mutual fund that does not have any sales commissions.

Nominal yield *See* Coupon yield.

Non-marketable security Security that cannot be easily bought and sold.

Normal growth firms Firms whose earnings grow at a constant rate.

Not-held orders (NH) Broker is not held liable if he or she is unable to trade.

Notional principal The basis on which swap interest payments are based, similar to the par value of bonds.

Objective probability The true unobservable underlying probability.

Odd lot Orders not in sizes of 100s.

Open-end fund A mutual fund that can issue more shares.

Open interest The number of futures contracts outstanding at a point in time.

Open market operations US Treasury transactions by the Federal Reserve used to influence bank reserves.

Opening transaction The transaction when the initial position is taken.

Opportunity line Represents portfolios that are achieved by combining different levels of borrowing and lending with a single risky portfolio.

Option A legal contract that gives its holder the right to buy or sell a specified amount of an underlying asset at a fixed price.

Option buyer The owner of the option contract.

Option premium The initial purchase or sales price of an option.

Option writer The person from whom the option buyer purchases the option contract.

Out-of-the-money An option that would generate negative cash flow if exercised now and liquidated.

Over-the-counter market A telephone-and computer-linked network for trading securities.

Participating preferred stock Dividends are tied to earnings.

Par value Lump sum paid at maturity.

Passive investment strategy An investment strategy in which the portfolio manager does *not* actively manage investments.

Payoff diagram A graph illustrating the value line or the profit and loss line.

Payment date Date dividend cheque is posted.

Peak The top of the business cycle.

Percentage financial statements The balance sheet and income statements converted to percentages.

Performance attribution A means to assess the sources of portfolio performance.

Performance index A risk-adjusted measure of how well a portfolio has performed.

Physical asset (also called **real** or **tangible** asset) Tangible assets, such as precious metals or land.

Pit A place where all buying and selling of futures contracts takes place.

Plain vanilla swap *See* Fixed for floating swap.

Point-and-figure chart A graph with *x*'s and *o*'s, used to plot price reversals without consideration of time.

Political risk The possibility that a country will take over a firm.

Portfolio A group of securities that are held together in an effort to achieve some future consumption desire.

Portfolio expected return A weighted average of the individual asset's expected return.

Portfolio insurance A strategy in which the maximum risk of loss is set in advance.

Portfolio variance A complex weighted average of the individual asset's variances and covariances (or correlations).

Preference share Preferred shares that have first claim to preferred dividends.

Preferred habitat hypothesis A hypothesis that suppliers and demanders of funds have a preferred region of the yield curve, but can be induced to move.

Preliminary estimates The second estimate of GDP released about two months after the measurement period.

Premium A closed-end fund trading above NAV, as a percentage of NAV.

Price continuity Minimal price changes due to transactions.

Price effect The impact on bond prices when interest rates change.

Price immunization Immunization strategies that focus on the current market value of assets and liabilities.

Price risk The risk that bond prices will fall when interest rates rise.

Primary market Where securities are first sold to the public.

Primary offering *See* Seasoned new issue.

Primary trend Long-term trends lasting 4 to $4\frac{1}{2}$ years in price data.

Principal *See* Par value.

Private placement An issue of securities that is not sold to the public.

Private placement memorandum Necessary information on a private placement.

Program trading Trading at least 15 securities at one time.

Prospectus A legal document containing a business plan and other information for investors regarding IPOs.

Protective put buying A strategy of holding a stock and buying out of the money option on this stock.

Purchasing power parity The relationship between two countries' inflation rates and their foreign exchange rates.

Pure yield pick-up swap Moving to bonds with a higher yield.

Put-call parity (PCP) Establishes the pricing relationship between the underlying security, the risk-free interest rate, call options and put options.

Put/call ratio A measure based on the volume of put and call option trading.

Put option A contract giving the right to sell a specified amount of an underlying asset during some period in the future at a predetermined price.

Put ratio backspread A complex spread strategy used when one believes the stock price will decline but fears the stock price might rise.

Quote rule Rule requiring market makers to publish quotations for any listed security when a quote represents more than 1% of the aggregate trading volume for that security.

Rally An overall rise in the stock market or in an individual security.

Random walk A statistical concept where future price changes are unpredictable, not based on prior outcomes.

Rate anticipation swap Positioning a bond portfolio based on the perceived direction of future interest rate moves.

Rate of return Profit divided by investment.

Rating agency A firm that assesses the credit risk of a bond.

Ratio analysis A method used to compare financial trends both between firms and for a given firm over time.

Real asset *See* Physical asset.

Real body On a candlestick line, it is the broad part consisting of the difference between opening and closing prices.

Real rate of return An inflation-adjusted rate of return.

Real GDP The inflation-adjusted measure of GDP.

Realized rate of return Rate of return that has already been earned.

Realized yield The holding period return actually generated from an investment in a bond.

Receive fixed counterparty The counterparty of an interest rate swap receiving payments based on the fixed rate and making payments based on the floating rate.

Receive floating counterparty The counterparty of an interest rate swap receiving payments based on the floating rate and making payments based on the fixed rate.

Recession Typically defined as two consecutive quarters of negative real GDP growth.

Registered competitive traders Members of an exchange who trade for their own account.

Registered equity market maker The title of the AMEX market maker.

Regulated investment company An investment company that satisfies Regulation M of the IRS in the USA and avoids taxes on security transactions.

Regulations Rules established by governments for the purpose of identifying unacceptable behaviour.

Regulatory risk The risk that governments will change the way a firm may operate.

Reinvestment effect The impact on the reinvestment rate when interest rates change.

Reinvestment rate risk The risk of not being able to reinvest coupon payments at as high an interest rate when rates fall.

Reinvestment risk The risk that future cash flows will be invested at a lower rate.

Relative strength A measure of the price performance of one index against another.

Repurchase agreement Sale of a money market security with an agreement to buy it back at a higher price at a specified time.

Resiliency Speed of new orders when prices change.

Resistance An upper bound on prices due to the quantity of willing sellers at that price level.

Revenue bond Backed by a specific project's income.

Reverse repos The opposite side of a repurchase agreement, where one buys securities with an agreement to sell them at a later day at a specified price.

Revised estimates The third estimate of GDP released about three months after the measurement period.

Risk *See* Uncertainty.

Risk averter Someone who dislikes risk.

Risk neutral Someone who is indifferent about risk.

Risk premium The higher return required to take higher risk.

Risk profile A mapping of the change in value or profits and losses to which an organization has exposure.

Risk seeker Someone who likes to take a risk and is even willing to pay for it.

Round lots A stock trade that is a multiple of 100.

Scalping Investment bankers buying up the good IPOs.

Seasonal anomalies Trading strategies that generate abnormal returns based solely on the time of year.

Seasoned new issue A new stock offering by a company that has sold stock previously.

Second market OTC trades on the OTC market.

Secondary market Where securities trade after they are issued.

Sector allocation The decision as to what proportion to invest in each sector.

Secured bonds Bonds with collateral backing them.

Securities Exchange Act of 1934 US Act that regulates the secondary market, established the SEC, gives the federal government authority to establish a margin and forbids insider trading.

Security An instrument that signifies an ownership position in a stock or a bond, or rights to ownership by an option.

Security market line (SML) The linear relationship between expected return and beta.

Security selection The decision as to what proportion to invest in each security; the process of determining the securities within each asset class that are most suitable.

Selective hedging Hedging during some time periods and not hedging during other time periods.

Semistrong form of the EMT Prices reflect all relevant publicly–available information.

Sentiment indicator An indicator of traders' opinions about the market.

Separation property *See* Separation theorem.

Separation theorem The decision of the optimal portfolio of risky assets (denoted *m*) is separate from the actual portfolio of the riskless asset and *m*.

Settle price An average of the trading prices that occur during the last few minutes of the day.

Shadows The thin lines above and below the real body on a candlestick line.

Share Unit of equity ownership in a corporation or mutual fund.

Sharpe's performance index A performance measure based on the CML.

Short position An agreement to *make delivery* in the futures market.

Short selling Selling borrowed securities.

Short-term trend Trends that last less than 3 weeks, and that are very erratic.

Simple interest The principal times the rate times the time.

Simple rate of return *See* Holding a period rate.

Single Index Model (SIM) A model by which all rates of return are generated by one factor, e.g. GNP, inflation rate or unemployment rate. This model dramatically reduces the computation load needed to derive the m-v frontier.

Sinking fund Money set aside to repay a bond principal in the future.

Specialist Appointed market maker on the NYSE.

Speculative Securities that involve a high level of risk.

Speculative grade bond Bonds with credit quality below BBB (or Baa).

Speculative stock Very risky stock.

Spot market A market where trades are made for immediate delivery (or within a few days).

Spot rate The yield to maturity of a zero-coupon bond with some stated maturity.

Spread An option strategy in which the investor holds long and short positions on the same type of option, but the contracts have different expiration dates and exercise prices.

Standard deviation A measure of risk, the square root of the variance.

Standard normal distribution A normal distribution with mean 0 and standard deviation 1.

Statement of cash flow An accounting statement showing the flow of cash through the firm.

Step-up swap An interest rate swap where the notional principal increases based on a predetermined schedule.

Stock split When a company issues more new shares in return for existing shares.

Stop order Order to trade if adverse price movement occurs.

Straddle An option strategy in which the investor buys or sells both puts and calls on the same underlying item with the same exercise price and expiration date.

Strike price The predetermined price to buy or sell within the option contract.

Strong form of the EMT Prices reflect all relevant publicly and privately available information.

Subjective probability One's beliefs regarding the actual underlying probabilities.

Subordinated bonds Bonds that stand behind other bonds in the credit line.

Substitution swap Selling overpriced bonds and buying underpriced bonds.

Supergrowth firms Firms whose earnings grow at a high rate for a period of time.

Support A lower bound on prices due to the quantity of willing buyers at that price level.

Swap A contract to exchange payments of some sort at a future date.

Syndicate A group of investment bankers who participate in an IPO, taking some of the risk.

Systematic risk The part of an asset's variance attributable to the overall market fluctuation; the risk related to overall movements in the market.

Tangible asset *See* Physical asset.

Technical analysis The process of identifying trends in historical price data and extending them to the future.

Tender offer An attempt to buy large portions of a publicly-held firm.

Term repos Repurchase agreements that have a longer holding period.

Term structure of interest rates *See* Yield curve.

Third market Exchange-listed issues traded off the exchange.

Time value Any option value in excess of intrinsic value.

Time-weighted rate of return Calculating returns that measure how invested wealth would grow.

Top–down approach A security selection approach that starts with asset allocation and works systematically through sector and industry allocation to individual security selection.

Treasury bills Short-term government securities issued at a discount.

Treasury bonds Over 10 years when initially issued, government securities.

Treasury notes 2 to 10 years when initially issued, government securities.

Trendline A line drawn on a bar chart to identify current trends.

Treynor's performance index A performance measure based on the CAPM.

Trough The bottom of the business cycle.

Turnover Value of securities purchased (or sold, whichever is less) divided by average NAV, a measure of transaction cost.

Unbiased expectations hypothesis (UEH) A hypothesis stating that the current implied forward rate is an unbiased predictor of future spot rates.

Uncertainty When more than one possible outcome could occur.

Underwriters These act as intermediaries between the firm and investors.

Underwriter's discount *See* Gross spread.

Unsystematic risk The part of an asset's variance attributable to the individual firm.

Upstairs market Trades arranged by a network of trading desks, usually large blocks.

Uptick Last price is above previous price.

Utility A measure of an investor's level of 'satisfaction' or preference.

Variance A measure of risk or the dispersion around the mean.

Weak form of the EMT Prices reflect information revealed by historical market-based data.

Wealth effect Investors reacting to interest rates' impact on bond portfolio value.

Writer *See* Option writer.

Yield curve The relationship between yield to maturity and maturity for similar bonds.

Yield to call The internal rate of return on a bond when it is assumed to be called on the first call date.

Yield to maturity The internal rate of return on a bond when held to maturity.

Zero beta An asset with zero beta has a zero correlation with the market portfolio. The expected return on such an asset in equilibrium equals the risk-free interest rate.

Zero-coupon bond Pays no interest and trades at a discount.

Zero-plus tick Last price is same as previous trading price, which was an uptick.

INDEX